ECONOMIC WARFARE

ECONOMIC WARFARE

*Sanctions, Embargo Busting, and
Their Human Cost*

R. T. NAYLOR

Northeastern University Press
BOSTON

Copyright 1999 by R. T. Naylor

Published in Canada in 1999 as *Patriots and Profiteers* by McClelland & Stewart, Inc., Toronto.
Published in the United States of America in 2001 by Northeastern University Press.

Library of Congress Cataloging-in-Publication Data

Naylor, R. T., 1945–
   [Patriots and profiteers]
   Economic warfare : sanctions, embargo busting, and their human cost / R. T. Naylor.
      p. cm.
   Originally published: Patriots and profiteers. c1999
   Includes bibliographical references and index.
   ISBN 1-55553-500-3 (cloth : alk. paper)—ISBN 1-55553-499-6 (pbk. : alk. paper)
      1. Economic sanctions. 2. Embargo. 3. International relations. 4. Political corruption.
   I. Title.
   HF1413.5 .N39 2001
   327.1¢17—dc21   2001040207

Designed by Ingrid Paulson
Printed and bound by Maple Press, York, Pennsylvania. The paper is Maple Eggshell, an acid-
free stock

MANUFACTURED IN THE UNITED STATES OF AMERICA
05   04   03   02   01   5   4   3   2   1

CONTENTS

FOREWORD

The people who shape foreign policy don't care much about economic history. To them, the important stuff is politics: the careers of politicians, the ebb and flow of political movements and parties. They're wrong: it is impossible to develop foreign policy without knowing about international trade and finance — where the money is and how it got there. Indeed, political history makes little sense without some knowledge of financial and economic history.

Policy makers could especially profit from an understanding of the issues that Tom Naylor focuses on in these pages. It is a history of misguided intervention and wrong-headed efforts at control and regulation in the international marketplace — and the mischief that has resulted. Evidence of that mischief is abundant everywhere.

I recently visited the American embassy in an African country. A political officer asked what I thought could be done about the corruption that was endemic there. I said the bribery and theft would end if the international community agreed to find and repatriate the money stolen from the Congo by former president Mobutu Sese Seko. I argued that the impact of such a coordinated campaign would be immeasurable: every other corrupt official on the continent would worry that his ill-gotten wealth was no longer safe.

The idea that the stolen money could be found, much less repatriated, had never occurred to this official. Nor did it occur to him to tackle the problem of corruption by tackling the infrastructure that supports it. To his way of thinking, the only solution to the problem was some form of punishment—

such as cutting off the (minuscule) flow of U.S. assistance or imposing some form of trade embargo.

Unfortunately, it is not just low-level officials in African outposts who think in these terms. It goes all the way to the top. Senior members of the Clinton administration, including Vice-President Al Gore and Deputy Secretary of State Strobe Talbot have chosen to ignore briefings on the extent and seriousness of organized crime in what remains of the Soviet Union. Instead, they want to focus on building a relationship with key figures in the Russian leadership. But it is impossible to understand the current situation — the economic collapse, the theft of state resources, and the emergence of various political parties — without first understanding the distortions afflicting the Russian economy as a result of the criminal activity associated with the old government.

As the twentieth century closes, war in the form of battling armies has become largely unthinkable. The weapons available are too destructive to be used by democracies. Their chief value is that their mere existence is a deterrent. Throughout the cold war, when both the United States and the Soviet Union maintained a powerful nuclear arsenal, the threat was of certain, overpowering retaliation. The doctrine of mutually assured destruction (MAD) changed the role of armies under democratic control to peacekeeping and disaster relief.

How, in these changed circumstances, can this or that errant government be punished for failing to live up to its commitments? How can regional or ethnic conflict be contained? Increasingly, the favoured response is to engage in some kind of economic warfare.

Thus, when the Republicans took control of the American Congress in 1994, the House of Representatives decided to "punish" the "rogue terrorist" state of Iran. Draconian sanctions legislation was introduced and moved forward at an appalling pace. I tried to tell members of the committee staff that sanctions would not work. I argued that they would anger other countries, make profits for crooks and create problems for legitimate businesses. The committee staff did not want to listen. Even to think about these issues would only slow down the process. I suggested that there were ways to improve the legislation to address some of the more obvious problems but even this offer was rebuffed. They knew!

The legislation is now in place. There is no sign that it made any difference to the Iranians.

This should come as no surprise. It's not the first time the United States has tried to force political change abroad by applying a trade embargo. If only the staff members had checked out the results of previous embargoes, they would have discovered for themselves the almost comically counter-productive effects they have had. To take just one example, when I worked for the Senate Foreign Relations Committee in 1988, I asked the General Accounting Office to assess the effectiveness of the economic sanctions the United States had imposed on Panama in order to oust the then-president, General Noriega.

The GAO reported that scores of American companies had complained that the sanctions would do irreparable harm to their business. These companies applied to the Treasury office that managed the sanctions for an exemption to one aspect or other of the rules. A large number of exemptions were granted, enforcement of the rules was lax, and the political impact on Noriega was limited. Noriega blamed the sanctions for all the country's problems and rallied the Panamanian population to resist Yankee imperialism. Ironically, the biggest financial problem Noriega had to deal with had nothing to do with the sanctions. The drug money that was being laundered through Panama's banks fled the country because the drug cartels were worried either that Noriega would offer to exchange their cash for peace with the United States or that their assets would be identified and seized following an American invasion. The sanctions themselves were clearly a failure.

The Helms-Burton bill, which targets those who do business with Cuba, is the most egregious of the current sanctions follies. Fidel Castro blames all of Cuba's economic problems on the sanctions and rallies patriotic Cubans to his support by pointing to the history of economic warfare conducted by the United States against his country. At the same time, the legislation has infuriated other governments whose companies are being punished for their failure to subscribe to American policy. The victims are the average people of Cuba.

If only our policy makers could have read this book, they might have had second thoughts. Tom Naylor's thorough account of failed embargoes and ineffective sanctions might finally have persuaded them — as it will surely persuade most readers — that economic warfare can work only when it is directed against an utterly helpless population in a limited territory.

As well as demonstrating the truth of this fundamental lesson, Naylor has provided a wonderful account of the infrastructure that has evolved to support sanctions-busters. Offshore banks, shell companies, flags of convenience and professional money-laundering operations are all part of the picture. Colourful international "traders," arms dealers and conmen cross the stage. This part of the story is told with wry humour.

It's funny, but also tragic, that misguided sanctions wind up producing difficult law-enforcement problems in other areas. The secret bank accounts, shell companies and flags of convenience that help the sanctions-busters also keep drug traffickers, ocean polluters and fraudsters out of the reach of police. Moreover, the people trying to get around the sanctions turn to the criminals for help.

Read this book to make the connection between economic and foreign policy. Find out why economic warfare almost always fails. Then join me in making the book required reading for anyone with an interest in how foreign policy is made.

Jack A. Blum
Attorney and former special counsel to the
U.S. Senate Foreign Relations Committee

ECONOMIC WARFARE

PROLOGUE

During his first term as president, Richard Nixon called for the United States to wage war against Chile. However, in retaliation for Chile's electing a Marxist chief of state and nationalizing American-owned businesses, Nixon did not unleash the Marines or call down the Air Force. His warriors carried attaché cases rather than assault rifles and wielded pens rather than bayonets. They attacked Chile's exports, assaulted its finances and blockaded its imports of food and spare parts. The point was, as Nixon put it, to "make the economy scream."[1] It did.

American mining companies tangled in lawsuits Chile's earnings from copper, its main export; U.S. pressure caused international banks to slash their loans to Chile; and, starved of parts, industrial and agricultural equipment eventually stopped working. Meanwhile, local allies spread stories that the financial system was about to crash to set off panic runs on the banks. They engaged in arson and sabotage. They hauled cash from secret Swiss bank accounts to finance a truck drivers' strike, especially disruptive in a country without rail transport.[2] At a time when unemployment was soaring and the inflation rate topping 1,000 per cent, Chile's military launched a coup in which the head of state died, and thousands of "subversives" were tortured, killed or exiled. It was war, despite the fact that no one had bothered to declare it and despite the seemingly unorthodox choice of weapons. That choice of weapons was really not so unusual, for today the economic component of warfare is at least as important as the military one. In fact, it probably always has been.

For centuries, belligerents have tried to sap the enemy's economic strength prior to, during or even instead of engaging the enemy directly. Usually the methods were crude — crops burned, storehouses sacked and irrigation systems ruined. Sometimes they were more subtle. Usury, for example, a mortal sin if practised among Christians, was approved by the medieval Church during the Crusades as a weapon of economic warfare. It was wrong to charge interest on loans to fellow Christians. But if draining the financial resources of the Muslim hordes advanced the cause of liberating the Holy Sepulchre, praise be to God. It was certainly not the last time that criminal acts would receive the seal of approval of the highest authority when committed in the name of "national security" or, in this case, its medieval equivalent.

It was precisely to dissect such a widely practised yet little understood aspect of statecraft that this book was written. It is less a study of economies at war than of war against economies.[3] To achieve everything from collecting compensation for expropriated property to forcing trade concessions, from disrupting military adventures to promoting the overthrow of a regime, one country or group of countries might attempt to ruin another's markets, block its access to strategic materials and destroy its credit rating.[4] The tools include export embargoes, import restrictions and financial sanctions. They can also include covert actions: counterfeiting currency to discredit state finances, using *agents provocateurs* to stir up labour disputes, or deploying rebel forces against strategic targets like electricity plants and oil refineries, roads, ports and railways, the food supply system and the main export industries. If those insurgents engage in a little extra-curricular activity — robbing banks, kidnapping wealthy citizens or trafficking contraband — that can reduce the costs of waging an economic war while increasing its effectiveness.[5]

Not all acts of modern economic warfare are undertaken as a means for one country to extract commercial or political concessions from another. Since World War II there has been a widely shared hope that economic measures could replace military coercion in enforcing international morality. The theory is that countries are now so interdependent, a "rogue state" excluded from normal trade and financial relations will be forced to reconsider its political options. Reflecting that hope, the same politically correct spirit that led to ministries of war being renamed departments of "defence" has meant that the aggressive sounding "economic warfare" has recently been laundered into the morally uplifting "economic sanctions."[6] But what often gets forgotten in the optimism is that the capacity of most states to weave their way around embargoes, dodge trade restrictions, and evade asset freezes has increased as rapidly as their economic interdependence.

Therefore a second objective of this book is to scrutinize the devices — shell companies, coded bank accounts, phoney documents and zigzag transportation routes — used to counter "sanctions," aided enormously by the fact that, in recent decades, financial secrecy havens, flag-of-convenience shipping centres and "free trade zones" have proliferated across the globe.[7] While everything from strategic metals to industrial diamonds, from black market gold to stolen computer chips, from Cuban cigars to Serbian brandy figures on their unwritten freight manifests, the most strategically important items are oil, arms and a third commodity whose peregrinations are cloaked in extra-thick layers of cover.

Oil is perhaps the most strategic of strategic goods. For every barrel traded for crude profit motives, there is another whose commercial purpose is much more refined. While representatives of producing countries and directors of global corporations meet at the top of skyscrapers to strike marketing deals, the real action takes place in the basement whence slick traders evade quotas, bust embargoes and play hide-and-seek with the fiscal authorities. Not least of their talents is arranging the secret swap of oil for arms.

Arms, too, are a commodity where the "black market" has always been an extension of diplomacy by other, covert means.[8] Typically arms traffickers, when not veteran army officers or ex-arms company executives, were (are) "retired" members of intelligence services. Not only do they keep in touch with former colleagues, routinely informing on customers, but, as the price of having a deal go through, might pay a sort-of covert action tax for funding intelligence operations. To a government the advantage of such "private" actors taking the initiative in a business theoretically subject to tight scrutiny is that they can always be hung out to dry if a particularly malodorous deal gets exposed.

But nowhere does the shady side of business intersect so neatly with the shadowy side of politics than in drug trafficking.[9] If weapons (or agents) have to be quietly moved, drug smugglers already have inside the targeted country the logistical apparatus, including safe houses and corrupted officials. The same routes and methods used for moving drugs can be adapted to strategic materials. Traffickers often pay "taxes" — cash, arms or supplies — to insurgent groups destabilizing targeted governments, or they kick back a share of their profit into an intelligence agency black treasury for financing deep-cover operations. And their products, infiltrated into the enemy's economy, can siphon off resources and undermine social stability. From at least the mid-nineteenth century when the British flooded China with opium, draining it of silver sufficiently to derange its national currency prior to demanding territorial concessions and sweeping trade deals, including the legalization of opium, drugs have played a role in economic warfare.[10]

Economic warfare inevitably promotes economic crime. That is the third theme of this book. When one side applies trade and technology embargoes, investment sanctions and asset freezes against another, the target responds by smuggling, industrial espionage and exchange control evasion. Therefore in times of economic war, agents of the state fraternize with, cater to and emulate the actions of underworld elements whom the state as trustee of the legal system is supposed to be committed to putting out of business, if not behind bars. If, on one level, the book seems an elaborate tale of cops and robbers, that tale is distinguished by the fact that during an economic war it is difficult, if not impossible, to tell them apart.

And the legacy endures. In medieval times each conflict left in its wake bands of mercenaries who, if not properly disposed of, took their talents freelance, plundering the countryside at will. Similarly, the winding down of economic wars today turns loose guerrilla groups who take to looting, extorting and racketeering, and unleashes a generation trained in smuggling, money-laundering and document fraud. In the final analysis, sanctions have done little or nothing to enforce international morality. But they have done a great deal to produce thriving black markets, criminalize legitimate business and create a class of economic war-profiteers that support a targeted regime, while the cost gets dumped onto those parts of the population least capable of making their political choices felt.

In attempting to tell a story so wrapped in deception and denial, secrecy and subterfuge, the first requirement is to pick through the misinformation and disinformation that are its common currencies. Often participants themselves are unable to differentiate reality from a three-whisky rumour.[11] All too frequently they also have a vested interest, financial or political, in exaggerating the importance of what they have to say. Veteran congressional investigator Jack Blum, godfather of the U.S. Foreign Corrupt Practices Act and the person who broke the BCCI scandal, ventured the opinion that an honest witness tells the truth 80 per cent of the time and makes genuine mistakes the other 20 per cent. However a fabricator, to achieve credibility, must also tell the truth at least 80 per cent of the time, while deliberately or reflexively misleading during the rest. The real skill of the investigator lies in being able to tell the difference. Generally it comes down to subjecting evidence in a particular case to instinct born of many.

Consider in this respect the career of Alberto Sicilia-Falcon. A Cuban refugee-turned-Miami street hustler, he was trained by the CIA to participate in the Bay of Pigs invasion. Like many veterans of that disaster, Sicilia-Falcon decided to put his education to better use. He set up shop in Tijuana, Mexico, and was soon living in luxury, surrounded by armed guards and boyfriends. The source of his new-found fortune was no mystery — his couriers regularly ran marijuana, heroin and cocaine in wholesale lots across the American border. He operated a tight ship, with accountants and lawyers to take care of business and to haul suitcases of cash for senior Mexican politicians and police officers. He also developed a sideline in weapons, some stolen from U.S. National Guard armouries, some bought on the world black market.

Alas, Sicilia-Falcon may have overestimated his strengths, reneged on some payments or merely outlived his usefulness. In 1976 he was arrested by the Mexican *federales*. Tortured, he told an incredible tale. He claimed to have been ordered by CIA handlers to run drugs to finance arms destined for guerrilla groups destabilizing central American governments. Among the recipients were rebels in Mexico's Sierra Madre del Sur mountains. At that time Mexican-American relations had been brought to a new low by Mexico's refusal to reduce barriers to U.S. investment and to open its oil fields. It was speculated by some Mexicans, prone to give the gringos more credit for machiavellian premeditation than they merit, that the United States wanted Sicilia-Falcon to arm the guerrillas to send the Mexican government a "message."

Perhaps it got the message in a different way. Sicilia-Falcon's arrest exposed a trail of corruption that led to a committed nationalist hand-picked by Mexico's ruling party to succeed the incumbent president. With him disgraced, the party opted for a weak alternative whose regime was distinguished by increasing servility to the United States in the area of oil and foreign investment, and by a dizzying increase in official graft.[12]

Sicilia-Falcon's story was outlandish, with a strong flavour of paranoid babbling by a trafficker fond of his own product and of panicked concoctions by a megalomaniac suddenly confronted with his own vulnerability. Spending time in a *federales* torture cell was likely further inspiration to flights of fancy. Everyone in authority, and later Sicilia-Falcon himself, denied the claims. And, contrary to conspiracy theory that, at least in North America, tends to dominate what passes for critical thought in the post–Cold War era, where there is smoke, there is rarely a raging inferno.

On the other hand, it would be quite a surprise if the presence of smoke did not mean that, once the layers of incombustible garbage are cleared away, there could be found at least a twig or two smouldering underneath. Exposing those twigs to view, and determining who rubbed them together, assuredly not members of a Boy Scout troop, is the fourth and final task this book sets out to achieve. The story it tells is not an edifying one, raking up the muck of several decades of often forgotten scandals. But it needs to be told, for those episodes are less aberrations than moments when the veil of hypocrisy gets lifted enough to allow reality to show its ugly face.

Part One

METHOD IN THE MAYHEM

Chapter I

MIGHTIER THAN THE SWORD?

In 1577 a little English fleet began pre-paring in deepest secrecy an audacious act of economic warfare. Queen Elizabeth I herself declared that anyone responsible for information reaching Spain's espionage service would lose their head. As further cover, once the flotilla set sail, the story was spread that it was a raiding party bound for Scotland. Three years later Francis Drake returned from looting Spanish treasure ships and plundering Spanish-American towns to declare a dividend of 4,700 per cent. Among the delighted investors was Elizabeth I. Her share sufficed to pay off the national debt, finance a more aggressive anti-Spanish foreign policy and invest in further foreign ventures. Yet this occurred when England and Spain were at peace. Indeed, one of the strongest arguments for the expedition had been that drying up Spain's supply of silver, even temporarily, would undermine its capacity to launch a war.[1]

The Prize Fighters
During Drake's time, and for centuries after, economic warfare was at the very heart of state-building. Political influence depended on military power and military power on economic strength. Yet the world and its resources were regarded as known and finite. Hence the only way to increase the wealth, and

therefore the power, of one state was to take something away from another. The most important strategic resources to be acquired at the expense of a rival were silver and gold, the "sinews of war."[2]

They could be acquired in two ways. One was through regulated trade. A state blocked imports that competed with its own industries, prohibited the export of raw materials useful for home production and banned the emigration of workers whose technical skills might build up a rival's economic strength. The ultimate goal was to ensure that exports exceeded imports in value, forcing trade partners to pay the difference in precious metals. If trade proved difficult, the alternative was plunder. The distinction was sometimes a fine one. When English privateers seized a Spanish colonial town, they demanded that local merchants buy their cargoes or see the town destroyed.[3]

There were risks, of course. Spanish ships could outgun English, and a merchant-adventurer whose privateering vessel was seized or sunk lost his capital. Furthermore, as long as England and Spain were nominally at peace, not only were English ports full of Spanish spies reporting the departure of privateers and the arrival of stolen cargoes, but Spain could press England to take legal action against the perpetrators. The answer to both dangers lay in forming corporations. Merchants pooled capital to finance multi-ship expeditions; that spread risks and increased chances of success. And they kept the shareholder list secret.[4]

Once the shooting started, there was no need to be coy. Looting enemy commerce helped war pay for itself, while it weakened a rival by driving up insurance rates, destroying ships on which maritime power depended and depriving the target state of precious metals. Naval ships and merchant vessels were equally armed for the task. The lure of booty was as much an incentive to service in the navy as with privateers. All a merchant ship needed to wage war was a letter of marque, a licence to steal without risking charges of piracy, provided a percentage of the loot was paid to the state.[5] Originally issued only by the king, letters of marque were soon sold openly by enterprising admiralty officers.[6]

Because no formal hostilities had been declared, on Drake's return, a debate briefly raged among Elizabeth's counsellors as to whether the treasure should be handed back to Spain. Those secretly holding shares were, not surprisingly, most strongly opposed. And the protesting Spanish owners were caught in their own dishonesty. To evade Customs duties it was common to under-declare, sometimes by as much as half, the value of a galleon's cargo. Consequently, the Spanish Crown had no idea how much Drake had stolen.

Drake's portion, along with that of his shareholders, was quietly removed, the rest set aside for possible restitution if Spain agreed to stop aiding a rebellion against English rule in Ireland. But ultimately none of the treasure was returned. Turning the tables, Elizabeth used part of her share to finance a rebellion against Spanish rule in Flanders.

Although the economic war seemed to produce spectacular and immediate financial benefits, it was never clear how much England really gained from Drake's voyage or from those of his imitators. Spanish commercial retaliation was severe enough to cause a depression in England's trade. And, far from seriously interfering with Spain's ability to launch a war, the privateers may have done much to provoke it. Fortunately for Drake, a weak Spanish armada, battered by storms and ravaged by fire, was no match for the waiting English fleet, and his honoured place in British history was assured.

When James I succeeded Elizabeth, he refused to issue letters of marque. English privateers briefly used flags of convenience, until James I decreed that any English subject serving on a foreign-flagged privateer was to be treated as a pirate. Shutting down privateering (like the end of a guerrilla war today) cast adrift thousands whose main skill was armed robbery. Many came together to form a pirates' cooperative, joined by adventurous landsmen, political refugees, or even legitimate sailors who found life among pirates more comfortable than a career with the English Navy. Piracy was a vocation that paid well while posing few risks. Merchant ships rarely resisted. And sanctuaries abounded. Much like modern Caribbean banking centres, Mediterranean city states competed to have the pirates and their money take up residence.

Unlike James I's England, most countries encouraged privateering. In France, Louis XIV and members of his court took shares. During the American Revolution, privateering attracted as many volunteers as the militia — the business was so well established that shares were discounted from hand to hand and used as collateral for loans.[7] By then the successors to James I had begun licensing privateers again.

Armies engaged in their own form of privateering. Like letters of marque, officers' commissions were a popular investment. Senior officers could expropriate resources from and impose "taxes" on conquered territories to finance wars (and their own lifestyle), while profiting by selling supplies to subordinate officers and speculating on price increases caused by their own actions.[8] For the ordinary soldiers, too, plunder was a right. Villages were looted, their inhabitants tortured to reveal their possessions. Merchants' caravans were pillaged. Enemy soldiers were stripped of personal effects, while those taken alive were ransomed. The richest pickings, though, came from major urban centres. By commonly accepted rules of engagement, if they failed to surrender before artillery was deployed against them, their inhabitants forfeited everything, including their lives.[9]

Looting performed three functions. The commander was spared the expense of paying adequate wages or providing sufficient supplies. The soldier was rewarded for a job well done. And the sponsoring country was able to hamper the enemy's war effort. Not until Napoleon's time was looting in European wars curbed, and then it was more to keep order than out of concern with the property rights of citizens.

Though plundering by land and sea was the most dramatic form of economic warfare, it was not alone. In the fifteenth century, the Duke of Milan faked the coins of his Venetian adversaries. During the next century, Charles IX of France did likewise to those of his German enemies.

The advent of paper money made counterfeiting much easier. During the eighteenth century, the American colonies, desperately short of both tax revenues and silver coin, began printing bills of credit, interest-bearing IOUs issued in small denominations that could circulate as currency. Samples ended up in the hands of professional counterfeiters in Europe, especially Ireland. Almost from the start, fake paper plagued the colonial finances. During the American Revolution, the Continental Congress, lacking power of taxation, also attempted to pay expenses with bills of credit. That gave an opportunity to the British, who hijacked several wagonloads of the paper on which the bills were printed, hired experienced Irish counterfeiters and auctioned the results to British sympathizers for circulation throughout the Thirteen Colonies. Within five years, official bills were being exchanged against silver at less than 2 per cent of face value. Although most of that depreciation was due to lack of faith that the Continental Congress could ever repay the notes, counterfeiting played its role. It permitted the British to finance part of their own war effort and helped bring their opponents' finances into disrepute.[10]

Although economic warfare was certainly present well before the eighteenth century, it did not become truly systematic until the Franco-British struggle at the end of that century. At that time, too, the main instruments began to shift from predatory measures such as raiding and pillaging to commercial ones such as embargoes and trade restrictions. Although Napoleon is celebrated more as a strategist of military than of economic war, his own priorities were actually the reverse. To the founder of the French cotton industry attempting to break the British stranglehold on the European market,

Napoleon explained, "We are both fighting the English, but yours is the better war."[11]

Beating the System

In 1793 France's Revolutionary Directorate banned all British-made goods, later extending the ban to any goods carried on British ships. It also decreed that if a neutral ship were caught carrying a British product, even something as innocuous as a blanket on the captain's bunk, the ship and cargo could be forfeited. Crew members were bribed to reveal contraband as a pretext for hauling the ship before a prize court. Prize courts, seated in French coastal towns, might be presided over by magistrates who were former privateers or who had a stake in the venture that seized the ship. The British responded with a "paper blockade," decreeing a trade embargo against many more ports than they could control, therefore justifying the seizure of any neutral ship bound for any enemy destination if the ship had not checked at a British port to have its cargo inspected and to purchase a licence.

When Napoleon took power, he curtailed some of the excesses of the previous regime. Shortly after, the two powers made peace. However, when war resumed, the British re-imposed their blockade with greater severity. Napoleon reacted by introducing his Continental System, which re-instituted most of the Directorate's measures while adding new ones.[12]

First, noting that the huge productivity gains of the early Industrial Revolution meant a growing dependence on export markets, Napoleon attempted to close Europe, by diplomacy or by conquest, to British products. He calculated that as goods piled up unsold, British workers would be laid off, and unemployment with the threat of mass starvation would provoke social upheaval.

Second, he tried to deny Britain strategic goods from the Baltic — especially timber (used for fuel, building materials and ships), hemp (for rigging and sails) and grain (when Britain had lost its food self-sufficiency).

Third, he set out to subvert Britain's financial system. The British had counterfeited bills of credit issued by Revolutionary France and attempted to circulate goldless *Louis d'or* gold coins. In turn, Napoleon ordered retaliatory counterfeiting of British paper. More importantly, he attempted to dry up Britain's sources of gold and silver — to throw its currency into disrepute, undermine its capacity to finance an anti-French alliance and hamper its ability to pay cash for strategic imports. Part of the job was done by cutting off British export markets in Europe and encouraging smugglers to drain precious metals out of Britain. However, the bulk of Britain's precious metals came from trade through the West Indies. There Napoleon attempted to eject the British, only to be ejected himself.

The British implemented countermeasures on each front. Faced with Napoleon's grain embargo, they banned distillation of grain to ensure bakeries got priority, passed laws encouraging the enclosure of fields and the conversion of small peasant plots into large capitalist farms to raise productivity, smuggled grain through Dutch and Baltic ports and imported some from Canada.[13] Similarly, they smuggled wood from Prussia and Poland while partially replacing Baltic timber with supplies from North American colonies. These responses to economic pressure — prioritizing use, increasing home production, diversifying sources and smuggling — became standard ways to beat embargoes in the years to come.

On the export front, the British were even more aggressive. As Napoleon seized large parts of Europe to stop the entry of British goods, Britain included more Continental ports within its own blockade. It grabbed Spanish, Dutch and Portuguese overseas territories as markets for goods no longer able to be sold in Europe. And it sought to destroy French overseas commerce.

For over 150 years, the two powers had contended for control of the world sugar market. France won. By the turn of the nineteenth century, sugar from its West Indian colonies cost 25 per cent of that from the older British plantations. The Napoleonic Wars gave the British a chance to strike back. First they attempted to capture St. Dominique (now Haiti), the source or destination of 75 per cent of France's colonial trade. Unsuccessful, they turned to indirect means. In 1807 Britain declared the abolition of the slave trade. When the British captured the African slave trade posts and committed the navy to stopping "illegal" traffic, they succeeded in cutting off the supply to the French islands, which required several thousand new slaves per year. It was perhaps the world's first economic blockade rationalized by "human rights" rhetoric. And it worked.[14]

Meanwhile, in the European theatre, the British encouraged (and protected) the development of smuggling centres — Gibraltar, Malta, Sicily, the Channel Islands, the Dalmatian coast islands and the Baltic port of Heligoland.[15] Again pioneering techniques that later became standard sanctions-busting practice, Britain provided traders with phoney certificates of origin attesting that cargoes were Dutch or German, and with papers showing that ships had just sailed from neutral ports when they had really come from British ones. British merchants became skilled in false labelling and packaging in sizes and forms convenient for smuggling. They sealed goods in watertight containers and threw them into the sea attached to buoys for French receivers to haul out. In the port of Hamburg, cargoes of cotton, sugar and coffee loaded in coffins were taken ashore in mock funeral processions. Small valuable commodities were carried across Europe in diplomatic valises legally immune from search.[16]

Prior to the Continental System, smuggling was a shady though popular profession.[17] During the Napoleonic wars it became more respectable and much better structured. As Napoleon himself described it, from top to bottom were businessmen who set up the operation (*entrepreneurs*); those, mainly in London, who insured loads against seizure (*assureurs*); people who invested for a share of profits (*intéressés*); on-site operations managers (*directeurs et conducteurs de réunions de fraudeurs*); and mules, who actually moved the goods (*simples porteurs*).[18] Napoleon should have added to the hierarchy two other essential layers.

One was the *financiers*. In Britain the war and blockade made the fortunes of merchant banks. They smuggled British government gold into Europe to finance the anti-Napoleonic alliance, they underwrote British war loans, and they negotiated bills of exchange to pay smugglers. They also used their far-flung networks of agents and correspondents to provide Britain with strategic intelligence.[19] The largest of these banking houses to combine espionage with money laundering was the Baring Brothers. But almost as important was the house of Rothschild. Originally bankers and merchants of Frankfurt, members of the family had relocated to Paris and London. Therefore they were well placed when Napoleon's embargo made Frankfurt one of the centres of European sanctions-busting. First achieving prominence as smugglers of British goods, in the last years of the conflict the Rothschilds also secretly ran enough British money into Spain and Portugal to permit the Duke of Wellington to buy supplies for his starving troops and to deal Napoleon his worst military setback before the disastrous march on Russia.[20]

There was one further layer essential to the contraband networks: *functionnaires pourris*. French customs officials, military commanders and consuls were bribed to issue phoney trade permits and faked certificates of origin. Raids were sometimes rendered worthless by tip-offs from corrupted police. Even when people were caught, they usually had little to fear. Local tribunals tried to acquit fellow citizens or, if they had to find them guilty, ensure that the offence was tax evasion rather than smuggling, which could carry the death penalty.[21]

Although Napoleon replaced corrupted functionaries with officers and used the army to raid warehouses, bribery was too institutionalized to eradicate. He finally made a virtue of necessity. Although he still banned British-made goods, colonial products such as sugar and coffee were admitted provided very steep taxes were paid. In practice the tariffs were so high there was still plenty of incentive to smuggle. But in principle it was an admission that the

Continental System had been severely weakened by leaks even before the defection of Russia in 1810 brought it effectively to a close.

Still, this first instance of modern economic warfare had its times and points of success. It forced a wave of land enclosures that drove hordes of British peasants into urban areas where they exacerbated an already severe problem of mass deprivation. It also led to heavy unemployment in British mill towns, setting off riots that Napoleon hoped were the precursors of mass insurrection. British commerce was further damaged when the United States, in retaliation for Britain's efforts to stop the flow of strategic goods to Napoleon, imposed its own trade embargo. Shortage of precious metals forced Britain to shift its currency from paper backed by gold to inconvertible paper. Although the great financial crisis of which Napoleon dreamed never occurred, in the later years inflation rose and the value of the British currency dropped sufficiently to shake confidence in the country's financial system. It took more than a decade after the wars for Britain to return to a full gold-based monetary system.

There were three important lessons strategists should have drawn from the Continental System and the British countermeasures. One was that economic warfare would work only if it completely sealed the target. The longer the embargo, the greater the leakage and the more time to diversify. And the more unpopular the embargo, the worse the corruption of functionaries and the greater the criminalization of businesses subject to it.

The second lesson was that the infrastructure of economic war is almost certain to outlive the war itself. Many Mediterranean and Caribbean islands, with official British encouragement, shifted their economic functions from plantations and pirates' lairs to smuggling posts, en route to becoming tax-evasion and money-laundering centres more than a century later.

The third lesson was that economic warfare for short-term gain can have unpredictable long-term consequences. Cutting off British industrial exports encouraged Europe to strive for greater self-sufficiency, while Britain was forced to depend more on the colonial market. That pattern persisted for the next century and a half.[22] In fact Britain's very success in seizing overseas territory, at the expense of its European rivals, was a central factor creating the jealousies that eventually exploded in the Great War of 1914–18.

Britannia Waives the Rules

For the century that followed the Napoleonic Wars, economic warfare played a relatively minor role in strategic thinking. With the exception of the American Civil War, conflicts among the Western powers were usually short-lived. War was left to professionals and financed out of tax revenues rather than by plunder — except in the colonial arena where the rules, if any existed, were quite different. It was recognized that failure to make a distinction between civil and military sectors could cause resentment among the victimized population, strengthening the position of the target government. Furthermore, failure to differentiate neutral and belligerent commerce could lead to neutrals siding with the enemy. The consensus became that non-combatants and their property should be spared, to whatever degree possible, war's side effects. Aptly capturing the new ethos, during the Crimean War pitting Russian armies against French, British and Turkish ones, Imperial Russia faithfully paid interest to its British and French bondholders.

At the same time, the world economy was evolving in ways that argued against economic warfare. Throughout the West, the cult of the "free market" triumphed, albeit briefly.[23] Rapid economic growth, industrialization and the opening of seemingly inexhaustible resource frontiers in the Americas, Africa and Australasia appeared to render embargoes less feasible. With the spread of the gold standard, most countries left printing paper money to private sector institutions: a state could no longer directly attack the credit of a rival by counterfeiting its paper. With the development of specialized ships of war, the practice of issuing letters of marque to armed merchantmen died out. In 1856 the great powers (except the United States) formally agreed to abolish privateering. In the future only naval vessels were permitted to seize merchant ships and even in those cases the property of neutrals had to be respected.[24]

The one major exception to this nineteenth-century trend towards separating military and economic issues came during the American Civil War. In 1861 the Union reacted to secession by the Confederate states with the Anaconda Plan, an attempt to squeeze the South with a naval blockade. The logic appeared impeccable. The South depended heavily on exports of cotton to finance imports of manufactured goods and of industrial equipment. Despite a drive to self-sufficiency, throughout the war the South relied on foreign sources for 60 per cent of its arms, 75 per cent of its gunpowder and at least a third of its lead, plus most of the cloth to make uniforms. Those supplies should have been grievously threatened by the South's inability to export cotton to pay the bills. Although the South had 3,500 miles of coastline, few of its ports could handle large amounts of modern shipping, and the most important of them, New Orleans, was soon captured by Union forces. Even worse, Britain, origin of most of the South's industrial equipment, arms and ships, and the main market for cotton, agreed officially to respect the Union's right under international law to impose an embargo.

The reality, though, was rather different. Private firms, in Britain, Mexico, Canada and even the North, found the profits of embargo-busting too rich to ignore. The price of Southern cotton, much superior to that from alternative sources like Egypt, shot up, making each cargo that did get through the blockade all the more valuable. Suppliers also accepted "cotton bonds," pledges of future delivery of cotton, in payment for merchandise. Cuba, the Bahamas and Bermuda bulged with goods bound for the Confederacy. British shipyards began turning out a new class of steamer, exceptionally fast and with a shallow draft ideal for dodging in and out of inlets and secondary harbours. Vessels approached the coast at night, blew off steam underwater, doused lights, muffled paddle wheels, flew the Union flag, burned relatively smokeless anthracite coal and fired off signal rockets of the type used by the Union Navy to send blockading ships searching in the wrong direction. Union efforts were further hampered by the fact that, once a blockade runner was spotted, the first Union Navy vessel to see it sometimes set off in pursuit without informing others to avoid having to share any prize money. At times blockade runners would jettison part of their cargo in the expectation that a pursuing Union warship would stop to pick up the merchandise — the remaining part was usually worth enough to still turn a profit. Goods also poured in across the Texas-Mexico border, although that was a route businessmen preferred to avoid — more than a hundred years before the modern drug boom, Mexican officials had already achieved notoriety for imposing *la mordida* as their price for allowing contraband to cross the frontier. Certainly not least important of the sources of supply were high-ranking Union officers who ran their own blockade-busting operations, or Northern businessmen, many of them political cronies of President Lincoln, who were licensed by the U.S. government to buy Southern cotton to keep Northern mills from collapsing. In the final analysis, it was shortages of manpower, not of strategic goods, that led to the collapse of the Confederate war effort.[25]

Apart from the period of the U.S. Civil War throughout the nineteenth-century, the commitment to protect private wealth from military conflict grew steadily. It culminated in the London Declaration in 1909 in which the British defined their policy in the event of another war. Blockades had to be formally declared, well publicized and limited to enemy or enemy-occupied ports. There had to be a genuine effort to enforce a blockade or else other states were free to ignore it without risking reprisals. And commodities were given a three-fold classification. Those purely military could be seized on sight. Those of mixed civil and military use could be taken only if bound for a "fortified" area. Those purely civil were immune no matter their destination.[26]

The London Declaration was never ratified by enough countries to become international law and was attacked at home as a surrender of Britain's strongest military asset, its capacity to bring an enemy's trade to a standstill. Nonetheless, when World War I began, there was an effort to respect the declaration's spirit. The British put almost all industrial raw materials on the non-contraband list. However, the major principles were soon abandoned.

When war broke out, it was expected to be short. When it bogged down into a military stalemate, the real struggle shifted to the economic front. Rationing and conscription muddied the distinction between civil and military sectors. While Germany at first accepted the principle that the property of citizens of occupied countries be respected, soon it began seizing cash in Belgian and French banks, grabbing inventories of raw materials and organizing conscript labour.[27] And as the war dragged on, the search for strategic commodities began shaping the very course of conflict.

Late in 1916 the Germans made a lunge for Romania. The prospect of Germany capturing the oil fields prompted the British to plug the wells, dynamite the derricks, smash the pipelines and set the equipment ablaze. Altogether seventy refineries and 800,000 tons of crude oil went up in smoke.[28] A year and a half later, the Allies followed up by denying Germany the oil fields of Azerbaijan. A precedent was set. In future conflicts, controlling fuel supplies became perhaps the single most important strategic objective.

In international trade, too, all pretence at differentiating civilian and military goods, or defending the rights of neutrals to trade, was abandoned. Goods could still move past the British blockade into Scandinavia, especially Sweden, then overland to Germany. Despite Britain putting guilty Swedish firms on a blacklist, the traffic via Sweden probably saved Germany from starvation. So much money could be made by selling to Germany that Scandinavia itself experienced food shortages. Similarly, petroleum from Britain (and, later, the United States) was sent to Scandinavia only once the consignee submitted guarantees that it would not resell to Germany. Since the guarantees were not legally binding in Sweden, some merchants signed whatever was required and carried on business as usual. Others were more circumspect. Ships arranged to be "intercepted" by the Germans en route. Others took fuel into Copenhagen's Free Harbour, then, while officials conveniently looked elsewhere, permitted German tankers to pull alongside.[29]

If the principle of protecting the civilian economy from the effects of war had to be tossed aside, so too was financial laissez-faire. Tight exchange controls prevented the free export and import of capital, gold convertibility was abandoned, and governments took over the business of printing money. This shift to government paper made officially sponsored counterfeiting once again feasible. The British used one of London's leading producers of stock and bond certificates to duplicate German and Austrian stamps and to counterfeit German imperial notes.[30] Far from the Crimean War notion of nuancing military conflict with financial peace, belligerent states froze foreign interest payments and impounded assets of enemy citizens. That precluded their use in the war effort and created a pool of capital that could be used for future "reparations" payments.

The Spoilers

The custom of imposing tribute payments on conquered populations has come down from antiquity. Under modern international law, it is supposed to be subject to certain limits. A conquering power can demand compensation for the costs of occupation. And reparations can be required as a condition of peace. During the Franco-Prussian War, for example, Prussia levied tribute payments on French cities, and after it, France had to make heavy reparations as well as ceding territory. However, the reparations imposed on Germany after World War I were enormous. They seemed to represent a regression to the ancient philosophy of making the total burden of war fall on the conquered areas and of stripping the defeated power of the means of exacting revenge.

Germany had to cede most of its ship tonnage and replace that lost by the Allied powers. It had to give up all its overseas possessions. It lost a third of its coal and iron while much of its future production from that remaining had to go in reparations. Its industrial heartland came under de facto French occupation. Scientific discoveries putting Germany at the forefront of the modern chemical industry were seized and turned over to leading firms in the United States. On top came a $20-billion direct bill for damages.[31] In another lesson that modern advocates of sanctions have still not fully absorbed, it was the economic and political aftershocks of the reparations bill that allowed the Nazi party to commence its ascent to political power.

All these departures from nineteenth-century rules had far-reaching consequences. Modern machinery for covertly moving money and hiding wealth that had evolved in response to wartime asset freezes and heavy taxes developed rapidly in the 1920s and 1930s. Europe was swept by financial, political and social instability, much of it the result of the arbitrary redrawing of the post-war map. For the wealthy, the desire to evade income taxes and exchange controls, to escape possible expropriation and to protect their money against inflation and depreciation sent them searching for neutral havens. During the post-war decades, Liechtenstein created its subsequently notorious instant-corporation manufacturing business, and it imposed severe penalties for revealing information about companies. Switzerland passed its infamous bank secrecy laws. Its bankers started employing professional couriers to ferry clients' cash and valuables past neighbouring countries' Customs officials and developed techniques such as anonymous mail drops. Across Europe the use of nominees and front companies came into vogue.[32]

German citizens, facing hyperinflation and growing political violence, were among the most enthusiastic users of these techniques. But so too were German businesses, encouraged by the government in its efforts to evade reparations and find the means to covertly reconstruct and rearm. German firms created secret subsidiaries elsewhere in Europe to manufacture forbidden products. They sent technical staff and machinery to affiliates in the Netherlands, Switzerland and Sweden, and exchanged patents with non-affiliated firms so that needs could be met away from the prying eyes of Armistice monitors. By one 1933 estimate, 80 per cent of Liechtenstein corporations were German-owned.[33]

In the meantime the world was struggling to avoid another conflict. After World War I, the League of Nations was established with a mandate to use collective economic warfare for the first time as deterrent to, rather than a complementary tool of, armed aggression. The theory was that states had become so economically interdependent that commercial sanctions alone, imposed not as a hostile act by one state against another, but as a moral one by the international community, might suffice to force dramatic political changes.[34] When Italy invaded Ethiopia in 1935, the League responded with a general embargo. It was an abject failure. The United States, not a member, ignored it; evasion was widespread; Italian vulnerability was overestimated; and strategic commodities like oil were exempted.[35]

Then came the World War II. This time unrestricted economic warfare was the rule from the start. No one made any serious effort to separate civil and military sectors, to distinguish types of goods or to economically differentiate belligerent and neutral parties. The core idea pushed by the Allies was that Nazi aggression was a crime against humanity. Therefore there was no inherent right of neutral parties to conduct commercial and financial relations with the aggressor.

Chapter 2

THE FORTUNES OF WAR

By 1918 the British blockade had brought Germany to the brink of starvation, while economic hardship caused massive walkouts in crucial industries and nearly set off a Communist revolution. Hence, at the start of World War II, the British were convinced that the best prospect for defeating Germany lay in a similar economic squeeze. It was a view Hitler shared. Germany was self-sufficient in only one strategic commodity, coal. And Germany had failed to stockpile strategic materials before 1939 because it had not expected the real contest to begin for several years. Seemingly over-stretched by its military success, Germany appeared an easy economic target.[1] However, appearances were deceiving.

Tricks of the Trade
The Allies declared a long list of contraband and intercepted cargoes on the high seas. They forced neutral ships to show certificates of clearing issued by Allied consuls to get service in Allied-controlled ports, which included virtually all the important ones. They blacklisted individuals and corporations who dealt with the enemy. Those on the lists might have their assets seized unless they cooperated in espionage and sabotage. The Allies also attempted to prevent Germany from gaining access to foreign-held assets of German citizens and firms or those of citizens and corporations of conquered countries. Their objectives were to hamper the Axis war effort and, later, to preclude any

fleeing Nazi leader from creating a nest egg to support a comfortable retirement or plot a comeback.[2]

There were also new techniques. Some, like strategic bombing, were dramatic. From the mid-1930s the British rearmament drive was centred on the long distance bomber, designed for use against targets that, in the nineteenth century, would have been regarded as civilian.[3] The prevailing theory was that because the Nazi war economy was strained to the utmost, it was particularly vulnerable.[4]

Some techniques were more subtle. To deny Germany tin, the Allies pre-emptively bought the ore. That set off an illegal tin rush in Portugal and Spain. When Portugal tried to stop wildcat mining, the Allies simply raised prices further and stationed agents inside Spain to collect tin smuggled over the border. Similarly, most of Europe's wolfram, the source of tungsten to harden steel, came from Portugal where many deposits were worked clandestinely by peasants. During the "wolfram war," Allied agents outbid German ones and paid in hard currency, permitting illegal miners to evade taxes, royalties and exchange controls.[5]

One particularly important target was industrial diamonds, used in cutting tools and in the jewelled bearings of guidance systems. Germany was estimated to require at least 500,000 carats annually, and Japan only a little less. Yet all the mines were in British-run (African) or American-influenced (South American) territory. From the early stages of the war, the British tightened controls in Africa. Later, American agents in South America undertook a three-stage offensive. They tried to outbid the Germans on the black market, planted agents inside smuggling rings, and, by monitoring black market prices for sudden run-ups, sometimes detected the imminent arrival of German buyers. If the price hikes coincided with the docking of a particular ship, the Allies could target more precisely which vessel to search, reducing tensions with neutral countries.[6]

In addition, the Allies covertly bought up and closed down, or sabotaged, mines and factories in neutral countries. They hijacked or blocked shipments bound for occupied Europe. Oil was a particularly important target. While Germany and the U.S.S.R. were at peace, the U.S.S.R. shipped oil to Germany. Therefore the British concocted a plan (never carried out) to sabotage the Azerbaijan oil fields.[7] Agents from Britain's Special Operations Executive (SOE) also attempted to buy all available means of transportation to stop deliveries of Romanian oil. Then, since most shipments went by tanker-barge along the Danube, they plotted with pro-Allied officials to dynamite the cliffs where the river narrowed, a scheme aborted when Romania swung to the Axis side.[8] When the Allies were unable to persuade Turkey to stop selling to

Germany chrome ore used for special steel alloys, agents of the American Office of Strategic Services (OSS) blew up the Balkan railway bridges over which most of the ore flowed.[9]

Inside German occupied areas, *agents provocateurs* incited work stoppages and wage demands. Others played the black market to discredit occupation currency, encourage hoarding and provoke capital flight. Yet others engaged in sabotage. Some planted bombs. Others infiltrated engineering sections of factories to falsify blueprints or induce malfunctions whose origins would be almost impossible to detect. Workers were encouraged to toss pebbles into machine works or lose essential components. And French Resistance members were given a special grease that wore down machine parts it was supposed to lubricate.[10]

On another front, the OSS secured or imitated official paper and inks, then recruited commercial artists from major magazines to fake passports and identity cards, to turn out imitation Axis stamps for mailing propaganda, and to counterfeit money. In the Philippines, the Japanese had introduced a special occupation currency, difficult to reproduce and, to better control population movements, stamped as valid only in specified areas. Yet the OSS duplicated it almost perfectly, determined the amounts for each district from pre-war census data, then distributed it to Filipino underground forces. However, in the European theatre it was decided that counterfeiting would be ineffective — too much was required; Germany could reissue too quickly; and in the tightly controlled German economy, almost every commodity was rationed. Instead, the OSS agents reproduced ration coupons to dump on German cities. Unlike so many others, these patriotic fabricators never lacked for cigarettes — whenever they ran out, they also counterfeited the required British and American ration coupons.[11]

The decision not to fake German currency meant that the Allies had to find alternative means to pay spies and finance guerrilla activity. People fleeing Germany and the occupied areas, friendly "neutral" diplomats, or American businessmen working in neutral countries sometimes came out with bundles of Axis or occupation currency, which the OSS could buy at a big discount. Some was reputedly obtained from the Istituto per le Opere di Religione, the Vatican bank. From its very establishment in early 1942, the IOR operated a huge, worldwide currency black market. Hundreds of priests, among the only people who could freely cross borders and ceasefire lines, acted as couriers to ferry hundreds of millions of dollars in cash, valuables and securities, for a fee, to safety outside occupied Europe.[12] Some currency, too, was acquired when resistance groups hijacked German payrolls. But perhaps the most important source was Tangiers.

Perched on the northwesterly tip of Africa facing Gibraltar, Tangiers had been an international city run by a consortium of Western powers since 1906. Politically detached from Morocco and surrounded by mountains, it was a virtual island without resources except geographic location, entrepreneurial energy and legal infrastructure. It hosted an instant corporation business, bank secrecy laws, a port zone where everything was welcome except drugs and guns, and a tax policy that made it cheaper to import luxuries like jewellery and silk (mainly for "international trade") than basic consumer goods (mainly for the local market). During the war those facilities attracted rich refugees, fortune hunters, criminals on the fly and agents of thirty-five countries sent there to monitor representatives of the other thirty-four.[13] Its freewheeling money market was an ideal source of exotic currencies. Anti-German resistors, corrupt German officials and refugees smuggled German or occupation currencies to Switzerland, where speculators purchased them cheaply, then sent them to Tangiers to be resold to, among others, the British SOE station chief. Because paying for the notes with British currency would attract attention and risk having the British currency fall into German hands, he ran his own black market, importing gemstones, expensive watches, even high-valued postage stamps to sell to criminals, smugglers or rich refugees for Moroccan francs. The francs were traded for Axis currencies, and those currencies were spirited into Europe to pay spies and finance sabotage operations.[14]

Beating the Blockade

All these tricks actually did little to diminish Germany's capacity to wage war. Although asset freezes worked against normal bank deposits and registered securities, they were much less effective when the money was held in cash or bearer securities, when third parties were used as cut-outs (fronts) or when the stuff was protected by bank secrecy laws. Prominent American and British firms continued to traffic with Germany. They worked behind the screen of corporate and bank secrecy laws, nominees and third-country subsidiaries, often set up for the purpose by Swiss lawyers.[15] While Standard Oil company officers worked with the OSS to watch Axis oil shipments and help plan a never-carried-out sabotage of the Romanian wells,[16] American fuel, much of it supplied by Standard Oil, flowed to Germany through Switzerland, Tangiers and the Canary Islands. While Ford, along with the rest of the American auto industry, grew fat on war orders at home, its plants in central Europe continued to make trucks for the German army. The communications conglomerate ITT not only had its Polish factories exempted from seizure by Germany, it used its good relations with Germany to win compensation when its

Romanian facilities were nationalized. ITT also assisted with communications and control systems for German fighter-bombers.[17] In Yugoslavia, whose regime collaborated with the Axis, the British-owned Trepca zinc and lead mines sold 70 per cent of their output to the government, which bartered it to Germany for arms, while the metallurgical complex associated with the mines produced batteries that powered German U-boats.[18] None of this was evidence of some pro-Nazi plot.[19] Rather, it was proof that big business intended to remain big and business-like, come war or peace.

Similarly, agreements between the Allies and neutrals to restrict exports to Germany to pre-war levels were thwarted by smuggling or under-declaring. In Sweden, the Allies recruited a shipping clerk in the main manufacturer of ball-bearings for German industry. Before the Swedish police arrested him for industrial espionage, he provided enough information for the Allies to shame Sweden into respecting the agreement. But by then Germany was making its own.[20]

The Allied blockade was particularly porous for items like platinum, medicines and quartz crystals (for radios). Such items were small in relation to their value even in normal times, and times were far from normal. Platinum from South America, for example, previously sold for $1,000 per kilogram. In Lisbon, one of Germany's main points of supply, it could fetch $11,000. While in London industrial diamonds sold for about $1 per carat, in Tangiers, the price ranged from $30 to $60. The result was thriving smuggling rings, some run by German agents, some purely entrepreneurial. The most important source of black market diamonds was the Belgian Congo. The security system at the main mines leaked, and illegal alluvial mining was almost impossible to police. U.S. agents posing as illegal buyers found diamonds moving in Red Cross parcels from the Congo to Belgium and thence to Germany.[21] Stolen diamonds were also turned over to Allied pilots who flew them to Casablanca, Cairo or Khartoum and passed them to Axis-linked diamond dealers.[22]

New tricks like pre-emptive buying were also of limited efficacy. By driving up prices, pre-emption may have encouraged suppliers to put more on the market, sometimes making it easier for Germany to obtain materials. More drastic measures such as blowing up railway bridges in the Balkans made a great deal of noise. But the Germans simply switched to trucks until Turkey, finally accepting that Germany was going to lose, bowed to Allied pressure and ceased selling Germany chrome ore.[23]

Even the much-touted strategic bombing campaign had no serious impact until late in the game when Germany was already in retreat, and then the damage was mainly from bombing synthetic oil plants. The campaign was premised on the myth that the German war economy was a tightly wrought machine humming with Teutonic efficiency. In fact, in the early years of the war, it was run by the Nazi top brass as a set of inefficient, non-cooperating and sometimes redundant industrial fiefdoms with enough excess capacity that the destruction had little effect on total production. With the high-profile bombing of ball-bearing and aircraft factories, it was later demonstrated that the campaign cost the Allies more in bombs, aircraft and manpower than it hurt the Germans in lost output. Nor was the aim very impressive. While the U.S. Air Force touted the accuracy of its bomb sights, the most vulnerable target often turned out to be open fields, coupled, in the last months of the war, with phoney airfields and wooden model planes. When cities like Hamburg were hit, there was huge damage to banks, shops, stores and residential areas, while factories and shipyards were largely unscathed. The Allied rationalization for heavy damage to areas with no military significance was that the pain would turn the population against the regime. The result was more often that people rendered unemployed in the civil sector reported angry and highly motivated for work in the arms factories.[24]

Therefore, despite Allied efforts, the Germans kept their war machine operational. Of all the German countermeasures, none was as important as measures to exploit the conquered territories. Although German invasions across Europe were undertaken primarily for political and strategic reasons, once seized, territories became economic assets.

Stockpiles of arms, foodstuffs, strategic materials and machine tools were the first target.[25] But the Germans went much further. Certain classes of citizens deemed enemies of the German people were targeted for expropriation: Freemasons, Communists, any Frenchman who had acquired wealth in the former German province of Alsace, and especially Jews. In the early days of Nazi rule in Germany, there had been boycotts in which customers of Jewish-owned businesses were harassed and business premises vandalized to drive the businesses to bankruptcy or into forced sale. These tactics were later replaced by outright confiscation. Initially, the expropriated resources were used to reward the party faithful. Later they were employed to bolster the war effort or to simply ease shortages by allowing ordinary citizens to bid openly for Jewish property. The same occurred in each country overrun by Germany. In Poland the confiscations were particularly ruthless. Strategic industries were taken for the war effort, general businesses were transferred to German owners, and personal property was confiscated for resale, often at very low prices, to German functionaries.[26]

In each occupied area Germany raised the value of the Reichsmark against local money from 30 to 200 per cent to purchase commodities at huge discounts.

It also required that their governments pay the costs of occupation. By setting the supposed cost well above actual, Germany could collect a surplus for local purchases.[27]

Those areas within the German sphere of influence could be paid in worthless IOUs or in Reichsmarks held in blocked accounts inside Germany. But trade with outside parties required gold and foreign exchange. The great majority came from the cash, foreign security holdings and gold reserves of the central banks of Czechoslovakia, Austria, the Netherlands, Belgium, Italy and Poland. Cash and bearer securities could be used directly, as could gold coins, which have no serial numbers. But the origins of gold bars had to be disguised. They were re-smelted, then shipped, accompanied by false documents, to neutral countries to be either sold directly or pledged for trade credits. In one clever laundering technique, some would be re-smelted and sold in Switzerland for Swiss francs. The francs would be transferred to another country — Argentina, for example — and converted into local currency — in Argentina's case, peso deposits. The pesos would be used to buy clean gold that could be safely pledged for trade credits or sold to finance imports from countries more inclined to ask awkward questions than was "neutral" Switzerland. To the loot of the central banks was added that from concentration camp victims. These assets were sold inside Germany or smelted at home or abroad. Part of the proceeds went to the Reichsbank, but much was used to set up a social security fund for families of SS members.[28]

All these methods of expropriating resources were applied across Nazi-held Europe. But nowhere were expectations so high, or the economic motive for war so impelling, as in the U.S.S.R. which was expected to fill the two most dangerous gaps in Germany's economic arsenal. The German leadership hoped that the black soil of the Ukraine would end an incipient food crisis.[29] Similarly with oil. In the early years, Germany depended on Romania (whose wells were rapidly depleting) or on imports from the U.S.S.R. Stalin had assumed that German reliance on Soviet oil would maintain peace between the two countries. But in 1941 Hitler invaded the U.S.S.R. precisely to seize the oil resources of Azerbaijan and to eliminate the threat a nearby Soviet military presence posed to the Romanian fields. The Red Army responded by stripping the areas it was vacating of food, materials and even factories and equipment, and it sabotaged the Azerbaijani oil wells. Before Germany could reactivate them, military disaster struck at Stalingrad, the city commanding the Soviet Union's oil supply route.[30] Germany's failure to capture Soviet oil resources forced it to step up efforts to promote self-sufficiency. That, in turn, had a direct impact on Germany's concentration camp policy.

Because Germany was much less successful than Britain or France in the nineteenth-century scramble for overseas raw materials, it had long been at the forefront of the search for synthetic alternatives. Ammonia, essential for both explosives and fertilizers, for decades had been derived largely from nitrate rock. Germany, with no indigenous mines, had to import it from Chile, the world's largest producer. During World War I, the Allies cut off the supply. However, German scientists had created a method of capturing atmospheric nitrogen and combining it with hydrogen from coal to make ammonia. In the decades following World War I, the German lead in synthetic-organic chemistry increased. During World War II, Germany relied heavily on products as varied as synthetic textiles and artificial rubber. And, after the loss of Soviet oil, nearly half its fuel came from coal liquefaction.

Given its strategic significance, the chemical industry was one of the most cosseted sectors in the Third Reich. It had priority of access to slave labour from the concentration camps. In fact, the industry's demands were one of the most important factors in shifting the function of concentration camps from internment facilities into slave labour establishments where millions died.[31]

The military reverses in the U.S.S.R. also had a more general impact. The less that could be plundered in the east, the more Germany had to take from central and western Europe. Apart from appropriating stockpiles of food, minerals and war materials, seizing personal wealth, purchasing goods at rigged exchange rates and running slave labour camps, Germany also tried to mitigate the adverse economic impact of the war on its own citizens through a clever use of the black markets in the conquered areas.[32]

The Home Front
During the war, governments on both sides pre-empted resources for the military, imposed price controls and rationing, and raised enormous amounts of money, mainly by taxation. With proliferating regulations and rapidly rising taxes, some black market activity was inevitable. But if too extensive, it could pose a double threat. The spectacle of war profiteers lining their pockets while the population was forced to pay heavy taxes and reduce consumption could undermine public support for the war effort. And illegal profits tended to be hoarded or frittered away in luxury consumption instead of reinvested in productive activity or appropriated by the government through taxes or war bond sales.[33]

In North America speculators diverted controlled commodities (especially meat and sugar) into black market sales, either by theft from warehouses or, more commonly, by the producer delivering the poorest quality to the state and selling the best illegally. Sellers evaded price controls by demanding extra cash payments, falsifying invoices to exaggerate quantity, or substituting inferior quality for goods specified in transaction records. Landlords violated rent controls by demanding cash on the side or by insisting on payment for fictitious services; recalcitrant tenants were illegally evicted.[34] Ration coupons, particularly for gasoline, were traded on the black market, stolen or counterfeited.[35]

Although there were many fakes, the real action was in genuine coupons. Gangs obtained new ones by break-ins or bust-outs at issuing offices, and used ones by having members take jobs in incineration firms. Because U.S. coupons bore serial numbers and were valid for limited periods, they had to be unloaded quickly. Wholesalers resold to retailers. Retailers peddled either directly to motorists or to gasoline station owners. If coupons were counterfeit, the gas station owners resold to trusted customers, insisting that they be negotiated at some other gas station. If genuine, they used them to sell fuel at a premium to motorists who had exhausted their own coupon book. There were efforts to combat the traffic by using special papers and inks to make counterfeiting more difficult, establishing shorter periods of validity and even making gas station owners responsible for outdated or counterfeit coupons. However, a partnership embracing drivers, retailers, fences, receivers and thieves, as well as employees of issuing offices and incineration stations, was impossible to eradicate.[36]

Similarly in Britain, ration coupons were counterfeited and stolen, subsidized commodities were smuggled to neutral Ireland where free-market prices were higher, and goods were diverted to the domestic black market. Some illicitly traded goods came from legitimate producers, urban and rural, who were happy to make extra, tax-free sales. Some came from underground manufacturing establishments. Some came from theft. Before the war most thefts were directed at homes of the well-to-do, and the most coveted objects were luxury items like jewellery. During the war, the action shifted to stealing basic goods from docks, trains and trucks, from businesses and warehouses and from military bases. Furthermore, the initiative was reversed. Instead of fences passively receiving what the thieves took, the fences gauged the marketplace, then placed orders.[37]

Still, black markets were little more than a nuisance to the Allies.[38] In the United States, enormous productivity gains meant that few suffered serious shortages, while in Britain, far more straitened, the same workers who bought cheap black market cigarettes were also putting in twelve-hour shifts at munitions factories for 37 shillings (about $10) a week. It was quite different in occupied Europe, where black markets were often a means of survival. In Poland, for example, the rations permitted each citizen were so low that only the black market kept the country alive, despite vigorous German efforts to stamp it out.[39]

In France black markets were particularly sophisticated. Each individual was issued a personal ration card for food, then given coupons for specific commodities. Some people travelled to the countryside to barter with farmers who hid part of their harvest or illegally slaughtered animals. Since farmers with family in the cities were permitted to send occasional parcels as gifts, a remarkable number of urban dwellers discovered rural relatives. People in cities would purchase what was supposed to be a gift, then resell it, sometimes from their homes, sometimes through shopkeepers who took a cut. Middlemen dealing in wholesale lots paid bribes to German soldiers and French police to facilitate passage, then resold them to markets or to restaurants whose clientele prominently included collaborators or black market *nouveaux riches*. Some deals were for cash, though bartering for other commodities might be preferable since currency could not be legally spent without ration coupons.[40]

Ration coupons of every type were stolen, counterfeited and illegally traded. Sometimes they were also ignored. If a customer offered the official price and a ration coupon, the commodity might be unavailable because the shopkeeper was holding back in hopes of a better deal. If a customer had no ration coupon, the price went up substantially. The transaction might be settled in cash or in coveted items like cigarettes. But the quickest service and the best quality went to a customer who could pay in gold. Although strictly forbidden, there was a large black market dealing in gold (and foreign exchange) catering to speculators, black marketeers looking for a safe place to park their earnings, refugees seeking the means to flee, Germans trying to set up retirement accounts in Switzerland, and various spies and Resistance fighters seeking the means to ply their professions.

Black markets could never have existed so extensively or for so long without official complicity. Some black enterprises like luxury restaurants worked only by pay-offs to German functionaries. Others operated with the collaboration of German agents. For example, when Germany had to purchase minerals from Spain and Spain refused to accept blocked credits, German agents told France's underground abattoirs they could stay in business only if they sold to the Germans for a low price animal hides that were then bartered to Spain at double what the Germans had paid.[41]

Most remarkable, though, were underground enterprises that existed because the Germans had created them.[42] While the French police were busy tracking and closing black markets catering to French citizens, the Paris headquarters of the Abwehr, German military intelligence, was advertising its willingness to buy all manner of goods at well above the legal price. Merchants and businesses wishing to sell were given *laisser-passers* to prevent French police from interfering. As further security, they were assigned pseudonyms to protect their identity even from German purchasing officers. On delivery, the seller was paid in bundles of newly minted French francs, making the transaction anonymous and tax free. Then the Abwehr office shipped the goods to Germany, commission and expenses on top, to help alleviate civilian shortages.

For a time it was fairly open. But the threat of reprisals made cooperating merchants demand better cover. Drug dealers, thieves and counterfeiters were released from prison to act as covert intermediaries and to staff a special police force charged with protecting the controlled black market, detecting Allied spies and ferreting out hoards of gold and foreign exchange.[43] The operation should have been expensive, for it relied on German officials outbidding normal black market buyers. But under the terms of the 1940 armistice, the government of France, like that of other conquered countries, had agreed to pay expenses of occupation, which the Germans inflated. France made payments into special accounts at the Bank of France from which the Germans could draw what they needed, including the freshly minted French notes required for black market operations.

In 1943 the Abwehr officially closed down its black market operation. Stocks were largely exhausted, and the building of a defensive wall along the Atlantic absorbed French resources that might have been diverted to Germany. Nonetheless while it had existed, the system of officially sponsored black markets had created and rewarded a collaborator class, provided financial support for intelligence operations and helped offset the impact of Allied economic warfare on German public morale.

There's No Life Like It

Germany struck back with a few tricks of its own. Its equivalent of the strategic bombing missions and naval blockade was submarine warfare against the supply line running to Britain from North America. It also infiltrated a few agents to conduct sabotage. It was (greatly exaggerated) fear of Axis agents that led the U.S. Office of Naval Intelligence to make its notorious deal with jailed Mafia boss Charles "Lucky" Luciano. In return for the promise of early release, he instructed his mobsters who ran the waterfront unions to conduct counter-intelligence in the main U.S. ports.[44] However, Germany's potentially most destructive act was Operation Bernhard, a plan to manufacture $630 million worth of British notes along with a smaller supply of American $100 bills. If the plan had been successful, Germany could have used the fake cash to make covert purchases and maintain intelligence networks abroad. And it might have dealt a severe blow to the British financial system.

The SS first approached the Reichsbank whose officials, though content to launder concentration camp loot, balked at the notion of aiding and abetting currency counterfeiting. The SS then pored over Interpol lists of known counterfeiters and scoured concentration camps for people able to forge currency (along with passports, ID cards and ration coupons). The key to the U.S. numbering system was located through a sophisticated piece of espionage — a German agent in Sweden located a copy of *Life* magazine containing an article about U.S. bank note manufacturing.[45] Apart from the poorest, which were junked, the notes were classified into three categories. Of the best quality notes, some were used to pay spies in enemy territory. Others were taken by diplomatic courier to neutral countries like Switzerland, Sweden, Spain and Portugal. There they were turned over to hotel managers and bank officers who could mix counterfeit with real bills and gradually put them into circulation. The next best notes were destined for collaborators in occupied areas who preferred British notes to occupation currency. Others of that class were exchanged in North Africa for gold, diamonds, dollars and Swiss francs. Yet others were used to buy weapons from Italian army units prior to their surrender to the Allies, or from peasants in Yugoslavia who had retrieved arms dropped for the Partisans. The third category was to be dumped by plane on Britain. This never happened, partly because the British took the precaution of withdrawing and reissuing the affected denominations, and partly because, before the final stage could be implemented, the Germans had lost mastery of the skies and were shortly in retreat.[46]

As the Allied soldiers marched through the liberated areas, most kept their eyes open for remnants of the Axis forces. But some focused their attention on opportunities for business. Sometimes they had local partners. In Sicily, for example, as an offshoot of the Luciano deal, Mafia bosses who had been driven into the hills by Mussolini provided assistance in the Allied landings, for which they were rewarded by being parachuted in as mayors of liberated towns. That permitted a consortium of Mafiosi, U.S. army quartermasters and gun-toting Franciscan priests already busy in loan-sharking, real estate speculation, extortion, looting and pornography, to team up to corner the black markets.[47]

Elsewhere in Europe, soldiers further liberated the liberated areas of cash, carpets, jewels and works of art the Nazis had not already grabbed. Some of the foreign currency stolen by the Germans was retrieved by the Allied forces, then promptly re-stolen by American troops — at least $30 million in cash, gold and jewels vanished along with $400 million in bearer bonds.[48] Automobiles were another favourite prize. A British division, ordered to make a fast advance into Germany, proceeded only at a snail's pace — the cars heisted en route made the column double its normal length. Some goods were "requisitioned" by the army and converted into the private property of officers or resold. Of 5,000 German automobiles taken by the Americans nominally for military use, only 1,500 were officially accounted for.[49]

One step up the entrepreneurial scale was trafficking in army-issue whisky, chocolate and especially cigarettes, which were not only desirable in their own right but functioned as a parallel currency for buying everything from sex to Persian carpets. Along with them was a traffic in material stolen from the army — medical supplies like opium, penicillin and radium; arms and ammunition; and especially gasoline.

Every other major armed force in the world used diesel fuel for its armoured vehicles. But, reflecting the power of the American automobile industry, U.S. tanks ran on gasoline. Two disparate sets of interests were delighted. One was German anti-tank gunners, since gasoline, unlike diesel fuel, explodes on impact. The second was European owners of passenger cars, starved of fuel for years. At one point General Patton's lunge towards the German border stopped not because of German resistance but because his tanks had run out of gas. In desperation, his troops impersonated supply officers of other units to divert their fuel, hijacked tanker trucks and railway cars, commandeered the gasoline that supply trucks needed to get back to base, and put aloft spy planes to scan the Allied sector for any fuel that could be seized. However, they apparently failed to call on the GI-run black market on the Champs Elysées to which gasoline by the trainload was being diverted.[50]

It was one thing to earn black market money, yet another to get the proceeds home. Valuables like gold and jewels could be sent back directly, but most profits went back through official army channels. To try to limit illegal activity, the army printed a special money supposedly valueless outside the war zone. However, soldiers had the right to exchange this occupation currency for dollar-denominated money orders to send home. Hence soldiers played the black market, earned profits in occupation currency and shipped them home through official channels. Even better, since the United States lent to the Soviet army the plates on which occupation currency was printed to permit it to pay its own troops, and since the Soviet troops did not have the right to reconvert occupation currency into Soviet roubles, American soldiers could sell valuables at high prices to Soviet soldiers and add the profits to their own home-bound hordes.[51] The obvious countermeasure — limiting the number of dollars each soldier could have to the equivalent of his pay in occupation currency — was not introduced until 1946. By then the "overdraft"— the amount by which dollars sent home exceeded total pay allocated to the American armies abroad — totalled $531 million, an astronomical sum at then-current prices.[52]

Beyond the Call of Duty

Despite British optimism at the start of the conflict, the German war machine was little inconvenienced by Allied economic warfare. The strategic bombing, for example, might have been, on balance, a net benefit to the Germans. It forced them to tighten their hitherto slack and corrupt economic organization so that output and productivity, notably in plants making aircraft and armoured vehicles, were higher after the bombing than before. In the final analysis, the amount of industrial plant knocked out was probably less than that built during the war, so that Germany finished the war with a net increase.[53] However, that was not the official line. The U.S. Air Force, then part of the army, exaggerated the impact of strategic bombing, using its "success" to secure the status of an independent service. In so doing, it set the stage for the emergence in the post-war world of a military-industrial complex in which a high-tech, high-cost, independent air force was the centrepiece.

Similar results followed from the clandestine component of the economic war. Its main significance had been to make American agents legends in their own minds. Veterans of the OSS, whose very creation had been largely the result of hysteria over non-existent German saboteurs, used hyped-up tales of their wartime exploits, augmented by a bogus Red Scare, to get permanent status in 1947 in the shape of the Central Intelligence Agency. The romance of covert economic action became an essential part of the agency's culture, and therefore of its operations agenda in the Cold War years that followed.[54]

Like all economic wars, that pursued during World War II left behind talent and infrastructure that were easily adapted to peacetime pursuits. In 1947 the U.S. Secret Service, the branch of the Treasury that tracks counterfeiting, discovered excellent reproductions of U.S. currency notes and American Express travellers' cheques arriving in the United States in the hands of refugees. Tracing the bills back to Paris, it uncovered an operation run not by ex-Gestapo agents taking their revenge, but by former French Resistance fighters. Production was handled by a Paris printer previously jailed by the Vichy government for making false ration coupons and identification cards for the Partisans, and distribution was run by a Marseilles gangster pardoned because of anti-German activities.[55]

Probably nowhere was this post-war transformation of patriotic duplicity into pure profiteering clearer than in Tangiers, wartime Europe's main centre of intrigue. During the late 1940s, many countries were struggling with reconstruction; inflation and depreciation were constant threats; the spectre of renewed war, this time against the U.S.S.R., spooked financial markets; governments desperately strove to conserve foreign exchange by tight controls on the export of hard currency and the import of gold; and states sought to replenish their treasuries by heavy taxes on commodities like tobacco, alcohol and luxury goods. Tangiers was ideally situated to help out. It offered secret accounts, anonymous shell companies and a freewheeling exchange market whose institutions ranged from staid name-brand banks to street peddlers shouting the latest rates. And its warehouses were stuffed with little gold bars, American cigarettes, Scotch whisky, Swiss watches and silk stockings for which the privileged class in Europe was pining. It boasted a population of former soldiers, sailors and spies from both sides eager to use their skills in private business. And its entrepreneurs helped Europe beat swords into cargo carriers, eagerly purchasing war-surplus small planes and speedboats. For a 100 per cent mark-up, the smuggling boats hauled cargoes of items like cigarettes to points just outside the territorial waters of France, Spain or Italy. For a 200 per cent mark-up, they guaranteed home delivery. And the banks flew gold over in decommissioned fighter planes, then parachuted it to certain isolated areas, such as those where the French Resistance used to take refuge during the war.

True, the days of Tangiers were numbered. As the late 1940s passed into the early 1950s, world gold markets reopened, taxes came down and exchange controls eased. Moreover, the city's unique legal position was about to end. Morocco, breaking free of its status as a French protectorate, insisted on formally reintegrating Tangiers. A grand exodus began. Far from reducing the world's supply of financial havens and free-trade zones, it had the opposite effect. From Tangiers, the French bankers left for Monaco or Switzerland, the British for the Caribbean and Gibraltar, the Americans for Panama. All these would-be rivals received a major infusion of talent just when the Cold War was about to cause an explosion of the world's population of sanctions-busters in need of their services.

Part Two

THE EAGLE AND THE BEAR

Chapter 3

SEEING RED

Because nuclear weapons had made direct military confrontation (almost) unthinkable, the Cold War was fought mainly on the economic front.[1] It should have been no contest. During World War II, the U.S. economy expanded enormously, while the Soviet one suffered appalling devastation. The United States gave western Europe massive reconstruction aid, while the U.S.S.R. received none. Although Soviet recovery was initially assisted by stripping capital equipment from occupied Germany and forcibly recruiting Axis technical personnel, as the Cold War intensified, the U.S.S.R. switched to building up rather than tearing down its satellites. Despite these disadvantages, in the early 1960s Premier Nikita Khrushchev could sum up Soviet economic progress with the bald prediction "We will bury you!"[2] It was a boast the United States was determined to render hollow.

Beans, Bullets and Trouser-Buttons

Economic warfare was not new to the history of Soviet-Western relations. The Bolshevik revolution had sparked a Western economic blockade as well as military intervention. Although relations were partially normalized by the early 1920s, residual suspicions and demands for the repayment of Czarist debts meant some sanctions remained. In fact, the threat they posed gave

Stalin a powerful argument for abandoning Lenin's market-oriented reforms in favour of "socialism in one country." One consequence of that policy was the vicious collectivization of agriculture, accompanied by the extermination of the well-to-do peasant class. And ongoing economic hostility may have been a factor prompting Stalin's first major retaliatory act.

Between the wars almost every major counterfeiting scheme was denounced as a Communist plot. Once, at least, it may have been true. When the U.S.S.R. unveiled its first Five Year Plan in 1928, it was desperately short of foreign exchange. Its position was exacerbated the next year by the collapse of the world price of wheat, its main export. Bypassing intelligence professionals who would (and later did) object, Stalin authorized counterfeiting of the U.S. $100 bill. The results were excellent copies, printed on paper that virtually duplicated the official material. To further bolster credibility, Stalin's agents bought a small private bank in Berlin from which notes would be shipped to other banks. Bogus bills eventually surfaced in China, Mexico, Cuba and Europe, though only by accident in the United States. When the Soviet intelligence services, worried that the scheme would attract attention to their networks and undermine the credibility of European Communist parties, bent Stalin's ear, the scheme was aborted, the remaining notes supposedly recalled to Moscow for destruction. But U.S. Communist Party members arranged to smuggle some out of Berlin to the United States to buy tear gas, stink bombs and small arms for strikes and demonstrations. They persuaded Chicago gangsters that the bills were genuine. When the crooks were caught passing them, the Communist Party members had to flee the ire of both U.S. Treasury agents and outraged mobsters.[3]

From 1941 to 1945, the Allies pumped supplies into the U.S.S.R. But after the fall of Nazi Germany, the anti-Soviet economic war resumed. The first weapon deployed was a denial of strategic goods and military technologies.[4] At first informal, the ban became systematic in 1949 with the creation of CoCom, the Coordinating Committee for Multilateral Export Controls, on which sat representatives of NATO countries plus Japan. From the start, CoCom ran up against a critical division of opinion — whether its prohibited list was intended to hamper general Soviet progress, as the United States wished, or simply to stop critical materials from reaching the Soviet military, as western Europe wanted. Nor was there agreement on what constituted a strategic good. Khrushchev pointed out that even buttons on a soldier's pants could be "strategic" since, without them, the soldier would be forced to use his hands to hold up his trousers in battle. The actual list therefore reflected bargaining based on national self-interest rather than consensus based on Soviet military needs.

Thus, the United States wanted rubber included, while the United Kingdom, whose Southeast Asian colonies were big rubber exporters, was opposed. The list, too, varied according to the self-interest of particular firms. The United States created an advisory committee to keep the selection of technologies requiring export licences up to date. According to protests by one electronics firm, a representative of its main competitor sat on that committee and deliberately steered the choice of what to restrict onto its rival's products.[5]

An early target on which all agreed was industrial diamonds. It looked easy. At least 80 per cent of the world's rough diamonds were controlled by South Africa's De Beers Consolidated, which refused to sell directly to the U.S.S.R. and threatened to cut off manufacturers who supplied diamond tools. Predictably the effect was to revive smuggling. Industrial diamonds were spirited from Zaire and Sierra Leone to Beirut, thence by diplomatic pouch to Moscow. The U.S.S.R. also pushed self-sufficiency, leading to both discovery of the world's greatest natural diamond deposits and important breakthroughs in synthesizing them. By the late 1950s, the world market saw the beginnings of a flood of Siberian gems that forced De Beers to shift from embargo to quiet cooperation. From then on, diamonds were one of the U.S.S.R.'s most dependable sources of foreign exchange. Further turning the tables, Soviet advances in artificial diamonds were so impressive, the trade was periodically shaken by rumours the U.S.S.R. was working through De Beers to market synthetic-gem-quality stones as natural ones.[6]

Like the diamond embargo, the effort to deny the U.S.S.R. strategic technologies was largely self-defeating. Placing something on the CoCom list immediately telegraphed to the U.S.S.R., always behind in the technology race, just what the West considered actually or potentially of military significance, helping the U.S.S.R. redirect scarce resources. In theory the list was secret. But the U.S.S.R. could deduce what was on it just by observing what the West refused to license. Furthermore, the embargo was politically advantageous to Stalin. Because the Soviet government favoured military production over civilian, living standards remained stagnant. But any resulting political discontent could be kept under control by pointing to the need for the U.S.S.R. to defend itself against Western economic aggression. Similarly, CoCom's existence gave Stalin a tool to pressure eastern Europe into closer integration with the U.S.S.R. The U.S.-led embargo therefore helped manufacture an iron curtain out of a wire-mesh fence.[7] Yet, in regard to impeding Soviet military development, CoCom was a failure. The U.S.S.R. produced its first atomic bomb within four years of the United States, and its first hydrogen bomb within months, and it put satellites into orbit years before.

By the late 1960s when détente was in the air, the restrictions were raising serious questions even in the United States. In 1969, the U.S. Export Administration Act heralded precisely the shift European allies had been demanding, from broadly based economic denial to narrowly defined strategic restriction. In 1972, the United States and the U.S.S.R. signed a treaty that, among other things, permitted the U.S.S.R. to buy American cutting-edge technology. However the pendulum was soon swinging back. The principal figure pressing for renewed restrictions was Democratic senator Henry "Scoop" Jackson. But working behind the scenes was his chief aide, Richard Perle, soon to be known in liberal circles as the ultra-right's Prince of Darkness. The result was a 1974 amendment linking Soviet benefits under the treaty to its willingness to grant exit visas to Soviet Jews. The U.S.S.R. reacted by cancelling the treaty. Détente started to die along with it. And it was buried in 1979 when Soviet forces marched into Afghanistan.

Claiming that the Red Army used trucks from an automotive complex built with American aid, President Jimmy Carter suspended all licences for restricted technologies and denied the U.S.S.R. access to American grain when Soviet harvests were poor. When Ronald Reagan came to power the next year, the economic war shifted into high gear.

The Reagan administration was obsessed with the perceived foreign policy reverses of the 1970s. Across Africa, country after country struck a Marxist pose. Victory of the North in the Vietnam War was followed by Communist takeovers in Laos and Cambodia. Pro-American regimes were ousted as far apart as Iran and Nicaragua. The Reagan administration was particularly traumatized by the Soviet military presence in Afghanistan. The first direct expansion of Soviet-controlled territory since World War II, it was also, according to Republican foreign policy experts who apparently had trouble reading maps or history books, the first step of the evil empire's march towards the oil fields of the Middle East.

Although the Reagan administration quickly surrendered to the farm lobby by abandoning the grain embargo, it moved ahead on other fronts. Leading the anti-Soviet economic campaign was the new director of Central Intelligence, William Casey. He was a veteran of both the U.S. Board of Economic Warfare and the OSS, where he had been responsible for recruiting neutral businessmen as informants, spreading false information on Allied strength and supervising counterfeiting of ID cards and ration coupons.[8] While his boosters claimed that his World War II job had been "pinpointing Hitler's economic jugular," it would be more accurate to say that Casey had struck a minor nerve in Der Führer's posterior. But he was ready to try again. Under his guidance, the United States attempted to undermine Soviet standing in world financial markets, attacked its export earnings, tightened the techno- logical blockade, forced the U.S.S.R. into a military spending contest and bled it through a proxy war in Afghanistan. The objective became, as Ronald Reagan himself stated in language Richard Nixon would have understood, to make the U.S.S.R. "yell 'uncle' or starve."9

Playing Russian Roulette with the Polish Debt
The U.S.S.R. seemed immune to direct financial attack. It possessed huge gold reserves and immense natural resource wealth. And it participated very little in international capital markets. Furthermore, to preclude an asset freeze, early in the Cold War it had moved its foreign exchange reserves out of American banks and deposited them in dollar accounts in London. Any attack on Soviet finances would have to proceed by indirect means.

Although the Polish economy had expanded rapidly in the 1970s, in 1980, burdened under $25 billion of foreign debt, it entered a crisis. National in- come plummeted while investment came to a standstill.10 That economic crisis was superimposed on a society with especially deep political schisms.

Unlike its counterparts in Czechoslovakia or Hungary, the Polish Com- munist Party had very weak indigenous roots, for it was largely the creation of the occupying Red Army. The U.S.S.R. had also imposed its central plan- ning model on a country whose economic structure was quite different. Agri- culture, Poland's largest sector, remained almost entirely in private hands. As well, although the Polish government followed the Soviet model in espousing official atheism, the population remained devoutly Catholic. By happy co- incidence, a Polish pope stood ready to cooperate with U.S. initiatives intended to return Poland jointly to international capitalism and the Catholic Church.11

Fed by secret subsidies from the Vatican and encouraged by agents of the anti–Communist American Federation of Labor, the dissident "Solidarity" trade union movement took root. Although it began in the shipyards, the main dan- ger it posed to the regime came from the coal mines. Poland relied heavily on coal for its own energy, bartered it to the U.S.S.R. for oil, and sold large amounts to western Europe. Protracted labour problems in the mines would have been financially catastrophic.

The Polish government responded, first by declaring martial law and later, faced with more labour agitation, by banning the union movement. That ban provided the United States with a pretext to stop further government-to- government credits, embargo exports of essential equipment and cease supply- ing grain, including animal feed essential for the agricultural sector. The next year the United States cancelled the low-tariff status enjoyed by Polish goods. Working through trading companies and religious foundations, the CIA funnelled money to the opposition.[12] The goal was to whip up enough labour unrest to bring Poland to the brink of default, or beyond. The ensuing panic would either force the Soviet Union into an expensive bailout or cause banks to refuse further loans to Communist countries. Even if Poland did manage to get its finances in order, it could do so only at the expense of another dramatic decrease in living standards. That would further discredit the regime in a country in which Communist governments had already been tossed out, twice, by popular unrest and food riots.

The United States also attacked Soviet exports. The significant point of weakness was not in manufactured goods. Thanks in part to how Stalin had reacted to CoCom, most Soviet manufacturered goods were sold in eastern Europe. The U.S.S.R. did sell plenty of strategic minerals and gold to the West, but they were too important to embargo. However, oil and natural gas were by far the U.S.S.R.'s leading foreign exchange earners. According to Republican cant, the reason revolutions in the 1970s carried off so many pro-Western governments was not the anger of desperate populations ruled by corrupt tyrants propped up by former colonial powers. Rather, it was because high petroleum prices permitted Moscow to buy allegiance and finance anti-Western agitation. Each one-dollar increase in the world price of oil meant another billion dollars of annual Soviet earnings. To this oil wealth would soon be added the returns from a massive pipeline project designed to haul Siberian natural gas to western Europe.

Apart from banning the sale of U.S. drilling equipment, there was little the U.S. government could do to slow down Soviet oil production or to prevent others from buying the oil — though a world petroleum glut and low prices in the 1980s did abundant damage. However, the gas pipeline was more directly vulnerable. The United States not only forbade employment of American equipment in construction of the pipeline, but, to the outrage of its European allies, banned the use all materials manufactured abroad by subsidiaries of U.S. corporations or by firms incorporating American technology in their products. The pipeline was eventually built, but with a single rather than the planned double strand, several years behind schedule and at a cost many billions of dollars above original estimates.[13]

Computer Cops and Techno-Robbers
The administration also tightened the techno-squeeze. It created a new agency in the Pentagon to screen foreign purchases of U.S. technology and launched

Operation Exodus, an undercover Customs investigation to stop covert sales. Appointed to protect America's high-tech military advantage was an interesting duo.

On Reagan's election, Richard Perle, the man who had helped Senator "Scoop" Jackson destroy détente, assumed the post of assistant secretary of defence for international security policy, the government's top techno-cop. Making the Pentagon's export control office one of Washington's most feared bureaucracies, Perle blocked hundreds of export permits, bullied civil servants and antagonized business executives.[14] He had help. The post of deputy assistant went to Stephen Bryen, also a former Senate aide, confirmed in his new public position of combating techno-espionage despite an FBI file in which the investigating agent had recommended convening a grand jury to determine if Bryen should be indicted for passing American military secrets to Israel.[15]

The new restrictions came at an awkward time. Although Soviet technology lagged, sometimes seriously, behind that of the United States, until the microelectronics revolution it was still possible for the U.S.S.R. to subscribe to its traditional doctrine that sheer numbers of planes, tanks and troops infused with "proletarian internationalism" would triumph over fancy avionics, space-age armour and fewer soldiers fed on an ideological diet of *Rambo* reruns and *Playboy* centrefolds. However, sophisticated communication, surveillance and targeting techniques, along with computer-controlled machine tools in military production, posed a new threat. That techno-menace was compounded by the Strategic Defense Initiative ("Star Wars").

The theory behind Star Wars came from Serbian engineering genius Nikola Tesla, who, in the early years of the century, had laid the foundations for modern electrical technology, including making possible the harnessing of Niagara Falls.[16] But the man who personified the initiative was Edward Teller, a strident anti-Communist, self-proclaimed father of the American H-bomb, unrepentant advocate of mass construction of air-raid shelters, enemy of nuclear test-ban treaties and apologist for the commercial nuclear industry. In 1980 two events gave Teller a new lease on scientific and political life. One was his conception of the idea of the X-ray laser. It would take the power of a hydrogen bomb, convert it to beams of intense radioactivity and flash it across space to knock out up to 100,000 separate targets. The second event was the victory of Ronald Reagan, mesmerized by Teller's vision of an anti-missile system that would eliminate the threat of Soviet retaliation and therefore remove the ultimate impediment to an American first-strike.[17]

From the start Star Wars was as much a defence industry boondoggle as it was serious science. The main driving force was the faith that, as Reagan's national security advisor put it, "when you turned the labs and companies loose with $26 billion, you knew they would come up with something." But the mere possibility it might work put the Soviet Union in a difficult position. If it chose to follow the U.S. lead, the project would be a huge economic drain.[18] Although enormous flaws eventually forced the abandonment of the X-ray laser — and Teller's subsequent idea of filling the skies with small projectiles that could smash Soviet rockets with kinetic energy — the Star Wars project did help frighten the U.S.S.R. into proposing to an uninterested Reagan administration sweeping arms reduction agreements, and into stepping up efforts to close the techno-gap.[19]

The U.S.S.R. had several options. The simplest were to have agents steal technology or buy it from professional thieves. During the go-go years of Silicon Valley, fierce competition made industrial espionage, burglaries, armed robberies, hijackings and insider diversions common. Drifting around the periphery were brokers who would buy surplus, scrap, used or stolen parts. They were not fussy about their customers.[20] With the Soviet Union willing to pay 250 to 400 per cent above market value, crooked brokers could order supposedly for delivery to a NATO country. Then they would have freight forwarding firms route the material to ghost companies elsewhere and take delivery in neutral places like Switzerland, Sweden or Austria. From there the equipment could be freely exported to China, eastern Europe or the U.S.S.R.[21] Thus, when Hughes Aircraft received an order for about $650,000 worth of electronic testing equipment, the largest from a private customer in the company's history, it tipped off U.S. Customs, who broke a ring of California businessmen that had diverted electronic materials supposedly worth "hundreds of millions of dollars."[22] (As with drug busts, the actual number is not important so long as it is large enough to catch mass-media attention.)

Alternatively, high-tech material could be purchased without licence as if for domestic use, then exported under false documentation. For several years, an American businessman filed Customs forms reporting television sets, video cassette recorders, typewriters and air-conditioners bound for Switzerland. In fact the cargoes were computers, oscilloscopes and a satellite image-processing system for customers like the Geological Institute of the U.S.S.R., the Soviet Space Institute and Minsk Computer Research Institute. His career as a techno-bandit ended in 1987 when he was arrested by the Royal Canadian Mounted Police while on a fishing trip in the Yukon.[23]

Yet another alternative was to bypass the United States and buy U.S.-style equipment from other CoCom countries whose firms were more concerned with the bottom line than the Iron Curtain. The most dramatic case involved ex-U.S. Navy officer, John Walker, who, in addition to passing to his KGB controllers information permitting the U.S.S.R. to crack U.S. military codes, also provided knowledge of how the United States had become successful in tracking Soviet submarines.[24] The U.S.S.R. then approached Toshiba Machines (51 per cent owned by Toshiba) to purchase special computer-controlled milling machines that it could use to turn out ultra-quiet propellers. It was turned down, so it went to a French firm. One day when Air France did not have sufficient freight to justify its regular cargo lift to Moscow, it diverted the material to Luxembourg for Aeroflot. But Luxembourg Customs opened the crates and alerted the French authorities, who quietly pressed the firm to stop sales.[25] So the U.S.S.R. went back to Toshiba. This time the Japanese firm was determined not to lose the order. By falsifying documents, it was twice granted export licences for the machines. Employees who expressed concern were browbeaten into silence. And when American pressure forced an investigation, the firm burned incriminating evidence.[26]

Toshiba had provided the machines, but, as its executives hastened to note, the computers came from Norway's Konisberg Vaapenfabrikk. From 1974 to 1984 this state-owned arms producer had shipped 140 such computers to the U.S.S.R. and China. Some went directly; others went to other NATO countries to be incorporated in their own products before being sent on.[27] Facing bankruptcy and already embroiled in another arms export scandal, Konisberg Vaapenfabrikk hardly needed the extra attention. When fingered, it tried to deflect attention by pointing in turn to firms in West Germany, Italy, Britain and France, all shipping prohibited technology to the U.S.S.R.[28]

Although Konisberg Vaapenfabrikk was suspended from Pentagon contracting and eventually collapsed, the real heat was put on the Japanese company. Navy spokesmen claimed that Soviet advances would cost $10 to $30 billion to counter. Consumer boycotts of Toshiba products were organized across the United States. Congressmen from constituencies whose industries faced serious Japanese competition took the heaven-sent photo-op to stand in front of the Capitol building smashing Toshiba VCRs with sledgehammers. And the U.S. Senate by 95–2 voted to ban Toshiba products for two years. The potentially devastating embargo was averted only by a slick public relations campaign and administration opposition.[29]

In the background, whispers were heard that maybe the fuss was a little overblown, that the military damage was actually minor because the United States still held a huge lead in the submarine race, that the navy was exaggerating the problem to bolster the case for a massive increase in spending for new subs and sub hunters, that the United States hoped to use the scandal to squeeze military base concessions from Japan, that the United States was really reacting to the rapid expansion of perfectly legal Japanese exports to the U.S.S.R. of which the United States was envious, and that U.S. legislators were pandering to anti-Japanese sentiment for short-term political gain. Not least, the United States stood accused of using the fiasco to implicitly threaten other countries with sanctions.[30]

Down with the Ship

In theory, CoCom restrictions applied only to NATO members. But the president could deny access to American technology to any companies and countries not cooperating with U.S. policy. That power permitted the United States to squeeze from Sweden, for example, a promise to try to end diversion of U.S. technology through Swedish free-trade zones, the assurance of better protection against pirating U.S. technology inside Sweden, an effort to deny the U.S.S.R. Swedish high-tech developments, and even a commitment to allow the United States to funnel through Sweden aid to Solidarity in Poland.[31]

Yet another country to come under heavy U.S. pressure was Austria. Neutral by the 1954 treaty under which Soviet forces withdrew, it was geographically tied to both western and eastern Europe, a position bolstered by historic links with Hungary, Czechoslovakia and Slovenia. Political leaders, at least of the long-ruling Socialist Party, were intent on defending Austrian neutrality and, along with it, the position of the Austrian brokers handling West–East transactions behind the cover of the world's tightest bank secrecy laws. They were certainly eager to defend Udo Proksch, long suspected but never proven kingpin of Austrian-based techno-banditry.[32]

Proksch's rise to power started in 1972 when the widow of the last family proprietor of Vienna's Konditorei Demel, former pastry makers to the Hapsburg court, decided to sell the firm. One person decidedly not an acceptable buyer was a hard-drinking, gun-toting, womanizing former pig farmer. However, with the joint assistance of a Swiss shell company and a pliable countess he was bedding, Proksch disguised his identity long enough to secure control of the imperial institution and the status it conveyed. He celebrated his coup by emptying his gun into a portrait of Emperor Franz Josef that graced the café's entrance. That same year Proksch created a secret society called Club 45, inspired by Italy's soon-to-be notorious Propagada Due (P-2) Masonic lodge. Among its roster of 300 members were top business people and senior political figures, along with the head of the Vienna police and the chief of Austrian intelligence, all linked to the Socialist Party. Two Club 45 members were soon elevated to the posts of minister of defence and minister of the interior. Aided by his political and intelligence connections and his portfolio of passports, Proksch soon had a reputation as one of Austria's most enterprising arms traffickers. And he will go down in the annals of gun-running as the architect of one of the most ingenious methods of getting around export restrictions.

Proksch arranged with a group of Club 45 friends to set up a non-profit cultural organization ostensibly to enhance Austrian national pride with a war museum. Since "airplanes are works of art," the minister of defence approved the gift of jet fighters and helicopters, along with tanks, rocket launchers, trucks and jeeps, parachutes, boats and even an American army fire-fighting unit. The only thing missing was the museum that Proksch and friends were too busy to build. When ten years later someone got around to asking what had become of the equipment, Proksch replied that it had been stolen. The thieves were so sophisticated that the fire-fighting unit ended up in Cairo and some of the trucks and jeeps in the hands of Polisario, the Western Sahara guerrilla movement Proksch supported. The rest of the usable material was scattered across the Middle East.[33]

Proksch's other enterprises also flourished. Back in the 1960s, before his entry into either the pastry- or political deal-making businesses, he had established a general trading, construction and technology development company to specialize in trade with the East bloc. When two of his associates, both skilled scientists and engineers, decided to set up on their own, Proksch invested money in their new firm, Sacher Technik Wien, whose purpose, defined on its office-door plaque, was to act as a "Laboratory for Technical Development." It kept one eye on what was happening in Silicon Valley and the other on East Germany's high-tech requirements. In 1973 the partners bought 50 per cent control of an American company whose founder specialized in reverse-engineering microchips, then quietly selling the blueprints. Among the happy customers was a front company in Vienna run by East German intelligence.

The relationship blossomed until 1978, when their American partner was arrested and charged with stealing data and parts from Intel. Police searches turned up the business cards of the partner's Austrian associates and the phone number of Udo Proksch's Konditorei Demel. Even before the case got to trial, a defector from East German intelligence arrived in West Germany with a list of agents and contacts, including, reputedly, the owners of the Sacher Technik Wien and their financial sponsor. But all the principals denied guilt. The American authorities traced stolen data to a shell company in Switzerland, whose business address was also that of the Swiss lawyer who had put together many of Proksch's deals. There was no way to follow the technology beyond Switzerland, or to prove that any participant had been involved in actually passing the material to East bloc interests. Proksch was never charged in the case, but another part of his past caught up with him.[34]

Proksch had incorporated in Switzerland a company called Zapata SA and used it to secure control of an abandoned coal mine. Machinery was removed, de-rusted and repainted, then marked Zapata SA. Various parts were shipped back and forth between Switzerland, Italy and Austria to cloud their origins, assisted by collaborators in Austrian Customs who altered the description on official documents. Proksch ordered from American manufacturers of uranium ore processing plants technical information about their machinery, which was copied onto documents bearing Zapata's corporate name and logo. Next, he set up a Hong Kong company whose officers signed a "contract" with Zapata to purchase uranium ore processing machinery. Some money was churned back and forth between different parties to simulate down payments. Meanwhile, Proksch's friends in the Defence Department allowed him to sign up for a military explosives course and to walk off with some samples apparently to continue his studies at home. Then it was time to charter a ship to carry the "plant" to the purchaser.

In 1977 everything was ready. An Austrian Customs official cleared the material. So did a Chinese cargo inspector sent out by the Hong Kong consignee to ensure that the shipment conformed to specifications. Then it was off by train to the Italian port of Chiaggio to stow the cargo with great ceremony aboard the M.S. *Lucona*. Proksch invited high-ranking Austrian officials to watch the loading of the crates, though not, of course, to witness 250 kilograms of high explosives artfully distributed on both sides of the vessel. Somewhere in the Indian Ocean, the freighter had an accident, sinking with six of its twelve crew members in waters more than 4,000 metres deep. Still, all was not lost. Knowing the dangers of the high seas, Proksch had insured the cargo for about $30 million.

Before paying up, the insurance company requested proof of purchase of the declared cargo. Proksch contacted a friend in the freight forwarding business in Switzerland who had experience complying with unusual requests for documentation — the friend had formerly run an Austrian oil trading company that specialized in moving Arab oil to Israel and busting the oil embargo against South Africa. Thanks to friends in Bulgarian intelligence, Proksch was able to produce delivery receipts and invoices attesting to the purchase of Bulgarian equipment. But the officious insurance company insisted that, based on the weight, product and price declarations, most of the declared parts could not have belonged to a uranium processing plant, and those that might have had been grossly over-insured. The firm refused to pay. Proksch launched a lawsuit.

From 1977 to 1985 the case bounced in and out of court. Over that period, too, prodded on by families of the deceased *Lucona* crew members, the police launched several criminal investigations, all blocked at the top. Meanwhile, the insurance company hired a private detective. In the course of the investigation, the Customs agent who had officiated at the send-off admitted he had been paid to fill out false documents, and died of a heart attack; the papers identifying the material as uranium processing equipment were shown to have been forged; and the "Chinese inspector" representing the Hong Kong consignee turned out to be a Japanese pastry chef specializing in cream rolls for Konditorei Demel. While these revelations were coming to light, the engineer who designed the *Lucona* fell off a highway bridge just before he was due to give evidence.

Nearly a decade after the sinking, criminal charges were finally laid against Proksch. The minister of defence who had covered for Proksch committed suicide. Proksch fled to the Philippines, from where he sent a telegram excusing his inability to return for interrogation by his need for urgent medical attention. The nature of that treatment became clearer a year later when he was recognized and arrested in the Vienna airport despite plastic surgery, a beard and a complexion darkened by make-up. Condemned to life imprisonment, at least Proksch finished his career without a charge of techno-banditry to blight his record.

Boot Failure?

Techno-banditry worked both ways. Although American intelligence operated purchasing rings in Bulgaria, East Germany, Czechoslovakia, Poland and Hungary, the most persistent efforts to track Soviet advances (and then devise countermeasures) were in Romania, with high-level assistance. For ten years, two brothers of dictator Nicolae Ceausescu ran a smuggling ring, passed on advanced Soviet equipment to U.S. military intelligence, and stuffed their pay into a Swiss bank account.[35] However, because it was the United States that was pushing outward the frontiers of the microelectronics revolution, American efforts to secure access to the other side's technology paled compared to those attempted by the Soviet Union, which the United States tried hard to counter.

Yet it was never clear that the 1980s' restrictions on technology transfers were any more successful than those of the 1950s and 1960s. There was the same dissension within NATO.[36] It was made worse in 1985 when the United States gave its Customs the power to investigate techno-banditry anywhere in the world, raising the spectre of American bounty hunting and juridical kidnapping already typical of global drug investigations. Nor was there a firm consensus at home. The Commerce Department, whose role was to promote American trade, found itself frequently at loggerheads with the Pentagon techno-cops whose zeal bordered on the absurd. In 1987, the Scottish subsidiary of a New Jersey firm was accused of shipping to the U.S.S.R. special carbon material used in the nose cones of missiles. The material had been placed on the restricted list even though it was basically the same stuff used to line coffee pots.[37]

Nor was it clear that the assumptions underlying the policy were based on rational deliberation. CoCom had been conceived in an atmosphere of near paranoia over Communist expansionism in the late 1940s, when the Soviet Union was still flat on its back. Similarly in the 1980s, the U.S. government saw techno-spies under its bed at night.[38] The policy, too, took for granted that it was feasible for the United States, in a world in which micro-technology was rapidly spreading, to police the manufacturing world. By the mid-1980s it was possible to find a non-U.S. source for almost everything on the prohibited list. Accordingly, much Soviet activity in acquiring technology had shifted to the Pacific rim, particularly to Hong Kong and Singapore. And by the end of the decade, computers with the power of those that designed U.S. nuclear weapons in the 1950s could be picked up in Radio Shack.[39]

At the same time, the U.S. government was caught in a contradiction. It promoted U.S. military sales all over the world, yet the spread of such weapons automatically carried the danger that they could fall into Soviet hands and be reverse-engineered. Furthermore, modern arms deals almost always carry agreements to offset part of the cost. Those arrangements often require that the seller agree to do part of the manufacturing on site. The more places using the technology, the greater the problem of industrial espionage, theft and technological diversion.

Even if it had been possible to completely staunch the flow, it was never proven that the U.S. lead in military technology could be seriously damaged by Soviet techno-smuggling. Technology is not a magic bullet. Successful application of advanced U.S. micro-electronics had as its prerequisite the infrastructure capable of using it and a military machine with enough flexibility to incorporate the results.

On the other hand, it was distinctly possible that, as in the early days of CoCom, the real agenda had little to do with Soviet military advances. Contrary to the rationalization offered to NATO allies, adversely affected neutral countries and afflicted companies, the actual reason for the techno-squeeze was more likely to disrupt the U.S.S.R.'s overall economic progress and attack the general standard of living of its population, with any negative consequences to military preparedness simply a bonus.

Chapter 4

WAR GAMES

Most of the devices by which the United States attempted to undermine Soviet economic strength — financial sanctions, export cut-offs and strategic import embargoes — were standard tools of economic warfare. However, the U.S.–U.S.S.R. contest was unique in one important respect: the most powerful weapon the United States employed was an arms race. It was based on a sound assessment of the difference in how the two economies would respond. In the U.S.S.R., military expenditures undertaken in a desperate attempt to keep pace with the United States imposed an increasingly heavy burden, while in the United States, defence spending was regarded as one of the keys to national prosperity.

Taking Root

For centuries the arms industry was economically marginal even in states involved in frequent conflict. Armies consisted of a small core of professionals to which were added, when the need arose, corps of peasants forcibly inducted and sent out to die for their lord's right to life, liberty and happy pursuit of more property. Gifted amateurs might dabble in military technology — Leonardo da Vinci may have taken as much pride in designing the world's first breech-loading cannon as in creating the *Mona Lisa*. But there was no science devoted strictly to military pursuits. With the exception of cannons, cast mainly in state-owned factories, an army's needs were met by civilian industries to which the state was merely one more customer, and probably slower than most to pay the bills. Typically the first to profit from war were those who fought it, financiers who lent to belligerent states came second, and makers of weapons ranked a poor third.[1]

Transformation came in four stages. First was the combined impact of Napoleon and the Industrial Revolution. Napoleon's "citizen-army" was premised on mass mobilization of freemen, while industrialization permitted large-scale armies to equip each soldier with the same type of weapon, using identical ammunition and interchangeable parts. By the middle of the nineteenth century, there were large, specialized arms manufacturers in Britain, France, Prussia, Russia, Japan and especially the United States. During the American Civil War, military demands for the first time took precedence over civilian. The war also set the standards of commercial morality still typical of the military supply business.

Contractors bribed officials to accept shoddy clothing, leaky tents and adulterated food. Because war disrupted normal commerce producing a glut of ships, owners connived with purchasing agents to unload their most antiquated or dangerous vessels onto the government. While his father, a powerful merchant banker, was selling U.S. war bonds in England, a young J.P. Morgan plotted to help the U.S. government dispose of the proceeds. When the government sold off a batch of defective carbines, Morgan, through a frontman, bought them for $3.50 each, "sold" them for $12 to another frontman to hide their origins, then talked a Union general into taking them, supposedly in perfect condition, for $22 a piece. After soldiers began blowing off their thumbs, the government cancelled the rest of the order and refused to pay. Morgan successfully sued for recovery of most of what was owing.[2]

Military contracting was only temporarily a path to quick riches. After the war, the business elite found that plundering the public purse in railroad jobs was far more lucrative than selling underweight measures of mouldy grain to a rapidly shrinking army. There was still the occasional chance to work "captains of industry" magic on weapons contracts. In 1893, steel tycoon Andrew Carnegie was accused by the Secretary of the Navy of conspiring to hide critical flaws in armour plate.[3] But by and large big business concentrated on civilian pursuits.

Carnegie's brief brush with the government in a naval contract signalled the second stage in the emergence of a modern weapons industry. For hundreds of years, the main difference between a merchant vessel and a naval ship had been who paid the sailors rather than in what they sailed. Towards the end of the nineteenth century, a race to build armoured warships began. Unlike small arms, such ships required sophisticated engineering, a long lead time and heavy overhead investment. The loss of the sale of even one unit could spell disaster. The result was a fundamental transformation of the relationship between supplier and customer. Instead of standing at arm's length, albeit with one party's hand sometimes dipping into the other's back pocket, in the future the two sides would be riveted together as surely as the steel plates on a dreadnought's hull.[4]

Not coincidentally, the twentieth century's first great arms scandals involved warships. In 1909 Britain's Coventry Ordnance secured a contract to build eight cruisers by publishing false figures about the size of the German fleet. In 1913 Germany's Alfred Krupp was discovered to be paying naval officers for information on secret government projects. The next year Britain's Vickers was caught attempting to bribe Japanese officials to win a battleship order. The affair culminated in the jailing of a corrupt Japanese admiral and the resignation of the Japanese prime minister.[5]

Such an environment produced the legendary Sir Basil Zaharoff. Born in the most notorious red-light district of Istanbul, he began business, appropriately enough, as a brothel tout before learning the art of black market money exchange. In a portent of his career as an arms salesman, he may also have been a member of a fire brigade notorious for setting blazes, then extorting bribes to put them out. Later in London, he cheated a business associate of £7,000, coaxed his rich wife to buy him out of trouble, then ran off to Cyprus to get into the arms trade. His big break came when he concocted a story about close relations with British intelligence and was appointed Balkans representative of Sweden's most important weapons firm just when the local political temperature was reaching the boiling point.

Zaharoff bribed purchasing officials and entertained politicians, sometimes in brothels and casinos in which he held a financial interest. He would sell to one side, tell the other what its enemy had acquired, then, after securing offsetting orders, return to the first to sell more. He played on ethnic tensions — for example, impressing on Greek politicians the need to rearm to "win back Asia Minor" from the Turks. He would claim for his merchandise the virtues of rival products. And he was among the first to realize the importance of persuading banks to lend for arms purchases, something they avoided in the past. Not least, during World War I, while he weighed in for Britain and France, his central European factories fulfilled their contractual requirements to the other side.[6]

During World War I the heaviest expenditures were for infantry and artillery. Therefore after the war, most industries easily shifted back to the civilian market for canned and preserved foods, synthetic textiles, automobiles, electrical products, and industrial and agricultural chemicals. Du Pont, for example, which accounted for 40 per cent of the shells fired by the Allied side, collected enough war booty in the form of German patents for synthetic chemical processes that it never again depended on the military for its prosperity. However, the previous mass involvement of industrialists in the war effort had a permanent effect on the relations of weapons producers and governments. The principle was established that, in a national emergency, governments were justified in handing out contracts without the nuisance of competitive bidding.

The next two decades were difficult for those firms still in the arms business. Revelations of pay-offs, extortion, bid-rigging, shoddy manufacturing, sabotage of rival's products and trading with the enemy put the industry under a moral cloud. Meanwhile, government orders shrank, and competition for what remained was vicious. Bribes became essential, not to help the buyer decide between alternative suppliers, but to convince officials they needed any product at all. Anticipating the spirit of the Cold War, in the 1930s the Romanian agent of Czechoslovakia's huge Skoda arms works was caught not only evading taxes, bribing officials and engaging in industrial espionage, but also fabricating evidence of a planned Soviet invasion.

The problem was that wars were episodic, enemies came and went, and resources committed to the military were seen as lost to the civilian economy. Ivory-tower economists of the inter-war era expounded before wide-eyed students about the "trade-off curve" between a society's capacity to manufacture guns and its ability to produce butter, before that commodity, too, acquired a lethal reputation. With the advent of World War II, arms makers could once again pose as distinguished corporate citizens. Still, the expectation was that peace would bring the usual reaction, moral and material. This time the expectation was wrong. The enemy did not go away. Preparation for war became a permanent phenomenon. And the war industry came to be viewed, not as a cost imposed on the civilian economy, but the font of prosperity. The third stage in the evolution of a modern arms industry had begun.

The new doctrine about the positive effects of military expenditure drew its inspiration from a misinterpretation of why Germany recovered from the Great Depression ahead of the rest of Europe. Although the driving force was the Nazi public works program,[7] a more convenient explanation, which also rationalized early French and British military reverses, was that Germany rose to prosperity on the crest of a rearmament wave. After the war the view became widespread that arms spending could stabilize the business cycle, ensure long-term economic growth and permit civilian industries to stay on the technological frontier by reaping spillovers from military research and development.

In reality, military expenditures have always made a poor stabilizer. Large projects require a long lead time and cannot be easily scheduled to start just when the economy is in a down phase. Furthermore, once the commitment is made to a big expenditure flow, it is difficult or impossible to turn it off, so that the spending peak may come after the economy has already started to heat up. The number of jobs typically produced is much less than in similar sized civilian projects, and they are almost always for people with skills that easily find employment elsewhere.[8] Even the technological benefits are exaggerated. While the U.S. military pioneered much modern aerospace, communications and electronics technology, not only could the civilian sector with the same amount of government support have done just as well or better (as Japan showed), but soon the military were borrowing from the civilian sector as much as or more than the other way around.[9]

Nonetheless, military spending had this striking advantage — no one could question it on ideological grounds. Everyone was in favour of "national security." And business interests that would viscerally oppose more spending on health, education and welfare, the obvious alternatives by which the government could stimulate the economy, were delighted to have so much public money lavished on a core part of the industrial structure. Nowhere was this better appreciated than in the post-war United States where the government, haunted by the twin spectres of another Great Depression at home and triumphant Communism abroad, broke with tradition and kept its military machine tooled up.

The Permanent War Contractors' Economy

In the early years of the "permanent war economy," the overall level of military spending, though remaining above previous peacetime norms, still rose during hostilities (like the Korean War) and fell afterwards. Furthermore, throughout the 1950s and 1960s, most money was spent in traditional ways, supplying large, mainly land-based forces with equipment that, while more sophisticated than that of the past, would not have seemed space-age to a World War II veteran. In the 1970s, both those features changed as the arms industry took its fourth, final step towards its modern form.

One of the main factors was Vietnam. To its heavy human and political legacy was added excitement in aerospace, communications and electronics. New equipment for the Pentagon, the world trendsetter, became increasingly complex, stressing science over manpower and war in the air rather than on land. Although the overall U.S. military budget declined sharply following the Vietnam War, for the first time in American history the part allocated to procurement of major weapons systems grew after a major conflict. With a few short setbacks, it kept growing for nearly two decades. While in the pre-World War I era the incestuous relationship between big arms contractors and government had been centred on the shipyards, by the 1970s it had pervaded the high-tech sector of American industry.[10]

The official rationalization seemed unchallengeable. The image of aggressively expansionist Communism had been contrived shortly after World War II, when the Soviet Union had lost 20 million people and most of its heavy industry, by an American intelligence apparatus desperate for a continued reason for existence.[11] It was reinforced with the outbreak of the Korean War. Though there was no direct Soviet involvement, the administration announced a Soviet threat to the American way of life, and Congress voted to treble the military budget over the next three years. Thereafter the idea that the United States was lagging the U.S.S.R. in military spending became a standard theme in presidential campaigns, hammered home with special force whenever the need arose to legitimize especially large increases. After the Korean War, Dwight Eisenhower revealed the "bomber gap." John F. Kennedy in his 1960 campaign discovered a "missile gap" when the United States had hundreds in service and the U.S.S.R. had deployed six. The process reached its apogee in Ronald Reagan's first State of the Union address when he announced a "spending gap" over the previous decade of more than $300 billion.[12]

To make such comparative calculations involving widely different economic systems, the CIA converted rouble figures into dollars at the official (instead of the more accurate black market) rate; used U.S. prices for thousands of items for which it could find no rouble value; imputed to Soviet soldiers, some with rags wrapped around their feet, the same standard of living as U.S. soldiers; included all Soviet military spending (about one-quarter of which was committed to the China theatre), instead of just that involved in confronting NATO; did not factor out of the Soviet numbers things like civil defence, internal security and building infrastructure in remote areas that had no equivalent in the U.S. military budget; and made no adjustment for the U.S.S.R. paying most of the costs of its Warsaw Pact allies while the NATO countries were self-financing. If the figures were duly modified, not only did the spending gap disappear, but the United States and its allies outspent the U.S.S.R. and Warsaw Pact countries by some $700 billion over that same decade.[13]

Still, the spending gap did its job, rationalizing the biggest arms build-up in U.S. peacetime history. During the 1980s the Pentagon was doling out, at peak, $28 million per hour, of which about 40 per cent (more than $100 billion per year) went to hardware. Not only did the overall amount shoot up, but the "black budget," the ultra-secret portion, grew so rapidly that it accounted at peak for $36 billion per year, a sum larger than the entire military budget of any other country except the U.S.S.R.. "Black" programs had one genuine purpose — to increase security around development of new weapons. But they also provided cover for funding covert intelligence operations; gave privileged firms a lever for extracting extra money, since few questioned how much was spent on supposedly state-of-the-art material; and covered up stupidity, waste and fraud, of which there was an abundance.[14]

Games Arms Manufacturers Play

In the early years of the permanent war economy the great scandals were the result of overseas sales tactics.[15] The Department of Defense, backed by a Treasury worried about the U.S. balance of payments, started pushing by the early 1960s for standardization of NATO forces around American models and for making sure that all allies who could afford to do so paid full cost for their U.S.-supplied weapons. Setting the tone was financially troubled Lockheed Corporation. In Italy, Lockheed hired as sales representative a former fighter pilot for Mussolini who had just been implicated in an ultra-right coup attempt. In the Netherlands, it contributed to the entertainment expenses of an impecunious Crown Prince who had trouble reconciling his wife's parsimony with his own taste for high-price-tag love affairs. In Japan it relied on a member of parliament soon convicted of embezzlement, former wartime intelligence officers purged by the U.S. occupation forces and two of Japan's most powerful gangsters. One had amassed his first fortune in the post-war gasoline black market. The other, Yoshio Kodama, began his political career as an ultra-nationalist agitator hired by wealthy industrialists in the 1930s to break strikes and battle Communists. He then graduated to become the military intelligence officer responsible for looting raw materials and running the heroin trade in Japanese-occupied China.[16] Jailed as a war criminal with a possible death sentence awaiting him, he was released as part of the War-on-Communism. With his new respectability and reputedly $175-million war booty, he funded the rise of the Liberal Democratic Party, which had a stranglehold on power until the end of the Cold War, and acted as money manager for the most important *yakuza* crime group before Lockheed employed him to launder its bribe money.[17]

These antics continued until a congressional investigation into the Watergate scandal turned up evidence of illegal donations to the Nixon re-election campaign by Lockheed's rival, Northrop Corporation. A closer look showed that election contributions followed the same trail through overseas shell companies and offshore bank accounts as corruption money to foreign sales agents. When Northrop was grilled, it pleaded in defence that its "consultancy system" had been modelled on Lockheed's.[18] When Lockheed was called to account (minus the officer responsible for the slush fund, who had shot himself), it had a telling rebuttal to its critics. Without bribes it could never best its French and British competitors, and since bribes were simply added to the price of the planes, taxpayers in the purchasing countries covered the cost. Even better, since Lockheed calculated its own mark-up on the basis of total cost including bribes, bribery actually raised its profit rate. So what was all the fuss about?[19] Although the scandal led to the passage of the Foreign Corrupt Practices Act, making bribery by American firms to secure foreign contracts a criminal offence, the effect was less to reduce corruption than to force corporations to use more sophisticated laundering methods.

Although most attention was focused on overseas sales tactics, domestic procurement had its share of scandals. The most notorious came when the Pentagon and Lockheed were caught jointly trying to falsify performance results and cost data to protect both the Pentagon's grossly inflated C-5 military transport-plane program and Lockheed's equally hyped stock market price. However, it was during the arms expenditure boom of the 1980s that fraudulent cost inflation, faked tests and bribed officials became epidemic.

Some contractors were caught billing for full cost but using inferior materials or only partially completing the job. Others loaded onto the Department of Defense totally bogus items — haircuts, golf-course fees, babysitters' wages, season's tickets to sporting events, parties to boost employee morale, and even charges from a kennel for minding an executive's dog.[20] Costs incurred on commercial contracts were dumped onto government ones, and if a contractor had over-budgeted for wasted, damaged and lost materials, the surplus could be used elsewhere for free. Sometimes cost-puffing took the form of aggressively padding labour costs. More often falsification involved component costs — the $7,622 coffee maker, $743 pliers and a $640 on-board toilet seat.[21] Summing it up neatly, a $10-million item on the bottom of a Northrop internal cost calculation for MX missile parts read "Room for Pad." Northrop also undertook an analysis of different methods of accounting, noting that one had the advantage of being more "honest"— the company picked a different one.[22]

Until 1986 the money flowed almost without interruption. But that year budgetary restrictions caused cutbacks while a public backlash led to an announced shift towards more competitive bidding. In fact, the "cutbacks" still left the military budget nearly a third above its pre-Reagan level, and the

Pentagon's definition of "competition" bore a greater resemblance to a back-room confab between golf buddies than a cut-throat price war between rivals.[23] To the extent the changes had any impact, it was not in reducing the amount of defence fraud, but shifting its nature. The real action became trafficking in inside information to ensure a firm either bested its rivals to secure a contract or arrived at an accommodation to rig the bid. And the key to success depended on "consultants" hired to wheel and deal, bribe and steal.[24]

The primary job of consultants was to collect information for client corporations about pending programs.[25] To do so, they had to open both office doors and bureau safes. They also developed a more proactive role. As more of the initiative for new weapons came from the private sector, consultants would pick up ideas from contractors and whip up enthusiasm inside the Pentagon. When the service involved drew up specifications, the consultant advised on how to write them to favour a particular company he or she was representing. Consultants could not have done their job without inside help.[26]

No one better personified this cosy arrangement than Melvyn Paisley, for six years head of the navy's procurement department.[27] Paisley used his influence to determine eligibility, write specifications to favour particular firms, and leak the contents of rival bids so that a firm could submit a superior offer.[28] In both his naval procurement position and his subsequent career as a freelance consultant, he secured confidential information and aided bids for many industry giants. Grumman, Boeing and McDonnell-Douglas were in his debt.[29] But nobody owed Paisley more than Unisys Corporation.[30]

The military's obsession with high-tech, high-cost solutions along with manufacturers' willingness to cut corners produced results that were sometimes comical — as in the case of an air force anti-tank missile that consistently missed tanks but proved lethal to telephone poles. Some, however, were tragic. The Aegis tracking system, for example, built by Unisys under a contract steered to it by Paisley, supposedly permitted a ship to detect multiple attackers, select and prioritize threats, and prime and fire missiles virtually automatically. The system inspired so much enthusiasm that positive results from testing under the most favourable conditions were issued to the public, while uniformly negative ones made under less favourable conditions were stamped "top secret" and buried. The system's moment of greatest glory came in 1988 when it decided that an Iranian civilian airliner with 290 people on board was a hostile F–14 fighter — even though the aircraft was only five miles off its designated flight path, was ascending instead of descending, and was moving 100 knots slower than would an F–14 in attack mode.[31]

Despite the 1970s Lockheed scandal, standards of deportment in selling weapons to foreign customers remained largely unchanged. In the late 1980s, Northrop, General Dynamics and McDonnell-Douglas got into a dogfight over who would provide fighter jets to South Korea. Northrop seemed to have the edge. Northrop's man in Korea contacted "Wheelchair" Kang, so-called because he had been partially crippled as a result of being shot in the back in a business dispute. Wheelchair Kang led Northrop to "Pistol" Park, former bodyguard to one assassinated president and lifelong friend of the incumbent one. While busy running a tavern in downtown Seoul where foreign business-men could meet expensive call-girls, Pistol Park (whose nickname apparently came from his practice of livening up his place on quiet nights by shooting out the mirrors behind the bar) remained close to the centres of power. He arranged for Northrop to funnel $6.25 million to the president under cover of "investing" in a hotel complex being built by the president's relatives.[32] When Pistol Park died, Northrop lost its access to the president. Its planes crashed on test flights. And, in the final indignity, the agent for General Dynamics, a retired Korean air force general who ran a consulting company aptly called Quick Riches, pumped enough money into the right hands to swing the contract.[33]

Justice for All?

There were many reasons for the resilience of a system based on crooks and cronies. The entire military-industrial complex was surrounded by protective constituencies. The companies had heavy economic clout. Senior officers pro-tected major suppliers both to ensure the flow of hardware and to enhance prospects of future corporate positions when their turn at the revolving door rolled round. And unions were committed to their members' job security in arms factories. After all, where else could people find jobs that permitted extra-curricular activities like manufacturing jewellery from strategic stocks of precious stones and metals, fabricating from military electronic components decoders to view cable TV without charge, and peddling insurance, real estate, diet foods and cosmetics over the long-distance phone at government expense?[34] Then there were politicians who found the arms industry a source of pros-perity for their constituents and for their election coffers.[35]

All those layers of protection made going after military procurement fraud a potential career minefield for investigators and prosecutors.[36] The highest-profile case involved General Dynamics, the country's largest arms maker. The prosecution contended that the company had, among many other things, committed multiple frauds in constructing a special anti-aircraft gun that blasted hundreds of millions of dollars' worth of holes in the defence budget without firing a shot, sunk a billion dollars of overcharges in its nuclear subs, and bribed foreign officials to buy its fighters. Yet the prosecution was never able to penetrate the buddy system, crack the codes, access secret defence department files or even understand convoluted contract requirements. General Dynamics was prosecuted, but the case ended with the government apologizing.[37]

Even when convictions were secured, the impact was negligible. The only really effective punishment would have been suspension from future participation in defence contracts. By the time the second round of cases ended in 1990, twenty-five of the hundred largest contractors had been found guilty of criminal offences, yet not a single one was barred from further Pentagon business. As so often happens in crimes committed by intelligence agents, each conviction was greeted with a plea that the company's work was essential for national security.[38]

Still, in all the storm and fury over procurement fraud, it was never clear why a clean Pentagon was more desirable. Much the way corrupt governments, whose leaders spend their time stuffing money into Swiss accounts, are sometimes an improvement over those capable of carrying out ugly agendas with brutal efficiency, arguably in military procurement, fraud could be a blessing. The accompanying cost inflation meant that fewer weapons would be bought, and those that were would often fail to kill people. But that aside, demands to clean up the system were based on a complete misunderstanding of the logic of U.S. arms expenditure during the 1980s.

Corporate crime and economic warfare had developed a symbiotic relationship. As the initiative for high-tech, high-priced weapons increasingly came from suppliers rather than users, as procurement jobs in the military became more desirable than operations ones, technical merit was a secondary consideration. On the micro level, the fundamental objectives were the profitability of the firms making the arms, and the benefits the purchasing officials could expect in the present or future. On the macro level, each time a gross fraud was committed, driving up cost, the practice of imputing U.S. prices to Soviet military spending automatically ratcheted up the estimate of that spending and provided a justification for the United States to lavish yet more on its own military the next fiscal year.[39] Once the main purpose of spending became destabilizing the Soviet economy, then, in a backhanded way, profiteering was patriotic.

Chapter 5

GRUDGE MATCH

The United States increased the military spending burden on the U.S.S.R. in two distinct ways. The first was to stoke the arms race. The second was to bog down the Soviet Union in an unwinnable guerrilla war. In 1979 the Soviet Union had blundered its way into Afghanistan. In a stroke, it undermined much of its credibility with the Third World; alienated Muslims everywhere, including in its own central Asia republics; frightened the Arab Gulf states into closer military cooperation with the United States; and consolidated a U.S.–China anti-Soviet alliance. Afghanistan drained the U.S.S.R. when its finances were already perilous and gave the United States an opportunity to observe in action Soviet military equipment as well as to test some of its own in the hands of resistance fighters. Not least, the Afghan debacle gave the United States a means to avenge the harshest blow the American military ego had ever suffered. In the eyes of Republican strategists, convinced of a global Bolshevik plot orchestrated from Moscow, the fact that the Soviet Union had avoided direct involvement did not lessen its responsibility for America's humiliation at the hands of Soviet-equipped forces in Vietnam.

Armed Robbery

In the beginning, it was not even America's battle. When World War II ended, France set out to reassert control of its Southeast Asian empire. But by 1954 the French, militarily humiliated and financially exhausted, conceded defeat in the north of Vietnam and handed the south over to the United States. Step by step, U.S. involvement moved from advising on counter-insurgency to limited participation by specialized units to total war involving hundreds of thousands of American soldiers. Like France, the United States was bled many times over. Apart from the human and political cost, the war stoked inflation, drained U.S. gold reserves and hit the dollar with waves of destabilizing speculation. The United States took resources that might have been directed against the U.S.S.R. and poured them into a corner of Southeast Asia with minimal strategic value. The drain was exacerbated by the fact that Vietnam witnessed racketeering at public expense that dwarfed World War II experience.

In addition to supplying its own troops and South Vietnam's enormous army, the United States ran a huge refugee aid program, greatly appreciated by black market dealers who stole much of the food, clothing and medicines.[1] The problem was partly sheer volume. Ports were so overcrowded that ships queued for months. Their captains sometimes could not resist the temptation to sell cargo to lighters that pulled alongside. Goods were stacked onto piers from which mountains of army-issue rations, clothes, combat gear, antibiotics and cigarettes would vanish. Although there was ample petty pilferage, the serious action was run by merchants from Cholon, Saigon's Chinatown and vice-racket centre. Sometimes official trucks were diverted by bribery or hijacked at gunpoint. Sometimes black market dealers loaded their own trucks. American soldiers guarding the docks were paid to look the other way or were distracted by prostitutes calling on their guard booths.

There was scarcely a shop or street stall in the major cities that did not sell stolen American PX stores, supplies looted from construction projects or diverted refugee relief aid. Some ended up as far away as China. The situation degenerated to the point where aid officials had to buy back stolen rice to feed refugees.

The same held true for military equipment. Some was stolen. Some was peddled by South Vietnamese soldiers who deserted in droves. M-16 carbines, officially worth $280 each, sold on the street for $40. Armoured personnel carriers, helicopters or even tanks were available with an advance order. South Vietnamese newspapers were forbidden to publish pictures of captured Viet Cong arms caches. The official reason was that it would compromise security. The real reason was more likely that so much material used by the enemy was American. On a more positive note, unlike World War II, there was no shortage of petroleum, thanks in part to big U.S. oil companies paying Communist guerrillas to not attack their facilities.[2]

American troops had access to military clubs, commissaries and R&R centres. Running some of them was a ring of sergeants who sold goods from their own businesses to the army and skimmed cash. Every post, too, had Vietnamese concessionaires. Officially they operated barber shops, laundries and similar services. Unofficially they used the concessions to import duty-free goods nominally for U.S. military use, then divert them to the Saigon black market. They also peddled sex and drugs.[3]

Among soldiers there was an enormous market for drugs. Locally grown cannabis abounded. Opium was produced by the hill tribes, processed into heroin by Chinese gangs in Hong Kong, then brought back to feed the GI market.[4] But the LSD was made-in-America. The most popular brand, Orange Sunshine, was the handiwork of the Brotherhood of Eternal Love, a California tax-exempt religious cult created by biker-gang members who peddled "acid" with equal enthusiasm to flower-power anti-war protesters at home and carbine-toting American soldiers abroad.[5]

Soldiers were also active as black market sellers. Periodically they received free from state-side manufacturers chocolate, alcohol, cigarettes and soap, which were snapped up by civilians. Each soldier, too, had a ration card to purchase similar items at cost at PX stores. The cards were sold from hand to hand and, in some cases, were counterfeited. Goods obtained could be diverted to illicit sale. Soldiers also received from the United States packages mailed at government expense. Some soldiers imported female clothing and cosmetics for sale to Vietnamese women; Saigon's tens of thousands of prostitutes formed an especially eager market. There was even a smuggling operation in which loads of heroin were stuffed into the gutted bodies of dead GIs, then shipped to the United States with code numbers so that conspiring officers could remove and market the drugs.[6]

Track of the Black Greenback

During World War II, there had been little problem getting black money back to the United States. But during the Vietnam War, illicit financial dealings were supposedly hemmed in by regulations. South Vietnam required that all funds coming in be converted into piastres at the official rate, and all going out secure official permission. And there were special U.S. restrictions. Since 1946 U.S. personnel abroad had been paid in dollar-denominated Military Pay Certificates (MPCs) that, in turn, had to be converted into books of chits before they were spent in military clubs, PXs and commissaries. To limit the temptation to use the currency black market to get money home, soldiers could choose to receive only part of their salaries in MPCs and have the rest deposited directly into a bank account back in the United States. If there was anything left over, they could convert a maximum of 80 per cent of salary received in Vietnam into money orders to mail back or, before themselves departing for home or for R&R, convert up to the same total into travellers' cheques.

On paper, the regulations looked effective. In practice, they were full of holes. Although it was technically forbidden, MPCs were widely accepted by Vietnamese base concessionaires and on the urban black markets. If someone hit the 80 per cent conversion limit, he could pay others to front for him. To get travellers' cheques, nominally available only on departure, it sufficed to use a cheap one-way air ticket as "proof" of pending departure. It was even possible for civilian employees to order a car in the United States using MPCs for payment, then cancel the order and ask the U.S. manufacturer to refund dollars to an American bank account.[7] Reversing the process, personnel importing money into Vietnam tried to avoid the poor official rate for piastres. They could swap dollars for MPCs on the black market at a 50 to 100 per cent better rate. NCOs running the clubs converted cheques or money orders into MPCs or even directly into chit books. Since chit books were often lost on missions into the jungle or the red-light district, the NCOs printed extra ones corresponding to the estimated loss. Since the overall totals issued and redeemed about balanced, the military accountants paid no attention. The NCOs then arranged to smuggle the cheques and money orders out of the country.

Underpinning the structure was an underground money market run by a syndicate of Indian Muslims with extended family connections throughout Southeast Asia and excellent working relations with major banks in Hong Kong.[8] The money changers would buy MPCs at deep discount rates from Vietnamese concessionaires or from urban black marketeers for piastres, greenbacks or deposits in a U.S.-dollar bank account in Hong Kong. To get rid of the MPCs, a money changer might buy from an American soldier cheques drawn on the soldier's bank account back in the United States and remit the cheques to Hong Kong for deposit into the money changer's account. Thus, the American soldier would get MPCs at the black market rate, and the money changer would move assets out of Vietnam, bypassing exchange controls. Or the money changers might hire deserters with real or fake ID and send them to the military post office to change MPCs into money orders.

If the war in Vietnam was about defending free enterprise, this parallel financial system was its spiritual embodiment. It catered to Americans dealing in contraband goods, Vietnamese officials salting away corruption money, speculators preparing for flight, and wealthy civilians evading taxes, escaping exchange controls or merely hedging against inflation and depreciation. Even the Viet Cong used the facilities. They imposed taxes on traffic through areas they controlled, collected in piastres, traded them for dollars and used the dollars to buy arms. Equally active was the CIA, which traded dollars on the black market to make its budget go further.[9]

The linchpin was Hong Kong. Created by the British as a base for running opium into China, Hong Kong had been a major smuggling entrepôt for a century before the Vietnam War made it an international financial centre. Among the appreciative users was a clique of currency dealers known as Saigon brokers because so many of their transactions were with Vietnam. Again the market transcended ideology. One broker was a Hong Kong bank rumoured to be secretly owned by Communist China, which needed dollars to pay spies and buy embargoed U.S. military gear. Another was the Hong Kong branch of an American firm whose business connections were decidedly spooky. Deak & Co. was founded in 1939 by a Hungarian émigré. The company had barely begun when patriotic instincts induced its founder, Nicholas L. Deak, to sign on with the OSS. After World War II, Nicholas Deak reopened his company, building the business into the world's largest bullion and foreign exchange trading firm. Deak was a pioneer of post-war trading in inconvertible currencies. Refugees from Communist regimes would swap their cash at Deak's company for dollars at deep discount rates, and it would resell to persons needing an untraceable bundle of Ostmarks, zlotys or forints to square some underground accounts on the other side of the Iron Curtain.[10]

Deak went from success to success. When the CIA needed to get funds to royalists plotting the 1954 overthrow of a nationalist government in Iran, it turned to Deak's Zurich and Beirut offices. Deak's Swiss branch also helped finance CIA mercenary operations in the Belgian Congo during the 1960s. His Hong Kong affiliate handled the bribe money Lockheed sent to Japan to secure orders for its jets, ran gold to CIA-designated recipients throughout Southeast Asia, and was the hub of the money-go-round that started with the vice trade in Vietnam. Deak in Hong Kong was banker for the sergeants running the club rackets, and serviced the big Indian money changers. As one witness before a U.S. Senate inquiry ungrammatically described it: "They [sic] was never any questions asked in Deak & Company whether it was a black market currency operation or what it was. Hong Kong don't care. If you get there with the money, they will accept it. They don't care how you got it."[11]

Alas, the firm seems to have taken its talents for financial discretion a step too far. Between 1976 and 1978, Deak's west coast branch was raided and fined for 377 different violations of the U.S. Bank Secrecy Act, notably the requirement that international transfers over $10,000 be reported to the U.S. Treasury. Much worse, in 1984 the President's Commission on Organized Crime accused Deak's New York office of accepting cardboard boxes containing

$97 million from Colombian cocaine traffickers, creating fictitious accounts, moving the money abroad and failing to report any of the transactions to the authorities.[12] The firm, it seems, just could not shake the legacy of its founder's old spy instinct for keeping things quiet.[13]

Up in Arms

Defeat in Vietnam was a shock to the United States. Yet it was only the beginning of a string of reversals over the 1970s. The year 1979 finally brought good news, including a chance to turn the tables and make Soviet regular forces face a U.S.-backed guerrilla army.

The U.S.S.R. had begun wooing Afghanistan in the 1950s. Soviet influence grew considerably after the 1973 overthrow of the Afghan monarchy and grew further after a 1978 coup by an awkward coalition of Marxist factions whose idea of political debate was to draw pistols during cabinet meetings. Worried over growing Islamic fundamentalism on its borders, in 1979 the U.S.S.R. sent in the army. The United States responded by providing aid to the Afghan mujahideen resistance.

In the first few years, the United States and Saudi Arabia split a modest annual aid bill of $30 to $50 million. But after Reagan's second presidential victory, the flows jumped, Saudi Arabia still matching the United States dollar for dollar. By the time the Soviet withdrawal from Afghanistan began, each country had kicked in $1.5 billion to create a guerrilla force of 200,000 to 300,000 fighters. The reason for the rapid cost hike was partly the increasing commitment to bleed the U.S.S.R. and partly the nature of the aid pipeline.[14] It not merely leaked, but gushed. By some estimates as little as half the allocated material actually reached the resistance.[15]

The first stage of the aid pipeline, directly controlled by the CIA, involved securing arms. The preference was for Soviet models, which were simple to maintain and worked well even if wet or dirty. Soviet weapons also provided the United States with "deniability," permitted use of captured ammunition, and gave a propaganda weapon to guerrillas who could claim their arms were taken in battle. Some arms came from CIA stockpiles. Some came from China, Egypt and Israel. Yet more were bought on the world black market from dealers whose own sources of supply were shrouded by layers of deniability. Communist Poland, with its desperation for foreign exchange, was rumoured to be a major source.[16]

In this first stage, some arms were stolen before they arrived. Some thefts may have been by the CIA itself. Skimming from the officially sanctioned Afghan account was an easy way to get around congressional bans on CIA aid to covert wars in southern Africa and central America. Some may have been the work of brokers and frontmen. In secret arms deals, bargaining over price, monitoring transactions and keeping formal records were difficult, if not impossible. Even the port duties in Pakistan were paid in cash. As a result, prices at source might be too high, dealers might substitute inferior goods, and those in charge of shipping could pad invoices while diverting the material (sometimes reported as "lost at sea") to their own customers. Theft was all the easier since no one at the point of arrival checked the contents against the original manifests.[17]

Of those arms arriving, quality varied greatly. China's factories turned out excellent models of Soviet equipment. Egypt, switching over to U.S. equipment, unloaded obsolete Soviet arms. An American congressman lobbied for the purchase of forty unwieldy anti-aircraft guns produced by a company in which he may have held a financial interest — six made it to the Afghans.[18] One load of mortar ammunition arrived with warnings not to use the shells after December 1944. When a batch of 50,000 British Army rifles, veterans of World War II, were obtained from an Indian arms dealer, an enterprising Pakistani broker persuaded the United States that he had secret stocks of ammunition overseas. He diverted 30 million rounds from Pakistan army stores, loaded them at Karachi, had the ship steam away, then turn around to unload the ammunition at a pier controlled by Pakistani military intelligence. Secrecy being so important, every round bore the markings of the Pakistan army's ordnance factory.[19]

Once arms arrived in Karachi, Pakistan's Inter-Services Intelligence (ISI) took over. Supposedly this was to prevent the Soviet Union from being able to accuse Pakistan of complicity. Since the U.S.S.R. could have read about Pakistan's role in the *New York Times* (or on shell casings!), a more convincing reason could be inferred from the fact that some generals involved in the arms pipeline retired rich.

Packed in containers with markings like "food" and "engineering parts," the weapons were hauled from Karachi northward. Some went by military train. Some went by trucks owned by the army's National Logistics Cell, outfitted with false and frequently changed licence plates and driven by soldiers bearing special passes to prevent Pakistani police or Customs from interfering. Moving in small fleets that mixed with civilian traffic, the trucks took weapons to special dumps near Rawalpindi. At that point opportunity again knocked, with both hands. Some weapons were reputedly diverted by the ISI to equip antigovernment guerrillas in the Indian states of Kashmir and Punjab;[20] others were sold on the black market.[21] Then the ISI arranged for more trucks,

bearing registration plates issued to Afghan refugees, to haul arms to Peshawar, capital of Pakistan's Northwest Frontier Province and Afghan exile headquarters, or to the border city of Quetta in Baluchistan, to be turned over to
the leadership of the seven major political tendencies of the resistance.[22] At that
point more diversion occurred. Much weaponry turned up in the Northwest
Frontier town of Dara. For centuries it had been the home of craftsmen who
could reproduce almost any basic weapon, but Dara businesses had shifted from
making their own to trafficking in CIA-supplied equipment, along with
alcohol, drugs, stolen cars, smuggled electronics and counterfeit currency.[23]

The final stage, entrusted to "private" contractors with business or family
relations with the Afghan exile leadership, required that weapons be hauled,
often by mule train, into Afghanistan. Once there, the arms were supplied to
field commanders, some of whom exaggerated quantities used or lost in battle
and sold off the difference.

Along with arms came a supply of "humanitarian" aid (much with covert
military functions) paid for by international organizations. It moved from
Pakistan to Afghanistan in the same convoys and caravans carrying ordinary
contraband. The Afghan capital of Kabul, even under its Communist regime,
was a Himalayan free port, with a wide-open bazaar and a freewheeling money
market. About $100 million worth of consumer goods flowed across the
Afghan-Pakistan border each year. Japanese electronics, Chinese silks, French
glassware and perfumes, British crockery and much more went from Karachi
nominally to Kabul, with a lot dumped in Pakistan en route. Back flowed
eastern European manufactured goods, cheap enough to undercut legitimately
imported or locally produced items in Pakistan.[24] The mujahideen aid flow
also permitted Afridi tribes on the Pakistan-Afghan border to extort protection money. Each clan demanded its cut. Some, too, were paid by the Afghan
government to attack the arms convoys, requiring the ISI to outbid the
Afghan government to buy the tribes' quiescence.[25]

The distribution of aid was subject to dual political control. The ISI determined which parties got what, allowing Pakistan to favour the growth of
factions with whose ideology it felt most comfortable.[26] Then party leaders
decided how much would go to individual commanders. The result was that
some resistance groups had to buy on the arms black market weapons already
purchased for them by American taxpayers. The same happened with humanitarian aid. In a replay of Vietnam, aid agencies scoured local bazaars to buy
back relief supplies. At one point so much grain sent by the United States
was stolen that the shipments were suspended. As to the 1,000 schools and
800 clinics supposedly built with international assistance in "liberated" parts

of Afghanistan, most existed only on paper. Meanwhile some Afghan leaders displayed a sharp eye for real estate investments and a taste for Peshawar villas and foreign bank accounts. There was even an obliging financial institution on hand that made a specialty of catering to those tastes.[27]

The Full Service Bank

The Bank of Credit and Commerce International (BCCI) had an unusual history, a unique mission and a curious clientele.[28] Although it was not founded until 1972, its spiritual roots go back to World War II when British intelligence infiltrated some of the Indian subcontinent's most important contraband networks. Apart from trafficking in gold, foreign exchange and rationed commodities, those rings smuggled Axis agents and Indian independence fighters. So the British made a deal. The smugglers got carte blanche to do their usual business, the British even opening special banking facilities for them on Madagascar. In return they had to identify for the British any Axis agents and Indian nationalist agitators who sought their services. They also used their network to move money to pay for espionage activities in Axis-controlled territories.[29]

In 1947 the British withdrew from India, taking the intelligence records and bequeathing a currency-smuggling apparatus just when India was trying to promote economic self-sufficiency. The chaos of partition further entrenched the underground bankers. British India became divided into two intensely hostile countries with a problem of resettling tens of millions of uprooted people. With no formal relations between the two states, people relied on underground bankers to liquidate property and move assets from one side to the other, the bankers gaining practical experience, political connections and public trust. In 1963 an Indo-Pakistani war gave yet more impetus. Attempting to conserve foreign exchange, discourage hoarding, reduce tax evasion and eliminate a major symptom of social inequality, India passed the Gold Control Act, banning imports except under extremely restrictive conditions. Among those taking advantage was Deak's Zurich bank, which used the proceeds of the Vietnam rackets to buy gold, reselling to smugglers who hauled it to India for sale at the black market price.[30]

Moving gold into India was simple: routes were long established and functionaries already corrupted. The problem was getting paid, since the Indian (or Pakistani) rupee was inconvertible. The crudest way was to smuggle out black market foreign exchange, looted antiquities or silver. But soon a more sophisticated alternative emerged.

During the 1970s the Arab Gulf states experienced an oil boom that attracted a huge labour force of Indians and Pakistanis. If they remitted earnings back to their families through the formal banking system, the money was converted into rupees at the official rate, and the authorities could trace the cash for tax purposes. At the same time, Indian and Pakistani gold smugglers in the Gulf had to buy gold for U.S. dollars but accept payment in rupees. Into the breach stepped the underground bankers. Earnings by émigré workers would be collected in the Arab Gulf states and used to buy gold. The gold would be spirited to India or Pakistan and sold for rupees. Then the gold importer would pay to the family of the émigré worker in rupees at the black market rate the equivalent of what the émigré worker had contributed in dollars. No monetary instrument had to cross borders or oceans. It was neat, efficient and almost untraceable.

It was in this context — the chaos of partition, the Indo-Pakistani war and the growing gold-and-remittances link — that Agha Hasan Abedi learned his banking skills. As he rose through the emerging Pakistani banking system, he cultivated the country's military leaders. Then in 1972, following another conflict with India, the military lost power to a civilian government headed by Zulfiqar Ali Bhutto. Bhutto nationalized the banking system, including the institution managed by Abedi, denounced Abedi as a CIA agent and put him under house arrest. Temporarily disgraced, Abedi dreamed of creating a genuinely international bank to serve businesses in the developing world that the big American, European and Japanese institutions neglected. He also wanted to ensure a bank of his would never again face hostile political takeover. Therefore he placed the nominal headquarters in Luxembourg. Capital came from several rich Saudis, and especially from the emir of Abu Dhabi whom Abedi had cultivated during visits to Pakistan. And in September 1972 the Bank of Credit and Commerce International was formally opened in a ceremony at the posh Phoenicia Hotel in Beirut. It was just in time to cash in on the oil boom that began late the next year.[31]

From the Middle East the bank spread around the world: to Africa, South America, Asia and Europe, with a toehold in North America. It worked both ends of the social ladder. It offered financial services to small businesses in developing countries and Asian minorities in Western ones. And its "protocol department" sought out the powerful, pandering to their weaknesses, be they money, high-profile charity, hot cars, young women or boys. Structured to take advantage of the world of offshore havens and having a widely dispersed network of branches and affiliates, BCCI attracted those elements for whom the bank's talents in unrecorded deposits, off-balance-sheet financing, doctored letters of credit, covert transfers and back-to-back loans would be so useful operationally.

During its short but spectacular career, BCCI aided capital flight, engaged in bribery, laundered drug money, assisted quota busting, abetted maritime fraud, facilitated techno-banditry and financed arms trafficking. It helped military dictators and commodity traders loot Nigeria's oil wealth. It bribed Peruvian central bank officials to get them to deposit the country's foreign exchange reserves in BCCI. It handled narco-payoffs in Panama. It ran tax evasion schemes for Asians in Britain and exchange control scams for people in India and Pakistan. While draining countries of foreign exchange and tax revenues, it was busy making payoffs to secure government business while providing recipient officials with a safe place to hide the money.

Despite its status as the world's largest privately owned bank, BCCI's soul remained in Pakistan. When the army deposed Ali Bhutto in 1977 and hanged him two years later, BCCI came in from the cold. In short order Abedi created between the Pakistani political elite and his bank a revolving-door relationship that would have made a Pentagon procurement officer blush. BCCI handled the remittances that many thousands of ordinary Pakistanis (and Indians) working in the Gulf sent to their families. Some of the money went through official channels, subject to taxes and official exchange rates. More went through informal channels with the advantage of secrecy and black market rates. Among those informal channels was the gold smuggling racket for which BCCI had the reputation of virtually being a central bank. At the other end of the social scale, members of the Pakistani elite put their confidence in BCCI to ensure their fortunes would be spirited to tax-free bliss abroad. And when capital flight threatened to precipitate a balance of payments crisis, BCCI was on hand to offer loans or, even better, to fake hard currency deposits to bolster Pakistan's reported foreign exchange reserves and therefore keep its foreign creditors from panicking.[32]

BCCI was also banker to secret state projects. When the godfather of Pakistan's nuclear program was arrested in the Netherlands in 1983 and charged with attempting to steal blueprints of a uranium enrichment plant, BCCI covered his legal fees. Four years later, BCCI financed an attempt by a Toronto-based Pakistani to smuggle special steel for a nuclear processing plant out of the United States. However, what really consolidated BCCI's position was the Afghan war.

For BCCI there was nothing unusual about hobnobbing with intelligence services. Among its most important early shareholders was Kamal Adham, long-time head of Saudi intelligence and chief CIA contact in the Middle East. The bank's relations with Pakistan's ISI were so tight that ISI swept BCCI's London office for bugs. The head of that London branch regularly liaised with

Britain's MI6 over the activities of some account holders. But above all else there was the CIA. BCCI could be especially useful in countries where the United States had few intelligence assets. It knew the leaders' darker secrets and where they had hidden the loot, opening them to blackmail. And, because BCCI often paid for them, it could monitor arms and military technology flows. CIA chief William Casey regularly chatted with Abedi on matters of mutual interest. And their main mutual interest was Afghanistan.

Most funds contributed by the CIA or Saudi Arabia to the mujahideen passed through CIA-controlled accounts in Switzerland. However, when money was spent on military supplies, BCCI often issued the letters of credit. Furthermore, private donations from rich Gulf Arabs were handled directly by BCCI. When CIA purchasing agents were unable to find material, BCCI stepped in as broker. BCCI scoured the world to find the mules the mujahideen used to haul supplies. Without BCCI's assistance, the entire transportation chain from the world arms black market to Karachi to the Northwest Frontier and on into Afghanistan might have broken down. Not least, BCCI was available to handle money generated from the return cargoes.

Smoking Russia Away

Afghanistan was less a country than a set of warring ethnic, clan and religious fiefdoms united in little beyond use of the same currency. Even in peace the government's writ barely extended beyond the three major cities. Early in the war, many field commanders could collect enough tribute from local populations to remain autonomous. Later Soviet forces destroyed local economies and sent millions fleeing to Pakistan and Iran. Commanders then became dependent on what was allocated to them by party chiefs in Peshawar or looked for alternatives.

Protection money could be extorted from smugglers' caravans, a practice sufficiently lucrative that gangs of thieves would pose as mujahideen to take a share.[33] One group was paid by the government to refrain from attacking Kabul's power plants and transmission lines.[34] The legendary field commander, Ahmed Mas'ud, was among the least favoured with outside aid. However, he made up the shortfall partly by collecting payments from the Red Army to permit supply convoys unimpeded passage along the highway linking the Afghan capital of Kabul with the Soviet border. The area under Mas'ud's control also boasted the world's finest deposits of lapis lazuli, from which a tax of 5 to 10 per cent went into his treasury.

Precious stones were not the only natural resource that Afghanistan offered for a good cause. "How else can we get money?" retorted the brother of one of the most important leaders when eyebrows were raised at poppy fields flourishing under mujahideen control. "We must grow and sell opium to fight our holy war against Russian non-believers." To the injunction in the *Qur'an* against drugs, there was an easy reply. "Islamic law forbids the taking of opium, but there is no prohibition against growing it." By the early 1990s, Afghanistan was the world's largest opium producer.[35]

It also had a prodigious cannabis crop. Growers made payoffs to resistance groups. They also showed solidarity by stamping bars of hashish with anti-Soviet slogans. "Crumble the Kremlin" was a favourite. Police in Britain also intercepted a shipment of 24,000 half-kilogram slabs, each emblazoned with crossed Kalashnikovs and the exhortation "Smoke Russia Away."[36]

Drugs may have helped pay for the war against the Russian non-believer. But they were a source of contention among mujahideen leaders who battled to control the richest crops or the roads over which the stuff was shipped. It was generally easier for one faction's drug caravans to get through government-controlled areas where a small bribe sufficed than through territory run by a rival mujahideen commander.

Cannabis required little preparation beyond pressing into hashish. However, opium had to be refined using somewhat complex chemistry before export. In the no man's land where Pakistan, Iran and Afghanistan connect, what was billed as the world's largest heroin refinery opened under the protection of the Hezb-i-Islami, the resistance faction that, despite being the most favoured in the distribution of outside aid, also had the worst reputation for looting aid flows bound for other groups.[37] Heroin was also refined in the autonomous tribal region of Pakistan's Northwest Frontier Province. The refineries, joint ventures of Pakistani merchants and Afghan leaders, yielded so much protection money that, when combined with the returns from gun-running, kidnapping and extortion, tribal chiefs could move from mud-walled forts guarded by a few kinsmen with bolt-action rifles to marble-floored Jacuzzi-equipped mansions protected by anti-aircraft missiles.[38]

From the Northwest Frontier, the drugs moved south, hidden in sacks of grain carried by the same National Logistics Cell trucks that brought the weapons north, still protected by the ISI against Customs and police probes.[39] Then some of the drugs were taken over by professional smuggling gangs linked to Sikh guerrilla groups already moving whisky (banned under Islamic law) into Pakistan and arms back into India. Inside India, drugs would go to Bombay where the underworld, rich on gold smuggling, arranged their export. Or they would head farther south where Tamil separatist guerrillas from Sri Lanka would move them out via their European courier system. Other shipments headed to Karachi where five families, each with a senior officer in their ranks, controlled exports and ran profits through accounts in BCCI. And some went westward by land. Baluchi tribesmen would carry drugs to Iran and transfer them to Kurdish groups to take across Turkey. There the drugs entered a smuggling complex of corrupted officials, political insurgents, career gangsters and intelligence agents who not only controlled much of the heroin entering western Europe, but were also the epicentre of one of the Cold War's most bizarre scandals.

Grey Wolves at the Kremlin Door?

The insurrection in Afghanistan threatened Soviet Central Asia, while the Soviet Trans-Caucasian republics had a potentially troublesome neighbour a little farther west. Turkey, the southern cornerstone of NATO, was (and remains) a country confused over three possible definitions of national identity. The official ideology, created after the fall of the Ottoman Empire, emphasizes a Western secular society. That self-image has always had to coexist with a sense of Islamic community that pulls the country closer to the Middle East. But there is a third definition, of Turkey as part of a pan-Turkic entity spanning central Asia all the way to China. The pan-Turkic idea first took practical form in 1942 when the Germans created Turkic-speaking units from Soviet prisoners, and "neutral" Turkey mobilized troops on the Soviet frontier, ready to invade if Stalingrad fell.[40] Pan-Turkism formally entered the political arena in 1960 when a military government purged from cabinet several officers noted for extremist views. One was the late Colonel Alparslan Türkeş, former Turkish military attaché to Washington and NATO liaison in Ankara, who then founded the virulently anti-Soviet Nationalist Action Party.[41] For a long time it represented only a neo-fascist fringe. But in the 1970s that changed.

Those were years of bitter transition. U.S. pressure forced Turkey to ban its opium crop, destroying the livelihood of many peasants as well as threatening some of the most powerful smugglers. A land reform program alienated big landlords who swung against the government. Political violence began to shake Turkish society. As the Nationalist Action Party gained strength, it created the Bozkurtlar (Grey Wolves), a paramilitary strike force established, in Colonel Türkeş's words, to "defend Turkey against Communism."[42]

Initially dependent on landlords for support, the Grey Wolves were soon financially autonomous. They drew money from extortion rackets and, aided by sympathizers in Customs, from running contraband for the drugs-and-arms *mafya*. For, far from ending the drug trade, the ban on Turkish opium broadened its reach. During the 1970s more and more opium, morphine and, finally, heroin from Iran, Pakistan and Afghanistan crossed Turkey en route to western Europe and the United States. The drugs blended with other contraband. Opiates moved westward, while gold, watches, counterfeit goods and weapons moved east. The linchpin was Bulgaria. Its complicity was more than just an accident of geography. Captured smugglers told Turkish police that Bulgarian officials collected 10 to 15 per cent of the value of the goods crossing the border in return for safe havens, military escorts and even rescue facilities for smuggling boats that ran into bad weather on the Black Sea.[43]

The smuggling networks were supported by a parallel banking system. After the suppression of opium production, some who left the drug-producing areas had emigrated to France, Germany and Switzerland to traffic in commodities as varied as hazelnuts and heroin. Others, often members of the same families, moved to Istanbul to take up black market money changing. The collection point was the Tahkatele section of the Istanbul Grand Bazaar. There, in a small inner courtyard beyond the gold and jewellery shops that acted as collectors, money changers would negotiate the hard currency proceeds of gun-running, drug trafficking, gold smuggling and the sale of stolen antiquities. From the vaults of the Tahkatele money changers came batches of dollars and Deutschmarks that were stuffed under false floors in buses and driven to the Bulgarian border. In Sofia the money was taken to a special warehouse owned by an import-export company controlled by Bulgarian intelligence. Bulgarian officials took a modest $1 to $3 per $1,000, and the remainder was turned over to couriers. Escorted to the airport by Bulgarian police, the couriers winged their way to Zurich airport, either turning the money over to other couriers sent by the Swiss banks or depositing it directly in branches those same banks kept inside the transit area. The Bulgarian nexus also worked in reverse. Money in the Swiss banks was used to buy gold. Armoured cars conveyed the gold to Zurich airport. Couriers with ten to twenty kilograms strapped around their bodies flew to Sofia. The Bulgarian police met and accompanied them to the safe house. The gold was weighed, the Bulgarians getting $60 per kilogram, then stuffed under the false floors of buses carrying back to Istanbul their share of the 60 to 100 tons of gold (worth more than $1 billion) annually smuggled via Bulgaria into Turkey.[44]

Over the 1970s, as political violence increased, the legal parts of the Turkish economy went into a tailspin, capital flight accelerated, tax evasion soared and smuggling ran rampant. Smuggling was a source of arms, as well as the profits to pay for them. In 1980 came a military coup. The army began rounding up weapons. It claimed over 750,000 pistols, rifles and machine guns, 23 rocket launchers, five anti-aircraft guns, two howitzers and 3.6 million rounds of ammunition. They were displayed each evening as a sort of catch-of-the-day on Turkish TV news to reassure the population that the military coup had saved the country from chaos. Astute observers noted, however, that the main difference in the picture from night to night was often how the weapons were arranged on the tables. Though arms were of disparate origins, some were still packed in crates belonging to Kintex, a Bulgarian state trading company. And even with weapons made elsewhere, most passed via Bulgaria en route to Turkey.[45]

After the coup the military government clamped down on smugglers and banned extremist groups. The Grey Wolves leadership went into exile, still preaching the need to liberate the Turkic-populated republics of the Soviet Union from Russian clutches. For the next decade most operations were conducted from Germany. There, sheltering among the large émigré Turkish community, the Grey Wolves raised money from extortion, alien smuggling and heroin trafficking while attacking left-wing and pro-Soviet targets. From this German exile, a member of the Grey Wolves launched the operation that would bring him worldwide notoriety and permit the United States to score its biggest propaganda coup of the Cold War.

Ali Agca and the Forty Spies

One day early in 1981, in St. Peter's Square, a young Turk named Mehmet Ali Agca shot John Paul II, the Polish pope, just when the U.S.–U.S.S.R. confrontation over Poland was heating up. For a year, Ali Agca sat in jail, bragging that he had done the dirty deed by himself. Ali had no lack of visitors. One was Francesco Pazienza who had run liaison between Italian military intelligence (Servicio informazioni sulla sicurezza militari or SISMI) and organized crime when the two had common interests. In 1982 Italy was shaken by the P-2 scandal, the exposure of a plot by a secret right-wing Masonic organization to subvert the Italian government. Among the members of P-2 was the head of SISMI. After the SISMI chief was fired, Pazienza also decided on a change of career. He became counsellor to Roberto Calvi, the head of Italy's Banco Ambrosiano, its largest private bank. A short time later the bank, buffetted by allegations it had been the centre of a massive capital flight, tax evasion and gun-running operation, crumbled with a $2-billion hole in its books. An international arrest warrant was sworn out for Pazienza, sending him hightailing for friendlier climes.[46]

Still, Ali was not lonely. Another visitor was a priest intent on converting him — though to what was never clear. The priest was later convicted under Italy's anti-Mafia conspiracy law.[47] Another caller represented Don Raffaele Cutolo, jailed boss of the Naples Comorra, Italian's second most powerful crime fraternity. The Comorra presented Ali with gifts, including the TV set from which he derived much of the "evidence" he later presented in court. When Don Raffaele objected to being transferred to another prison, too far away to allow him to supervise his cigarette-smuggling business, he cut a deal. In return for being left where he was, Don Raffaele would try to persuade Ali to tell the truth, the whole truth and nothing but the truth about what had happened in St. Peter's Square.[48]

Like others before him, Ali Agca accused Bulgaria's secret services of running contraband both to bolster the foreign exchange earnings of a bankrupt Stalinist state and to destabilize Turkey, a key NATO ally. But, according to Ali, those Bulgarians, acting on orders from Moscow, had committed even worse deeds. One of their targets had been a Polish pope committed to liberating his homeland from the claws of the Russian bear. As Ali told it, Bulgarian intelligence had called in debts from the Turkish *babas*, the godfathers of the drugs-and-arms *mafya* who had had fled Turkey after the coup and holed up in a luxury hotel in Sofia. There were two point men. One was Abuzer Uğurlu, the most notorious of Istanbul's crime bosses whom Ali Agca insisted was an agent of Bulgarian intelligence.[49] However, far from enjoying a Bulgarian exile, Uğurlu was then sitting in an Istanbul prison cell. Therefore he had needed help. His second-in-command was Bekir Çelenk. For much of the 1970s, Çelenk had been living in Switzerland, running a shipping company and smuggling watches and weapons into Turkey. Named as a possible drug trafficker in 1979, he fled to Bulgaria leaving behind 8 million Swiss francs in debts.[50] While in exile, Çelenk on behalf of Uğurlu on behalf of Bulgarian intelligence on behalf of the KGB supposedly recruited Ali Agca for the hit.

Ali Agca was well trained for the job. Raised in Malatya, a town that was a major contraband centre and a breeding ground for ultra-rightist groups, Ali worked as a driver for a local drug-and-gun runner before being recruited into the Grey Wolves. In 1979 he was jailed for murdering a left-wing Turkish journalist who had published an exposé alleging close ties between the CIA and the Nationalist Action Party.[51] After a remarkably easy jailbreak, Ali celebrated his liberation with a letter to the largest circulation newspaper announcing his intent to kill the pope.[52] Apparently the U.S.S.R. decided that Ali was advertising for sponsors. According to Ali, the price was set at 3 million Deutschmarks; Uğurlu moved the money from his secret smuggling-cum-intelligence accounts and gave it to Çelenk; Çelenk was to pay Ali when the job was done. Agca was provided with a stolen pistol, and was turned over to his handler, Sergei Antonov, a senior Bulgarian intelligence operative posing as the Rome manager of the Bulgarian state airline.

When Ali laid it all out, it was truly a story "heard round the world." The U.S. Senate froze funds earmarked to promote trade with Bulgaria. Italy recalled its ambassador to Bulgaria, blocked further commercial and financial relations, arrested several Bulgarians, including Sergei Antonov, and began a three-year odyssey to prove the "Bulgarian Connection" in court.[53]

The case seemed to be very strong. The fact that Antonov spoke only Bulgarian and Italian and Agca only Turkish and a smattering of English apparently did not deter the two from getting together in private to plot the deed. Ali's story about visiting Antonov's apartment checked out: during interrogation he reproduced the address perfectly, right down to the misspelling of the street name in the Rome telephone book. He identified Antonov's wife who, he insisted, had greeted him at the door, on a day when a hotel registration form showed her staying in Yugoslavia. And he knew a great deal about the layout of the apartment, which, by an odd coincidence, was identical to one in the building inhabited by a priest later accused in the Italian press of being a CIA informant.

Although it seemed an open-and-shut case, there were a few snags. Once extradited to Turkey to stand trial for drug smuggling, arms trafficking, exchange control violations and tax fraud, Bekir Çelenk admitted to dealing in Bulgarian arms but denied he sold weapons to the Grey Wolves or that he knew Ali Agca.[54] One of his business partners backed up the story, insisting that, while Çelenk was a smuggler and, like all the big ones, had close ties to Bulgarian Customs, he had never dealt in drugs and had no connection with Agca. Similarly, the moneybags of the plot, Abuzer Uğurlu, told the Italians that he had indeed arranged for Ali to receive money, a grand total of $750, at the request of a friend who wanted to help the impoverished fugitive because they came from the same town. As to the rest of the story, Uğurlu insisted that Ali was conning everyone. Of course, there was no way the prosecution would take the word of two jailed smugglers over that of a bank robber, extortionist and assassin who had seen the error of his ways, particularly given his courtroom performance.

When the "trial of the century" began, Ali Agca did everything he could to improve his credibility. He repeated his frequent claim that the U.S.S.R. was the political and financial centre of global terrorism, but, just to maintain a balance, he also accused the White House and Vatican of conspiring to dominate the world. He spoke of his many plots, including those to kill the heads of state of Tunisia and Malta and the leader of Poland's Solidarity union movement. Apparently to assuage any doubts he was capable of such deeds, he proclaimed himself Jesus Christ and announced that the world was about to end, although he hastened to reassure the court that he had the ability to bring the dead back to life.[55] The trial ended with the prosecutor advising the jury to find the defendants not guilty.[56] Still, this ignominious finale occurred nearly four years after the traumatic event. By then the tale of the Bulgarian Connection had entered the public consciousness as further proof that there was no limit to the dastardly deeds the evil empire was prepared to commit to bring capitalism to its knees.

Chapter 6

RED SUNSET?

Historically, the economic spectre haunting America was overproduction, the possibility that industries would turn out more than consumers could absorb, precipitating a depression. The (short-sighted) answer, accepted after World War II, was to step up military expenditure. That pumped incomes earned in the military sector into the hands of consumers, enabling them to buy more civilian goods and services.

Meanwhile, the Soviet system was plagued not by inadequate demand for consumer goods but a chronic inability to produce enough. That was a direct consequence of the arms race. Based on its wartime experience, Soviet military doctrine assumed that sheer mass would triumph over fancy technology. As a result, its arms industries absorbed huge amounts of precisely those resources desperately needed for consumer goods. In a capitalist economy, an excess of spending power over available goods would have produced inflation. But in the U.S.S.R., basic goods were rationed and prices of essentials kept low to ensure everyone could buy them, if they were available. Extra money therefore had nowhere to go except the black market. While in the United States the mirror image of the arms race was industrial espionage, accounting fraud and public sector corruption, in the U.S.S.R. it was theft of materials, underground manufacturing and illicit trafficking in consumer goods.

Inside the "Empire of Evil"

The most important difference between a centrally planned system and a capitalist one is how decisions about what and how much to produce are made. Planners, not entrepreneurs, determine production targets. And those targets are set in terms of quantities of goods, rather than expected profits. Prices, too, reflect political decisions rather than market scarcity. Since the purest forms of socialism permit no private ownership of capital, all income is earned by "labour." Therefore the state can directly determine who gets how much, and influence where they spend it, by using its power to fix both wages and prices.

However, even in the U.S.S.R. where central planning originated, and to a greater extent in East bloc countries, the system was never pure. Enterprise managers were given monetary incentives to meet targets. But unless they were in a privileged sector like military production, those managers were rarely allocated sufficient resources. Often they could achieve their legal targets (and earn their bonuses) only by illegal means. From as early as the 1930s, they started to rely on professional wheeler-dealers (*tolkachi*) to bribe, barter or buy on the black market the extra labour and materials required. Since this involved diverting illegally obtained materials to legal ends, the authorities were prepared not merely to tolerate but to subtly encourage the practice.[1] From the start, economic crime in the U.S.S.R. was essential to the survival of the political system.

Soviet economic crime differed from that of the West in other ways. An offence like price-fixing was impossible when all prices were set by a central political authority. Nor were there any capital markets to defraud through stock market swindles. Social benefit fraud was rare because, in theory, unemployment did not exist, benefits were distributed through the workplace and major social services were free. On the other hand, Soviet economic crimes included "speculation" (buying with intent to resell at a profit) and "exploitation" (private hiring of labour outside the household), which are the heart and soul of a capitalist system.[2]

Nonetheless, some economic crimes were similar. One was bootlegging. Alcohol was deeply entrenched in the popular culture of the Slavic republics. Although there were periods when the market was free, the general rule since Czarist times was that production and sale of vodka (since the sixteenth century the tipple of choice) was state-controlled and highly taxed. During some years in the nineteenth century, it yielded nearly half of state revenues. The Bolsheviks, convinced that drunkenness was a Czarist plot to keep the working class in an apolitical stupour, tried to discourage consumption. They were quickly defeated by tradition, police corruption and the peasantry's need for extra income from home brewing. Soon the U.S.S.R. had more state shops selling alcohol than food. Yet with high taxes and prodigious consumption, bootlegging continued to flourish.[3]

There was also some drug trafficking, though it was marginal. In the central Asian republics, cannabis had historical roots, while in more urbanized areas the main drug problem was the diversion of medical barbiturates. Reflecting official atheism, there was also an underground trade in religious icons. And perhaps the most lucrative manifestation of underground capitalism was the work of professional smugglers in league with state officials who moved enormous quantities of art and antiquities stolen from churches and museums, to join the loot from Italy, Greece, Turkey, Egypt and Southeast Asia that graced private collections and museums throughout the West.

Therefore, although enterprise crime for personal profit was present, at least until the end of the Stalinist era, it was not very serious.[4] It was almost impossible to manage large sums of illegally obtained money. The banks were monitored closely; there were no private businesses through which to launder cash; large sums in hoards could rot before safely converted into coveted goods like fine cars or large apartments; and, since the victim could scarcely complain to the police, illicit earnings were vulnerable to common thieves. Furthermore, access to the good life in an environment where goods were scarce and rationing tight really depended on political position, not on income. On the disincentive side, the KGB and the OBKhSS (the police responsible for combating economic crime) were powerful and ruthless. While political dissidents were subject to internal exile, committed to psychiatric hospitals or sent to the Gulag, economic dissidents who committed serious offences were shot.[5]

As a result black market entrepreneurs were relatively few and lived modestly. To the extent they did accumulate substantial sums, they were more likely to fritter them away in underground gambling houses or blow them on vodka than spend them on luxury goods or reinvest them in illegal businesses. Even the underclass of professional thieves, the Vorovskoi Mir, avoided enterprise crime. Impelled by an anti-materialist ethic, they disdained "trade," including its illicit forms, in favour of pure predation, principally against the state.[6] However, by the late 1960s, a major change was evident.

The Red and the Black

In the West, the economic system is very effective in providing consumer goods for those who can afford them, and mediocre in providing collective ones. In the East, the opposite tended to be true. When the state was the sole customer — for machine tools, steel and coal and military — the system worked reasonably well. But it was patently inadequate in supplying ordinary needs. Facing constant shortages, consumers with surplus income could save it, hoping desired goods would be available in the future. Or they could use it to obtain the goods immediately through illegal channels, something rendered easier by the nature of socialist distribution.

At the bottom of the multi-tiered retail system were ordinary stores selling often limited quantities of basic goods quite cheaply. Next came better-stocked commission stores, open to all who could pay higher prices; these were also the only places citizens could legally resell their possessions, subject to a commission paid to the state. There were also *kolkhoz* (farmers' markets) in which part of the output of the collectivized agricultural sector was sold at prices more closely reflecting relative scarcity. Further up the ladder were "closed" stores patronized by senior bureaucrats and a few others like holders of certain military and state honours, where better-quality goods were more readily available. These stores were important because in the U.S.S.R., the main factor differentiating economic classes was not income but privileged access to places in which to spend it.[7] At the top were *berizoka* (foreign currency) stores, open only to foreigners, politically privileged people or citizens who had earned hard currency abroad. Such citizens were required to surrender their hard currency for *kupon* at a better-than-official exchange rate, and they could spend those coupons in the *berizoka* stores.[8]

Commodities leaked out for illegal sale from all four layers. To obtain goods from ordinary or commercial stores, a bribe might be required. Those allowed to use closed and foreign exchange stores might divert goods to intermediaries who would resell the goods (or, in the case of the *berizoka* stores, foreign exchange coupons) on the black market. Even the right to use those facilities could be a commodity bought and sold. While the direct monetary value of state and military honours was derisory, the access they provided to closed stores (or elite hospitals) was sufficiently appreciated to create a black market in medals and fake biographies to go with them.[9]

A second, more politically dangerous, source of illegal consumer goods came from production facilities specifically geared to the black market. For decades workers would moonlight, sometimes using materials stolen from their regular jobs, or spend time on the job producing items for private sale. However, that small-scale activity was mainly motivated by the needs of survival. Much more serious were operations involving management. As always, managers could barter for extra inputs to produce more output and therefore achieve or better their targets to earn bonuses, a tactic that lubricated the system. They could over-report output to get bonuses, paying off bureaucrats to cover for the falsification, a tactic that left the system nominally intact but corrupted it. Or they could under-report their output and divert the residual to black market sales, challenging the system both materially and morally. This could be complemented by actually setting up inside the plant a parallel production facility. At its most extreme, illegal production could involve diversion of state-supplied materials to underground factories completely off-site in order to produce directly to order for the parallel economy.[10] While underground factories existed across the U.S.S.R., they were especially prevalent in the southern republics. There they were protected by political pay-offs and by tight clan and family structures. Their operations were scarcely secret. But Moscow was afraid that cracking down would trigger a nationalist backlash.[11]

The spread of illicit production meant a profound change in the nature of economic crime, from being symbiotic with the planning system to corroding it. While the superficial cause of the transformation was the failure to provide enough consumer goods, deeper down it reflected a process of moral decay. By the end of the 1960s, with the exception of a handful of aging figures at the top, the U.S.S.R. was run by a new generation of leaders, distant from the Revolution, materialistic in outlook, forming a privileged and socially segregated caste and susceptible to corruption.[12] Below them was a population that combined rising expectations with disenchantment from decades of deprivation. If the officialdom could take bribes, the population at large could steal — for direct use, for resale or for inputs to feed underground production. Stealing from an individual was still abhorrent, but stealing from the state came to be quite normal. Furthermore, stereotypes about totalitarian police states notwithstanding, there was rarely adequate security for state property.[13]

Corruption and underground production complemented each other. Since it was still dangerous to display too much wealth, income earned from bribes in the legal economy would be diverted to the illegal one. When illicit goods were obtained by pay-offs to store employees, the acts, however frequent, were isolated and affected only the retail distribution system. But illicit goods stolen from state warehouses or produced by underground factories usually required the cooperation of officials. This alliance of underground businessmen and corrupt functionaries the Soviet population referred to as "the mafia," a term picked up from American gangster movies. The "fishing mafia" and the "fruit and vegetable mafia" diverted goods away from state distribution outlets onto the black market. The "hotel mafia" refused to book rooms, even in largely empty establishments, unless "service" payments were made. The "transportation mafia" similarly controlled access to airlines and trains.

The growth of these cabals at first invoked relatively little official alarm. Partly that reflected the growing number of functionaries profiting from them. But there were deeper reasons. In the early years, when the system was failing to satisfy consumer demand, the hope was that part of the discontent could be appeased by the black market. Then, over the course of the 1970s and into the 1980s, the "second economy" came to be seen as, though not publicly admitted to be, a means of sopping up some of the theoretically non-existent unemployment that particularly plagued the southern republics, and of channelling into commerce the energies of ethnic minorities left out of the power structure. That proved to be a monumental miscalculation.

During the late 1970s and 1980s, the U.S.S.R. was rocked by major black market scandals. The greatest was the Uzbek Cotton Scandal.[14] The racket was not particularly novel. For years central planners had demanded ever more from the cotton farms of Uzbekistan, while chemical toxification and erosion were rapidly destroying the soil. The local authorities faithfully reported they had met their quotas, and corrupt officials in Moscow, for a kickback, approved payments based on exaggerated claims. While raw cotton was over-reported, output from cotton factories was under-reported and the surplus diverted to the black market. What made the affair especially important was not just the sums embezzled (about 4 billion roubles, at a time when the rouble was officially about $1.50) or the extent and scale of the bribery (from point of delivery right up to Moscow bureaucrats). Rather it was the direct involvement of the leadership of a republic in which a nascent nationalist movement was stirring. Nor was Uzbekistan alone.

The Soviet Union was a potentially explosive mixture of more than 100 officially recognized ethnic groups. Many from southwest and central Asia harboured long-standing grievances against Moscow, and they were characterized by tight family and clan loyalties. The grievances provided a justification and the kinship networks a support mechanism for black market dealings. Not only were the southern republics poorer, but their peoples felt cut out of a system dominated by Slavs. With their upward mobility through legal means restricted, the alternative was the "second economy." With the growing involvement of the political leadership, it was only a matter of time before black market activity ceased to be merely an act of economic dissidence and became inextricably bound up with political insurrection. A rising class of politicians eager to expand their power relied on black marketeers for muscle and financial support, and in exchange provided protection. When Moscow, which still had a relatively clean criminal prosecution arm, cracked down, as in Uzbekistan, shaking up the republic's leadership and executing a number of principals in the cotton scandal, the result was not popular gratitude but nationalist outrage.[15]

These growing problems meant that by the mid-1980s, the Soviet leadership was desperate for a renewal of détente. Facing economic stagnation, popular discontent and rising nationalism, the leaders knew that saving the system, and themselves, required a massive shift of resources into the civilian sector. But the Reagan administration, sensing weakness, turned up the heat.

Holy War, Unholy Mess

The Afghan mujahideen certainly needed all the help the United States could give them. They were racked by political, theological and ethnic infighting that got worse the more foreign aid or racket money there was over which to argue. As well, their traditional concept of warfare was antithetical to modern guerrilla tactics. They preferred noisy public exchanges of fire and grabbed the first opportunity to loot.[16] Under American and Pakistani tutelage, some groups were trained to attack economic targets. In government-run areas, power supplies were disrupted (unless there were pay-offs), factories sabotaged, the main bakery serving Kabul subject to frequent attacks, and government-run health clinics and schools (deemed un-Islamic since they educated girls) destroyed. Once the Soviet Union, attempting to offset part of the military cost, began pulling minerals and gas out of northern Afghanistan at prices well below world market, mujahideen were taught to sabotage mines and pipelines.[17] The CIA also supplied counterfeit Afghan currency to buy supplies and help discredit the government.

Still, their performance was dramatically out of sync with their propaganda. During the disastrous 1988 campaign for the strategic city of Jalalabad, for example, the resistance news agency at various times reported the capture of 637 government posts out of the 30 that existed.[18] Even the economic squeeze turned out to be exaggerated. Despite its Marxist ideology, the government freed trade and turned smugglers loose — the same people who had made fortunes trafficking weapons and running dope switched to trading imported fuel and food, keeping the cities supplied despite attempts by the mujahideen to close the routes.[19]

Part of the problem was that the resistance forces were vulnerable to Soviet air power. For a time, the mujahideen had Soviet-model anti-aircraft missiles. However, those acquired from Egypt were old and defective. Others surreptitiously bought from Poland through the front of a private arms dealer were sabotaged by the KGB.[20] The CIA arranged for Short's of Belfast to sell its Blowpipe missiles overtly to Chile, and for Chile to sell them covertly to the CIA. But the

Blowpipe required the person firing it to expose himself to guide the missile to target.[21] Finally militant congressmen lobbied hard, against Pentagon and CIA opposition, to equip the Afghans with the state-of-the-art Stinger missiles.

When the Stingers started arriving late in 1986, they were more than merely a new weapon. The United States had broken the most fundamental rule of covert war. There was no denying who had supplied them. And the U.S. administration crowed about the results. Its official line would soon be that the Stinger, massive defections by Afghan government troops and striking victories by the mujahideen combined to force the U.S.S.R. to pull its forces from Afghanistan. The reality was a little different.

Apart from the fact that the U.S.S.R. had announced its pending disengagement months before the first Stinger arrived, most Soviet aircraft were downed by ordinary anti-aircraft weapons. More might have fallen victim to Stingers. But of the 1,000 allocated to the mujahideen, many were stolen by Pakistani officers, and others were sold by the mujahideen on the black market. Far from defections draining the Afghan government, as long as Soviet subsidies permitted it to buy loyalty with money, land and guns, defections from the mujahideen to the government were as common as the reverse. The government further curried favour by playing down Marxism, ending land reform, freeing political prisoners and adopting an Islamic veneer.[22] As to mujahideen victories, in ten years the resistance captured five small provincial capitals out of thirty-one, and never succeeded in holding an airport or a road for any significant length of time. By the end of the 1980s, the Communist government actually controlled more of the country than a decade before when the insurgency had barely started.[23]

In addition, the Kabul regime got lucky. In 1988 the United States and the U.S.S.R. signed an accord ending outside military aid. Prior to its taking effect, they both made last-minute deliveries. As usual, those bound for the mujahideen were turned over to the ISI, who stashed them in a secret base outside Islamabad. Explosives, missiles and shells, piled up in the open camp yard, provided a final opportunity to skim. Rumours of embezzlement reached the United States government, which dispatched a team to investigate. Four hours before the Americans landed, a massive explosion levelled the camp. Some said the blast had been an accident, caused when a soldier dropped a phosphorus shell or when a truck caught fire. Others countered that it was sabotage by the Afghan secret service. But the most logical explanation was that the Pakistani officers who had been stealing material planned a small explosion to cover their tracks; they could report to the American team that the missing items had been destroyed by accident. However, in the packed conditions, the initial blast triggered a cataclysmic explosion that devastated the camp and the environs, incidentally wiping out 75 per cent of the supplies sent by the CIA for the final topping up of the mujahideen arsenal.[24]

Ultimately it was not victories scored by the "freedom fighters" that precipitated the fall of the Afghan government, but the collapse of the U.S.S.R. With the end of Soviet financial aid, the government could no longer bribe regional militias to keep them loyal.[25] Afghanistan disintegrated into ethnic fiefdoms dominated by warlords deriving their financial support from contraband, drug trafficking and gun-running. Thousands of Islamic volunteers attracted by the propaganda of the Holy War returned with their CIA-financed battlefield training to foment armed dissent across the Indian subcontinent, North Africa, the Middle East, the Balkans and even into Southeast Asia. Algerian and Egyptian Islamic insurgents, Bosnian Muslim paramilitary forces, Moro separatists from the Philippines, Islamic guerrillas in Kosovo and even a Muslim rebel movement in Burma all drew training, arms and experience from the Afghan cauldron.[26] Indeed, "blowback" from Afghanistan eventually played a critical role in the bombing of New York's World Trade Center in 1994, American military installations in Saudi Arabia in 1995 and U.S. embassies in Kenya and Tanzania in 1998. Meantime, the CIA had to engage in a worldwide hunt to try to buy back off the black market all the diverted Stinger anti-aircraft missiles. Whatever their real record against Soviet military aircraft, they were sufficiently dangerous that for years after the fall of the Communist regime in Kabul, civilian airlines had to run up heavy extra fuel costs by veering away from the affected area lest some "freedom fighter" decided to see if the battery packs in his Stingers were still functioning.[27]

The Criminal Ethic and the Spirit of Capitalism

The Afghan war was an enormous economic, political and moral drain on Soviet society, exacerbating the impact of the other measures of economic warfare. However, in the final analysis, the disintegration of the Soviet Union was mainly the result of inherent problems of the system. The most critical was the endemic shortages — in 1989 a complete absence of soap sent several thousand Siberian coal miners out on a strike that quickly spread across the U.S.S.R.[28] Added to the problems caused by shortages were entrenched corruption, rising ethnic nationalism and, not least, a mounting wave of economic crime.

Until the Afghan war, illicit drug dealing consisted mainly of selling morphine stolen from hospitals or pharmacies, or, in the southern republics, trafficking local cannabis. But with the war, Soviet soldiers of Uzbek, Tadjik and Turkomen nationality contacted ethnic kinfolk in Afghanistan producing drugs, supposedly to raise money for the anti-Soviet war effort, though usually just to enhance some local warlord's military power. Apart from feeding Soviet demand, drugs from central Asia began crossing the U.S.S.R. en route to western Europe and North America, swelling the coffers of criminal groups.[29] Some 5,000 kilograms of hashish hidden in bales of camel hair were seized by the first-ever joint Soviet-Canadian police operation in the port of Montreal in 1987. The next year, British Customs, on a Soviet tip-off, grabbed three and a half tons of "Afghan black" packed in sacks of licorice root and shipped to England via the U.S.S.R.[30]

Another impetus to criminal enterprise came from the burgeoning arms black market. When the U.S. troops lost weapons in Vietnam, they were thousands of miles from home. Soviet losses occurred only a short drive from a border crossed daily by hundreds of military vehicles. Inside the U.S.S.R., there were sales by disaffected (and impoverished) soldiers; theft from army, police and KGB armouries; diversion from state-owned factories; and smuggling of NATO-issued weapons into the U.S.S.R. by way of eastern Europe. The supply of illegal weapons accelerated as financial difficulties plagued the Red Army. The end of the Cold War left more than a million demobilized soldiers without housing or jobs. Meanwhile, commanders of bases slated for dismantling sold off stocks to whoever had the means to pay.[31] On the other side of the market were criminals, ethnic insurgents, even ordinary citizens alarmed at the deterioration of the security situation, all eager to buy the means of offence or defence.

Yet another opportunity for Western-style crime came with the initial steps towards Western-style incentives. The perestroika campaign introduced two important new initiatives, a 1987 law encouraging individual small enterprise and a 1988 one designed to promote cooperatives for the first time since the 1920s. Three groups took advantage. Some were state managers testing private waters. Some were underground businesses who took the occasion to surface. And some were mobsters able, for the first time in sixty years, to extort money from the legal business sector or use co-ops and small businesses for laundering the take from other rackets.[32]

Perhaps the most important impetus to large-scale criminality came from an attempt to deal with the national scourge. By the middle of the decade, some 27 million workers were reported to have serious alcohol abuse problems. Pushed by public opinion, Premier Mikhail Gorbachev ordered a drastic cut in vodka production, sharply restricted sales hours, doubled the price and started a public education campaign. The result was disaster.

On the demand side, people diverted more sparse income to black market alcohol, neglecting food; before the campaign was abandoned, at least 18,000 people died from drinking poisonous bootleg brews in addition to everything from anti-freeze to shoe polish. To the extent the restrictions did inhibit people from buying vodka, the results with regard to productivity were not necessarily favourable. For some, alcohol-related absenteeism and bad work performance might have been reduced. But for other people, the work ethic was eroded when they were deprived of one of the favourite goods on which they used to spend their pay.

On the supply side, the campaign shifted bootlegging from a cottage industry run by peasants and old-age pensioners into a large-scale racket operated by career criminals. It doubled the black market price, the profits of which poured into criminal coffers. It accentuated an acute sugar shortage when speculators cornered the market to sell sugar to illegal distillers. It certainly stimulated thirsty imaginations; the MiG 25 fighter-bomber, which needed half a ton of alcohol for its braking system, became known in the air force as the flying restaurant.[33] Not least, it helped undermine the public finances.

In the 1970s, alcohol revenues had matched — occasionally even exceeded — defence expenditures. Granted, bootlegging was common, but the state still collected at least two-thirds of the income from legitimate alcohol sales. In the late 1980s, the ratio was reversed in favour of the bootleggers at a time when the budget deficit was already soaring. That, in turn, forced the government to cover some of the gap by printing money. With prices in the legal economy still fixed, the new money fed the black market. And a last-ditch effort to tackle the monetary overhang helped precipitate the final fracturing of an increasingly fragile union.

The authorities had two options to neutralize the threat from a huge amount of cash and liquid savings. One was freeing official prices, a move that would have produced too much hardship and generated too much social unrest to contemplate. The second was to directly reduce the monetary overhang. Citing the need to attack black market hoards and prevent roubles that had illegally left the country from flooding back, the authorities decreed demonetization of the 50- and 100-rouble notes, accounting for nearly one-third of the value of all the cash in circulation. Workers could exchange up to 1,000 roubles (about one month's average wages) without condition, while pensioners were restricted to the equivalent of one month's payments. Anything above required holders to present themselves at their workplace to a committee of union officials and KGB agents to explain the origins of their savings. The rules also restricted cash withdrawals to a maximum of 500 roubles in an effort to stop further black market transactions.[34]

What had been forgotten was that, given the history of shortages and the absence of consumer credit facilities, ordinary citizens routinely kept at home large amounts of high denomination notes so that when goods finally did arrive in the shops they could buy them quickly. Yet black marketeers held their savings only minimally in local currency; most were in gold, jewellery, foreign exchange and even religious icons.[35] To the extent that black marketeers had large denomination notes, some took advantage of leaks to dump them before demonetization, while others laundered them through legitimate businesses. Those with the ability to run the notes through business accounts sometimes bought notes from desperate and worried people for a fraction of their face value. The result was a transfer of income away from those who resorted to illegal activity for survival and towards big-time speculators and black marketeers.[36]

Not least of the scheme's failings was the government's inability to predict the reaction. Fear among the population at large was matched by the outrage of republican leaders. Some denounced it as an affront to the sovereignty of the republics. Others insisted on imposing their own rules, including longer redemption periods and higher conversion thresholds. The opportunities for laundering, together with the softening of the restrictions, meant that ultimately the vast majority of large denomination notes were exchanged at full value, making only a small dent in the monetary overhang. The operation did, however, make a huge dent in the central government's authority. Russian leader Boris Yeltsin, who had already consolidated his political position by supporting the 1989 strikes, seized on the rouble conversion for a high-profile defiance of the Kremlin, setting the stage for Russia's de facto secession from the U.S.S.R. a short time later.

Towards Mob Rule?
Immediately after the fall of Communism, stories surfaced about a secret party treasure trove. Supposedly party officials had salted away $12 to $180 billion — the amount depended on the mood of the teller and the credulity of the audience — from skimming arms sales revenues, ripping off resources and looting the Central Bank gold reserves. The money was reputedly hidden in a system of 7,000 foreign, mainly European, bank accounts. That the only thing ever found was 500 million roubles (then worth a few million dollars) stashed at 4 per cent in a local bank was taken simply as proof of how well the loot was hidden.[37]

There were also mass-media warnings of an emerging alliance of ex-Party apparatchiks, former KGB types and mobsters intent, for greed and revenge, on undermining Western civilization. Meanwhile a new global Crimeintern led by Italian and Colombian mobsters was reportedly moving trunks of drug cash to Russia to trade on the black market for roubles, using the roubles to buy mountains of minerals, forests of timber, and wells of oil at cut-throat prices, selling them abroad at huge mark-ups and stuffing the money into Swiss or Cypriot banks.[38]

There was certainly criminality aplenty. Speculation, suddenly legal, took the form not merely of buying with intent to resell, but of contriving artificial shortages by hijacking trucks, blocking supply channels, looting inventories and diverting goods wholesale from manufacturers to underground depots. When Russia issued privatization vouchers to citizens, permitting them to take a stake in former state-owned enterprises, cabals drove down the prices on the secondary market to grab the vouchers cheaply and gobble up prime assets. The free-enterprise frenzy even hit taxi drivers, who became notorious for running mobile money-changing bureaus, while some had prostitutes ensconced on their back seats for the benefit of customers eager for a different kind of lift. Fiscal fraud became so bad that Russian tax collectors set off to work, not with pocket calculators and scratch pads, but night-vision goggles and bulletproof vests.

However the Party treasury story was largely the work of a beleaguered government intent on blaming the previous regime for an empty treasury and depleted gold reserves. Most of the dollars entering Russia came, not tainted with cocaine and packed in suitcases, but still wrapped in Federal Reserve seals and flown in by cargo plane. They were swallowed up by the black market and then spirited out again in capital flight. The result was that the U.S. government, which paid a few cents to produce each $100 bill, rather than some Colombian-Sicilian cartel, was the biggest promoter of and profiteer from the monetary chaos. Privatization did produce huge illicit gains, but not because of the connivings of mobsters. Most people, facing impoverishment and mounting unemployment in a society that formerly provided (albeit modestly) from cradle to grave, sold their vouchers out of sheer desperation. The rapidity at which the state was willing to dump assets, at prices far below what they were worth, reflected the regime's commitment to ensuring that if a backlash ever put the Communists back in power, they would find the cupboard bare. And tales of the new Russian-based Crimeintern were mainly the work of the flotsam and jetsam of the Western Cold War establishment, desperate to find a rationale for continued existence, along with police forces who had run out of Italians to harass. The rash of speculation, looting and profiteering was less evidence of a new criminal *nomenklatura* than the inevitable consequence of a rush to capitalism after seventy-five years of banishing business to the fringes.[39]

Part Three

THE MUCH-PROMISED LAND

Chapter 7

OUT OF THEIR LEAGUE

In 1945 World War II ended. In 1946 the post-war world's first formal act of collective economic warfare began. The Arab League banned Israeli goods and services. It prohibited from dealing with Arab countries any individual, company or organization supplying Israel with weapons, setting up subsidiaries inside Israel, assisting exploitation of natural resources in Israel or carrying Jewish immigrants to Israel.[1] On paper the embargo looked tough. But Arab states put little effort into policing it — in fact, some violated it blatantly. It gained no outside support; some countries subjected citizens and firms who respected it to criminal charges. And Israel mobilized an impressive sanctions-busting apparatus. Fifty years later, the Palestinian Authority agreed to try to bring the boycott to a close even though none of the issues leading to its imposition had been resolved.[2]

Creating a Land Without People

The notion of a Jewish homeland in Palestine was first given official sanction by Napoleon as part of his effort to destroy British trade with the Orient. To that end, he occupied Egypt, which commanded the Red Sea route between India and Europe. Then he called for European Jews to settle in Palestine, through which the main caravan route ran from the Persian Gulf to the Mediterranean.

Though Napoleon was quickly expelled from Egypt, others took up the notion of Palestine as a strategic asset. British policy-makers in the late nineteenth century were worried that the Suez Canal would fall into hostile hands. That would force British trade with the East to go the long way around Africa. Because Palestine was a possible alternative route for a canal, leaders of the emerging Zionist movement attempted, without success, to convince Britain to seize Palestine from the Ottoman empire and re-populate it with friendly colonists.[3]

There had been a small Jewish population in Palestine for centuries, but most chose to live there for religious reasons. Although more Jews facing late nineteenth-century pogroms in Czarist Russia fled to Palestine, their numbers were still small, and conflict with the existing population, though certainly present, was the exception. The situation changed dramatically after World War I.

During that war Britain and France had promised the Ottoman-ruled Arab areas independence in return for military assistance, while plotting secretly to divide the Turkish territories between themselves. Simultaneously, the British tried to woo some central European Jewish leaders away from Germany and Austria-Hungary by promising a Jewish homeland in Palestine.[4] As the number of Jewish settlers grew, they purchased land from émigré Arab landowners and frequently evicted the Palestinian peasants. Inter-communal relations deteriorated. There were a series of bloody clashes, the worst the 1929 anti-Jewish riots in Hebron.[5]

During the 1930s, economic collapse followed by the rise of Nazism sent many more central European Jews fleeing. With doors closed in much of Europe and only half-open in America, British-ruled Palestine was one of the few possible refuges. But the indigenous population saw its national existence increasingly threatened. In an effort to deprive Jewish colonists of the means to buy more land and weapons, the Arab leadership called for Arabs to boycott goods made in Jewish-owned factories and to refuse to buy from Jewish-owned stores. The boycott was backed by sporadic attempts to block Arab customers from entering those stores or, if they did, to intimidate them into returning the merchandise. Meanwhile the Zionist leadership conducted its own campaign to force Jewish colonists to buy only from Jewish-owned businesses even if prices were higher, and to hire exclusively Jewish workers at better wages than the Arabs they displaced. Simultaneously, Jewish businesses were encouraged to sell to Arabs. In the decades to come, both sides would carry over the spirit of these informal commercial boycotts into their formal policies of economic war.

In 1946 the ban on the products and businesses of Jewish Palestine was codified into law by the handful of independent Arab states. It was a flop. After wartime shortages, few were inclined to forgo purchases, whatever the source of the goods. In a foretaste of what was to come, networks emerged that smuggled into Arab countries Jewish products with their origins disguised.[6] By then, too, it was clear that the decision as to who would live in Palestine would be made not in merchants' shops but on the battlefield.

Before the war, the British had crushed a Palestinian rebellion, arresting, deporting or liquidating its leadership, and disarming the population, while raising obstacles to further Jewish immigration. The Mufti of Jerusalem, titular head of the Arab resistance, fled to Germany, where he spent part of the war making Axis propaganda. In the meantime, radical political Zionism had taken inspiration from Benito Mussolini. Menachem Begin, for example, future leader of the Irgun Zvei Leumi terrorist group and, decades later, Israel's prime minister, in his native Poland joined a brown-shirt organization whose chief wrote a newspaper column that lauded fascism. But when Mussolini, anxious for German aid to bolster fascist forces in the Spanish Civil War, began to cosy up to Hitler, the mainstream Zionist leaders patched up their quarrels with Britain.[7] Even the Irgun kept its head down during the war. Once it even hired on with the British for a sabotage raid into Iraq, then ruled by a pro-Axis regime.[8] But soon after the war, the Irgun went on the offensive, against the British and the indigenous population.

The Irgun had units raising money, locating arms and training members in twenty-three countries.[9] The most important of these was the United States, where fund-raisers worked by persuasion, guilt and intimidation on religious congregations, businesses and households.[10] Sympathetic gangsters also kicked in money. Mafia hit man Jimmy "The Weasel" Fratianno described one Irgun fund-raising rally with the words "I've never seen so many Jewish bookmakers in one place in my life." The organizer boasted of raising $800,000 to buy a ship and load of weapons. The ship supposedly went down in a storm en route to Palestine, though Jimmy "The Weasel" suspected the operation was a mob scam from the start.[11] In addition to outside aid, the Irgun benefited from hold-ups of banks, post offices and a payroll train, as well as extortion from Jewish businesses in Palestine.[12] In all these activities, it had competition.

The Irgun decision to tone down anti-British activities during the war had caused a split. Out of it emerged the Lohamei Herut Israel terrorist group led by Avraham Stern, who had gone to Palestine in the 1930s committed to creating the kind of totalitarian movement he had admired in Europe. Stern and his followers blamed the Zionist mainstream for alienating Mussolini. They tried to convince the Nazis to create a Jewish state militarily aligned with

Germany on the French colony of Madagascar. They later proposed, equally unsuccessfully, that they be permitted to arm and train Jews in the Warsaw ghetto and move them to Palestine to fight the British.[13]

In 1942 the British killed Stern, opening a succession contest. One night Yitzhak Shamir, another future Israeli prime minister, went for a stroll with his chief rival for the vacant position and came back alone. His rival was later found with a bullet in his head.[14] Under its new boss, the Stern Gang expanded its operations. Externally, there were contributions from much the same sources that aided the Irgun. Internally, money came from robberies (of banks, government offices and the paymaster handling relief funds for Jewish refugees from Poland), from extortion, and possibly from taking advantage of one area where the British actively supported Jewish immigration. When the Nazis overran Belgium, world centre of the diamond trade, the British subsidized the movement of Jewish diamond cutters to Palestine. And the Stern Gang, or its imitators, seemed to find their precious stones a prize too rich to resist.[15]

Although the Irgun and Stern Gang received the most notoriety, mainstream movements were not strangers to similar fund-raising methods. Across Europe and the Americas, in French-ruled North Africa and white-dominated South Africa, the Haganah, the principal political and paramilitary organization, mobilized millions of dollars and tons of arms.[16] Its bagmen courted American mob boss Meyer Lansky, who staged a fund-raiser in one of his casinos and arranged through his wartime black market contacts to divert or sabotage arms shipments bound to Arab states.[17] Inside Palestine, the Haganah raised money by imposing "taxes," by playing the currency black market and by counterfeiting: a British raid on a safehouse turned up equipment for forging British government bearer bonds along with £50,000 worth ready for circulation.[18] This *may* have been supplemented by another source. While the U.S. army's Criminal Investigation Division and Counter Intelligence Corps were investigating a massive theft of cash, gold and bearer bonds from the former hoards of Nazi Germany, those same agencies were reputed to have in their ranks a number of Americans sympathetic to Zionism. There were allegations that those sympathizers had engaged in an exercise of pre-emptive reparations, taking some of the loot to Palestine.[19]

Arms came from many sources. During the war, the British had commissioned weapons from Haganah arms factories in Palestine. Part of the output, paid for by Britain, was siphoned off by Jewish irregular forces. Those militias also purchased black market weapons from corrupt British quarter-masters in North Africa. When the war ended, Haganah gun-runners raided American army depots in Europe and scoured the United States for war surplus material.

Arms, machinery, ships and even squadrons of fighter aircraft were available at less than scrap value. It was technically illegal to export the material without a licence, but that obstacle was overcome by pay-offs to mob-run longshoremen's unions, mislabelling or hiding shipments and working through cut-outs abroad who would attest to a legal destination while cooperating in diversion to Palestine. For a decade, one of the most important was Nicaragua's strongman, General Anastasio Somoza Garcia. For a price — a $200,000 deposit in the New York branch of the Bank of London & South America, plus gifts like a large diamond — Somoza allowed Haganah gun-runners (the most important of whom carried a Nicaraguan diplomatic passport) to claim weapons were destined for Nicaragua, and signed fake affidavits attesting to their arrival. The Haganah also purchased weapons from British forces who were about to withdraw from Palestine, outbidding Palestinians vying for the same arsenals.[20]

By 1948 Czechoslovakia, under its new Communist government, had become the most important source of arms. The Czechs provided not just weapons but also reconditioned fighter planes that were moved, sometimes painted with American insignia, through the American-occupied zone in Germany to Palestine. It was a mutually beneficial alliance. The Czechs took payment in hard currency, gold and stolen American military technology that Warsaw Pact countries could study and copy. And the new weapons, especially aircraft, arrived in time to be decisive against the Arab side.[21]

As the Israelis gained the military upper hand, the Palestinian peasant population fled, prodded on by massacres or by rumours, deliberately spread by Irgun radio, of typhoid and cholera epidemics. Emptied of their Palestinian inhabitants, some 380 towns and villages were demolished or handed over to Jewish colonists who then gave them Hebrew names.[22] The countryside secured, the Israelis could more easily attack major urban centres. The commander-in-chief of their elite forces declared, "We must strike at their economy" by choking off supplies and systematically destroying transportation facilities, stores and manufacturing plants, forcing the urban population to also take flight.[23] Afterwards, another facet of the economic war became paramount.

One of the earliest laws of the new state of Israel proclaimed that all who fled (750,000 people) forfeited their property: houses, farmlands and personal possessions along with about 10,000 shops, stores and factories.[24] To lose property under this law, the population did not have to pass the frontiers of what became Israel. Those who simply sought refuge in a neighbouring village also lost everything left behind. In areas where the population was slow to leave, Israeli soldiers evicted people from their homes or blocked farmers from cultivating their lands, therefore making the property forfeit under the law. In Haifa, the commercial and financial centre of Palestine, a billion and a half (Palestine) pounds worth of Arab deposits were sequestered. In later years, Arabs were recruited as Israeli spies by a promise to release their frozen bank accounts.[25]

All seized assets were supposed to be turned over to the Custodian of Abandoned Property. In practice, Israeli soldiers broke into homes and took jewellery, cash and oriental carpets. The army carted off truckloads of household goods that were never delivered to the Custodian. In an effort to stop the drain, the Custodian began paying a 10 per cent commission to soldiers who brought in looted goods. But even when goods were placed in the Custodian's hands, they sometimes disappeared again. Israel's "founding father," David Ben-Gurion, expressed disgust at the theft by individuals of property the state had intended to take. The loss of those assets would, he felt, interfere with the new country's ability to attract and support Jewish immigrants to farm the lands, tend the orchards and staff the factories and shops whose previous owners had been driven into refugee camps in the surrounding countries.[26]

Others, whose consciences were not as selective, were also upset. Among them was Count Folke Bernadotte, the UN mediator in Palestine who insisted that the first priority in a peace settlement be the repatriation of those who had fled. In 1948 he was murdered by the Stern Gang.[27] World pressure to restore to the Palestinians their land and property largely died with him, even though no one had been able to satisfactorily respond to King Abd el-Aziz Ibn Sa'ud of Saudi Arabia. When, in the last months of World War II, U.S. president Franklin Roosevelt personally brought to the king's attention the sufferings of Jews in Europe, the king had suggested that the morally correct solution was to compensate them with land in Germany. When Roosevelt noted that Jews seemed to prefer Palestine, the king's reply was simple. "Amends should be made by the criminal, not the innocent bystander."[28]

The League Beleaguered

From the start, the Arab League was at a major disadvantage. Most Arab countries were still colonies or protectorates. And the boycott attracted no outside support. While Israel was busy creating a national economy and developing commercial links with the United States and western Europe, the direct trade ban was of little consequence. The indirect boycott and blacklist, too, were easy to ignore. Most firms conducted business relations with Israel with no fear of losing the Arab market. The machinery of enforcement was limited. And, in any event, loss of Arab trade was not much of a threat. Arab countries, including the oil producers, were small and poor. For the first two and a half decades of Israel's existence, it may even have welcomed the boycott because it reinforced the image of David under siege by swarthy Kalashnikov-wielding Goliaths.

Furthermore, Arab states had no means of employing several traditional forms of economic warfare. There was no prospect of financial sanctions. Arab countries had no clout on international financial markets. And Israel would have been immune, for most of its outside capital came in government-to-government grants and concessionary loans. From 1948 until the mid-1960s, Israel's most important source of funds was West Germany. Funds allocated as reparations to Holocaust survivors went directly into Israel's state coffers. On top came private contributions, some open, others under the table.

In the early years, most people emigrating to Israel were destitute. They arrived from refugee camps in Europe, fled from increasingly hostile Arab states or, later, came from countries with repressive regimes. However, some were wealthy. Since their host countries often had tight restrictions on the export of money (in Syria it was a capital offence), certain financial institutions, mainly in Geneva, emerged to handle their needs. The pioneer was Société financière Mirelis, set up in 1949 by two Iraqi Jews to promote Jewish capital flight from Arab states. Later it diversified. In 1972 it landed in a British exchange control scandal after Scotland Yard bribed two employees to get the client list. And the firm's name subsequently figured in investigations by the Italian Financial Guard into the destination of money accumulated by tax evaders and drug traffickers.[29]

There was also the Trade Development Bank set up by the Safra family. Formerly money changers and bullion dealers in the Syrian city of Aleppo, then bankers in Beirut, the Safras made their fortune buying refugees' banknotes for a pittance and selling Gulf state magnates gold at inflated prices. After 1948 they fled Beirut, establishing their main business in Brazil and their bullion dealership in Geneva. Until the introduction of airport security machines, professional couriers working for the Safra bank were winging their way around the Middle East, and the world beyond, with up to twenty kilograms of gold strapped around their midriffs.[30]

Probably the most important conduit for covert money movements to, and sometimes from, Israel was Geneva's Banque de crédit international. Its guiding hand was Rabbi Tibor Rosenbaum, formerly chief Haganah procurer of Czech weapons. Rosenbaum's main public function was to act as banker to joint ventures between the state of Israel and European Jewish businessmen. But he also ran a more discreet portfolio of assets. One was Jewish flight capital, some from South America, most from France, a country where, contrary to stereotype, the most important status symbol of the well-to-do male was not a flashy mistress but a coy Swiss account. Rosenbaum's bank treated depositors exceptionally well. Its couriers handled the mechanics of moving money past French Customs, it paid higher than market rates, and it pioneered the practice of paying interest on accounts denominated in ounces of gold. The bank also arranged for Jews (and Communist Party officials) to smuggle money out of the East bloc. And it was the institution to which American mob boss Meyer Lansky directed his profits from skimming casinos. Nor were official functions neglected. Rosenbaum's bank financed Israel's covert military purchases at a time when many countries had imposed an arms embargo. And it acted as European paymaster for Mossad, Israel's external intelligence service.[31]

Incapable of applying financial sanctions, Arab states were also in no position to deny Israel strategic imports such as arms and food. Israel's major weapons suppliers, France and the U.S.S.R., were openly hostile to the Arab position. After being chased from Southeast Asia, France became embroiled in a bitter struggle to keep control of its North African empire against Algerian rebels backed by the Arab League. To the U.S.S.R. Arab states were allies of Britain in blocking Soviet influence in the Middle East. As to food, Israel was a net exporter of agricultural products; its earliest success was citrus fruit grown in orchards seized from the Palestinians.

One potentially serious weakness was oil. In 1948 Iraq, the traditional supplier, cut off the flow through its pipeline to Haifa in Palestine and built a new one to the Lebanese port of Tripoli. While Israel acquired oil from non-Arab producers, the costs were higher and the oil lifeline in danger from war. In the years to come, finding a secure source of oil was a central strategic consideration. That concern particularly affected Israeli policy towards Egypt, which had not only oil in the Sinai desert but also the Suez Canal through which, until 1967, much of the world's tanker fleet passed.

Egyptian efforts to deny Israel use of the canal dated formally from its 1950 Embargo Act, which declared certain goods war contraband and therefore subject to automatic seizure. After nationalist officers led by Gamel Abd el-Nasir overthrew the monarchy, Egypt tightened its blockade. Originally targeted at weapons, in 1953 the Embargo Act was broadened to include anything that contributed to Israeli military strength. And Egypt began refusing ships that dealt with Israel access to Egyptian port facilities. The threat became more serious in 1956. The United States offered Egypt financial aid for its Aswan Dam project, deemed essential for agricultural and industrial progress, if it would sign a peace treaty with Israel. When Abd el-Nasir balked, then compounded the offence by extending diplomatic recognition to the People's Republic of China, the United States, apart from plotting his assassination, withdrew the offer of assistance and pressed its allies to do the same. At that point Abd el-Nasir began eyeing the revenues of the French- and British-owned Suez Canal. When he nationalized the canal, Britain, France and Israel invaded, Israel taking the occasion to occupy the Sinai peninsula.[32] Although forced back by U.S. pressure, in 1967 Israel seized on the pretext of an Egyptian blockade of the Strait of Tiran to strike again. It grabbed the parts of Palestine that had eluded it in 1948, Syria's Golan Heights with its rich soil and aquifers, and Egypt's Sinai peninsula. The Sinai was a double boon. By closing the canal, Israel could deny Egypt its main source of foreign exchange. At the same time the Sinai meant oil.

In rushed American wildcatters. Leading the charge was resource-fund speculator John King, who had the financial backing of Bernie Cornfeld, a former B'nai Brith activist turned Trotskyist turned advocate of "people's capitalism." Using his Investors' Overseas Services, a shady offshore mutual fund operation, Cornfeld went looking for crooked money on the assumption that the dirtier the funds invested in his stocks, the less likely they were to be withdrawn in a hurry. Where IOS went — from Europe to Africa to the Middle East to South America — scandals over money laundering, tax fraud and exchange control evasion followed. For a time Cornfeld banked the black money his salesmen collected around the world in Tibor Rosenbaum's Banque de crédit international. But in 1967 *Life* magazine published a photograph of a courier who worked jointly for the Meyer Lansky mob and IOS, carrying cash to Rosenbaum's institution. IOS wisely set up its own Swiss bank.[33]

With IOS money and Israeli government support, John King arranged for a drilling rig to be hauled around the African cape and into the Red Sea. When it stopped over in the Côte d'Ivoire, Egyptian saboteurs planted dynamite charges. The explosion did little physical damage, but it was loud enough to attract the U.S. State Department. Fearing reprisals against American oil interests elsewhere in the Middle East, the State Department leaned on American companies to stop helping exploit the Sinai wells.[34] Although King was forced out, other American firms simply hid their identity behind foreign subsidiaries. And Sinai oil proved to be such a bonanza that it set off Israel's first stock exchange boom. As long as Israel held the Sinai wells, it seemed insulated from a direct squeeze with respect to the one commodity in which Arab countries could exercise some influence over world markets. But in October 1973, Egypt, brought to the brink of bankruptcy by the loss of Suez Canal revenues, and Syria, smarting over the loss of Golan, combined to launch a new war. During that war it seemed that the Arab side for the first time had an economic weapon that could really hurt.

Over a Barrel?

Oil is the most strategic of strategic goods. Its omission was, by Mussolini's assessment, the main reason that League of Nations sanctions failed against Italy, while denial of oil supplies had been the most effective act of Allied economic warfare against Germany. The importance of oil had increased greatly in the post-war world. It had become the foundation of mass consumption societies, fuelling automobiles and fertilizing grain fields, spinning synthetic fibres and distilling industrial solvents. Even if the Arab states could not affect Israel directly through oil, they should have been in a position to pressure other countries that dealt with Israel.

Yet limited oil embargoes in the 1956 and 1967 Mideast wars had been failures. The United States produced enough for its own requirements and a surplus for export, sufficient to fill any shortages felt by France and Britain during the 1956 war. Furthermore, the very nature of the international oil business worked against its use in economic warfare. For decades after World War II, seven giant American and British companies dominated production, distribution and refining, setting prices at each stage to maximize profits and minimize interference — from smaller competitors, producing countries and fiscal authorities. As late as 1973, the "spot market" on which oil was openly traded accounted for less than 10 per cent of international sales. Operating through colonial-era concessions making them de facto sovereign powers in large areas of the Middle East, the major oil companies could determine the state of public finances of producing states and therefore their pace of economic development. Since the "seven sisters" also controlled marketing, they could seriously impede any country that dared take control of its own production from selling oil. Behind them stood the American and British intelligence services, ready to stage coups against leaders of oil-producing countries who got too big for their burnooses.

That power also seemed to preclude Arab states from wielding an effective oil weapon. The companies could respect an embargo in theory while undermining it in practice by simply moving more Arab oil to non-embargoed customers and supplying more from non-embargoing producers to embargoed locations. The futility of previous efforts had not only given Arab producers an excuse to resist pressure from Egypt and Syria to use an oil embargo in the event of another conflict, but led to the conviction it would never be deployed. Hence, consternation during the October War of 1973, when the "oil weapon" was unsheathed.[35]

For more than twenty-five years after World War II, oil prices had been falling, while prices of most other major commodities trended upward. By the early

1960s the purchasing power of a barrel had dropped in half. To resist further cuts, in 1962 the Organization of Petroleum Exporting Countries (OPEC) was born, but for nearly a decade it was ineffective. Since oil was almost all priced in dollars, producers were hurt further when financial pressures caused by the Vietnam War forced a major devaluation of the dollar in 1971. However, by then the balance of market power was shifting. Rapid economic growth in the West had driven up demand, while the United States was running out of surplus capacity. As the market tightened, more buyers bypassed the companies to deal directly with producers. Led by the Shah of Iran (Israel's main supplier), in the autumn of 1973 OPEC producers demanded a quadrupling of prices.[36]

Although the hike was denounced in Washington as an anti-American plot, the jump had at least the implicit assent of politically powerful business interests inside the United States. American economic and political power was shifting from the northeast, where the industrial structure centred on the automobile, to the southwest where the giants of the military-industrial complex (and the American oil industry) were situated. Therefore the traditional concern of government with ensuring that domestic consumers could buy cars was increasingly tempered by its interest in ensuring that foreign governments, especially in oil-producing countries, could buy weapons. Moreover, to protect high-cost U.S. producers from cheap Middle Eastern oil, the United States had quotas on imports. The result was that U.S. industries bought oil at a much higher price than Europe and Japan, who secured a cost advantage just when they were invading American markets. A jump in oil prices combined with elimination of the quotas imposed higher energy costs on Europe and Japan, while it permitted the major international oil companies, mostly American, to rake in more profit. Even better, the entire exercise could be blamed on the machinations of the wily Orientals of the Oil Cartel.

While the negotiations that would eventually result in the quadrupling of oil prices were in progress within OPEC, the October War broke out. That set off a quite different chain of events by the Organization of Arab Petroleum Exporting Countries (OAPEC). Saudi Arabia, the most important Arab producer, resisted the notion of an embargo as long as it could. It sent a secret message to the United States begging it to avoid being too blatant in its support of Israel. But in a flurry of publicity, the United States announced a massive weapons airlift and flew the arms directly to Israel on its proud new C-5 cargo planes. This neat ploy permitted Lockheed and the Pentagon to sweep out of the minds of a public concerned over Israel's fate the huge plane's history of fraudulent cost-padding and faked test results.[37] Saudi Arabia was forced to act, the other Gulf producers following suit, by proclaiming, first, a general

5 per cent per month production cut and, second, a total embargo against the United States.

It was a farce. U.S. domestic production still covered the overwhelming share of domestic needs and could, in a pinch, take care of all of them. At peak, only 6 per cent of the small amount of oil the United States imported came from Arab countries. The disruption of supply proved to be minor and transitory.[38] During the first three quarters of 1973, oil production by OPEC countries had been running much higher than the previous year. All the OAPEC "embargo" did was to adjust the last quarter down to compensate for the previous excess.[39] Once oil was in transit, there was no means of monitoring its final destination. And other non-Arab producers, including Iran, Nigeria and Mexico, made up any shortfalls. The U.S. government declared oil import information to be classified, making it difficult to tell from where it was coming. That permitted the United States to hide sanctions-busting by its oil companies and to still publicly proclaim that the embargo was "100 per cent effective," enabling those companies to blame gasoline price increases on Arab ill will. While the "embargo" was supposed to last until Arab lands occupied in 1967 had been freed, it formally ended in six months with none of its objectives achieved.[40] In its aftermath, a former ambassador of the United Arab Emirates scoffed, "There was no embargo. There was no actual shortage. That was all said for local consumption. . . . You want to use oil as a weapon? You shut down the fields. That is the only way."[41] Needless to say, no one took his advice.

Pockets of No Resistance

The 1973 Mideast war had ended in a military stalemate. It was followed by an increasing commitment from the United States to ensure that Israel always possessed the armed strength to best its Arab foes. Thanks to the efforts of the most powerful foreign policy lobby in Washington,[42] Israel not only became by far the largest per capita recipient of U.S. direct economic assistance,[43] but received an even larger sum in military aid. Military aid to Israel was an excellent investment for the U.S. defence establishment. Each time Israel tested U.S. weaponry on live targets, the Pentagon and U.S. military contractors used the (often exaggerated) results in a worldwide sales campaign.[44] By the end of the Cold War, U.S. military aid was running at an annual rate of $1.8 billion, about $10,000 per Israeli soldier.[45]

Therefore, for the Arab states, a military resolution to the Arab-Israeli dispute was out of the question. That did not prevent them from spending lavishly on arms or maintaining a repressive security apparatus. However, the motivation was as much or more to suppress internal dissent as to prepare for war. Any pressures they could bring to bear on the question of Israeli-occupied land really had to come from the economic front.

On the surface, prospects for economic pressure seemed much better than before 1973. Even though the Arab "oil weapon" was largely an illusion, the OPEC oil price increases brought a flood of cash into Middle East producing countries. That had three potentially powerful effects. One was to enhance Arab political influence by giving oil-rich states more clout in international financial markets. Commercial banks scrambled to be the happy recipients of "petrodollars," and Arab contributions to the World Bank and IMF shot up. The second consequence was to strengthen the Palestinian diaspora. Led by the Palestine Liberation Organization, Palestinians abroad could use their access to oil wealth to build a government-in-exile and to support the struggle for self-determination of those under occupation at home. The third was to raise the stakes for any company caught violating the Arab League Boycott. Buoyed by oil money, the Arab market was no longer negligible.

In fact, the much-vaunted cash surpluses disappeared very quickly. Some, the part on which most media attention was focused, was frittered away by Gulf-state princes setting new records for *parvenu* vulgarity in Monaco casinos and London department stores. But the really serious money went elsewhere. Some was spent on American arms. After the price hikes, the United States set out to recapture, through arms sales to oil producers, $20 billion of the money it spent on oil. However, none of those weapons went to countries confronting Israel. During the 1970s, by far the largest buyer was Israel's ally, the Shah of Iran. Every weapon he bought put more pressure on nearby Arab states to shift military strength from the Arab-Israel front to their eastern frontiers. The next-largest buyer was slavishly pro-Western Saudi Arabia, whose armed forces were incapable of using the equipment loaded on them; the arms were purchased more for the fat commissions Saudi princes were collecting than for any notion of national defence.[46]

Some of the surpluses were spent on huge construction projects in the Gulf states, many having more to do with opportunities for local businessmen to skim than genuine development. The largest contractor was Bechtel Corporation, the American engineering giant. It was never clear in its Middle Eastern operations where the company ended and the Company (the CIA) began.[47]

Some of the excess was parked in U.S. banks. The largest recipient of Arab petro-deposits, Chase Manhattan Bank, was soon, quite publicly, one of the largest American sellers of State of Israel bonds.

And some was stashed in special U.S. government treasury bills with the unique feature of not being redeemable on demand by the country that owned them. It was as if rich Arab states went out of their way to give the United States the ability to freeze *their* assets should they engage in foreign policy actions of which the United States strongly disapproved.

PLO Inc.

The second impact of the oil price hikes was potentially more serious. Oil wealth facilitated the growth of Palestinian diaspora institutions. In 1964, the Arab states had created the Palestine Liberation Organization, nominally to support the armed struggle, in reality to keep the Palestinian refugees on a short leash lest they precipitate a conflict the Arab states knew they would lose. Yet several guerrilla factions, divided sharply by ideology and tactics, already existed outside the control of the PLO. Most important of these groups was Yasir Arafat's Harakat Tahrir Filistin, better known as Fatah.

At first it was a guerrilla group like the others. Its first military strike occurred under Syrian auspices. The 1948 ceasefire had awarded Israel and Syria joint control of some border areas designated demilitarized zones. Israel sent in soldiers disguised as farmers who slowly but methodically extended furrows farther towards Syrian territory. When the Syrians started shooting, Israel replaced ordinary tractors with armour-plated ones and hit back by air and artillery raids. By 1965 Israel had control of the entire area. Unable to match Israel's devastating strikes, Syria deployed Fatah in an ineffective attack on an Israeli irrigation project in the disputed area. When that helped provide Israel with a pretext for seizing Golan two years later, Syria's leadership concluded that irregular forces were at best irrelevant, at worst dangerous in a dispute that only conventional armies and/or diplomats could resolve.[48]

When the Arab armies were smashed in the 1967 war and the regimes discredited, the old Arab League-controlled PLO also fell apart. A new organization emerged, dominated by Fatah. Arafat's ability to transform Fatah into a political force, and the PLO into an independent voice, was mainly the result of his financial resources. In its early years Fatah was financed on a shoestring by occasional contributions from Palestinian businessmen and by money raised among Palestinian students in West Germany. Gifts from Arab heads of state, apart from the emir of Kuwait, were rare. Yet from the start Arafat recognized the political power of money. During his efforts to entrench the PLO in Jordan, Arafat vied with King Hussein to buy the allegiance of Bedouin tribes. It was in part to ensure that the king could outbid the PLO that the CIA put Hussein on its payroll. In fact the opening round of what eventually became a civil war in Jordan took the form of a clash between Arafat and King

Hussein over Arafat's attempts to independently tax the Palestinian refugee population in Jordan.

There had been sporadic attempts by the PLO to directly tap the region's oil wealth. In 1970, for example, the future PLO intelligence chief, Ali Salameh, reputedly leaned on some oil companies to kick in money — those that did not had their facilities bombed. But in 1973 the situation was transformed. The Gulf states agreed to impose a Palestine Liberation Tax on the salaries of the hundreds of thousands of expatriate Palestinian workers; those states also kicked in money. The biggest part was raised in Saudi Arabia and paid directly to Fatah. Smaller factions had to find their own sources. Some engaged in kidnapping, skyjacking and extorting money from Gulf state rulers.[49] Some depended on subsidies from Arab government intelligence agencies. A breakaway group, the Fatah Revolutionary Council, headed by Sabri el-Banna (Abu Nidal), collected most of the contents of its war chest from black market arms deals.[50] However, none could match Fatah.[51]

In 1970 the PLO was ejected from Jordan, its former headquarters, in a bloody civil war. Lebanon then became to the Palestinian diaspora what Pakistan's Northwest Frontier Province would shortly be for Afghan exiles. From Lebanon, the PLO supported all the accoutrements of a state: worldwide information and diplomatic services, an army and social security (pensions, medical care and educational subsidies) for the refugee population. Lebanon was also home to the bulk of the PLO's armed forces, the core of its communications facilities and the main industrial investments designed to train a generation of skilled workers and entrepreneurs.[52]

Some of the PLO's expenditures were made abroad. Each time a house in the Occupied Territories was razed by the Israeli army, the family would get a PLO subsidy to rebuild. Even the small Arab population still in Israel benefited. Israel neglected Arab institutions and infrastructure, leaving the job to the PLO on the tacit understanding that none of the money would support political violence.[53] However, most expenditures were made in Lebanon. At peak, PLO economic activities may have accounted for 15 per cent of the country's GNP, converting the Palestinian presence from a band of dispirited refugees into a veritable PLO Inc.

A Run for Their Money
The third impact of the huge oil revenues should have been to make the Arab market, at least in the Gulf states, too rich for companies potentially facing the Arab League Boycott to shrug off. To Israel, the danger was that foreign

business partners might be inclined to sacrifice the Israeli market for the Arab one. Furthermore, as Israeli businesses expanded in size and scope, they also coveted the Arab market.

However, the creation and enforcement of the blacklist of foreign firms was quite spotty. Some companies that did deals in Arab markets subcontracted their Israeli business to others already on the blacklist. Some handled their dealings with Israel through divisions or affiliates with names that disguised their links to the parent firm. Some that cultivated good relations with the heads of Arab states, American Express or Hilton Hotels, for example, were left free to do business in both Israel and the Arab countries. So, too, Coca-Cola. It had not only set up a bottling plant in Israel, but had publicly fêted the outcome of the 1967 war by handing out celebratory free samples to Israeli soldiers.[54] Yet Coca-Cola operated openly in Tunisia and Morocco. Even if a firm was placed on the boycott list, it could sometimes hire agents to lobby or buy its way off. Such selective enforcement reflected the fact that, while the terms of the boycott were collectively set, actual application was left to each member country. Certain Arab leaders put the demands of economic development, their personal asset portfolios or the need to appease powerful interests ahead of their pan-Arabist sentiments.[55]

On its side, Israel created its own blacklist of firms who respected the embargo, not just banning them from Israel, but circulating their names worldwide to discourage Jewish-controlled businesses from dealing with them. And Israel's supporters pressed Western governments to make it a criminal offence for their firms to adhere to the boycott. Some countries passed such legislation, then simply did not bother to enforce it. But in the United States the Israel lobby went looking for American firms who violated the anti-boycott law and pushed the government to prosecute them.[56]

One of the biggest catches was the U.S. medical supply group, Baxter Corporation, which had been added to the blacklist because of investments in Israel. When Baxter tried to establish a joint venture with a Swiss firm, it was told by its would-be partner that getting off the blacklist was a precondition. Baxter hired a Syrian lawyer to lobby the boycott office and offered to invest the same sum in an Arab country. To no avail. Bans were supposed to be lifted only when firms provided documentary proof they had withdrawn from Israel. Luckily, another firm offered to buy out Baxter's Israeli plant, and it could then supply the boycott office with proof of compliance. Unluckily, a recently fired employee decided to get even by leaking information to Israel's supporters. They reported to the U.S. government, which launched a criminal investigation.[57]

Nor was the direct trade embargo difficult to evade. Israel deployed many effective counter-measures with sufficient success that, by the late 1980s, the Boycott Office estimated that between $750 million and $1 billion worth of Israel's goods, about 10 per cent of its total exports, were reaching Arab markets each year. Agricultural produce led the list as the population of Arab states rose while their food production lagged, though agricultural equipment, pharmaceuticals, office supplies and furniture were all part of the flow.[58]

Front companies were set up in third countries to import goods, then re-export them with false labels and phoney certificates of origins. Sometimes only the paperwork got "imported" and "exported." Thus, if a Jordanian agricultural consortium wished to buy irrigation equipment from an Israeli manufacturer, the two partners would set up a dummy company in Cyprus, for example, to pose as the seller, and another in Mexico to act as buyer. The equipment would be sent to the Israeli port of Eilat and loaded on a false-flagged ship secretly owned by the Israeli national carrier. The ship would sail into international waters, then turn around and land at Aqabah, the Jordanian port within a stone's throw of Eilat, to show fake certificates of origin and bills of lading provided by the Israeli shipping company.[59]

Sometimes companies would buy Israeli technology and/or partially finished materials, complete the goods, then export them to Arab countries without informing the customers. Origins could be further clouded by trans-shipment through various ports. Israel worked out arrangements with U.S. firms that had Israeli affiliates for Israeli products to pass through different subsidiaries and re-emerge posing as American-made goods.[60] Such devices often involved the connivance of Arab importers and even Arab trade commissioners in third countries.[61]

For a long time, Greece and Cyprus, with their convenient location, multilateral trade connections, large but discreet shipping fleets and, in the case of Cyprus, corporate and bank secrecy laws, were the most popular places from which to smuggle Israeli goods into Arab states. But there were others. After the 1979 Camp David peace accords between Israel and Egypt, Israeli goods could be legally shipped to Egypt, then relabelled as Egyptian. However, Israeli-Egyptian trade never reached the great heights the framers of the peace treaty expected. And the treaty made other Arab countries suspicious of "Egyptian" products. Still, there was another neighbour whose potential as a spring-board into the regional market was much greater. It was also the main host to the increasingly restive Palestinian diaspora.

Chapter 8

FROM CEDARS TO CINDERS

In 1948 Haganah militiamen destroyed the economy of the Palestinian port city of Haifa, then emptied it of its Arab population, ending its role as the business capital of the Mashreq (the Arab East).[1] The heir was Beirut.[2] Lebanon's loose import rules made Beirut the main transit point for goods heading for Arab markets, while its tight bank secrecy laws, better than 100 per cent gold reserves, and zero tax on interest earned by foreign depositors permitted it to also become the region's premier financial centre. Among the institutions it attracted was a field unit of the Office of Finance of the CIA.[3] Such attributes, along with luxury hotels, the world's largest casino and a lax, often corrupt government apparatus, made Beirut a favourite haunt of the idle rich and the ambitious not-so-rich, the cream of the international press corps and the dregs of the international hustler brigade. Also among those enjoying its charms was the elite of world spookdom. They gathered daily in the bar at the St. George Hotel to plot coups, hatch revolutions and strike arms deals with political exiles.[4]

A Bank for All Reasons
Nothing better symbolized these forces at work than the rise of Yusef Beidas. Shortly after fleeing Palestine in 1948, he founded Intra Bank, soon Lebanon's largest bank. More than a bank, Intra owned the national airline, the television

and radio network, the casino, port facilities, a luxury hotel and the largest system of refrigerated warehouses in the Middle East.[5] Catering to kings and commodity traders, speculators and spies, Intra also acted as banker (accepting deposits and making loans) for Yasir Arafat's Fatah. Just for balance Beidas also helped the local CIA station-chief run black market foreign exchange deals to stretch the CIA budget for covert operations in neighbouring states.[6]

In 1966 Intra got into trouble. Partly the problem was an interest rate squeeze. Its investments, though solid, were not paying enough to meet all current obligations. But mainly it was a depositors' run of mysterious origin. Some muttered of dark plots by gangsters coveting control of the casino to launder heroin money, by Soviet agents seeking the national airline for smuggling strategic goods, by Arab potentates trying to score points in arcane political disputes. Inevitably some Palestinians blamed a conspiracy of New York Jewish bankers. But the real reason may have been completely fatuous.

Rumours about the bank's condition had been circulating in the St. George Hotel bar. Eventually they reached the ears of the emir of Kuwait, summering in Beirut. To check if his money was safe, the emir insisted on withdrawing $5 million. Beidas promptly arrived at the emir's villa with the cash. When the embarrassed emir asked him to take it back, Beidas suggested the emir might find a more appropriate place to stuff his money. Other rich Kuwaitis felt they had no choice but to support their monarch's injured pride by pulling their own deposits out of Intra, which collapsed shortly after in the greatest bank failure since World War II.[7]

Sifting through the wreckage, investigators turned up all manner of oddities: "dividends" paid by money-losing subsidiaries; violations of insider loan limits; faked deposit records; diversions of funds; abuses of trust funds; unsecured loans to politicians, newspaper reporters and the bank's own auditors.[8] Yet Intra Bank was solvent. It fell not because of the depositors' run or management frauds, but because the Lebanese central bank refused to lend it money to ride out the crisis. And that reflected the Lebanese establishment's resentment of the power of a Palestinian upstart.

After the collapse, control of Intra passed to the government along with the bank's stakes in the port, television and radio stations, the airline and the casino. The government put out an international warrant for Beidas, who died in Switzerland before he could be deported. The real causes of his downfall he himself had summed up: "I only made one mistake, but it was a big one. I made myself economically greater than the government."[9] It was a "mistake" the Palestinian community would repeat on a grand scale in the years to follow.

Revolutionaries and Racketeers

There was a dark side to the Palestinian presence in Lebanon. When the initial refugee wave poured into the south, the area was very backward. The influx, almost all farmers, meant cheap labour for the local agricultural economy, while Palestinians used their earnings to set up small businesses in the refugee camps or nearby towns. Hence, for two decades the Palestinians were regarded as an economic benefit. But following the organization's expulsion from Jordan in 1970, the PLO moved in, in force.

The PLO offered local Palestinians who joined the military considerably more than the agricultural wage. Where that did not force landowners to pay more, organizers from leftist groups like the Democratic Front for the Liberation of Palestine did. Shopkeepers faced competition from Palestinians who smuggled duty-free goods through ports controlled by the PLO. Contractors throughout South Lebanon had to buy construction steel from one large factory owned by a senior official of the Popular Front for the Liberation of Palestine who was accused of driving out competitors, then jacking up prices. The largest bank in Sidon was Palestinian-owned, ran the PLO investment portfolio, and earned the nickname "Fatah Bank"; the biggest construction company in that city belonged to a close associate of Arafat who was suspected of fronting for Fatah.[10]

As the PLO settled down in Lebanon, the attractions of consumerism to its cadres became often too powerful to resist, and officials became cavalier about the distinction between the organization's assets and their own. Aptly summing up the transformation induced by the lethal combination of oil money and a secure base, Ali Salameh, the PLO intelligence chief, married Miss Lebanon, cultivated good relations with the CIA Beirut station chief and took to racing hot-rods in the company of the spoiled sons of the country's Christian elite — until his career as a playboy-revolutionary was abruptly terminated by a bomb planted by the Mossad.

Meanwhile ordinary people were robbed, merchants had goods taken without payment and cars were stolen by young Palestinian militiamen waving AK-47s. With increasing frequency, Lebanese families faced death and destruction wrought by Israeli air raids and were only partially compensated by PLO subsidies for rebuilding homes and businesses. And Lebanese police and functionaries found their actions subject to PLO approval.[11] As the Palestinian infrastructure took on an aura of permanence, relations with the Lebanese hosts, or at least with the dominant community, deteriorated.

In 1975 political tensions exploded into a vicious civil war.[12] On one side was a loose alliance of Palestinian and Lebanese factions ranging from

Communist to Muslim fundamentalists, whose main point of common interest was to challenge the entrenched power of the Maronite Catholic elite. On the other side, there was a medley of rival paramilitary groups, based on ideology, family loyalties or merely the geography of the rackets that sustained them.[13]

Onward Christian Soldiers

In the southern-most part of Lebanon, Sa'ad Haddad, an army major later cashiered for treason, gathered a ragtag collection of smugglers and army deserters, subsequently renamed the South Lebanon Army, that would be Israel's principal proxy force in decades to come. Armed and trained by the Israeli army, the militia drew financial sustenance from Israeli military intelligence as well as what it could extort from villages under its control. Using powerful transmitters contributed by American Christian fundamentalists (who deducted the cost as a charitable and religious contribution against U.S. taxes), Haddad's people broadcast as far as Iran and Saudi Arabia, sending out a mixture of country and western music, gospel messages read with a Texas drawl, and snatches of the world news according to Haddad. On occasion, Haddad himself took to the airwaves to announce to villages behind on their protection payments the pending delivery of overdue notices by his Israeli-supplied artillery.[14]

Farther north, the most powerful Maronite faction was the Kata'eb (Phalange) party, created by Pierre el-Jemayel after he returned from Europe inspired by Hitler's 1936 Olympics. Like a good patriarch, he decreed that his oldest son, Amin, would go into politics while the youngest, Bashir, would follow a military career. Bashir's main responsibility was to use the party's paramilitary arm to knock out the competition.[15]

Prominent among the competitors was Suleiman Franjieh, Christian warlord of the northern fiefdom of Zghorta, who had begun his political ascent by killing a rival leader in a Church shoot-out. In 1970, with the approval of the United States, which chose to ignore CIA reports tying the Franjieh clan to the hashish trade, he had become president, elected by the Lebanese Chamber of Deputies after his bodyguards pulled guns on recalcitrant members. As president of the entire country, Franjieh was, naturally, concerned about communication. Therefore he appointed his son minister of telecommunications with a licence to shake down companies seeking government contracts. Nor did he neglect more local concerns, creating in Zghorta the Maradah militia force, most of whose weapons were paid for by exports of drugs or by a $100 "tax" on every truckload of cement sold in Lebanon.

Another competitor was Kamil Nimer Sham'un. His own term as president in the 1950s had been distinguished by Sham'un personally drafting Lebanon's bank secrecy laws and just as personally receiving a CIA subsidy. Pushed from the presidency by an insurrection that frightened the United States sufficiently for it to send in the Marines, Sham'un created his own political party and a paramilitary force. His Tiger militia soon earned a reputation for undisciplined thuggery outstanding even in Lebanon. Among its jobs was aiding the expansion of the Sham'un family business empire and protecting its smuggling rackets.[16]

With its forces split among those and several more factions, the Maronite side was at first at a military disadvantage. At one point, its opponents collectively controlled 80 per cent of the country. In 1976 two factors turned the tide. First, Syria, alarmed at the prospect that a triumphant Palestinian-led coalition would drag it into war with Israel, sent in its army. Although the Syrian intervention was initially designed to block further gains by the leftists, in the years to come the main concern of Syrian forces would be less military action than looting and racketeering. Troops loyal to Rif'at el-Asad, brother of Syria's president, displayed such an appetite for oriental carpets as to earn Rif'at the derisory nickname "the Persian." Over the next two decades, villages on both sides of the border shifted from agriculture to smuggling, and Syrian officers and non-coms began paying bribes for a posting to Lebanon in hopes of making a fortune.[17]

The second factor changing the military balance was the success of Bashir el-Jemayel in merging the Maronite militias into one unit. It was not an easy job. When the Phalangists attempted a takeover of the Franjieh clan's hashish and building supply rackets, they were beaten back, though not before murdering the patriarch's son, along with the son's wife and two-year-old daughter. However, a similar lunge against Sham'un was more successful. The Phalangists captured his smuggling business, murdered some of his wealthy supporters and won a nasty firefight with the Tiger militia. Among the victims were Pakistani workers in the Sham'un business empire that both sides used for target practice during lulls in the fighting.[18]

The result of the merger of the Christian factions (except Franjieh's) was the Lebanese Forces, which enjoyed two coy bedfellows. In a dress rehearsal for the Iran-contra scandal more than a decade later, Saudi Arabia, fearful of the possibility of a radical regime in Lebanon, put money into Cyprus bank accounts for the Lebanese Forces who used it to buy $100 million worth of weapons from Israel.[19] To avoid embarrassing the Saudi government, Israel worked through intermediaries; one of its favourites was EOKA, an anti-Muslim Greek-Cypriot terrorist group.[20]

The Gang's All Here

Virtually all groups relied on outside sources for arms and money. Most also engaged in local fund-raising. In the early stages, when the territorial division was still fluid and various factions even on the same side operated with limited coordination, they relied on simple predatory acts. One target was the port of Beirut, pillaged by the Phalangists with such enthusiasm that troops defending one of their most important strategic points abandoned battle stations to join the fun, leaving the position to be overrun by the other side. Although the value of the goods might have been in the hundreds of millions of dollars, the militia force got only a tiny fraction. Initially the militia had charged merchants a flat fee of about $6,000 to load up a truck, only later learning to set aside valuables like carpets, cars and jewellery for public auction.[21]

Yet another target was the banks. During the spring of 1976, eleven were robbed. One, the British Bank of the Middle East, earned a place in the *Guinness Book of Records* for bank heists when the pro-Syrian Saiqa militia, aided by professional Corsican safe-crackers, walked off with about $2 million in cash and travellers' cheques from the bank vault plus anywhere from $20 to $50 million from the safety deposit boxes. Apart from cash and bearer bonds, the boxes contained much of the gold inventory of the Beirut jewellery district. Belying the principle of honour among thieves, the boss of Saiqa welched on the Corsicans. They assassinated him in Nice a short time later.[22]

Later, as weapons got heavier and militia groups better coordinated, zones of control tended to stabilize and fund-raising became more systematic. In West Beirut, fiefdom of the Muslim-leftist-Palestinian coalition, there was little difference between taxation and extortion. Businesses might be shaken down several times by different groups claiming fiscal sovereignty, and bombed if they resisted. In East Beirut, centre of the Maronite district, taxation was far better controlled. The Lebanese Forces' equivalent of a ministry of finance levied hearth taxes on every household, sales taxes on cinema tickets and restaurant meals, excise taxes on tobacco, "visa" fees on outsiders coming into the territory, and transit duties on goods. Gasoline was taxed three times: at the import, wholesale and retail stages, albeit much of the money appears to have been skimmed by a el-Jemayel cousin who ran a wholesale fuel firm and the Lebanese Forces' petroleum department. When cars began stalling, he was asked by his customers to stop putting so much nail polish remover in his gasoline.[23]

The most important source of income came from taxing the import trade in a country that, in normal times, had to buy abroad at least 50 per cent of the goods it consumed, and whose prosperity depended on its role as a transit station for goods moving from Europe to the Gulf. Militias either took control of ports or built their own and applied a much lower rate of duty than did the Lebanese government at the legal ports. Militia control of ports, too, coincided with a worldwide epidemic of maritime fraud; an increasing number of hijacked cargoes made their way to no-questions-asked Lebanese havens.[24] And it facilitated an inflow of arms as well as outflow of one of Lebanon's best-known products.

Lebanon had long been a major producer of high-quality cannabis, protected selectively by politicians who pointed the police towards plantations funding their rivals' election campaigns.[25] During the 1950s and 1960s, most of the crop was sold in Egypt. Even the state of Arab-Israeli tensions did little to disrupt business. Drugs (mainly hashish) were hauled from Lebanon, across Syria and into Jordan (then including the West Bank). There they were turned over to Bedouin groups who carried them across Israel, first by camel caravan and later by truck, along illegal tracks protected by Israeli military intelligence, and into Gaza, then under Egyptian administration. After pay-offs to Egyptian officers, the drugs passed into Egypt proper. For Israeli military intelligence, it was a means of ensuring good relations with the Bedouin who acted as informants, a tool of economic warfare against Egypt, and possibly a means of accumulating a black budget for covert operations.[26]

Although the 1967 war upset the marketing arrangement, it was re-established within a short time, albeit with the routes shifted. Drugs from Lebanon would move into Israel, be transferred to Gaza and then infiltrated into Egypt by boat. The final leg was handled by the same Palestinian networks that plied the gold and cigarette smuggling trade with licence from the Israeli occupation authorities to put to sea at night.

Although by the 1960s cannabis cultivation had become widespread in Lebanon, it was really civil chaos after 1975 that caused it to explode and the market to become truly global. And it soon had an even more valuable competitor. A small amount of opium poppy had been grown in Lebanon since the middle of the nineteenth century. But prior to the civil war, the country's role in the world heroin trade had been mainly as a transit point for Turkish morphine bound for Sicilian refineries. True, some had gone farther. One former cigarette smuggler turned Phalangist gun-runner, Sami el-Khoury, a sometime business partner of Charles "Lucky" Luciano, set up heroin refineries to supplement his hashish exporting and cocaine importing business. He became important enough to be singled out by the UN in 1955 as the most important trafficker in the Middle East.[27] Still, Lebanon's share of the total heroin market was small. However, from the mid-1970s, cultivation of opium, and its transformation into heroin, spread rapidly.

There were several reasons for the drug boom. War disrupted markets for normal crops and made it more difficult for farmers to obtain fertilizers and pesticides. However, opium poppy and cannabis are hardy plants that do well under difficult conditions. After being processed into morphine or heroin, hashish or hashish oil, they are also very valuable in relation to bulk and therefore easy to move even when infrastructure is poor. Moreover, state authority was replaced by rule of the militias, who saw in the drug trade an opportunity to tap a hard currency market to support their operations. While much of Lebanon was riven by inter-confessional bloodbaths, drugs actually maintained a modicum of ethno-religious tolerance. In the central highlands and the south, growers were mainly Shi'a Muslims who had their own paramilitary groups to protect their turf. However the morphine-heroin refineries, the source of the serious money, were owned by Maronite militia leaders who also ran the principal gateways through which the product was exported. Initially, Bashir el-Jemayel, seeing drugs as a threat to military efficiency, tried to crack down on the traffickers. They reacted by offering financial support and assurance they would not sell in the Christian areas. But that accommodation was short-lived. Lebanese Forces officers began knocking off the traffickers to take control of the trade. Henceforth, between Shi'a grower and Maronite exporter there was peace, brokered by Syrian military intelligence officers who controlled the central highlands and demanded a cut, while bitter wars between different Maronite factions were fought at least partly to control drug exports.[28]

Apart from the mellowing effect of drugs, the civil war disrupted transit trade, wrecked factories, destroyed luxury hotels and damaged the public finances as taxes went unpaid and militias siphoned off Customs duties. Hundreds of thousands of people were uprooted and thousands killed in ethno-religious cleansing campaigns. Yet, after the initial shocks, most of the economy still functioned. Partly this reflected the huge inflow of money. Tens of thousands working abroad, especially in the oil-producing states, repatriated earnings to families in Lebanon. There were also subsidies to various factions from foreign governments and intelligence services. Similarly, there were the enormous expenditures of the PLO. Thus, while the shells rained down and the bodies piled up, the Lebanese pound actually rose against the dollar.[29] Furthermore, fiscally handicapped though it was, the state continued to provide essential services. The telephones and electricity usually worked, even if bills went unpaid. The ministry of finance still subsidized bread and gasoline. The central bank continued to issue banknotes whose value was secured against huge gold deposits safely out of reach in the United States. Although there was racketeering aplenty, most economic activity still followed legal channels. That would all change after the summer of 1982.[30]

Break-ins and Bust-outs

As the PLO entrenched itself in southern Lebanon, bringing northern Israel within range of its rockets, Israel intensified shelling and bombing. In 1978 it briefly invaded, sending nearly half the population of the area fleeing, either abroad or into the "belt of misery," the mixed Palestinian-Lebanese Muslim refugee camps and slums that ringed Beirut.[31] In 1982 it again rolled across the border, with one-third of its army. Before the carnage was over, some 50,000 Lebanese and Palestinians were dead, maimed or wounded, 85 to 90 per cent of them civilians, and some 600,000 to 700,000 people were displaced. In the aftermath, the Lebanese government estimated the reconstruction bill at a minimum of $8 billion, excluding damage to Palestinian infrastructure, while others put the total as high as $27 billion.[32]

The invasion damaged 350 major buildings as well as thousands of residential units. While the Israeli armed forces bragged of pinpoint accuracy, they shelled the Beirut mental asylum and orphanage and blew apart the hippodrome, killing forty Arabian racehorses.[33] The last of the luxury hotels not yet damaged was shelled though there was no military activity near it. Eight hospitals were heavily damaged, some after combat in the vicinity had ended. Although Lebanon's air force consisted of two 1950s-vintage jets, the runways were bombed and civil aircraft blown up. Israel thoughtfully opened El-Al offices in Tyre and Sidon and began bussing passengers to and from Ben-Gurion Airport.[34]

The Palestinian refugee camps were especially contested war zones. After PLO forces were evicted, several were razed. In Sidon, whose outskirts had hosted one of the largest refugee camps flattened by the Israeli army, Israeli manufacturers of prefabricated houses exhibited model homes to potential buyers.[35]

The 1982 invasion also wreaked havoc on the manufacturing base. Twenty-five major plants were destroyed and scores of smaller ones damaged. Much of the damage was caused when Israeli forces blew up facilities that survived the actual conflict, though sometimes not before their machinery was removed. Overall, Beirut-area industries, the worst hit, had to curtail production by 75 per cent. After the destruction, industrialists received letters from Israeli businesses offering to supply the goods they could no longer produce locally.[36]

Agriculture in the Israeli-occupied areas suffered disruption of markets, loss of labour through flight, death or kidnapping, destruction of irrigation works and razing of citrus orchards, swathed, the army said, for "security" reasons. Armoured invasion was followed by an assault by fresh fruit and vegetables — assisted by a military order that urban markets could put local produce on sale only after 10:00 A.M., by which time most demand had been met by heavily subsidized produce from Israel. Similarly, the hours during which fishermen were allowed to take out their boats were cut back, and the markets flooded with Israeli seafood.[37]

Another strategic objective was Lebanon's tight-lipped banks, raided by Israeli intelligence officers in search of financial records. Although the Lebanese government ordered the banks to resist, the Israeli probes shook depositors' confidence. At the same time, Israeli banks sent mobile offices into the occupied areas to exchange dollars and gold-backed Lebanese pounds into Israeli shekels. The Israeli Hapoalim Bank opened a permanent branch at the Lebanese border town of Naqoura, forgetting to apply for a Lebanese banking licence.[38] By insisting on the use of Israeli currency in occupied areas, the Israeli authorities were able to manipulate the exchange rate so that the Israeli currency traded at nearly double the value it should have against the Lebanese lira.[39]

During the occupation, Israeli soldiers went on house-to-house searches. Some took the occasion to seize objects that posed a security threat: cash, jewellery, art collections and electronic goods. Troops abandoned jeeps in favour of Mercedes-Benzes and BMWs. Research institutions, Arab embassies and electrical product stores on Hamra Street, heart of the West Beirut commercial district, were ransacked, trashed and looted. On top of individual acts of pillage, not much different from those already perpetrated by Syrian soldiers, Lebanese militiamen or Palestinian guerrillas, came officially sanctioned acts. The Israeli army grabbed stocks of weapons from the PLO (much of whose heavy equipment was more fit for military museums than battlefields) and from Lebanese government armouries.[40] Medical equipment was taken from hospitals. The airport lost computer and telephone equipment, vehicles and a helicopter. Equipment was uprooted from an agricultural research station. The inventories of the PFLP-owned steelworks were declared "enemy property" and loaded into Israeli army trucks. Archaeological artefacts from Tyre and Sidon were hauled away. Not least important of the prizes were the archives of the Palestinian diaspora collected to preserve the historical record and maintain hope of someday going home.[41]

Trading Places

The 1982 Israeli invasion of Lebanon quickly accomplished one major objective: the eviction of the PLO. Even before that was completed, the Israeli authorities were pressing on a second front, demanding from the Lebanese government a peace treaty that would open the border to Israeli goods.[42] The invasion had been timed to coincide with a change of government in Beirut. Aspiring to replace the incumbent president was Israel's military ally, Bashir el-Jemayel, who was assured of victory by the Israeli army rounding up deputies and hauling them to work on the day the legislature was to vote for a new president.

However, while Israel's Lebanese allies were delighted with the eviction of the PLO, they could not accede so easily to Israel's second objective. In some years Saudi Arabia alone took more than 50 per cent of Lebanon's exports. If Israeli goods were allowed legally to cross the border, Lebanon might be cut off from the Gulf market. Furthermore, remittances from émigré workers in the Gulf were the main thing keeping the Lebanese financial system afloat. If, in retaliation for Lebanon signing a deal with Israel, the Gulf states expelled Lebanese workers, the economy would sink like a stone. The Gulf states could also do severe damage by withdrawing bank deposits and refusing reconstruction aid.[43] And when Bashir el-Jemayel was killed in a bomb blast before he could take office, the presidency passed to his elder brother, Amin, whose commitment as president was less to appeasing Israel than to earning his nickname "Mr. Ten Percent." Faced with the economic realities, the Lebanese prime minister was categorical: "Even if all Arab countries make peace with Israel, Lebanon should be the last."[44]

Under international pressure, Israel gradually pulled back to a "security belt" in the south where it consolidated its hold. Mixed groups of Israeli soldiers and local militiamen went from home to home collecting "taxes" or demanding payment for the release of men held in local prison camps. People in the region were sometimes forced to sell their land cheaply to Israeli-designated buyers on pain of being expelled from their homes, which holdouts sometimes were.[45] And a smuggling apparatus flooded Lebanon with Israeli products.

Smuggling actually had a long history. Even before the establishment of Israel, goods used to leak across the Palestine-Lebanon border past a Customs post emblazoned with a sign reminding travellers that "importation of Zionist goods is strictly forbidden." During the 1948 war, while Lebanese troops fought alongside other Arab contingents in Palestine, Lebanese gun-runners spirited Czech arms across the border to supply the Israeli forces. By the mid-1950s a contraband network, controlled by the same Lebanese political figures who ran the hashish trade, was moving Israeli products the other way. The little southern village of Khiam, run by a Shi'a patriarch on the Mossad payroll, drew most of its financial sustenance from shipping cigarettes to Israel and bringing weapons back. While smuggling withered during the early 1970s, when the PLO had strongly entrenched itself in southern Lebanon, by the middle of that decade it began to accelerate. Israeli goods poured into both Sa'ad Haddad's "Free Lebanon" enclave in the south and the Phalangist zone of control around East

Beirut. With the 1982 invasion, almost all of Lebanon came under economic siege. In the first year alone Israeli exports to Lebanon, all paid in hard currency, totalled more than ten times the amount sent to Egypt as a result of the Camp David peace accords.[46]

About half the goods were Israeli products, the rest imports through the port of Haifa. As Israel's director of international commerce explained to one of the groups of Lebanese businessmen wined and dined by Israeli government officials, Haifa could be restored to its old grandeur as the commercial gateway to the entire region. Port duties were dropped to negligible levels making it cheaper to import through Haifa than through the Lebanese pirate ports. Goods were trucked across the border protected by the Israeli army from Lebanese nationalist saboteurs. After a 1 per cent tax was paid to support Sa'ad Haddad's militia, loads were transferred to other trucks owned by collaborating Lebanese merchants. Helping the process were Israeli trade officials, stationed in Phalangist-run East Beirut with catalogues and addresses of Israeli suppliers. When not dumped on the Lebanese market, the goods, equipped with phoney certificates of origin, mixed with the regular flow of Lebanese exports to Arab countries. Sometimes Lebanese merchants did not even remove the Hebrew lettering from packing cases. In one instance, a merchant tried to persuade Syrian Customs officers that the writing was really Russian.[47]

Israeli goods were soon turning up across the Middle East: biscuits in the storehouses of the Iraqi army, textiles in Syria, bags of onions and plastic furniture in Saudi Arabia. In an effort to pressure the Lebanese government to clamp down, Saudi Arabia and Jordan briefly banned goods from Lebanon.[48] The prime minister warned that any Lebanese caught trading with the enemy would be stripped of his citizenship, and he threatened to deploy the army to seize contraband stocks and arrest smugglers. In vain. The Israeli military protected the flow at source, the militias who drew much of their income from smuggling defended the apparatus, and influential political figures were compromised in the traffic. Furthermore, in the post-invasion period, it was difficult to persuade people traumatized by war, impoverished by destruction and facing acute shortages to pass up cheap essentials. When queried about the Israeli products on display in his stall, one West Beirut fruit seller observed, "I asked my sheikh and he said it was all right as long as 'Israel' was not written on the boxes."[49]

Officially this was a one-way flow.[50] The fifty or sixty trucks per day that rolled into the "security belt" were searched carefully on their return to ensure no Lebanese products went back. There was some smuggling in vehicles specially fitted with secret compartments. Israeli soldiers brought home videos and cigarettes, highly taxed inside Israel.[51] At one point a Druze sheikh with fifty Casio watches stashed under his turban and in his robes was caught when one of the watches began a wake-up chime as he was crossing the border checkpoint. However, the only Lebanese product that got through in any great quantity was one that never showed up in trade statistics.

Most drugs still headed out from the pirate ports to Cyprus, site of the regional U.S. Drug Enforcement Administration (DEA) headquarters, where bagmen from the militia groups would hatch deals with international traffickers.[52] But increasing amounts went south. During the late 1970s, the stuff could move across the border only in vehicles with military clearance, and Haddad's militia charged transit fees. With the invasion, all order broke down. Israeli soldiers bartered their weapons for hashish and opium, then reported the arms lost in action. Military vehicles carrying bales of marijuana made their way back across the border.[53] While much was for the local market or for trans-shipment to Egypt, ex-Israeli soldiers started being picked up by police in Europe plying the closely linked drug and weapons trades.[54]

Thus, the Israeli incursion into Lebanon struck a double blow against the Arab economic weapon. Israeli goods flowed across the border en route to Arab markets. And the PLO presence was reduced to a shadow of its former self, its military smashed and its finances battered by massive destruction of businesses and institutions.[55] The PLO was forced to slash subsidies to the Occupied Territories as well as cut salaries to its armed forces. Combined with resentment over cronyism and corruption, the salary cuts precipitated a brief but bloody rebellion against Arafat's leadership.[56] However, while the PLO's eclipse was supposed to weaken resistance inside Palestine, paradoxically it was the factor that finally goaded the population into open revolt.

Chapter 9

HOW THE WEST BANK
WAS WON

When Israel seized the West Bank and Gaza in 1967, its leaders were ambiguous about whether the new acquisitions should be exploited for their economic value or used, along with Golan and the Sinai, in land-for-peace deals. The balance of opinion in the long-ruling Labour Party favoured the second. But in 1977, with the ascent to power of ex-Irgun boss, Menachem Begin, the ambiguity vanished. His government sought to clear the best land of Arabs; divert the territories' water resources to Israel or to new Jewish colonies; collect tax and foreign exchange surpluses from the occupied population; turn the area into a dumping ground for Israeli goods; and, not least, use the territories, particularly the West Bank, as a base for breaking the Arab League Boycott.[1] All of this required dealing firmly with economic resistance from the indigenous population.

Creating a People Without Land

Virtually all public land was expropriated by military order. Then the Israeli government began seizing private land on the pretext of security, the owners sometimes finding out only after bulldozers had arrived to flatten their houses. The Israeli authorities also employed an Ottoman-era law that reserved all unregistered and uncultivated land for "public" purposes, like building a road to service a Jewish settlement. And they grabbed land by declaring it a nature preserve. If neither Israeli security regulations nor Ottoman law sufficed, they could apply various British or Jordanian regulations.[2]

In addition, the new government opened the territories to private developers. Despite the smashing of the PLO in Lebanon, nationalist resistance was still a serious obstacle. Therefore private speculators had to work through collaborating Arab dealers (*simasra*). The *simsar* would approach the land-owner, posing as the ultimate buyer. If a deal was made, the *simsar* would resell to the Jewish developer. If not, Israeli buyers might arrive with cash to make landowners offers they could not refuse. If they still resisted, they might be beaten, threatened with deportation or, on occasion, shot. More commonly they were simply conned. One enterprising *simsar* secured the agreement of a blind Arab owner by telling him he was signing an appeal to the military authorities for the release of his jailed son. Alternatively, a *simsar* could forge the owner's signature and take the document to the local *mukhtar*, the village leader who had the power to certify local land deals. Most *makhateer* had been parachuted into their positions by the occupation authorities. Armed and paid by Israel, they were usually happy to certify the deal. With the purchase authenticated, the *simsar* resold the land to Jewish developers, who arranged to evict the original owner.[3]

In 1983 the Israeli State Comptroller reported that as much as 80 per cent of sales involving the state showed irregularities. Two years later the Israeli Citizens' Rights Movement noted of private transactions, "Most of the land deals in the area are rooted in forgery, deceit, pressure and threats." Still, in 1986 then-prime minister Yitzhak Shamir shrugged off a land fraud scandal with the words: "Sometimes tricks and schemes were needed and unconventional means used to purchase and redeem land."[4]

When residents of the occupied territories faced the "redemption" of their land or in some cases just its topsoil ("redeemed" when settlers arrived with bulldozers and pick-up trucks to steal it), or when their olive trees, some hundreds of years old and the living symbol of Palestinian attachment to the land, were uprooted by the army and left to die, they could appeal to Israeli justice. In 1985 over 100 defrauded residents of the Bethlehem area went to the local police. They were told that the West Bank police could not accept complaints against Israelis. When they took their complaint to Jerusalem, the police there refused to accept it on the ground that they had no jurisdiction over West Bank cases.[5]

Until the early 1980s, it was possible to have recourse to civil courts staffed by Israeli-appointed Arab judges charged with administering land law according to pre-conquest rules. In 1982 a sixty-five-year-old Palestinian landowner waved such a court order in front of settlers advancing on him with a bulldozer — and was shot dead. The next year the military authorities transferred power to handle land disputes to a review board staffed by Israeli officers. By 1990 the Military Appeals Court had reversed a grand total of four out of five thousand confiscations, by which point Palestinians stopped bothering to appeal.[6]

Once the land was "redeemed" it had to be settled. Initially, the lead in colonizing activity was taken by groups like Gush Emunim. This American blood-and-soil cult, supported financially by ultra-conservative synagogues, was committed to carving out and defending, with Torah and Uzi, a frontier of Jewish settlements sporting ancient Israeli place names and modern American swimming pools. Its members were joined by members of the late Rabbi Meir Kahane's Jewish Defense League, some of whom settled in the West Bank ahead of American arrest warrants for murder.

Over time, the nature of the settler class began to change. Religious zealots were joined by *Homo suburbanus*. Some were Israelis attracted by heavy subsidies for internal migration. Others responded to advertisements in the North American Jewish press extolling the chance of a dream home in commuter communities with excellent links to the major urban centres.[7] A West Bank condo seemed a good investment. Prices were very moderate. Utility and mortgage costs were heavily subsidized by the state. Labour was cheap; Israeli developers could use as construction workers uprooted Arab farmers denied workplace protection because aggressive unions were banned and union leaders were jailed or "deported."[8] And part of the cost was covered by the U.S. government.[9]

Faith, Hope and Tax-Exempt Charity
On top of official economic and military aid, the United States heavily subsidized Israel through charitable, religious and educational institutions whose tax-deductible status made them another burden on the American public purse. Throughout the 1980s and 1990s such transfers to Israel were running at about $1 billion per annum. Among those that benefited was Rabbi Kahane's Institute for the Jewish Idea. In one of its flyers, the institute charitably and educationally observed that "a Jewish state can never make the Arab equal" and that Israel "must create nuclear, biological and chemical weapons for mass deterrent [sic]."[10] It is illegal for funds raised in the United States by a tax-exempt body to be used for military purposes. Nonetheless, every time a war strained the Israeli government's budget, it asked Diaspora organizations to take over more funding of education, health and welfare, permitting the government, legally, to use money saved on social services for military operations. Since contributions were tax deductible, part of the cost of the war ended up being loaded onto the U.S. taxpayer. Similarly, while the most important charitable organizations refrain from spending directly in the West Bank, the more

relief they provide the Israeli public purse, the easier for Israel to divert regular revenues to colonization.[11]

Along with land came water. In the Middle East, water has a strategic significance approximating that of oil in the West. This is especially true in Israel, which consumes per capita five times as much as its neighbours. When Israel captured the West Bank, it took control of two aquifers that, by the 1980s, were supplying 40 per cent of its domestic needs as well as those of its West Bank colonies. Palestinian farmers were forbidden to drill new wells or to use mechanical pumping devices on old ones. Some existing artesian wells were seized and capped. Yet American drilling companies were hired by Jewish settlements to drill new wells, sometimes adjacent to old Arab-controlled ones, bringing the threat of desertification to Arab-owned farm land.[12]

Elsewhere in the Middle East, deserts mean oil, something Israel still lacked. With the Israeli-Egyptian peace treaty, Israel lost control of the Sinai Peninsula. Although Egypt was obliged to sell oil to Israel, it did so at the world market price payable in hard currency, and there was always the danger of an unfriendly regime shutting off the flow. Worse, a short time after the return of the Sinai, a new revolutionary government in Iran imposed on its customers a pledge never to resell oil to Israel on pain of being cut off. Israel was forced to obtain one-third of its oil for cash on the spot market. Some of Israel's American supporters thought the Occupied Territories could fill the gap.

Among Israel's 1967 prizes were East Jerusalem and other Biblical cities like Bethlehem. They attracted hundreds of millions of dollars per year from religious tourism. They also attracted members of American evangelical churches who toured the West Bank using the scriptures as a guide to oil deposits. One investor in a biblically based drilling venture enthused, "We believe that when the oil comes in, Jesus will return and the Jews will turn back to God in fulfilment of the prophecy." That result was assured, another contended, because "oil will anoint the chosen people and they will become believers." Neither geological realities nor, it seems, the need for fancy equipment stood in the way. A U.S. radio ad touting shares in one venture stated, "We believe that God will open a shaft into the abyss and the blessings within will begin to flow."[13]

Gathering the Harvest

Seizures of land, uprooting of olive trees and capping of wells placed Palestine's agrarian society under siege. Israeli trade measures threatened to destroy it completely. Immediately after the conquest, the Occupied Territories were placed inside Israeli tariff walls and opened to Israeli-government subsidized products. Yet Palestinian farmers were forbidden to ship products into Israel without a licence, which was granted only if there were serious shortages of a particular crop. Nor could Palestinian farmers export to any other country if such exports threatened the markets of Israeli goods. One way to enforce the rule was by forbidding Palestinian farmers to spray with wax, which was widely used in Israel to keep produce from rotting quickly. As a result, Palestinian produce was inhibited from reaching distant markets while inspectors in Israeli markets could more easily spot unwaxed "contraband."[14]

The uprooted Palestinian farmers found little alternative employment at home. The development of local industry was blocked by regulations requiring a licence for virtually all economic activity. Receipt of such a licence depended on two criteria. One was that the activity pose no threat to Israeli business. Thus, the importation of most machinery was banned, and import licences were routinely refused for materials coming from anywhere but Israel. The second was that the licensee pass the scrutiny of the security forces, ensuring prosperity to either traditional leading families who accommodated the occupation authorities or outright collaborators.[15]

The abundance of collaborators made it easy for Israel to administer the territories. Some were recruited through intimidation. Many were recruited simply by money. And some were criminals, arrested by Palestinian police officers, only to have the Israeli authorities turn them loose, on the excuse that the prisons were full (of persons held for political offences). The grateful criminals resumed normal business and repaid their benefactors by political collaboration.[16]

Collaborators usually started as undercover informants and graduated to a more open role as agents of influence who would, for payment, use their connections to secure licences and permits. Those granted licences subsequently became dependent on the Israeli security forces to maintain those licences. In Gaza, for example, the only people ensured of permits to pursue the deep-sea fishery were those who agreed to be informants. Some took the permits as a licence to smuggle gold, cigarettes and drugs to Egypt.[17]

Even where permits were granted, indigenous enterprise was crippled by the need to compete with Israeli firms who received tax exemptions and subsidies at home and even more privileges if they set up in the territories. Palestinian businesses were also severely hampered by the absence of proper credit facilities. In 1967 the occupation authorities had shut down the local banks, freezing their deposits and seizing their records. Into the void came two large Israeli banks who accepted deposits, collected foreign exchange but refused virtually all business loans.[18] To obtain credit, local businessmen had to rely on money changers who charged high rates for small, short-term loans. Those money lenders in turn relied on cash and gold that their couriers were able to bring from Jordan.

And that depended on constantly changing Israeli regulations and on whether the border officials or police chose to confiscate the money on "security" grounds.[19] To reduce the chances of confiscation, money changers used priests as couriers. But even that was not foolproof. In 1987 the Greek Orthodox patriarch was stopped, his car searched and $1 million in gold seized, on the pretext that the patriarch was also smuggling heroin.[20] Even if the authorities let the money through, some Israeli citizen might decide on a form of citizen's arrest — of the money rather than the courier. In 1985 a Nablus money changer arrived at the frontier, dutifully reported to Israeli Customs some $350,000, then climbed into a taxi for the trip home. It was cut short by three men in Israeli army uniforms who relieved him of the cash at gunpoint.[21]

As the industrial and agricultural base withered, the population was left with two options. One was working in Israel in unskilled low-wage jobs. Some were illegal; virtually the entire economy of Gaza came to depend on the "black" labour market in Israel for its sustenance. Others were legal — and beholden to the Israeli security services. Israeli employers would apply for a certain number of permits to import workers. The permits would be turned over to *makhateer* who acted much like mob labour bosses making sweetheart deals with employers. The *makhateer* would grant work permits to friends, relatives or whoever would pay most, while denying them to potential troublemakers.[22] Once in Israel, these workers were subject to income taxes to help support Israeli bombing of refugee camps in Lebanon. They paid social security charges used to ensure a decent social safety net — for Israelis only. They had deducted from their pay (half the Israeli average) fees to help the Histadrut, the Israeli central trade union, protect Israeli standards of living, even though the Palestinians had only temporary labour status, which permitted them to be fired at will. After 1982 they paid a special 2 per cent surtax imposed on wages to finance the war in Lebanon.[23]

The other option was to seek work elsewhere. The émigré Palestinian population in the Gulf states peaked just before the 1991 Gulf War at 500,000. Their remittances back to Palestine reached an officially recorded $250 to $300 million per annum, most ending up in Israeli banks, with perhaps another $50 to $100 million coming back through black market channels. And this financial gain highlighted another critical role of the Occupied Territories in the Israeli economy.

During the first two decades of occupation, the Israelis introduced forty-five amendments to the old Jordanian tax code, including the right to seize productive equipment to cover arrears, and they added an entirely new value added tax, even though that was contrary to international law governing occupations.[24] Yet the authorities pumped little back into the economy. They deliberately neglected roads and telephones to reduce intra-communal communications. In fact, for many years Israel was happy to let PLO money, at least a half billion dollars, into the territories to finance social infrastructure — though it took the precaution of also letting anti-PLO Muslim fundamentalist groups send in subsidies, particularly to Gaza, to offset any political gains the PLO might obtain.[25] Although the government refused to publish the balance sheet, Israeli opposition groups calculated that throughout the 1980s taxes on the territories not only covered the cost of occupation plus all social services but left a surplus never less than $150 million per annum. Thus, the Palestinians helped finance Israeli settlements on their land.

In the meantime, Israeli firms with government subsidies established themselves in the territories. They acted as a magnet for settlers who had guaranteed high-wage jobs while the Palestinians had an unemployment rate from 25 to 50 per cent. Their presence also consolidated the role of the Occupied Territories as a base for breaking the Arab League Boycott. Israeli companies could register "offshore" in Ramallah, free from many Israeli taxes, and use their supposed location to export to Jordan Israeli goods parading as Palestinian merchandise. Thus, Israeli citrus fruit left packing centres unmarked, was put in boxes with West Bank markings, loaded onto trucks with West Bank licence plates indicating Arab ownership and taken to Jordan for distribution throughout the Arab states. Dairy products from Israel's largest producer were handled the same way, unmarked at the point of production, then with stickers and stamps put on at the point of trans-shipment. When it was realized that kosher meat met the same standards demanded in Muslim states for *halal* produce, one Israeli firm started sending unmarked truckloads from the West Bank to the Jordanian port of Aqabah for delivery to nearby Saudi Arabia, which had an enormous demand for *halal* foodstuffs, especially during the Haj.[26]

The Last Stand

Fertile land and irrigation water, biblical cities to attract religious tourism, a largely docile population riddled with collaborators that formed both a cheap labour pool and a captive market for Israeli goods, an excellent means to tap Arab oil wealth by capturing foreign exchange remitted by émigré workers and the PLO, a back door for smuggling Israeli goods to Arab markets, and a fiscal profit through taxes — it was too good to last forever. In December 1987, a vehicle loaded with Palestinians returning from work in Israel was (accidentally) rammed by an Israeli army truck. The next day when mourners at the funerals were surrounded by Israeli troops, riots broke out. Though there had been confrontations in the past, this was the beginning of a genuine grass-roots revolt that took Israel, the traditional Palestinian leadership in the territories and the PLO equally by surprise, threatening the authority of all three. The intifada was much more than ragged children throwing stones at armoured vehicles. It grew out of blind rage after years of being abused by Israeli employees, cheated on wages, and harassed and humiliated by the security services. In the early stages, the targets were not just the Israeli army and colonial administration but, at least in Gaza, even traditionalist and well-to-do Palestinian merchants.[27] But it soon took on more nationalist overtones, becoming an intensified replay of the pre-1948 economic boycott campaign. It had three major components.

One was an attempt to persuade workers not to cross into Israel. By the late 1980s Israel was heavily dependent on cheap Arab labour for agriculture, construction trades, sweat shops and cheap service industries like municipal street cleaning and garbage collection. But the labour boycott was largely a failure, as the organizers themselves recognized when they abandoned the general labour withdrawal and replaced it with periodic strikes. With the destruction of alternative employment at home, the Palestinian population was desperately dependent on income earned in Israel for nearly 75 per cent of earnings in Gaza and 40 to 50 per cent in the West Bank. Indeed, Israel periodically put the boycott in reverse by closing its borders to Palestinian workers.

That made all the more important the second aspect of the intifada: the refusal to buy made-in-Israel products along with the promotion of Palestinian enterprise. In the past, about 80 per cent of Palestinians' savings typically went into housing. But during the intifada it became patriotic to invest in producing commodities for local consumption. Initially the embargo was sweeping. But soon the leadership understood the importance of making boycotts selective, targeting those items from Israel that local industries could replace. This part of the uprising was enforced by *mulathameen*, masked and armed activists, who, apart from killing collaborators, destroyed merchandise from Israel. Networks of self-sufficiency were created. Some Palestinian firms grew rapidly. Some even became adroit at reversing the traditional dumping, labelling their goods "Made in Israel," marking them with Israeli flags or labelling exclusively with Hebrew writing so they could be sold illegally inside Israel.[28]

The third, perhaps most important part of the intifada, which struck directly at the heart of occupation economics, was a massive tax revolt. Already impoverished by steadily rising taxes, the population often put a patriotic mask on the simple fact that they had not the capacity to pay. The leadership exhorted them to fiscal resistance by stressing the illegality of the tax regime and the failure of the revenues to be reinvested in the territories. It also put pressure on Palestinians working for the occupation tax departments to resign.

Although the intifada began spontaneously, it soon required outside assistance. The PLO and various Islamic movements began fund-raising; Arab leaders made their usual pledges of support, few of which were honoured; and Palestinians in the Gulf states and Jordan began paying part of their salaries into a Fund for the Uprising. The need for money to maintain the families of those who lost jobs in Israel, resigned from the colonial administration or were imprisoned or killed or had their homes razed, gave the PLO a chance to reverse the rapid erosion of its standing. However, raising the money solved only half the problem. The money had to be moved into the territories. And the Israeli rules were strict. Prior to the intifada, no organization could import funds without permission, granted only after security forces had investigated the intended use of the money. In theory, individuals could import any amount. But sums above $5,000 had to be declared on arrival, then deposited in one of the Israeli banks within forty-eight hours, at an exchange rate 25 per cent inferior to that on the black market. If the money was not declared, it could be seized. If it was declared and suspected of "hostile" origins, it could also be seized.[29]

Once the intifada began, the Israeli authorities made stopping the inflow of support money a top priority. Organizations requesting permission to import funds were subjected to extra scrutiny; bank accounts were monitored regularly; new regulations further restricted the activities of money changers; and the limit for individuals to import money without a declaration was cut to $1,000. The regulations were further strengthened by an amendment to the Prevention of Terror Ordinance. It created a new offence of receiving or bringing into Israel or the territories property known to be connected to a "terrorist organization," permitted the seizure of any property received directly or indirectly from such an organization, and allowed the Israeli registrar of companies to refuse to register a corporation suspected of being illegal. The target was not just money sent in by the PLO or Arab governments. It also aimed at contributions by non-governmental organizations and wealthy Palestinians abroad who might have no connection to the PLO.[30]

The population responded by taking the money movements underground. Since about 1 million people per year rode the buses between the West Bank and Jordan, money could be distributed among many potential couriers. Some chose to smuggle in more gold instead of cash, or to convert money into very high-denomination banknotes to facilitate concealment. Following the lead of the professional money lenders, those responsible for aiding the intifada employed as cash couriers Muslim and Christian clergymen in the hope that they were less likely to be searched. Tourists and Arab Israelis were recruited to buy travellers cheques abroad, cash them in Israel and cross into the territories with the money. There were even instances where sympathizers purchased Israel bonds in the United States and cashed them in Israel, turning the money, including interest, over to support the intifada. Another method was for the PLO to put into reverse Israeli capital flight routes.

Israel was a country whose very creation had depended on the ability of its founders to smuggle in people, arms and money. However, after the 1973 war it had faced a growing problem of emigration, not just of people, but also of money. In an attempt to reverse that drain, one of the policy initiatives of the Begin government in 1977 had been to turn Israel into a financial haven. His minister of finance declared, "Israel wants to become the Switzerland of the Middle East." The government pushed up interest rates, legislated new tax breaks for foreign investors and generally rolled out the welcome mat. There were even signs at the international airport calling on Jews living elsewhere to open a foreign resident deposit. The currency denominations were flexible, the term to maturity adjustable to the requirements of the depositor, and the interest rate quite competitive with that offered by other havens and free of withholding tax. The private banking departments of the big Israeli banks, or their Cayman Islands and Panama subsidiaries, would also set up instant corporations and foundations for the depositor and manage trust accounts. Not least of the attractions, Israeli banks, like those of other financial havens, were unconcerned about other countries' tax and exchange control laws. One banker replied to a query about the scrutiny to which he subjected new clients and their money, "We don't ask questions."[31]

However, those measures failed to solve the problem of capital flight. Exchange controls remained in force, but they could be evaded. People would buy dollars on the currency black market, then either carry the cash out of the country themselves or entrust it to courier networks. In 1982 a former Israeli of Swiss nationality was caught by Customs with a list of sixty Israelis for whom he had smuggled out between $50,000 and $1,250,000 each. Most were listed only by code or pseudonym and the courier refused to break the code, citing the requirement of "discretion" imposed on him by Swiss bank secrecy law. While most courier systems were strictly secular, at least one had a more religious vocation.

The Mea Shearim district of Jerusalem was and remains home to Naturei Karta, a Hassidic sect that long refused political recognition to the state of Israel on the grounds that scripture calls for the recreation of ancient Israel as a theological not a political phenomenon, and only *after* the coming of the

Messiah. Denouncing the legitimacy of the state of Israel, members of this sect also refused to use its currency. Some combined political protest with financial convenience by smuggling in theologically acceptable substitutes, usually dollars or Swiss francs. The same pipeline could, for a price, be made available to those whose differences with the state of Israel were less its existence than its exchange control laws.

Yet another technique for smuggling cash was through Jordan. Many West Bank entrepreneurs kept bank accounts in Jordan and crossed the border frequently to sell goods, purchase materials and conduct financial affairs. Israelis could arrange for those businessmen to carry cash or gold on their behalf, stuff it in accounts in Amman and then wire it elsewhere.

Many of these same techniques were reversed to run money to support the intifada. Dollars were smuggled in by obliging individuals, members of Naturei Karta reputedly put their Swiss-Israel pipeline at the service of the PLO, and West Bank businessmen with bank accounts in Jordan could simultaneously assist Israelis to get money out and help supporters of the intifada to get it in. The PLO and the Islamic charities would deposit money in the Jordanian accounts of the West Bank businessmen who would use the funds to finance imports, then make the equivalent sum available inside the territories to intifada leaders.[32]

Some of the money was lost in transit through theft by PLO officials or couriers. One Israeli soldier recruited in Lebanon to take $500,000 to the territories decided to unilaterally raise his service fee from 10 to 30 per cent. Even when the money got to the territories, the problems did not end. Much more was lost through corruption, passed out to cronies or used to re-establish the old PLO-linked patronage networks that the intifada had temporarily eclipsed.[33] And there was never enough to offset the damage the Israeli countermeasures were imposing.

The Reckoning

When Israel closed charities receiving money from abroad and confiscated their funds, it damaged the financial lifeline of the intifada.[34] Other forms of counter-attack were equally or more effective. Collective punishments including curfews and mass arrests meant crops could not be tended or harvested, leaving them to rot in the fields, and people could not get to their jobs. There were further impediments on exports to Jordan. Access to the sea for the Gaza fishing industry was blocked by a security fence, passage through which required special clearances and additional fees. New trade regulations hampered the flow of goods between Gaza and the West Bank. There were arbitrary withdrawals of permits, closure of factories and farms, destruction of crops, uprooting of orchards, and confiscation of industrial equipment. Israeli banks, who rarely made long-term loans to Palestinian firms, also reduced short-term credit: they refused to make advances to suppliers or to clear cheques. Villages where resistance was especially strong, or where collaborators had been murdered, were subject to siege, their supplies of water, electricity or even food cut off.[35]

Israel also curtailed the right of Palestinians to work in Israel. Their places were taken by labour from southern Europe or by Soviet Jewish immigrants. This dealt a harsh blow to the standard of living of the territories and simultaneously undercut the local market for the new intifada-era industries. Jewish Defense League gangs invaded Jewish businesses in Jerusalem, threatening the owners until they fired their Arab workers and posted signs: "No Arabs employed here." [36]

But of all the countermeasures, none was as powerful as the use of tax commandos. Palestinians were already paying higher rates than Israelis or Jewish settlers. The burden was increased by new levies, forfeitures and fines, for example, for wearing a T-shirt with a "subversive" slogan or for writing anti-occupation poetry. Parents of children caught throwing stones were fined and imprisoned if they failed to pay. Regular tax assessments were also arbitrarily raised. People were told they should pay first and appeal later.[37]

To collect the taxes the Israelis stationed income, sales and property tax officers behind military roadblocks. After the soldiers checked IDs, the tax commandos went to work, using unpaid bills as an excuse to arrest people or just seize cars and contents. When soldiers raided a village, kicking down doors, the tax commandos were right behind, arresting people for non-payment and grabbing what they could. Sometimes, before dawn, soldiers would seal an entire village or town, then go door to door, ordering residents to a local school. There the tax collectors presented bills for overdue taxes and future estimates, while the army confiscated cars, appliances, furniture and valuables from anyone resisting immediate payment, and inventory and machinery from businesses judged in arrears. In some raids the Israelis made little attempt to match property seized with persons supposedly delinquent; the goods taken might belong to family, employers or even friends. The taxmen then hauled the booty to Tel Aviv for auction. Even those Palestinians who had money to buy back their property might be refused a permit to cross into Israel. The confiscations reached such proportions that the UN Security Council proposed a resolution calling for the return of the property — only to have it vetoed by the permanent member whose founding principle was "no taxation without representation."[38]

For an economic war to succeed, it must impose a relatively higher cost on the target than on the sender. In the intifada, the reverse was true. The Israeli GNP dropped by 1.5 per cent in 1988 and 0.5 to 1.0 per cent the next year. How much was due to the intifada was never clear. But the situation alarmed Israeli industrialists enough for them to press the government for a deal that would reopen the territories as a market and labour pool and to push towards more open access to the Arab market beyond.

For the Palestinian economy, though, the impact of losing external markets and labour income in Israel was catastrophic. In 1988 income dropped 30 to 40 per cent. The final blow came with the Gulf War of 1991. In response to Arafat's support for Iraq, Saudi Arabia and the Gulf States cut off funds to the PLO and expelled nearly 400,000 Palestinian workers. They also stepped up funding of radical Islamic groups opposed to the PLO's nationalist line. As its financial reserves dwindled, the PLO had to severely curtail subsidies to the territories. Threatened with total eclipse, the PLO accepted a "peace" agreement that included the formal recognition Israel had long sought. With that recognition came de facto acceptance by the PLO of Israeli laws, including the ones that had stripped the Palestinians of their property, in exchange for a limited "self-rule" that left Israel with control of the arable land and water of the Occupied Territories, the monetary system and most of the taxes. Nothing better summed up what the Palestinians were offered under "self-rule" than the spectacle of Palestinian Authority immigration officials subsequently checking documents at the Jordan border in booths equipped with one-way glass walls. Unseen behind those walls sit Israeli security officers who monitor proceedings and authorize or reject each would-be visitor. Under "self-rule" the pace of land seizure accelerated, and more houses were razed. Buoyed by an influx of Russian Jews fleeing economic chaos and rising anti-Semitism in the former Soviet Union, colonization continued. The economy of the territories stagnated further. Promised international aid came in only in dribs and drabs.[39] But President Arafat had the consolation of being able to choose the design for new Palestinian postage stamps, wisely deferring to those who counselled him to avoid issuing one bearing his own likeness.[40]

Part Four

BLACK, WHITE AND
SHADES OF GREY

Chapter 10

SLICK BUSINESS

$\mathbf{W}$hile the Arab League Boycott of Israel was the longest-running instance of economic warfare in the post–World War II era, the campaign against South Africa came a close second. The Arab League Boycott was ignored or denounced outside the Middle East. By contrast, over time a wide consensus emerged in favour of using sanctions against South Africa. Initially imposed to protest gross human rights violations, the world's commitment to sanctions grew as South Africa compounded the offence by military aggression against its neighbours and efforts to acquire weapons of mass destruction.[1]

On the surface the results looked impressive. By the early 1990s South Africa had dismantled the apartheid system, ended its occupation of neighbouring Namibia and renounced its nuclear arsenal. But how much this had to do with sanctions was far from obvious. Economic warfare against South Africa was actually spotty, sloppily enforced and countered through a well-oiled sanctions-busting machine. South Africa started with a big advantage, experience, for which it could thank its neighbour to the north.

Rule Britannia?
After Rhodesia's unilateral declaration of independence (UDI) in 1965, it should have been a perfect candidate for sanctions. Its currency was linked to the

British pound, and Britain was custodian of its exchange reserves. It was highly dependent on exports, and most of its trade was with Britain. It was land-locked, and it had no oil.[2]

Britain responded to UDI by freezing the colony's foreign assets and stopping all financial transfers on the assumption this would provoke capital flight, inflation and financial panic. Far from it. Since Britain had guaranteed its colony's borrowings, Rhodesia defaulted and left the British to pick up the tab. By banning payment of interest and dividends abroad, Rhodesia encouraged businesses to reinvest more profits at home. Rhodesia produced enough gold to offset the freeze on its foreign exchange reserves. Even the fact that its banknotes had been printed in England was only a temporary inconvenience: West Germany secretly sent a printing press permitting the rebel state to make its own notes. The only really discernible effect of the first stage of British sanctions was a shortage of Scotch whisky and port in the most prestigious whites-only clubs.[3]

Then the British tightened the screws, banning British companies from selling oil or purchasing tobacco and sugar, the colony's leading foreign exchange earners. The UN followed with a total trade ban.[4] It was supposedly mandatory. That was news to several countries, among them Italy, still recalling its own experience with League of Nations sanctions; France, always eager to make trouble for Britain in Africa; Portugal, committed to perpetuating white rule in its African colonies, one of which, Mozambique, commanded Rhodesia's primary access to the sea; and South Africa, which provided the alternative route and was fearful that success against Rhodesia would encourage sanctions against South Africa in turn.[5]

The core of the sanctions-busting apparatus was a set of parastatal organizations supervised by a special Customs adviser to the prime minister and managed by the intelligence service. Shell companies, easily replaceable if exposed, were set up in Liechtenstein and Luxembourg. Bank accounts were opened in Switzerland. And the apparatus was further protected by a law forbidding citizens from discussing the country's economic problems with foreigners.[6]

Since Britain had absorbed up to 70 per cent of the crop, sanctions on tobacco, Rhodesia's top export, should have been especially damaging. However, the quality of the crop ensured that there were many other buyers who asked only that their anonymity be guaranteed. The government wrapped the trade in a security blanket, created secret warehouses, replaced open auctions by covert deals, and shipped tobacco to Europe and Asia labelled as the product of Mozambique.[7] More effective was the ban on sugar, which the world had in abundance.

Rhodesia also produced minerals. Some, like chrome, deemed strategic, were exempted from sanctions. Others went to market with phoney certificates of origin claiming they came from Mozambique or Malawi. Yet others were co-mingled with South African ores.

Sanctions worked little better on the import side. To increase agricultural self-sufficiency, the government encouraged tobacco and sugar farmers to diversify into food crops. The country began growing cotton, and the government subsidized the emergence of a textile industry.[8] Although Rhodesia had no military industries, South Africa provided assistance directly, while also permitting weapons from other countries to transit. Italian-made planes with Rhodesian Air Force markings soon patrolled the skies. The Israeli government sold arms to Rhodesia. Israeli mercenaries joined French and British ones in the Rhodesian army. An Israeli corporation headed by a reserve general constructed a 500-mile mined security belt along the Mozambique and Zambia borders to keep guerrillas at bay.[9]

One point of vulnerability was oil. Formerly, crude oil had been shipped to Mozambique's port of Beira, unloaded into storage tanks owned by the major oil companies, pumped through a pipeline owned by Lonrho Corporation, a private conglomerate with interests all across Africa, then refined in Rhodesia. With the embargo, the majors refused use of their storage tanks, and Lonrho closed its pipeline. However, the refinery, though largely owned by the majors, stayed open, sparking the epic voyage of the *Joanna V*.[10]

Early in 1966, a tanker called the *Arietta Vezielos* left Iran with oil for Rotterdam. En route a Greek trader bought the cargo, then arranged through a Panama shell company to purchase the tanker for double its value. He changed its name to *Joanna V* and altered its course for Beira, where a Rhodesian front company was building storage facilities. The British Navy intercepted the ship, but was powerless to stop it. Meanwhile, the Greek oil trader sent another tanker in its wake.

The UN Security Council convened an emergency meeting out of which, for the first time since the Korean War, an incident was declared "a threat to international peace." That absurdly inflated designation gave member states the right to use force. The British Navy turned back the second tanker, and the Greek consul in Beira informed the *Joanna V* that its registration had been lifted. Unfazed, the owner re-registered the ship in Panama. But the episode had attracted so much attention the Panamanian government revoked the registration, leaving the *Joanna V* a pirate ship. Finally Rhodesia backed down. The ship, still loaded, sailed off for other destinations. And the British triumphantly slapped on a naval blockade. But Rhodesia's oil needs were already taken care of by another route.

The same oil companies that cut off Rhodesia still sold to subsidiaries in South Africa and Mozambique. Those subsidiaries resold to South African brokers, who marketed the oil to a Rhodesian government front company. That company then sold to Rhodesian subsidiaries of the same oil companies that initiated the process. Some was hauled by truck via South Africa; most went by rail from Maputo in Mozambique into Rhodesia. The sides of the tanker trucks or tanker cars were still emblazoned with the logos of the oil companies. Two-thirds of the sanctions-breaking oil was supplied by Shell Oil and British Petroleum, the first partly and the second completely owned by the British government, whose warships were publicly watching for embargo-busting tankers off Beira.[11]

By the early 1970s the Rhodesian economy was one of the world's hottest. Immigration was rising and investment increasing. But the party was about to end. In 1973 oil prices quadrupled; in 1974 came a slump in world prices of primary products like tobacco and minerals; and in 1975 Portugal abandoned its African empire. Upon independence, Mozambique sealed the border to goods while opening it to guerrillas. Finally, South Africa decided that, with the independence of Mozambique, Rhodesia ceased to be a buffer against black Africa and became a vulnerable finger pointing into hostile territory.[12] In 1980 Rhodesia capitulated.

When South Africa's turn came, its ministry of trade and industry set up the Secretariat of Unconventional Trade staffed with veterans of the Rhodesian operation to run parastatal corporations, shell companies and secret bank accounts.[13] The apparatus included Freight Services Inc., jointly owned by Safmarine, the government shipping line, and Anglo-American Corporation, the giant conglomerate that dominated the country's export trade.[14] Freight Services created holding companies in Panama, Amsterdam and Jersey, and used them to buy British firms in freight forwarding, procurement, air and maritime cargo. By linking this infrastructure it became possible to order restricted goods, for example, in the United States through a London-based procurement company, have a freight forwarding company fly them to Tel Aviv, load the goods on a freighter, and move the cargo from port to port in the Mediterranean to throw any investigators off the trail, before passing through the Suez Canal or the Straits of Gibraltar. Then the goods would go to some neutral country from which South Africa's fleet of merchant ships and cargo planes would complete the odyssey.[15]

All Pumped Up

South Africa, like Rhodesia, should have been vulnerable to an oil embargo. It was technologically advanced with high per capita consumption, yet had no wells of its own, though not for want of effort.

The affair of the *avion renifleur* (literally, sniffer airplane) began when a Belgian count with a passionate belief in alchemy and UFOs teamed up with an Italian TV-repairman-turned-self-proclaimed-nuclear-physicist to set up a Geneva company to finance "scientific discoveries." One of their projects was a device mounted on an airplane to catch the scent of underground reserves of fresh water. It was a flop. Undiscouraged, they reasoned that if their device could not smell water, perhaps it could sniff out oil, especially in a besieged bastion of Western civilization. They picked up their apparatus and headed for South Africa.

The timing was propitious. Oil prices had shot up in 1973, and the Organization of Arab Petroleum Exporting Countries slapped an embargo on South Africa. The French state-owned oil company Elf-Acquitaine was happy to help a project that might give it a new source of crude, freeing it of dependence on the potentially hostile former colony of Algeria and possibly propelling it into the ranks of the world majors. With a nod from the French president and a wink from the intelligence services, work got under way. While unable to sniff oil, the device had a fine nose for French francs, some 800 million of which were subsequently refined through Swiss bank accounts. For a time the French government kept the affair buried. But in 1983 a tax department clerk, investigating the route by which so much money left France in defiance of exchange controls, blew the cover. France had a major scandal, and South Africa was still oil-less in the face of the embargo.[16]

In the early years, when only Arab states and Nigeria boycotted South Africa, the embargo was of little consequence. On a visit to South Africa, the chairman of BP stated categorically that the big companies had "intentionally set out to thwart Arab attempts at enforcing embargoes on countries like South Africa."[17] The companies sold oil from non-embargoing sources to South Africa and made up the shortfall to other customers by selling them more Arab oil. However, in 1978 the UN General Assembly asked members to cut off oil. The next year the Iranian Revolution brought down the Shah, principal oil supplier to South Africa, and replaced him with a mullah-cracy that banned further sales. Over the 1980s more producers announced adherence to the embargo.

There were countermeasures. South Africa introduced an energy substitution program that promoted hydro power and made great strides in coal liquefaction. The resulting fuel was dirty and cost well above the world price, but it took care of a third of requirements.[18] For the other two-thirds, South Africa had a barrel of tricks.[19]

Throughout the 1980s when the oil embargo was supposedly being tightened, the market was glutted, prices were dropping and traders were anxious to dump whatever they could wherever they could. South Africa bought heavily while prices were low until its strategic reserves were five times Western norms.[20] Furthermore, the key to the burden oil imposed on South Africa was not its price, but that price relative to gold, source of 50 per cent of South Africa's foreign exchange. When oil soared in the late 1970s, so did gold — and diamonds and platinum, which South Africa also had in abundance. Although gold (and diamonds) dropped subsequently, oil fell farther. Gold was more than just a lucrative export. Many countries seeking to build up reserves were happy to exchange off-the-books oil for anonymous gold. Of course discretion is guaranteed only if both buyer and seller respect it. South Africa made it a criminal offence, punishable by stiff fines and imprisonment, to reveal information about its oil policy.[21] On the other side, too, there were ample motives for keeping mum.

Preventing Oil Spills

While the world was mesmerized by unsustainable price hikes in 1973, the really important change was in marketing. Bypassing the big companies, producing countries sold more of their oil either in direct state-to-state deals or on the spot market. In theory OPEC negotiated production quotas. But it lacked any independent monitoring or enforcement powers. Member countries cheated repeatedly. Oil produced outside OPEC quotas could then be diverted at will.[22]

Sometimes the motive for the diversion was personal profit. This was common in Nigeria, which, during the mid-1980s, was "losing" up to $4 billion worth per annum. Oil was pumped out and shipped without reporting, with the complicity of government ministers or officers of the Nigerian National Petroleum Company. Typically, the captain of a tramp tanker would arrive, pay dollars to a local official for crude or refined fuel oils, and sail off, perhaps with a load of Nigerian marijuana thrown in for good measure, while the official would collect doubly by converting the dollars on the black market. Alternatively, he could deposit the dollars in the local branch of BCCI, much of whose profit came from running a capital flight operation for corrupt Nigerian officials. Although stolen Nigerian crude and fuel oil could end up anywhere, South Africa was one destination.[23]

So dirty did the Nigerian oil business become that it was soon a breeding ground for some of the world's most skilled fraudsters. They sought out customers for cut-rate oil, telling them that it was from special presidential or armed forces "liftings," the industry's apt term for pumping oil, or that it was a gift from the president to a crony. By also claiming it was surplus to OPEC quotas, they could increase the credibility, and confidentiality, of the deal. Unlike other internationally traded commodities, oil is paid on delivery rather than on loading. So fraudsters demanded advance payments plus a few hundred thousand dollars to pay port charges and bribes. They sold the same oil to a number of customers, all sworn to secrecy. They further increased the customer ranks by reselling the cargo once the tanker was en route, with the result that when it arrived a veritable army of "owners" descended to claim it. In the neatest version, there was no oil at all — the entire operation was based on inside information about tankers with loads already owned by the big transnational companies.[24]

Personal profit was only one reason for oil diversion. During the last years of the Shah of Iran, an analyst at the National Iranian Oil Company discovered that 10 per cent of the country's production was being siphoned off into secret accounts at Chase Manhattan Bank to create special political contingency funds in anticipation of the need to finance a counter-coup.[25] Oil might also be diverted to finance covert military acquisitions. Oil-for-arms swaps are state secrets in Saudi Arabia, where the rule is, the more controversial the project, the more likely it is financed with oil to better hide the trail.[26]

The post-1973 trading environment saw another fundamental change: the emergence of networks of slick traders who were skilled in "selling" oil back and forth between dummy companies to hide its origins, dexterous at manufacturing phoney bills of lading to disguise its destination, and adroit at making the payments vanish through coded bank accounts. For those traders, oil in excess of OPEC quotas was especially desirable. Once a country had busted its quota, it was hardly in a position to object, if it wanted to, when the oil ended up in some embargoed destination.

The star of this business was Marc Rich, boss of the world's largest commodity trading firm. While he dealt in virtually everything, his heart and his fortune were in oil.[27] Where others saw an embargo as a manifestation of the international community's desire for social justice, Marc Rich saw it as a profit opportunity too good to be missed. He sold Saudi oil to Israel, Soviet oil to western Europe, and Nigerian oil to South Africa. In 1979, when the United States banned all trade with Iran, Marc Rich & Co. was on hand, buying Iranian oil and passing it through subsidiaries handling Nigerian, Peruvian and Argentinean oil before marketing it to desperate refiners. Simultaneously, when the United States reacted to the dramatic price hikes by slapping price controls on oil from old wells (on the rationale that the owners had already met their overheads and therefore had no excuse for price-gouging), Marc Rich & Co. bought oil from old wells at capped prices and passed it through a daisy chain of intermediate "sales" before unloading it as new oil at the free-market price. By manipulating the price at which oil was moved from one shell company to another, Marc Rich & Co. could make the profits disappear into Switzerland. The firm's skills eventually earned it and its principals criminal charges for trading with the enemy on top of making them targets in the most massive tax evasion case in U.S. history.[28] Rich, safely ensconced in Switzerland to avoid a potential three and a half centuries of jail, remained a favourite business partner of the Iranians. He alone of the major traders had not abandoned Iran at the time of the Revolution, he made sure that prices contained enough room to divert "chocolates" into the secret accounts of officials, and he was ready to arrange arms-for-oil barter deals.[29]

The Iranian revolution had initially shaken South Africa. The new government made a great show of cutting off the apartheid regime, threatening customers with blacklisting should they be caught reselling. Within a year of Iran publicly joining the embargo came an attack by guerrillas of the military wing of the African National Congress on South Africa's most important coal-liquefaction complex. The resulting fears sent South Africa on a Caribbean cruise.

In 1978 Patrick John had led Dominica to independence from Britain. His dream was to "industrialize" an economy hitherto based on bananas. The plan was that small farmers would be coerced into selling land to an American consortium, the area would be closed to locals, the Americans would build a "free port" into which crude oil would be imported, and the South Africans would secretly finance a refinery. When the news became public in 1979, Patrick John was deposed.[30]

Out but not down, the ex-prime minister was approached the next year by a group of Ku Klux Klan types who offered to put him back in power in exchange for a place to establish a white-supremacist enclave complete with offshore banking facilities and a gambling franchise. Hired to assist were the Dreads, marijuana-trafficking members of a Rastafarian sect who, unlike most of their mellow co-religionists, periodically ventured down from the hills to rob banks and shoot up government installations. However, ten heavily armed Klansmen were arrested in New Orleans before they could set sail; Patrick John and local ringleaders were jailed; the Dominican government passed a new anti-terrorism law targeted at the Dreads; and South Africa's grand plan for a Caribbean sanctions-busting oil facility went bust.[31]

Still, there was another prospect. In 1970 Robert Vesco, soon-to-be-crowned king of American white-collar crime, had taken over Bernie Cornfeld's Investors' Overseas Services and looted it, so the Securities and Exchange Commission (SEC, the main regulator of American financial markets) charged, of $225 million. Before fleeing the United States he tried to diversify his interests. For example, Vesco hired the ex-CIA Beirut station chief to help in a vain effort to get control of the recently collapsed Intra Bank, along with its casino, airline, mass-media holdings and port facilities.[32] While on the lam from the American authorities, he also decided to try his hand in the oil business, attempting to secure control of a Bahamas refinery owned by the government of Libya so he could use it to smuggle refined oil products to South Africa. But the scheme fared no better than his Lebanon ventures.[33]

Despite these setbacks, relief was in sight. Within a year of the Shah's overthrow, Iran began a long and bitter war with its neighbour, Iraq. Iran faced an international arms embargo that South Africa was happy to ignore, while South Africa faced an oil embargo that Iran was content to contravene. Aided by the ever-helpful Marc Rich, the traffic continued until the mid-1980s, when South Africa opened a covert arms-for-oil relationship with Iraq, one of the conditions being that South Africa cease further dealings with Iran.

But Marc Rich found alternative sources. Brunei had been one of the last major producers to sell openly to South Africa. In 1985 it was pressed into joining the embargo. The next year it reported thirty tanker-loads "missing." At least twenty-five had been bought by a Japanese company and resold to Rich, whose ships, publicly told to haul the oil to the west coast of the United States, had got lost and ended up in South Africa.[34]

Although Marc Rich was probably the leading supplier, there was competition, especially from John Deuss, a Bermuda-based former used-car dealer, whose Transworld Oil was responsible for shipping nearly 100 tanker-loads to South Africa. Much came from Saudi Arabia, which, despite the embargo by Arab producers, not only was eager to do business with South Africa, but willing to undercut the official OPEC price, guarantee long-term deliveries and split the sanctions-busting premium with Transworld.[35]

To hide the trail, tankers could leave the Gulf with papers showing their destination to be the Far East or Europe, then, once outside territorial waters, change course; new instructions sometimes arrived in code over the radio while ships were en route. They would later file phoney discharge certificates with the country of origin. Or they could quietly offload to smaller tankers to complete the run. Geography lent a hand. During the sanctions era, the world's tanker fleet was carrying annually about $175 billion worth of oil.

Until the 1967 Middle East war, much of that fleet had passed through the Suez Canal. When Israel captured the Sinai, the canal was closed. By the time it reopened, the greatest share of the sea-borne oil trade was carried in super-tankers. Too large to pass through the canal, they made their way from the Persian Gulf to Europe and the Americas down the Indian Ocean and around the Cape of Good Hope, leaving South Africa sitting astride the world's main tanker lane. The result was that a series of tankers changed their names en route or just arrived in South African ports with a blanket draped over the parts of the hull where their names were painted.[36]

Alternatively, a tanker might call on its legal destination, acquire documents attesting to the fact, then, without unloading, double back and head for South Africa. With a glut of tankers and rapidly falling charter rates, a deal could easily bear the cost of the extra mileage, especially since South Africa paid a premium. Another possibility was multi-porting. The oil could be declared for a certain destination or destinations that wanted only a portion of it, the rest offloaded in South Africa.[37] Yet further cover for off-the-books sales came from the fact that, by the mid-1980s theft of oil from tankers was estimated to be costing $7.5 billion per annum. Some tankers had false bottoms, permitting them to drain off and sell on the black market part of the cargo, then report it as lost or evaporated or the result of a mistake at the loading end.[38]

Of course, any shipping company caught violating the embargo faced possible fines and its officers could be imprisoned. But as soon as one was exposed, it closed down and reopened in another location, leaving few clues about the identity of the owners.[39] The ships themselves had, as the saying went, more lives than a cat and more names than a Spanish duke. An embargo-busting ship was usually "owned" by a shell company whose only asset was the tanker, the ship could be "sold" from one shell company to another in a matter of minutes, and the ship could be chartered and sub-chartered often enough that it was almost impossible to follow the vessel's peregrinations. All this occurred thanks to the unique infrastructure of the world's shipping business.

During World War II, Panama had reflagged the U.S. tanker fleet to allow it to legally evade the American neutrality laws and deliver oil to Britain. For a short time Panama had a virtual lock on the flag-of-convenience business. But in 1949 it woke to find Liberia a serious competitor. There a ship could be naturalized in forty-eight hours. Nor did it have to be "owned" by a Liberian company. Aided by bank and corporate secrecy laws, Liberia became home to 20 per cent of the world's tanker fleet and close to half the ships running oil to South Africa.[40] Among them was the *Salem*.

The *Salem* epic began in 1978 when the *Alexandros K* picked up on behalf of a Spanish company 3,000 tons of steel bars bound for Bulgaria. En route the ship received word the steel had been resold. The Egyptian buyer flew to Piraeus to inspect the load. That was the last time he saw it. The ship, renamed the *Leila*, was diverted to one of the Lebanese pirate ports where the steel was sold.[41]

A couple of years later, two men approached the South African oil procurement agency. Identifying themselves as oil traders, they claimed to know of a huge tank farm in Kuwait where evaporation and leakage were so great, it would be easy for the manager, in league with them, to exaggerate the loss and deliver oil at a very special price. Since there would be no record of the oil's existence, there was no need to fake documents. And since South Africa would pay only on delivery, the venture seemed risk free. The one drawback was that the traders did not have a tanker. They coaxed the South Africans into financing the purchase of the *South Sun* (née *Sea Sovereign*), a barely seaworthy vessel already experienced on the South Africa run. To wipe out its record, they renamed it the *Salem* — and insured it for twice the purchase price. A Greek shipping agent, who himself had wisely given up sailing when two well-insured vessels sank under him, located an experienced captain, the former skipper of the *Alexandros K*. And they found a cargo: a shipment of legitimate Kuwaiti oil purchased by an Italian oil trading company, then resold to Shell Oil for delivery to France. The *Salem* went to Kuwait, picked up the oil and set off to fulfil its contract.

Unfortunately, as the tanker made its way up the West African coast it had an accident. Fortunately, the captain and crew had time to change into street clothes and load their belongings along with thousands of cigarettes into lifeboats before giving the distress signal. Even more fortunately, West Africa was spared a major ecological disaster by the captain's foresight in unloading his cargo in South Africa, then refilling the tanks with seawater to make the ship appear fully loaded. To South Africa, the cargo was worth $44 million. Once the South Africans deducted $12.3 million for the advance on the tanker, they wired the rest to Switzerland. A short time later black limousines pulled up in front of the bank, had the cash loaded into their trunks and disappeared across the Italian border — leaving marine insurance companies to wrangle in court with Shell about whether insurance against "taking at sea" applied if the pirates were the captain and crew.[42]

Actually, the *Salem* affair was a disaster for South Africa. Another British tanker had unexpectedly arrived at the "accident" scene and noted both the absence of a serious oil slick and the sang-froid of a crew fresh from such a traumatic experience. Eventually most of the principals, including the captain, were jailed. And South Africa had to reimburse Shell $26 million, thus paying twice for the load.

All these schemes — diversion, thefts, multi-porting and zigzag transportation routes — had their role in a business where variety is the staff rather than merely the spice of life. But the most reliable method of securing oil worked by third-country diversions. Some were episodic. At one point the father-in-law of Haiti's Jean-Claude ("Baby Doc") Duvalier was rumoured to be involved in buying a shipment of oil nominally for Haiti, at concessionary prices appropriate to the island's poverty, then diverting it to South Africa for sale at the market price plus sanctions-busting premium.[43] But some were systematic. One accommodating third country assumed its oily vocation through a set of intrigues that, if submitted as a script to any respectable film studio, would have been summarily rejected as too fantastic to be believed.

Strangers in Paradise

The setting was the Seychelles, a group of beautiful coral islands in the Indian Ocean. Originally a supply station for British sailing ships on the East India run, the Seychelles was eclipsed by the rise of steam and the opening of the Suez Canal, and remained a colonial anachronism until the June 1967 war. Then, with Suez closed, much of the world's oil began rolling down the East African coast. With the islands basking in their new importance, the chief minister, James Mancham, dreamed for them a brilliant future as a tourist Mecca and a trade entrepôt, as well as a tax haven and offshore banking centre modelled on the Channel Islands. And if prostitution, smuggling, fiscal fraud and money-laundering were not enough to brighten the Seychelles' prospects, there was also its growing role as a CIA post monitoring Soviet activities in the Indian Ocean.[44]

Despite those prospects, the Seychelles was not a happy place. Politics was riven into two main factions. One, led by Mancham, a right-wing anglophile, long resisted independence in favour of a coddled status vis-à-vis Britain; René Albert led a radical leftist party, secretly supported by France, advocating independence and ties with black Africa. Britain finally forced independence in a compromise deal in which Mancham became president and Albert prime minister. But Albert ousted Mancham, who retreated to Britain, still dreaming of luxury hotels, casinos and offshore banks.

The coup led to a panic flight of capital. Arriving in the midst of the turmoil was Giovanni Mario Ricci, a millionaire Italian businessman, who set up the modestly named GMR Corporation and began wooing the Seychelles government with tales of big investments.[45] There was a catch: the government had to make the islands into a tax haven and allow him to launch the first offshore banking facility. In response, the Seychelles abolished taxes on offshore companies, passed bank and corporate secrecy laws and even legalized casino gambling. Although René Albert continued to profess Marxist principles, there was really little to differentiate the course the Seychelles took under his leadership from that which Mancham had plotted, beyond the names of the guilty parties. And even they came close to changing back again.[46]

One day in 1981, an all-male group of tourists landed, sporting on their T-shirts a picture of an overflowing tankard of ale. It was the symbol of the Ancient Order of Froth Blowers, a British fraternal order devoted to good cheer and the assistance of children deprived of a decent life, perhaps by alcoholic fathers. When an overcurious Customs officer opened a piece of hand luggage and discovered a machine-gun, the group transmuted from vacationing British football hooligans to mercenaries (ex-Green Berets, former British SAS troops and Rhodesian army veterans) led by Colonel T.M.B. "Mad Mike" Hoare, survivor of many of Africa's civil wars and coups. After a shoot-up in the airport in which their own plane was wrecked, most of Mad Mike's merry band hijacked an Air India jet to South Africa. They left behind a shaken head of state, suddenly aware of South Africa's growing interest in his island home.[47] Soon he had two new visitors with more ideas on the subject.

One was South African master-spy Craig Williamson, who achieved renown for infiltrating and manipulating the African National Congress during the 1970s. Williamson arrived to secure the release of the handful of Mad Mike's men whom the Seychelles had captured, and to arrange a deal: trading an indemnity against repetition of the incident for René Albert's willingness to be more reasonable in his foreign policy.

The second new arrival came with some practical notions about just what constituted reasonable behaviour. Francesco Pazienza had been in his remarkably varied career to date an agent of SISMI (Italian military intelligence) who had handled its liaison with the Mafia; the man who first tried to coax the jailed Ali Agca into implicating the Bulgarians in his attempted assassination of Pope John Paul II; confidante of Licio Gelli, grand master of the P-2 Masonic lodge whose plan to subvert the Italian government precipitated the greatest political scandal in Italy's post-war history (no mean feat); and counsellor to Roberto Calvi, head of the collapsed Banco Ambrosiano, found hanging under London's Blackfriar's Bridge in one of the most acrobatic suicides in forensic history. All of this professional activity had put Pazienza under indictment for subversion, embezzlement, fraudulent bankruptcy, forgery and terrorism by the time he decided to take a well-earned vacation in a tropical paradise. It was from Pazienza that the idea emerged of setting up in the Seychelles a bunkering station to fuel aircraft and ships plying the Indian Ocean routes, and to provide cover for moving crude oil to South Africa. Marc Rich himself turned up to give the scheme his blessing.[48] To assist, the Seychelles government decided to grant the main architects diplomatic status. Henceforth they would be accredited as representatives to the Seychelles.

Contrary to widespread belief, the world's smallest country is not the Vatican, a few hundred square metres in the heart of Rome, but one building within the Vatican City housing the headquarters of the Sovereign Order of the Knights of Malta. An ancient chivalric order, the Knights are recognized as an independent country by twenty or more jurisdictions. Those holding the order's diplomatic passports, including some former CIA directors, could saunter past Customs officials without the indignity of a baggage check.[49] That privilege inevitably inspired pretenders with the result that by the mid-1980s there were about two dozen Knights of Malta organizations in existence. One of them, run by "Prince" Arnaldo Petrucci of Vanone and Sienna, claimed sovereign rights over a group of coral islands in the South Pacific, at least at low tide when the physical rather than diplomatic existence of the country could be verified. Prince Petrucci's order did have its problems — its London plenipotentiary had to hightail it to Panama from his suite in London's Ritz Hotel leaving behind a £55,000 tab. And his order spawned a breakaway group, the Sovereign Order of Catholic Copts/Knights of Malta, incorporated in New York by Francesco Pazienza with Mario Ricci, a.k.a. Iohannes Marius I, as its president-for-life.[50] In this capacity Ricci received ambassadorial recognition from René Albert and was soon regarded as the doyen of the Seychelles diplomatic community. Ricci's GMR company moved its headquarters into the "embassy," hiring as general manager another diplomat named Craig Williamson, who retired from the intelligence services for a new career in "private" business. When queried about what GMR was up to, all Williamson would say is that it was engaged in international trade in "strategic commodities."[51]

Francesco Pazienza would not be around to get credit; he was arrested in New York and deported to Italy. But step by step, his idea was put into practice. In 1985 René Albert showed his commitment to Marxist principles by nationalizing the local subsidiary of Shell Oil. And he showed his commitment to South Africa by turning it over to Mario Ricci's oil subsidiary to manage.[52]

Thus, one way or another $4 to $5 billion worth of oil ended up in South Africa every year. Once there it was resold to the local subsidiaries of five of the world's largest international oil companies, the same ones that had been active in Rhodesia. When queried about the origins of the oil their South Africa affiliates were refining, the headquarters of those companies disclaimed all knowledge, insisting that their subsidiaries were completely autonomous. Indeed, no better proof of that independence existed than the fact that the local subsidiary of the oil giant Caltex operated under a completely different name. In South Africa it was called "Con Oil."

Chapter 11

SHOOTING HOLES IN
THE ARMS EMBARGO

Oil was not South Africa's only strategic weakness. It also needed to import weapons. Therefore the arms embargo raised high hopes among the regime's opponents, though a glance at history should have deflated their expectations. The idea of ensuring peace by collectively denying arms first emerged at the end of World War I when a population traumatized by the slaughter and politicians desperate to deflect the heat found a simple explanation: the war had been caused by the "merchants of death," a cabal of arms suppliers who deliberately fostered conflict, then sold arms to all sides. Some countries nationalized the industry, others began introducing mandatory export licensing, and the League of Nations set up the first registry of international arms transfers.[1]

An excellent opportunity to test the viability of arms controls came in the early 1930s during the Chaco War between Bolivia and Paraguay. Both were landlocked and neither manufactured weapons. Argentina publicly announced adherence to the ban, while privately slipping Paraguay arms, fuel and money. Uruguay scrupulously respected a pledge not to sell weapons made by its own (non-existent) arms industry, while permitting its shipping companies to run other countries' guns to Paraguay. For balance, Chile permitted Bolivia to transship arms, while Peru sold Bolivia weapons from its own stockpiles.

The great powers showed a similar commitment to the embargo. Establishing the principle of arms-market neutrality for which it would later be renowned, France sold Bolivia weapons for cash, while allowing Paraguay to negotiate a loan to buy French arms and build its first weapons plant.[2] U.S. restrictions were described in Congress as "a joke. . . . If you want to get anything out — just ship it. They are all doing it." Only two American companies were charged with evasion, and the United States made no protest when Standard Oil paid royalties earmarked by the Bolivian government for arms purchases.[3]

At the end of World War II, prospects for supply-side control seemed better. The great majority of countries required their firms to apply for export licences. And they refused to issue a licence unless would-be buyers presented an "end-user certificate," a pledge by responsible officials that the weapons were for use only by the buying country's armed forces and would not be transferred without express permission of the original vendor. Just how effective the new control system was became evident in Africa during its 1960s decolonization struggles.

Gun-Shy?

Algeria's Front de libération nationale (FLN) initially had few weapons to oppose French occupation. It located some caches the United States had left behind in North Africa after World War II. It set up underground factories to make bombs out of odds and ends. But mostly it relied on material stolen from the French army. Later, a few shipments arrived from Egypt, paid for by the Arab League out of solidarity with an Arab people struggling for independence — and out of embarrassment about the League's failure in Palestine. However such support was minimal. When the war got into high gear, the FLN had to rely on the black market, and that required money.

The FLN imposed "war taxes" on Algerian businessmen and collected contributions from émigré workers. The more Frenchmen were conscripted to fight in Algeria, the more jobs in France were filled by Algerians. For several years, until French intelligence broke it up, an émigré network ran cash in suitcases to Geneva's Banque Commerciale Arabe, which then paid the gun-runners.[4]

Most were career smugglers who had plied the cigarette and gold traffic out of Tangiers in its heyday, or ex-SS officers, or, as in the case of Georg Puchert, both. After World War II Puchert (nicknamed Captain Phillip Morris) established a fleet of "fishing" ships to net customers for his cigarettes. When Puchert diversified into weapons, the FLN granted him a monopoly to supply one of their six military districts.[5] His most popular item was the German Mauser. However Germany's post-war arms industry was still very small, and Germany closely monitored foreign customers. Therefore Czechoslovakia was the main source. For a while the Czechs sold guns that had been seized from the retreating German army. When those inventories were run down, they set up their own factory to turn out perfect imitations, right down to the Swastikas emblazoned on the stocks.

Although some weapons reached Algeria directly, usually gun-runners loaded arms on German or Yugoslav ships, then sent them via Morocco or Tunisia. In an attempt to staunch the flow, the navy tightly patrolled the coast while the French army tried to seal the frontiers. Much of the job of interdiction fell to the intelligence service, which set up mock factories to sell faulty weapons to the FLN in order to trace the smuggling rings. French intelligence also used more drastic methods. It hired professional killers from the Corsican underworld to track the bagmen, and it sponsored a terrorist organization (*la main rouge*) to collect information on FLN activities, infiltrate networks and assassinate gun-runners. Among the victims was Captain Phillip Morris. He was first sent a quiet warning, then had one of his boats blown up, then was put permanently out of business.[6]

France eventually acceded to Algerian independence, and more than a million embittered French colonists went home. Among the conflict's more enduring legacies was a supply of French mercenaries, largely Algerian veterans, who sold their services across Africa and the Middle East, and an intelligence service riddled with Corsican gangsters who divided their energies between planning assassinations and peddling heroin.[7] The obvious lesson of the conflict was that, faced with sufficient political will, arms-transfer controls accomplish little. However, when the next major conflict stalked Africa, there was an even more ambitious attempt to embargo arms, this time by the UN General Assembly.

The Nigerian civil war began with a failed coup attempt by junior officers. The fact that many were Ibos, resented because of their disproportionate representation in the administration and army, provided a pretext for a pogrom by Yoruba and Hausa senior officers and officials. The country effectively split in two. Initially the Ibo forces had the upper hand: at one point they threatened the federal capital. However, after a series of setbacks, the Ibo objectives shifted from contesting control of the federal state to setting up the independent Republic of Biafra.[8]

Biafra needed weapons, and to acquire weapons it needed money. Initially the nascent republic seemed well placed. Biafra contained most of Nigeria's oil wells, and Shell agreed to pay royalties into the new regime's British bank accounts. Nigeria protested that this constituted de facto recognition. When Biafra, anticipating trouble, tried to shift the money to Switzerland, the British froze the funds.[9]

The Biafrans had other sources. Just before the break-up, the Biafran regional authority, without Nigerian federal consent, had transferred £6 million sterling to Switzerland. The Biafrans also seized the cash in local banks and federal offices. While their forces were threatening Lagos, they grabbed a plane-load of money the federal authorities had tried to send to safety. But the federal government struck back. It demonetized the old currency, issuing replacement notes only to people living within federally controlled territory. In desperation, Biafran agents carted suitcases to the world's money markets, offering to unload the cash at deep discounts. A plane-load nominally worth £7 million landed to refuel in Togo, where the money was confiscated and the pilot stuck in jail. Another load was stowed on a plane en route to Geneva, where the Biafra representative and an officer of one of the Swiss banks were waiting — they may still be. Ultimately, only a few of the last-minute conversions were successful. Stacks of old currency were later found abandoned in European capitals.[10]

After the demonetization, Biafra's sources of financial support became murkier. Some were churches and missionary services who would, in return for newly issued Biafran currency that they could use for local expenses, deposit hard currency in Biafra's foreign accounts. And there were rumours, vehemently denied, that Banque Rothschild in Paris lent the republic $16 million in return for mineral concessions.[11]

In addition to buying arms, both sides, though mainly the Biafrans, hired mercenaries, recruited on the Brussels market and paid through Swiss banks. Some were genuinely committed to the Biafran cause. But most were thrill-seekers, fugitives from justice or maladjusted products of previous wars. Nor were they always a bargain. The leader of the French contingent billed the Biafrans for 100 soldiers, collected payment in full, then turned up briefly on the battlefield with less than half the contracted number.[12]

The Biafrans were also ripped off by arms traffickers. One consignment of Swiss artillery was too rusty to use. Biafran buyers laid out £100,000 for an American plane that took flight to another destination. Two French fighters, paid in advance, arrived minus their wings. Once the head of the Biafran government authorized a business acquaintance to draw £75,000 from London and Paris accounts to buy arms — the acquaintance withdrew both the money and himself from the Biafran cause.[13]

The UN arms embargo not only leaked, but, when convenient, gushed. To maintain deniability, governments backing Biafra would sell "demilitarized" aircraft and vehicles that, on arrival, could be quickly reconverted. They would also use circuitous routes. British and American small arms given to the Netherlands at the end of World War II were sold to a French gun-runner who claimed to have contracted for a British manufacturer to "recondition" them. The British government granted the company an import licence. This was presented to the Dutch government as proof of destination, so the Dutch issued an export licence. A cargo plane carrying the weapons approached Birmingham, circled without landing, then announced to the tower it had been ordered to Majorca. From there it began hopping southward through Africa. It crashed in Cameroon before it could reach Biafra.[14]

The most important source of support for the Nigerian federal side was Britain, eager to keep control of Nigeria's oil in the face of rising nationalist sentiment in the Middle East. In the early stages, Britain remained coy, leaving the arms supply business largely to a "private" dealer named Sam Cummings. Cummings had formerly worked as a buyer for a CIA proprietary company that specialized in acquiring non-traceable weapons for mounting coups and revolutions. Once the CIA began handling most of those matters in-house, he went private, with the quiet backing of the United States and Britain, buying and selling war-surplus arms. He once bragged that he could equip straight from his warehouses forty infantry divisions. Since his was an international operation, he could act as a cut-out for embargo-busting operations. With a nod from Washington, for example, he ran arms to Pakistan during its 1963 war with India. Hence, the British initially left to Cummings the job of supplying the Nigerian federal army, obliging him with any export licence he requested and making sure that he never had any hassles with Customs.[15]

Once the tide turned in the federal government's favour, Britain took over the arms supply directly, rationalizing official participation by such convincing arguments as the need to support a Commonwealth country, the moral obligation to continue to serve a regular customer, the fear that failure to support the federal side would encourage secessionist movements elsewhere, and the contention that as long as Britain supplied arms, it could use the threat of a cut-off to moderate federal behaviour.[16] Apparently that behaviour was always impeccable.

The federal side had other suppliers. One was Switzerland's Oerlikon-Buehrle AG. Switzerland was not a UN member and therefore not obliged to respect the embargo — which was, in any case, voluntary. However, it did have laws forbidding arms exports to trouble spots. As Oerlikon interpreted those laws, islands of tranquillity included Israel, Egypt, South Africa, Saudi Arabia — and Nigeria. Using end-user certificates supposedly from Ethiopia, Oerlikon shipped to the federal forces anti-aircraft weapons they reputedly used to fire on Swiss Red Cross planes carrying relief supplies to Biafra.[17]

Biafra, too, had sources of outside support. The French government put Biafran buyers in touch with arms merchants operating with the blessing of

French intelligence. Israel sold Biafra arms to weaken the pan-African influence of Nigeria's large Muslim population. Portugal, angry over Nigerian support for independence movements in Portugal's African colonies, hosted the main Biafran arms-buying mission and allowed gun-runners to refuel their planes at Lisbon, Port Guinea and the island of São Tomé.

Building a Behemoth

South Africa, like Portugal, supported Biafra in order to weaken other potential opponents. However, it played only a minor role in arms supply. That was partly through lack of ability. Although South Africa would end the sanctions era as the continent's military giant, it started as a midget. After World War II, it had dismantled virtually all its weapons-making capacity, preferring to rely on cheap British surplus for its army and to shift onto the Royal Navy responsibility for defence by sea. Still, the first UN arms embargo in 1963 caused little concern. The embargo was voluntary — so many ignored it. The country's most pressing requirement was for easy-to-acquire counter-insurgency equipment, rather than modern heavy weapons. And to the extent it needed major systems, it could rely on France, which claimed that it sold weapons only for external defence and not for internal repression. Nonetheless, as a precaution, in 1968 South Africa created Armscor, a state-owned corporation charged with importing arms and weapons technology and building up domestic arms plants.[18]

Things turned more serious in 1977 when the arms embargo became mandatory. South Africa could still use the black market. Thousands of assault rifles, mortars, recoilless rifles and ammunition, originally sent by the United States to Taiwan, had been reclassified as scrap and supposedly dumped in the sea. In reality, they were sneaked off to Thailand, sold to "Jack" Frost, a CIA-officer-turned-arms-dealer, then resold to an Armscor buyer and shipped to South Africa.[19] South Africa could also still rely to some degree on traditional suppliers. On five occasions from 1978 to 1980, the Danish-owned, Panamanian-registered and Marbella-managed *Tinemura* loaded French arms at Bordeaux, watched over by French intelligence agents. When the operation was exposed, the Danish owner fled to South Africa after the Danish police neglected to impound his passport or freeze his bank accounts; the ship was sold off to a business associate to see more gun-running business under another name.[20] Although South Africa could always use such channels to smuggle arms, the embargo still raised the costs and lowered the probability of acquiring any particular item. And South Africa's needs were all the greater because the arms embargo became mandatory when it was facing a military crisis.

After protracted insurgencies in its colonies of Mozambique and Angola, in 1975 Portugal threw in the towel. While in Mozambique the FRELIMO guerrilla movement was the only possible successor to the colonial authorities, in Angola three rebel forces battled the Portuguese (with various degrees of enthusiasm) and each other (with more consistency). The Soviet-backed Popular Front for the Liberation of Angola (MPLA) took the title, besting its two CIA-supported rivals. That prompted South African intervention, which in turn led to Cuba aiding the MPLA. After South African forces were badly mauled by Cuban pilots flying Soviet MiGs and Cuban troops using Soviet hardware, South Africa responded in three distinct ways.

One was to step up support of the insurgent groups battling the new regimes in Angola and Mozambique. To equip its proxy forces with the same material as the governments they were fighting, South Africa went searching for Soviet-style equipment. Some cheap knock-offs were purchased from China. The same Danish shipper who had bought the *Tinemura* from its fugitive owner may have had another ship, the *Thaven* (later to be the *Stephanie*, and even later the *Jutlandia*), pick up a cargo of Chinese weapons from Shanghai, deliver them to Zaire to be passed on to the South African-supported rebels in Angola, then head back to South Africa to pick up yet more weapons and deliver them to South African-supported rebels in Mozambique, while changing its name to the *Avenia* en route. Others arms were smuggled out of eastern Europe. Poland sold several cargoes to trading companies secretly owned by Armscor. With Bulgaria, the most loyal of the Soviet Union's eastern European allies, the approach had to be more circumspect.

During the late 1970s, a Liechtenstein corporation secretly owned by Armscor placed an order with a London firm owned by a Frankfurt gun-runner already notorious for supplying the IRA. He in turn called on a Viennese businessman with a contact in Kintex, the Bulgarian state trading company. The gun-runner arranged for his Luxembourg bank to open a letter of credit with a Bulgarian bank. Then he supplied an end-user certificate (EUC) signed by the military attaché of the Nigerian embassy in London. To improve credibility, he had the signature and seals on the EUC backed up by a British Foreign Office guarantee. The signature and the seals were indeed authentic: he had bribed the Nigerian embassy employee to provide them. The guarantee was forged. After several transactions, the Viennese broker tried to claim his share of the commissions only to see the gun-runner abscond with all the money to a well-fortified retirement near Miami.[21]

A second result of the Angolan war was for South Africa to search for state-of-the-art hand-held anti-aircraft equipment. It almost got lucky in 1985 when the Ulster Defence Association (UDA), the largest Protestant paramilitary force in Northern Ireland, came asking to buy light arms. Reputedly with an okay from British military intelligence, South Africa passed the UDA onto Israel. Israel contacted its Lebanese Christian allies, and they agreed to sell a large batch of rocket-propelled grenade-launchers and AK-47 assault rifles. The UDA paid in cash, £250,000, which had been withdrawn — at gunpoint — from an Ulster bank.[22] A short time later the UDA had a chance to return the favour. The target was Short's of Belfast, a factory with a largely Protestant workforce full of UDA sympathizers making the most advanced British anti-aircraft missiles. From his Paris hotel, a South African agent contacted the UDA, offering a million pounds sterling in cash or the equivalent value in weapons. UDA sympathizers stole a demonstrator model and a training simulator. But when they arrived to deliver, so did French police, who arrested the agent, three UDA men and a South African diplomat.[23]

The third result of the Angola campaign was to send South Africa in pursuit of a means to counter the range of Soviet rocket launchers and artillery. When the State Department balked at the suggestion that the United States directly violate the UN arms embargo, the CIA came up with a "private sector" alternative. In so doing, it launched South Africa's largest and, perhaps in the long run, most significant sanctions-busting deal.[24]

Going Ballistic

For the majority of armies, the most important artillery piece is the 155 mm howitzer. Such guns usually had a range of fifteen to twenty kilometres. As an artillery shell is propelled down the barrel, it produces a partial vacuum behind itself that creates a reverse drag. NATO forces eventually solved the problem by adding rocket boosters to their heavy shells. But before that, a Canadian ballistics expert, Gerald Bull, came up with a solution that was simpler and cheaper. His shells emitted from the base a gas that filled the vacuum. Subsequently combined with a special howitzer of his own design, Bull's shells had a range of forty kilometres, permitting his guns to compete directly with larger, more expensive ones for long-distance bombardments.[25]

Bull's infatuation with artillery began accidentally when, as a graduate student at the University of Toronto, he set out to increase the velocity in a wind tunnel. Rather than having wind blown on a stationary object, his solution was to fire the test object down a cannon barrel. Later, he became the guiding light in McGill University's High Altitude Research Program, which used a huge cannon to fire meteorological research satellites into space. At the time it was much cheaper than using rockets and set a still unsurpassed altitude record of 175 kilometres.

For a time, money flowed from the Pentagon, which was intrigued by the possibility of using Bull's guns to fire anti-ballistic missile projectiles. However, by the end of the 1960s, American interest was waning. Prevailing doctrine called for using rocket-propelled missiles for long-distance strikes, leaving artillery to handle things closer up. So Bull went private, creating Space Research Corporation straddling the Quebec-Vermont border. To keep his projects going, he relied on consulting fees from foreign military engineering projects, principally dealing with artillery, for other countries viewed Bull's research more positively.

The 1973 Middle East war had ended in a stalemate. Because the ceasefire terms required Israel to pull back in the Sinai and Golan, its heavy artillery could no longer threaten certain strategic targets. In his first major overseas contract, Bull provided Israel with special ammunition that put Damascus in range. It proved its worth during Israel's 1978 invasion of Lebanon when Bull's shells blasted the centre of the biblical city of Tyre. Then Bull's involvement in the murky world of international arms dealing went one big step further.

In 1976 an Armscor representative, CIA gun-runner Jack Frost and Gerald Bull met in Brussels to work out a way to meet South Africa's needs. Bull would place an order for shell casings with a U.S. army forge, truck them into Canada labelled "rough steel forgings," then send them to Barbados, where Space Research had a test site. From Barbados the shells would go to Israel. Israel would fill the shells and export them to South Africa. Its reward would be the right to manufacture Bull's shells for use by the Israeli armed forces. And Armscor would secretly invest in Bull's company, buttressing its capital base. However, four successive calamities struck the venture.

First came elections in Barbados in which the government, implicated in a bribery scandal, was defeated. Members of the successor government claimed that Bull had plotted against the new regime, and they kicked Space Research off the island.

Antigua was a good choice for a new home. In later years, U.S. government planes could land there without a Customs or Immigration check, making it an excellent base for covert operations. Indeed, its relationship with U.S. intelligence is likely the main reason the island managed to stay in business throughout the 1980s and 1990s as one of the Caribbean's most notorious way stations for dirty money.[26] However, back in the mid-1970s, Antigua was still a sleepy place with few banks. Only an occasional salvo from Space Research's heavy guns disturbed its peace. In theory those guns should have been booming almost constantly, so large was the supply of shells arriving for "test" purposes.

Bull obtained a letter from the U.S. Office of Munitions Control stating that, because the shell casings he was buying from the U.S. army forge were shipped without explosive charges, he did not need an export licence. The casings were sent to Quebec to be finished. The shells then went by rail to Saint John, New Brunswick, thence by commercial carrier to Antigua. But another disaster struck.

The Israeli government, pressed by the new Carter administration to cut back military relations with South Africa, backed out. Hence, when the first shipment arrived from Saint John, it spent two weeks on the quay guarded by the Antiguan Defence Force, then was reloaded onto the *Tugelaland*, a German-flagged vessel chartered by Safmarine, the South African maritime agency responsible for much of the sanctions-busting, and hauled directly to South Africa. Later, the same ship called at Saint John, picking up thirty-two containers of which ten were empty, and took them to Antigua. The freighter discharged twelve containers, all ten empty ones and two with ammunition for the test site, and carted the rest away to South Africa. A follow-up trip planned by the *Tugelaland* had to be aborted because of a third stroke of bad luck.

During the ship's previous trip to Antigua, a crane had fallen into its hold and broken open a container, causing artillery shells to spill out. The local opposition papers figured out the ship's destination, and a Canadian news team picked up the story. Both U.S. Customs and the Royal Canadian Mounted Police opened investigations, but the principals took little notice. They were sure they had official, if covert, approval. Hence it was business as normal with one twist. The third and fourth loads were nominally sold to the Spanish army. A shipping agency used regularly by the Spanish government took the shells to Barcelona. Two months later they were quietly moved to South Africa.[27]

In the meantime the investigation made little headway. When Space Research was asked to account for nearly 60,000 shells, it stated, waving the shipping documents, that half had been sold to the Spanish government. The other half, it claimed, were fired off at the Antigua test site. The RCMP decided to check the gun barrels to verify that the company did test-fire all those shells. It was told that the burnt-out barrels had been dumped in the ocean.[28] It seemed to be a stand-off. But shortly after, a fourth mishap brought more unwanted attention to Space Research's activities.

In September 1979 a U.S. spy satellite, apparently off course, recorded a curious explosion off the coast of South Africa. While the U.S. government attempted to fudge the results, one persistent theory was that the explosion was a joint Israeli–South Africa test of a long-range artillery shell with a tactical nuclear payload.[29] Although Bull played no role in the South African or Israeli nuclear programs, the event put pressure on the U.S. government to appear to be doing something serious about embargo-busting. Gerald Bull was the perfect fall guy, particularly when Jack Frost, angry about having been denied commissions in the South Africa deal, started leaking information.

Bull was pressured or conned into a quick guilty plea that aborted further probes, then spent four months in a minimum security prison. The plea and the sentence sent out the right message: it was Bull who was guilty of breaking sanctions, not the CIA, which set up the deal; not the U.S. Office of Munitions Control, which endorsed it; not the U.S. Army, which willingly participated. Bull emerged bitter about being made a scapegoat and shifted his base of operations permanently to Brussels. For the next decade, he undertook artillery projects for a number of Third World countries. Among his prophecies was that some day soon, Western forces would be confounded by a technology they had rejected.[30]

In South Africa, though, there was greater cheer. Bull's weapons revolutionized its arms acquisition program. South Africa obtained not only shells, but, much more important, the capacity to make its own. Using a British engineering company as go-between, Armscor obtained French shell-turning lathes. Then it made a deal in which a German steel and engineering works sold to "Paraguay" a complete plant for filling and priming artillery shells but somehow misaddressed the shipment. When Armscor also obtained from Bull rights to produce his revolutionary 155 mm artillery piece, it was set to enter the world market, no longer as just a (covert) buyer, but increasingly as a major seller.[31]

Bull's artillery, in conjunction with the Iran-Iraq War, solved much of South Africa's oil supply concerns. Downgrading its ties with Iran, South Africa supplied Iraq with 155 mm artillery and huge amounts of ammunition in exchange for oil. Oil tankers with their tanks partly full of water and partly with ammunition unloaded the shells in the Jordanian port of Aqabah from where they were trucked to Iraq. Then the ships sailed to Kuwait to load oil, donated by Saudi Arabia and Kuwait for the Iraqi war effort, and hauled it back to South Africa in payment for the arms.[32]

Helping Those Who Help Themselves

Securing rights to Bull's artillery was a crucial step in Armscor's strategy of shifting from smuggling weapons to making its own. However, to obtain other advanced weapons technology, South Africa needed a special back channel into the Pentagon. And there was no channel that ran deeper than Israel.

For the first two decades of Israel's existence, its needs for sophisticated weapons had been met largely by purchasing, first from the Soviet bloc, then from France. After the 1967 war, the French slapped on an embargo. Hence Israel began a drive for military autonomy. Development of cutting-edge weapons requires the commitment of big money for long periods. Therefore, Israel set out not to create them from scratch, but to monitor their evolution elsewhere, especially in the United States, then acquire them once they were ready for application.

One method was through formal "sharing" agreements in which Israel got U.S. technology and the United States got to pay the bill.[33]

A second was by exchanging personnel. Until recently, the United States permitted dual citizenship with only one country, Israel. Hence a number of military engineers and scientists could move back and forth with ease. One such individual, a veteran of running guns into Palestine, developed drone aircraft for Israel that were used in its Lebanon war. So impressed was the United States that it decided to have drones built for the U.S. Navy. Competition took the usual forms: the contract specifications were so written that only one Israeli firm could possibly meet them. Few drones got off the ground and most of those that did soon crashed. Still, it was an excellent bargain for the principals, including naval procurement czar Melvyn Paisley, who arranged for the Israeli firm to get the contract.[34]

A third way to secure technology was through cross-investment. U.S. military firms setting up branches in Israel could still have unrestricted access to U.S. weapons technology while taking advantage of lower wages, subsidized interest rates, and the fact that Israel was relaxed about arms embargoes. Israeli firms could also form joint ventures in the United States with American ones, access technology and secure Pentagon contracts to develop it.

However, all of these had a major drawback: the technology was owned by U.S. firms with an interest in protecting their overseas markets. Therefore, as Israel's emphasis shifted from its own needs to exports, many of its technological acquisitions had to be made by less obvious means.

A fourth approach was to reverse-engineer a U.S. weapon. Once an item was "sold" to Israel, it could be broken down and copied, a few modifications added, then placed in the Israeli sales catalogue. The Israeli MAPATS anti-tank missile, for example, was so close to the American original, it could be fired from the same launcher.[35]

A fifth method was outright theft.[36] Although there had been black bag jobs in the past, most run by Mossad, really systematic Israeli techno-banditry began in the 1950s with the creation of LAKAM, a special scientific espionage unit.

LAKAM's original mandate was to help create a nuclear arsenal. Most of the early Israeli nuclear program was developed with assistance from France. However after the 1967 embargo, Israel searched elsewhere. Nuclear power and nuclear weapons production are closely interlinked: fission in power plants leaves plutonium as a byproduct and enriching uranium to bomb grade requires huge inputs of electricity. Therefore all exporters of nuclear technology require a pledge from importers, verified by international inspection, about how it will be used. Israel was the first country to break those pledges.[37] It diverted into its arms program heavy water supplied by Norway for civilian power plants. It staged techno-thefts in France and Britain. It hijacked a freighter loaded with uranium off the Italian coast. And in 1968 it set up NUMEC, a front company in the United States to drain off bomb-grade material using as cover the claim that the firm was making food irradiation equipment. The firm was later fined for "losing" the uranium.

By the time of the NUMEC affair, LAKAM had branched out. It was involved, for example, in paying a Swiss engineer $200,000 to steal blueprints for the French engine powering Mirage jets — which Israel copied and marketed under the trade name Kfir.[38] But most of LAKAM's activities were in the United States. In the 1980s, it began to overstep itself.

By working through a front company, Israel obtained from Napco, a U.S. military engineering plant, the technical data for chroming tank barrels to prolong their life. It even got the United States to pay for construction in Israel of a plant to use the smuggled designs by telling the Pentagon that it was going to build hydraulic cylinders.[39] A short time later Recon, an American manufacturer of airborne surveillance equipment, signed a contract with the Israeli Air Force, which sent three officers to the plant as "liaison." When the Israeli officers, constantly interfering, were finally ordered out of the plant, plant security caught them leaving with fourteen boxes of documents, including letters in Hebrew detailing plans to steal the technology. Some had already gone to Israel and ended up in the hands of a competitor seeking its own Pentagon contracts.[40] There was actually little scandal from the Napco or Recon affairs. By then public attention was focused elsewhere, on a case so big that, as one investigator put it, "this one can't be buried."[41]

Jonathan Pollard, a U.S. Navy employee, was recruited by a senior Israeli air force officer at an Israel bond drive in New York. He was offered a large Swiss account as well as an Israeli passport and new identity if things got sticky. Hardly the perfect spy, he spent lavishly to wine and dine and bestow expensive presents on his wife, bragged to friends that he was engaged in high-level intelligence work, and claimed the rank of colonel in the Mossad with particular responsibility for running Israeli guns to Rhodesia and South Africa. In a telling comment on either the ineffectiveness of American counter-intelligence or the effectiveness of friends in high places, Pollard was assigned to a navy anti-terrorism unit where he had virtually open access to the Pentagon's secrets. Some seem to have been passed on to his friends in the investment business, but the great majority were destined for LAKAM. By the time Pollard was caught, he had fed his employers enough material to fill to the ceiling the jail cell he later occupied. His effectiveness was accentuated by the fact that his controllers could order documents by their top-secret code numbers. The information included data on U.S. ship placements, navy training and port facilities, weapons systems possessed by other Middle Eastern countries, the layout of the PLO headquarters in Tunis (used in an Israeli bombing raid) and information on Indian nuclear facilities (traded to Pakistan for data on Saudi Arabia). On top were two especially choice morsels. Pollard passed on to Israel a manual, whose intelligence classification was beyond top secret; it explained how the United States had broken Soviet codes and was soon winging its way to Moscow. He also provided Israel with information on a U.S. spy ring in South Africa, permitting South Africa to smash the network.[42]

Thick as Thieves

With almost unlimited access to American military technology and a generous flow of U.S. military aid money, Israel had a problem. In its early decades, it had been almost exclusively a weapons importer, its exports limited to small amounts of surplus or refurbished light arms. But, starting in the mid-1970s, it became increasingly dependent on export sales — at peak about 40 per cent of export earnings came from arms and "security" services. To reduce costs to its own military, to generate jobs and to earn foreign exchange in a world marketplace largely divided between the two superpowers, it had to seek special niche markets. Those, among many others, included Chile after the United States cut off military assistance in retaliation for the murder in Washington of an exiled opposition leader; Argentina during its Falklands/Malvinas War with Britain; Taiwan when the United States opened relations with China; and Guatemala when the United States stopped selling arms to protest gross human rights violations. What all these niche markets had in common was the need for secrecy and preference for weapons from a supplier that did take end-user restrictions seriously. Where there was an arms embargo, there was an opportunity for business, with premium prices and no questions asked. And who was better placed to pay premium prices or keep quiet about it than apartheid-era South Africa?

From Israel to South Africa went aircraft engines, recoilless rifles, armoured personnel carriers, anti-tank missiles, cluster bombs and air-to-air missiles, all direct copies of U.S. equipment with, at best, minor modifications, and all in theory non-transferable without American permission. South Africa also invested in the creation of an Israeli facility to manufacture gunboats based almost entirely on U.S. technology, in return for which it got the first five ships completed.

Inevitably objections were raised. In 1986, the U.S. Congress, over President Reagan's veto, passed the Comprehensive Anti-Apartheid Act, which demanded that all U.S. allies reveal their military relations with South Africa on pain of losing their aid payments. Israel admitted to a trade worth hundreds of millions of dollars per annum. It included riot control equipment to put down black disturbances, refuelling planes that permitted South Africa's air force to bomb at will across sub-Sahara Africa and components for nuclear weapons delivery systems.[43] Congress showed its outrage by once again increasing the amount of aid money to Israel. Four years later when the U.S. government found that, in spite of promises to freeze existing military relations, Israel had illegally exported American-made ballistic missile parts to South Africa, the administration was finally aroused to impose trade sanctions — on the South African firm involved.[44]

The results of the partnership were dramatic. In 1963 when the first (voluntary) restrictions were imposed, South Africa spent 70% of its limited arms procurement budget abroad. Two decades later it spent almost all of a vastly increased budget at home. Indeed, South Africa's military self-sufficiency program was so successful that in 1984 the UN had to pass a new sanctions measure. This one added weapons to the list of items member states were requested not to *buy* from South Africa.

Chapter 12

FRIENDS AND NEIGHBOURS

No matter how porous the embargoes on oil and arms, nothing would have got through had South Africa been unable to pay above-market prices. The sanctions-busting premium on oil, for example, was $4 to $6 per barrel, costing an extra $500 million a year. To meet the bills, South Africa had to sell more abroad or attract foreign money. Both responses were supposedly hampered by other sanctions.

True, there were no sanctions on strategic metals. The West required them for defence industries. There were occasional calls for an embargo on gold, of which South Africa was by far the world's leading producer, usually from lobbies funded by Canadian, American and Australian mining companies eager to drive up the price. But implementation would have been extremely difficult. Fully 90 per cent of South Africa's gold was flown to Switzerland, escorted to vaults without passing Customs, and sold to clients whose anonymity was tightly protected. Ultimately only krugerrands were affected; they were banned in some countries because of the high-minded pressure of places like Canada that produced competing gold coins.[1]

While gold led the export list, the jewel in South Africa's financial crown was diamonds. Here, too, sanctions were never seriously considered. India, the first to impose a trade embargo, remained studiously silent about the origins of so many of the rough diamonds that made it, by the mid-1980s, number one of world diamond-cutting centres.[2] Diamonds, too, consummated South

Africa's commercial and military marriage to Israel. For decades after the British had shifted the world diamond-cutting centre from German-occupied Antwerp to Palestine, cut stones were Israel's most important export, eclipsed only by weaponry in the 1970s. Sanctions were further hampered by the fact that diamonds are almost made to be smuggled — an entire month's output of Namibia, for example, could be sneaked to market in a small attaché case. In any event, who would police the sanctions?

The Carat and the Stick

While South Africa's own share of world production fell sharply over the twentieth century, the diamond world remained under the sway of De Beers Consolidated, corporate twin to Anglo-American.[3] De Beers owned partly or completely the biggest mines in South Africa and some neighbouring countries, and managed state-owned mines in others. Its marketing arm, the Central Selling Office in London, controlled 80 per cent of the world's rough stones. That dominance was particularly remarkable given that, until the 1980s when Australia became a major producer, the great majority of diamonds were from either the rhetorically anti-apartheid U.S.S.R. or black Africa. All producers cooperated because, without the De Beers-run cartel, prices would have plunged. Instead, from 1948 to 1990, they rose 1,800 per cent. De Beers also provided countries nominally antagonist to South Africa with an alibi by running their commercial relations through front companies in Switzerland, Luxembourg and Bermuda.[4] On the other side, if any producing country refused to cooperate, the cartel could use its muscle with London banks to attack its credit, from its huge stockpiles dump particular kinds of diamonds to ruin its market, and encourage smuggling to drain its foreign exchange.

However, control of the diamond market also required tight control of the mine sites. True, the great majority of stones are industrial rather than gem quality; much less valuable, they are also much less vulnerable to theft and smuggling. Many diamonds, too, come from deep mines in closely confined areas that are relatively easy to police, particularly if close to South Africa. Botswana's main mine consists of one huge hole in the ground in an isolated, easily policed area. Although Namibia's stones are spread over a large seafront and heavily tilted towards gems, they are quarried under conditions that make security at the Pentagon look lax. However, West African deposits, far enough from South Africa to avoid direct pressure, are in vast alluvial fields worked by masses of small-scale miners, and in some the proportion of gems is exceptionally high.

In Sierra Leone, De Beers initially had its own concessions as well as the right to buy everything others produced — yet it still had problems. Its miners were poorly paid, and theft was common. In the early post-war decades, its very success in driving up prices caused illegal miners to flood into the diggings, scraping with shovels and hoes, frequently at night, protected by alarms, informants and camouflage techniques some of them had learned in British irregular warfare units. Behind the miners were "investors" who advanced supplies, bought the product and smuggled the stones. Most were Lebanese, the product of a turn-of-the-century mass migration in which many had headed for the New World in a vain search for streets lined with gold while others opted for West Africa, where they found alluvial fields seeded with diamonds.[5]

For a time Lebanese smugglers took diamonds to Lebanon. From there, industrial stones went to Moscow, while gem-quality ones crossed the southern border to the Israeli gem-cutting industry, evading both the De Beers monopoly and the Arab League Boycott.[6] However, by the 1960s virtually all were marketed in Monrovia, capital of Sierra Leone's neighbour, Liberia. Sierra Leone's stones along with those from Côte d'Ivoire, Guinea, Ghana and the Central African Republic — could enter Liberia duty free, and leave again subject to a much lower export tax than their own governments imposed. Furthermore, in Liberia the national currency was the U.S. dollar, the universal medium of exchange in the diamond trade. As Africa's principal tax haven and offshore banking centre, Liberia understood the need for discretion. Phoney diamond mines were set up in the jungle so that everything purchased could be marketed internationally as "Monrovian" in origin.

To strike back at the smugglers, De Beers hired the former wartime chief of British military intelligence. His agents infiltrated rings to monitor prices, plot routes, then, like narcotics cops, do "buy-and-bust" operations. Sometimes they "turned" those caught, allowing them to stay in business in exchange for information about the higher-ups. De Beers also paid a gang of bandits run by a Lebanese storekeeper from the backwoods of Liberia to hijack smugglers' caravans crossing the border.[7] Finally De Beers made a deal with Jalil Said Mohammed, an Afro-Lebanese who was Sierra Leone's most powerful "investor," to act as covert agent, buying up stones from diggers and smaller smugglers and reselling them to De Beers.[8]

However, by the early 1970s, the main threat to De Beers came not from smuggling but nationalist resentment. De Beers lost its mines, then its purchasing monopoly. With De Beers sheared of direct influence, power lay with a handful of officially designated diamond traders of which the strongest was Jalil Mohammed. Using his diamond profits, he became by far the most powerful force in Sierra Leonean business — and politics. His close relations with the country's aging president enabled him to put together a corporation to which the government conferred a monopoly of the purchase of all diamonds (and gold) along with the right to use the foreign exchange they earned. As the largest shareholder and managing director of that unique purchasing agency, Jalil Mohammed ran de facto a parallel central bank and a shadow finance ministry. Since the big banks in Sierra Leone refused to advance loans to any diamond dealer operating outside the De Beers circuit, Jalil also set up in partnership with BCCI, the International Bank of Trade and Industry, to handle diamond trade financing.[9] All this was alarming enough to De Beers, but it also had implications far beyond the regional diamond business.

The original Lebanese migration to Sierra Leone was mainly Christian. But the most recent wave was Shi'a Muslim when Islamic militancy was on the rise in the Middle East.[10] The flow went both ways. Nabih Berri, a child-hood friend of Jalil Mohammed, left Sierra Leone, his birthplace, for Lebanon to become boss of Amal, its largest Shi'a militia force and Syria's main military ally against Israel. Through Berri's influence, revolutionary Iran chose Sierra Leone as its window on West Africa — to the consternation of the CIA, whose main listening post was neighbouring Liberia. Iran reciprocated by providing Sierra Leone with cheap oil, sold exclusively through a company run by Jalil Mohammed. And Jalil Mohammed, whose home was protected by anti-aircraft guns, rocket launchers and light machine-guns manned by a special security force trained by the PLO, persuaded the president to arrange a state visit by Yasir Arafat.[11] But in 1985 the president was ousted.

The architect of the coup was Shabtai Kalmanovitch, a Soviet Jew who had migrated to Israel in the early 1970s, then headed abroad in search of greener pastures. He first landed in Bophuthatswana, one of the tribal homelands whose political "independence" only South Africa recognized. Apart from an attempt to rationalize apartheid, "Boph" was a sweated labour reserve for South African, Israeli and Taiwanese businesses, a staging point for sanctions-busting, and an offshore sin centre for whites leaving the puritanism of South Africa to enjoy a dirty weekend "abroad." Less a country than a commercial concession, Bophuthatswana was really run not by its South African–appointed president but by a group of Israeli carpet-baggers attracted by what a "Boph" trade delegation to Israel described as the "highly competitive" level of wages (about $9 per week) and the lack of "legislation that could distort free wage competition," that is, no unions or social security.[12] Kalmanovitch set up LIAT Finance Trade and Construction Corporation, whose main contribution to economic development was to win public contracts, sublet the actual work to other companies whose own bids had been lower, then kick back part of the profits to the president. To make sure he got paid, Kalmanovitch also arranged for "Boph" to borrow abroad, specifically from Kredietbank in Belgium, the institution through which South African intelligence financed its European espionage activities.[13] When "Boph" started running out of money, Kalmanovitch sought greener pastures. He landed in Sierra Leone at a time of acute economic crisis. Smuggling had become so pervasive that Customs caught the vice-chancellor of the university attempting to export books with diamonds and gold stashed inside.

Enthusiastically supported by Sierra Leone's new president, who offered tax concessions and subsidies, Kalmanovitch quickly supplanted Jalil Mohammed, who was forced into exile. From LIAT's Freetown headquarters, protected by Israeli-trained paramilitary units, Kalmanovitch ran farms, public transportation systems and mines. He planned low-income housing and hatched a plan with Marat Balagula, a Russian mobster, ex-KGB informant, and diamond-and-drug smuggler, to import whisky and gasoline from the United States. This scheme ended abruptly when Balagula was jailed in the United States for his part in the biggest excise tax scam in American history. Kalmanovitch further schemed to open banks and insurance companies and to take over the national airline. There was even a plot with a West German firm with a reputation for nuclear smuggling to dump radioactive leftovers in Sierra Leone. LIAT also secured a licence to deal in diamonds, along with the privilege of being the only buyer that legally did not have to bring the money back home.[14] Meanwhile, Kalmanovitch's Tel Aviv office was run by a retired deputy chief of Israeli military intelligence who apparently preferred working for Kalmanovitch to his previous private-sector job as head of security for President Ferdinand Marcos of the Philippines.[15]

LIAT seemed to have all bases covered. Sierra Leone's new president used it to undermine the Afro-Lebanese elite. Israel saw it as a tool for commercial penetration of West Africa and to block PLO plans for a training base in Sierra Leone.[16] South Africa regarded its duty-free shops, export licences, freedom from exchange controls and tax breaks as instruments for sanctions-busting. LIAT could import South African goods and re-export them marked "made in Sierra Leone." It could also import strategic goods, then slip them south. But late in 1987 British police arrested and jailed Kalmanovitch on charges of having passed over $2 million in forged cheques in the United States.[17] Extradited to the U.S., he was later released on bail, given back his passports and allowed to hightail it for Israel. Once there, Kalmanovitch was promptly charged again, this time with espionage for the U.S.S.R. The United States was incensed over information Jonathan Pollard had stolen that had ended up in Moscow. Kalmanovitch's close relations with his former homeland made him a perfect scapegoat. Imprisoned, his knowledge of Israeli and South African covert operations was safely out of reach.[18] Still, Sierra Leone's potential as a sanctions-busting centre had been compromised just when South Africa needed it most.

Breaking Conventions

Although diamonds, gold and strategic metals were exempted from sanctions, basic goods like coal, steel, food and textiles with many alternative suppliers, were not.[19] Even so, with phoney certificates of origin, false labels, co-mingling and third-country diversions, effectiveness of sanctions ranged from weak to hopeless.

The export of coal, after gold South Africa's most important export, should have been easy to stop. It is extremely bulky in relation to value, its origins can be readily identified, and there were many alternative suppliers. Furthermore, over half went to one destination, the European Economic Community (EEC). And it was largely handled by a few giant oil companies whose activities, in theory, could be monitored. For a change, theory seemed substantiated by statistics showing by the late 1980s a one-third drop in South Africa's coal exports.

Of course statistics can be subject to interpretation. For example, in 1987 Dutch data showed coal exports to Britain of 1.1 million tons. That was curious, given that the Netherlands had not mined coal since the 1960s. South African coal was sent to Rotterdam in bulk carriers owned by Shell Oil, whose captains were instructed not to admit that South Africa had been a port of call. In Rotterdam, the port authorities ceased recording the movement of bulk carriers to and from South Africa so that the paperwork cited the Netherlands as the country of origin. South African coal was mixed with Chinese and marketed around the world as "Dutch blend." Similarly, South African coal was marketed by way of Belgium and labelled Australian.[20] In total, the coal sanctions, which could have cost South Africa markets for 10 million tons, ended up reducing its exports by no more than 3 million. By the time sanctions were abolished, a plan was afoot to restore part of that loss by stocking South African coal in Israeli ports where it could be mixed with Colombian, then re-exported.[21]

Similarly with steel. Many countries who refused to buy South African products had no objection to steel produced by a Swiss company that possessed no plant and equipment, but was owned jointly by the South African Steel & Coal Corporation and the Israeli Histadrut.[22]

Although minerals and metals were much more important, South Africa also wanted its manufactured goods to win global acceptance. The primary target was the United States. With the front door closed, South Africa relied on friends to hold open the back one. Under the U.S.–Israel Free Trade Agreement, a product with a minimum of 35 per cent Israeli value added qualified for duty-free entry into the U.S. In theory, the U.S.–Israel trade deal, and that between Israel and the EEC, did not apply to products of Occupied Palestine. In practice, countries turned a diplomatically blind eye. South African firms could manufacture components using sweated black labour in or from the Bantustans and finish production in plants owned with Israeli partners in the West Bank, where wages were from one-quarter to one-third of the Israeli level. The savings on labour more than offset any extra costs from round-about transportation. The goods, labelled "made in Israel" could then achieve tariff-free entry into the U.S. market or preferential entry into the EEC.[23]

Of course, the goods still had to pass the 35 per cent value-added rule. Chambers of Commerce in Israel handed out certificates of origin that attested that the 35 per cent requirement had been met but were otherwise left blank. When the commercial attaché at the American embassy in Tel Aviv was queried about verification, he explained, "All this is done on a lot of faith."[24] One company sharing that faith was Voyageur Corporation of Tel Aviv, which placed advertisements in a South African business publication baldly announcing, "Any sanctions impediments can be circumvented through our offices for modest percentages," and offering such "unconventional trade" services as trans-shipments, re-invoicing, bartering and buy-backs.[25] Through the Israeli bolt-hole, South African steel, chemicals, fertilizers, kitchenware and processed foods, among others, made their way to markets in the United States and around the world.[26]

In 1987 Israel, under pressure from black congressmen in the United States, finally agreed to its own sanctions. The government of Israel, a country where ownership of 93 per cent of the land is legally barred to anyone who is not Jewish, publicly denounced apartheid.[27] It promised a suspension of military contracts, a freeze on tourism, the end of oil deals and an embargo on kruger-rand coins. Yet military cooperation continued.[28] South Africa remained by far Israel's leading trade partner in Africa. Tourism actually rose after the Israeli "sanctions." The number of flights between the two countries doubled. And South African bank loans to Israeli companies increased. Nor did South Africa seem inconvenienced by losing access to Israel's famous oil wells. And its dis-appointment over the banning of the krugerrand was perhaps tempered by the realization that for decades Israel had restricted any import of gold coins.[29]

There was also abundant demand much closer at home for South African–manufactured exports. Although black Africa was poor per capita, it was vast in numbers. It was also (with a few minor exceptions) supposedly closed to South African goods. However, in sub-Sahara Africa no one really knew how much trade there was or where it was going. Shortages of funds and corruption of functionaries made border controls almost non-existent.[30] The confusion helped cover the infiltration of South African products. It became so blatant that in Zambia, for example, while leaders were vehement about avoiding commercial contagion from the apartheid state, South African goods lined shelves of government-owned stores whose managers publicly praised their quality, price and ready availability.[31]

Sub-Sahara Africa's importance went beyond its direct capacity to absorb goods. South Africa surrounds and economically dominates Lesotho, Swaziland and Botswana. All three were locked into a Customs union with their powerful neighbour and depended heavily on exporting cheap labour to South Africa, mainly to the mines. In the 1980s they found a new role. Thus, a Taiwanese firm manufactured textiles in South Africa on one of the Bantustans and sent the finished products to Swaziland where "made in Swaziland" labels were sewn on. The goods went back to South Africa accompanied by Swaziland government certificates of origin for export to places like the United States. The caper was so good that the firm started importing Taiwanese-made textiles for the same treatment, evading both the U.S. ban on South African textiles and U.S. quotas restricting the amount allowed in from Taiwan.

Sometimes the process involved a little more than labels. One firm set up in Swaziland a plant to put wooden handles on steel pots made in South Africa, thereby qualifying for tariff-free export to the EEC. Swaziland certificates of origin accompanied South African beach sandals to vacation spots around the world. "Product of Swaziland" labels appeared on South African avocados in the Middle East, apples in Europe, wine in Canada and timber, maize and industrial plastics in Iran.[32]

Swaziland was not alone. "Botswana" grapes and "Lesotho" apples found favour with European and North American consumers trying to avoid South African produce. And a "Lesotho" airline, created by Mario Ricci and Craig Williamson, flew from South Africa to the Seychelles bearing goods to be trans-shipped to an export processing zone in Mauritius. There they were finished and labelled "Made in Mauritius," before winging around the world.[33] In fact, the potential for using island states in the Indian Ocean as sanctions-busting centres provided an opportunity for one of Africa's most legendary mercenaries, Robert Denard, to bring his career to a spectacularly bloody climax.

Gun-smoke and Glory

After his term as quartermaster for the forces battling in vain to preserve the French empire in Southeast Asia, Robert Denard flirted with the Organisation d'armée secrete, the settler and army-backed terrorist group that tried to block Algerian independence and assassinate President Charles de Gaulle. After being arrested and held for a brief time, he headed for black Africa in the mid-1960s when decolonization struggles were rocking the continent. He sold his sword to secessionists in Shaba province of the Belgian Congo, to Biafran separatists, to the white-settler regime in Rhodesia, to counter-revolutionaries in Angola and to coup-plotters in Benin, all with the quiet backing of France's external intelligence service, which was happy to have "Bob" take the heat if things went sour.[34] With all this and more under his web-belt, it seemed only natural that Bob might at some point consider retiring to a set of Indian Ocean islands once described by Mark Twain as the place on which Paradise was modelled.

Robert Denard's first foray into the convoluted politics of the Comoro Islands came in 1975 when he was hired by presidential aspirant Ali Soilih to oust the incumbent, Ahmed Abdullah, who had angered the French by a unilateral declaration of independence. Once president, Ali Soilih himself nationalized French property and threatened war over France's refusal to cede control of a neighbouring island. After three years, during which Ali Soilih went from a flamboyant Marxist to a psychotic voluptuary, it was ex-president Abdullah's turn to hire Bob to reverse the previous coup's results, killing Ali Soilih in the process.[35] Restored to the appearance of power, Ahmed Abdullah found himself "protected" by a special force calling itself the Presidential Guard, the core of which was a group of French and Belgian mercenaries who took orders from Robert Denard. Bob, who by then could count to six when asked about either his war wounds or his wives, decided to take advantage of the islands' hospitality. He and his mercenaries controlled local politics and external diplomacy, and ran most of the island's foreign trade. Bob himself managed a plantation, an import-export firm and a private security company that hired itself out to protect South African investments.

Island life was not entirely idyllic. When the army chief-of-staff was caught running a cigarette and liquor smuggling operation without cutting in the Presidential Guard, Denard pressed President Abdullah to fire the officer. Then, suspecting that Abdullah was plotting to oust him, Denard and his forces launched a pre-emptive strike, with Abdullah meeting the same fate as his predecessor. South Africa and France both cut off aid, and, after negotiations, Bob left for South Africa before heading off to France a while later to "clear his name."[36]

However, until that unfortunate denouement, South Africa had been sufficiently happy with its little neighbour to meet the payroll for the Presidential Guard.[37] It found the islands almost as useful as the Seychelles for smuggling South African goods. They were favoured destinations for South African investments in agribusiness and tourism. And the Comoros were a way station through which South Africa supplied paramilitary groups destabilizing other neighbouring countries as part of its own program of regional economic warfare.

Into the Heart of Commercial Darkness

South Africa's economic clout against its neighbours was enormous. It could curtail food and energy supplies, deny transportation rights, suspend investment, block tourism, arbitrarily change trade regulations, and refuse work permits.[38] Against various neighbours at different times it did most of those things. With two of them, it tore yet another leaf from the book of classical economic warfare.

One target was Mozambique. After independence, the revolutionary government had closed the Rhodesian border to trade and permitted anti-regime forces to strike across it. To hit back, Rhodesian intelligence created an irregular unit later named the Mozambique National Resistance (RENAMO), many members of which were recruited from those rendered unemployed by the collapse of Mozambique-Rhodesia trade. After the fall of Rhodesia, RENAMO was adopted by South Africa, provided with money, training and arms and put to work. It attacked mines and agricultural projects, bombed transportation and power infrastructure, wiped out crops of sugar, cotton and cashew nuts, and destroyed rural schools and health clinics. It pillaged rural and village stores, selling the loot in neighbouring Malawi. It raided convoys carrying emergency aid to afflicted areas. It attacked Mozambican workers coming back from South Africa, stealing their savings, which it could then spend in South Africa for supplies. But its main objective was the Beira corridor, the transportation route from the central part of southern Africa to the east coast, which could have given black Africa an alternative outlet to the Indian Ocean. With that shut, trade had to go through ports in South Africa, which used control of the traffic to divert, mislabel and smuggle in defiance of sanctions.[39]

The Beira corridor had yet another function. After white-ruled Rhodesia became black-ruled Zimbabwe, the oil pipeline from Beira, closed by UN sanctions, was reopened. Once Zimbabwe became a base of operations for anti-South African guerrillas, South African forces raided oil storage tanks in

Beira, while RENAMO attacked the pipeline. When Mozambique began moving oil by rail from Maputo, the railway became a target. Ultimately, Zimbabwe could secure oil supplies only by importing from South Africa along the same land route formerly used to bust sanctions against Rhodesia. Any sanctions-induced increase in the price of oil to South Africa could be partially recouped by South Africa charging even more to Zimbabwe, or to other southern African countries dependent on South Africa for energy supplies.[40]

Much the same transpired in Angola. After independence, the MPLA guerrilla army wiped out one of the opposition groups and came close to doing the same to the second, the National Union for the Total Independence of Angola (UNITA).[41] Subsequently, South Africa resurrected UNITA and re-oriented its strategy. Instead of attempting to overthrow the government, UNITA targeted the economy.

To disrupt trade, it shut the 1,200-mile railway and road link that ran from the mineral-rich Shaba province of Zaire to the Angolan Atlantic port of Lobito. That forced almost all of Angola's trade, and that of several neighbours, to go through South African ports. The result was direct earnings to South African transportation facilities and more transit trade that could be mislabelled and re-routed.[42] To ruin the food supply, UNITA launched the "manioc war." To deny the government foreign exchange, it disrupted the coffee harvest and sabotaged the country's main iron mine.[43] It attempted, without success, to wrest from government control Cabinda, the oil-rich enclave where Cuban troops guarded American-owned oil installations from guerrilla attacks that in later years were financed partly by the American taxpayer.[44] UNITA's greatest success came in the diamond mines.

Angola is probably second only to Russia in the richness of its gemstone deposits. Controlling them had always been a problem. During the 1960s, European gun-runners dealt with guerrilla bagmen carrying their revolutionary treasuries in small canvas sacks around their necks. After the 1974 revolution in Portugal, when it was clear imperial rule would soon end, the main source of contraband became fleeing Portuguese colonists. To get their wealth to safety they would sell local assets and use the proceeds to buy black market diamonds. Portugal then waived normal smuggling penalties and permitted sale of stones with no questions.[45] This was supposedly done as a short-term measure to promote resettlement of Portuguese refugees. In fact, the law stayed on the books to become one means by which anti-government guerrillas could finance arms and supplies.

The new government of Angola faced two distinct problems. In government-run mines, miners stole stones, sold them to illegal dealers, many

Portuguese, who turned the gems over to corrupt diplomats to smuggle. From Lisbon, the diamonds went to Antwerp or Tel Aviv.[46] Meanwhile UNITA raided mines, killed technical personnel, destroyed equipment and stole diamond stocks. Yet more dangerous to the government's control of the diamond market, by the mid-1980s UNITA began to encourage illegal alluvial mining, then taxed what the miners dug up. Sometimes UNITA soldiers themselves became miners.[47] By the late 1980s UNITA had an independent budget of about $200 million per annum of which fully a third came from selling stolen and illegally mined diamonds. Some went to Portugal. Most went to De Beers.[48] It was a perfect arrangement for all parties — except the Angolan government. UNITA had independent financing. De Beers was able to control gemstones that would otherwise have made their way onto the black market. And South Africa could conduct economic warfare against Angola through UNITA without having to pick up much of the tab.

The guerrilla groups had other sources of money. Apart from official donors (the United States for UNITA, South Africa and Saudi Arabia for RENAMO),[49] there were corporate sponsors. Lonrho Corporation in search of future mineral concessions backed UNITA, while trying to protect its pipeline by bribing RENAMO to keep away. Elf-Aquitaine, still "sniffing" around for African oil, kicked in money in the hope of obtaining oil contracts. RENAMO received contributions from a shadowy network of former Portuguese colonists and black marketeers spread across southern Africa, Brazil and western Europe, and from a collection of U.S. right-wing tax-exempt foundations. Evangelical Christians and political nutcases kicked in money. One ultra-right group even struck a commemorative RENAMO silver coin, which it sold to raise money for the cause. There were also various rackets. Shortly after independence, counterfeit money started turning up in Angola.[50] Perhaps inspired by that example, a group of RENAMO boosters counterfeited $100 and 50-rand notes.[51] UNITA support units trafficked in cocaine and in Mandrax, a synthetic drug provided to them by South African intelligence front companies that manufactured it as a tool for "crowd control" back home.[52] To further fatten their treasuries, UNITA and RENAMO poached animal hides, rare hardwoods and ivory.[53] In that, too, they had help.

In 1980 South African Military Intelligence created Frama Inter-trading (Pty) Ltd., a commercial front company, to supply UNITA. The company purchased trucks and reviewed all tenders for UNITA supplies and verified delivery. Although it was originally set up with "private" cut-outs, in 1986 military intelligence discovered that the directors were skimming the profits and took direct control of Frama. Much like ISI trucks plying the Karachi-Peshawar route during the Afghan war, Frama's vehicles were immune from search. Therefore they were ideal vehicles for contraband, including ivory and rhino horn, which were packed in boxes labelled "Arms" or "Dental equipment."[54]

UNITA (and likely RENAMO) collected ivory from elephants killed by their own troops or purchased it from freelancers. They passed it to South African military intelligence teams at special drop points. For UNITA the main staging area was occupied Namibia. For RENAMO it was the triangle where Mozambique, Zimbabwe and South Africa meet. There the ivory came not only from RENAMO, but also from the Zimbabwe army, which poached tusks from the country's game parks.[55] By blaming the poaching on RENAMO infiltrators, the army could then justify its continued presence in the parks and continue poaching. Other units of the Zimbabwe army were stationed in Mozambique, ostensibly to help protect trade routes from RENAMO. Those units would receive poached ivory and resell it to RENAMO buyers, who would pass it on to South Africa.[56] South African military units delivering weapons would truck or fly back ivory to buyers in South Africa, Lesotho, Swaziland or Botswana.[57]

At first the existence of this traffic was strenuously denied by the South African government. Yet the head of UNITA publicly confirmed that he regularly traded ivory through South Africa to pay for weapons. Similarly, when Mozambique government forces captured RENAMO headquarters, they found nearly 20,000 tusks ready to be loaded onto South African military planes.[58]

Taking Credit

One way or another, trade sanctions were circumvented. On the sending side, certain countries profited from violating them, while others were unable and/or unwilling to police them. On the receiving side, South Africa skilfully used the infrastructure of evasion and held its neighbours' trade flows captive. Still, there was one final way in which South Africa might have been subject to serious pressure.

Financial sanctions fell into two categories. One was a campaign to get transnational corporations to cut back or pull out. Some responded by reducing their shares in local operations to below 50 per cent. That was the tactic chosen, for example, by the two big British institutions that dominated banking. They subsequently claimed they could no longer tell their local affiliates what to do — a surprise to most of the world's great corporations, which are controlled with far smaller blocks of stock. Reducing equity participation also permitted corporations to insist that violations were no longer their fault. Thus did General Motors disclaim responsibility for GM vehicles that wound up in the hands of the South African police and army.[59]

Other firms genuinely cut their share positions to zero. They therefore won plaudits for standing up to apartheid while doing something they had planned to do for strictly commercial reasons. All over the world during the 1980s, transnational corporations substituted licensing for direct ownership and collected royalties instead of profits. South Africa was no different. Any assets sold by transnationals could be bought cheaply by locals, along with a long-term agreement to use the technology, trade marks and industrial designs. The impact was neatly summarized by IBM, which sold to a local firm, then took a full-page ad to assure customers, dealers, employees and suppliers that the company's commitment to service would remain unchanged.[60] In the only cases where transnational corporations shut down completely, their South African subsidiaries were losing money.

The second type of financial sanction was imposed after 1985 when commercial banks ceased to renew long-term loans to the South African government.[61] Once more the actions were accompanied by a public relations blitz. Yet the real question was not why they chose to pull out of South Africa, but why they had stayed so long when everywhere else in the world they had been cutting back loans to shaky governments for several years. The answer was written in gold, source of half of South Africa's foreign exchange. As long as the price of gold was high, South Africa was an attractive customer. But in the early 1980s it began to fall sharply, causing banks to reclassify South Africa as a bad credit risk. The apparent financial "sanctions" had less to do with the banks' moral revulsion against apartheid than with their practical revulsion against losing money.

To be sure, dramatic political changes did take place in South Africa after 1990, though with no real shift in the distribution of wealth or economic power. And sanctions likely played some role in prompting the changes: by driving up the cost of oil, by forcing South Africa to discount goods it was selling, by imposing a pariah tax on foreign borrowings and by making it more awkward for growing South African businesses to participate in a global economy. However, sanctions were far from the whole story. They may even have been marginal.

Much as with Rhodesia two decades before, the changes were partly the result of shocks quite unrelated to sanctions that hit the very heart of the economy. Production from South Africa's old and expensive gold mines peaked in 1970. For a time, high prices disguised the danger. But after 1980, South Africa was caught in a squeeze. Costs were rising at home, while abroad, new and cheaper mines were coming on stream and new technologies even permitted the extraction of gold from slag heaps around previously abandoned sites. The result was that prices kept falling, undermining the country's financial foundations and setting off a slow-motion meltdown. It reached crisis proportions in the 1980s, just when the sanctions movement was attracting the most media attention.[62]

Furthermore, the business class was changing in ways that undercut much of the former support for the regime's policies. Apartheid had been implemented partly to maintain a supply of cheap labour for mines and farms, and partly to insulate Afrikaner workers from the competition of blacks, who were paid far less. But by the 1980s the typical Afrikaner was no longer a hard-hatted mine worker or a red-necked farmer. There had emerged a broad urban middle class that had not only less ideological stake in the status quo but an economic interest in changing it. And for that, credit went less to sanctions than, in a backhanded way, to South Africa's success in contravening them.

The economic strategy of self-sufficiency meant that, especially as gold sagged, the driving force of the economy had to come from the internal market. That depended on a black consumer population growing rapidly in numbers and purchasing power — impossible as long as wages were kept low by institutional discrimination and massive unemployment. Meanwhile the nature of the internal challenge faced by the regime changed ominously.

The African National Congress's military wing had launched its first sabotage campaign in the 1960s on the standard theory that attacking transportation and communications infrastructure would disrupt production, precipitate capital flight and threaten white living standards, so forcing the government to negotiate. The campaign fizzled very quickly. It resurfaced in the 1980s with little more effect. There were attacks on coal-liquefaction plants, railway lines, power systems and oil depots. Once again, the state was able to smash the guerrillas, although at much higher cost.[63]

By then the stage was set for a South African intifada launched by a subclass of unemployed black youth. It took the form of economic actions organized at the grass-roots level. Much like during its Palestinian equivalent, though ultimately with more effect, there were consumer boycotts, policed by gangs who forced those who purchased in white shops to destroy the goods. There were rent strikes that functioned like the fiscal intifada, striking at the finances of local governments. Labour action, too, became more common. Strikes were held to protest not just wages and working conditions, but also dismissals.[64] Against such mass unrest, South Africa's military might was largely useless. That was why, in desperation, military intelligence employed top white scientific and medical personnel to manufacture drugs like Mandrax and Ecstasy to incapacitate the black population. It later rationalized the traffic by the notion that drugs were a much more "ethical" form of crowd control than bullets.[65] While never a decisive blow against the system or the regime, collective economic actions were another sign that an era was drawing to a close and that, regardless of the success or failure of sanctions, apartheid and the economic autarky it fostered were no longer in the financial interests of the class that had created them.

Part Five

BELLUM AMERICANUM

Chapter 13

CIGAR–ENVY

Sanctions are usually touted as a sign of the world's displeasure at outlaw behaviour by a pariah state. However, most programs are initiated by one country against a weaker one for strictly political reasons, though, to add a fig leaf of international moral authority, third countries are sometimes bribed or bullied into enlisting. That has been true in the many cases from the 1960s to the 1990s when the United States imposed its hemispheric will, usually with the Organization of American States wagging its tail in affable assent. While countries as varied as Chile and Nicaragua, Panama and Haiti were at the receiving end, nothing could so easily drive American politicians into a rage as a bout of cigar-envy caused by the sight of an unrepentant Fidel Castro puffing on a Habano while delivering an epic anti-gringo tirade on prime-time TV.[1]

Sugar and Vice and Everything Nice
Prior to the 1959 revolution, Cuba was a joint venture of two sets of U.S. business interests: the sugar companies and the mob. During Prohibition, it was a transit station for foreign alcohol running into the United States. After Prohibition ended, mobsters continued to smuggle liquor via Cuba to evade taxes and used Cuban molasses to make rot-gut booze bottled with brand-

name labels. Later, heroin and cocaine were added to the freight list.[2] Close to Florida but without the nuisance of U.S. law enforcement, the island became the premier playground of the idle rich. In 1952, when their U.S. gambling operations were under scrutiny, the mob helped return to power former strongman Fulgencio Batista.[3] He repaid with enough tax breaks and subsidies that the island soon hosted mob-run hotels, resorts and casinos, serviced by the hemisphere's most notorious red-light district.[4]

After Castro's victory, the elite and much of the professional class fled. Not all intended to suffer in exile. When asked how he got $20 million out of the country in merely two years, a former minister of education replied, "In suitcases."[5] This diaspora of skilled people and their money allowed Miami, until then a torpid backwater, to compete with Panama for the position of financial centre of Latin America. In 1980 virtually the entire population of Cuba's jails (which hosted many more common criminals than political dissidents) was released on condition that it would leave the island. Most headed for Florida. The combined effect permitted Miami to take its place as the primary North American distribution centre for drugs, arms and dirty money, and as a major launching pad for U.S. covert action throughout the Americas.[6]

Although Castro quickly appointed overseers for U.S.-owned businesses in sensitive sectors like sugar milling and public utilities, it was oil that first fouled bilateral relations. Previously, U.S. companies in Cuba had imported and refined Venezuelan crude. But in 1960 Cuba bartered sugar for Soviet oil. The United States ordered local refineries to refuse to process it. In retaliation, Cuba nationalized their properties.[7] The U.S. responded by banning imports of Cuban sugar, in the hope of drying up the country's foreign exchange and forcing big wage cuts among the sector's 500,000 workers, turning them against the regime. Cuba replied by negotiating a sugar deal with the U.S.S.R. and by nationalizing all other U.S. economic interests, including the hotels and casinos run by Meyer Lansky and his associates.[8] In a fever of un-American activity, Castro went on to raze the brothels and convert the red-light district into an area housing museums to socialist achievement.[9]

In reaction, the United States banned all trade to and from Cuba, a particularly harsh blow since Cuban ports and shipping facilities were equipped to handle only the short Cuba-Florida run. Switching trade partners required Cuba to pay higher freight costs and to upgrade its infrastructure. The United States also blacklisted non-U.S. firms and ships that did business in Cuba. An American warship patrolled to monitor the vessels that came and went. By strong-arming neighbouring countries into imposing sanctions, the United States further drove up freight costs. Blocked from other stops in the region, a ship wishing to call on Cuba often had trouble securing a full cargo and had to charge the entire cost to the Cuban portion. Later, the United States attacked the island's tourist revenues by prohibiting Americans from visiting, and it pressed U.S. banks and international agencies like the World Bank and the IMF to cut off credit. Once Cuba announced its formal adherence to Marxism, the United States could deploy CoCom, forcing even those member countries who continued to trade with Cuba to ban items the United States managed to get classified as strategic.[10]

Even before sanctions were fully in place, the United States began plotting Castro's assassination and moulding Cuban exiles into a military force. In 1961 the invaders waded ashore at the Bay of Pigs and into disaster. The survivors were ransomed for $10 million cash and $53 million worth of food and medicine. After this debacle, U.S. policy shifted from direct assault to Operation Mongoose, a CIA-run program of low-intensity warfare and economic sabotage.[11]

Led by OSS veterans of the glory days of World War II, the CIA set up in the Miami area gun shops, travel agencies, shipping companies, air charter services, radio stations, boat and car dealerships, real estate firms and detective agencies as fronts for paying agents, providing supplies or, on occasion, granting pensions to widows.[12] Bank accounts were established in Miami and across the Caribbean on islands making their first moves towards becoming bank secrecy centres. Working in Miami, CIA officers and contract agents were unable to hide behind the cover of employment at an embassy or wave diplomatic passports when caught in every act from possession of illegal explosives to violations of the Neutrality Act. But with the connivance of the major law enforcement arms, the agency kept its protégés out of jail long enough to train thousands of Cuban exiles in paramilitary skills, while their support staff learned smuggling and money-laundering. "Sterile" weapons, untraceable to the U.S. government, came from special CIA stocks, from agency-supported gun-runners or from the Miami black market. Nothing better summed up the process than one 20 mm Finnish cannon. It was sold off after World War II to an Italian arms dealer who peddled it to the Haganah. After a few years with the Israeli army, it was sold back to the same arms dealer who unloaded it on Costa Rica, which eventually resold it to another arms broker working for the Algerian Front de libération nationale. After Algerian independence, the cannon wound up in Panama, supposedly in unusable condition, entered the United States classified as a deactivated war trophy, magically acquired a new barrel, and was sold by a Miami black market arms merchant to the anti-Castro guerrillas for $300.[13]

These preliminaries — training, arms and supplies — taken care of, it was time to get down to business. And in Cuba, there was no business like sugar. American intelligence officers plotted bacteriological and meteorological warfare to destroy the crop, while agents burned fields, bombed sugar mills, contaminated cargoes en route to market and sabotaged milling equipment bound for Cuba. Once the CIA persuaded a London broker to short-sell sugar in an effort to drive down the price and dry up Cuba's foreign exchange earnings.[14]

Next in importance to sugar was a huge nickel-copper mining complex, the target of several sabotage campaigns. Even when such raids failed to achieve their direct objectives, they forced Cuba to divert scarce resources into coastal defence. At the same time there were efforts to destroy economic infrastructure. A covert CIA-run navy (operating from Nicaragua) and air force (flying from abandoned fields in Florida) conducted shelling and bombing expeditions against oil storage facilities, power plants and transportation centres.

The CIA also blocked Cuba's access to American machinery and spare parts, causing a severe problem of breakdowns. When Cuba sought replacements outside the United States, American agents sometimes secured the cooperation of manufacturers in delivering defective merchandise. A German firm, for example, sent Cuba ball-bearings that were off centre. Alternatively, they directly sabotaged parts and machinery in transit. Inability to obtain basic industrial equipment was one reason Cuba abandoned plans to diversify away from sugar. Apparently according to U.S. government logic, forcing Cuba to depend on sugar and therefore on the Soviet market, while simultaneously cutting off all sources of oil besides the U.S.S.R., was an effective way to check the spread of Communist influence in the Americas.[15]

To supplement the financial boycott, there was a scheme to flood Cuba with counterfeit money, first, to finance the underground purchase of supplies by anti-regime activists, and, second, once the sums got large enough, to induce a flight from the Cuban currency. Initially, staff of the U.S. Bureau of Engraving and Printing helped make plates to run off flawless-looking ten-peso notes. However, bad luck intervened. Many who fled Cuba had taken loads of currency with them. To neutralize the overseas hoards, the Cuban government demonetized the old currency, exchanging old notes for new only for residents. That made the bogus notes useless. Furthermore, the U.S. administration forbade official participation in further counterfeiting schemes. So the plotters turned to private enterprise. A wealthy Miami contractor whose Cuban properties had been seized offered money to hire private counterfeiters. But the contractor was killed in an airplane crash (some blamed Cuban agents, some the U.S. government) and the U.S. Secret Service arrested the others involved in the scheme.[16]

The economic war was to be the prelude to another invasion. But the U.S.S.R. brought the island under its nuclear umbrella. After the most dangerous confrontation of the Cold War in 1962, the U.S.S.R. agreed to withdraw its missiles, and the United States pledged not to invade. In theory that deal also ended paramilitary raids, though leaving the trade and credit sanctions in force. While the United States insisted that further attacks were strictly freelance, and occasionally arrested the perpetrators, many were still officially sponsored with deeper cover. CIA assets were buried inside private commercial companies.[17] Money to finance operations came via private sector fronts or sources, seemingly substantiating the official claim that the guerrillas were mere mercenaries. Contracts to assassinate Fidel Castro were sublet to U.S. mobsters still smarting from the loss of their Cuban rackets.[18] Ultimately it was the demands of Vietnam, as well as the realization that Cuban strength made the raids largely useless, not any deal with the U.S.S.R., that brought officially sponsored action largely to an end.

For the United States, Operation Mongoose had a series of important repercussions. First was the subversion of law enforcement. Agents consorted with mobsters and rang up violations of trade, tax, firearms and neutrality laws, while their handlers perfected the plea of "national security."[19] This not only created an exempted criminal class, but sent a message to strictly private sector entrepreneurs that one way to beat a smuggling or gun-running rap was to claim some association with the CIA. That would put the prosecution in the unenviable position of having to prove that the defendant was not an agent of an organization whose modus operandi was based on denying the identity of its hirelings.[20] It would also help spawn a conspiracy industry among American radicals and, on occasion, Hollywood producers, that imputed everything from the assassination of JFK to the future crack epidemic to dark CIA plots.

A second repercussion was to bring home to the United States the "disposal" problem that has plagued sponsors of proxy war since at least medieval times when decommissioned mercenaries ravaged the countryside at large. Left behind when the "secret war" was wound down were Cuban exiles trained in assassination and sabotage, along with a generation of smugglers, money launderers and counter-surveillance experts whose skills were perfectly adapted to the drug, arms and alien smuggling boom to follow. In the decades after the end of the "covert war," veterans of Brigade 2506, the anti-Castro Cuban paramilitary force, would rack up an impressive list of drug-trafficking and money-laundering arrests.[21]

Third, as always, the infrastructure of an economic war outlived it. The same Caribbean islands used by the CIA as safe havens and supply depots became in later years contraband storage and refuelling bases for smugglers. Financial havens boasting bank and corporate secrecy laws, once in place, could cater to all manner of clients. Indeed, even while the secret war was in progress, the same institutions used by the CIA had to keep up the appearance of normal business by servicing insider traders, commodity fraudsters and tax evaders just like any offshore bank.[22]

Fourth, the failure to separate private and public interests created great potential for corruption. Sometimes training and supplies were paid for directly by the U.S. government. However, sometimes they were paid for by Cuban exiles or American mobsters who had their own agendas.[23] Moreover, actual operations were often run by an old-boys' network of retired agency personnel and their sympathizers in private business over whom public scrutiny was weak or non-existent.[24] An ex-president of United Fruit posed as the nominal owner of a radio station that ran anti-Castro propaganda and broadcast coded instructions to operatives in the field while drug traffickers shared their boats with guerrillas en route to mission. The legacy of this confusion of public and private, between covert and criminal, later culminated in the Iran-contra affair in which the same methods, and some of the same people, were involved.

Behind the Smokescreen
During the 1970s Cuban-American relations were at a stand-off. There were even periodic hints of rapprochement. The Carter administration terminated reconnaissance flights, cracked down on raids by Cuban exiles, and relaxed rules on sending goods and money to Cuba. It also tried, without success, to barter Cuba's withdrawal of military support of revolutionary regimes in Africa for lifting the ban on medicine and on equipment for the nickel industry.[25] But in the 1980s, as part of the Reagan administration's worldwide anti-Communist crusade, the United States renewed its economic offensive and the Cubans went on the counter-offensive.[26]

Of the formal trade sanctions, the U.S. ban on Cuban goods was, in the long run, the least important. Once the initial shock had been absorbed, there were ample alternative markets. For the next three decades Cuba sold most of its sugar to the U.S.S.R. on excellent terms, taking much of the payment in oil, simultaneously undercutting the U.S. fuel embargo. That permitted Cuba, on occasion, to buy super-cheap sugar on world markets, deliver it to the U.S.S.R. at a far higher price, receive subsidized oil, and divert part to foreign sales at the commercial rate — while publicly decrying the immorality of creeping capitalism in East bloc countries.[27] Although the sugar–oil swap was the most important, Cuba and the U.S.S.R. negotiated other barter deals with the terms-of-trade similarly twisted in Cuba's favour. All together they meant a Soviet subsidy that, at peak, amounted to 20 per cent of Cuba's national income and underwrote its dramatic growth during the early 1980s when most of Latin America was hurting.[28]

Other Cuban products found easy markets in Canada, Latin America and Europe. Tourism from around the world expanded. And Cuba also found a number of techniques to sneak its products into the United States. Initially, Cuban embargo-busters were inexperienced, and a few agents sent out to establish secret trading facilities just disappeared with the money. But once Cuba began selecting its commercial agents on the basis of business training rather than revolutionary ardour, the results were much more impressive.

The simplest technique was the old-fashioned one. It began when exiles working fishing boats from Florida discovered that running shoes, blue jeans and electrical appliances made the best bait. Decreeing their own truce with fishermen from Cuba, they swapped goods in short supply in Cuba for banned seafood that brought premium prices in the United States, under the watchful eye of a Cuban gunship.[29]

A more sophisticated technique was co-mingling. Nickel ore, until the new tourism boom second only to sugar as a source of foreign exchange, could be sent abroad, mixed with ore from other countries and shipped to the United States. Alternatively, nickel would be refined from Cuban ore, manufactured into finished products in Canada, Europe and Asia, and similarly sent to the U.S.[30] However, another commodity smuggled into the U.S., though counting for far less in dollars, was much more important in the defiance it symbolized. For this product was as indelibly associated with Cuba as fine champagne with France, high fashion with Italy and bad food with Britain.

Part of the cigar trade left Cuba directly. Fast boats struck out from southern Florida to pick up cigars in Cuba or off larger ships, then scooted back, mixing with the huge number of pleasure craft moving between Florida and the Bahamas chain. Much more of the trade followed a round-about route, relying on the fact that among the exile community are the families that used to dominate the cigar business inside Cuba. With an intimate knowledge of the trade, they took over cigar manufacturing in Honduras and the Dominican

Republic, the countries that inherited (legally) Cuba's cigar trade with the United States; they also controlled distribution in Spain, which takes 50 per cent of all Cuban tobacco exports. To get cigars back into the United States from Spain or other European distributing centres, individuals hid them in personal luggage or arranged for mail order delivery (in unmarked or mislabelled packages). Even larger lots came through commercial channels. Cigars went from Spain to Switzerland, for example, then under false labels to cigar distributors in the United States who repackaged them with Cuban labels for underground sale. Much the same occurred with cigars consigned to Canada.[31]

Profits could be huge — up to 1,000 per cent.[32] Though most gains accrued to smugglers and middlemen, for Cuba the financial returns were far from negligible, and the political ones much greater — provided it could maintain consumers' faith. For that reason Cuba, which refuses in the name of socialist solidarity to recognize international copyright, strenuously defends the trade marks under which its cigars are sold worldwide.[33]

About 20 per cent of "Cuban" cigars marketed illegally in the United States are fakes. Some are made in Honduras or the Dominican Republic, whose tobacco is close enough to Cuban to fool someone smoking cigars more for the prestige of their name than the taste of their tobacco. Some are the work of Cuban émigrés in the Miami region who buy ordinary cigars, strip off the wrapper, affix fake Cuban labels, then sell to neophyte puffers. But a lot of the fakes are made in Cuba. Underground manufacturers collect the floor sweepings in government-run factories or buy illegally from tobacco farmers (who are supposed to sell only to the state), roll low-quality imitations and pack them in boxes used for legitimate cigars. The cigars are sold either to professional smugglers who run them, along with the real products, into the United States, or to unsuspecting tourists. Cuban police sometimes raid the underground factories or arrest street peddlers, while airport officials scour outgoing tourist luggage for fakes and demand proof of legal purchase — all to assure the world's fops of the aristocratic purity of socialist Cuba's most prestigious product. However, those security measures have little effect on underground traffickers who can also counterfeit receipts issued by the legal sales outlets.[34]

In various ways Cuba was able to evade the impact of the American ban on its products. Its chief difficulty was on the import side. The principal concern was not the three commodities traditionally subject to embargo. Cuba was close to food self-sufficiency, and the U.S.S.R. supplied oil and arms. Rather, Cuba had to find American machinery and spare parts, and, a little later, computers, banned under CoCom. As its dependence on tourism grew, it also began shopping for American consumer goods to resell at handsome mark-ups to foreign visitors, especially from the Soviet bloc. To meet some of those needs, one of Cuba's more notorious long-term visitors tried to lend a helping hand.

Robert Vesco was a man with a mission, and a record. He had been accused of looting Investors Overseas Services of nearly a quarter of a billion dollars. (Actually, the number appears to have been puffed up by 200 to 800 per cent to sensationalize the theft, and most of the missing money was quickly recovered.) On the run — from outraged investors, the FBI, SEC and Watergate investigators probing illegal contributions to Richard Nixon's re-election campaign — he hopped from exile to exile — Costa Rica, the Bahamas, Antigua — pursued by American law enforcement and bad publicity, and worse. In his increasingly paranoid mindset, he became convinced during a brief Nicaragua stopover that his capture was one of the objectives of the U.S.-armed contra rebels then fighting the Soviet-backed government. Eventually he settled in Cuba. Vesco's welcome was based partly on his claims to be an expert on real estate development when Cuba was expanding tourist facilities, and partly on stories that he had huge amounts of money stashed in various financial havens. In reality, by the time he arrived in Cuba, he appears to have been almost broke, and he soon had to earn his keep.[35]

For years Vesco had been trying to sell one Caribbean destination after another plans for tapping the flows of hot and homeless money washing through the region. At one point he teamed up with an Italian film star to attempt to convince the family dynasty ruling Antigua to cede them part of the neighbouring island of Barbuda as the site for the (Knights-of-Malta-inspired) Sovereign Order of New Aragon. This chivalric enterprise planned to sell "knighthoods," diplomatic passports and financial secrecy to the rich and infamous, while running the usual array of casinos, free trade facilities and offshore banks. The plan was aborted when the Italian partner was arrested on gun-running charges. Not discouraged, Vesco came up with an even wackier scheme for the governments of Nicaragua, Cuba and Grenada (then run by a leftist party in Washington's bad books) to take advantage of the Swiss relaxing their bank secrecy laws by creating a new monetary bloc, passing tight bank secrecy laws and issuing their own currency backed by Soviet gold. The countries concerned, he suggested, would not only gain by attracting the region's underground money, but could use it for economic warfare against the United States. While the Cubans showed no inclination to take his advice on money matters, not even a scheme for offshore banks on the island of Cayo Largo, Vesco did have talents and associates the Cubans felt they could use.[36]

In his most notorious caper, Vesco arranged for some confederates to order American machinery, along with a decade's worth of spare parts, that would both refine sugar and manufacture fuel pellets from the leftover biomass, creating a fuel source that would permit Cuba to cut its demand for imported oil. As the machinery was loaded on a plane for Mexico, nominally en route to Costa Rica, a tip-off about the real destination led to a U.S. Customs raid. Vesco's colleagues were charged with trading with the enemy. Ultimately only one stood trial. While free on bail, another died of a massive heart attack, though he had no previous history of coronary disease, and two others were murdered.[37]

As the scheme showed, one of the ways Cuba obtained U.S. machinery was by subcontracting with brokers in Mexico, where Cuba had at least a dozen agents and front companies, or in Canada, Brazil and western Europe.[38] To reduce further the chance of being caught and blacklisted, intermediaries might purchase U.S. parts, incorporate them into their own products and export the completed items to Cuba. If the final product had more than 10 per cent American content, the procedure was technically contrary to U.S. law. But the scam could be broken only by dismantling the questionable item. Or Cuba could set up shell companies in financial havens and have them place the order with the supplier who could then remain blissfully ignorant of the identity of the ultimate customer. Incorporation in haven countries also meant that insta-companies could be easily replaced should they be identified and blacklisted.

For that reason, Cuba did a remarkable amount of business with Liechtenstein, whose chief manufactured products are sausage skins, false teeth and shell companies. However, the preferred business location for embargo-busters was central America's biggest financial haven and smuggling centre. Obliging Panamanian companies, some secretly owned by Cuba, some independent, would import from the United States goods like cigarettes, televisions, electrical appliances, tires, jeans and cosmetics that were in high demand both for the regular economy and for sale through dollar-based shops and tourist facilities. The same companies also exported Cuban-made rum, tobacco, textiles, costume jewellery and sporting equipment back to the United States. Cuban seafood, labelled "product of Panama," found U.S. markets. Panama also handled the financing. Among its 130 banks was a branch of the Banco Nacional de Cuba. For extra cover, European investors in Cuban tourist facilities would made deposits in their own banks on behalf of Cuba. Cuba would draw down lines of credit from those banks to pay the Panamanian companies. And those companies would pay the American suppliers through their local bank accounts.[39] In fact, it was by playing such a role as the financial base for smuggling operations that Panama helped precipitate the biggest political scandal in Cuba's revolutionary history.

Snow Job?

Since the early 1980s the United States had been publicly claiming that Cuba was providing sanctuary and trans-shipment facilities for Colombian cocaine barons, with the pay-offs used to buy weapons for leftist insurgent groups in Latin America.[40] Furthermore, helping to launder the take was supposedly one of the services offered to his hosts by Robert Vesco.[41] Cuba is surrounded by drug transit countries and countless boats and planes, including those carrying drugs, inevitably skirt its territorial waters and airspace. Hence charges about Cuban drug operations were easy to make. They were believed largely by those already predisposed to believe them, and shrugged off as more American disinformation by everyone else — until 1989 when Cuba arrested, and eventually executed, several senior officers, including respected veterans of the Revolution, on charges of, among other things, drug trafficking.[42]

In 1986 Colonel Antonio de la Guardia had returned from service with the Cuban military mission in Ethiopia and was put in charge of Departamento MC, the top-secret division of the Ministry of the Interior, responsible for evading sanctions. While on business in Panama, de la Guardia supposedly made contact with a representative of Colombian cocaine baron, Pablo Escobar. At the time, the traffickers' Bahamas-based route into the United States was coming under pressure. One alternative was through Cuba. Drugs were flown into air force bases or into the tourist resort of Varadero, often in IBM boxes, a good cover given that Departamento MC's priorities included acquiring American computers. The drugs were stuffed into crates of tobacco and cigars, the covert export of which was also high on the department's task list, and handed over to fast boats from Miami. The alliance with senior Cuban officials also gave the Colombian traffickers an opportunity to dream up (though never implement) an even more audacious plan to refine cocaine and manufacture counterfeit U.S. dollars in Angola.

Heading the Cuban military mission to Angola was General Arnaldo Ochoa, one of Fidel Castro's original small band of revolutionaries. His duties involved raising hard currency to defray costs of the mission. With official approval he arranged barter deals in Cuban products and set up foreign currency stores in Angola to peddle Cuban goods to airline crew members, diplomats and other foreigners. His officials sold Cuban sugar, rum and fish for local currency, then traded it on the illegal foreign exchange market for dollars. In addition, Ochoa and General Patricio de la Guardia, brother of "Tony" de la Guardia and representative of the Ministry of the Interior in Angola, trafficked in ivory and diamonds, made money selling military equipment (some of it smuggled out of the United States courtesy of a Cuban-American ex-CIA agent[43]) to the Angolan government, and even peddled anti-aircraft missiles on the central American black market. Some of the profits were shipped to Panama for deposit in a secret account, apparently the same one into which pay-offs from using Cuba for cocaine smuggling were being stashed. Some of the profits were brought back and held in the form of stashes of high-denomination peso notes in the participants' homes.

That the rackets existed seems incontrovertible. Cuban officers dabbled in Angolan black markets, especially diamonds, from the very start of the military mission in 1976.[44] Why they existed is another question. Had General Ochoa, darling of the Revolution, and the only marginally less distinguished de la Guardia brothers, simply become personally corrupt? It would hardly be the first time in the history of covert economic warfare that principals used the officially approved smuggling apparatus for self-enrichment. The de la Guardias had been born to wealth and perhaps had a yearning for the good old days, while General Ochoa had evidently developed a taste for high living.

Or was General Ochoa, supposedly growing dissatisfied with the regime's policy in Angola and its refusal to decentralize economic controls, using black market dealings to build up a war chest for a coup? That, too, would hardly be unprecedented. It has long been part of the hidden craft of intelligence to use contraband profits to finance covert operations. And the regime was quite aware that their role in embargo-busting dramatically increased the power of senior officials in the Interior Ministry. Furthermore, Cuba, along with most Socialist countries, maintained a watchful suspicion of top military figures lest they use their position for political purposes. Indeed the scandal provided the regime with a pretext to thoroughly purge Departamento MC and even to jail the minister of the interior on charges he abused his own power and covered up for his officials.

Alternatively, was General Ochoa, as he claimed in his trial, simply carrying out orders to earn hard currency for government projects, particularly to finance expansion of the tourist facilities, only to be made a scapegoat? The regime's motives for singling him out might be both to curry favour with the Americans through a public crackdown on drug trafficking, and to remove the popular general before he became a lightning rod for dissent. Ochoa's black market operations, even if state-sanctioned, would have been conducted in such a way that he could be made the fall guy if the operation were exposed. That, too, is normal in the intelligence trade.

Or were the charges real? And was it possible that the exemplary punishment was a desperate attempt to stop the rot as the regime successfully combated the American embargo but lost its ideological soul in the process? That was particularly true in the 1990s when the fall of the U.S.S.R. put the Cuban economy into a tailspin and forced the regime to take huge steps back to capitalism in its worst form.

Semper Fidelis?

Back in 1959, the revolutionary government had imposed price controls on food. Each household received a *libreta de abastecimiento* and was to register with the retail outlet of its choice from which it could draw rations at prices everyone could afford. The next year the state strengthened its grip by nationalizing retail outlets, starting with stores owned by Americans or Cubans who fled or had been caught hoarding and profiteering.[45] As the controls tightened, black markets emerged, fed from all along the distribution chain. Private farms and co-ops diverted output to unofficial markets; thieves stole from state warehouses; officials running warehouses sent the poorest quality goods to the state stores and sold the best to the black markets; retailers, especially of meat and other higher-priced products, cheated on quantity or supplied second-class merchandise at the rationed price while selling the rest or the best for cash on the side; consumers bought at state stores at low, fixed prices, then resold at a profit.

In the 1970s to try to defeat the black market, the regime introduced an official parallel distribution system in which more luxurious items could be sold at prices far above controlled levels. Black markets still existed, but they ceased to appear serious enough to threaten the system. Indeed, a few years later, the parallel market was discontinued. And in the early 1980s, with the economy thriving and food shortages seemingly a thing of the past, the regime tightened the degree of centralized control and purged officials who argued for market-oriented reforms.

However, by the late 1980s illegal trafficking was again widespread, not just in food, but in construction materials, motor parts and fuel. It was a replay of Soviet experience packed into a much shorter time frame. Some of the goods trafficked were produced in underground factories, using inputs, tools and raw materials stolen from the state. Some were illegally imported. Some came from managers of state stores who would under-report deliveries, over-report losses or simply short-change customers.[46] Probably the most important source, not in volume but in portent, was diversion onto the local market from the *diplotiendas*, foreign currency stores stocked with desirable imported goods. They were legally open only to diplomats, foreign technical personnel or Cubans either returning with hard currency from authorized trips abroad or waving receipts from government stores where Cubans were allowed to sell valuables like gold and jewellery at state-fixed prices. These *diplotiendas* were a running sore in a society committed to wiping out economic class distinctions, particularly when it faced, in the early 1990s, its deepest crisis in thirty years.

Before its demise, the U.S.S.R. had begun insisting that Cuba pay world prices in hard currency. That caused Cuban trade to plummet, drove up the price of essential goods and eliminated the massive subsidies that had underwritten Cuban prosperity. On top came the decision by American presidents to pander to the powerful exile community in Florida by further tightening the screws. George Bush, facing a tight re-election contest, pushed through the 1992 Cuban Democracy Act. This law extended the trade embargo to overseas subsidiaries of U.S. firms, who accounted for nearly 20 per cent of all Cuba's non-Communist imports. It also attacked trade and tourism by tightening the shipping embargo until it was as rigorous as in the 1960s. Any foreign vessel, including cruise ships, docking in Cuba was banned for the next six months from American ports.[47] Taking their signals from the administration, officials took sadistic delight in strictly applying the provisions. Thus, they ruled that Colombia was not permitted to ship chickens to Cuba because the American chicken feed on which they had been raised accounted for more than 10 per cent of their total weight.[48]

George Bush's successor, Bill Clinton, favoured reconciliation. So did one faction of the Cuban-American community and a growing number of U.S. businesses, worried about the inroads into Cuba made by Canadian, European and Latin American firms. But the anti-Cuba lobby prevailed. Therefore the Clinton administration further squeezed Cuba, reducing below the low levels set by previous Republican presidents the remittances Cuban émigrés and exiles were permitted to send to their families.[49]

With the end of the Soviet subsidies and the tightening of the U.S. embargo, the economic situation deteriorated rapidly. Masses of rural girls left home to take up streetwalking in front of the foreign-run tourist hotels, a situation the Cubans found particularly humiliating given the pride they had taken in closing the notorious red-light district in the 1960s.[50] Food shortages meant that stores selling price-controlled goods went empty. Theft, hijacking and looting of state property escalated. Part of the crisis was met by moving resources out of sugar and into basic food crops, while resurrecting the legal parallel market where farmers could sell freely anything in excess of their quotas. Small urban businesses outside the state-controlled sector were also legalized. These measures were harmless enough. But the next step had heavy consequences. The government formalized use of the U.S. dollar.[51]

The immediate objective was to encourage people in Florida to circumvent restrictions on remittances by sending over money in cash. Thousands of exiles began flying to Havana carrying greenbacks, while thousands more Cubans emigrated to the United States on temporary visas to hustle for work and ship money to family back home. As U.S. Customs forced ever more outbound Cubans to submit to strip-searches, travel agencies, remittance companies and freight forwarding firms advertised their expertise in getting money to Cuba. By the mid-1990s the result was an influx of dollars put conservatively at $500 million per annum. To capture the greenbacks, the government opened across Cuba dollar stores selling everything from imported luxuries to basic foodstuffs. Indeed, the suspicion arose that the government was starving the ordinary stores to divert commodities to the dollar stores from which it could collect foreign exchange. The government also permitted people with dollars to swap them for a special convertible peso, with the right to trade them back when they wished.[52]

While implemented as a measure of immediate economic survival, legalization of the dollar effectively divided the Cuban economy into two parts and the population into two classes. The first, where prices were set and transactions effected in pesos, remained in deep depression, with the state in disorganized retreat, and the population losing faith. The second, dollar-based sector, flourished as tourism and foreign investment grew. The government also began paying workers in key sectors — nickel mining, sugar, steel and fishing — productivity bonuses in peso certificates convertible into dollars.[53] The corrosive effect of the new dollar dependency was aptly summed up in 1993 when Cuban police broke a ring that had used the graphic arts unit of the Ministry of Culture to counterfeit U.S. currency.[54]

Washington remained susceptible to bouts of cigar-envy. This would produce periodic legislative outrages like the 1995 Helms-Burton Act, which permitted the U.S. Treasury to harass with lawsuits and prosecute as "Cuban agents" non-U.S. companies that continued to do business with Cuba.[55] And the United States discovered a new method of bullying foreign business people dealing with Cuba. While foreign citizens could hardly be charged with trading with the enemy, they could be arraigned on charges of laundering the money so earned if at any point it passed through an American-owned or affiliated bank.[56] Yet years after pundits confidently predicted the end was nigh, Fidel was still in power.

However, if U.S. economic warfare had failed to oust the regime, it had helped set the stage for a dramatic transformation of Cuban society. An economy dependent on tourism and the dollar reproduced many ills of pre-Revolutionary Cuba. Black market hustling, bureaucratic corruption and property crime became the new growth sectors.[57] The beach areas were blighted by chintzy hotels, surrounded at night by legions of young prostitutes. Across the country a new elite emerged, made up not of veterans of the Revolution or pioneers of Cuba's embargo-defying, world-class biotechnology sector, but of hotel clerks and bartenders who strutted the streets flashing dollars. Nothing better symbolized the new Cuba than a special limited-edition cigar storage box. It bore on the top a facsimile of a carving by Ecuadorian revolutionary artist, Guayasimin, and it contained inside a certificate of authenticity jointly signed by Fidel and the artist. The box was available for anyone with $20,000 to contribute to the cause of maintaining socialist purity in Cuba.

Chapter 14

OLD PROS AND NEW CONTRAS

Although the regime resisted U.S. economic pressure, Cuba had been quarantined. Its early dreams of exporting revolution were utter failures. Not until the 1970s did American paranoia about Communist threats in its own backyard induce it to take similar action against another neighbour. Unlike Cuba, neither Chile nor Nicaragua was particularly secure. They lacked external protectors, were financially vulnerable and faced powerful internal opposition. Both, therefore, were easy targets of economic warfare.

The Big Chill

In response to the nationalization of American-owned property in 1971, the U.S. government's Export-Import Bank stopped guaranteeing loans to finance exports to Chile, and American commercial banks ceased to lend. Since 80 per cent of Chile's trade credit came from U.S. banks, it could no longer import American parts for industrial and agricultural equipment or for its copper mines, the main foreign exchange earner. At one point nearly a third of all trucks at the major mine sites, 30 per cent of city buses and 20 per cent of cabs stopped running. American pressure also led the World Bank to refuse all loans and to the Inter-American Development Bank cutting back. The private sector did its share. A successful court appeal in the United States by Kennecott Copper froze the bank accounts of nine Chilean-owned companies, including the new state-owned copper company. Lawsuits in France and Germany permitted the U.S. firms to seize ore cargoes. That frightened off potential customers, who feared they would pay, then lose the shipment.[1]

The economic war was well timed. While the Chilean government, naturally, denounced a CIA plot to drive down copper prices, Chile had nationalized its mines just when there was a worldwide glut and its mines were badly in need of new equipment. Furthermore, U.S. actions were amply supplemented by internal protests. The Chilean elite financed a crippling truckers' strike and paid farmers to refuse to plant.[2] Explosions wrecked industrial plants, and mining equipment inexplicably broke down. As the environment deteriorated, hoarding led to shortages, which the population blamed on the government and the government blamed on the CIA. Finally, one week before General Augusto Pinochet led a military coup that overthrew the regime, the United States refused a request by Chile to purchase 300,000 tons of U.S. grain on soft terms at a time when the country's foreign exchange reserves had largely disappeared and it faced a bread shortage. Shortly after the coup, the United States acceded to an identical request from the new military regime.

Yet the outcome was scarcely a brilliant success. The widely publicized bloodbath following the coup generated world sympathy for the ousted government. It also precipitated a major scandal in the United States that hung out in public much of its intelligence establishment's dirty linen. Relations between the U.S. and the military regime soon degenerated to the point where the U.S. imposed against it an arms embargo. When a new opportunity arose for the U.S. to apply an economic squeeze to oust a target regime, the results, from a public relations point of view, were much more satisfactory.

All in the Family?

President Anastasio Somoza Debayle, last patriarch of the American-installed dynasty ruling Nicaragua since the thirties, was convinced that the business of government was his business. At the time of his overthrow in 1979, he owned, among other things, 25 per cent of the arable land, the national airline and shipping companies, the cement factory, textile manufacturing plants and sugar mills whose value had shot up after Washington transferred to Nicaragua part of the sugar quota of pre-Castro Cuba. He owed his power to four principal bases of support.

One was the CIA, which reciprocated the assistance he or his father had lent to various endeavours: supporting a coup against the government of Guatemala when it angered the United Fruit Company with land reform in the 1950s; making Nicaragua a base for anti-Cuban operations in the 1960s;

and threatening Omar Torrijos, nationalist military boss in Panama, with a Nicaraguan alternative to the Panama Canal if he did not tone down his anti-gringo rhetoric in the 1970s.

A second pillar of support was Israel. The older Somoza had earned its grati-tude, first by fronting for arms purchases by Zionist paramilitary organizations in Palestine, then by providing weapons and diplomatic cover to Israeli agents. The support was reciprocated in the 1970s when his son's military went to Israel for training, and Israel continued selling weapons right up to two weeks before the end, long after the U.S. government had cut the regime off.[3]

Third was a shadowy network of ultra-right business and political figures from around the world. Somoza's Nicaragua played a curious role in the oper-ation of Italy's Propaganda Due (P-2) Masonic lodge. Although centred in Italy, P-2 had tentacles across Europe and throughout Latin America. It was under Somoza's wing that Banco Ambrosiano, the Italian private bank that functioned as virtual paymaster of the P-2, opened a Managua branch to facil-itate exchange control evasion, political pay-offs and arms trafficking in Italy and abroad. Right to the end, the bank helped Somoza buy weapons and it assisted his supporters in creating offshore retirement accounts.[4]

Fourth was the National Guard. It ran military security, the police, customs and immigration, the national radio, and the postal and telephone system. It was also a business in its own right with de facto control of the black markets in liquor, arms, cigarettes and prostitutes. Members paid lower taxes, secured priv-ileged access to credit, got food and clothing at subsidized rates, had special rights to housing and schooling and were well positioned to collect bribes.[5] In return, the National Guard functioned as an anti-insurgency force, with sufficient effec-tiveness to kill 50,000 people before the Sandinista insurgency triumphed.

As the end drew nigh, Somoza began liquidating his assets, mortgaging them to a bank he controlled, and shifting the money abroad, leaving the debts for his successors to worry over. After a final looting party in the Central Bank, he hopped on his private yacht and sailed off to exile, stopping at the Bahamas with trunk-loads of cash to try to buy a residence permit.[6] Rebuffed, he headed for Paraguay where a prosperous retirement among his peers — warlords in exile, retired cocaine barons and ex-Nazis — was terminated by a fatal bomb blast. Meanwhile, members of the old elite were taking similar preparations, siphoning assets off to safety in Miami. And National Guardsmen retired to neighbouring countries to ply the arms and cocaine trade while plotting a comeback. When Ronald Reagan came to power in 1981, prospects of such a comeback brightened considerably.[7]

Fidel's Cuba was a geographic and ideological island in a politically hostile sea. Sandinista Nicaragua was very different. Some of its leaders professed Marxism-Leninism, but the operating ideology was far from Communist. Opposition political forces, led by anti-Somoza businessmen who dissented from the radical turn the revolution took, were harassed by the junta. And the anti-Sandinista media were subject to censorship (usually rationalized on "national security" grounds). But both continued to function. Nor were there any prisons packed with political detainees. Some sectors (banks, mines and power companies) were nationalized, with the pledge of compensation at book value, although the government never had the money to fulfil its promise. But, apart from seizures because property was abandoned or imposed as a penalty for capital flight, the only confiscations without compensation were of assets of the fugitive dictator and his henchmen. Although businesses complained of increasing state regulation, 60 per cent of industry and 75 per cent of agriculture, the sector in which most of the population was employed, remained in private hands.[8] This meant that, unlike Cuba whose neo-Stalinist orientation dimmed its appeal, Nicaragua was a serious challenge to the status quo in Central America at a time when bitter insurgencies were raging in Guatemala and El Salvador. With its history of extreme dependence on the United States (which took 70 per cent of exports and supplied most capital equipment) and a government with plenty of revolutionary ardour but little business sense, Nicaragua was also a soft target.

The first sanction imposed was a credit cut-off. The new Reagan administration cancelled foreign aid payments, blocked loans through the multilateral lending institutions and lobbied private sector banks to stop lending.[9] In subsequent years, American commercial banks would form a special task force to trace and seize Nicaraguan government assets around the world.

Financial sanctions were followed by an oil embargo. Formerly, the country's refinery, owned by Exxon, imported crude from Mexico and Venezuela to produce fuel, while most petro-chemicals came from the United States. The U.S. banned the export of refined products, forcing Nicaragua to purchase from more distant locations at greater cost. Eventually it also succeeded in pressuring Mexico and Venezuela to demand cash for oil formerly sold on credit. Apart from contributions from Iran, Nicaragua had to rely on the U.S.S.R. for oil, which enabled the United States to claim that Nicaragua had become just another Soviet satellite.[10]

Another measure was a drastic cut in the amount of sugar, Nicaragua's largest export, allowed into the United States. Yet another was to cut off the landing rights of the national airline whose only profitable run was to and from Miami. All this was for starters. In 1985, CIA director William Casey told his officials, "Take a look at what a total boycott will do."[11]

The impact of complete sanctions was mitigated by the fact that, for several years, Nicaragua had been diversifying its trade relations. Europe and Canada became markets for most foodstuffs formerly sent to the United States. The Soviet Union provided oil and arms. Even financial sanctions were partially off-set by contributions from places like Libya. But, as with Cuba and Chile before it, the ban on spare parts, industrial inputs and machinery had an immediate impact. Agriculture was damaged as tractors and spray planes wore down, and as the supply of fertilizers and pesticides was cut back. The fishery was hurt by an inability to keep motors and trawling equipment in repair. The cotton mills and mines were forced to drastically reduce production. The pharmaceutical industry was soon operating at 40 per cent capacity. Even Exxon had to scramble for alternative suppliers of equipment.[12]

The Sandinistas were able to take some countermeasures. American machinery was purchased in Canada from subsidiaries of U.S. corporations, until U.S. pressure put an end to it. American-made spare parts, chemicals and pesticides were bought through Mexico. Honduran and Costa Rican vessels were licensed to fish in Nicaraguan waters: they exported the catch to the United States labelled as their national produce. Front companies in Panama bought U.S. goods, particularly machinery and parts, and even on one occasion, old military aircraft, or exported items like bananas and seafood to the United States. Though somewhat successful, these measures exacted a heavy price. Finding alternative markets meant extra transportation costs. Nicaragua could sell its sugar elsewhere but at a loss, and its beef at a much reduced profit. Working through third countries and front companies drove up the acquisition cost of essential items, sometimes substantially. And neither trade diversification nor smuggling could counter the most important part of the American strategy.[13]

Divert and Dissemble, Deal and Deny

The contra rebels began with the September 15 Legion, a collection of National Guard exiles, ex-Guatemalan intelligence agents and professional criminals specializing in robbery, kidnapping and extortion. The original core was combined with aging Bay of Pigs veterans, CIA contract agents posing as Nicaraguan exiles, British soldiers-of-fortune, Israeli government-approved rent-a-Rambos and American paramilitary thrill-seekers, along with an assortment of drug smugglers and cattle rustlers. This disparate band was knocked into the semblance of a military unit. Or rather, several military units, fraught with internal tensions and divided by old grudges, new jealousies and disagreements over objectives, strategies and how to share the loot.[14]

Initially, the United States subcontracted to Argentina the job of arming and training the rebels. That was a wise choice. Argentina was run by a vicious military dictatorship that had honed its skills on bringing about mass disappearances of political dissidents and leftist guerrillas at home, and on its support of the 1980 "cocaine coup" in Bolivia. That event brought to power a clique of drug-trafficking senior Bolivian army officers who repaid Argentina with drug money to support Argentina's central American counter-insurgency efforts. But in 1981 Argentina and Britain came to blows over the Falklands/Malvinas Islands. When the United States supported Britain with advanced weapons and military intelligence, Argentina pulled the plug on the contras and the CIA stepped in directly.[15]

However, intervention in Central America was far from popular at home. In 1982 Congress sharply restricted the amount of money the agency could spend. In 1984, following a CIA-sponsored raid on Nicaragua's main harbour in which several ships of neutral countries were damaged, Congress cut funds off completely. During those periods of restricted official funding, other methods to finance the war had to be found. They added up to a virtual encyclopedia of white-collar crime.

Some of the tricks directly involved U.S. agencies. Funds authorized by Congress for the Afghan mujahideen and money earmarked by the State Department for "humanitarian" assistance to Nicaraguan exiles may have been diverted into contra coffers. Arms were loaded onto planes supposedly carrying non-military supplies and the entire freight cost charged to the "humanitarian aid" account. Some of the job was offloaded onto the U.S. army, which could obtain funds from its own burgeoning covert operations budget or skim them from foreign military aid allotments to Honduras, El Salvador and Guatemala.[16]

Some covert support techniques involved foreign governments. Countries ranging from Singapore to South Korea, from Taiwan to Brunei were lobbied to help the contras in exchange for political favours, trade concessions or just the prospect of putting the U.S. administration in their debt.[17] Israel offered the CIA obsolete Soviet-bloc equipment (claiming to have captured it from the PLO in Lebanon). But instead of a pay-off by a direct increase in military aid, it asked the United States to sell to Israel warplanes at reduced prices, therefore avoiding embarrassing its congressional boosters.[18]

Israel's largesse was more than matched by Saudi Arabia's. In fact, the two, who had formed an implicit alliance during the Lebanese civil war, worked in tandem again: Saudi money was used to buy Israeli arms for the contras. While officially Saudi Arabia maintained cordial relations with the Nicaraguan government, under the table it kicked in at least $30 million to oust it, passing the money through Caribbean and Florida banking connections set up by Nicaraguan exiles. Then, in a remarkable scheme apparently the work of CIA chief Casey, Saudi Arabia was asked — and *may* have assented — to do a double double-cross. Saudi Arabia was already covertly exceeding its OPEC quota. Part of the excess was covertly sold to South Africa. In Casey's scheme, part of the profits from the South African sanctions premium were to be contributed to a secret fund run by American intelligence to buy Soviet-bloc weapons to arm anti-Communist guerrilla forces around the world, including those in Nicaragua.[19]

On top came "private" financing. American political voyeurs with more money than taste were asked for support in exchange for a handshake from, or even the chance to pose in photographs with, Ronald Reagan. Religious cults from the Christian Broadcasting Network to the Moonies were praying for the contras' success by preying on their followers' pockets. Eager to enlist were aging arm-chair soldiers, weekend warriors and wanna-be mercenaries. Added to them were "public interest" associations with edifying names like the National Endowment for the Preservation of Liberty, which solicited tax-deductible contributions and diverted them, less 30 to 35 per cent for "administrative costs," into the contra coffers. In fact, so many tax-exempt "religious, charitable and educational" foundations stood ready to pony up there was even a plan to cut out the middlemen and have the contras themselves decreed a tax-exempt charity.[20]

The world arms black market offered a special opportunity for collecting secret funds. The United States had imposed an arms embargo against Iran, and the Iran-Iraq war had driven the world black market price for certain types of American weaponry to dizzy heights. The Pentagon sold cheaply anti-tank and anti-aircraft weapons to "private" American and Israeli gunrunners who resold at a fat profit to Iran. Part of the profits were used for military supplies for the contras. This was the foundation of the infamous Iran-contra affair, numerous official investigations of which would generate enormous amounts of heat but, by design, shed little light.[21]

There was also potential in playing American financial markets. One opportunity came from the ongoing crisis rocking and roiling the American savings and loan bank system. When changes in government regulations facilitated the takeover of shaky banks by a new generation of cowboy capitalists, most were eager to plunge the deposit money into high-stakes real estate or financial market speculations. However, some had more inventive ideas. Individuals linked to the contra aid program would either secure control of ailing

S&Ls or, working through bent insiders, obtain loans on fraudulent terms. The borrowers would default, leaving the public deposit insurance fund to pick up the tab. Meantime the money ended up swelling Cayman Island bank accounts, filling garages with luxury automobiles, or, on occasion, pulling off an arms deal.[22]

The 1980s was also the decade of junk bonds, high-interest corporate IOUs used to finance takeovers of companies whose assets were then milked to repay the debts. That seems to have inspired "Nicaragua Freedom Bonds" to finance the ultimate hostile takeover bid. Backed by "the full faith and credit" of the contras and bearing 13 per cent, the bonds were repayable out of the treasury of Nicaragua once it was "liberated." The prospectus assured would-be investors that buying them would not constitute a violation of the U.S. Neutrality Act and that losses were likely tax deductible. To avoid the possibility that the SEC might snoop, the bonds were to be sold privately only to a select group of rich investors who would send their money to an opaque company in Delaware, from where it would be passed on to the contra leadership.[23]

In addition to collecting outside aid, the contras could use their business acumen to become partially self-sufficient. Contra field commanders rented troops to local landlords to keep unruly tenants in line. Contra treasurers played currency black markets, earning up to 30 per cent on cash the U.S. government or "private" donors supplied, though it appeared that the profits ended up in the pockets of the officials who ran the scheme rather than in the contra treasury.[24] And there was money to be picked up from the region's main growth industry.

Founding Fathers?

There were many reasons for drug traffickers to make common cause with the anti-Sandinista guerrillas. Both were plying their crafts in the same general area. Linking up with the contra struggle provided access to clandestine airstrips and cover for flights carrying drugs into the United States and money back. Some planes airdropped drugs to small boats, which then ran the stuff into Florida. Some flew directly to U.S. military bases where no one would inspect a contra supply flight. On the return flights, some planes carried cash for deposit in Panama from where it might be wired to Costa Rican banks to pay for contra supplies.[25] Aiding the contras also permitted traffickers to play the "national security" card if things got tough. Once the U.S. government returned $36,000 seized from a convicted cocaine trafficker in San Francisco after he produced a letter from contra leaders stating that the money was for the "reinstatement of democracy in Nicaragua."[26] Drug traffickers happily kicked in cash, planes or supplies paid for out of drug profits, paid fees to use contra airstrips, hired contras to guard trafficking installations, and employed them as couriers. There was even a scheme to murder a former U.S. ambassador to Colombia, collect the $1-million reward offered by drug barons, and divert the money to the contra cause, while blaming the murder on the Nicaraguan government. Despite dozens of reports of contra drug deals, the top echelon of the CIA kept using known traffickers in the war effort.[27]

Thus, one way or another, the contra war coffers were kept well topped up even when Congress severely restricted or banned official aid. As the money flowed in from embezzlement, tax evasion, political influence peddling, bank fraud, currency black marketeering, gun-running and drug trafficking, Ronald Reagan publicly extolled the contras as the "moral equivalent of our founding fathers," perhaps an allusion to the number of fine old New England families whose fortunes were based on slave trading and opium trafficking. The proceeds piled up so quickly that, at one point, contra treasurers, like conscientious corporate executives, invested their surpluses in thirty-day certificates of deposit.[28]

On the other side of the ledger, the money was spent on supplies, apart from arms, mainly in southern Florida. The Miami area played the same role in the contra war it had twenty years earlier in the "secret war" against Cuba. Committed to proving the superiority of free-market capitalism, contra officials siphoned off aid money by inflating invoices, substituting inferior for specified goods or diverting supplies onto black market sales.[29] There was even greater opportunity for fun and profit in the arms supply pipeline.

Some weapons were taken from U.S. army stocks. These weapons were declared obsolete or surplus, their value deliberately under-reported to remain within congressional aid limits. Some were stolen from National Guard armouries. As cover, they were recorded as destroyed or scrapped.[30] But most had to be Soviet models, for the usual reasons: to cloak the American role, to permit use of captured ammunition and to allow the rebels a propaganda coup by claiming their weapons had been captured from the Soviet-equipped Nicaraguan army.

Initially, much of the responsibility for arms supply went to Major General John K. Singlaub. An OSS man during World War II and head of a CIA-run clandestine warfare unit during the Vietnam War, after a public clash with President Carter over American plans to cut troops in Southeast Asia, Singlaub took his talents elsewhere. He became a director of an arms company and head of the World Anti-Communist League, a global umbrella organization of ultra-right political cults and paramilitary groups, as well as of the Council of World

Freedom, its U.S. affiliate.[31] Singlaub's council used its tax-exempt status to provide the contras with "freedom fighter kits" and Spanish-language bibles, while Singlaub lobbied for financial support and helped the contras spend the proceeds. He scouted up Soviet bloc equipment in Israel and Poland before conceiving a scheme to permanently circumvent congressional mood swings. Singlaub proposed to his old OSS buddy, William Casey, that the United States provide to Israel advanced military technology for free. Israel would manufacture it into sophisticated weapons and pass them on to China. China would then provide a continuous supply of Soviet-model light weaponry to a Singlaub-run offshore company, which would resell them to U.S.-supported anti-Communist forces all over the world.[32] Apparently no one had explained to the general that Israel already got the technology for free, courtesy of either the American taxpayer or its efficient techno-espionage apparatus.

In the meantime, acting in competition with Singlaub was another coterie of U.S. veteran military men, former spooks and career arms dealers headed by General Richard Secord. Secord, too, had had an illustrious military career, working with the CIA during the "secret war" in Laos and Cambodia in the 1970s, then heading the American arms sales mission to Iran during the regime of the Shah. His subsequent career as head of the entire Pentagon arms sales program was intended to be a stepping stone to the post of Air Force Chief of Staff. But those hopes were aborted when he came under suspicion (though he was never formally charged), along with a group of ex-CIA and naval intelligence officials, of participating in a scheme to swindle the U.S. government out of several million dollars in a deal to deliver arms to Egypt.[33] In "private" business along with several of his former military and intelligence colleagues, Secord managed to outmanoeuvre Singlaub and win the bulk of the business of supplying weapons to the contras. However, before he could fill his contracts, Secord had to obtain access to Soviet model equipment. And that required keeping some curious company.

Among the more curious was Munzer el-Qassar. A member of a Syrian diplomatic family, el-Qassar started his business career by smuggling stolen cars into the Middle East and hashish out again. Arrested and jailed on narcotics charges in Denmark in 1972 and in Britain in 1974, he narrowly escaped a third incarceration in 1977 when Interpol tried to talk to him about arms-for-drugs swaps between the Sicilian Mafia and the Lebanese Christian militia forces. Apparently seeing the error of his ways, el-Qassar was soon running a respectable arms-dealing operation out of Vienna while living in Marbella, on Spain's Costa Del Sol (whose extradition-free environment led to it being popularly called the Costa Del Crime), with forty Filipino servants and a fleet

of custom-built Mercedes-Benzes and Rolls-Royces. In addition to outstanding drugs charges, there were accusations he had provided weapons to
Palestinian terrorists, including the group that had hijacked the Italian cruise
ship *Achille Lauro* and murdered one of its passengers, an elderly Jewish-
American confined to a wheelchair.[34] Still, el-Qassar carried on business as
usual. He seemed well protected by his role as intermediary and informant for
various Western intelligence forces, and by his growing fan club in and around
the U.S. government. That new-found respect in the United States was in part
due to the privileged relations el-Qassar had with Cenzin, Communist
Poland's state arms company that was always eager to sell Soviet-model equipment for U.S.-sponsored covert wars against pro-Soviet regimes all over the
world. In his first deal for the contras, el-Qassar bought 158 tons of AK-47s
and ammunition and resold them to Secord. After many peregrinations, they
arrived more or less at their destination.[35] The same could not be said for
el-Qassar's second shipment.

In conjunction with an official British Ministry of Defence contractor
(which afterwards insisted it had no idea who its notorious partner was), he
placed an order with the government of Yugoslavia for Soviet-style assault rifles,
rocket-propelled grenade launchers and anti-aircraft missiles supposedly bound
for the Honduran army, which has always been equipped with American
weapons. To move the merchandise, el-Qassar chartered the *Silver Sea*, a
Panamanian-registered freighter "owned" by a Channel Island shell company
that, under previous ownership, had already gained notoriety as a gun-runner.
It was outfitted with an on-board crane, a sure sign it was planning to unload
off a deserted beach or near a mangrove swamp rather than in a modern port
where crane facilities would be available. And, as cover, the story was floated
that the ship was going "treasure hunting" in the Caribbean. Just before the
departure, British Customs arrived to verify that nothing was amiss. Then,
after the Customs officers left, trucks arrived to load aboard the *Silver Sea*
camouflaged jeeps, inflatable boats, communications equipment and various
jungle-warfare gear. Lifting anchor, the ship headed south towards Gibraltar en
route to Yugoslavia to pick up the weapons shipment that el-Qassar had
arranged. The plan was that, once those weapons were loaded, the ship would
head for the Caribbean, protected against mishap by U.S. Air Force surveillance.

Unfortunately, there was little the air force could do about bad weather or
a green crew who spent hours spewing into the rolling seas before the ship
made an emergency stop in Brest. Boarded by French Customs, who found
the British military equipment, the ship and its crew were arrested. Since the

captain had taken the precaution of obliterating marks on charts indicating Costa Rica as a destination and displaying other charts with a course plotted for West Africa, the authorities initially concluded the ship was part of a plan to support a mercenary coup in Sierra Leone. However, eventually the captain decided there was no reason for secrecy. To him, "supplying the contras would have been just another job."[36]

The Second Casualty

Despite the flood of money, the weapons supply was erratic. General Secord's offerings prompted unfriendly suggestions that "end-users" paid overcharges of as much as 300 per cent on some items while getting stuck with dud grenades and artillery shells manufactured in 1954.[37] The pipeline was drained by pay-offs to Guatemalan and Honduran officers. Even where weapons arrived, contra officers sometimes dumped them on the black market — among the happy recipients apparently were left-wing guerrillas in El Salvador battling a U.S.-backed junta.[38] While supplies were plundered by agents in Miami, contra units had to "requisition" food from farmers and villagers. Nor was the contra military performance exactly the stuff of Hollywood epics. They were badly mauled time after time by government forces. Still, they did their job. For the real objective was not to overthrow the Nicaraguan regime, but to undermine the Nicaraguan economy.[39]

The contras blew up bridges and boats and mined roads to impede the movement of goods. They attacked cooperative farms, destroying or stealing farm machinery, sabotaging irrigation works, and burning mills and storage facilities. They wiped out crops, focusing particularly on the biggest potential foreign exchange earners: sugar, tobacco and coffee.[40] Over 3,000 farmers who had benefited from land redistribution were killed, and many thousands more were driven into the cities, simultaneously depriving rural areas of manpower and burdening the government with the cost of refugee relief.[41]

Another important target was oil. Like the situation in Mozambique and Zimbabwe, Nicaragua was served by a triple system. There were oil storage tanks in the Pacific port of Corinto and a refinery near Managua. A pipeline linked the two. Since the refinery was a difficult target, the United States used the same strategy as did South Africa. Contra forces attacked the pipeline, while armed speedboats staffed by Latino mercenaries (trained and paid by the CIA, but with instructions to call themselves contras if caught) were unleashed to destroy the fuel storage facilities, along with goods awaiting export. A short time later they returned to blow up an underwater section of the pipeline.

Finally, in an effort to directly disrupt the fuel supply, and to drive up insurance rates to reduce tanker traffic, the main port was mined, damaging nine ships, including a Soviet tanker and a Japanese freighter.[42]

Ordinary citizens were encouraged in sabotage. While the American liberal media raised a commotion over the discovery of a CIA manual calling on the contras to recruit by blackmail, incite violence at demonstrations, shoot people trying to leave captured towns and hire professional criminals to deploy their unique skills,[43] they overlooked a second manual that told people how to wreck machinery and vehicles, improvise explosives, steal documents, harass officials, call in false alarms to police and fire stations, and encourage theft and hoarding.[44]

Combined with the sanctions, the result of the contra war was to cause Nicaraguan exports to plummet and essential imports to either dry up or rise dramatically in price. The pressures of war forced the government to shift resources to the army, which, at peak, claimed 60 per cent of the budget. At the same time, tax revenues collapsed, leading to cutbacks in food subsidies, literacy campaigns and rural development programs. As foreign exchange and tax revenues dried up, the fiscal crisis forced the government to finance more spending by printing money, increasing the dangers of hyperinflation.[45]

The combination of a depreciating currency, acute shortages, soaring unemployment and falling real wages encouraged the spread of black markets. In the early years of the Sandinista regime, when few commodities were rationed, black markets had been of little importance. If anything, they were seen by the authorities as a modest safety valve to fill in shortages of consumer goods. But with the tightening of the blockade, the increased drain of resources into the war effort and the collapse of legal production, the economy quickly became a dual one. In the legal sector, a few basic goods were cheap, though often not available. In the illegal one, there were plentiful supplies, at prices few could afford. The goods sold on the black market came from the usual sources: smuggling, underground production, diversion out of the legal sector, theft from state enterprises and corrupt government functionaries selling goods that had arrived as foreign aid.[46]

The government attempted to mitigate the damage by a currency conversion. The theory was that withdrawing the old currency would neutralize illegal hoards, hurt black market dealers and reduce inflationary pressures caused by the surplus of cash. In 1988 the old *córdaba* was demonetized and replaced by a new one, with three zeros lopped off. Any household could change up to 10 million old *córdabas* for new ones with no questions asked, and owners of legal businesses another 10 million. Anything above had to be held in a bank, pending investigation. As in any currency exchange, there were tricks.[47]

Those with excess cash would hire others, especially the urban poor, to exchange it. However, at the end of three days, 80 per cent of the currency was replaced, 10 per cent immobilized in bank accounts and another 10 per cent wiped out.[48] But the hope that this would seriously dampen inflation proved a vain one. For the most important cause of the inflation was not "excess" money in the hands of the public. Rather it was shortages, the drain of resources into the military, and an atmosphere of crisis that put a premium on speculation and price-gouging over investment in producing essential goods and services.

To truly alleviate the shortages, the government had to find the money to import basic commodities. One possible source was the burgeoning underground traffic in U.S. dollars. Every year about $130 million entered the country, mainly illegally, in remittances from family members living in the United States. To tap it, the government opened foreign exchange stores to everyone who had hard currency. That move gave the government access to more foreign exchange, but at a high moral cost. Much as in Cuba, the policy created two classes of consumers in a country ostensibly devoted to eradicating the worst forms of income disparity.[49]

The Nicaraguan economic warfare campaign was ultimately a great success.[50] By the end of the decade the income level was hovering at its 1930s level, making Nicaragua even poorer than Haiti.[51] As the standard of living dropped and the social programs that were the ideological *raison d'être* of the revolutionary regime dismantled, the popularity of the government sank. The United States, which periodically explodes in outrage at revelations of illegal foreign contributions to its election campaigns, covertly funded the opposition. In the 1990 presidential elections, the Sandinista government was defeated, and the political experiment it represented brought to an end.

Chapter 15

SHORT CIRCUITS AND
BACK CHANNELS

$\mathbf{M}$uch of the sanctions-busting by Cuba and Nicaragua worked through Panama, the hemispheric super-haven. The country had been created in 1903 when the United States, seeking a location for a canal to span the isthmus, sponsored a revolution in the northernmost province of Colombia. The next year legislation to entrench the U.S. dollar as the new country's currency was drafted, appropriately enough, by the American Secretary of War.[1] Panama subsequently put in place the infrastructure for offshore banks, instant corporations, free trade facilities and a flag-of-convenience ship registry on which its prosperity was based.[2] An embargo-buster's paradise, Panama suddenly found itself on the receiving end of an economic war when the United States decided that Panama should have its banking system wrecked, its trade ruined and its shipping business undermined, and bear a full-scale invasion, to rid itself of a renegade CIA agent whom Washington itself had contrived to put in power.[3]

At Who's Service?
The "services" orientation of Panama's economy was partly the result of geography. The American-controlled canal accounted at peak for nearly 7 per cent of GDP and paid the government about 12 per cent of its total revenues. Around that canal was the world's second largest (next to Hong Kong) free trade zone in which enterprising merchants broke down large consignments

into small packages suitable for smuggling. Along the canal, too, ran a trans-isthmus pipeline that carried Alaskan oil to Mexican Gulf refineries while spouting transit fees for the government. There was also SouthCom, a large American military presence that paid trebly: the government collected rent, soldiers' spending buoyed the local economy, and the Pentagon connection reassured foreign investors.

Panama's service sector was also encouraged by the country's legal infrastructure. It offered to shipping companies cheap registration fees, quick name changes and the chance to hide the real ownership of the ships on which its flag proudly fluttered.[4] Experts in clandestine commerce claimed that it was possible to register in Panama a ship that almost anywhere else would be ordered to the scrapyard. Even better, if it proved impossible to find a captain willing to risk his life aboard, some official could usually be induced to issue a shipmaster's licence to the owner even if his previous nautical experience consisted of floating rubber ducks in his bathtub.[5]

Panama also boasted corporate secrecy laws as tight as Liechtenstein's. It first created tax-exempt offshore companies in 1927. But the real impetus came during World War II, when Allied economic sanctions sent companies around the world scrambling for cover. In 1941, the year the United States declared war, Panama passed fifty-nine different statutes facilitating the creation of shell companies and increasing financial secrecy. In susbsequent years, local lawyers manufactured companies in job lots, peddling them to customers that varied from Fortune 500 corporations "avoiding" taxes to Colombian drug smugglers evading detection. One brokerage firm, Interseco, for example, in the course of fifteen years, created 2,000 shell companies, including some involved in the Iran-contra scandal. One of its chief officers ended up admitting in a U.S. court to laundering money for a Cuban-American drug ring headed by a Bay of Pigs veteran and to helping the ring invest its surpluses in the take-over of a Florida bank, which collapsed under the weight of fraudulent loans a few years after.[6] Neutrality, though, was the watchword. While the United States armed the contras through Panama companies, Sandinista Nicaragua worked through another Panama company to buy aircraft and parts from a Miami supplier.[7]

Above all else there were banks. Panama passed its first bank secrecy law in 1917, tightened it in 1941, reinforced it with Swiss-style coded accounts in 1959, and strengthened it further with offshore banking legislation in 1970. Panama became not just the largest offshore centre in the Americas, but almost a central bank to other countries' offshore banks. When offshore banks in those other jurisdictions accepted deposits, they would often redeposit the funds in Panama. The official status of the U.S. dollar was further assurance of financial stability. And it provided cover. Since 20 per cent of the annual $9 to $10 billion of Free Trade Zone business is normally done in cash, suitcases of dirty dollars that arrived in Panama became indistinguishable from the proceeds of normal activities like cigarette smuggling or embargo-busting. Panama's banks were as committed to neutrality in world affairs as were its instant-corporation manufacturers. Among their satisfied customers were members of the El Salvador military junta who financed anti-leftist death squads through a kidnapping ring that deposited ransom money in Panama. At the same time, El Salvador rebel groups hid in Panama the proceeds of the extortion rackets that financed much of their war against that military junta.

Standing Guard

For all its apparent prosperity, Panama was politically an unhappy place. In earlier decades it had been run by a white planter class whose most popular political representative, Arnulfo Arias, actually resisted American pressures to turn Panama into a commercial and financial brothel. Elected to the presidency in 1940, Arias attempted to issue a national currency and refused an American request to allow Panamanian flagged vessels (including the bulk of the U.S. tanker fleet) to be armed against Axis raiders. In 1941 the United States accused him of being pro-German and arranged his ouster.[8]

Over the next several decades, the economy increasingly moved from agriculture to services. In tandem, the old elite shifted from a planter to a banker aristocracy while keeping a lock on government. Arnulfo Arias even staged a political comeback. But in 1968 he was ousted again, this time by Omar Torrijos Herrera, head of the Panamanian National Guard, an institution dominated by lower-class, darker-skinned mestizos. The constitution was re-written to give the National Guard power equal to that of the executive or legislative branches, though in reality it was the National Guard that governed the government. For a time the new regime was shaky. However, two unlikely allies stabilized its position. The coup got a belated nod from the U.S. government, concerned about rising nationalism and the fate of the canal. And Fidel Castro agreed not to support an anti-government insurgency in exchange for the new regime's assistance in undercutting American sanctions. Lending further support was an Israeli, Schlomo Glicksberg. A former adviser to Arias, Glicksberg deserted to Torrijos right after the coup. He quickly proved his worth by persuading the rabbi who ran United Fruit Company to tide the coup-makers over with a million-dollar contribution. And he later persuaded the merchant banking firm of Goldman, Sachs to grant the new regime Panama's first-ever foreign bank loan. In future years, Panama's appetite for foreign loans would bring it the dubious honour of being the most heavily indebted country in the Americas. Equally portentous, most of the Goldman, Sachs money, nominally slated to finance heavy equipment purchases by the Ministry of Public Works, was skimmed off in official graft.[9]

Over the next two decades the country's presidents, though drawn from the old elite, served at the National Guard's pleasure. And National Guard chief, Omar Torrijos, struck appropriate poses. While spouting populist rhetoric, he repaid his debt to United Fruit by smashing a potentially damaging strike by banana workers and replacing the militant workers' organization with a compliant company union. While thundering in public about the need to protect Panama's sovereignty, he reported regularly to American intelligence. While waxing eloquent about social justice, he encouraged the National Guard to get rich through racketeering.[10]

For a time the Guard had stuck to traditional ventures: prostitution, gambling and a little drug trafficking, mainly to cater to American military personnel. After the coup, its reach spread. National Guard officers imposed taxes on smugglers and sold business licences to (and collected protection money from) merchants in the Free Trade Zone. Guards officers formed joint ventures with merchants to import goods, supposedly for re-export, then sneak them off to Panama's own central business district for tax-free sale. They took shares in firms running the *contrabandista* system. At a time when Latin American countries typically imposed high tariffs on consumer goods, planes left Florida carrying American cigarettes, booze, auto parts and electronics, landed in Panama, were supplied fake manifests stating they were departing empty, flew south to isolated airports often run by Paraguayan generals, unloaded their material for local black markets and went on to a regular airport where inspection would confirm they carried no cargo. On the way back, they refuelled in Panama before continuing to the United States, some with hidden consignments of heroin and cocaine.[11]

Among the earliest Guard-run businesses was Transit SA, an import-export company originally set up to smuggle liquor into Costa Rica. Among its later games, it imported coffee from Colombia, relabelled it as Panamanian, and shipped it to the United States, thereby permitting Colombian coffee producers to bust their quotas under the international coffee agreement even if at the expense of Panamanian planters. Extra income could be generated by hiding cocaine in the coffee, whose aroma threw off drug-sniffing dogs. Since the Guard also ran immigration, another lucrative business was peddling passports to Asian and Cuban refugees. Cubans in the United States bought visas for their families for $7,000 to $10,000 a head, wiring the money directly to Panama, where the National Guard split the proceeds with Cuban military intelligence. Diplomatic passports were also for sale to, among others, Taiwanese and Israeli intelligence agents and Colombian cocaine barons. Another lucrative operation was Panama Marinexam SA, a firm that, for $45 to $100 a head, certified the seamanship of 250,000 sailors and officers who manned Panamanian-flagged ships all over the world.[12]

By encouraging officers to participate in or skim from businesses, Torrijos gave them an independent source of income, increasing their loyalty while reducing their inclination to take bribes, and he made the National Guard financially autonomous of the government.[13]

After entrenching the position of the Guard, Torrijos's top priority was to regain sovereignty over the canal in the face of American resistance. He was helped in 1971 when agents of the U.S. Bureau of Narcotics and Dangerous Drugs (predecessor of the DEA) lured the chief air traffic controller of Panama's international airport into the U.S.-controlled Canal Zone and arrested him on heroin charges. That set off an outburst of nationalist anger. Torrijos eventually secured a treaty by which the canal and surrounding real estate would revert to Panama by the year 2000, while Panama's canal revenues immediately increased. Shortly after the treaty was signed, canal politics claimed as a victim a not-so-innocent bystander.

The 1968 coup had won immediate sympathy from Anastasio Somoza. But relations soon soured. Whenever the United States balked in negotiations, Torrijos threatened to follow Gamel Abd el-Nasir's example and unilaterally nationalize the canal. The United States responded by sending Somoza to Panama to threaten Torrijos with the spectre of an alternative canal through Nicaragua, one with supertanker capacity. Somoza also irritated Torrijos by undermining another Panamanian initiative. Torrijos was the proud father of the Union de Países Exportadores del Banano, a cartel of Latin American banana producers accounting for 65 per cent of world output. In 1974 members decided on an OPEC-inspired production cutback and price hike, only to have it sabotaged when Nicaragua refused to cooperate. Torrijos never forgot or forgave.[14] As the Sandinista insurgency picked up steam, Torrijos permitted Cuba to open an arms pipeline via Panama, scoured his armouries for spare weapons, fronted for the purchase of arms abroad and had them flown to the rebels on Panamanian military planes.

After the canal treaty was signed, Torrijos, whose political vision was increasingly clouded by an alcoholic fog, lost interest in running Panama.

Day-to-day supervision passed to a military intelligence protégé named Manuel Noriega, who had already proven himself a remarkable survivor. In the early 1970s he made the all-star list drawn up by the U.S. Bureau of Narcotics and Dangerous Drugs of foreign political figures who should be assassinated for trafficking. A few years later, U.S. Customs came close to indicting him for organizing a Sandinista gun-running operation out of Miami.[15] Yet the CIA did not hesitate to pay him for information, including reports on his own gun-running operations and, perhaps, delicacies from Noriega's blackmail files on prominent Panamanians.

In 1981 Torrijos died in a plane crash, leaving the National Guard with no clear succession. In 1983, with the blessing of Washington, Noriega agreed to back the presidential candidate of one of his rivals, if the rival would concede to him, Noriega, the post of National Guard commander. Within a year of assuming command, he had contrived the ouster of the president and forced a new election. Noriega's own candidate, to whom Washington gave the nod, was victorious in a tight contest, ensured by Noriega's party stuffing the ballot boxes. Shortly after taking over the National Guard, Noriega was in Washington for his first official meeting with William Casey. Out of it came American money to modernize the National Guard, and a commitment from Noriega to support U.S. efforts to reverse the Sandinista victory his predecessor had done so much to ensure. In further consolidating power, Noriega was ably assisted by a man whom Omar Torrijos himself had described as "my mentor."

Whose Man in Panama?

In the early 1970s a Mossad hit squad scoured Europe for Palestinian targets, particularly future PLO intelligence chief Ali Salameh, whom Israel held responsible for killing Israeli athletes during the 1972 Olympics in Munich. In Norway the squad scored one of its most impressive blows against terrorism by gunning down a Moroccan waiter out strolling with his pregnant wife. In the ensuing uproar, the architect of the operation, Michael Hariri, was reassigned as Mossad station chief in Mexico City. A short time later Hariri "retired" into private business as a security consultant to Omar Torrijos and set up an import-export firm in the Canal Zone.[16]

Hariri arrived at the right time. Torrijos, to help undercut the power of the traditional white aristocracy, had been encouraging the economic ascent of the country's Jewish community (into which he had married), which reciprocated with strong support for his regime.[17] After the death of Torrijos, Hariri and Noriega became close associates, and Israel's links to Panama widened and deepened. Israeli banks, watching a flood of Latin American flight capital bound for Miami, set up branches in Panama to help divert part of the flow to Israel. Much of Israel's trade with Latin America, too, passed through Panama, while Israelis came to compete with, and beat, Lebanese traders for domination of the central business district. It was a development not without controversy, as the older, long-established Sephardic community became uncomfortable over the business behaviour of the *parvenu* Israelis, and the success of both groups made them increasingly a target for resentment by the Panamanian masses.[18]

Panama's importance to Israel went beyond trade and capital flows. Back in the 1940s it had been a base for smuggling U.S. war surplus weapons to Zionist forces in Palestine.[19] In the 1970s and 1980s it became a base for selling Israeli weapons throughout the region.[20] During the 1970s, when the Carter administration had stopped most American official arms sales to military juntas in Central and South America, Israel had stepped into the breach. But under Reagan, U.S. deliveries of large-ticket items started again, and Israel's role shifted to supplying light arms and training services. Those were areas where the expertise of someone like Hariri came in handy.[21]

In 1980 Hariri rejoined Mossad. During the next few years, he was the driving force behind reorganization of the Panamanian military, converting the National Guard, with its American-inspired name, into the Defence Force, with its Israeli-inspired one. Using the big increase in American aid money won during Noriega's 1983 pilgrimage to William Casey's office, Hariri acquired for Panama modern Israeli weapons. He also became de facto head of the air force, diverting its purchase orders to Israeli firms, some owned by the government, some by Hariri.[22] Equipment would be ordered from an Israeli government-owned distributorship in Miami, and Panamanian air force planes would fly the materials back home, sometimes accompanied by containers labelled "aircraft parts" that were stuffed with money seeking a wash job in Panama's banks. Hariri also trafficked in Panamanian end-user certificates. And he bought East bloc arms, then arranged to airdrop them to the contras.[23]

With his own position as military chief secured, his man in the presidency, support from the CIA and the Pentagon, and Hariri's backing, Noriega seemed to have all bases nicely covered. He collected public citations from the United States for his role in the War-on-Drugs and private citations from the War-on-Communism. He fought both wars with equal zeal. He turned in traffickers and launderers who had outlived their financial or political usefulness. And he permitted the contras to set up a secret training centre in Panama, reported to Washington the results of his own spying in Nicaragua, and made Panama a principal conduit for contra arms shipments. Simultaneously, he collected pay-offs from drug dealers still in his favour and he permitted Nicaraguan and Cuban front companies in Panama to break the U.S. trade embargoes.[24] But by the mid-1980s, Noriega's political tightrope act was getting harder to sustain, his enemies were accumulating faster than his Swiss bank balances and the quality of his service in both of America's favourite wars was being called seriously into question.

Backfire

When Noriega flew to Washington to enrol in William Casey's crusade against Communism, at the controls of the plane had been one of the hemisphere's leading marijuana smugglers. Stephen Kalish had started by peddling grass in dime bags to fellow high school students and graduated to importing hundred-ton lots, eventually accumulating so much cash that his Cayman Island bankers were unable to handle it. In Panama, one of Noriega's business associates offered armoured cars to ferry cash from the airport and discreet bankers to receive it, all with the protection of the National Guard, provided the proper tithe was paid to its commander-in-chief. While planning his career triumph — moving 1.4 million pounds of merchandise through the canal in a container protected by Panamanian Customs seals — Kalish was nabbed by American narcotics agents. Convinced Noriega had sold him out, he started to sing, if not for his supper, then at least for a reduced sentence. At least one chorus had to do with a Panamanian general with a taste for leather briefcases stuffed with cash.[25] His refrain was taken up by Ramon Milian-Rodriguez. A Cuban exile trained as a money-launderer by the Bay of Pigs gang, Milian-Rodriguez had decided to make his talents available to the private sector, first to Cuban exiles who gave up paramilitary action for freelance smuggling, and then to Pablo Escobar and his associates. Like Kalish, he had found Panama most obliging with banks, security and diplomatic passports. Arrested in 1983, he confessed, albeit with the sums he claimed to have laundered growing in geometric progression with every iteration. His performance culminated in 1988 before whirring TV cameras when he bragged of washing $11 billion through Panama while paying $320 to $350 million to Noriega. To further bolster his credibility, he went on to claim that the dirty money cycle was a Communist plot and insisted that the emerging Colombian heroin industry was run by the PLO.[26]

By the time Milian-Rodriguez sang his swansong before a U.S. Senate committee, Noriega was in serious trouble. Even his friends in the CIA and Pentagon had abandoned him, thanks in part to the ill-fated voyage of the *Pia Vesta*.

The problem began in the early 1980s when El Salvador's Faribundo Marti National Liberation Front (FMLN) tried to diversify its weapons supply. Until then it had relied on what it could steal from the U.S.-equipped Salvadorian army or buy on the local black market using money raised by kidnapping landlords and businessmen. After the overthrow of Somoza, the Sandinista regime in Nicaragua had briefly supplied arms. But with the coming to power of the Reagan administration, Nicaragua cut off its fellow revolutionaries. That was only a minor blow to the FMLN. Since it was fighting a government equipped with U.S. weapons, it wanted a source of the same kind of arms, and Nicaragua used Soviet models. It was, however, a considerably greater blow to the Reagan administration, which desperately needed a propaganda weapon to use against the Sandinistas. Despite periodic American denunciations that the Sandinistas were the main arms supplier to the FMLN, almost all of the group's arms and ammunition, when not obtained from corrupt Guatemalan or Honduran officers, were purchased legally in the United States from some of that country's 250,000 licenced gun dealers, then smuggled back home via Mexico.[27] But if the Reagan administration could not find the smoking gun, it could try to invent one.

Back in 1985, when the U.S. administration was officially forbidden to back the contras, CIA chief Casey had one of his brainwaves. He persuaded South Africa to pick up the tab for a shipment of East German small arms. As cover the money was pumped through a Liechtenstein shell company. The arms were sold through a Swiss-based dealer connected to French intelligence, to a Miami-based broker supposedly working on behalf of the Peruvian Navy. Loaded on the *Pia Vesta*, a dilapidated (and dispensable) old Danish vessel, the cargo of "rolling stock and spare parts" headed through the Panama Canal en route to Peru. The plan was that, once the arms arrived there, instead of being discharged, the load would be topped up with Blowpipe missiles contributed by the government of Ecuador to the contra cause. The entire lot would then be sent up the Pacific coast to El Salvador where the military junta would "seize" it and announce they had interdicted a shipment from the Sandinistas to the El Salvador rebels. This would finally provide the "proof" the Reagan administration needed of Nicaragua's efforts to export revolution throughout the Americas and might embarrass Congress into lifting its ban on official support for the contras. In the final stage, the "seized" arms were to be quietly passed on to the contras, leaving Casey chuckling over his diabolical brilliance.[28]

However, the plan failed to take account of General Noriega's bad temper. In 1986 tales of Noriega's sidelines — laundering drug money, selling embargoed

U.S. technology to Cuba and running guns to everyone with the means to pay — were splashed across the front page of the *New York Times*.[29] Convinced it was a U.S. government leak, Noriega reacted by seizing the *Pia Vesta*, then riding at anchor off Panama. Neither threats nor bribes convinced him to release it. Indeed, the general may have indulged his sense of humour at American expense by renaming the vessel *Iran-Contra*, sailing it back and forth through the canal, then selling some of the weapons to the El Salvador guerrillas.[30]

With relations between the United States and Panama deteriorating, a strange coalition came together inside the U.S. to push for action. It combined liberal elements repelled at the regime's criminality with right-wing elements looking for an excuse to renounce the canal treaty. It also included Miami. The city's development officers had calculated that if Panama's role as a banking centre could be undermined, Miami stood to gain 10,000 white-collar jobs, consolidating Miami's position as the financial centre of Latin America.[31]

The erosion of external support encouraged internal dissent. When one of Noriega's best-known political opponents who claimed possession of a drug-trade dossier that would bring the general down, was found dead, his headless body battered almost beyond recognition, public protests forced the president to open an enquiry. This prompted Noriega to oust the man whose election he had rigged and to replace him by a compliant sugar planter whose Jewish origins, the general hoped, would rally the Israel lobby in the United States to Noriega's side should the going get rougher. It got much rougher indeed. Noriega was soon facing for the first time an organized opposition, every prominent member of which was drawn from the banking community, which, in turn, was dominated by descendants of the old white planter class still itching to get back into power. In early 1987, as Noriega's own regime began to fracture, the opposition launched street demonstrations, followed by consumer boycotts of businesses owned by people close to the regime. Stores owned by Michael Harari's relatives were singled out for vandalism. When Noriega dismissed yet another president, the U.S. government, reluctantly, imposed sanctions.[32]

Panama should have been extremely vulnerable. Its economy was already in deep crisis. The canal was old and increasingly rendered redundant by containerized rail traffic across the United States, while the usefulness of the pipeline was threatened by a direct connection between the U.S. west coast and the Gulf of Mexico.[33] Because most of Latin America had still not fully recovered from a major depression in the early 1980s, commerce through the Free Trade Zone had been dropping. Because hemispheric trade was becoming freer, the zone's attractions as a smuggling centre were declining. The quick ship-registry business, too, was slumping; old rivals like Liberia, Cyprus and the

Bahamas and new ones like mighty seafaring Luxembourg were luring away clients. Not even the insta-company business was safe. Traditional competitors like Barbados cashed in on fears that a confrontation between Noriega and Washington might undermine Panama's secrecy laws. But the most vulnerable sector was the banks, the core of the service sector. Their reputation had been hurt by American pressure for Panama to sign a special treaty for cooperation in criminal investigations that would punch a big hole in the protective wall of bank secrecy.

The United States imposed some commercial sanctions: a partial trade embargo and the traditional suspension of the sugar quota. But mainly the U.S. relied on financial action, to which Panama was especially vulnerable. Forbidding American companies in Panama to pay local taxes and refusing to remit payments for using the canal, pipeline or military facilities threw the Panamanian public finances into chaos. Refusing clearing rights through U.S. banks and cutting off the supply of U.S. cash crippled the monetary system. Meanwhile the ousted president ordered consuls around the world to refuse to send back to Panama payments for shipping services; he filed suits to freeze $50 million in Panama government deposits held in U.S. banks. The mere possibility of the United States blacklisting the entry to U.S. ports of Panamanian registered ships was sufficient to send many seeking re-registration elsewhere. They were encouraged by rival flag-of-convenience centres that scrambled to lower fees.[34]

In a year, Panama's GNP dropped 22 per cent and salaries 50 per cent, while unemployment soared, starvation stalked the poor, soup kitchens found their lines growing daily, and the banking system was drained. People rushed to convert bank deposits into cash. When the reserves ran out, the banks were ordered to close. Ordinary cheques and credit cards ceased to function, so that more and more trade took place by barter. The speed with which the Panamanian banking system ran out of cash was partly due to the actions of several U.S. banks who packed $100 million into green garbage bags and smuggled it to safety on the U.S. military base. It was never clear if this was ordered by the United States or simply a precaution in case Noriega's National Guard decided to make a few large withdrawals.[35]

Simultaneously, Panama, formerly the premier hemispheric haven for money evading other countries' taxes, exchange controls, police probes or social disorders, was swept by a massive wave of capital flight. Miami, as that city had hoped, was a major beneficiary. On top came a fiscal crisis. With virtually no sources of revenue, the government could not pay the civil service, except by means of government cheques which, being uncashable, circulated from hand to hand at discounts. Some speculators bought them, along with passbooks for frozen savings accounts, at a small percentage of their worth from people either desperate for money or anxious to flee.[36]

Yet economic sanctions failed to bring down the regime. It was reasonably sure of the loyalty of most officers, who stood to lose their privileges should an American-sponsored counter-revolution prevail. Therefore while unpaid civil servants rioted and traffic police tried to collect their overdue salaries in the form of bribes from motorists, the regime wisely used what cash it could find to pay the army. Although the regime was widely unpopular, it could still occasionally appeal to the poor mestizo against the white elite. And although Panama had been in crisis before sanctions were imposed, they permitted the regime to blame all the economic woes on gringo aggression.

The regime did take some countermeasures. It searched for revenue sources that the United States could not block: levies on the racetrack, the national lottery, special taxes on the Free Trade Zone, money earned from selling passports and end-user certificates by embassies run by diplomats loyal or beholden to Noriega. The government's dollar deposits in non-U.S. banks were safe from the freeze, and non-U.S. banks and businesses continued to bring money into the country. Cleverly, the regime made the uncashable government pension and social security cheques legal tender for payment of fees and taxes, therefore helping to keep their value. Furthermore, the cash squeeze imposed by the United States was undermined by its own economic presence. Every month the U.S. government sent 45,000 paycheques to its employees, civil and military; the cheques were cashed at banks in the Canal Zone; and the money was largely spent in Panama proper where most U.S. government employees lived and shopped.

There was also covert assistance from sympathetic foreign governments. No country was eager to follow the American lead. Most of Latin America regarded the American actions as hypocritical, while Asian countries like Japan and Taiwan were happy to use the crisis to improve their business position in Panama at American expense.[37] Not least resourceful of the regime's defenders was Michael Hariri, who supervised the installation of electronic espionage equipment to keep tabs on internal opposition, arranged for Noriega to have a team of Israeli-trained bodyguards, helped the general purchase a "retirement" home in Israel, and directly took over Panama's military intelligence in 1988 when the American pressure provoked a coup attempt.

A year after the economic sanctions were imposed, Panama's economy actually started to improve. Trade quickened, financial aid and investment from Asia flowed in, and some of the funds that had fled began trickling back. Reporters were taken on tours of the central business district to show that opposition calls for a merchants' strike were being ignored—at least by businesses owned by those closest to the regime. American corporations active in Panama lobbied the U.S. government to resolve the impasse. In fact so discouraging were the results that the Reagan administration, its term rapidly drawing to a close, began easing sanctions and preparing the political ground for eliminating them entirely, on the assumption that they only served to draw public attention to a foreign policy failure.[38] Then U.S. Customs put Noriega back in the spotlight by going after his favourite bank on money-laundering charges.

Who's Banking on It?

Panama had special advantages over other financial havens. One was simply experience: it was the hemispheric pioneer. A second was its (usually) privileged relations with the United States which seemed to ensure security. A third was its unique geographic situation. In 1980 these advantages had brought Panama yet another addition to its distinguished roster of international banking institutions, one so prominent that the incumbent president himself turned up at the welcoming party.

By the time the Bank of Credit and Commerce International moved into Panama, it had become perhaps the fastest-growing institution in the world, eventually with branches in seventy-six countries. However, much of the impetus to growth came from desperation. At the end of the 1970s, over half its loans had been to a single set of borrowers, themselves in deep trouble. BCCI backing had turned the Gokal brothers' Gulf Group into the world's largest private shipping company, engaged in everything from running illegal oil to South Africa to smuggling embargoed arms to Iran. But the fleet was rapidly sinking into a sea of red ink. The Gulf Group deficit meant that BCCI was caught in the classic bankers' dilemma. To maintain loans to customers unable to repay, it had to obtain more deposit money. Managers across the world were told to pursue new deposit business by hook or, quite often, by crook. BCCI's depositors therefore ranged from central banks of indebted countries trying to hide their meagre assets from their international creditors to Colombian narcos trying to hide their ample assets from American law-enforcement officers. They included town councils and tax evaders, charitable foundations and commodity fraudsters, small-scale Asian entrepreneurs and international terrorist organizations as varied as the Abu Nidal group and the CIA. They also included General Manuel Noriega.

BCCI Panama spent two years trying to coax Noriega into using its services. In 1982 he agreed, requesting that the bank open a secret military intelligence account over which he would have sole signing authority. For additional security, he had the account moved to London. Thereafter his Panamanian banker would accept Noriega's cash, then phone London to have the account credited, neatly precluding any formal records that could fall into the wrong hands. Into the account went bribes paid to Noriega by drug dealers, profits from inflating invoices on air force deals run with Hariri and the general's retainer from the CIA. Out of it was paid personal expenses for the general and his family on foreign junkets and shopping trips, the bills for intelligence operations and miscellaneous charges for things like rigging elections.[39]

After Milian-Rodriguez wowed the senators with his claims of megabillions washed through Panama and hundreds of millions paid to Noriega in service charges, others regaled the press with stories that Noriega was part owner of a heroin refinery along the Colombia-Panama border, that he ran an illegal steroid manufacturing operation in Mexico, and that the enterprising general controlled an airline smuggling money weekly from the United States. All this created the right ambiance for the U.S. Justice Department to indict Noriega on drug-trafficking charges.[40] However, this time there was an additional target. BCCI's longevity had depended on the support of the powerful and that depended on errands it could run for them. In 1987 William Casey died. In 1988 the U.S.–Soviet standoff in Afghanistan ended. BCCI's cover was gone. That cleared the path for an indictment of BCCI and a string of officers, including the one who had formerly handled Noriega's account. With the spotlight back on Panama and a new U.S. administration about to assume office, the general made perhaps his costliest blunder. In a bid to relegitimize the Panama government, he decided to stage a new presidential election.

The CIA offered $10 million to the opposition for electoral expenses. Unfortunately the CIA's courier was arrested by the DEA on drug-dealing and money-laundering charges before he could get the money to Panama to help oust the drug-dealing, money-laundering general.[41] On the other side, Noriega and the National Guard stood ready to stuff ballot boxes and bust skulls. Not only did the regime steal an election in which all legitimate opinion polls showed the opposing slate to be a 2–1 favourite, but it followed up by beating up the opposition team in full view of TV reporters. Because sanctions had already been proven a failure, the U.S. government had to either retreat or take serious action.

In the final analysis it took a full-scale invasion in which a densely packed slum neighbourhood was burned to the ground, Jewish-owned stores in the central business district were massively looted and 300 civilians were killed to overthrow the general.[42] In his hour of need, Noriega was deserted by his Israeli protector, who was quickly whisked away, with his files and records, by U.S. forces before the media could locate him. The general himself was kidnapped for a show-trial back in the United States. As the court proceedings made clear, tales about his role in drug trafficking had been grossly exagger-ated — he was just another corrupt cop.[43] After the invasion, drugs and dirty money, smuggling and embargo-busting were at least as important to the Panama economy as before. But the stories had done their job in justifying the American action that brought Noriega's regime and the political power of the mestizo National Guard to a noisy end. They were replaced by a government drawn from the old planter aristocracy that took its oath of office, appropriately enough, on an American military base.

Part Six

TROUBLE ON OILED WATERS

Chapter 16

ARMS AND THE AYATOLLAH

$\mathbf{I}$n 1911, Winston Churchill, First Lord of the Admiralty, ordered the British Navy to switch the fuel in its boilers from coal to oil, a decision that would help make oil the world's most important strategic commodity. Two years later the Anglo–Persian Oil Company obtained control of Iran's oil fields, which contained 25 per cent of the world's proven reserves. For the next four decades the government of Iran operated like an administrative arm of the company. Angered at the fact that the company could unilaterally determine Iran's export earnings, yet paid the British government three times as much in taxes as it paid to Iran, in 1951 a nationalist regime took over the petroleum sector. After a series of clashes with his prime minister, the monarch, Mohammed Reza Shah Pahlavi, fled. The British responded by sending warships and imposing an oil boycott.

Denied 95 per cent of its export revenues, Iran faced financial catastrophe. When the new government opened trade talks with the U.S.S.R., the CIA sponsored a coup, had the prime minister jailed and brought back the Shah, who was greeted by crowds paid to cheer his return.[1] In one blow, the Americans ousted the nationalists, blocked rapprochement with the U.S.S.R. and bested the British for control of Iran's oil. The grateful monarch ceded 40 per cent of production to American firms. And he shortly began shopping for top-of-the-line military equipment to try to prevent the indignity of another precipitous departure.

The Gusher

The Shah had good reasons for concern. The British had installed his father as monarch shortly after World War I to keep watch over their oil concessions. Much like his role model, Mustafa Kemal Ataturk, the military strongman who turned post-Ottoman Turkey into a modern, westernized state, Reza Khan had attempted to secularize education, emancipate women and undermine the power of the traditional clergy by stripping them of land and wealth. To promote secular nationalism as a counterweight to Shi'a Islam, he purged the Persian language of Arabic words and changed the name of the country from Persia to Iran, land of the Aryan. However his efforts to offset British influence by promoting close relations with Germany proved disastrous. In 1941, when Germany invaded the U.S.S.R., the Allies decided to use Iran as a supply line to the beleaguered Soviet forces. Therefore the British Navy and Red Army combined to force the old Shah into exile, replacing him with his weak playboy son, Mohammed.

After the war, as oil fields opened up across the Middle East, Iran's command of the Persian Gulf increased its strategic importance. In fact the first major clash of the Cold War occurred in 1946 when American pressure forced Soviet troops to vacate Iran's Azerbaijan province. To further curb Soviet influence and undercut the popularity of the Tudeh (Communist) Party, in 1963 the U.S. pressured the Shah into launching the White Revolution. Similar in spirit to the Alliance for Progress cobbled together for Latin America in the wake of Castro's takeover of Cuba, the White Revolution called for the promotion of private enterprise, profit-sharing for workers in a few visible industries and land reform to create a small-holder class loyal to the Shah's regime. Simultaneously the Shah stepped up his father's efforts to curb the power and influence of the clergy. Leading the opposition to the White Revolution was a respected legal scholar and theologian, Ayatollah Ruhollah Khomeini.

Despite mounting opposition from both clerics and leftist forces during the 1960s and early 1970s, the Shah's grip on power tightened. Internally, he alternately bought off and killed off dissidents. Externally, he cultivated the Western powers. When post-imperial Britain decided to withdraw its forces east of Suez, the Shah offered to fill the void. When post-Vietnam America faced a shrinking market for arms and the need to protect its Middle East interests without risking American lives, the Shah offered a solution to both. After the 1973 oil price hike, his purchasing power shot up, and the United States for the first time gave a developing country carte blanche to buy any non-nuclear item in the American arsenal.[2] Over the 1970s, Iran's army nearly trebled in size. It was to be strengthened further by Operation Flower, a billion-dollar military technology-for-oil agreement with Israel that was meant to lead, among other things, to joint production of a nuclear-capable missile. However, before Operation Flower could bloom, storm clouds gathered.[3]

As oil revenues poured into Iran's coffers, happy faces had lit up American corporate boardrooms, particularly of aerospace giants suffering post-Vietnam combat fatigue. By the time of his second ouster in 1979, the Shah had bought $17 billion worth of American arms and had another $12 billion on order. Construction projects transferred billions more to American engineering firms. Of all his American beneficiaries, none was more grateful than Chase Manhattan Bank, depository of the Shah's personal wealth and of the national oil company's receipts.[4]

Back home the reception was not so favourable. Critics objected to the waste of national wealth on arms and prestige projects, and to the rampant corruption, while the masses remained mired in poverty.[5] The backbone of the opposition was a coalition of bazaar merchants and radical clergy. Traditionally in control of both domestic and foreign trade, and even most banking functions, the *bazaari* were threatened by the emergence of a westernized business class and the spread of U.S.-style supermarkets. They became convinced there was a government plot to undermine them. That conviction was strengthened when the government imposed price controls, then arrested, fined and jailed *bazaari*, or closed their shops, on charges of profiteering. The Shah also angered the radical clergy, already irked by his father's secularization of education, by seeming to tolerate libertine behaviour. The clergy took up the cause of the *bazaari,* who reciprocated by financially backing the clerical opposition.[6] Meanwhile land reform had proven a disaster. It bequeathed to peasants plots too small to be viable, replaced old landlords who advanced seeds and equipment with rural loan sharks who ran virtual extortion rackets, and discouraged maintenance of the traditional irrigation system. Masses of rural poor thronged into the urban slums where they could hear radical clergy simultaneously opposing land reform and blaming the farmers' problems on the corruption of the Shah and his U.S. backers.

The Shah struck back. The most serious dissenters found themselves in exile or in the hands of the Sazman-e-Ettelaat va Amniyat-e-Keshvar (SAVAK), the secret police whose ministrations many failed to survive. It was first from Iraq, then later from Paris, that Ayatollah Khomeini shaped the awkward combination of nationalists, leftists and fundamentalists whose revolution would shake global politics and, incidentally, transform the world arms black market.

Hostage to Whose Fortune?

When spreading strikes and military mutiny forced the Shah to flee the country, there were sporadic anti-American protests, including a brief takeover of the U.S. embassy. But they were quickly dispersed. The overall climate still seemed positive for American interests. Nonetheless, anticipating trouble, the United States began coordinating with its oil companies plans for a worldwide boycott. Trouble soon came.

After the Shah was diagnosed with advanced cancer, his American supporters intrigued to have him admitted to the United States for medical treatment supposedly unavailable elsewhere. In reaction, a mob, goaded on by radical clergy, stormed the American embassy in Teheran and took the staff hostage. When the United States tried to find the Shah another sanctuary, Omar Torrijos, with big debts to President Carter for the Panama Canal treaty, was in no position to refuse. The prospect of the Shah investing a chunk of his fortune in Panama was another attraction. And any residual reluctance dissolved when the Shah passed out $12 million in bribes. But revolutionary Iran had its own methods of persuasion. It offered to make Panama the first beneficiary of a scheme to sell oil at a discount to Third World countries suffering under American imperialism and to finance an oil refinery, something that would have been a real coup for Torrijos in his efforts to assert greater economic independence from the United States.[7] Smelling a double-cross, the Shah fled Panama. He died in Egypt a few months later.

Meanwhile U.S.–Iran relations deteriorated badly. The original revolutionary government had talked about the illegitimacy of certain debts the Shah had negotiated with U.S. banks and threatened to move Iranian deposits out of Chase Manhattan. Still, it had taken no concrete action inimical to U.S. economic interests. But following the embassy takeover, the United States blocked shipments of military equipment for which Iran had already paid, banned Iranian oil and froze Iranian assets in U.S. banks, preventing Iran from issuing letters of credit to pay for imports.[8] For the first time, such a freeze was extended to foreign branches of U.S. banks, prompting a court battle that the United States deliberately stretched out to maintain the freeze as long as possible.[9] The U.S. also attempted to get the UN to impose mandatory trade and investment sanctions. Although stymied by a Soviet veto, some U.S. allies imposed sanctions unilaterally. Over the next few months, the United States embargoed all exports except food and medicine and introduced measures to permit private American claims against Iran to be paid out of frozen assets. However, its most severe pressure came from a wink in the direction of Iran's bellicose neighbour.

Relations between Iran and Iraq had long been tenuous. In the early 1970s, Iran, the United States and Israel ran an arms pipeline to Kurdish insurgents in Iraq, turning an insurrection into a veritable civil war. Fearful of losing a third of its territory, including one of its main oil fields, Iraq signed a 1975 treaty with Iran that settled their border on Iran's terms. Although the treaty permitted Iraq to crush the Kurds, Iraq interpreted the agreement as a national humiliation. Then in 1980 radical elements in the Iranian armed forces began random attacks along the border, while Teheran broadcast anti-Iraq propaganda. Taking the absence of a red light from Washington as equivalent to a green one, Iraqi strongman Saddam Hussein plotted with forces inside Iran loyal to the Shah to open the border posts to an Iraqi invasion. But the plotters had been infiltrated. They were neutralized and the invasion quickly blunted.[10]

The onset of the Iran-Iraq War pushed Iran into a deal with the United States. The hostages were released, Iran's assets unfrozen and most trade sanctions (except the arms embargo) terminated. But the settlement came too late to save Jimmy Carter. A triumphant President Ronald Reagan welcomed the hostages home. His administration spent the next eight years stoking the most intensive and expensive conflict since World War II.

The Prophet's Profiteers

The war presented the Iranian clerical elite with a multiple challenge: guarding against a repetition of the 1950s counter-coup, purifying the society of Western ills, mobilizing resources for the struggle against Iraq, and circumventing the arms embargo. The main instrument was the Pasdaran. This corps of "Revolutionary Guards" was established as a popular army, with its own command structure and supply networks to defend the new regime at a time when the traditional armed forces had been humiliated and partially demobilized. The Pasdaran's role in maintaining internal security increased in importance once war with Iraq forced the regime to restore to duty officers purged for royalist sentiments. The Pasdaran was also given the task of enforcing Islamic economic principles in a society straitened by war. Because it had control over borders and the distribution of key commodities, the Pasdaran, originally idealistic and committed to the revolution, soon attracted a different class of recruit.[11]

As wartime shortages got worse, Pasdaran racketeers extorted money from bazaar merchants caught evading price controls and diverted commodities for black market sale at prices up to ten times the legal ones. The regime had combined Koranic purity with wartime austerity by banning alcohol, foreign cigarettes and Western video cassettes. That provided another source of income to those Pasdaran members who controlled the airports, ports and border crossings. Sometimes Pasdaran units accompanied smugglers' caravans to protect them from hijackers, police or Customs.

Drugs were another lucrative sideline. During the Shah's regime, the traffic had been open. Even his brother secured permission to grow poppy for pharmaceutical purposes, then reputedly under-reported his crop to divert the surplus to the black market.[12] The new regime decreed death sentences to traffickers and banned opium cultivation. However, those Pasdaran in charge of moving arms and relief aid to the Afghan mujahideen were equally well placed to move drugs from Afghanistan and Pakistan. Pasdaran elements at the border could use the harsh anti-drug law to eliminate would-be competitors or those who failed to pay appropriate transit duties.

Emigration restrictions also created a racket in rich refugees. Since refugees wanted to take their wealth with them, that traffic interfaced with the black markets in gold, foreign exchange and antiquities from which Pasdaran members collected a tithe. Assets could also be taken out in the form of Persian carpets. The government had cracked down on smuggling, forcing all sales through a state monopoly. Official exports dropped catastrophically in the early 1980s, while smuggling protected by corrupt Pasdaran officers boomed.

On top of running internal security and the distribution of goods, legal and illegal, the Pasdaran, along with the intelligence services, had another weighty responsibility: to ensure the supply of weapons in the face of the American-led embargo.

Ghost Companies and Phantom Cargoes
Although it inherited one of the world's most powerful arsenals, the new government was vulnerable to shortages of spare parts and U.S. instructors. While Iraq had only a third the population of Iran and also faced an embargo by the Soviet Union, its principal arms supplier, France, was happy to fill the gap. Furthermore, within two years the U.S.S.R. again started supplying. However, the United States maintained its embargo against Iran, at least publicly, and pressed its allies to do likewise. So Iran went underground.[13] Because it lacked experience in black market deals, it was a sitting duck for every con artist in the trade.

Some pulled off advance-fee frauds. A convicted heroin trafficker, after failing to sell Exocet anti-ship missiles to Argentina during the Falklands/ Malvinas War, copied official documents from a sale of fighter planes to Jordan to bilk the Iranians out of a multimillion-dollar down payment.[14]

Some tried "phantom cargo" dodges. An Iranian expatriate in London offered 8,000 TOW (Tube-launched, Optically tracked, Wire-guided) anti-tank missiles that were supposedly waiting on a ship across the Channel.

Three Iranian officers sent to inspect the "weapons" (thirty-four containers of scrap iron) were kidnapped and ordered to send messages to the London branch of Iran's Bank Melli authorizing payment. When they refused, the architect of the scheme forged their signatures. When the head of the London bank balked, he too was kidnapped. The officers escaped, and Scotland Yard released the banker before any money changed hands.[15]

Some pulled off bill of lading scams. In Paris in 1981 an Iranian who had worked for the Shah, been imprisoned after the revolution, then released to take up his old trade for the new regime, arranged for a Lebanese merchant with a Panama "oil trading" company to supply rockets and launchers. In most trade deals, letters of credit are cashed once the bank holding the LC receives a bill of lading attesting that the specified cargo has been stowed in good order on a commercial carrier. The Lebanese merchant produced such a bill of lading showing the arms had been loaded in Rio de Janeiro; the Paris branch of Iran's Bank Melli paid $56 million. But the "office" issuing the bill turned out to be a construction site. The ship, too small to carry the cargo specified, underwent a quick change of ownership. And the purchase money vanished through a Geneva bank. The Lebanese merchant also vanished, with an Iranian hit squad on his tail. Although the Iranian buyer was condemned to death, he turned up happily on the Côte d'Azur where he had invested in a villa, a restaurant and some nightclubs. One explanation offered for his nonchalance was that $20 million of the missing money had been kicked back to senior Iranian officials.[16]

Some fraudsters played all these games, and more. In 1981 Sadegh Tabatabai, a former deputy prime minister sent to Germany to set up a supply line, was approached with an offer of fifty American tanks by a group of "arms dealers" headed by an ex-laundry worker who saw a chance to really clean up. The gang had no tanks. But they did have a crooked Portuguese broker with forged invoices, bills of lading and a cargo manifest for a ship then sitting in dry dock. The documents were presented to Tabatabai's banker along with an insurance certificate for a cargo of "heavy diesel equipment." Unlike the other documents, the insurance certificate was genuine — the conspirators planned to scuttle the ship. Some 90 million Swiss francs (about $43 million) was paid into a Luxembourg account, then whizzed off to Zurich. By a fluke, Swiss police arrested one of the conspirators on an unrelated offence and found forged documents. They alerted the Zurich bank. When one of the gang tried to withdraw funds, the bank informed the police. Four Germans, three Swiss and an Iranian were arrested. But 30 million Swiss francs were never recovered. And by the time the arrests occurred, Tabatabai had legal problems of his own, thanks to his relations with another would-be weapons supplier.[17]

George Perry, born in Prague and raised in the United States, was truly a citizen of the world. By the early 1980s, the wealthy businessman had three passports and six languages to ease his passage, and the CIA to debrief him when he came home. What was to be his greatest coup was also his last. He offered Sadegh Tabatabai a billion-dollar deal for weapons from Brazil. After meeting with Perry in Zurich to finalize details, Tabatabai returned to Teheran, secured approval, authorized a $20-million down payment, then headed back to West Germany — only to be arrested at the airport with two kilograms of raw opium (probably planted) in his suitcase. After considerable confusion over whether he had diplomatic immunity, he was "urgently recalled" to Iran. A little later, New York State police pulled George Perry's body out of a lake with three bullet holes in its head and weights attached to its legs. Subsequently the New York manager of the Brazilian company that was to supply the arms was arrested for conspiracy to sell cocaine, his business partner was murdered, and the presumed assassin of the partner turned up dead a short time later. Of the $20-million down payment, there was no trace.[18]

After being burned so often in the black market, Iran tightened procurement procedures. Throughout most of the war, the bulk of Iranian purchases were negotiated from a building in London that jointly housed the National Iranian Oil Company (generating the money) and the Iranian Logistics Support Centre (spending it). Although Britain banned arms to Iran, it permitted its many arms dealers to operate freely provided they had a licence and the merchandise did not originate in Britain. Many just ignored the first requirement. And since Britain had been, after the United States, the most important supplier to the Shah, the government performed semantic gymnastics to get around the second. Engines for tanks and aircraft, for example, were cleared on the grounds that they were not themselves "lethal"— true enough, unless Iranian soldiers were planning to drop them on their enemies' heads. The permissiveness was fostered further when Margaret Thatcher's government went on a worldwide hunt for arms markets. Besides having English, the *lingua franca* of the arms business, as its mother tongue, London was the most important international banking centre and the hub of world commodity trade. Whether arms were paid for by oil or bank instruments, London was likely involved. Although the United States and Arab states supporting Iraq pressured the British to close the Iranian purchasing mission, Margaret Thatcher resisted, insisting that it would do nothing to reduce the arms flow and merely cost Britain legitimate trade. She was probably correct. When, late in 1987, she capitulated, the expelled Iranian officials continued business as usual elsewhere in Europe. In fact they may have been happy to move; by the time they left, the walls of their London office probably housed more bugs than the bedding of a Tijuana brothel.

Iran narrowed its preferred dealer list to about a dozen. It also tightened up on financing. Some deals involved commodity swaps. For example, in 1986 a British arms dealer pulled off a double sanctions-busting coup — he bought TOW missiles from Israel and sold them to a shell company on the Isle of Man for delivery to South Africa, which traded them to Iran for oil.[19] Similarly, when Theodore Shackley, who had run the CIA's "secret" war against Cuba, went into private business as consultant to John Deuss, one of South Africa's main oil suppliers, he tried to set up an arrangement in which Iran would barter crude to Portugal for weapons, Portugal would refine the oil, and Deuss's Transworld Oil would purchase it for resale to South Africa.[20] There was also reputedly at least one major deal in the works using for payment a commodity that revolutionary Iran supposedly no longer produced.

In 1986 a Swiss banker whose name had figured in the financial flow charts of the Pizza Connection, the largest heroin trafficking conspiracy in the United States in the 1980s, received a Turkish visitor seeking advice on how to handle money from a pending deal.[21] The banker immediately phoned the police. They arranged for an American narcotics officer to infiltrate the ring. After the DEA agent won its boss's confidence, he was told about a scheme to purchase, on behalf of Iran, fifty Oerlikon anti-tank batteries worth 1.2 billion Swiss francs, paying for them partly in cash and partly with 3,000 kilograms of top-grade heroin. The first shipment, 100 kilograms of heroin and morphine, left Istanbul stashed in a truckload of plate glass bound for a Swiss window manufacturer. When police at the border grabbed the truck and arrested one of the principals, they inadvertently triggered a political explosion that rocked the Alps.

A year before that arrest, an Armenian from Turkey had purchased a ticket on a Pan Am flight from Los Angeles to Europe and attempted to check in two large suitcases, only to face a demand for overweight luggage charges. After a brief altercation, the man agreed to pay. But his belligerence had stamped his face in the ticket agent's memory. When she saw him, a few minutes later, buying a ticket for a Europe-bound KLM flight, she was alarmed. However, in his checked luggage police found not a bomb but $2 million in small bills from the local cocaine trade. The courier confessed that the money was destined for a Zurich money-changing firm run by two Armenian brothers. When, the next year, the police at the Italian-Swiss border arrested the traffickers with the truckload of morphine and heroin, they found a business card bearing the same names.

The Magharian brothers had begun business in Aleppo, moved to Beirut because of Syrian exchange controls, then shifted during the Lebanese civil war to Switzerland. There, they came under the sponsorship of Mohammed Sharkachi, whose firm of bullion and exchange dealers had four marks of distinction. It had created a small gold bar especially popular among Middle Eastern smugglers; it had sold the CIA at least 25 million Swiss francs worth of Afghan and Pakistani currency at black market prices to make its Afghan war budget go further; it had briefly welcomed as a client a Turk who later fled Switzerland just ahead of an arrest warrant for heroin trafficking in the Pizza Connection case; and it had a prominent, politically connected vice-president who had intervened to get the firm's bank accounts unfrozen after the identity of that client had been revealed. Mohammed Sharkachi was also a man with a conscience when it came to assisting fellow refugees from the conflict in Lebanon. He had lent the Magharians use of his courier network, which had direct access to the tarmac at Zurich airport without passing Customs; gave them a start-up loan; and provided introductions to the big Swiss banks. It was more than a labour of love. The Magharians were the largest Swiss recipient of the masses of banknotes smuggled via Bulgaria from Istanbul's "Takhatele Central Bank," while Sharkachi's firm was one of the main suppliers of the gold being smuggled back into Turkey along the same route. When news of the investigation reached the Swiss minister of justice and police, she telephoned her husband, vice-president of the Sharkachi firm, to advise him to resign in a hurry, precipitating the greatest political scandal in Switzerland's post-war history and costing her her job.[22]

Although barter deals, usually for oil, perhaps occasionally for drugs, had a role, for the great majority of deals Iran insisted on using proper banking channels. Typically the seller would deposit a performance bond worth 10 per cent of the deal with Iran's banker, usually Bank Melli; Iran's banker would issue an irrevocable letter of credit in favour of the seller. Although letters of credit are usually cashed (and performance bond voided) once appropriate documents are presented to the bank holding the LC, Iran demanded that its own designees inspect the load. Until Arif Durrani's career was brought to a close by a ten-year prison sentence in the United States, the Iranians would send this son of a former chief of procurement of the Pakistan army to verify cargoes. On his arrival, local officials would whiz him past Customs and immigration without pausing for formalities or tell-tale passport stamps. If the cargo checked out, he would call a number in Frankfurt and have someone there relay the call to Teheran. On receipt of his okay, the Iranians would clear payment.[23]

But even that was not always enough. Most banks refused to negotiate letters of credit for arms deals. Hence the documents usually stipulated "heavy machinery," "auto parts" or "oil drilling equipment." One London broker selling Iran anti-tank missiles secured from BCCI an LC stipulating that the cargo consisted of "fork-lift trucks."[24] This procedure opened up the intriguing possibility that arms could be loaded, the bill of lading presented, the LC paid and the performance bond voided, and then the cargo switched or diverted en route. Those pulling it off could collect twice, then vanish. The Iranians would discover the deception only after they took delivery of containers of bricks or scrap iron or nothing at all. At that point they had no legal recourse — the money had been properly paid out by the bank.[25] For that reason, Iran began insisting to suppliers that payment be cleared only on actual delivery to an Iranian port.

Delivering the Goods

Delivery often required careful cover to disguise the nature of cargoes and indirect routes. Portugal performed several roles. It sold its own weapons and peddled EUCs. In fact it linked the two — it would provide an EUC-of-convenience if the dealer agreed to source half the load in Portugal. In arms trade morality, half a lie is better than a whole one, and for the weapons-producing country much more profitable. In addition, Portugal made available its free-port facilities for trans-shipments, for which service officials were reputed to demand 1 per cent of the value of the load.[26]

If material was urgently required, it went by air, either directly or through Frankfurt, Brussels or Lisbon. If the source was central or eastern Europe, the load could go by truck, train or even barge along the Danube. Weapons arriving in Bulgaria were turned over to state-owned Balkan Transport, loaded on trucks, sealed by Customs and dispatched through Turkey. Since Bulgaria was officially neutral, once inside Turkey the convoy divided, one part heading east to Iran and the other south to Iraq. Meanwhile the textile industry of equally neutral Turkey was working overtime manufacturing burial cloth for its two neighbours.

The great majority of arms went by sea. That required the right registration, since countries banning arms sales might also forbid their ships to carry weapons even if they originated elsewhere. When the West German *Gretl* was hired by a Danish shipbroker to haul Portuguese arms to Iran, the sailors tipped off Bonn, which sent a message to the vessel ordering it to return to Portugal. When it got back, the Portuguese, objecting to German interference, refused to allow it to discharge. The *Gretl* spent some time wandering back and forth before a compromise was worked out: the Germans permitted the ship to offload the weapons to another vessel, which completed the delivery, though at a cost three times the original contract price.²⁷

Although usually registered in flag-of-convenience centres, most ships hauling weapons to Iran were Danish-owned. Using lucrative tax breaks, the Danish government encouraged everyone from industrial tycoons to small-town dentists to invest in shipping. A high proportion of Danish ships were designated by the International Maritime Bureau as suitable for high-risk cargo. And Danish ships had a reputation for success gained from busting sanctions on South Africa. That embargo-busters might collect fees up to four to five times normal was undoubtedly another incentive.²⁸

To evade detection, ships would leave Israel, Portugal or Belgium with freight manifests misrepresenting the cargo and destination. Once at sea, the original manifests would be replaced by others identifying the real ports of call. Circuitous routing provided an alibi and made countermeasures more difficult. China, for example, was one of Iran's most important suppliers, providing over the course of the war $2.5 billion worth of equipment, including Silkworm anti-ship missiles that Iran could use to attack oil tankers leaving Iraq or Kuwait. China's objectives were both financial and strategic. The People's Liberation Army, which ran the arms industries, was facing deep budget cuts and searching for customers. By selling arms to Iran, China reduced the chances of Iran patching up relations with the U.S.S.R. Still, the Chinese were careful to maintain deniability. They worked through a Hong Kong intermediary, who in turn dealt with Iranian-appointed brokers in France and Germany; they shipped via North Korea, which was happy to earn commissions and content to have its reputation as a rogue state reinforced.²⁹

Ships, too, might pick up weapons in one place, then go from port to port loading and discharging innocent merchandise before heading to Iran. Sometimes they changed course en route. In South Korea, the Honduran-registered, American-owned *OK Rita Ann* loaded weapons nominally for Spain. While at sea it received a message from the company chartering the ship to make for Iran. The captain took the precaution of informing the American owner, who instructed the ship to return to South Korea. ³⁰

The business was not without risks. In 1982 the *Sarah Jane* called at Portugal to pick up bomb fuses for Iran, docked in Valencia to load artillery and mortar shells for Iraq, then headed for Greece to take on grenades for Iran. The first stop in the Gulf was a Saudi port where the artillery and mortar shells for Iraq were unloaded. Then the ship headed for Bandar Abbas. There the Iranians removed the grenades but, outraged to find American markings on the containers of fuses, ordered the captain at gunpoint to take them away.

Short supplies forced him to put in at Dubai, where Customs found the fuses, impounded the ship and arrested the skipper. After several months in jail, he had to sell the ship for a fraction its value to meet the fine and port charges. In the final indignity, the Iranians never paid for the fuses.[31]

Another Kind of Deficit Spending

In the early years, the Iranians could still obtain some supplies in the United States despite the embargo. The U.S. government seemed to take the view that when a radical Arab regime and a fundamentalist Islamic one got into a spat, the more of each other's citizens they killed, the better — especially since it would wear down both arsenals and facilitate future U.S. arms sales to chastened successor regimes. But by the end of 1983, American concerns about the consequences of an Iranian victory led to Operation Staunch, an undercover program to cut the leakage. U.S. Customs was overjoyed to be assigned responsibility. For that gave Customs a chance to one-up the DEA, which had been getting all kinds of favourable press for its lead role in the war on drugs. Subsequently there were prosecutions for smuggling everything from missiles to infrared sensors to aircraft parts.[32]

Leakage still did not end. By the Pentagon's own admission, at least $1 billion worth of material got "lost" each year. Among those helping to misplace equipment was an American insurance salesman who recruited U.S. naval personnel to steal parts for F-4 planes, then fake the computer records to hide the trail. The ring was broken when a Customs officer opened an outbound container of "automobile parts" and spotted an inertial guidance system. Despite the occasional conviction, a few Americans were still eager to try their hand at gun-running. Tracking their efforts sometimes turned up curious connections.

When George Perry's body was fished from a New York lake, his death not only aborted his own billion-dollar project, but complicated another supposedly worth double that sum. It started modestly when an informant led agents of the Bureau of Alcohol, Tobacco and Firearms to the New York office of United States Motors, whose owner was offering MAC-10 and MAC-11 submachine guns with silencers but without serial numbers. Posing as an IRA arms supplier, one agent offered to buy 10,000 of them for $15 million. The owner of the company then upped the stakes, claiming he could supply 60 attack helicopters, 4 military transport planes, 200,000 RPGs, 40,000 hand grenades, 10,000 MACs and some M-48 tanks. Assured by the ATF agent that customers could be found for the hardware, they concluded a $100-million deal, with the prospects of another $2 billion worth if all went well.

The would-be vendor had a problem. To date, his only successful foreign deal had been a U.S. government-licenced sale of ten rifles to a Belgian company. With potential billions staring at him, he contacted Abbott Van Backer, a former shoe salesman who had toured the Middle East and North Africa for American engineering firms and occasionally peddled military supplies. Bragging of contacts with Israeli generals, close relations with the late Shah's entourage and friendship with William Casey, the ex-shoe salesman seemed the right person to cobble together a big deal.

To get end-user certificates they first tried George Perry, who had friends in Brazil, but, alas, mortal enemies elsewhere. Still, Van Backer had other sources. For paper from Liberia, he claimed, the price was a new Mercedes-Benz. From Saudi Arabia it was much more expensive but much more credible. Finally they decided on a middle course — Egyptian EUCs were sufficiently respectable and, at 8 to 12 per cent of the value of the load, more reasonable. Van Backer also promised a ship with a captain not likely to be surprised at course changes in mid-voyage, though he advised his partners that they would also need enough loose cash to ease any concerns foreign port officials might have over unscheduled stops.

Any such deal required that both sides prove their bona fides. Van Backer flashed to the ATF agents a purchase order for $162 million worth of American helicopters signed by "Marshall General Zaglaviras," a supposed Greek general staff officer who turned out to be an unemployed former military adviser to the late Anastasio Somoza. For their part, the ATF agents took Van Backer to a private bank vault and displayed a 250-pound stack of $100 bills, the $10 million Van Backer claimed he would need to bribe U.S. government officials. Van Backer had also told them that his syndicate had as "paid legal consultant and adviser" a former cabinet secretary ready to doctor export documents and run cover in emergencies. Though Van Backer refused to allow a face-to-face meeting with his supposed protector, he was, as usual, not shy about dropping the name.[33]

Robert B. Anderson's political career began with his election to the Texas legislature in 1933. As bagman for Texas oil wealth, he was later instrumental in persuading Dwight Eisenhower to seek the Republican presidential nomination. Since Anderson came from landlocked Fort Worth, he was a natural choice as Ike's Secretary of the Navy, one of the biggest holders of oil reserves in the United States. In fact, so great was the esteem Eisenhower had for the new secretary that he sent Anderson to Egypt in 1956 to try to bribe Gamel Abd el-Nasir into making peace with Israel in exchange for U.S. aid for the Aswan dam project.[34] After a stint in government, Anderson returned to private business. Although Eisenhower was unsuccessful in having him replace Richard Nixon as running mate in 1956, Ike did offer another cabinet appointment. To tempt Anderson back into politics, oil industry chums arranged a $1-million trust, astutely granted in the form of Texas land whose value depended on the domestic price of oil. In 1957 Anderson became Secretary of the Treasury, where he sired an import quota system that for a decade and a half protected domestic producers from cheap Middle Eastern oil. And he kept so tight a watch over the national currency on which his signature appeared that his policies helped precipitate the 1960 recession, which, together with ballot-box stuffing, tilted the presidential election to the Democratic candidate, John F. Kennedy.[35]

During the Democratic interlude, Anderson was never far from power. Fellow Texan Lyndon Baines Johnson treated Anderson as the most important member of his informal "kitchen cabinet." But freed of formal public responsibilities, Anderson threw himself into consulting, advising Kuwait on how to use its oil wealth, helping with the Panama Canal treaty negotiations, and working as a part-time informant for the CIA, particularly after his golf buddy, William Casey, took over.[36] Then, perhaps because Anderson's Manhattan office sported both a picture of Jesus Christ and signed testimonials from several past presidents, in 1983 he received a visit from the Reverend Sun Myung Moon of the Holy Spirit Association for the Unification of World Churches.

Moon needed two services. The Moonie cult was investing heavily in Uruguay. Besides a hotel and newspaper, it had acquired one of the largest banks in a country famed for its secrecy laws. But the cult's reputation was causing international banks to balk at renewing a credit line. In return for Anderson's intercession, the Moonies endowed Anderson with a $240,000 annual salary, offices and money to pay the staff of his Global Economic Action Institute, whose modest objectives included an international conference to reconstruct the world monetary system.[37] Moon also solicited from Anderson help with a domestic problem in which Anderson had some expertise.

During his service as Eisenhower's Secretary of the Treasury, Anderson had vehemently opposed a tax cut. However, his views on lowering taxes had evidently undergone some change. For his second task was to lobby the Reagan White House to get the Supreme Court to review Reverend Moon's conviction for tax fraud. When the White House refused to support Moon, Anderson's views on America's financial future seemed to turn sour. He advised clients that they were better off depositing their savings in the same institution where he banked his Moonie consulting fees, namely his own Anguilla-based Commercial Exchange Bank and Trust. There they could find the benefits of "absolute client anonymity" in a "tax-free environment." Others had been eager to take advantage of the bank's services, including one drug dealer who deposited his money, then had it recycled back into tax-free investments in an energy project run by another of Anderson's business associates. Alas, in 1985 the Anguillan bank's co-owner was convicted of money laundering; in 1986 the manager of the energy venture pleaded guilty to defrauding depositors; and in 1987 Anderson himself was convicted of tax evasion and violations of banking law.[38] However, at least he had kept the record clean in one department.

Tapes made by the ATF agents had recorded Van Backer saying, "Anderson would like to have a piece of the profits. He's already declaring himself in." Of course there was no free lunch. According to Van Backer, Anderson, among other services, would structure payments to ensure secrecy. But efforts by the ATF undercover agents to get a meeting with Anderson were fruitless. Anderson later insisted his contacts with Van Backer had been limited to a few casual minutes that came to nothing.[39]

Holes in the Dike

If the Customs or ATF net ever became too tight, Iran could often find U.S. equipment abroad. It could, for example, locate a country with a stockpile of American equipment willing to openly flout U.S. restrictions. North Vietnam had captured at least $5 billion worth, including 73 F-5 fighter planes, some still in their packing cases, 550 tanks and 1,300 artillery pieces. Since North Vietnam used Soviet equipment, it was happy to sell the booty, but only to those with whom it felt an affinity. It rebuffed, for example, an offer from Sam Cummings to buy the lot for $500 million.[40] In the early stages of the war, supplies from Vietnam were essential to Iran's ability to blunt the Iraqi offensive.

Similarly, Iran was eager to obtain the much-touted Stinger anti-aircraft missile. When the missiles started turning up in the hands of the Pasdaran, an embarrassed Pentagon claimed that they had been seized at gunpoint from an Afghan mujahideen truck that had broken down near the border. A more credible explanation was that they had been allocated to Hezb-i-Islami guerrillas who simply sold them to the Iranians.[41]

A second approach was to find a country to serve as a front. In 1984 a chief of staff of Paraguay decided, as he put it, "to guarantee the defence and security of our country." To do so he requested that the Pentagon supply fifty M-48 tanks, four military transport planes, twenty-three F-4 jets and ten attack helicopters, and topped it off by requesting from West Germany fifty Leopard tanks. Despite a history of conflict with their little neighbour, neither Argentina nor Brazil protested to Washington the upsetting of the regional balance of power. Perhaps that reflected Paraguay's remarkable sense of discretion. The only visible sign inside Paraguay of its new military seems to have been a $5-million commission that the general split with the president.[42]

Another option was to rely on Israel with its never-ending stream of U.S. weaponry, acquired for free, courtesy of the U.S. taxpayer, then sold off at war-inflated prices.

When the Shah was ousted, Israel lost a strategic ally that threatened Arab states from the east, a guaranteed source of oil and a large market for its military industries. When the war broke out, Israel wasted little time re-establishing relations, sending technicians to refurbish the Iranian air force and, through a French front, selling spare parts for combat planes. The Carter administration had attempted to take advantage of the Iraqi invasion by secretly offering arms in exchange for hostages in the American embassy. But with an alternative source of U.S. equipment, the Iranians could ignore Carter's overtures.[43]

Once the Iranians had their air force sufficiently operational to blunt the Iraqi advance, they sought to get their tank force up to muster. That required replacement engines, barrels and ammunition. To keep the supply line secret, the Israelis hired two American freelancers who purchased in Buenos Aires an old cargo plane from a firm with a reputation for not asking questions. When it landed in Amsterdam, police, working on a tip-off, searched the plane for weapons, but found nothing. Next stop was Tel Aviv, where tank engines were loaded. Then to Cyprus where the papers were changed prior to flying to Teheran with a load of "pipes." On their third trip, the plane wandered into Soviet airspace and was either shot down or collided with a Soviet fighter.[44]

Despite that setback the Israeli-Iranian arms relationship flourished. While the Ayatollah Khomeini routinely thundered in public about Zionist plots, each week an Iranian agent delivered a list of needed supplies to the military attaché of the Israeli embassy in London for transmission to Tel Aviv. There the requirements were fed through armed forces' computers tracking availability of U.S. and American-compatible weapons systems worldwide.[45] If the Israelis (usually through the front of Swiss- or London-based dealers) were able to meet Iranian needs, they might mark up the price as much as 500 per cent. If not, location data was transmitted to the Iranian agent in London for forwarding to Teheran. Israel collected a finder's fee.[46]

Chapter 17

EXPLOSIVE REVELATIONS

In the early years of conflict, Iran's main objective was to get its American-supplied arsenal in shape to blunt, then reverse the Iraqi thrust. When that was accomplished, the fighting bogged down into a war of attrition. Both sides required enormous supplies of basic ordnance — explosives, mines, shells and artillery — to sustain the most intense confrontation of stationary infantry forces since World War I. While Iraq relied largely on the U.S.S.R. and France, over eight years of war Iran bought annually $2 to $3 billion worth of hardware from the four corners of the world.[1]

Nobel Sentiments
Neutral Sweden typified the world's attitude towards the Iran–Iraq War. While its prime minister, Olaf Palme, was acting as UN special commissioner to end the war, its most important arms conglomerate, Bofors-Nobelkrut, was the centre of a pan-European plot, not merely to fan the flames, but to pour on the combustibles. This was a fitting vocation for a firm whose founder had been both the pioneer of modern military explosives and the patron of the peace prize that bears his name.

Sweden had been wrestling with the same dilemma for nearly half a century. In 1936 it had unveiled the 40 mm Bofors gun, soon the most popular in the world. That same year it passed laws sharply restricting weapons exports. During World War II, when Germany occupied Norway and Denmark,

Sweden could import arms only from the one country that threatened it. That led to a post-war decision to invest heavily in manufacturing arms. However, it also tightened its export rules to prohibit sales, not just to areas of conflict or potential conflict, but also to countries using armed force to suppress human rights. As a further constraint, well before the United States adopted its Foreign Corrupt Practices Act, Sweden made it a criminal offence to pay bribes to secure foreign orders.

Of course, the Swedish government had to be realistic. As the industry grew, Swedish forces could not absorb all its output, forcing Swedish arms makers deeper into the export market just when it was getting particularly nasty. Bribery was therefore understandable, and even tax-deductible, where it was impossible to conduct business without it. And the government was prepared be equally reasonable about those tough export restrictions. Arms could be shipped abroad if the government saw a need to maintain Sweden's "credibility" as a supplier, or to respect decisions of previous Swedish governments even if they were wrong, or just to remain faithful to a history of supplying a particular area. Assuming all that failed to justify a sale, the authorities could rely on a "general evaluation." That was used, for example, to override the embarrassing finding that the United States was among the countries Swedish criteria would have made off limits. Such reasonableness ensured that, from 1950 until scandal erupted in the late 1980s, the government authorized exports to at least thirty countries fighting wars, putting down insurgencies or crushing political dissidents.[2]

By the end of the 1970s, Bofors-Nobelkrut had fallen on hard times. The Swedish military was cutting purchases and civilian divisions were losing money. But prominent in the Bofors inventory was the RBS-70, a cheap, effective ground-to-air missile with which the company might relive in a modest way the glory days of its 40 mm gun. When the government insisted on classifying the Persian Gulf as a zone of conflict, Bofors' disappointment was partially assuaged by its evolving relationship with Singapore, which had the twin attractions of being at peace and possessing a voracious appetite for weapons. By then it was a standard joke in the trade that if Singapore had kept all the weapons for which its officials signed, it would have sunk into the sea.[3]

After the Gulf War began, there were recurrent reports that the RBS-70 missile was showing up in Iran. Confronted in 1981 by the inspector of war material exports, Bofors denied all. There the matter ended for four years until a disaffected insider leaked documents to a peace research group, who took the matter to the police. The government charged two Bofors executives and banned sales to Singapore, which launched legal proceedings against the ex-manager of the local Bofors affiliate for bribery and forgery.[4] That, too, might have put the matter to rest, but for a piece of bad luck.

While the inquiry into how Bofors missiles guided themselves to forbidden places was still in progress, Swedish Customs received a message from its West German counterpart. Railway wagons loaded with gunpowder had been sent from Nobel, the explosives arm of the group, via Germany nominally bound for Austria. They had got as far as the border, turned around and headed for the port of Hamburg. Further investigation revealed that, although Nobel had a licence to export to Austria, shipping and insurance documents stipulated the powder be mixed with water, a normal precaution when explosives are sent by ship. The real destination turned out to be Syria en route to Iran. Six months later Swedish Customs got around to raiding Bofors-Nobelkrut and seizing documents that exposed a Nobel-led, pan-European cartel pouring military explosives into Iran and Iraq.

Bofors' ties with Iran dated at least to the early 1970s when it was contracted to build an armaments factory. After the revolution, the Swedish government proclaimed Iran off limits. But Bofors-Nobelkrut needed export markets, and Iran, whose military strategy was based on infantry assaults preceded by massive artillery barrages, needed powder. It seemed a perfect match, blocked only by cumbersome export restrictions. The chances of the government applying its customary reasonableness seemed slim when not only was the greatest conflict since World War II raging on the TV news, but the prime minister was Olaf Palme, still collecting kudos for his peacekeeping mission. Of course, there were ways around such obstacles: military products could be disguised as civilian; deals could be run through multiple layers of intermediation; EUCs could be faked; circuitous transportation routes could be employed; arms could be diverted through third countries; and factories could be built in embargoed places. Most embargo-busters used some of these techniques. Bofors-Nobelkrut used them all.

Bofors-Nobelkrut worked through the European Association for the Study of Safety Problems in the Production and Use of Propellant Powders, a name so cumbersome that members thought it best not to try to fit it into the telephone directory. This group of European majors, including several foreign subsidiaries of Nobel, was originally created to counter a public relations disaster arising from a series of plant explosions.[5] But once the Gulf market started demanding two-thirds of Europe's explosives-making capacity, members found happier things about which to chat. They began to meet regularly to divvy up orders, rig bids and inflate prices.[6] Initially, Nobel would accept requests from Iran for much larger amounts than it could manufacture, then subcontract to other members. The subcontractors would export to Sweden, and Nobel would move the entire shipment to Iran, claiming it was for civil purposes. Although some chemicals had dual uses, the size of the orders combined with their destination was an obvious clue about their real purpose to anyone asking any but pro forma questions. Furthermore, some material had only military uses. That, too, was shipped without licence, the trail clouded by a simple device — when Nobel received an order from the Ministry of Defence, it would reply to the Ministry of Economic Affairs.

Over time the cover deepened. Because Italy had not yet joined the embargo, in 1982 an Italian firm, which in the past had fronted for sales to South Africa, bought from Nobel and the others and resold to Iran. In 1984 Italy bowed to American pressure, catching 250 tons of cartel powder in transit. At that point, Karl-Erik Schmitz, owner-manager of Scandinavian Commodities Corporation (Scanco), entered the picture.

Back in the early 1970s Karl-Erik Schmitz had found Iran to be among his biggest markets for fertilizers, and South Africa his largest supplier. Shortly after the war began, he went back to Teheran to sell precursor chemicals for explosives: many were the same as those used in fertilizer. He impressed the Iranian defence ministry enough that in 1984 it asked him to handle a series of orders. He turned first to his old fertilizer partner. Iran would deposit funds from oil sales in the London branch of Bank Melli; that bank would pay into Scanco's account in a Luxembourg branch of Belgium's Kredietbank, the institution that usually handled South Africa's quiet dealings; Kredietbank would make payments to an Armscor front company in London; and that company would remit the funds to South Africa.

In 1984, the same year Italy banned sales to Iran, South Africa struck its arms-for-oil deal with Iraq, part of the agreement being to cut off Iran. The cartel was left without an Italian intermediary and Schmitz without a supplier. Nature took its course. Yugoslavia's defence ministry would buy from Nobel and resell to Scanco, collecting a 3 per cent commission. Then, to move the stuff from Yugoslavia to Iran, Schmitz bought from officials in the Kenyan defence ministry end-user certificates for a flat fee of $10,000. The payment methods were equally circuitous, from the London branch of Bank Melli, to Scanco accounts in London and Luxembourg, to Yugoslavia, then back to Nobel, which distributed money to subcontractors.

A second route for moving cartel power worked by Schmitz placing an order for $164 million dollars' worth, enough to produce 900,000 large-calibre shells, with Nobel. It subcontracted with French, Belgian and West German companies, collected the powder and shipped it to Pakistan, where Nobel had a joint venture with the government. Pakistan resold the powder to Iran. The transaction was perfectly proper. All necessary documents had been obtained — and then some. When Customs officers, following the German tip-off, raided Nobel, they found a supply of legitimate Pakistani end-user certificates, blank but for the bona fide signatures of responsible Pakistani officials. Yet a third route used as straw-purchaser a Greek company, suspected of being secretly owned by Armscor. The company charged 5 per cent for the service — until an explosion, possibly set by Iraqi agents, wrecked its factory. Subsequently Portugal became country-for-hire in the transiting cartel powder.

Meantime, back in Sweden, the police raids forced Nobel to lower its profile. Hence in 1986 Schmitz began dealing directly with the Belgian, Dutch, Spanish and French companies. Later, when the heat on the European companies was getting too intense, Israel picked up part of the slack.

In the powder business, as in the regular arms trade and for the same reasons (experience and discretion), Danish vessels handled most of the transportation. Once, when much of Europe's shipping was idled by industry holidays, Schmitz sent explosives by air. His choice was St. Lucia Airways. In retrospect, it seems lucky the airline had the time to ferry his powder, so busy was it normally kept flying CIA-supplied weapons to central America for the contras, to Zaire for UNITA, and eventually to Iran.[7]

Schmitz was also helping Iran prepare for the day when all suppliers might cut it off. He scoured Europe for the machine tools, parts and precursor chemicals Iran needed to build its own huge ammunition plant. He broke the project requirements down into 200 separate orders supposedly bound for places like Nigeria, Greece and Yugoslavia to prevent any outsider from figuring what was afoot.[8] But the Iraqis did. They bombed the complex out of existence several months before it was due to open.

Curious Company

When Italy cut off military relations with Iran, the news took a long time to reach one of the powder cartel's Italian customers. Italy has long held a reputation as Europe's centre for top-quality, high-fashion goods, a reputation as true in arms as in men's clothing. Notable among the haberdashers of hardware was Valsella Meccanotechnica, which could display before entranced clients top-quality lines of anti-personnel, anti-ship and anti-tank mines. One of those clients was the Islamic Republic of Iran.[9]

To be fair to Valsella, it was not alone in appreciating Iranian taste. Many top designers, including firms owned by the Italian government, were anxious to see Iran decked out with everything from pistols to night-vision scopes to aircraft parts. Shortly after the revolution, Iran received a visit from Stefano delle Chiaie, perhaps Italy's most notorious right-wing terrorist, who continued to operate largely because the intelligence services found his activities, including a 1980 bombing of the Bologna railway station that killed eighty people, useful for protecting Italy from "communism." He channelled Western arms, including spare parts and missiles for Italian-made Agusta helicopter gunships, to Iran, until news of his extra-curricular activities back home prompted the Iranian government to send him packing.[10] Even after Italy joined the boycott, arms were shipped to military bases for packing, then loaded on Danish ships under the myopic eyes of secret service agents and the congested noses of Customs officers.[11] Among the suppliers was the Italian branch of Switzerland's Oerlikon. On nine occasions from 1984 to 1986, it secured licences to send Iran machine-guns and anti-aircraft cannons. Valsella did things a little differently.

When it came to making cargoes disappear, Aldo Anghessa was a proven master. The Italian-Swiss shipping broker had once been convicted in a maritime fraud case when he claimed $500,000 insurance on a cargo lost when a very peculiar storm sank a freighter in an area blessed by balmy weather. Fortunately, only the ship and cargo went down. The captain and crew found ample time to load their belongings in a lifeboat and land safely in Cyprus. Duly lightened, the ship refloated itself and sought refuge from the storm in one of the pirate ports of Lebanon, where it was repainted to see service again under a new name. Sentenced to four years, Anghessa had an opportunity to put his experience in the quick freight business to more personal use when he escaped from a Swiss prison with an ease at first difficult to understand. Shortly after, he surfaced in Lebanon, displaying new-found wealth and offering to arrange arms deals. He assured would-be customers that Swiss banks stood ready to handle the money. Each of the Greek ships he chartered was doubly registered in Honduras and in Lebanon, permitting them to change identity on demand. And he claimed he had the backing of the Syrian secret services. Anghessa found two especially distinguished clients.[12]

The 1984 ban had been a harsh blow to Valsella. But its directors, confronted with the need to diversify their client list, rose to the challenge. In 1986 they presented to the government EUCs specifying Nigeria as the proud buyer of 30,000 anti-personnel mines, and called on Aldo Anghessa to do the rest. Although most nautical charts showed Nigeria lying southwest of Italy, one of Anghessa's double-identity ships headed east. On arrival in Syria, it unloaded the mines for trans-shipment to Iran. A year later he routed 2 million mines to Syria via Barcelona using a Spanish end-user certificate. In the undercover freight business, no less than with legitimate loads, the best way to give good service at reasonable rates is to secure cargoes coming and going. So while Valsella started preparing its next shipment of mines, Anghessa went looking for a load of in-bound merchandise. The story of how he found it started in 1985.

Palestinian renegade Abu Nidal had a busy schedule. He bombed airlines and blew up synagogues. He killed PLO aides and ran guns for Iraq. He jetted between Tripoli, Damascus, Madrid, Beirut, Baghdad, Algiers, Caracas, and Warsaw; he even made an appearance in a Paul Erdman novel.[13] Still, he managed time off to launch a grenade and machine-gun attack on Rome's Fiumicino Airport, leading to an intensive investigation by the *carabinieri*, the paramilitary police, into the routes by which small arms were reaching terrorist organizations. In the course of that investigation, they tapped Aldo Anghessa's telephone and noted his contacts with arms suppliers around the world. Even better, they learned about the pending arrival in the port of La Spezia of a tramp steamer, known as the *Boustany-I* in Lebanon and the *Good Luck* in Honduras. But they were also embarrassed to discover that Anghessa had secret partners.

As the *Boustany-I* (a.k.a. *Good Luck*) steamed towards La Spezia, the *carabinieri*, Aldo Anghessa and his secret partners all waited anxiously. But they were upstaged by the Guardia di Finanzia, the treasury police, one of whose helicopters, suspecting smuggling, forced the ship to put into the port of Bari on the heel of the Italian boot. Everyone rushed to the scene. As local TV cameras whirred, the police searched the ship and came up with nothing. Eventually a tip-off from a guest in a nearby hotel allowed them to locate two types of hidden cargo. One was a load of grenade launchers and rockets of Italian manufacture that had been sold to a Barcelona company using a Spanish end-user certificate, diverted to Syria, passed on to Iran, then run back through Lebanon to be passed on to urban guerrilla groups in Europe. They also found a stash of heroin and hashish for delivery to local mobsters. Then, in the hotel where their informant had been hiding, they spotted a briefcase giving interesting information about the return cargo the ship had been expecting to pick up in La Spezia.[14] In the aftermath, thirty people were arrested, although the case against the Valsella executives was later dropped. In all the excitement, one person not picked up was Aldo Anghessa, the former tenant of the hotel room, who had, for the last three years, been working as a paid informant for both the Italian and Swiss secret services in arms and drug smuggling cases.[15]

Shell Game

While cartel explosives were being stuffed into Valsella's mines prior to their reporting for duty in the Gulf, Valsella's propellant powders found consumers elsewhere in Europe with much the same idea. Hundreds of tons of explosives moved from Nobel in Sweden to its Austrian affiliate, thence to a straw-purchaser in Finland acting on behalf of a curious patron.

In 1966 East Germany's intelligence service, the Stasi, set up Kommerzielle Koordinierung (KoKo), to traffic in Western military technology and East German weapons. Working through a network of European front companies controlled via Liechtenstein and the Netherlands Antilles, KoKo had no lack of customers. One of them was the CIA. KoKo supplied assault rifles and ammunition that were passed on to the Afghan mujahideen and Angola's UNITA, both battling Soviet-armed governments. It also sold advanced Soviet weapons, including radar equipment, fighter planes and control mechanisms for missiles, which the CIA turned over to the Pentagon to study. Indeed, the entrepreneurial KoKo even managed to steal the march on an East bloc competitor. When, in the wake of the Bulgarian Connection scandal that followed the 1981 papal assassination attempt, Spain suspended commercial relations with Bulgaria, Munzer el-Qassar had to find another source of Soviet-model arms for the Nicaraguan contras. KoKo was pleased to pick up the slack.[16]

KoKo also had a long and profitable relationship with Iran. Its chairman had formed a joint venture with Sadegh Tabatabai and Ahmed Khomeini, the Ayatollah's son, to overtly export Iranian caviar, carpets and frozen food to West Germany, and to covertly smuggle East German arms to Iran. But its most important role was as a front for the powder cartel. Using fake paperwork provided by KoKo, cartel powder was exported via West to East Germany where it was pumped into shells, bombs and grenades en route to Iran — though just to keep things balanced, KoKo did the same for Iraq. East Germany's participation in the munitions trade to the Gulf remained a state secret until the end of the Cold War, whereas the same antics in France blew up in its government's face.

From tiny, American-subsidized roots after World War II, by the 1980s, France's war industries had blossomed into third place, behind the United States and the U.S.S.R., in the world market. Although for decades most production had been absorbed by the French military, France's big break in the export business came after the 1956 Suez War when Israel, facing a de facto embargo, went looking for a supplier with plenty of arms but not much conscience. This marked the start of a dedication to exports strong enough for France to be the last major Western power to formally embargo South Africa.[17]

The French were fully aware of the dangers of proliferation. France had long banned unlicensed exports. And its monitoring machinery was arguably the tightest in the world. Unlike most countries, France requires its arms manufacturers to apply to the government even before they negotiate a contract. Once permission is given, they make their deal. Then they submit their application for an export licence to the Ministry of Defence, complete with end-user certificates. If the application is in the least contentious, it goes to the Commission interministerielle pour l'étude des exportations de matériels de guerre, made up of representatives from defence, foreign affairs, industry and finance. The CIEEMG recommendation is passed on to the prime minister for a final decision. Nor does the control stop there. On the way out the weapons are checked by Customs. Then French consular officials are expected to confirm they reached their proper destination. For a time it was also necessary for exporters to post bonds to guarantee the weapons would arrive where they should.[18] Finally, for many years, including those of the Iran-Iraq War, France had exchange controls giving finance officials some scope to monitor the payments. So much for theory.

The control apparatus made sense when France was a minor exporter selling arms mainly for geo-strategic reasons. But by the 1980s, it had to deal with thousands of applications for export licences, a world glut threatened to cause French exports to nosedive, and, although the Socialist party took office in 1982, committed to reducing government promotion of arms sales, it inherited a military-industrial complex that directly employed 300,000. Perhaps another 700,000 found their livelihood indirectly dependent on arms production.[19] Political pressure for sales sent a clear message to the control apparachniks. Hence once a firm passed its first scrutiny, its applications for renewals or new licences were endorsed more or less automatically. With annual exports sometimes exceeding $5 billion, the CIEEMG moved from screening mechanism to cheerleader.

Granted there was a "red list." But the extent to which France takes embargoes, even its own, seriously was shown in 1968. In retaliation for Israel's use of French helicopters to raid Beirut airport and destroy several Lebanese civil aircraft, France publicly cut off shipments, while privately making sure Israel got adequate spare parts to keep its fighter planes in the air. That provided a portent of what was to happen during the Gulf War.

The French were strategically wedded to Iraq. But, being French, they soon indulged in a bit of hanky-panky on the side. The fact that Iraq was having trouble paying its bills was another incentive to infidelity. When Iran ordered Chinese Silkworm anti-ship missiles, and China was coy about providing them directly, a French arms dealer placed the order with a Chinese military front company in Hong Kong, nominally on behalf of Libya, while the missiles were shipped via North Korea to Bandar Abbas. The payments went from the Iranian central bank to its correspondent bank in Frankfurt, then to the French arms dealer's bank. He deducted his commission and wired payment to China. Since these were big-ticket items, at least $1.5 million each, the deal was virtually impossible without at least tacit approval of French intelligence. As well, at least three times during the early 1980s, air force planes secretly carried French-made missile systems to Iran.[20] Still, the really explosive action involved artillery shells.

When Daniel Dewavrin took over Luchaire, a conglomerate making automobiles, aeronautics and munitions, it seemed at death's door. Interestingly for a company whose main shareholders were life insurance companies, Dewavrin decided that the weapons sector would lead the turnaround. Iran was, of course, an unacceptable client. Fortunately, many others were enthusiastic about Luchaire's products. Thus, when Iraq could not pay for an order of 155 mm shells, Luchaire was fortunate enough to find a Belgian gun-runner with a sure market in Greece and Peru. However, the cargo got lost en route, and Iraq was soon taking delivery of its shells the hard way.[21] Israel and Pakistan, Yugoslavia and Portugal also placed orders, though, in the interests of discretion, with Luchaire's Italian subsidiary. Thailand, too, bought 100,000 203 mm shells even though it did not have an artillery piece big enough to fire them. Ecuador stockpiled enough 155 mm stuff to repel an invasion from the People's Republic of China. The advantage of multiple paper designations was that if all had been consigned to a single place, it would have been a tip-off that the real buyer was a country at war. In addition, the legitimacy of the sales was confirmed by EUCs. The Thai one was authentic — the bribed officials could confirm that. The Portuguese one, though, was signed by an officer who had never bothered to pick up a paycheque from the armed forces. The CIEEMG subjected all of them to its usual close scrutiny and gave positive recommendations. It seemed that Luchaire's stock was rising, both politically in light of its cosy relationship with the French Socialist party, and financially as its shares shot up from 70 francs in 1982 to 750 four years later.

During the first three years of the war, most of the shells were taken to Cherbourg to be loaded under the supervision of a senior Luchaire official. To make sure the job was done properly, also present were representatives of the secret service, military intelligence and the investigative branch of the police. Swelling the growing crowd of witnesses to the top-secret operation were Iranian officials sent to inspect the cargo. They were probably on duty day and night — they refused to stay in the hotel Luchaire had booked for them. Apparently they suspected that it was a brothel in which French intelligence agents planned to photograph them in compromising positions.[22]

From Cherbourg the preferred route was via Suez, until the last day of 1983 when a Cypriot ship was boarded by Egyptian Customs officials who were fascinated by a manifest stating that Iran, in the midst of a nasty war, was in the market for a shipload of casserole dishes. A short time later, the chief of France's external intelligence service confirmed directly to the president that Luchaire's shells were reaching Iran. Not only were the EUCs phoney, but, of the certificates of arrival supposedly filed with French Customs, some were fakes, others provided by bribed officials at the nominal ports of destination, others simply nonexistent; and no one had bothered to telex the French consuls for confirmation.[23] The president decided to treat the conversation as strictly confidential.

After the Egyptian scare, Luchaire (apart from kindly agreeing that Iran would not have to pay for its lost cargo of casserole dishes) changed customers. Orders started arriving, ostensibly on behalf of Brazil, from an instant corporation in the Caribbean. Instead of relying on French ports, the shells were trucked to Bulgaria, Spain and Portugal for loading on freighters flying flags of convenience.

If the deals had been normal, Iran's Bank Melli would have issued LCs and sent them to France's Banque Worms, banker to and 23 per cent shareholder in Luchaire. And Banque Worms would have provided the performance bond. But since they were routed through Luchaire's Italian subsidiaries, Bank Melli would order its Italian correspondent banks to issue LCs on behalf of Luchaire's Italian subsidiaries, which sent them to Italy's Banca Nazionale del Lavoro. BNL would provide the performance bond. And BNL would use the original LCs as security to issue its own LCs in favour of the Luchaire parent firm in France. That firm sent the LCs to Banque Worms for negotiation. When the goods were loaded on board ship, Banque Worms would present its LCs to BNL for payment, and BNL would do likewise with the correspondent banks of Bank Melli. This use of back-to-back letters of credit was a simple but effective device for breaking up the money trail.[24]

In the final stage, Banque Worms would put the money, less its fees, in Luchaire's account. And Luchaire reputedly made a few payments of its own. According to a subsequent official investigation, some was skimmed through a Panama shell company for bagmen of the French Socialist party. Another payment went to a Swiss BNL branch, ostensibly as commissions to Iranian middlemen, though the inordinately large amount led some to conclude that much of that payment ended up in another Swiss bank where a prominent member of the French Socialist party had an account.[25]

While these subterfuges for a time ensured there was no public scandal, there was internal disagreement. No official was more unhappy than General René Audran, director of international affairs of the defence ministry, so partial to the other side he was nicknamed "Monsieur Iraq." However, the general's chance to register dissent ended abruptly in 1985 when he was gunned down by Action directe, a French urban guerrilla group.[26]

After elections in 1986 returned a conservative government, the lid blew off the casserole dish. Luchaire's boss, Daniel Dewavrin, was bewildered at the fuss. After all, he insisted, fake EUCs were standard in the arms business. Still, the new prime minister ordered a public enquiry, which led to criminal charges. But the general who had originally provided evidence of pay-offs to the Socialist party later decided that he had been misunderstood. And a court eventually acquitted Dewavrin, citing lack of evidence. The new French government, having achieved its immediate goal of blackening the reputations of a few opponents, stopped further investigations to protect "national security."[27]

The Search for the Smoking Gun

Arms brokers had trouble keeping up with the Iranians, who tended to fire off enormous amounts of ammunition, then go desperately shopping for more. Suppliers had to scramble constantly to find existing stocks instead of being able to feed a steady flow of orders to producing factories.[28] Meantime, the Iraqis were blasting back. Initially the Iranians had the advantage. They had more guns, and their top-of-the-line American artillery outdistanced the best that the Iraqis had from the U.S.S.R. At that point, fate in the form of a Lebanese-Armenian wheeler-dealer lent a hand.

For a while, Sarkis Soghanalian had worked as a "translator" at the American embassy in Beirut. During off-duty hours, he built a reputation as a freelance gun-runner. His role in arming the Tiger militia of Lebanese warlord Kamil Sham'un led to a quick decision to relocate to New York ahead of the hit squad from a rival group. Even in his new home he kept in touch with old friends. His continued assistance in arming rightist forces in Lebanon won the appreciation of the CIA.[29] Still, Sarkis was not inclined to put all his hand grenades in one basket. In 1977 while living in Florida, he met the representative of Boca Investments, a Channel Island company that had just won a contract to supply machine-guns to Mauritania. Sarkis persuaded the rep that he, Sarkis, was the director of a firm making the desired material. The Boca representative turned over an end-user certificate along with a letter from the

Mauritania ambassador to the United States attesting to its authenticity. Soghanalian gave the representative certificates of origin for the weapons, an airways bill showing they were ready for shipment and a copy of the insurance policy on the cargo. On the basis of these documents, a Belgian bank paid $1,153,000 into Soghanalian's bank account. For months he stalled Boca, while putting its money to good use: paying off his large and long-overdue American Express bill, settling on himself a fine salary as a reward for his hard work, putting a down payment on his first airplane and investing in a genuine gun-running operation.

The customer, Anastasio Somoza, was then under siege from the Sandinista insurgency and facing an arms embargo imposed by the Carter administration. Since it was illegal to send American material, Soghanalian with a partner in Lisbon ran Portuguese weapons to Managua. As long as the arms flowed to Somoza's tottering regime, Boca's repeated complaints, to federal and state authorities and even to the CIA, were ignored. It was not until Somoza was facing certain ouster that action was taken and only then after Boca started civil proceedings. Soghanalian was eventually charged with thirty-eight counts of fraud, though none of gun-running, and, after another two years of legal manoeuvring, was sentenced to five years' probation and ordered to repay the money. If, as rumour had it, he had earned about $25 million running guns to Somoza, it was not a great hardship.[30]

In the years following his Florida coup, Soghanalian added new customers including (so he claimed) the Argentine junta during the Falklands/Malvinas War, the Nicaraguan contras, and both Iran and Iraq. In 1981 Soghanalian connected Iraq to France's new Socialist government in a potential 10-billion franc contract.[31] The centrepiece was the new GCT (*grande cadence de tir*), billed as the fastest and most accurate 155 mm gun in the world. What the French did not advertise so loudly was that it was also the most expensive. The price drove Iraq to search out other suppliers with a success due in large measure to the misfortunes of Gerald Bull.

While Bull was serving his brief jail sentence for smuggling artillery and shells to South Africa, his legal bills were piling up and Space Research Corporation was facing possible bankruptcy. Financial desperation led him to a licensing deal that amounted to almost giving away manufacturing rights to Noricum GesMBH, the military subsidiary of Voest-Alpine, Austria's largest steel and engineering firm. Since the mid-1970s every division of Voest-Alpine except its commodity trading subsidiary had been losing money. In 1981 the government, which owned the firm, poured in $200 million and a new management team. The best prospects for revival seemed to be in pushing Noricum's military sales, provided certain marketing obstacles could be overcome.

Austria, like Sweden, is a small country whose own military could not possibly absorb at reasonable cost the full output of a modern firm making major systems. Austria, also like Sweden, has strict laws regarding exports. Following a scandal over armoured cars sent to the Chilean junta in the 1970s, it became illegal to sell to areas of conflict or places that consistently violated human rights. Facing Swedish-type obstacles, Austria found Swedish-type solutions. Iraq was clearly on the prohibited list, but there was nothing to prevent Voest from selling 200 weapons to "Jordan."

When the first 100 of the Voest-Wunderkanone arrived, Iraq was delighted. Much cheaper than the French competitor, it could carry for forty kilometres while the French weapon had a top range of twenty-four. But under continuous fire, the barrels started to melt. Iraq cancelled the remaining 100. Then Sarkis Soghanalian got busy again, putting Iraq in touch with Bull. He in turn steered them to South Africa, the first country to license his technology, assuring them that the South African weapon came equipped with a hardened barrel.[32] For Iraq it was a stroke of rare luck. It not only bought hundreds of artillery pieces, but scored an additional coup in getting South Africa to agree to cease supplying Iran. Voest-Alpine was left in the lurch. But then it got a break.

Keeping up with the Khans

In 1977 Pakistan had received from the United States 155 mm howitzers that easily out-ranged those in India's arsenal. Although Pakistan received only thirty weapons, India interpreted the delivery as a U.S. "tilt" in Pakistan's favour. India's concerns were alleviated when the Carter administration, in protest over Pakistan's nuclear program, cut back military assistance. But the Reagan administration, as a reward for Pakistan's role in supplying the Afghan resistance, not only turned the tap back on, but opened the spigot to full. Spooked by a sale of advanced American fighter jets to Pakistan and emboldened by the return to power of the bellicose Indira Gandhi, India let out word it was in the market for big guns. It soon found several European manufacturers knocking on the door while their local agents tried to slither under it.[33]

Trials began in 1981. The British entry was quickly eliminated. The American one fared better, but was knocked out because the U.S. government refused to throw in some missile guidance systems. That left three contestants. The initial consensus favoured Voest-Alpine. Bull's weapon, with the barrel problem rectified, was widely accepted as the most advanced. It easily out-ranged the others; it was simple to maintain, more mobile, easiest to camouflage and cheapest. Of a fifteen-member investigating committee, fourteen, including five of the six military reps, backed Voest. The French weapon came second. The Bofors gun ranked third. Its range was much inferior to the Austrian weapon. It was difficult to maintain, had an unsuitable traction system, had a high silhouette that made it an easy target, and was expensive. And in early trials, among the deadly projectiles the Bofors gun shot off was its own firing mechanism. The contest seemed so lopsided that Voest fronted the money to permit Noricum to start producing the guns, not only before the ink on the India contract was dry, but before anyone had uncapped their pens. Then strange things began to happen.

Back in Sweden, Prime Minister Palme was under pressure. Swedish army orders were running out, Bofors had just missed a Pentagon contract, and the company announced lay-offs in an area where unemployment was already heavy. In 1985 Palme called on Rajiv Gandhi, who had recently succeeded his assassinated mother as India's prime minister. Gandhi ordered new trials. In the meantime, the technical specifications were rewritten, and press articles emerged denouncing the Austrian gun, which was dropped from the shortlist. Yet more secret discussion followed until the announcement in 1986 that Bofors had won the largest single defence deal in Indian history.[34] Initially, Bofors was to supply for $1.3 billion 400 howitzers, enough to keep its Swedish plants fully employed for three and a half years. Another 1,100 guns, worth $2.2 billion more, were to follow, some produced from two new plants Bofors would construct in India. The Swedish government was again prepared to be reasonable about those meddlesome arms sales rules. It signed a memorandum of understanding that guaranteed delivery even if India were at war.[35]

There were two reasons given for the shift. One was that Pakistan had just acquired from the United States a special radar permitting it to home in on (and direct artillery fire to) India's guns forty-five seconds after they opened fire. That supposedly tilted the balance in favour of Bofors because its gun could fire three shots in thirteen seconds, then pack up and move, while the competition took two seconds more. But since artillery almost always needs several ranging rounds before it finds its target, the capacity to fire a three-round burst at the push of a button, then run away, was of little military consequence. In any event, the key to a successful "shoot and scoot" strategy was not a two-second difference in burst firing, but how long it took to fold up the gun-trails from the firing to the moving position — about two minutes with all weapons under consideration.

The second supposed reason for the change was the price. Gandhi claimed he had an agreement with Palme to bypass middlemen. Eliminating commissions, along with a price cut, reputedly tilted the advantage to Bofors. But once the numbers were adjusted for exchange risks, probable interest rate variations and the fact that Bofors wanted 20 per cent up front, whereas the French would accept 10 per cent followed by another 10 per cent several months later, the French weapon was probably a better buy. And both were inferior to the Austrian. Furthermore, claims about the absence of commissions were bogus.

One of Rajiv Gandhi's great boasts was that his government had struck a blow against corruption in Indian public life by making it riskier for local businessmen to funnel slush funds to party bagmen. Rather than improve Indian democracy, the result was to shift the burden of financing elections from local businessmen to contract-hungry foreign corporations, especially in the defence sector at a time when India was engaged in its greatest ever military build-up. Although Gandhi made a show of ordering agents of foreign defence firms away from his office, a ruling party had a massive advantage in collecting election funds from foreign corporations.

Gandhi had also announced a more rigorous enforcement of tax and exchange control laws and delegated the job to his finance minister, V. P. Singh. To aid the offensive against "black money," Singh put together a strike force of financial sleuths led by the Fairfax Group, an American economic investigative agency. Singh's raiders hit at least 5,000 businesses. But then the finger started pointing in a very sensitive direction.

BCCI had broken into the Indian market in its usual way. To neutralize opposition from the central bank, it cultivated close relations with the Gandhi family, using cash, jobs, donations to designated charities and a few other favours.[36] The year before it secured its licence, there had been a nasty battle for control of a textile conglomerate whose owner was a crony of the Gandhi clan. The government had introduced a program that encouraged non-resident Indians to invest back home. So the company supporters set up a series of Channel Island corporations and used them to buy up the stock, while pretending that the money was coming from non-resident Indians. It worked nicely both to keep the company out of the hands of corporate raiders and to illegally transfer a controlling interest offshore. Loans to finance the transaction were guaranteed by BCCI.

Once up and active inside India, BCCI got busy with the capital flight trade. Customers would pay BCCI in rupees at the low black market rate and collect the equivalent in dollars abroad, while BCCI would use the rupees for local loans. In reverse, any Indian needing to repatriate money could deposit hard currency with a BCCI branch abroad and collect rupees in India. To cloak the transaction, the person would go to BCCI Bombay, take out a loan without collateral, then default. BCCI, already compensated in hard currency abroad, would happily write it off.

The set-up began to unravel by accident. The textile conglomerate to which BCCI had lent a helping hand had grossly undervalued for import duty purposes machinery imported from the United States. Those low invoices attracted the attention of the Fairfax investigators. During the investigations, the head of Fairfax was offered a million dollars to ensure the Gandhi family was absolved, with the option of having his chopped-up body tossed in the Potomac River. A raid on BCCI Bombay discovered several hundred thousand dollars in undeclared hard currency and phoney foreign exchange permits. Several bankers were arrested.[37] A panic visit by Agha Hasan Abedi led to Gandhi having charges against the BCCI staff dropped, closing out the Fairfax contract and shifting the principal sleuths to less sensitive posts. V.P. Singh had already been moved from finance to the defence ministry.[38] But, ironically, that made matters worse.

Singh latched on to rumours that, during a $450-million deal for West German submarines, the German company had made a little extra on the side by covertly selling to South Africa the intelligence data, including the blueprints, breaking the UN arms embargo and rendering the Indian subs vulnerable. Furthermore, there was a little matter of $30 million paid, with Gandhi's okay, to the Hinduja family. These ultra-religious commodity traders who had moved to Iran early in the century did not let their strict vegetarianism stop them from feeding the Shah's carnivorous appetite for modern weaponry in the 1970s, or deter them, once they had decamped to Switzerland, from collecting supposedly non-existent commissions on the submarine contract.[39]

While the submarines controversy was raging, Swedish radio revealed that Bofors, to procure the howitzer contract, had also paid commissions to agents. One of them was Wineshwar Nath Chadha, a former peddler for transnational pharmaceutical firms who evidently decided there was more money to be made in selling the means to kill people than in peddling potions to cure them. Bofors was not his sole responsibility. In 1980 he arranged for an Italian firm to sell India $35 million worth of torpedoes that twice turned around and homed in on the ship launching them. For this, Chadha was paid a 6 per cent commission. The behaviour of the torpedoes did not mean Chadha lacked a sense of responsibility. When the naval officer who made the choice was forced to resign, he found a new job, with Chadha's consulting firm. And in 1987 the Italian company was given another contract, for the same sum but requiring delivery of fewer torpedoes, with Chadha again cut in for 6 per cent. Although Chadha was happy to help himself to such side dishes, Bofors was his main meal ticket.

Rajiv's public opposition to middlemen meant the payments flow went underground. Chadha insisted that he was not an agent, an individual who acts on behalf of a company for a percentage, but a representative who runs errands for a fixed salary. In fact he was both. His representative's salary was paid publicly in India, while commissions were paid secretly in Switzerland.[40] They were split into three components. One part was paid into the Geneva account of a company called Svenska, set up for Chadha by Interseco, the same Panamanian company broker to which Richard Secord and his associates had turned in the Iran-contra affair. Another part was deposited in Geneva accounts owned by the Hindujas, who were quietly rooting for Bofors, a firm they had represented in Iran during the 1970s. A third part was paid into the Zurich account of a London company called AE Services (a big public relations improvement over its former name, Target Practice Inc.). AE Services in turn was owned by a Liechtenstein trust company that supposedly numbered among its officers a lawyer for the Gandhi family trust.[41]

To Chadha the scandal over the commissions was a plot by the disappointed French competitor to cause the cancellation of the Bofors contract. For Gandhi, it was much darker — the entire affair, he insisted, was a conspiracy, probably of Pakistani origin, to destabilize the government and destroy India's capacity to defend itself. He referred the matter to a parliamentary committee. In its eagerness to investigate, it insisted on having as technical adviser a senior military man, selecting the only one of the fifteen on the original committee to rank the Bofors gun ahead of its competitors. In the meantime, the shrinking number of Congress party members loyal to Gandhi took up the refrain that the Bofors contract had been awarded, not by graft but purely on military and financial merit. Among those sceptical of such claims was the former managing director of Voest-Alpine. He described to a committee of the Austrian parliament the process by which weapons were sold in India. "There was not a single day when someone did not come to me asking for money." Indian politicians sent trusted aides to say, "If you work with me, you will get the contract." Asked why that honour finally went to Bofors rather than Voest, he answered, "Obviously they offered to pay more than we did."[42]

Too Much Sachertorte?

After the Bofors scandal, V.P. Singh, already forced out of cabinet over the subs affair, mobilized an opposition coalition to defeat Gandhi. But despite the pessimistic musings of Win Chadha from exile in the United States, the Bofors contract was never reopened. Voest-Alpine, again left alone at the altar, faced difficult times. Weapons were stockpiled, waiting for buyers. There were major commitments to suppliers of propellant powders. The situation was described by the boss of the Noricum division as disastrous. Big job losses seemed in the offing. Misfortune had also befallen Voest's hitherto star-performing commodity trading wing. Once one of the ten most important oil traders in the world, with a reputation for being able to get oil to odd places, South Africa among them, in 1984 it had blown $200 million in a deal that sent several executives to jail. What was bad for Voest-Alpine was worse for Austria, or at least its Socialist party government, which faced the prospect of either another massive bailout or a radical downsizing that might cost it heavily at the polls.[43] However, there was one way things could be put right — another major weapons deal. The problem was finding the right customer.[44]

That customer could not be Iran, even though it was being very persuasive. Early in 1983 an Iranian representative called on the minister of foreign affairs to complain about delivery of 100 Voest wonder-guns to Iraq. To make its discontent clear, Iran started its own sanctions campaign. Voest's chief executive counted the potential cost: elimination of Austria from a competition for 8,000 train cars; exclusion from participation in a new ship-works at Bandar Abbas; suspension of a major truck contract; curtailment of Iranian commodity deals with Voest's trading arm, etc. He laid this sombre tally before the government along with Iranian insistence that restoration of normal business was contingent on its getting the same consideration, or better, than Iraq.[45] There were others pushing, including imperial pastry maker, Udo Proksch, who (prior to being charged in the *Lucona* affair) had led a visiting Iranian military delegation, posing as Kuwaitis, to view Austria's tastiest offerings.[46] Austria refused to bend — it would not sell arms to Iran. But it would sell to Argentina, Brazil, Bulgaria, Cyprus, Egypt, Poland and Thailand, a virtual alphabet soup of countries suddenly clamouring for wonder-cannons. Confirmed orders totalled 350 units with another 150 possible, potentially worth $800 million over the next three years. That represented enough potential profit to restore Voest-Alpine to financial health.

Iran, knowing that Voest was desperate, drove a hard bargain. Fasami Corporation, a Hong Kong-registered, Tokyo-based trading company secretly owned by Iran, placed the order. Voest was required to post a performance bond of 800 million Austrian shillings (AS) (about $75 million); Fasami opened a letter of credit for 2 billion shillings and sent it to a bank in Frankfurt with instructions to pay instalments to Voest as the contract proceeded. Once the account was drawn down to 20 per cent, Iran was to top it up with another

2 billion. Voest had to deposit in the Swiss account of a Panama company 337 million Austrian shillings (about $28 million) for kickbacks to Iranian intermediaries. After the deal was negotiated, Iran discovered that Voest was charging per weapon 20 per cent more than offered to India. Iran insisted on a drastic price cut and backed up its demands by having the Pasdaran kidnap Voest's Iranian sales manager. He was released after the firm's managing director flew to Teheran, agreed to the price cut and squared away the Pasdaran with a suitcase containing a million dollars.

Early in 1985 Voest-Noricum applied for a licence to export 200 cannons to "Libya," presenting an end-user certificate for which it had paid AS 320 million to a Liechtenstein front company. The government obliged with an export licence. It also granted several company officers special passports identifying them as persons travelling on government business, freeing them of most visa requirements as well as making their itinerary difficult to reconstruct. Weapons started moving. But problems soon began.

In June of 1985 the Austrian ambassador to the United States told his government that he had been shown U.S. spy satellite photos that revealed Voest-Noricum wonder-cannons at a military base in Iran. Then in July the Austrian ambassador to Greece received similar information from an exiled Iranian arms dealer who claimed he had been instrumental in setting up the deal but been cheated out of his commission. The ambassador in Greece sent a series of telexes to Vienna. The government ordered further exports to be stopped pending an investigation. The ambassador announced that he was about to meet with the arms dealer to get concrete proof the weapons were going to Iran. The night before the meeting, the ambassador died of a heart attack. A few days later the government pronounced the Libyan end-user certificate valid and told Voest-Noricum to proceed with the exports. The late ambassador's informant was later reconciled with AS 35 million.

Alas, the course of arms dealing, like true love, seldom runs smoothly. Reporters discovered some forty cannons waiting for a ship in a Yugoslavian harbour. Although the guns were nominally destined for Libya, their instruction manuals were written in Farsi rather than Arabic. Even worse, Libya itself soon ceased to be an acceptable destination. That problem began early in 1986 when the United States decided to protest Libya's support of "international terrorism" by dropping bombs on Colonel Mu'ammar Qadhafi's eighteen-month-old daughter. Under American pressure, the Austrian government banned sales to Libya and restarted its probe.[47]

Voest in its hour of need found friends in strange places. One of the stranger places was Marbella, on Spain's Costa Del Crime. And the friend turned out to be someone who, when not running his Vienna-based arms brokerage house, preferred life on the Spanish Riviera to facing heroin trafficking charges elsewhere. Munzer el-Qassar's name had already surfaced in a remarkable string of shadowy arms deals. In the late 1970s he had been accused of brokering arms-for-hashish swaps between a Lebanese Christian militia and Italian Mafiosi. Among his subsequent deals was a sale through a British arms merchant of £43 million worth of missiles, tanks and artillery to Chad during its civil war.[48] El-Qassar also managed a complex deal in which friends in the Portuguese Ministry of Defence bought old anti-tank missiles from North Korea and sold them to a British-based arms dealer who shipped them to Iran using a Nigerian end-user certificate. The arrangement was financed by BCCI. These and similar episodes attracted the interest of the U.S. National Security Council cowboys who used el-Qassar to obtain East bloc weapons for the Nicaraguan contras.

Apart from solid experience in the covert arms trade and a close relationship with Udo Proksch (who made el-Qassar an honoured guest at Club 45 meetings), another thing that made el-Qassar a wise choice for the Austrian firm was his Argentine diplomatic passport, the result of connections with members of the family of President Carlos Menem, himself a descendant of Syrian émigrés to Argentina.[49] Hence 41 million shillings paid to el-Qassar's Overseas Trading Company to secure an Argentine end-user certificate seemed well spent. It mattered little that its Ministry of Defence stamp was a crude forgery, or that it was "signed" by someone who had already left the relevant position in Argentina's foreign office.[50] After all, Voest's ammunition-making subsidiary had filed a Bulgarian end-user certificate written on the same typewriter as the order for the guns. No one objected, certainly not Munzer el-Qassar, who pocketed the commissions on that sale, too.

Voest managed to get 140 of its wonder-cannons and spare barrels to Iran before police raids blocked the rest. Iran cashed out 350 million shillings on the performance bond. Together with the bribes, kickbacks and manufacturing losses, the deal that was supposed to be the firm's financial salvation produced nearly 2 billion shillings in losses. That eventually forced the Austrian government to break up the firm and sell off the pieces. Among the politicians implicated, only the minister of the interior was ever convicted — of obstruction of justice. Several Voest-Alpine executives were found guilty of various offences. One person not among them was the former managing director. If he did not have his day in court, he did have his day before an Austrian government enquiry where he made his rueful observation about Voest's failure to understand sufficiently that the route to an Indian politician's heart is through his wallet. He might have had much more to say. But he died of a heart attack the next day.

Those Who Live by the Sword . . . ?

Meanwhile back in Sweden, although some Nobel officers had been charged in the powder case, Bofors had remained largely unscathed. Two officials had admitted running RBS-70 missiles to Iran and been acquitted. A government enquiry concurred that whoever else had been at fault in the Indian artillery deal, it was not Bofors. However, the official resolution to another, perhaps related scandal, failed to quiet public concern.

For a country like Sweden, whose weapons have graced so many battlefields, the 1986 gunning down of Prime Minister Olaf Palme was a shock. Although a homeless psychotic was picked up, Palme's role in delicate international affairs encouraged speculation that there were deeper causes.[51] These suspicions were accentuated in January 1987, when the chief inspector of war material stepped in front of a Stockholm subway train on his way back from a meeting with the president of Bofors–Nobelkrut.[52]

For a time the investigation focused on militants of the PKK, Turkey's Kurdish Workers' Party, who had for a time enjoyed political exile in Sweden. One possibility was that they wanted revenge after Palme, under pressure from Turkey, ordered that several of them be expelled. A variation on that theme was that the killing had been a contract hit carried out by PKK people but paid for by Iran. This theory was backed by a claim that the very day of his murder, Palme had promised the Iraqi ambassador to cut off Swedish arms to Iran. The PKK theory permitted police to spend eighteen months harassing people on the basis of their ideological passions and tinted complexions, both of which stood out against the political and physiological blandness of Sweden, but no one could find any real evidence.

Another hypothesis was that the murder had been paid for by one of Bofors' competitors in a last-ditch effort to derail the India deal. There was talk, too, that the assassination was the work of members of Sweden's own intelligence services, at that time riven between left-wing (pro-government) and right-wing (pro-American) factions. In later years there would even be a claim it was crafted by South African super-spy, Craig Williamson, to silence a fervid critique of the apartheid regime. Just why Williamson would take time out from his successful sanctions-busting businesses to knock off someone whose anti-apartheid endeavours had been as fruitful as his efforts to mediate in the Iran-Iraq War was never really explained.[53] When these theories led nowhere, the police fell back on the "lone nut" explanation. Karl Gustaff Christer

Pettersson, an alcoholic and drug addict with a history of violent, anti-social behaviour and petty crime, was arrested and found guilty, though the conviction was later overturned for lack of evidence.[54]

Olaf Palme's overt struggle to make peace had been balanced by his covert fight to sell the tools of war. The most deadly conflict since World War II dragged on until 1988 when the Iranians finally agreed to Iraq's requests for a ceasefire. The United States and its allies were quick to claim credit. Peace was the result, they insisted, of the economic and military-supply squeeze put on Iran. In fact, whatever else might have driven Iran to the bargaining table, it was not lack of access to weaponry, not even the most advanced items in the U.S. arsenal.

Chapter 18

LEADING THEM INTO TEMPTATION

Missiles from Bofors, heavy artillery from Voest-Alpine, explosives from Nobel, artillery shells from Luchaire and mines from Valsella warmed the Ayatollah's heart and scorched the enemy's soul. But by themselves they could not turn the tide. Nor could masses of youngsters chanting Koranic verses as they raced across minefields brandishing plastic keys to Paradise. To move from a war of attrition to a serious offensive, Iran needed to counter the Iraqi advantage in armour and air power. The search for the means began in the chaos of Lebanon.

The Lower Depths

For several years after its civil war began, Lebanon maintained a semblance of normalcy. The financial system continued to function and the currency remained strong. While smuggling, tax evasion and unpaid electricity and phone bills plagued the government, the militias recognized the need for basic public functions. Even the main groups running cigarette smuggling struck a deal with the state tobacco monopoly to split the revenues. But by the early 1980s the PLO and its money had been driven out. Low oil prices caused workers' remittances to plunge. Enormous sums were required to restore public infrastructure, but 80 per cent of import duties were unpaid as goods sneaked in through the pirate ports or the contraband networks in the south. Even the deal over cigarettes broke down — the country was flooded with American brands, while smugglers blew up the factory that made cheap local cigarettes.[1]

While tax evasion crippled revenues, fraud ravaged government spending programs. Racketeers imported expired or fake medicines, or made contraband versions, and sold them to clinics, who demand full reimbursement from the state health service. To keep down the price of bread, the state subsidized flour. Fictitious bakeries then diverted the flour to Syria to sell at market price. Similarly, state-subsidized fuel oil was smuggled to Syria and Israel where prices were three times as high.[2]

The financial situation, too, sharply worsened. As inflation accelerated, the local currency depreciated and the dollar steadily replaced it. Each major military operation led to another flight from the Lebanese lira. With the connivance of bankers, speculators in league with militia groups got huge credits and used them to bet against the lira just before the shooting began. They broadcast exaggerated reports over their radio stations (every major militia group had one) to scare the population into buying dollars. On occasion they sent their own troops onto the streets, firing in the air to drive up the exchange rate. With the discrediting of the lira, the population became divided between those with access to dollars and those locked into the rapidly declining, lira-based domestic sector.[3]

Apart from a brief rash of robberies, the banks had been relatively unscathed during the civil war. Now they were hit from all sides. Their trade and remittance business with the Gulf dropped sharply, while currency instability scared off depositors. Bank officers plundered deposits, using the money to finance speculation abroad. Major banks crashed. The cost of bailouts was loaded onto the central bank, while the perpetrators fled for comfortable retirement in France. The largest victim was Banque el Mashreq, the name given to Intra Bank when it was seized from Yusef Beidas twenty years before.[4]

The economic geography became increasingly cantonized. New paramilitary forces emerged and old ones splintered. Each had its own fiefdom within which it imposed taxes, extorted from businesses and ran rackets. In the past membership in militias had been part-time, and the main reward was from looting. But an increasingly destitute population came to depend on subsidized food, clothing, housing and medical care dispensed by the militia chiefs whose power accordingly increased.[5] Across the country, militias came to serve the financial objectives of racketeers, rather than vice versa, as politics conducted through criminal means gave way to crime conducted behind a façade of political purpose.

That drugs were the best source of quick cash became such an article of faith that in 1987 a Greek-Orthodox archbishop was caught in Rome airport with three kilograms of heroin under his cassock.[6] But drugs were not the only lucrative form of contraband. By the 1980s Lebanon was so awash with weapons that every district had its hawkers of pistols, rifles, sub-machine guns and rocket launchers. Some had dealers specializing in bombs and detonators, such as the popular mercury tilt-switches that could be set off by the movement of a car. Beirut became a global weapons supermarket catering to everyone from gangsters to insurgent groups to intelligence agencies hunting for untraceable weapons.[7]

Another burgeoning racket was maritime fraud. Gangs established fictitious shipping companies that bought old ships cheaply and over-insured them. Working through crooked brokers in Greece, Cyprus or Hong Kong, they advertised for cargo, then diverted it to Lebanon either for the local market or for the transit trade. Afterwards the ship might be scuttled and an insurance claim filed. However, if the ship were sound, the scuttling was metaphorical. With a quick paint job and name change, the ship lived to sail again. Piracy became sufficiently pandemic that the International Maritime Board, which monitors the world shipping business, made a deal with the Lebanese Forces, the most powerful militia group, to stop hijacking and start rescuing cargoes taken by other factions for a fee rumoured to be about 20 per cent of the recovered cargo's value.[8]

Another favourite enterprise was trafficking in luxury cars stolen from Europe and North America. Bringing them by road was risky — too many borders to cross. Better by sea. At the pirate ports, cars were assessed import duty proportional to their internationally recognized second-hand value. Some were chopped up for parts. Most were sold intact with serial numbers changed. The more sophisticated gangs contacted European police to report serial numbers they planned to use to make sure they did not correspond to those on a hot list. With a new paint job and paperwork, many were resold abroad, even in the countries from which they had been originally stolen.[9]

Another of the emerging industries achieved particular notoriety. In a little over a decade, some 14,000 people were kidnapped and another 17,000 just vanished.[10] Originally, victims were almost always of a different religious or political persuasion, and kidnappers frequently murdered them. But during the 1980s the dominant motive became ransom. The prime targets in West Beirut were well-to-do businessmen no matter what religious faith or political creed, and foreign nationals.[11] Most kidnappings were carried out by radical Shi'a groups. Though proclaiming solidarity with Iran in its struggle against various Satans — the United States, France, Israel or even the U.S.S.R. depending on whim and opportunity — the gangs operated independently and had different, rapidly changing demands. Hence securing the release of hostages was no simple task.

France, whose citizens were at first the most popular targets, entered a series of complex deals to free hostages. Often Iran acted as intermediary. However, some deals were apparently brokered by Munzer el-Qassar in hope of a pardon for an eight-year sentence in absentia for terrorism, gun-running and drug trafficking.[12] Typically the kidnappers walked off with cash and/or pledges for France to moderate its support of Maronite militias. Iran's rewards took various forms. France clamped down on Iranian exile opposition groups, repaid debts owed Iran since the Shah's days, abolished a short-lived oil embargo against Iran, cut back arms sales to Iraq, and allowed the covert flow of French arms to Iran.[13] The French negotiations set a precedent the United States would attempt to emulate a short time later.

American targets were even more popular than French. All Americans were assumed to be rich. Victimizing Americans was seen as a way to repay the United States for its support of Israel. And when the U.S. sent the Marines into Lebanon and bombarded Muslim militia forces to support the Phalangist government, it became a de facto partisan in Lebanon's civil conflict, inviting retaliation. Most American victims were ordinary civilians: missionaries, university professors or reporters. But when a pro-Iranian group grabbed William Buckley, the act sent shock waves through the U.S. intelligence establishment. Buckley was not merely the CIA's Beirut station chief, but the former point man for American aid to the Afghan mujahideen. Futile efforts to rescue Buckley led the United States directly into the notorious Iran-contra scandal.

Citizen Khashoggi

A strange alliance formed to advocate the notion that the United States could use the sale of high-tech weapons to Iran to free American hostages in Lebanon. One participant was Yaacov Nimrodi, formerly Mossad liaison with and military attaché to the Israeli embassy in Iran. When Nimrodi left his official duties, the Shah rewarded him for training the SAVAK secret police by letting him get rich in the arms trade. With the fall of the Shah, Nimrodi decamped, leaving several millions in investments behind him. In his subsequent career, Nimrodi joined what Israeli tax officials call Commando 181, so-called because its members remain out of the country for more than 180 days a year to gain a tax exemption. He set up shop in London near the Iranian procurement mission to run two types of businesses. One was smuggling Israeli goods into Arab countries in violation of the Arab League Boycott. The second was intermediating the movement of Israeli weapons to Iran.[14]

Iran had turned to Nimrodi early in the hostilities. When Iraq offered an armistice in 1980, the Iranians seriously considered it, until Nimrodi assured them that weapons to beat back the Iraqi assault would be forthcoming. True to his word, in 1981 he brokered a deal for $135 million worth of missiles and ammunition. Exported from Rotterdam with a false bill of lading, they proved crucial when the Iranians broke the Iraqi siege of the oil port of Abadan, then started pressing the invaders back towards the border.[15]

In 1984 Nimrodi and another arms dealer, Al Schwimmer, the man most responsible for smuggling U.S. war-surplus planes into Palestine during the 1940s, linked up with a former SAVAK agent turned arms supplier named Manuchehr Ghorbanifar.[16] At the time an Iranian advance on Basra was blocked by Iraq's armour and aircraft superiority. Hence the Iranians wanted American TOW anti-tank and HAWK anti-aircraft missiles. But Israel was loath to run down its supplies without guarantees the United States would replace them. To win U.S. cooperation, Israel dangled the bait of American hostages, particularly William Buckley.[17] When the Reagan administration finally agreed, the only problem was money. The Iranians refused to pay before weapons arrived, while the Israelis refused to ship before payment was received. To bridge the gap, the architects of the scheme called on an ebullient Saudi influence-peddler fallen on hard times.[18]

Initially, Adnan Khashoggi had been just another commercial agent for foreign firms trying to understand the mysteries of business in the desert kingdom. Then his star began to rise. In the early 1960s a civil war in neighbouring Yemen pitted Saudi-backed royalists against radical republicans supported by Egypt's Gamel Abd el-Nasir. Khashoggi was delegated to sneak arms to the royalists without leaving a trail traceable to the House of Saud. Mission accomplished, Khashoggi was well positioned when, in the late 1960s and early 1970s, the United States began a big drive to sell arms. Major firms appointed him as their Saudi agent. Even Lockheed added Khashoggi to the list of impecunious monarchs, war criminals and career gangsters hired to peddle its wares around the world.

Saudi arms deals were even more of a honey pot than those in Iran. In the Shah's Iran, the arms acquisition program generated commissions and kickbacks as an incidental byproduct. In Saudi Arabia commissions and kickbacks were the point of the exercise, and the equipment little more than a pretext.

Public sector purchasing systems in much of the world work by agents for both seller and buyer collecting commissions and agreeing on how much to kick back to influential persons. In Saudi Arabia there was also inevitably at least one fixer in alliance with a powerful prince to square away. But there were also skimmers, princes with even more power, to share in and sometimes inflate the take. The intervention of a skimmer in a 1980s deal for nuclear, bacteriological and chemical warfare suits, for example, led to the contracted number being raised from 20,000 to 1 million, enough to suit each Saudi soldier ten times, at a total cost of $450 million. The overall result was less an air force, army and navy than huge undermanned installations, parks of trucks with no drivers, far more arms systems than men capable of operating them, and incompatible weapons platforms.[19]

During the 1970s Adnan Khashoggi was the linchpin for many of the fattest deals. He was soon a citizen of the world. He owned banks in California and South Korea, plantations in Brazil and Malaysia, a Utah industrial park, a Kenyan ranch and much more.[20] However, he spent as fast as he earned. His twelve homes, one hundred Mercedes-Benzes, three planes and $76-million yacht cost about $250,000 a day to maintain. And not all of his business ventures were great successes. A plan for mass tourism in the Seychelles was aborted when René Albert's coup ousted Khashoggi's friend, James Mancham. Equally unsuccessful was a scheme in Egypt in which he and a group of Canadian promoters were to turn the area around the Pyramids into a glitzy casino-and-hotel complex. Although enthusiastically supported by Egyptian president Anwar el-Sadat, whose son-in-law was to secure the construction contracts, the outrage of those sensitive to Egyptian history caused even the normally docile Egyptian Parliament to object.[21]

During the 1980s, Khashoggi fell on hard times. The decline in oil prices hit his Saudi businesses hard, while factions in the Saudi ruling family found his prodigal lifestyle increasingly out of line with the image of Islamic asceticism they projected in public and grossly violated in private. Revelations in the Israeli press that Khashoggi had been partners with Yaacov Nimrodi in busting the Arab League Boycott probably did not help. When Saudi Arabia led other Arab states to protest Zaire's establishment of diplomatic relations with Israel by cutting off investment in Zaire's mineral wealth, Khashoggi tried to sneak in the back door — and got caught. A grand scheme for taking control of the Sudan's huge and virtually untouched natural resources earned him a denunciation by rebel forces fighting to win independence for the resource-rich south. Then came a military coup in Khartoum, which ousted the head of state whom Khashoggi had in his pocket, and the new government cancelled Khashoggi's mineral concessions.[22] The final disaster came when Khashoggi was successfully manoeuvred out of his share of commissions in the "deal of the century."

After the Iranian revolution, a fearful Saudi royal family had to make a show of beefing up the military, more to persuade its own population that the regime was prepared to defend itself than to deter a serious aggressor. It would not risk stiffening the army, a breeding ground of religious and secular opposition. The alternative was to modernize the air force, which had been so thoroughly purged of potential troublemakers that most of its senior personnel were members of the extended royal family or of tribes whose loyalties were certain. When the word got out, squadrons of hustlers flew into the country. The competition narrowed to three: the United States, France and Britain. At first most bets were on the United States, to whose every wish the Saudi regime was normally obedient. But the Israel lobby in Congress objected, successfully, to such a major sale of modern American arms to Saudi Arabia.[23] The contest then came down to British Aerospace versus France's Dassault Aviation. At the beginning, Adnan Khashoggi had signed on with the British. However, when he heard that the Saudi Air Force favoured Dassault's product, he deserted to the French camp just when it was running into serious problems.

Running the British campaign was the "Savoy Mafia," a group of arms brokers, veteran intelligence officers and bankers specializing in arms deals who gathered in a suite in the Savoy Hotel to talk weapons. Among their recruits was a thrice-failed accountant named Mark Thatcher who had given up his youthful ambitions as a racing driver for a mature vocation as a defence industry procurer. Meanwhile his mother, Maggie, lobbied the Saudis and talked Ronald Reagan into doing likewise. Despite technical indicators favouring the French, the British clinched the deal. The $30-billion contract (carrying the Orwellian name, El-Yamamah — the dove) for top-of-the-line fighter jets, attack helicopters, minesweepers and two huge military bases vaulted Britain to the position of the world's number two arms supplier.[24] The planes, choppers and ships were soon rolling one way while the money flowed back the other, literally by the barrelful.

When oil revenues were abundant, Saudi Arabia had paid cash. But by the 1980s, barter had become more common. Because oil-for-arms deals were secret, they provided a means for members of the royal family to cash in while everyone else was told to tighten their belts. They were also a neat way to bust OPEC quotas.[25] To pay for the El-Yamamah deal, the Saudi government allocated oil to BP and Shell; the oil companies placed the proceeds in a special account administered by the British Ministry of Defence; ministry officials dished out money to British Aerospace as the contract proceeded; and British Aerospace covered its own costs, paid off other contractors and transferred money to brokers and dealers, fixers and skimmers. Mark Thatcher pocketed £12 million.[26] While commissions for the main European participants were washed through Liechtenstein, those destined for Saudi principals, far greater in amount, had to be handled more carefully. Some were paid directly into secret foreign bank accounts. Some were paid by awarding "subcontracts" for non-existent work to Saudis. Everyone exited smiling — with one exception. Cut out of the El-Yamamah action and with his enterprises around the world bleeding red ink, Adnan Khashoggi's financial desperation got him embroiled in the Iran-contra affair a short time later.

Cutting a Deal

In the initial stages the arms-for-hostages deal seemed straightforward. The United States wanted to extricate American kidnap victims, starting with William Buckley (who died of heart disease before he could be sprung), while the Israelis sought to sell U.S. arms to Iran. The only complication had been finding the bridge-money. Israel demanded payment in advance, Iran would pay only on delivery, and the two sides to a deal that had to be wrapped in many layers of cover could hardly ask a commercial bank to cover the gap with a letter of credit. That was where Khashoggi entered the picture. He deposited money for TOW missiles in a Swiss account controlled by Ghorbanifar, taking as security post-dated cheques for the sum borrowed plus a 20 per cent commission. Ghorbanifar transferred the money to an Israeli Ministry of Defence Swiss account managed by Nimrodi. The weapons were then released. Al Schwimmer applied his proven talents in the quick freight business by having a Belgium-based air freight company with the interesting name International Air Tours of Nigeria haul the missiles to Iran. When they arrived, the Iranians wired payment to Ghorbanifar's account. And Khashoggi cashed his cheques through his account at the Monaco subsidiary of BCCI. Since Israel charged $6,000 per missile while Iran paid $12,000 a unit, there were plenty of profits — to be shared by participants, to pay kickbacks to Iranian officials and, perhaps, to contribute to an Israeli intelligence black treasury. When the first load was followed by the release of one American hostage, the U.S. administration took it as confirmation the Iranians controlled the Lebanese militias. None of the other participants were inclined to disabuse them.

A few months later the team tried it again, this time with HAWK anti-aircraft missiles. Nimrodi and Schwimmer agreed to pay Israel $140,000 for each missile. They would sell them to Ghorbanifar for $225,000 each. He would charge Iran $300,000 a unit. So pleased had the Iranians been with the first deal, this time they made an advance payment into Ghorbanifar's account of $24 million for eighty HAWK missiles plus an extra $20 million towards future shipments, obviating the need for Khashoggi's bridge financing. But the first shipment of eighteen missiles was a disaster from stem to stern.

To start with, the HAWK missiles were too long for standard cargo airplanes, and, once freight companies with 747s learned of the nature and destination of the cargo, they demanded a $50-million security deposit for each plane. Israel refused. At that point the CIA offered the use of a cargo plane from St. Lucia Airways, which it secretly owned, to carry "oil drilling equipment" from Israel to Iran. The decision to use a CIA proprietary line represented a serious breach of security. It was the first time a U.S. government agency had got directly involved in the supply chain.

Even then the problems had not ended. When the Iranians inspected the HAWKs, they discovered that the Israelis had unloaded on them old models. Worse, they bore Star of David insignia. The Iranians demanded their money back. In reaction, security was further compromised. Instead of Israel supplying the weapons, then having the United States replace them, the U.S. decided to sell directly out of its own stocks, using Richard Secord, chief supplier of arms to the contras, as its agent, and employing Israel only as the transit point.

When the next missile deal came round, the Iranians again insisted that payment occur only on delivery; now it was the U.S. government that refused to release missiles unless paid in advance. Once again Khashoggi stepped into the breach. He deposited $10 million in Ghorbanifar's Swiss account. The Department of Defence then sold 1,000 TOW missiles to the CIA for $3.7 million; the CIA, working through Richard Secord, sold them to Ghorbanifar for $10 million. Ghorbanifar sold them to Iran for $12 million. As soon as the money was paid, Khashoggi retrieved his loan plus the usual 20 per cent for interest, expenses and commission. This new arrangement created a direct link between the United States and Iran. It also meant a number of people, Nimrodi and Schwimmer notably among them, were cut out. And it left Richard Secord sitting on $6.3 million in profit. In Washington, nimble wits were busy calculating the interesting things to which some of those funds could be applied. One of the things to which their imaginations turned was the hole in the contra treasury caused by the congressional ban.

Soon a new deal for HAWKs was in the works. But Adnan Khashoggi had trouble working his usual magic. All over the world his creditors were pressing him. In the ultimate indignity, a London casino sued over a $2-million bounced cheque.[27] According to a disgruntled former aide, Khashoggi considered raising the money from his chums, Ferdinand and Imelda Marcos. After the former first family of the Philippines had beaten an undignified retreat, leaving behind several thousand pairs of Imelda's shoes and accusations that they had looted billions from the treasury, they obtained Khashoggi's assistance in hiding assets from the new government. One of his plans, apparently, was to pose as the real owner of their holdings of real estate and old-master paintings, liquidate them and hide the cash in various tax havens, while borrowing from the Marcos family nest egg enough funds to finance the HAWK shipment.[28] However, that scheme, too, came to naught. Finally, in desperation, Khashoggi borrowed the necessary bridge-money from two Canadian financiers who demanded a mortgage on his best remaining American properties. If the HAWK anti-aircraft missile deal misfired, Khashoggi could be shot down in flames.

By then the U.S. sponsors had even more grandiose objectives, which required direct negotiations with Iran. For these plans to work, the Iranians had to need the Americans as much as the Americans needed them. While the American team was putting together a new HAWK shipment, others, apparently with the backing of Israeli military intelligence, were busy with a rival $2-billion arms package that would include two batteries of HAWKs, 3,780 TOWs, 18 F-4s, 46 Skyhawks, heavy artillery, Hercules transport planes and much more. Fortunately for the U.S.-sponsored arms deal, this potentially dangerous competitor had already been compromised by a fifth column.

A CIA informant since the mid-1970s, Cyrus Hashemi had fled Iran after the fall of the Shah, then signed on with the new regime as a weapons supplier. In 1984 he earned a criminal indictment for smuggling embargoed communications equipment out of the United States, though it was never clear if the indictment was genuine, or just a ploy to deepen his cover. Despite the seriousness of the allegations, he was let out on $100,000 bail, given back his passport and permitted to jet off to London where he had businesses to which to attend. One of them was the World Trade Group, a company he set up with Adnan Khashoggi and Roy Furmark, an American oil broker and chum of William Casey, to buy oil from and sell commodities, including weapons, to Iran. Abandoned by Khashoggi as soon as the Saudi procurer sniffed out better prospects elsewhere, Hashemi found alternatives. Some old business associates approached him for help in setting up mega-deals with Iran. He happily agreed, then sneaked off to the New York attorney's office to offer his services as an informant.[29]

To his would-be associates, Hashemi held out irresistible bait. Iran, he claimed, had $500 million in a New York bank just waiting to be spent on arms. Iran had also committed to Hashemi 100,000 barrels of oil a day to pay for even more weapons. Among the big fish ready to snap was General Haim Bar-Am, former deputy commander of the Israeli forces in Lebanon. Israel later insisted that the operation was strictly the work of "freelancers." Perhaps so. But one of the conversations Hashemi secretly taped caught General Bar-Am saying that the deal would provide for Iran a full armoured division, and that "we are simply going to take it out from our division, put in on the boat, send it over. . . . You can put your people inside and go to the war."[30] Israel would certainly seem to be the promised land for "private" arms dealers.

The mass arrest was a public relations coup, well appreciated by the head of U.S. Customs who publicly denounced a conspiracy of "brokers of death who organized a terrorist flea market." Other U.S. officials, notably in the Reagan White House, must have been equally delighted. The month after the sting smashed the Israeli ring, sending to Iran a message that the United States could seriously interfere with the Iranian weapons supply line, a high-ranking U.S. delegation was on a St. Lucia Airways plane to Teheran.

There were many things on the agenda for discussion. One was Nicaragua. This time the plan was for more than just to use profits from arms sales to aid the contras. Iran supplied oil to Nicaragua on soft terms, and the United States hoped to persuade Iran to cut off the supply. Furthermore, weapons sales had the potential to secure Iran's help on another, much more important Cold War front.

The original Marxist government in Afghanistan had been run by rigid Stalinists who had alienated traditional landlords by land reform and traditional clerics by social emancipation of women. In preparation for pulling Soviet troops out of Afghanistan, the Kremlin had parachuted in as head of state Mohammed Najibullah, former chief of the Afghan security services. He purged the government of orthodox Marxists, called a halt to land reform and wooed the religious establishment. Hailing from the border tribes through which the arms pipeline from Pakistan ran, Najibullah knew how to manipulate clan alliances through nepotism, bribery and bullets. For the first time, the United States began to fret that the flow of arms would be hampered, and that the war would tilt in favour of the Afghan government. That fear sent the United States off to persuade Iran to take a more active role in Afghanistan. Iran had close relations with certain Afghan mujahideen factions that operated too far from Pakistan to be supplied directly by the U.S. and who, to date, had taken little part in the war. Therefore the U.S. delegation planned to request that Iran pass on 20 per cent of the U.S.-supplied missiles to those groups.[31]

The American team arrived bearing gifts — a Reagan-autographed Bible, two Colt pistols, a chocolate cake and a verse from the *Qur'an*. The choices accurately reflected the team's sensitivity to and understanding of the Middle East. Defacing a Holy Book (including the Bible) is, to Muslims, a sacrilegious act. Colt revolvers arriving in conjunction with the Bible baffled the Iranians, who had always been taught that Jesus Christ (whom Muslims revere as a prophet) preached non-violence. The cake was presented during the month of Ramadan when good Muslims fast from dawn to dusk. And the Koranic verse chosen by the U.S. administration with very tight military and political relations with Israel, denounced Jews for calling themselves the chosen people. While the gifts convinced the Iranians that Reagan and his officials were stupid, the fact that the plane arrived minus most of the promised HAWK missile parts probably convinced them they were also deceitful.[32] Furthermore, the Iranians had got hold of a Pentagon price list and discovered the huge overcharges. In a fury, they refused to pay for what had arrived. That left Khashoggi in the lurch, trying to hold off his creditors while sending emissaries to threaten William Casey that the whistle would be blown if the U.S. government did not cover the bill.

Still, the Americans did not give up. To set the stage for further deals, they began pressuring the Iraqis to unleash their hitherto hesitant air force and to strike oil installations deep inside Iran.[33] At the same time, they reopened negotiations with Iran. The Iranians responded with a new shopping list. The CIA sold missiles to Secord's company for $3,469 each and he resold them to the Iranians for $7,200. But each time a U.S. hostage was released, at least one more was grabbed, often by another previously unknown faction with completely new demands, leaving the Americans convinced that they were victims of an Iranian double-cross.

With so many players entering and exiting, the intermingling of personnel, the confusion of bank accounts and the mixing together of covert operations around each of which there should have been a firewall, leaks were inevitable. By the autumn of 1986, they had started to assume the epic proportions that had sent Noah fleeing to his ark. The administration was trebly embarrassed. It had been caught subverting the congressional ban on aid to the contras, contravening its avowed policy of never negotiating with terrorists over hostages, and violating the very arms embargo it tried so hard to get its allies to respect. It also found its efforts to stop private arms initiatives seriously compromised. That the U.S. government was openly admitting to underground traffic provided those accused in more than a dozen pending cases with a virtually iron-clad defence.

First to fall was the rap against the "brokers of death." When the defendants insisted that they had been sure their scheme had U.S. government backing, the only hope for the prosecution was Cyrus Hashemi's rebuttal. But shortly before the trial could get under way, he contracted an odd form of cancer that killed him within a week of diagnosis.[34] Some claimed that he was poisoned by "a certain American government agency" because he knew too much. Others were more inclined to give epidemiological credit to Iran's intelligence service, angry over his betrayal in the "broker of death" case.[35] However, Iran also had reason to be grateful to Hashemi. For his intervention in a quite different set of intrigues may have helped them finally score a $325-million victory in a long dispute with one of the U.S.'s leading oil companies.

Ashland to Ashland, Bust to Bust

By the time of the Iranian revolution, Ashland Oil had grown from a small regional refinery into the largest independent in the United States. It had help. In 1975, under pressure from the Securities and Exchange Commission, the CIA admitted to using Ashland as a conduit for money to support foreign covert operations. At the same time Ashland was found guilty of pumping $700,000 illegally into various election campaigns, including both of Richard Nixon's presidential runs, and it faced a scandal over bribe money piped to politicians in Gabon.[36] Still, the oil refining business was prosperous — until 1979 when the U.S. embargo on Iran cost Ashland 25 per cent of its crude supply. There were compensations — Ashland patriotically decided not to pay Iran $283 million owed for its last seven tanker-loads. However Ashland had to search for alternatives sources. One reputedly under consideration was Newfoundland, where Ashland eyed a defunct refinery project with an option on offshore oil deposits. The problem was that others also coveted the refinery, including its founder.

John Shaheen, a Lebanese-American and OSS veteran whose job had been monitoring Axis oil flows, emerged from World War II convinced that the West had to defend its energy lifeline. His plan involved creating a network of oil depots and refineries in places relatively safe from enemy (i.e., Soviet) action. Only two were ever built. One was in Puerto Rico and the other in the Newfoundland fishing village of Come-By-Chance.[37] Newfoundland was on the short ocean passage from northern Europe to North America. It was a good location for large tankers to dump their oil, leaving smaller ones to haul refined products to North American markets. Furthermore, there was geological evidence of major offshore oil deposits. There were substantial risks, though, and whoever was going to bear them, it would not be John Shaheen. During the 1960s Shaheen had got an ambitious lawyer named Richard M. Nixon to draft plans for a deal based on a simple cost-benefit calculation: Newfoundland would bear the costs and Shaheen would collect the benefits. To build the complex, Newfoundland would establish a state-run company capitalized with 2,000 shares, each with a par value of $1. If all went well, John Shaheen would have the right to buy those shares at par — in short, he would acquire the entire complex, on which the government finally spent $155 million, for $2,000. When Newfoundland accepted his scheme, Shaheen's reaction was characteristically frank: "I thought they were out of their tree."[38]

More charitably, Newfoundland was at that point run by a long-serving premier who had manoeuvred the impoverished British colony into Canada after World War II in the hope that union would bring prosperity. It did not. The only other plan of which the premier could conceive was a massive giveaway of the island's resource wealth to any carpet-merchant who happened by. In 1970 the province guaranteed the refinery project's construction debts, granted it an option on the first 100,000 barrels a day once offshore oil started to flow, and threw in a vast tract of timberland. After the terms became public, newspapers were singularly unflattering — until Shaheen slapped each that dared be critical with massive lawsuits. In Newfoundland cabinet ministers resigned in protest and the opposition howled in outrage. But when the government changed in 1972, the new premier found himself jetted around by Shaheen to high-profile public functions and attending the Liverpool launch of a new ship in the Shaheen fleet that proudly bore the premier's name. When the new premier's enthusiasm raised eyebrows back home, he explained that his previous concerns as opposition chief had never been the deal per se but just making sure Newfoundland got the best from it.

In 1973 the first part of the complex had a spectacular opening, highlighted by a visit from the *Queen Elizabeth II* luxury liner, which discharged 1,000 guests at a $23-million special dock paid for by the Canadian federal government. Despite that promising start, cost overruns accelerated, geological obstacles kept offshore oil from flowing, the only thing passing through the refinery was taxpayer subsidies, and a paper mill promised by Shaheen continued to exist only on paper. By 1976 the operation was bankrupt.

Efforts were made to resuscitate it. In 1977 the Canadian federal government tried and failed to coax the Shah of Iran into buying the derelict refinery. Two years later a company called First Arabian Corporation put in a bid.

Its general manager, Roger Tamraz, was the man on whom the Lebanese government had bestowed responsibility for Intra Bank in the wake of the 1966 crash. He was still in charge when its successor, Banque el Mashreq, was plundered into insolvency by insiders twenty years later. The two main shareholders of First Arabian were rich Saudis, one of whom, Kamel Adham, had been founder of the Saudi intelligence service and the CIA's main liaison throughout the Middle East, and both of whom would subsequently achieve notoriety as frontmen for Agha Hasan Abedi in the BCCI scandal. Their bid for a bankrupt refinery in the backwoods of Newfoundland looked a little odd. John Shaheen thought he found the explanation: First Arabian was a stand-in for Ashland, whose somewhat soiled reputation inclined it to keep its own name out of the scenario until the deal was done.

But in the end, First Arabian's bid was turned down. So too was a competing offer by John Shaheen. And the complex passed into the hands of Petro-Canada, the state-owned oil corporation. After a few years in mothballs, the refinery was put back on the auction block by PetroCanada. One of those bidding was a Haifa firm fronting for the Israeli government, still searching for oil security. Another was John Shaheen. His hopes for a last-ditch comeback died along with him a few months later — but not before his former right-hand man at Come-By-Chance, New York oil broker Roy Furmark, had introduced him to Cyrus Hashemi. Hashemi told Shaheen about his grand schemes for oil deals with Iran and prevailed on Shaheen to carry a proposal for an arms-for-hostages swap to his old OSS buddy, William Casey.

While all this was happening, Ashland was still searching for alternative sources of oil. After Newfoundland, it tried Oman, where it landed itself in another scandal over pay-offs to an adviser to the Sultan. In the aftermath, the company tried to exorcise the past by firing Orin Atkins, the CEO who had presided over its fortunes and misfortunes for two decades. Atkins was not one to take that sitting down, unless it was in a back room, plotting revenge. But he accepted the company's offer to serve as a consultant and bided his time, watching its difficulties mount. Ashland was found guilty of bid-rigging on a construction job. Two executives fired for refusing to participate in covering up the Oman scandal collected $25 million for wrongful dismissal. The SEC again accused it of illegal payments abroad. A storage tank burst, dumping 500,000 gallons of diesel oil into a river. And the Iranians launched a $500-million lawsuit.

During his work as a consultant, Atkins continued to have access to company documents. The year after he was fired, he sent his good friend, Roy Furmark, to meet lawyers for the National Iranian Oil Company in Cyrus

Hashemi's London office. He offered information in exchange for 20 per cent of whatever the Iranians recovered from Ashland. The lawyers were interested. Equally interested was the American Justice Department, tipped off by a private investigator that Ashland had put on its ex-CEO's tail. When Furmark was arrested in 1988, he did the honourable thing by turning informant and agreeing to trap Atkins — who in turn was arrested. He pleaded guilty the next year. Whether because of the purloined documents or simply because the rip-off had been so blatant, Ashland buckled. It agreed to pay $325 million of the $500 million in costs, interest and damages the Iranians were seeking. The money was sorely needed. For by that point Iran's fortunes of oil were going as badly as its fortunes of war.[39]

Chapter 19

THE SECOND FRONT

At the start of the Iran-Iraq War, former U.S. Secretary of State Henry Kissinger defined an ideal American policy — helping both sides lose. Until other objectives (supplying the contras and turning up the heat in Afghanistan) interfered, the United States left to Israel the job of supplying Iran with enough American weaponry to stop the Iraqi assault. When the tide turned, the job of keeping Iraq from being overwhelmed was more complex. Saudi Arabia and Jordan were given the nod to selectively divert U.S.-supplied arms. But since Iraq relied mainly on Soviet and French systems, most American aid took indirect forms.[1]

Pipe Dreams
Initially Iraq was at a profound economic disadvantage. It is almost landlocked. Its oil was exported by sea via a very narrow strip of coastline where the Shatt el-Arab meets the Persian Gulf, or by pipeline across Syria to the Mediterranean. Early in the war, the Iranians blocked the first and Syria, allied with Iran, shut down the second. When Saudi Arabia and Kuwait started shipping their own oil and crediting the money to Iraq, Iran used its Chinese Silkworm missiles to attack Kuwaiti oil facilities and departing tankers. Iraqi planes struck back, damaging pumping facilities on Kharg Island and some tankers carrying Iranian oil. However, with its long coastline and series of harbours, Iran was much less vulnerable.[2]

Iraq exhausted its foreign exchange reserves, borrowed heavily from Saudi Arabia and Kuwait, and then began pushing alternative pipelines. One passed through Turkey. A second linked to existing lines through Saudi Arabia. Running the show in Saudi Arabia was Khaled Ben Mahfouz, a senior (soon-to-be-indicted) shareholder in BCCI. Ben Mahfouz was no stranger to banking; his family controlled the National Commercial Bank, the institution through which the Saudi royal family ran its more discreet business deals, including funds for the Afghan mujahideen. Ben Mahfouz and his Saudi partners sold Iraqi oil and collected a commission. Then they used the money to buy weapons on the world market that they resold to Iraq for another fat mark-up. The Iraqis were furious at the double rip-off, but had no option other than to accept the arrangement — until Bechtel Corporation came along. Bechtel proposed building another pipeline through Jordan to the port of Aqabah. That would free the Iraqis from the Saudi grasp. The route had another advantage. Most Iraqi imports were already shipped to a sealed-off part of Aqabah controlled by Iraqi Customs, then trucked to Iraq. The downside was that a pipeline so close to the Israeli border would be a sitting target. Iraq hesitated.

But Bechtel had "friends in high places."[3] Two of its former senior officers sat in the Reagan administration as Secretary of State and Secretary of Defense. In 1984 the United States obtained from Israeli prime minister Shimon Peres verbal assurances that Israel would not attack Bechtel's pipeline. For Iraq, these kind words were not enough. So in 1985 Bechtel found a partner for the proposed venture, Bruce Rappaport, a Swiss-based businessman who owned oil wells, tankers and refineries around the world, as well as banks in useful places like Switzerland, and who was tight with Israeli intelligence.[4] Rappaport was to get rights to market about $200 million per annum of Iraqi oil coming through the Bechtel pipeline provided he could deliver an Israeli agreement to let the oil flow unmolested. Israel had a powerful incentive to play along.

Under the Camp David peace accords, Israel had to withdraw from Sinai. Egypt had guaranteed unrestricted passage through the Suez Canal for tankers bound for Israel and agreed to sell oil to Israel on the same terms as to other customers, while the United States pledged that Israel would never want for oil. Still, the loss of the Sinai wells haunted Israeli leaders, causing several, including Yitzhak Shamir, to oppose the treaty. The ink was barely dry when the Iranian revolution underlined Israel's oil vulnerability. Therefore an opportunity to ensure supplies from the very country that had led the anti-Israel economic war in 1948 by cutting off oil formerly provided to Palestine seemed too rich to pass up. For a guaranteed ten-year supply of cut-rate oil, worth $70 million a year (and, allegedly, a hefty one-time kickback to his

Labour Party), Prime Minister Shimon Peres was willing to issue a formal letter of assurance that Israel would refrain from bombing the pipeline.[5] It was still not enough. Jordan and Iraq, publicly staunch supporters of the Arab League Boycott, demanded a $400-million irrevocable letter of credit from Israel. Matters seemed deadlocked. So Rappaport laid out $150,000 to hire a man already familiar with Washington back rooms.

Full Metal Fabricators

E. Robert Wallach, former classmate of and personal lawyer to Reagan's attorney-general, Edwin Meese, had already built a reputation for winning product liability cases on behalf of injured clients, then walking off with most of the money, when Washington beckoned. There his first client was not Bechtel, but WedTech Corporation.[6] And WedTech's objectives were not to build an Iraqi pipeline to bypass the Persian Gulf, but to cash in on a Pentagon project to defend the West's oil lifeline through it.

WedTech began as a little metal-working shop in the South Bronx, an area heavily burned out by landlords seeking to evict tenants and defraud insurance companies. An equal partnership of a Puerto Rican born-again-Christian and a Romanian veteran of the Stern Gang, WedTech got its first big break by falsifying the bookwork to make it appear to qualify for a program, slapped together after race riots in the 1960s, setting aside federal contracts for minority-owned businesses. In 1975, on receiving their first small military contract, the partners began learning what business schools neglect to teach. They set up a secret bank account to collect kickbacks from suppliers and to pay bribes to Teamsters' officials to guarantee labour peace, then put on their payroll the local congressman, a former cop turned latter-day robber who was eventually convicted of bribery and extortion. They were ready for serious action when Ronald Reagan came to power and the Pentagon spending spree began.

But as outsiders, they were unable to breach the Pentagon walls. So they hired a former commanding officer of the New York National Guard; his duties involved keeping two wives, earning a consulting fee and limousine from *Penthouse* for ensuring that militia stores had enough copies to meet any military emergency, running a loan-sharking operation among lower ranking officers, and exempting himself from taxes on his WedTech lobbying fees. But that did not help.[7] Convinced that some Pentagon official had it in for them, the WedTech partners engaged a private detective to pinpoint the individual and dig up some dirt to change his mind. Instead, what that detective recommended was E. Robert Wallach. WedTech eventually paid Wallach a total of $1.3 million plus a block of stock to carry its message straight to the White

House. By taking local people off welfare through private sector initiative, WedTech claimed it could provide a working example of the Reaganite creed, and give the administration something to combat rude insinuations about its lack of concern for visible minorities who usually voted Democrat. Meese's chief deputy, who later left government to become WedTech's Washington representative, browbeat Pentagon officials on WedTech's behalf. In 1982 it was granted without competitive bidding a contract for electrical pumps at double what the army wanted to pay, received a $3-million grant from the Small Business Administration despite a rule normally restricting such grants to $100,000, and $6 million in loans.[8]

Despite long delays in delivering the engines and repeated cash crunches (solved by means ranging from accounting fraud to borrowing from loan sharks), WedTech went from success to success. One contract followed another, without the nuisance of bidding. One functionary after another was recruited through cash or stock to sing praises and sign approvals, or be shunted aside. Top Wall Street lawyers and investment bankers collaborated to take the company public. Everyone found it expedient to ignore the fact that public companies did not legally qualify under the set-aside program. After auditors discovered fraud in billing methods, the problem was resolved by having the auditors join WedTech as directors and shareholders. Then, as proof the firm had hit the big leagues, WedTech decided to issue junk bonds. But to reassure would-be buyers it could pay the interest on the paper, Wed-Tech needed a juicy new contract.

One objective of the Reagan build-up was to greatly enhance the Rapid Deployment Force, a special combined-services unit established in the Carter era to move quickly to trouble spots like the Persian Gulf. That force was deemed more essential after the Red Army rolled into Afghanistan. From that location it was supposedly poised to march across hundreds of miles of inhospitable desert and mountain through the world's fiercest guerrilla fighters to block the West's oil supply at the Straits of Hormuz. One necessary component of the plan was a set of pontoon-causeways to ferry supplies to troops ashore.[9] That was a tall order, worth perhaps $1 billion. When WedTech tried to sign up, the navy, like the army before it, had serious reservations about the new recruit. But collegial chats between Edwin Meese and the Secretary of Defense, and pay-offs for inside information to a navy official, secured the contract. Then the fun began.

WedTech insiders leased the company one of their own buildings, permitting them to inflate rental costs, then arranged for renovation, opening yet more opportunities for skimming. They found a supplier willing to substitute second-hand for new machinery, billing for the full sum and kicking back part of the overcharge. They needed water frontage. So they bribed a Bronx city official to evict a tenant on a suitable property. Because no one in the firm possessed the expertise to actually build pontoons, they were bled by cost over-runs. These were temporarily staunched by nimble bookkeeping — their accountants invented income from non-existent contracts. Then, to clear the road for a new stock issue, E. Robert Wallach located two professional touts. One was a former globe-trotting encyclopedia salesman turned hot-shot investment adviser who ran Edwin Meese's personal investment portfolio.[10] The second was a self-proclaimed successful gambler and author of several books on how to beat the odds at blackjack — who also knew how to beat the odds on a tax audit by stashing royalties in Switzerland. The stock-puffing operation was so successful that, in the last few months before WedTech went on the scrap heap, insiders dumped $11 million "worth" on an unsuspecting public.

The end result of WedTech's foray into defence contracting was to force the Pentagon to downgrade sharply, albeit quietly, the amphibious landing capabilities of the Rapid Deployment Force.[11] Recipient of $500 million in government contracts, most military, WedTech defrauded hundreds of share-holders, bilked institutions holding its junk bonds of tens of millions, left 1,500 workers unemployed, and led to the criminal indictment of twenty politicians, government officials and company principals. E. Robert Wallach joined their ranks, but not before he had time to press the Aqabah pipeline project on his old school chum's colleagues.[12]

Wallach won over senior administration officials, including CIA chief Casey by promising that the project would at one and the same time help Iraq buy weapons, guarantee oil to Israel and ensure pipeline royalties for the shaky finances of Jordan. For the plan to succeed, someone had to come up with money for the guarantees Iraq and Jordan demanded. The Overseas Private Investment Corporation (OPIC), a government agency that insures foreign investments of American firms, balked at Bechtel's request for $360 million of coverage. With Wallach's lobbying, OPIC proposed a compromise. It would insure the package provided that, if Israel did knock out the pipeline, Bechtel and Rappaport would each kick in $150 million to repay part of what OPIC would have to pay Iraq. When Bechtel and Rappaport refused, Wallach proposed that the Pentagon advance $375 million disguised as additional military aid to Israel, but put the money in an escrow account and use it to repay Iraq should the worst come to pass. Under that scheme, the cost of guaranteeing that Israel did not use U.S. taxpayer-financed weapons to destroy a U.S. government-supported initiative would be covered by the U.S. taxpayer. But

Justice Department lawyers questioned the legality of the arrangement, and the National Security Advisor denounced it as a protection racket. The project died.[13] However, the administration had already found another way to use government insurance agencies to buttress Iraq's finances.

Giving Credit Where It Isn't Due

The United States, almost alone of the world's major powers, has granted its executive branch tools for arbitrarily initiating economic warfare. One of the most potent consists of designating a country uncooperative in efforts to eradicate drug trafficking. That permits the United States to withhold aid to, and suspend trading privileges with, countries of whose political or commercial behaviour it disapproves. An even more flexible tool, since unconstrained either by geography or agronomy, is designating a country supportive of international "terrorism."

Iraq had long been on the unofficial index. One of the reasons given was its close relations with the notorious Abu Nidal. A former money launderer for Fatah, when he broke with Arafat, Iraq gave Abu Nidal all of Fatah's Iraq-based assets: money, weapons, training facilities, a radio station, and more. He reciprocated by pulling off hits for Iraqi intelligence, including an attempted assassination of the Israeli ambassador to Britain in 1982 that provided Israel with a pretext for its Lebanon invasion. And he plied the arms market on Iraq's behalf.

However, Abu Nidal had poor relations with Saddam Hussein. For a few years, Abu Nidal survived because the U.S.S.R., to protest Iraq's invasion of Iran, slapped Iraq with an arms embargo. Abu Nidal's connections in eastern Europe made him a useful alternative source of Soviet-style weapons. Once the Soviet embargo was lifted, his days were numbered. In 1983 he got into trouble over some Iraqi funds missing from a Swiss account and was formally expelled.[14] Quietly welcomed by Libya and Syria, Abu Nidal raised money by extortion from Gulf states and continued to run guns, sometimes to Iraq, and sometimes, in the interests of fairness, to Iran. Most of his arms deals were handled from London where his partners had accounts in BCCI. Through BCCI Abu Nidal tried one of his most intriguing scams. As part of the secret U.S. program to acquire Soviet weaponry, the United States planned to send American weapons to Poland, and a Polish general would send back Soviet equipment. Before shipping himself to the United States in exchange for $1 million, the Polish general would sell the American arms to Abu Nidal, who would resell them in the Middle East.[15]

The departure of Abu Nidal from Iraq provided the pretext for the United States to remove Iraq from the terror-sponsoring list, opening the way for trade credit guarantees. The way they worked, an importer of U.S. goods opened a letter of credit with its banker and sent it to the U.S. exporter who, in turn, lodged the LC with its banker. Once the goods were shipped, the U.S. bank would pay the exporter and present the LC to the importer's bank. U.S. government agencies like the Export-Import Bank and the Commodity Credit Corporation (CCC) guaranteed the U.S. bank against default, permitting it to reduce the fees it charged.

However, lifting Iraq's ban did not change its reputation as a bad credit risk.[16] For a time, the Ex-Im Bank resisted administration pressure. Finally capitulating, it guaranteed $227 million. This was a pittance compared to the Commodity Credit Corporation. By 1991 the CCC offered exporters of American agricultural products to Iraq over $5 billion in guarantees. Among those pleased by the arrangements were American agribusinesses, who found a new market; bankers, who collected trade finance profits virtually without risk; and Iraq, which could divert some of the money earmarked for food imports into military procurement.

For that, Iraq owed thanks to an enterprising banker. In 1984 Chris Drogoul became manager of the Atlanta, Georgia, branch of Banca Nazionale del Lavoro (BNL).[17] The largest of Italy's state-run financial institutions, BNL was more than just a bank. It also provided a venue where members of Italy's principal underworlds — the Mafia, the Freemasons, the secret services and party bagmen — could hobnob. BNL was at the centre of many of Italy's covert arms deals. It issued letters of credit and performance bonds to run Luchaire's artillery shells to Iran. It arranged financing when Valsella Meccanotechnica, already selling mines to Iran, decided to balance the scales by selling some to "Singapore" that ended up in Iraq. BNL was active, too, in financing the sale to Iraq by Agusta, Italy's soon-to-be notorious state-owned aviation firm, of "civilian" helicopters, which Iraq promptly fitted with machine-guns and missiles.[18]

When Drogoul took over, BNL Atlanta was losing money. Encouraged by BNL Rome, which targeted trade financing as a growth sector, Drogoul decided to get in on the CCC action. By the time the dust of scandal settled and the desert storm began, Iraq had one-sixth of all outstanding CCC guarantees, and BNL Atlanta had handled nearly 40 per cent of the Iraqi business. At first their business was conducted in the open. Iraq's foreign trade bank would issue letters of credit for agricultural goods. BNL would accept the LCs and pay the exporters, financing the transaction by borrowing on the New York interbank market. Once Iraq honoured the LCs, BNL would repay the interbank loans. Soon Drogoul had run the Iraqi account up to $600 million. But when Italy and Iraq got into a scrap about overdue payments on military equipment, BNL Rome told Drogoul not to allow the Iraqi balance to exceed $100 million.[19]

Drogoul knew better than to take the ceiling seriously. The more loans he made, the higher the bank's earnings, and the brighter his future. To disguise the extent of interbank borrowing, he began getting more money from local Georgia institutions, so there was no report by the lender to BNL's American head office in New York. He deposited the borrowed funds in his clearing bank, then immediately paid exporters so that the daily balance in the account, the only thing inspectors normally monitored, usually showed zero. Aided by the incompatibility of the computer systems used by Atlanta and New York, he "skipped" the loans — removing them from the books when BNL New York came to inspect, and putting them back when the danger passed.[20]

In principle, CCC credits should have been difficult to abuse. The LC is for a fixed sum; the money is paid into the account of a bona fide U.S. agribusiness firm; and the exporter's bank collects from the Iraqi bank, with the CCC getting involved only if a default occurs. Until political relations between the United States and Iraq broke down, there was no default.[21] The improprieties occurred elsewhere.

The CCC program is supposed to insure only the basic commodity. But Iraq got American firms to swallow freight costs, throw in items that bore no relationship to the contract, and cover after-sales services. The extras were loaded into the price insured by the CCC. Smart operators seem to have imported foreign commodities, then sent them to Iraq posing as American, while qualifying for CCC guarantees that lowered the credit costs. Firms selling goods to Iraq were required to overcharge, then either purchase militarily useful supplies or kick back the extra into a slush fund to be spent elsewhere. When the U.S.S.R. faced a grain shortage and was banned from CCC credits, grain bought from the United States with subsidized credit was swapped by Iraq to the U.S.S.R. for weapons.[22] Emboldened by that success, BNL also began financing grain deals directly for the U.S.S.R., paying exporters and assuming the risks itself, while hiding the loans by booking them (along with fake telexes, faxes and loan documents) as if they were part of credit lines authorized by Rome for major U.S. corporations. BNL was later accused of providing export credits using a CCC guarantee for wheat diverted to Cuba.

Throughout it all, Rome was sufficiently impressed with Drogoul's performance, and his branch's profitability, that it began using BNL Atlanta for a subterfuge of its own. Iraq was so far behind in paying Italian suppliers, there was a danger that, if BNL in Italy agreed to new export finance, old suppliers awaiting payment would sue for the collateral posted for new LCs. Italian firms were told that, even though their deals involved direct export from Italy to Iraq, trade financing should be handled through Atlanta.[23] This encouraged Drogoul in his boldest caper, offering Iraq unsecured lines of direct credit that it could spend without restriction.

To raise the money, Drogoul again turned to the interbank market with the trail hidden in the usual way. To keep inspectors from examining the disbursements, Drogoul shifted from "skipping" (removing then restoring loans to the books) to maintaining a parallel set of "grey books" that he kept stuffed in the trunk of his car. Sometimes Iraq would designate a supplier and Drogoul would issue the appropriate LC. Sometimes the money would be credited to the Central Bank of Iraq, which would transfer funds to third banks in the United States or Europe with instructions to pay particular suppliers.[24]

All of this activity — billions in interbank loans, wire transfers for many millions at a time from the United States to Iraq, thousands of LCs issued against goods that often required export licences, and reams of telexes between Atlanta and Baghdad — was conducted supposedly in total secrecy. It went apparently undetected by the State Department charged with reviewing export licence applications, the CIA monitoring the world arms market, the U.S. Treasury overseeing financial transactions, and the National Security Agency listening in on every electrical and electronic transmission in the world. Nor did anyone in Rome apparently take note, despite the burgeoning business of its newest U.S. branch. Instead, one "rogue banker" in Atlanta was allowed to finance development of the ambitious program of military industrialization that would play a major role in turning the tide of war in Iraq's favour.

Superdollars and Nonsense

Meanwhile, according to a Republican Party task force on terrorism and unconventional warfare, while the United States supported the Iraqi war effort through quiet financial diplomacy, Iran had devised a nasty means to strike back through an especially odious form of covert economic warfare.[25] Although the U.S. $100 bill had long been the prime target for counterfeiters around the world, most of their handiwork had been amateurish. However, the "supernote," first discovered in London in 1989, supposedly could escape the critical scrutiny not just of commercial bank staff trained to detect fakes, but even of the electronic detectors of the U.S. Federal Reserve. It also provided for perhaps the most egregious exercise in "black propaganda" since the tale of the Bulgarian Connection.

The origins of the supernote reputedly lay in the early days of the Lebanese civil war when the Phalangists, short on money and weapons, linked up with Armenian underworld printers to fake U.S. large-denomination notes. While not especially impressive, the results sufficed when Phalangist officials took a few suitcases to Prague to buy Czech weapons. Sometime in the 1980s, Syrian military intelligence took control and requested Iranian aid in upgrading the project. During his last years, the Shah had harboured ambitions for Iran to be not merely the regional military superpower but also its banking and financial centre. As a step towards making the Iranian riyal the Gulf area's premier currency, he bought the best American equipment and had his engravers trained in the United States. When he was overthrown, this infrastructure fell into the hands of a mob of mad mullahs frothing with hatred against the "Great Satan." With Syria's prodding, and assistance from East Germany (which provided the "plates"), by the early 1990s, the Iranians had reputedly flooded the world with at least $10 billion worth of bogus U.S. $100 notes.

Once a week the foreign operations directorate of the Iranian intelligence service flew the product, along with other forms of "terrorist" paraphernalia, to Damascus, where Syrian intelligence, supervised by top-level people with the ear of the Syrian president himself, handled distribution. Part was passed directly to the main Pasdaran base in Lebanon's Biqa' Valley, where it was used to finance global terrorist activity by the Iranians and their Lebanese allies. Part went through Lebanese drug-trafficking networks that worked hand-in-glove with the Syrians, to be exported through the Lebanese port of Junieh. Part was trucked into Turkey, then beyond. Later, to deepen their cover, the Iranians also moved the actual printing plant to Lebanon.

Much like Operation Bernhard, the notes produced were of variable quality, depending on the type of paper available. The poorest headed for the most distant and least suspecting locations: they were used in developing countries or, after 1991, in the ex-Soviet Republics, to buy political support and to finance terrorist operations. The mid-range went to Middle Eastern countries, whose money changers have some experience in detecting fakes. The very best, of course, were destined for the good old U.S. of A.

The purpose of the counterfeiting operation was not just to cover a temporary balance of payments shortfall, or to buy tickets to Disney World. Much worse. The primary objective was to attack the U.S. financial system. A massive infusion of counterfeit would cause loss of faith in the U.S. currency. This could lead to Third World banks and leaders shedding their huge dollar holdings in favour of gold or other currencies and prompt the world financial system to downgrade drastically the central role of the U.S. dollar. But that was not all. The Iranian–Syrian enterprise was also intended to undermine Israel's heavily dollarized economy, and to give perpetrators the financial means to shop for an off-the-shelf, ready-to-use nuclear weapons system. The task force reported that "Syrian military representatives have been traveling in Czechia, Slovakia, and the Ukraine with some $800 million in cash trying to buy strategic weapons, including nuclear warheads and high performance weapons systems for immediate delivery. . . ." Undoubtedly those military representatives felt that they could cut freight charges by using the same cases required to cart all that cash to haul back the nuclear arms they purchased.

The sources for this truly disturbing tale were impeccable. In addition to Israeli intelligence reports, known for objectivity in informing the United States about the schemes of Israel's neighbours, there was independent confirmation from two Lebanese drug dealers jailed in Massachusetts in 1992. They were eager to repent their former misdeeds by revealing details about the plot, before throwing themselves on the mercies of the American justice system.[26]

Nonetheless, there were a few problems with the notion of Iran engaging in a numismatic jihad. For a start, it was never clear just how super the supernote really was. To the Republican task force, the only thing it lacked was Abe Lincoln's fingerprints, but to Secret Service agents it had all manner of visible flaws.

Nor was it ever clear just how the Iranians had got their hands on the equipment necessary to do the job. The Shah's Iran had acquired its fancy printing equipment not from the United States, as the story went, but from the Swiss firm de la Rue-Giori, the world's principal manufacturer of fancy intaglio presses. The firm had been contracted to create a complete printing plant, install the equipment and train the staff. Then the revolution intervened. For years afterwards, the equipment sat incomplete and unopened, while Iran, desperate for new banknotes, was forced to overprint old ones to remove the Shah's head and emblazon them with revolutionary slogans.[27]

Another curiosity was how Syria had persuaded the fanatically anti-Syrian Phalangists to fold their own counterfeiting networks into the emerging Irani-Syrian one, and to permit the Syrians to export counterfeit through the port of Junieh around which the Phalangists were still exchanging gunfire with the Syrians until as late as 1991. Apparently, too, when the Iranians moved the printing operation to Lebanon, into areas controlled by their Shi'a and Syrian allies, they hid it so carefully that the only counterfeiting equipment ever found when the civil war ended and government authority was restored was crude offset presses whose product would have scarcely passed the scrutiny of a street-corner ice-cream vendor.[28]

Nor could anyone explain why eastern European countries with nuclear arsenals would be any keener than those of western Europe to promote proliferation, particularly if their reward took the form of container-loads of American counterfeit currency. And it was never revealed how spreading lousy counterfeit was likely to win friends and influence leaders in the countries where Iran was attempting to raise its political profile.

As to the purported effects on the U.S. financial system, and especially on the international role of the U.S. dollar, by the time the supernote surfaced, the total amount of U.S. currency in circulation outside America's borders was around $400 billion. This delighted two classes of people — international criminals whose deals were done in hard cash and U.S. Treasury officials. The ability to print for a few cents a copy the principal bill used in global black markets saved the United States up to $25 billion a year in interest payments on money it would otherwise have had to borrow. Yet, despite the undoubted popularity of U.S. currency notes, the world's elites were more likely to keep their savings in U.S. dollar-denominated securities rather than in cash stuffed in socks under their beds. And to carry out financial transactions, the world monetary system relied not on the attaché cases filled with banknotes — that is more the province of Republican Party bagmen — but on trillions in dollar-denominated interbank transfers. If there really were a great crisis of confidence in the U.S. currency induced by the discovery of massive amounts of counterfeit, presumably the main losers would be drug dealers and tax evaders caught counting their cash rather than people who had already managed to deposit their money safely in obliging banks.

Interestingly, at the very time the Iranians were supposedly pumping out almost undetectable bogus American bills, their own economy was awash with fake riyals. The official currency was apparently very easy to copy because Iran's printing facilities were so primitive. And that spate of counterfeiting reflected the profound economic crisis nearly a decade of war had produced.

Down But Not Out?

When the shooting stopped, the United States rushed to take public credit for the outbreak of peace. However the end of the war had little to do with arms embargoes. After the Iran-contra scandal, not only did major arms smuggling cases then before the courts crumble, but many countries that had hesitated to sell to Iran, or had done so surreptitiously, came out of the closet. Furthermore, thanks to the Pasdaran, Iran's own arms industry had made great strides, greatly reducing its need for imports, saving foreign exchange and insulating itself against future embargoes. By the end of the war, Iran could make at least

80 per cent of its ammunition requirements. Its factories, often converted from civil use, were turning out passable imitations of American spare parts. It had a fledgling missile and naval shipbuilding industry. And it had begun full-scale production of its own fighter planes using a hodge-podge of Soviet and U.S. parts.[29]

However, Iraq was more than matching Iran's performance. Its success in building new pipelines offset Iran's ability to block its oil exports. That coupled with the increasing effectiveness of the Iraqi air force against Iranian oil platforms and tankers meant that by the end of the war Iraq was able to export more oil, and therefore earn more foreign exchange, than Iran. Although both suffered when prices sagged badly in the face of a glut and OPEC quota-busting, Iran was hit hardest.[30]

While Iraq had kept up civilian as well as military spending, though it drove the country deeply into debt, Iran had avoided borrowing, even managing to reduce its foreign debt over the course of the war. But it paid a price. The Iranian Revolution had raised dramatically economic expectations among the poor. The Ayatollah Khomeini had insisted that proper housing, education and medical care were Islamic rights. His regime made a special effort to meet the needs of the poor. Yet as the war dragged on, an increasing share of the population was displaced to urban slums. Rents skyrocketed. In spite of rationing and price controls, food prices soared while black market rackets created a visible class of war profiteers. Meanwhile, the luxury housing in the highlands north of Teheran ceased to accommodate representatives of foreign corporations as in the Shah's era, instead becoming home to rich clergy and their black market cronies.

Even more important, though, were developments on the military front. While Iraq had started the war with untested armed forces struggling to master weapons systems from new suppliers, over the course of the conflict, its military capacity sharply improved. Lightning victories by its conventional forces in the marshy southern areas where Iran's superiority in numbers could not be effectively brought to bear shook the morale of the Iranian army. Iraq developed a long-range missile that struck terror into the citizens of Iran's capital, hitherto too far away to be directly affected by the war. So did Iraq's willingness and ability to use poison gas. The war ended with little territorial change, but with a potentially new military power in the region. There was clearly some unfinished business in the Gulf to which the Western powers had to attend.

Part Seven

HELLFIRE AND SADDAMNATION!

Chapter 20

PLOWSHARES AND SWORDS

Many developing countries, Iraq among them, regard the military sector as the technological base on which to build a modern economy. Almost alone, the military seemed to have the required organization, skills and infrastructure. Nor are military-controlled enterprises as susceptible to either labour disputes or the notorious propensity of developing country capitalists to favour Swiss bank accounts over new machine tools.[1]

Iraq also had strategic reasons for seeking self-sufficiency. Through bad experience it realized that, in time of need, weapons from abroad might fail to be forthcoming or arrive with humiliating conditions attached. Its first efforts at military industrialization came in the early 1970s when the U.S.S.R. took exception to Saddam Hussein's urge to purge un-American activities by the arrest, torture and murder of Communist Party activists. The U.S.S.R. used a similar embargo to show disapproval at the start of the Iran-Iraq War. Although French supplies minimized the damage, the lesson was clear. Twice burned, Iraq ceased to be shy about its ambition to reduce reliance on the U.S.S.R. Although the United States wooed Iraq during the war, it never sent military equipment directly. And the sincerity of its overtures was thrown seriously into doubt by the Iran-contra affair. Iraq preferred the route of self-reliance.

Although Iraq had started building arms factories before the war with Iran, during that conflict most of its military expenditures had to go to buying abroad completed weapons systems. After peace returned, a larger share of resources could be committed to military industrialization. However, even if it still needed to purchase particular items off the shelf, and foreign suppliers slapped on embargoes, experience showed Iraq that where there was a strong will, there was a devious way.

The Banker, the Faker, the Cluster-Bomb Maker
One of the more delectable items on the Pentagon menu, widely used as an "area denial device" during the Vietnam War, is the cluster bomb. Delivered by artillery or by air, its casing is designed to open in flight to spread hundreds of tiny bomblets over an area that could be the size of several football fields. Each bomblet in turn spews metal or plastic darts. Cluster bombs, naturally, were subject to tight export restrictions. They were given by the United States to Israel, for example, on strict condition they be used only if Israel were under attack by two or more Arab states. Many people in Lebanon shorn of limbs in 1982 could attest to the scrupulousness with which that condition was respected. Undoubtedly Iraq, facing Iranian "human wave" assaults, was also impressed by the cluster bomb's potential as a crowd-control device. Iraq could not buy directly from the United States. France offered a competitor. However, at $27,000 a copy, it was beyond Iraq's budget. Fortunately, the legacy of previous U.S. embargoes had created a bargain-basement supplier elsewhere.

In 1977, Chile's secret service had assassinated an exiled opposition leader in Washington. In response, the United States banned arms sales. For Chile, then involved in a nasty territorial dispute with Argentina, the timing was especially bad. Hence Chile offered Carlos Cardoen, a local manufacturer of mining explosives, low-interest loans and tax breaks to diversify. He started making bombs and shells, later expanding into armoured vehicles. Subsequently, he licensed from South Africa the rights to a mobile version of Gerald Bull's howitzer.[2] Rumours that Cardoen was also planning to export to Iraq a helicopter incorporating restricted British technology brought a British reporter to Chile to investigate — until he was overcome by an urge to commit suicide in his hotel room.[3] Cardoen's biggest coup, though, was in the cluster-bomb business. His product, at $7,000 per unit, was too attractive for Saddam Hussein to resist. By the mid-1980s 95 per cent of the output of Industrias Cardoen was destined for export, three-quarters to Iraq, transforming Industrias Cardoen into South America's biggest arms maker.

To get his business up and running, Cardoen shopped across the United States for arms plants to be stripped and shipped. In theory they had first to be demilitarized. In reality, over the objections of U.S. Customs, they were reclassified as scrap metal and sent whole to Chile. It was less a turnkey than a COD operation. In addition to machinery, Cardoen needed zirconium, a metal that increases the power of explosives. Since zirconium also plays a role in nuclear weapons, its export is subject to official control. When Cardoen requested 100 tons from Teledyne Industries of Oregon, an executive reported the order to the CIA, and the Commerce Department warned that it was too large for the mining explosives industry. Nonetheless, the State Department issued an export licence. It was still possible to check on how the material was used. The U.S. ambassador to Chile made so many visits to Cardoen's Chilean munitions factory that he was later hired by Cardoen as a consultant while serving on the CIA's Senior Review Panel.[4]

Before making cluster bombs, Cardoen needed exact technical specifications. For that he owed thanks to a Bible-thumping spy whose idea of Christian charity was to give to the needy at home while pulling off billion-dollar financial scams abroad.[5] After leaving a managerial post at Lockheed, James Guerin opened International Signal and Control Corporation (ISC) inside a chicken coop. In the early 1970s he hooked up jointly with South Africa's Armscor and U.S. intelligence. Under the auspices of the National Security Agency and the Office of Naval Intelligence, Guerin set up Gamma Systems Associates, a front for running communications gear to permit South Africa to eavesdrop on Soviet warships in the South Atlantic. Although such cooperation was supposedly banned in 1977 in response to the UN arms embargo, the intelligence-sharing ("Project X") was simply taken over by the "private" sector.

Riding the wave of excitement over military electronics in the years that followed, Guerin was soon making chemical weapons components, bomb parts and electronic warfare equipment for aircraft — some of which he smuggled to South Africa. In 1982 he was ready to take ISC public, choosing to offer the stock in London where scrutiny was much looser. The drawback was that, to continue to qualify for Pentagon contracts, some Americans had to join the British firm's board of directors. Guerin recruited three former senior officials, including a man who had been head of Naval Intelligence and deputy director of the CIA. That same year, ISC acquired a California firm that made cluster bombs. That deal brought Guerin into contact with Carlos Cardoen. With ISC providing technology, bomb fuses and an agreement to divide the world market, the Chilean upstart soon had his cluster-bomb factory going. Later an Armscor front company in the Channel Islands contracted to redesign Cardoen's cluster bombs for use at low altitudes and to manufacture them in Iraq. Meanwhile, Guerin did not neglect his old clients. He sneaked off to South Africa guidance systems for anti-aircraft and ballistic missiles, some of which navigated their way to Iraq.[6]

In the late 1980s, as Cold War tensions receded, military budgets were slashed. ISC's finances deteriorated. So did those of Ferranti International Ltd., one of Britain's biggest military electronics firms. Ferranti, too, had a problem fending off hostile takeover bids. When Guerin proposed a merger, Ferranti listened. Combined, they would be too big to be easily swallowed. Furthermore, with Guerin bragging about his CIA connections and waving around ISC's burgeoning order books, a merger promised much new business. The fact that, in the post-Cold War climate, no new orders really existed was scarcely a problem. Working through a network of thirty-eight Panama companies and fifty-one Swiss bank accounts, some created for Project X, Guerin invented customers, booked phoney orders complete with receipts and shipping documents, shipped money to one part of the world nominally in payment for supplies, then brought it back in the guise of receipts from sales. Nearly a billion dollars of fake business was invented to puff ISC stock and lure Ferranti into the merger.[7]

When Ferranti discovered the fraud, the cover was also stripped from Guerin's arms smuggling. A disgruntled company employee tried to use information about the South Africa deals to squeeze a severance package from ISC. Rebuffed, he went to the law. Guerin faced criminal charges. The Armscor executives named in the indictment ignored their American subpoenas. Carlos Cardoen was also charged, but no effort was made to force him to tell his tale in an American courtroom. Although South Africa offered Guerin political asylum, he returned to the United States to face a fifteen-year jail sentence. Still, the "private" arms dealer was not alone. Also sentenced in a separate case was a "rogue" banker named Chris Drogoul, whose letters of credit had paid for Cardoen's Chilean plant and much more of Iraq's military industrialization program.[8]

Helping Those Who Help Themselves

To save foreign exchange, create jobs, transfer technology and profit locals who have political connections, most developing countries insist on offsets in arms deals. The supplier must not merely provide off-the-shelf equipment, but undertake part of the assembly in the customer country. Sometimes the customer requires the supplier to build turnkey plants and train technicians. Iraq went a step further. It created a procurement network to buy components and technology to build armaments factories by itself. That reduced the capacity of the West to monitor Iraq's drive to self-sufficiency or to control the results.[9] Worse, Iraq appeared to be acquiring the know-how to manufacture "weapons of mass destruction." Although what falls into that category depends more on political convenience than military impact, the implication was that tinted types were making technological strides into fields the West had long regarded as a combination of birthright and Divine right.[10]

At the top of Iraq's procurement network was the Military Industrialization Board. It set overall goals while delegating to the Ministry of Industry and Military Industrialization (MIMI) the job of fulfilling them. If an Iraqi company needed equipment or components, MIMI officials passed the order to the Iraqi embassy in Germany, which communicated with "front" companies, some Iraqi owned, some just hired as agents. Support companies would locate suppliers and solicit bids. A bid was passed back to the Iraqi factory initiating the order, and it would indicate to MIMI if the bid was satisfactory.[11]

Typical was the experience of Matrix-Churchill, a troubled British machine-tool firm. Baghdad-based El Arabi Trading Company set up a British subsidiary called the Trade and Development Group (TDG) to purchase both computer-run machinery and, on occasion, actual companies. Matrix-Churchill was one of its acquisitions. As a TDG subsidiary, Matrix-Churchill trained Iraqi engineers, exported lathes to machine 155 mm shells with special stabilizer fins Gerald Bull had designed for greater accuracy and range, and sold computer-controlled machine-tools, some to Carlos Cardoen, some to Iraq for a missile plant and a chemical complex. Export financing was handled by BNL-Atlanta backed by guarantees from the U.S. Export-Import Bank and the British government's export credit insurance agency. The shipment of lathes was cleared through the British Ministry of International Trade, the minister himself suggesting that the application for an export licence emphasize civilian rather than military uses. The firm's managing director, experienced as an intelligence informant while working in eastern Europe, reported to MI6. Meanwhile, the Ohio subsidiary of Matrix-Churchill was similarly exporting "dual-use" technology with State Department clearance long after it had been identified as part of the Iraqi procurement network.[12]

Iraq was later accused of maintaining "front" companies to deal with a host of suppliers in order to break orders down into small units that were more difficult to trace.[13] In fact, the Iraqis went out of their way to make most of their purchasing visible and legal. For the bulk of their needs, there was no need for secrecy; most of their "fronts" were well known; and when they sought to buy from a multiplicity of sources, it reflected concern with cost-cutting rather than duplicity. Nor was the focus on "dual-use" technologies merely a conspiracy to muddy the trail.[14] In Iraq, giant state-owned companies were the norm for both civil and military sectors. The complementarity of civilian and military projects was reflected in the very name, Ministry of Industry and Military Industrialization, which was, quite publicly, the most powerful in the country. When turnkey plants were built in Iraq, in most cases there was little effort to disguise their function. American and British businesses involved reported quite proper business relations.[15] Although their critics later claimed that such firms were putting short-term gain ahead of long-term responsibility (as if that were not what capitalism is all about), some had a different explanation for why they preferred doing business with Iraq rather than other countries in the region. Saddam Hussein, in a bid to reduce prices and clean up the bureaucracy, executed those caught taking bribes.[16] However, the media-fête accompanying the later Gulf War crisis popularized the theme that Judeo-Christian civilization had been placed in mortal peril by a coalition of hook-nosed spies and grasping arms merchants.[17]

Acquiring dual-use technology was not always easy. Although the United States often obliged Iraq by supplying export licences, some transfers were hampered by a Cold War between the Commerce Department, which favoured exports, and the Pentagon, where the techno-cops, Stephen Bryen and Richard Perle, or their successors, tried to block militarily useful material for Arab countries.[18] Iraq could sometimes sidestep the United States by purchasing competing items from European suppliers. Or it could source American technology outside the U.S. Although foreign companies using restricted U.S. technology were supposed to apply to the United States for export licences, many did not. Such an unlicensed export to Iraq of equipment later used to make night-vision devices earned a Dutch supplier a criminal conviction in 1992.[19] Or the material could be obtained the old-fashioned way, as when Iraq and Egypt went shopping for their intermediate-range ballistic missile project.

The Condor missile project was actually initiated by Argentina, still smarting from its defeat by Britain in the 1982 Falklands/Malvinas War. Had it not been for Anthony Divall, that war, and the future course of Italian politics, might have had a quite different outcome. After a tour with the Royal Marines, Divall launched a public career as a Hamburg-based arms broker and a private one as an agent of Britain's MI6. He built up credentials by peddling his wares to insurgents in Algeria, secessionists in the Nigerian state of Biafra and anti-government guerrillas in the Sudan and Angola. In 1973 he proved his worth by helping MI6 bust an arms pipeline from Libya to the IRA. His biggest coup came in 1982 when Argentina was desperately seeking more Exocet missiles that had proven devastating against British warships. Divall's job was to pose as a credible enough supplier to divert Argentina's arms-buying mission away from anyone who might actually deliver before the war was over, and then to monitor Argentina's future arms purchases in case it was preparing another lunge for the disputed territory.[20] His success proved fatal to more than just Argentina's territorial ambitions. For financing of the abortive Exocet deal was supposed to have been provided by Italy's Banco Ambrosiano.[21] In the aftermath of Argentina's defeat, the bank's boss, the overweight, unathletic and vertigo-prone Roberto Calvi, managed to clamber down the scaffolding of London's Blackfriar's Bridge, load rocks in his pocket and hang himself, helping to set off a scandal that shook Italy to its roots and brought down the government. Not that Anthony Divall's fate was much better. A few years later, one of his old partners was busted in Hamburg for running anti-aircraft missiles to South Korea. The police raid turned up Divall's name. When he came under regular surveillance from West German police, his career as an arms dealer ended. So did his usefulness to his intelligence handlers, who dumped him unceremoniously after four decades of service, refusing even to cover expenses from the Exocet double deal let alone provide the aging spook with a pension.

While Argentina took the lead in trying to get the Condor project off the ground, it soon had partners. In 1981, in the run-up to an Israeli election, Israeli prime minister Menachem Begin ordered the bombing of an Iraqi nuclear reactor. He impressed the Israeli public enough to win re-election, and he impressed front-line Arab states enough to convince them of the need to offset Israel's air superiority.[22] When Argentina approached Egypt for technical assistance, it not only said yes but, a few years later, brought in Iraq, which was seeking to upgrade Soviet-supplied Scud missiles to reach deeper inside Iran. As the project took shape, Argentina's president, Carlos Menem, was sufficiently enthusiastic about its prospects to turn the job of marketing over to Munzer el-Qassar, along with a passport and residency permit. Although American pressure caused Argentina to back out, the other two partners proceeded, until a major embarrassment also forced Egypt to withdraw.

The job of developing the basic hardware had been assigned to Consen, a group of companies nominally headquartered in Zug, Switzerland, with branches across Europe, ultimately answering to the German engineering giant, Messerschmitt-Bolkow-Blohm (MBB).[23] However, the carbon phenolic fibre necessary to keep nose cones from melting on re-entry into the atmosphere and certain chemicals for the solid fuel required by the first stage motor were available only in the United States. And they were tightly restricted.

Not so tightly restricted was an Egyptian-American who instructed his purchasing agents to claim that the chemicals were for benign use, and for delivery inside the United States, therefore obviating the need for an export licence. The agents changed the labels, falsified the manifests and sent the material to freight forwarders who arranged to fly it out on a military plane provided by the Egyptian embassy in Washington. After Customs grabbed the plane, the Egyptian minister of defence lost his post, and Egypt renounced any further role.[24] But Iraq persevered. And in 1989 it shook the West by launching a multiple stage rocket into space. It was far from an unqualified success, and there is a big difference between a spacecraft and a successful ballistic missile. However, the launch drew dramatic attention to the technical progress Iraq had made, particularly when the prospect of intermediate-range missiles could be linked to its chemical warfare program.

Petrochemical Warfare

Although it has never been adequately explained why it is worse for a soldier to die in a fit of convulsive coughing as his lungs are seared with poisonous gas than for him to bleed to death after his abdomen has been shredded by shrapnel, nonetheless, since World War I, chemical weapons have acquired notoriety as especially loathsome instruments of war. In reality mustard gas, the most common chemical weapon in the early years, was not particularly lethal. Useful only against fixed masses of unprepared troops when weather conditions were ideal, chemical weapons (including the more dangerous but less common chlorine gas) accounted for a very small percentage of World War I casualties. Most victims recovered completely. Still, clouds of toxic fumes, especially when invisible, delivered a psychological blow out of all proportion to their military significance and led to the first efforts to ban "unconventional" weapons. The stigma remained so strong that a public backlash during the Vietnam War forced the United States to stop using emetic gas to incapacitate and facilitate the capture of enemy soldiers — so it went back to simply killing them.[25]

Gas has two distinct military functions. First, it can be a deterrent. The threat it posed was, in a twisted way, the origin of the doctrine of mutually assured destruction. Although Nazi Germany developed highly lethal nerve gases like tabun and sarin, they were never used for fear of provoking Allied retaliation — concentration camps used cheaper, low-tech alternatives. In the same spirit, some developing countries came to see chemical weapons, which cost little and are easy to make, as the great equalizer.[26] When the superpowers scrambled to match each other's capacity to incinerate the globe hundreds of times over, the resulting balance of thermonuclear terror was credited with keeping the world from a fatal collision. But when Saddam Hussein attempted to use chemical weapons to counter Israel's nuclear arsenal, he was depicted as a satanic demagogue hell-bent on unleashing a toxic apocalypse.[27]

Gas has a second possible function. Despite formal treaties and moral strictures, it has continued to be employed where retaliation is impossible. Long before Iraq built a chemical arsenal, it had been made aware of the potential of poison gas to terrorize defenceless opponents. In 1923, when mass protests demanding Iraq's independence were a menace to British rule, Winston Churchill authorized the first-ever use of poison gas in the Middle East against those whom he referred to as "recalcitrant Arabs."[28] Perhaps inspired by Churchill, Saddam's most notorious use of gas was against thousands of Iraq's own citizens. The gas attack on the Kurdish town of Halabja was, like the Allied firebombing of Dresden in 1945, an act of pure military terrorism. However, unlike those responsible for Dresden, the perpetrators of the Halabja attack made no efforts at self-justification — they just claimed it did not happen. It will remain for philosophers to debate which course was the more dishonest.

The attractiveness of chemical weapons to Iraq also reflected the fact that the country was abundantly endowed with basic raw materials, petroleum and phosphates. Chemical weapons production, too, fitted the strategy of mixed civil-military industrialization. Almost all petroleum-derived synthetics start with ethylene, propylene and a few other products of the catalytic cracking process. These feedstocks are then chemically combined with sulphur and chlorine to make about 200 other substances called in the trade "evergreens." The evergreens are converted to yield pharmaceuticals, pesticides, plastics, synthetic fibres, construction materials and many more essentials of modern existence. Not only are a huge range of modern industrial chemicals toxic in their own right, some virulently so, but the difference between civil and military production processes is minor. With some it is a matter of simply moving one step up the chemical chain.[29] Thus, thiodiglycol, commonly used in such things as ink or textile dyes, when reacted with hydrochloric acid makes mustard gas. With others it is merely a question of degree. The difference between an organophosphate insecticide and a nerve gas is little more than concentration of the dose. Even the notorious tabun gas is made from four commonly used industrial chemicals.[30]

The result is awesome control problems. A modern chemical plant is a giant mixing vessel of pipes, valves, tubes and pressurized containers logically and technologically difficult to differentiate from a chemical weapons facility. Any modern pharmaceutical factory, fertilizer manufacturer or pesticide plant, sometimes even a brewery, can be readily converted to military use. There is no need to set up a clandestine facility. It is easy to make restricted substances inside a normal civilian facility, to divert from it into military use large amounts of supposedly benign chemicals, or to experiment with chemical compounds not yet on an internationally banned list. When Western firms were accused of assisting the development of a chemical weapons plant in some "rogue state"—prior to Iraq, Libya was the toxic flavour-of-the-month—they could declare, occasionally with honesty, that they thought they were building something benign.[31] The only way to stop chemical weapons proliferation is to deny developing countries the right to take the first steps towards industrialization based on synthetic organic materials, the very foundation of modern mass consumption society.

In 1978 Iraq took that first step, requesting that a U.S. firm develop plans for a pesticide plant. When the U.S. government blocked the technology, Iraq turned to European (mainly German) suppliers.[32] Before the plants could turn out weapons, Iraq had to find certain precursor chemicals. To secure thiodiglycol, for example, it hired a Dutch chemical broker with the right equipment—two Panamanian corporations operating from Switzerland. The broker placed an order with Alcolac International of Baltimore. It consigned the cargo to Antwerp, care of the Dutch broker's Swiss company, with a bill of lading on which the chemicals were described by the brand name Kromfax, which few Customs officers would recognize, instead of the generic name of thiodiglycol, and with a freight manifest describing the cargo as goods-in-transit without specifying a final address. Then it was a simple matter of persuading Belgian Customs to clear the load through to Aqabah. Just to keep things balanced, another chemical broker in Germany was buying the same material from Alcolac and running it, via Singapore and Pakistan, to Iran.[33]

Just how much progress Iraq had made was a matter of speculation. It was through his attempts to solve the riddle that Farzad Bazcroft wound up at the end of a rope. A person of dubious background—convicted of bank robbery, he then turned Scotland Yard informant—Bazcroft secured a job with a prominent British newspaper, which dispatched him to Iraq. Though posing as a reporter is a common cover in the intelligence craft, Bazcroft was certainly no model spy. He was of Iranian origin. He was caught taking soil samples to test for chemical contaminants at the site of an Iraqi military complex that had recently been destroyed by a massive explosion. And in his possession was an address book in which appeared the name and phone number of Israeli master gun-runner and Mossad agent Yaacov Nimrodi. All in all, Bazcroft's behaviour appeared less duplicitous than simply dumb.[34] And if there were any truth to his "confession," his main concern was not chemicals per se, but the methods by which Iraq might deploy them. Apart from missiles, there was the work of the man Bazcroft singled out in his "confession" as the main target of his espionage, Gerald Bull and his "supergun."

The Mother of All Artillery Pieces

It began with the Paris Gun, used by the Germans in World War I to bombard the French capital from 120 kilometres. It was an inaccurate weapon and carried a mere seven-kilogram payload. And the prototypes were dismantled after the war. Although Germany had a similar project in World War II, it was soon accepted that the airplane was the key to long-distance delivery, and by the end of the war the missile had made its debut. The central lesson of twentieth-century warfare was that, barring the existence of masses of immobilized troops to target, big fixed guns were largely useless and very vulnerable.

Gerald Bull dissented. He tracked down the surviving engineers of the Paris Gun and obtained from the widow of the designer some of the blueprints. The problem was to find someone to take his vision seriously. After multiple frustrations, Sarkis Soghanalian entered the picture.

Soghanalian had pulled off a number of deals for Iraq, all, he insisted, with CIA backing.[35] His most notorious coup involved Iraq delivering late-model Soviet equipment to the CIA for study, and the CIA greasing a deal in which Soghanalian brokered the sale of "civilian" helicopters, then scoured the black market to equip them with anti-tank missiles. This arrangement secured for Soghanalian yet another criminal conviction and a six-and-a-half-year jail sentence.[36] However, long before that denouement, Soghanalian, who had the ear of Saddam Hussein, managed to whisper into it Gerald Bull's name.

In the past Saddam Hussein's armed forces had encountered Bull's handiwork only indirectly, through the 155 mm artillery pieces purchased from Armscor and Voest-Alpine. In 1988 they brought Bull to Iraq to work on making their guns mobile and on developing larger weapons. Bull seized the occasion to prove at last the feasibility and cost-effectiveness of his method of launching satellites.

Project Babylon was one of military history's most closely guarded secrets. After pestering the Pentagon, Bull had taken the supergun idea to Israel in 1983 and been turned down. When he resurrected it in Iraq, he reported what he was doing to the U.S. Office of Munitions Control. He also appears to have briefed British intelligence —MI6 was fully aware of progress at least a year before the supergun became an international *cause célèbre*. At least half a dozen well-known European companies were contracted to make various sections, increasing geometrically the chance of information getting loose. Indeed, the supergun was so secret there was even a scale model displayed at the Baghdad trade fair in 1989, along with an engineer to explain Project Babylon to the assembled military attachés, reporters and spooks. Just to stiffen security further, Bull had published a manuscript describing the project in technical detail two years before.[37]

All that secrecy was necessary given the supergun's military significance. Weighing 5,000 tons — the barrel alone was 2,000 — it was to be locked in place on the side of a mountain, incapable of being elevated or traversed. Any artillery piece requires several rounds to home in on target. Normally that takes, at most, a few minutes. But the supergun in Iraq could fire perhaps twice a day with a flame so long it would be immediately spotted by spy satellites, and with a recoil that could be picked up on a seismograph as far away as California. Every sophisticated military force in the world would get an exact fix within minutes. The alignment of the barrel, welded together from sections of specially reinforced steel pipe, would have been so fragile that a small bomb dropped five kilometres away would throw it out of sync. But no one had a chance to try. Project Babylon had got no further than a few test rounds through a small-scale version pointing horizontally into an uninhabited stretch of desert by the time extreme prejudice terminated the experiment.

In 1990 Bull was shot in the back of the head with a 7.65 mm pistol in the corridor outside his Brussels apartment. The murder was the signal for an international media frenzy as supergun components were dramatically seized in the United Kingdom, Spain, Greece, Italy and Turkey, apparently on the principle that the more strung out the pieces and the places, the more publicity.[38] The point of the project was exactly what Bull had always claimed, to launch satellites from big guns, something attractive to Iraq, partly for prestige and partly because at the end of the Iran-Iraq War, it had lost access to U.S. satellite data. But the supergun was quickly transmogrified into a device to launch chemical warheads against Teheran, Tel Aviv and even New York.

The murder provoked a plethora of conspiracy theories. Some said it was a revenge killing by the Iranians, whose quaint views on arms control had already been blamed for murders ranging from René Audan in France to Olaf Palme in Sweden. But given the use Iran had already made of Bull's weapons, it seemed more likely they would first try to hire him away.[39] Some said it was the Iraqis themselves, perhaps out of anger over contracts unfulfilled.[40] This was improbable in light of the public homage Saddam Hussein made to the deceased Bull. Others imputed it to a blood vendetta among arms dealers. But Bull's market niche was sufficiently unique to preclude the most obvious forms of rivalry. Others imputed it to the CIA, which feared Bull would take revenge for being made a scapegoat a decade before by revealing all about the

South African smuggling episode. That seems dubious when the Guerin scandal had already highlighted more recent CIA complicity in getting even more dangerous weaponry to South Africa. Some imputed it to British intelligence seeking to cover up official complicity in the arming of Iraq. [41]

The main suspect was Israel. Bull had reputedly been warned off his Iraqi work by Mossad some time before. And Israel had committed similar acts. In 1980, for example, Israeli agents had used a prostitute to set a trap for an Egyptian nuclear scientist helping Iraq and, failing to recruit him, beat him to death in his hotel room, then apparently murdered the prostitute to keep her from talking.[42] Still, it was not obvious why the Israelis would bother. Not only had they refused the supergun five years before Bull went to Iraq, but in subsequent appraisals they had written it off as militarily useless. In fact Israel may have welcomed it as a waste of Iraqi money that might otherwise be spent on something dangerous.[43]

There was one further theory, propounded by Chris Cowley, ex-engineer-in-chief of Project Babylon. After Bull's murder, Cowley began sending information to André Cools, former deputy prime minister of Belgium, regarding Poudrières réunies de Belgique (PRB), the main contractor for the propellant powder for Project Babylon. PRB, along with other subsidiaries of Belgium's La Société générale de Belgique, had been involved for years in Iraqi (and Iranian) procurement programs. PRB was one of the few companies in western Europe able to make ammunition for Iraq's Soviet-style artillery. And the Belgian air force had been hired to regularly fly PRB shells to an Iraqi-run ammunition dump near the Jordanian capital of Amman. Belgian politicians were apparently collecting rake-offs to conceal the traffic.[44] When PRB was sold off to Astra, a British arms conglomerate, its books revealed contracts for shells and ammunition to countries that did not have the guns to fire them. Astra had also picked up two British subsidiaries, in each of which it found evidence of illegal sales to Iraq, all with the complicity or active participation of MI6, which set up the directors to take the fall if the ruse were exposed.[45] Just before his death, Bull had agreed to help Astra's owners in legal action out of which PRB's deepest secrets (and the covert British arms pipeline to Iraq) might be exposed.

All this was probably welcome news to Cools, eager to pursue a long political vendetta against La Société générale de Belgique, PRB's former owner, and a company long seen as a *bête noir* by the Belgian left. But a short time later, Cools was assassinated in Liège, shot, like Bull, with a 7.65 mm pistol, in the head and throat.[46] While the investigation ultimately showed that Cools was not, as some suspected, yet a further casualty of the supergun, it did expose the antics of another of Iraq's more infamous arms suppliers and claimed a string of prominent new victims.

The Gunships of Agusta

At the time of his assassination, André Cools had supposedly left politics. In fact he kept his fingers in every pot. Some were simmering, some were stewing and some were threatening to bubble over. Once more there were no lack of theories about the murder. The most interesting emerged as an accidental offshoot of a huge political scandal rocking Italy.

Italian politics had a public face, consisting of democratic contests between parties of disparate ideologies, and a private face, consisting of secret service plots, pseudo-Masonic conspiracies, Vatican conniving and acts of corporate corruption. As the Cold War thawed and the plea of national security ceased to work as cover for egregious political acts, more and more of the ugly secrets were exposed. This culminated in a massive anti-corruption probe. One of the things revealed in this "Clean Hands" investigation was the connections between the Socialist Party, BNL and Agusta, a firm that manufactured helicopters. A firm with a long history in the arms business, Agusta had prospered during the 1970s, thanks to the Shah of Iran and a network of secret bank accounts from Curaçao to Panama to Hong Kong. When the Shah fell, the company was badly hurt. Saddam Hussein's appetite for arms permitted a partial recovery. But it still went bankrupt and was taken over by the state. The network of secret bank accounts was left intact, partly to grease its order book and partly to serve as a vehicle for Socialist Party financing at home and, interestingly enough, abroad.[47]

When the Belgian army decided to let a contract (worth 12 billion Belgian francs —$400 million) to replace its aging fleet of helicopter gunships, three machines were in the running.[48] The German entry was strongly favoured by the military; the French by the Finance Department. Despite the firm's dubious capacity to deliver, Agusta's helicopter was the choice of the ruling (and chronically cash-short) Socialist Party.[49] All three competitors had to submit confidential offers. Both the French and the German bids were superior to the Italian. Hence, the *chef du cabinet* of the minister of economic affairs phoned Agusta to tell it to spruce up its bid. After Agusta promised more offsets, including a major investment in the minister's home constituency, the minister announced publicly his "slight preference" for the Agusta proposition. For its part, Agusta announced privately a slight preference in the form of 1 per cent of the value of the contract for Socialist Party coffers.[50] The minister of defence agreed to the terms, and the contract was signed.

Agusta's man in Belgium received three kinds of commissions. One, his own, was paid into his consulting company's Luxembourg account. The other two reflected the fact that in bi-national Belgium, ethnic tension is kept under control by making sure that politicians from both French- and Dutch-speaking constituencies get their cut. Therefore the second payment went into another Luxembourg account held in the name of a Jersey shell corporation appropriately named Downhole, and from there wound its way to the Wallonia wing of the Socialist Party.[51] For the third, a lawyer created a Panama instant corporation, Kasma Overseas Ltd., with a company account in Zurich. Party bagmen opened accounts in the same bank in the name of two insta-companies called Katin and Kater. Agusta's agent ran some 51 million Belgian francs into the Kasma account. The funds were withdrawn by a middleman, who could not be easily linked to either side, then redeposited in the Kater and Katin accounts.[52] Most of the money was then sent to Belgium by bank transfer, routed through Luxembourg to cloud the trail. Once in Belgium, some went to clear the debts of a Flemish Socialist Party newspaper; some was funnelled to owners of a recreation centre favoured by party workers; some went into bolstering the financial position of the Flemish party machine. The rest came home by a simpler route. The lawyer who ran Kasma drew a bearer cheque and handed it to a bagman who cashed the cheque, carried the cash to Brussels and stuffed it in a safety deposit box. It was eventually hauled back to Switzerland again to pay lawyers fighting (unsuccessfully) to keep the Swiss government from waiving bank secrecy laws and opening bank records to the Cools murder investigation.[53]

According to the theory the investigators were following, Cools was threatening to blow the whistle on secret commission payments unless Agusta honoured its commitments to industrial investments in the Liège area that Cools long represented. Supposedly people tied to Agusta had too much at stake to lose the contract and too little in the bank to meet the commitments. The response was to hire a Mafia assassin to silence Cools.[54] Once the investigators got the bank records, they found something odd. Agusta had deposited only 51 million francs into the Kasma account. Yet a total 111 million francs had passed through it. The discovery of the identity of the second secret benefactor of the Socialist Party triggered yet another political scandal.[55]

At the time Agusta's helicopter deal was being negotiated, also up for grabs were contracts to upgrade fighter planes. Some were French Mirages, some American F-16s. France's Dassault Aviation, the manufacturer, had the inside track in the Mirage contract, while the betting favoured a U.S. firm for the F-16s. As expected, the first deal went to Dassault, but so did the second. The story had a familiar public face: Dassault agreed to certain off-sets and the use of Belgian subcontractors. And it also had a familiar private face — contributions to the Socialist Party welfare fund. Showing sufficient professional negligence to merit a malpractice suit, the lawyer acting for the Socialist Party had stuffed both kickbacks into the same account.[56]

Although Belgium now had two arms contracting scandals, they were of no help in explaining the Cools murder. Ultimately, that turned out to involve something much more mundane. The personal secretary to the senior minister of the Wallonian regional government had been using his office as cover for a gang stealing securities, credit cards and paintings. When Cools pressed for an investigation, the official hired a Mafia assassin to curb his ardour for clean government.[57]

Meanwhile, the scandals mowed down politicians. In Italy the former Socialist Party prime minister fled to a Tunisian exile ahead of an arrest warrant, while the former head of the state holding company, who had initiated the Agusta-Belgium negotiations, was found near Rome, a cocked pistol in his pocket and his head half eaten away by wild animals.[58] A former chief of staff of the Belgian air force committed suicide, and eventually a string of Belgian ministers and former ministers faced criminal indictments. So, too, did the head of Dassault.[59] In France, however, matters were taken in stride. At the peak of the uproar, the minister of external trade had publicly praised Dassault and deplored the fuss. Commissions, he said, had been for many decades "*aides naturelles*" in international trade. "This," the minister insisted, "has nothing to do with corruption."[60]

That was not the opinion of others in the trade. According to a former lobbyist for Aérospatiale, one of the losers in the helicopter contract, bribes were "the rule of the game in the aerospace industry." Still, there is a right way and a wrong way. "The way these Agusta commissions were transferred to the SP was done so amateurishly that it simply cries out to be sanctioned.... Who puts down in writing that he has been promised bribe money?... Usually one is smart enough to settle these transactions in cash."[61]

Chapter 21

SAND–STORMS

In 1990 Iraq invaded Kuwait. If there was ever a case of the bully kicking desert sand in the face of the runt, this had to be it. The international community mobilized as never before. Sanctions were total, immediate and nearly unanimously endorsed.[1] Since extreme actions called for tough responses, the "Allies" also hit Iraq with the most devastating strategic bombing attack since World War II. Kuwait, the world insisted, must be liberated — returned to a family dynasty that had accorded partial civil rights to about 10 per cent of the country's population, then been so upset at the results that it suspended Parliament.

The Big Euromac Attack
By the time it invaded Kuwait, Iraq had become convinced there were anti-regime plots everywhere. First was the dramatic bust of BNL, producing wide publicity about Iraq's military industrialization. Then came the Bazcroft affair, followed shortly by the murder of Gerald Bull and a series of high-profile arrests of British and American businessmen engaged in the supposedly covert arming of Iraq. That was the fate of the Iraqi-born founder of Euromac, a small trading company established in Britain in 1987 to take advantage of the U.K. government's public drive for more business with Iraq. He was arrested for attempting to smuggle to Iraq krytons, a genre of electrical capacitor.[2]

Though they have a variety of civil applications, krytons can function as high-speed electronic switches to time nuclear explosions. Their export from the United States was subject to strict controls. In the early 1980s Israel had needed them for its Jericho missile. Designed to explode over cities or armoured formations, the Jerichos were to be Israel's ultimate "deterrent," provided certain technical limitations were overcome. Lending a hand was Arnon Milchan, who combined careers as a Hollywood mogul, gun-runner and spook. In the 1970s he had laundered money through Belgium's Kredietbank that South Africa's Bureau of State Security used to buy magazines in Britain to silence their anti-apartheid line. He was also Israeli representative of North American Rockwell, the defence giant that employed Richard Smyth, the second key figure.

While at Rockwell, Smyth diverted to Israel a chemical compound for the Jericho fuel system. Then he left Rockwell to join Milchan in enterprises that became conduits for siphoning U.S. military technology to Israel. The high point came in 1985 when Smyth was caught by Customs exporting to one of Milchan's Israeli companies over 800 krytons. Curiously enough, a few months before, CoCom had considered dropping krytons from its control list. They were, Stephen Bryen insisted, a "trivial technology." That opinion did not reassure Smyth, who jumped bail and hightailed it to Israel. Nor was Bryen's uncharacteristically liberal attitude universally shared. When a Pakistani agent was arrested later that year for trying to obtain krytons, Brooklyn Representative Stephen Solarz demonstrated his outrage by sponsoring a bill under which any country found to have illegally acquired technology useful for nuclear weapons would be subject to a cut-off of American aid.[3] Of course Solarz's concern with justice precluded the punitive provisions being made retroactive. Later, Israel returned 469 of the krytons, reporting the rest destroyed during experiments.

Three years after the Solarz bill, an Iraqi procurement company approached Euromac to check the availability of a type of kryton with civilian applications and subject to no U.K. export regulations. Though not the kind of business Euromac normally did, it agreed to accommodate an existing customer. Euromac asked a California firm named CSI Technology if they had the type of capacitor the Iraqi firm wanted. CSI was already in trouble with U.S. Customs and, as recompense, had agreed to cooperate in fishing expeditions. It informed Customs that there might be a nibble on its dangling hook.

Alas, it seemed that this sucker was about to get away. The Euromac employee who had initiated the request left for another job, and Euromac showed no further interest. At that point CSI took the lead, persisting even when Euromac told CSI to deal directly with Baghdad. CSI also suggested that they should be negotiating not over the kind of krytons used in laser photography, which they had requested, but over a different kind with military applications in which the Iraqis had shown no interest. In fact the Iraqis were picked up on tape stating that "we want to go to the original specifications," a phrase later mistranslated and fed to the press as "we take our orders from the very top." Eventually they worked out a deal for forty capacitors worth a staggering $10,500. Euromac still attempted to get CSI to ship directly to Baghdad. But CSI persisted in working through Euromac. When the krytons arrived in London airport for transfer to Iraq, the Euromac principal was arrested. The type of kryton seized would have been useless in a nuclear program, though arguably of assistance in the separation of a two-stage rocket. In any event, within a few months of the affair, Iraq was making its own krytons. They were publicly demonstrated by Saddam himself when he generously announced that the British and American governments were free to apply to MIMI for a licence if they wanted to import some.[4] Still, the head of Euromac was put through a show trial in London. Although eventually found not guilty on appeal, the damage — to the individual, his company and hopes that public opinion would rally against the winds of war blowing in the Gulf — had already been done.

From Bazcroft to Bull to Euromac, these events were taken in Baghdad to be parts of a program of psychological warfare. If they were, the architects had judged their target well. After Bazcroft was hung for espionage, the Israeli press began to discuss the need for pre-emptive strikes against Iraq's chemical weapons plants. During a eulogy for Gerald Bull, Saddam thundered his response: if Israel had a missile, Iraq wanted a missile; if Israel struck Iraq with nuclear arms, Iraq would reply with chemical weapons. This was quickly transformed by the mass media from an example of Saddam's less-than-subtle notion of deterrent diplomacy into an unprovoked threat.

All this played out against a deteriorating financial climate that, on top of sagging oil prices, included the BNL affair and the introduction of an anti-Iraq sanctions bill in the American Senate. An exasperated Saddam Hussein explained to the American ambassador to Iraq, "Military war kills people by bleeding them, while economic war kills their humanity by depriving them of their chance to have a good standard of living."[5] The immediate target of his anger, though, was not the United States, but the country Saddam regarded as America's principal ally in a deliberate campaign of economic sabotage.

As-Saddam Aleikum

Kuwait was first settled as a fishing and trading port by peoples from the Nejd, the northeastern part of what is now Saudi Arabia. They were later joined by an influx from southern Iraq that quickly outnumbered the original Nejdi settlers. Not only are there family ties on both sides, but the Kuwait–Iraq border has long been a subject of contention. After World War I the French and the British, in their carve-up of the Ottoman empire, marked the boundaries to detach the major population centres of the Mashreq from the coastal areas to better use the second to control the first. The French drew the Syrian-Lebanese and Syrian-Turkish borders to deprive Syria of its main ports, while the British delineated the Iraqi-Kuwaiti frontier to narrow to a small strip Iraq's direct access to the Gulf. For Iraq the resulting strategic vulnerability was one reason it blundered into war with Iran. In fact, during a 1981 meeting between the head of Iraqi intelligence and the CIA's William Casey, the Iraqis stated their intent to gain better access to the sea by annexing Iran's Arab-populated Khuzestan province, an area that had been part of Iraq (historical Mesopotamia) until the mid-nineteenth century. When the Americans objected, the conversation turned to Kuwait, this time with no American protests, leaving the Iraqis to surmise that the United States was indifferent to the emirate's fate.[6] When the Iran-Iraq conflict ended with no territorial change, the Kuwait border issue became more important. It was compounded by a financial dispute.

While Iraq, as a result of the war, was running deeply into debt, Kuwait was building up huge investments abroad. A big part was the private stash of the emir and his family. There were also official holdings, most managed by the London-based Kuwait Investment Office, whose main responsibility was the $80 to $100 billion Reserve Fund for Future Generations meant to maintain the country once the oil ran out. On top was the foreign portfolio of the Kuwait Petroleum Company (KPC). Over the 1980s, KPC focused on the downstream part of the oil business, setting up not just refineries but a European-based chain of retail gasoline stations cutely called Q-8. When oil prices fell in the 1980s, in part due to Kuwait and Saudi Arabia busting their OPEC quotas, Kuwait could well afford to ride out the dips. Earnings from its investment portfolio could sustain it, and much of the revenue lost by low crude prices could be offset by increased profits from refining and retailing.[7] To the outside world that seemed a clever investment strategy. To Saddam Hussein, it was another plot. "We cannot tolerate this kind of economic warfare that is waged against Iraq," he thundered, particularly since part of the oil that Kuwait overproduced came from a field straddling the border.

Kuwait took a high-stakes gamble. Iraq and Saudi Arabia had signed a non-aggression pact in which Saudi Arabia had formally forgiven $40 billion in debts incurred during the war. Iraq offered Kuwait a similar treaty, requesting the wiping out of $14 billion in debt, fresh cash and the lease of islands in the Gulf to help resolve Iraq's problem of lack of strategic depth. The emir refused. After the invasion, Iraqi intelligence claimed to have found a document confirming that Kuwait, with the support of the CIA, had been using Iraq's financial weakness to wring out a border agreement in Kuwait's favour.[8]

As the dispute festered, Kuwaiti "provocations" piled up: the denial of over-flight rights to Iraqi civil aviation; "secret" talks between Kuwait and Iran's foreign minister; an offer by Kuwait of reconstruction assistance to Iran; and a demand that Iraq immediately repay war debts. When Iraq replied that it had no money, Kuwait initiated discussions with bankers in London about the possibility of selling Iraqi notes at a heavy discount, an act that might have destroyed Iraq's remaining credit standing. Finally, after an inter-Arab consensus to raise oil prices, Kuwait announced it would abide by the agreement only for three months, helping to precipitate a sharp depreciation of the Iraqi dinar.[9]

Iraq probably exaggerated its financial crisis, imputable as much to grandiose post-war designs as to a shortage of cash to meet genuine needs. But after several months on the receiving end of what it presumed was an American-Kuwaiti plot, Iraq made its move. The Kuwaiti armed forces immediately retreated, lock, stock and gun-barrel, to Saudi Arabia, the commander-in-chief reputedly fleeing in his underwear.[10] The only resistance came from a handful of armed Shi'a, the class of citizens the Kuwaiti establishment treated most shabbily. The emir and those wealthy Kuwaitis not already summering in their European villas similarly bolted, though not before contacting their bankers to make sure their money was safe. And the world reacted with sanctions.

Iraq seemed a vulnerable target. Its finances were extremely weak. It produced one export of significance, which could be easily blocked, especially at a time of oil glut. Its industries were dependent on imported parts. It was self-sufficient in one product: dates. It had land borders with five states. Iran and Syria were implacable enemies. Turkey was engaged in a bitter dispute with Iraq over water. Saudi Arabia quickly invited in a large American military contingent. And Jordan could be easily closed off at the Gulf of Aqabah. Iraq's own outlet to the sea was but a sliver, any gains from the seizure of Kuwait negated by an American and British naval blockade.

With borders and seafront sealed, Iraq's oil exports ground to a halt. Its overseas assets, and those of Kuwait, were frozen, preventing Iraq from issuing letters of credit. Any food, capital equipment and spare parts it still obtained were expected to dry up quickly, since smugglers want premium prices, cash up front. The country was battered by the mass flight of foreign skilled workers while much of its own economically active population had been inducted into the armed forces. Therefore, unlike so many other cases, experts insisted, sanctions should work to get Iraq out of Kuwait.[11] However to George Bush and Margaret Thatcher the real objective was not the evacuation of Kuwait, but to apply to Iraq a version of the Morgenthau Plan. This scheme, devised in World War II by the U.S. Treasury secretary, called for dismantling German heavy industry, busting up concentrations of economic power, and imposing heavy reparations on the defeated state. Only the advent of the Cold War, in which a divided Germany was the front line, prevented its implementation.[12] When Iraq's turn came, there was no longer an East-West confrontation to deter those intent on converting it from an aspiring new Prussia into a land of hewers of dates and drawers of goats' milk.

There followed a PR campaign of remarkable effectiveness. Broadcast around the world were tales of pillage, rape and even atrocities against babies of the type that have been the stuff of war propaganda at least since the 1915 German invasion of Belgium. In televised hearings before Congress, a Kuwaiti "nurse" related, in flawless English, how she had witnessed premature babies torn from incubators and left to die on hospital floors while the incubators were shipped to Iraq. When the Iraqis were evicted from Kuwait, the missing incubators were discovered locked in the hospital basement, babies were found to have died because foreign doctors had fled, and the brave "nurse" turned out to be the daughter of a Kuwaiti diplomat in the United States.[13]

There was looting. Some occurred after disciplined elite units that launched the invasion were replaced by peasant draftees to whom Kuwait was a consumers' wonderland. Some, too, appears to have been the work of Asian servants suddenly abandoned, unpaid, by their fleeing masters. In addition, people caught in the invasion sold valuables cheaply to Iraqi soldiers to gather money for flight. However, several soldiers were shot or hung for looting. (Pictures of the executions were published in the West with captions identifying the victims as Kuwaiti resisters.) And the new Iraqi-imposed quisling regime forbade the export from Kuwait of any merchandise without a government certificate attesting that it was not stolen. That rule was imposed less out of concern for the property of people in Kuwait than to ensure that the great majority of the looting would be officially sponsored. Banks were emptied of about $2 billion worth of foreign exchange and gold. Government buildings, factories, warehouses and the university were stripped of useful equipment and materials, partly out of pique, partly to compensate for sanctions, but in either case an indication that, from the start, the Iraqis assumed their occupation would be brief.[14]

The Iraqis were scrupulous in assuring the United States that none of its economic interests would be affected, and avoiding any action that Saudi Arabia might find provocative. Even assuming the occupation was protracted, it was hard to argue that the West's oil lifeline was threatened. There was already a glut; the United States and Europe drew only small percentages of their oil from Kuwait; the invasion would not eliminate production so much as change the identity of who did the pumping. This made a pretext for war hard to find. Furthermore, although the U.S. had, over the course of the previous decade, constructed enormously expensive bases in Saudi Arabia to support U.S. intervention in the region, a powerful wing of the ruling family was loath to be too tight with Washington.[15] Yet war needed the full cooperation of Saudi Arabia.

If the Iraqi occupation of Kuwait did not pose an economic threat to the world, surely an invasion of Saudi Arabia would? With satellite photos purporting to show a massive Iraqi presence in Kuwait pointing to Saudi Arabia, the trick was done — even though Iraq had only half the number of troops the United States claimed, it had already started to pull out of Kuwait and had made not the slightest move towards the border. Then, after Representative Solarz, still working himself into a selective lather over Middle East aggressors, introduced a war resolution into Congress, the way was clear for Desert Shield, a huge U.S. build-up to "protect" Saudi Arabia. However, before the next stage, Desert Storm, an actual offensive action to expel Iraq from Kuwait, could be undertaken, it was necessary to secure a UN fig leaf. And for that Kuwait's overseas wealth may have played a useful role.

During the 1980s the managers of the Kuwait Investment Office (KIO) had begun looking not for safety and long-term return but short-term speculative gains. One of the hottest markets left after the 1987 world stock-market meltdown was, appropriately enough, in the land of the bull. After linking up with a matador-capitalist who had just been fired over a $1-billion loss by a bank holding company he been running, KIO began pumping billions of Kuwait's oil wealth into Spain. Soon its Grupo Torras was the country's largest privately held industrial conglomerate. But as fast as the money flowed into Spain, it leaked out again through a system of shell companies and vanished. Eventually $5 billion was lost. According to a later Kuwait government lawsuit, about $4 billion was blown through stock puffing operations that benefited insiders, while another $1 billion was simply stolen. Perhaps, but by whom and why? Wagging tongues later suggested that somewhere between $300 and $500 million had been siphoned off on orders of the emir to buy votes in the UN to support the war option.[16]

It was perhaps history's greatest act of vandalism. A larger tonnage of high explosives was rained down on Iraq than had been dumped on Germany during all of World War II. Not just military installations, but metallurgical and electronics plants, warehouses, oil refineries, fertilizer and chemical firms, water treatment and electrical facilities, transportation networks and even a baby food factory were smashed. As one American officer explained calmly, strategic bombing by its nature is aimed at "all those things that allow a nation to sustain itself."[17] Although the public rationalization was that sufficient damage would make the population rise up against the regime, the real reasons were elsewhere. Iraq's modernization drive had been premised on technologies that might have been partly civilian but also had military applications. Hence, to wipe out Iraq as a military power, the Allies destroyed civilian facilities. And it was assumed that desperation to restore public infrastructure would force Iraq to beg for international reconstruction aid, which would be granted only on terms dictated by the United States. The sole important economic target untouched was the oil fields from which Iraq could pay reparations.

Yet Desert Storm was only the beginning. After a mass flight of Iraqi forces from Kuwait, and a last flourish of machismo in the form of Scud missiles fired at Saudi Arabia and Israel, the war ended. Defeated abroad, the regime faced rebellions at home in the Shi'a southern areas and the Kurdish northern ones. Yet economic sanctions voted with the avowed objective of securing the Iraqi withdrawal from Kuwait were tightened.

Damage Control

The regime showed remarkable resourcefulness. The southern revolt was crushed, the northern one tamed and the mass of population kept in line by the fact that their survival depended on subsidized rations handed out by the regime. Within two years, hundreds of miles of road and railway track as well as electrical grids and communication facilities were operating again. Most industrial fixed plant and equipment, too, were operational once more. In a drive for agricultural self-sufficiency, Iraq desalinated millions of hectares of land, in the process wiping out marshes where many of the regime's political enemies used to hide.[18] Still, the recovery was illusory. The reconstruction of some sectors was based on cannibalization of others. The regime was forced to divert into replacing destroyed plant and equipment resources that should have gone to support the population at large, whose living standards suffered a massive decline. And shortages of spares and materials kept the restored factories operating well below capacity. Furthermore, during the oil boom and Gulf War, rural areas had been depopulated, leaving Iraq dependent on imported food. Although the regime under sanction encouraged a massive shift back to the countryside, the country's fertilizer plants had been bombed flat, its ability to make pesticides stopped by bans on the import of chemicals, and its fleet of tractors grounded by the embargo on spare parts. The spectre of famine haunted the country for the next seven years.[19] Yet, despite enormous pressures, the regime held on, giving here and there on tactical issues while staying strategically defiant, aided by sanctions-busting.

To provision the private sector, Iraq lifted many controls on trade and released convicted smugglers from jail.[20] It provided some with trucks and Jordanian passports to better ply their profession. Turning smugglers loose not only helped contravene the blockade, but, typical in sanctions-busting situations, created a *nouveau riche* class of black-marketeers beholden to the regime.[21] To provision the state, the regime drew on the existing network of secret companies set up for military procurement, owned and operated by trusted aides, many of them members of Saddam's clan.[22]

Evading sanctions was a three-stage process. First, it required locating foreign suppliers willing to take the risk. Second, and much more difficult, was finding the means to pay. Private sanctions-breakers seeking consumer goods paid with gold bought cheaply from desperate people inside Iraq or counter-traded with Iraqi products or sometimes found merchants willing to accept Iraqi cash at heavy discounts. But those attempting to supply the state with strategic goods needed something more solid.

One option for payment was to pledge gold reserves against secret trade credits. Although Iraq had ceased reporting its holdings in 1977, they had then stood at nearly 130 metric tons. To that was added some gold looted from Kuwait.

A second option was to scoop up black market foreign exchange. The government printed dinars massively and, working though street money-changers, bought up dollars coming in from secret émigré remittances and private sector smuggling.[23]

A third option was to issue government bonds secured against future oil revenues. The bonds were either traded directly to suppliers or purchased by speculators at discounts in expectation of big capital gains once sanctions were lifted. They were supplemented by sales of goods against the security of frozen assets, again with an eye to capital gains.[24]

A fourth option *may* have been to earn money secretly from the oil futures market. Each time progress was made with UN negotiators in oil-for-food swap deals, the spot price of oil plunged, while each setback caused it to rise. No insider trader was better equipped to predict progress and regress of the talks than members of the Iraqi inner circle, who could tip off brokers in Europe and Hong Kong on which way to place their bets.[25]

Yet a fifth option came from the proceeds of smuggling. Fuel oil was sent in small boats from southern Iraq, hugging the Iranian coast to evade sanctions monitors. It was also driven to Jordan, which was officially allowed to import a certain amount of Iraqi oil, in fleets of tanker-trucks whose contents exceeded the legal allowance. And it was hauled across the Turkish border. From each of those places, Iraqi fuels could be sold locally or trans-shipped to world markets.[26]

The sixth option, supposedly the most important source of foreign exchange, was for Iraq to draw down funds from an underground treasury, spread through bank accounts or held in shares of publicly traded corporations, and managed from Geneva by Barzan el-Tikriti, Saddam's half-brother.[27]

The origins of the secret treasure trove were subject to much speculation. From the end of the 1970s Saddam Hussein had allegedly been skimming 5 per cent from the national oil revenues, building a nest egg that by 1990 might have totalled $20 to $28 billion. The treasury had reputedly been topped up by kickbacks from foreign businesses securing contracts in Iraq. Those firms inflated bills, collected from the Iraqi government and remitted the difference to Saddam's secret accounts.[28] Yet another source supposedly was an abortive $2.65-billion deal with Italy to provide Iraq with an instant navy, few of the sailors in which ever had to worry about getting seasick.

Late in 1980 Iraq ordered four frigates, six corvettes and a supply ship. Fincantieri Navali Riuniti, a government-owned shipbuilder, was the lead contractor. BNL handled the financing. The timing was bad. Iraq invaded Iran when only two of the General Electric engines for the ships had been delivered to Italy, and President Carter embargoed the rest. That problem was resolved two years later when the Reagan administration authorized sale of the engines provided the export licence stated that the customer was the Italian navy. Although the ships were eventually completed, none made it to Iraq. First they were blocked, sometimes with Iraqi crews aboard, by Italy bending to U.S. pressure and joining the arms embargo — unlike a shipment of mines, it would be hard to claim that a fleet of warships newly built by an Italian state company arrived in a forbidden location because of the unauthorized machinations of some "private" arms dealer. Then, after the war, delivery was stopped by a quarrel over money, still unresolved when UN sanctions killed any prospect the ships would reach Iraq.[29]

When the Italians first acted to embargo the ships, Iraq pulled $800 million out of BNL in protest. Publicly BNL struck back by imposing a $100-million limit on Iraq's CCC credits handled by its Atlanta branch. But privately it moved to conciliate Iraq by turning a blind eye when Chris Dragoul, manager of its Atlanta branch, switched from CCC-backed lending to unsecured credits that Iraq could spend at will. In 1988, when the war ended, the financial dispute turned more bitter. Iraq threatened to cancel the contract and cash more than $3 billion in performance bonds if Italy did not renegotiate the terms; Italy refused to deliver until existing debts were paid. The Italian shipbuilder claimed that to date, it had received only a $441-million down payment. Not true, insisted Iraq, which showed deposit slips for nearly $2 billion paid into two Zurich bank accounts.[30]

The accounts had been in the name of Kapital Beratung AG, an investment company liquidated shortly after receiving the Iraqi payments. And Kapital Beratung had been owned by a Swiss venture capital firm called Trans-KB. Until it collapsed with a 50-million Swiss franc hole in its books, one of the owners of Trans-KB had been a prominent lawyer and businessman named Hans Kopp, who eventually earned a conviction for fraudulent bankruptcy.[31] Kopp had other business interests. He was the vice-president of the Shakarchi bullion dealing and currency exchange firm fingered in the Magharian brothers money-laundering investigation, and the husband of the Swiss minister of justice and police who was forced to resign over the scandal. Kopp also acknowledged another, less public career. As a student he had created an anti-Communist secret political society while as a young lawyer he set up the Schweuzerische Arbeitsgemeinschaft für Demokratie, a public propaganda network committed to warning Switzerland about the international Bolshevik menace. He later spent a term as head of the psychological warfare department of Swiss military intelligence. But he denied any personal knowledge of or participation in the fate of the Iraqi money. "Maybe it was one of my partners," he suggested.[32] Perhaps. But an alternative theory suggested that, once Trans-KB collapsed, the money found its way to safety in Barzan el-Tikriti's network of secret bank accounts.[33]

Like others of the ilk — the Marcos family silver, Pablo Escobar's stash, ex-President-for-Life Mobutu's unregistered retirement plan and many more — Saddam's treasure chest increased in value with each iteration. Yet no one was ever successful in tracking it down, not even after Saddam's son-in-law and former boss of MIMI bolted to Jordan and began spilling what he knew. (Later he returned to Baghdad, begged forgiveness and was promptly shot.) The nest egg was either brilliantly hidden or was largely the product of the

imaginations of three groups: Iraqi defectors eager to convince future protectors of their importance, Kuwaiti prospectors hyped up about potential
reparations payments or financial investigators trying to justify their fees.

In addition to having to find unscrupulous or uninformed trade partners
and the means to pay, the Iraqis had a third requirement; they needed the
means to sneak goods in and out. At the beginning the main seepage point
was Jordan. Since it depended on petroleum from Iraq, UN sanctions permitted hundreds of Iraqi tanker-trucks to enter daily. Some of their contents were
secretly re-exported. Iraq's non-oil exports used the same route; they exited
via Aqabah using fake certificates of origin stating they came from Turkey,
Syria, Lebanon or Jordan. Since Jordan was the main entrepôt for food and
medicine permitted under the UN sanctions, on the way back Jordanian officials permitted Iraqi agents to fake cargo manifests and add in strategic goods,
before sending the sealed trucks to Iraq.[34] The reward was Iraqi oil at half the
world price. Under U.S. pressure, Jordan later officially cracked down on un-
authorized cargoes. But the main result was to drive the trade further underground. Jordanian traders and industrialists whose main market had always
been Iraq began relying more on Bedouin who knew the terrain intimately
to find uncharted tracks across the border.

At the start of the sanctions, evasion through Lebanon and Syria was made
easier by the fact that the Lebanese government had no control of the militia-
run ports. From Lebanon goods could be trucked through Syria, then either
cross directly into Iraq along established smuggling routes or move into Jordan to join regular truck convoys.[35] The traffic was abetted by the fact that, to
cause problems for Syria, Iraq had provided money and guns to Christian
militias battling Syrian forces in Lebanon. Even though Syria eventually brought
the Christian militias to heel, their warlords repaid their debt by smuggling
strategic goods to Iraq, with the connivance of Syrian border guards. Loads of
Iraqi dates, sulphur and urea would then pass back again through Syria with
phoney certificates of origin, to be sold at discount prices, mainly in the Far
East. Although over the early 1990s the Lebanese government gradually took
control of the pirate ports, corruption was so bad that smuggling, including
of goods bound to and from Iraq, continued with little interuption.[36]

Another porous border was the one shared with Iran. At the start of the
Gulf War, Iraq had rushed to offer a peace treaty that gave Iran almost everything for which it had asked. Soon sacks of grain marked "Iran" were prominent in Iraqi warehouses and markets. Iran began purchasing Iraqi oil for its
own refineries.[37] By the mid-1990s, it was facilitating the sale of Iraqi gas-oil
products. Tugs hauling barges set off from Iraqi ports, hugging the shore to

avoid detection. They quickly arrived inside Iranian territorial waters that were closed to ships enforcing sanctions. Assuming the barges, many unsuited for liquid cargoes, did not spill their loads en route, they discharged into small tankers. After paying off the Pasdaran and picking up fake Iranian certificates of origin, the tankers crossed to Dubai, the Gulf's traditional smuggling capital and domicile of Iraqi businessmen dealing in food, medicine and strategic commodities. From there the fuel would go mainly to India in dhows, the rugged little sail-and-motor boats that have long plied the Indian Ocean carrying everything from gold (banned until recently in India) to whisky (forbidden in Saudi Arabia) to ivory and rhino horn (subject to worldwide embargoes). In reverse, forbidden goods like auto parts and industrial equipment made their way from Dubai into Iraq using bills of lading specifying Iran, or, ironically enough, Kuwait as the destination.[38]

From the start the key to making sanctions bite was to seal the border with the country that had been Iraq's largest trading partners, and that therefore had the most to lose. Turkey's willingness to enforce sanctions depended on the strategic situation in Kurdistan.

A Kurd in Hand

With the break-up of the Ottoman empire, the Kurds had been promised their own state, then left divided between Iran, Iraq and Turkey. Another chance came at the end of World War II with the emergence of the Mahabad Republic in the Kurdish parts of Iran. But the Cold War led to the Western powers strengthening Iran, and the U.S.S.R. refused to give the Kurdish entity military assistance. Subsequently, the Kurds either fought against their hosts or were used by those hosts to make mischief against neighbours. Invariably, their sponsors dumped the Kurds when their immediate usefulness was over.[39]

The Mahabad Republic had encouraged the Iraqi Kurds led by Mullah Mustafa Barzani to organize the Kurdish Democratic Party (KDP). But it soon split between those from the north, agrarian, traditionalist and loyal to the Barzani clan, and those from farther south, more urban, attracted by Marxist rhetoric and eventually following Jalal Talabani. In the late 1960s, fed weapons by Iran, Israel and the United States, the Kurds began a protracted guerrilla war. However, the factional split was so deep that Talabani's men sometimes joined with the Iraqi army against Barzani's forces. Fear of Barzani's growing strength led Iraq to grant autonomy to the Kurds. But the 1975 agreement between Iran and Iraq cut off Iranian aid. The Kurdish movement collapsed; Talabani retreated to Syria to form the rival Patriotic Union of Kurdistan (PUK); and Barzani fled to Washington where he died in 1979.

By then the strategic balance was swinging back. The revolutionary regime in Iran refused to enforce the 1975 agreement and encouraged infiltration by armed Kurds. During the Iran-Iraq War, the Iranians used the Kurds to attack the main highway and supply route from Iraq to Turkey and to sabotage oil installations. But the division between the Iranian-backed KDP and the Syrian-supported PUK continued.[40] Further complicating the scene was the rise of yet another Kurdish insurgent group.

Among the paramilitary groups active in Turkey during the turbulent 1970s was the Kurdish People's Party (PKK). After the 1980 coup, Turkey responded to the Kurdish rebels with a vicious counter-insurgency campaign. Over the next decade hundreds of villages were destroyed or depopulated, and an area, already denied industrial development, was further depressed. Driven abroad, first by heavy unemployment, then by military action, Turkish Kurds formed in Germany, France and Sweden, a growing diaspora. More and more of the diaspora organizations fell under the PKK's sway. Money to support the struggle came partly from donations, partly from social benefit fraud and partly from extortion against émigré businessmen. Meanwhile PKK units inside Turkey collected war taxes, kidnap ransom and profits from running heroin. At peak the PKK could support 10,000 armed men.[41] Yet the Turkish Kurds never coordinated operations with their Iraqi and Iranian kinfolk. Just the opposite. In addition to its struggle with the Turkish army, the PKK found itself embroiled in contraband wars with the Iraqi Kurds. Meanwhile divisions among the Iraqi Kurds worsened. Partly it was politics; the PUK demanded total independence, while the KDP was willing to strike a new autonomy deal. But even more it was money.

After the Gulf War, the United States had encouraged the Kurds to establish a regional government in northern Iraq. At the start it was less a public administration than a system of rackets. Outside the main towns, local militias manned checkpoints and charged "tolls" to anyone using the roads. Across Kurdistan everything from heavy engineering equipment to high tension wiring was stripped to be sold in Iran along with thousands of municipal vehicles, including most of the police cars. Farmers defied demands by the Kurdish regional administration to give Kurdish areas priority access to their harvests and sold their produce in the big cities controlled by Iraqi forces. However, under American guidance, the situation began to stabilize; tens of millions of dollars' worth of relief poured into the area, while the rest of Iraq was left bereft. The United States even paid to stop farmers from selling their crops to the Iraqi-controlled areas. And it coaxed the two warring factions into a 50-50 power-sharing agreement. But Saddam struck back, cutting off supplies of food, medicine and fuel, and blocking funds, leaving the civil service unpaid.[42] Then he found a simple but powerful way to bring the autonomous zone to heel.

Sanctions had badly shaken Iraq's financial system, drying up its foreign exchange and depriving the government of its main tax revenues. But by accident they also provided some relief. Formerly Iraq had imported bank-notes from Europe. With sanctions it was forced to make its own. Printing money permitted the government to cash in, literally, on the hyperinflation racking the country. Apparently taking seriously the notion that the pen is mightier than the sword, a UN embargo supposedly intended to impede re-armament also banned fine paper and high-quality inks. Hence new Iraqi banknotes were crudely photocopied reproductions. That made the job of counterfeiting much easier. In 1991 Baghdad accused Turkey, Saudi Arabia and Iran of flooding Iraq with bogus notes.[43] The next year it claimed that counterfeit 100-dinar notes along with $100 bills were dumped from Allied helicopters in a CIA operation code-named Laundry. Iraq made counterfeit-ing a capital offence, then recalled and reissued all 100-dinar notes.[44] A year later it came up with a more interesting tactic.

The Iraqi population distrusted the new notes, which circulated at a heavy discount against the old, European-printed ones. Those older notes were either hoarded or picked up by refugees and smugglers and taken illegally out of the country. Many ended up in Kuwait and Saudi Arabia where they posed a double threat. Those enemy states could release them en masse to further destabilize the Iraqi economy, or speculators could use them to take advantage of Iraq's prostrate economy when sanctions were lifted.

In 1993 the government announced the withdrawal of the old European-made 25-dinar note, the most important in circulation. And it sealed the borders. Iraqis living in areas under the regime's control were given five days to exchange old notes for new with no questions asked. But notes that had fled abroad into the hands of merchants, speculators or intelligence agencies were wiped out. Since Kurdistan was outside government control, one-third of its cash in circulation was demonetized without compensation. The result was financial panic. When efforts to substitute Turkish currency were blocked by Ankara, the Kurds decided to simply ignore the demonetization, keeping in circulation a currency that was legally valueless outside their enclave.[45]

Borderline Business

Sanctions unexpectedly provided an opportunity for the Iraqi regime to reach a truce with the rebellious northern territories. Smuggling across the Iraqi-Turkish border through Kurdistan was an old story. All the villages participated, and the Turkish government, more concerned with buying support for its war against the PKK than with the revenue lost to smuggling, turned a blind eye. The Gulf War converted regular smuggling into a gold rush.[46]

One of the targets of Allied bombing had been oil refineries. The surviving plants produced too much diesel and aviation fuel for Iraq's own consumption. In theory sanctions strictly limited the amount of surplus that could be exported. Although some extra fuel found its way out via Jordan or Iran, the most important route lay through Kurdistan. Truckers then picked up loads of foodstuffs and building supplies in Turkey where they were relatively cheap and hauled them to the border at the Khabour-Abu Khalil Bridge. On the Turkish side, truckers paid off Customs officials. From 500 to 1,000 trucks crossed daily through checkpoints manned by militiamen representing the Kurdish autonomist authority. Here truckers paid another toll of about $130 each.[47] Heading south into Iraq they sold their cargoes, sometimes for gold or cash but usually for barter: one ton of flour might be exchanged for 6,000 litres of diesel fuel. Tanker-trucks legally limited to four tons of oil then routinely hauled back ten, part of it pumped into special tanks slung underneath the trucks — welding tanks was one of the few growth industries in Kurdistan. On the way home they again paid transit charges. In Turkey, they offloaded fuels to special bunkering stations, from which it was pumped into large tanker-trucks and taken to market elsewhere in the country.[48]

It was a brilliant example of the power of the profit motive to transcend political strife. Iraq got to sell diesel fuel and import essentials despite the embargo. Although the fuel entering Turkey evaded taxes and undercut legal distributors, the Turkish government was willing to ignore the sanctions and swallow the tax losses for fear that a crackdown would hurt the depressed regional economy and provoke more sympathy for the PKK.[49] But it made its accommodation of the trade conditional on Iraqi Kurds cooperating in blocking efforts by the PKK to use Iraqi bases for raids across the border. The KDP was happy to oblige. It kept a hot line open to Turkish intelligence and stamped on PKK activity. Although the two Iraqi factions were supposed to share power, control of the revenues permitted the KDP to dominate the autonomy authority.[50] The PUK, strongest near the Iranian border, had its own contraband routes. It taxed the smuggling of carpets from Iran into Turkey and the flow of cigarettes, alcohol and weapons back again. However, that trade was far less lucrative. The KDP's greater financial resources soon translated into muscle. Assisted by Iraqi forces, it chased the PUK out of the area. A delighted Saddam Hussein formally recognized the victorious KDP's rights to the diesel transit revenue.[51]

To the Victor, the Spoils?

The invasion of Kuwait was an appalling act. By attacking a virtually defence-less neighbour to overthrow its government, try to capture its ruler, then grab the country's assets, Saddam Hussein showed as much disrespect for inter-national law as had George Bush when he ordered the invasion of Panama, the kidnapping of its military chief and the withholding of reconstruction aid in hopes of blackmailing the new government into opening the books of its banks to American probes. After the Iraqi invasion, Kuwait compiled a list of 300 political assassinations by the occupation forces.[52] In Panama the bodies of about the same number of collaterally damaged civilians were dumped en masse into unmarked graves.

To such appalling acts there should be an appropriate response, though just what it is is the subject of contention. Some had argued for use of the eco-nomic weapon alone. Others had seen economic war only as a complement to military action. Many deplored the decision to rush to combat. But at least one set of powerful corporate interests was overjoyed.

Most military activity on the ground was a sideshow in which American forces slaughtered demoralized Iraqi conscripts already in flight. The main event was staged on prime-time TV where people could watch in awe as "smart bombs" zeroed in on target, helicopter gunships chewed up Iraqi armour and Patriot anti-missile missiles knocked down the infamous Scuds. A shiver of pride went up the spines of American defence industry workers. The result was to wipe from the collective memory a decade of Pentagon scandals, of faked test results and fraudulent cost inflation, and to give U.S. weapons makers, until then in trepidation over the post-Cold War shrinkage of the market, a resounding victory over their Russian and French competi-tors, who had supplied most of the Iraqi hardware.[53]

Once the hype was stripped away, most of the damage to Iraq's armour was found to have been done by the cheapest and oldest equipment in the Amer-ican arsenal, particularly a slow and ugly cannon-firing aircraft the air force, fixated on svelte missile-dispensing planes setting double records for speed and cost, had strenuously resisted deploying. The vast majority (over 90 per cent) of shells fired and bombs dropped were of the old-fashioned "dumb" type that produced a civilian toll about double the number of people ever permit-ted to vote in a Kuwaiti election. As to the Patriot anti-missile system, brought on line six years and $2 billion over schedule, its greatest moment came when George Bush used it as a backdrop to a victory speech. Though deployed against the easiest of possible quarries, the ancient Scud, which was slow, had a single warhead and lacked any capacity for evasive action, the Patriot may well have made the situation worse, by chasing bits and pieces of already destroyed missiles, then following debris into the ground, thus helping to strike the target. Scuds were more consistently the victims of sloppy engineering than of anti-missile defences.[54] Still, in poured the orders. The U.S. assistant secretary of defence in charge of international affairs declared Desert Storm "the world's biggest fund-raiser, which raised $60 billion for U.S. military forces alone," while the 1991 Paris Air Show featured U.S. pilots, paid by the Pentagon to stand beside planes and regale visitors with war stories.[55]

One casualty was the Arab League Boycott. Gratitude to their benefactor provided a pretext for Saudi Arabia and the other Gulf states to remove all U.S. firms from the boycott list without approval from the Arab League.[56] They even offered, via the U.S. Secretary of State, to renounce their boycott entirely if Israel would only ameliorate a little the conditions of the Palestinians under occupation — Israel refused.[57]

Thus another casualty was hopes for Palestinian independence. Caught between the fact that Iraq was the principal supporter of the Palestinian armed forces while the Gulf states, where 500,000 Palestinian refugees worked, were the main source of financing for the PLO, Arafat leaned to Iraq. That provided the Gulf states an excuse to cut off funds at a time when the PLO was already in rough financial shape. Badly hurt by the Israeli invasion of Lebanon, by severe losses on its worldwide investment portfolio and by some of its surrogates who disappeared with assets that (for security purposes) had been held in their own names, the PLO had been further drained of $340 million for financing the intifada.[58] The Gulf states also expelled Palestinian workers en masse. Financially and politically crippled, Arafat and his entourage agreed to a "self-rule" deal in which the PLO took over from the Israeli security forces much of the job of keeping a lid on political dissent in the Occupied Territories while Israeli colonization continued unabated.[59] To drive home the advantage, the United States sent Iraq a broad hint that it might lift sanctions if Iraq would allow 600,000 Palestinian refugees in Lebanon to move to Iraq. The deal was that, by settling the Palestinians in the north, Iraq could dilute the Kurdish majority and so relieve pressure on the United States to do something for the Palestinian refugees that might invoke Israel's ire.[60]

The wartime destruction of oil wells and pipelines, telecommunications, roads, buildings and factories cost Kuwait $160 billion and Iraq $190 billion.[61] For Iraq the immediate price was only the beginning. The sanctions cost it many years of direct revenues in addition to the impact of depreciation of its remaining capital equipment. Its legal exports of oil were fixed by the UN supposedly at a level sufficient to buy essential food and medicine. In fact, the level of permitted oil exports was really set more with a view to keeping the oil market from flooding. The proceeds were never sufficient to meet Iraq's food and medicine requirements. A country formerly priding itself on free medical care was trapped in epidemics of cholera, typhoid and gastroenteritis. The infant mortality rate trebled. By mid-decade less than a third of the hospitals were functioning normally. Imports of medicine had fallen from $50 million per annum to $500,000. While UN inspectors went on search-and-destroy missions against "chemical warfare" agents, there was no chlorine in the country to sterilize an increasingly contaminated drinking water supply, and the ban on "dual-use" equipment cost chemotherapy units their supplies of replacement materials. A universal and free school system was reduced to using ten-year-old books, when any were available. Investment in industry and agriculture ground to a halt. About 30 per cent of children suffered from malnutrition as the poor were forced to scavenge in the garbage, traffic on the black market, or survive by petty crime or by selling off family possessions and gold jewellery. The only parts of the legal private economy that flourished were pawn shops.[62]

Even the cultural fabric of the country was systematically destroyed. Iraq, heir to Mesopotamia and Assyria, contains more archaeological treasures than any other place on earth. Before the war its sites and its museums were superbly maintained. Since then, with the breakdown of order in the countryside and the withering of the government's resources, there emerged a massive traffic in looted artefacts. First there were random attacks on museums and storehouses. Then there were organized raids by gangs equipped with fake official licence plates and lists of items to take, probably supplied by brokers in Europe. Finally there were night-time assaults on archaeological sites by armies of Bedouin and peasants, hired for virtually nothing as diggers. The relics were spirited out by professional smugglers, government functionaries or, allegedly, UN diplomats, through Saudi Arabia or the Kurdish autonomist zone, paying transit fees to corrupt Customs agents or guerrilla groups, then laundered through Switzerland, before being marketed in London, New York and Tokyo.[63]

Faced with the toll, human and cultural, exiled opposition groups called repeatedly for the end of the sanctions, the results of which far exceeded in sheer criminality the impact of Saddam Hussein's many accumulated sins. The protests became so serious that in 1998 the U.S. State Department authorized $97 million to support an umbrella opposition organization. It was headed by a man who had fled from Jordan in the late 1980s in the face of accusations of bank fraud and money-laundering. He responded to the U.S. initiative by supporting the maintenance of sanctions against Iraq until his group took power. And he further won hearts and minds in Washington by stating that among the first acts of the successor regime would be reopening the Kirkuk-Haifa pipeline whose closure by Iraq in 1948 had heralded the start of the serious Arab economic war against Israel.[64]

Despite several years of an unprecedented economic squeeze following history's most intensive strategic bombing, Saddam and his associates (those not murdered in fits of pique and paranoia) have stayed in place, buttressed by a *nouveau riche* class of profiteers while the living standard of the population at large, the real victims of the Baathist regime, has been reduced to that of Calcutta or Haiti.

In 1990, based on 1987 data, the UN Human Development Report classified Iraq's standard of human welfare as "high-medium," ranking fifty-fourth of UN member states. Iraqis had a life expectancy of sixty-five and an adult literacy rate of 89 per cent. In 1998, based on 1995 data, Iraq ranked one hundred and twenty-eighth. Its population had a life expectancy of fifty-eight and an adult literacy rate of 58 per cent.

As to the impact of the destruction and the destitution on the infamous weapons of "mass destruction," the last word will forever rest with Jafer abu Jafer, father of Iraq's nuclear arms program: "You can bomb our buildings. You can destroy our technology. But you cannot take it out of our heads. We now have the capacity."[65]

Part Eight

YUGOSLAVIA, HUMPTY DUMPTY AND THE BERLIN WALL

Chapter 22

BALKANIZING THE BALKANS

From the end of the Napoleonic Wars and to the start of World War I, the great powers carved up the globe into rival spheres of influence. Yet during that century they rarely had recourse to economic warfare. Trade became progressively more open, capital flows freer and property rights better protected even during conflicts, which were usually of limited scope.[1] In 1914 the trends suddenly reversed. Total war required mass mobilization of resources by the state; attacking a rival's economic strength became, once again, as important as directly confronting its military power.

The precipitating event was the assassination of the Crown Prince of Austria by a Serbian nationalist in Sarajevo, capital of the Austro-Hungarian province of Bosnia. That the fuse was lit in the Balkans was no accident. It was the strategically vital land bridge between Europe and Asia, the traditional route for conquering armies moving both ways, and, for a long time, a cockpit for Russia, Austria-Hungary and the Ottoman Empire. In part to reduce the danger that the region's ethno-political rivalries might again serve as a catalyst for war, the victors in 1918 created an independent Kingdom of the Serbs, Croats and Slovenes, uniting several flashpoints. Though partitioned again during World War II, afterwards it was restored as modern Yugoslavia,

Communist in ideology though open to the West and committed to independence from both sides in the geo-strategic divide.[2]

Countdown to Catastrophe

The country's most important task was to reconcile national communities with constituent republics. At the top, geographically and economically, was Slovenia with a Catholic population of (almost all) Slovene ethnicity and generally uncontentious borders. At the bottom, geographically and economically, was Macedonia. The majority of its population were Orthodox Christians speaking a language sufficiently similar to Bulgarian to encourage revanchist sentiments in Bulgaria. It also hosted a large Albanian–Muslim minority. And its very name sent neighbouring Greece into paroxysms of chauvinist rage. Just north of Albania was Montenegro, clannish by nature, Serbian by speech and Orthodox by religion, though also with a big Albanian–Muslim minority. In between was an ethno-religious quagmire.

Catholic Croatia had borders drawn on the fly just after the war to incorporate an Orthodox Serbian population that, by 1990, totalled 600,000. Its more nationalist politicians, egged on by fanatical members of its Cold War diaspora, made little secret of their desire to redraw the frontier with Bosnia-Herzegovina to incorporate the 20 per cent of that republic's population of Croatian ethnicity.

Bosnia-Herzegovina itself hosted Orthodox Serbs, Catholic Croats and a Yugoslavian concoction called Muslims. Long regarded as backward Serbs or Croats who had converted to Islam while Bosnia was under Ottoman rule, the self-consciousness of the Muslim population received an important boost from the Yugoslav-Soviet split. Seeing military self-sufficiency as the sine qua non of independence, Yugoslavia located its main arms industries in mountainous Bosnia out of reach of a potential invader. The result was to bring industrialization and modern technical education to a previously isolated and backward area. In 1963 the Muslims were recognized as a constituent nationality within Yugoslavia. Thereafter Bosnia functioned politically on the basis not of popular vote, but of consensus among representatives of its three ethno-religious communities.[3]

Then there was Serbia, the largest and most populous republic, albeit with substantial national minorities whose political position was anomalous. While Bosnia's Muslims were accorded constitutional recognition, national status was never given to the Albanian–Muslim population forming the overwhelming majority of the Serbian province of Kosovo, or to the large Hungarian-Catholic minority of its province of Vojvodina. Instead a 1974 constitutional overhaul made Kosovo and Vojvodina autonomous. Not only did they have equal status with republics in the federal presidency, where decisions were made on the basis of one vote per republic, but any law passed by Serbia had to be ratified by the two autonomous provinces before it applied to them, while none of their laws had to be approved by Serbia. As a further irritant, more than 25 per cent of the Serb population lived as minorities in Croatia and Bosnia without formal recognition.[4]

For a long time the political balancing act worked. Apart from the status enjoyed by Marshall Josip Broz (Tito), post-war architect of the modern state, until his death in 1980, there was the unifying influence of the Communist Party and of the Yugoslav National Army. Unity was further encouraged by fear of the U.S.S.R., mistrust of neighbours and shared memories of World War II in which ethnic strife claimed more victims than had the Germans. More positively, Yugoslavia's economic achievements were exceptional in eastern Europe. Although it went through economically difficult times in the mid-1970s, its open borders to the West worked as a safety valve. Yugoslavs moved en masse to work abroad and sent money back to their families. Tourists from western Europe poured into the Dalmatian coast. And Western governments leaned on their banks to open their vaults.

The problem was that, in Yugoslavia's unique system of worker-managed companies, employees naturally preferred wage hikes to investment in machinery, causing productivity to stagnate. For a time businesses hid the problem by borrowing abroad. But in the early 1980s, the entire international financial system was shaken as heavily indebted developing countries flirted with default. When the United States, as part of its economic war against the Soviet Union, tried to precipitate a financial crisis in Poland, the panic spread to eastern Europe. Yugoslavia slide into recession. Its government was forced, for the first time since the immediate post-war period, to impose rationing, badly shaking faith in the system. Under intense pressure from international banks worried about repayment, the federal government agreed, after the stormiest session in its parliamentary history, to guarantee all foreign debt no matter which republic, bank or corporation had borrowed the money. It agreed that the country's assets, no matter in which republic, could be seized by foreign creditors if debts were unpaid. And it assumed authority to control further borrowing wherever in the country the borrower was located. Ambitious political leaders in the republics would later use those emergency financial measures to denounce federal intrusion on their sovereignty.

As austerity and recession took its toll, fresh blows landed. The end of the Iran-Iraq War killed the main market for arms, Yugoslavia's most successful export. The end of Communism wiped out markets for other goods in eastern Europe, while few Yugoslav businesses could compete in the West. When bad times hit Germany, Austria and Switzerland in the late 1980s, émigré workers drifted home to face unemployment. Commercial bank lending dried up. Then Yugoslavia landed in the middle of the BNL scandal. LBS Bank, the American subsidiary of Ljubaljanska Bank, one of Yugoslavia's biggest, was BNL Atlanta's second-largest customer. LBS lent BNL money to finance its loans to Iraq. Worse, it had taken over from BNL the loans to cover embargo-busting grain shipments to Cuba, and it had lent money to the trading company later caught swapping CCC-subsidized wheat for Soviet arms on behalf of Iraq. This embarrassment came in the wake of Operation Flying Kite in which the FBI had indicted several of the bank's senior officials and declared persona non grata Yugoslav consular personnel for laundering drug money and smuggling restricted technology.[5] With the financial system falling into ruin, in came the IMF and World Bank. They demanded a restructuring that added up to a complete abandonment of the principle of worker-managed firms, imposed a bankruptcy law that pushed countless enterprises over the brink and sent unemployment soaring, and forced the central authorities to divert into paying off external debts money that should have gone in transfer payments to the various republics and autonomous provinces.

As the economy spiralled down, the richer republics of Slovenia and Croatia increasingly objected to the transfer of resources to the poorer republics in the south. They responded by denouncing the terms on which they had to buy tariff-protected products of the north. The Yugoslav National Army had been the most important institution transcending the ethnic divide. But without a Soviet threat to justify its bloated existence, it became an easy target for accusations of waste and corruption.

The first shots were fired not between Muslims, Croats and Serbs in Bosnia, or in the Serb-populated parts of Croatia, but inside Serbia. The province of Kosovo, although poor and almost void of resources, had a special significance as the site of the fourteenth-century battle between Orthodox Serbia and Muslim Turkey, a conflict that nationalists took as the defining point of Serbian history. When Albanian riots sent members of the Serb minority fleeing, Slobodan Milošević used the Serbian national question to capture the republic's presidency. In the face of bitter resistance, Milošević imposed a state of siege on Kosovo, wiping out its autonomy, along with that of Vojvodina. That coup upset the political balance on which the Yugoslav consensus was based. For Serbia could now control three of the eight votes in the federal presidency and, with Montenegro almost always taking a pro-Serbian position, usually fully half.

The rising tide of nationalism caused the Communist Party to disintegrate. So, too, did economic unity. Slovenia and Serbia imposed trade restrictions on each other, followed shortly by Serbia and Croatia.[6] Encouraged by Italy and Austria, in 1991 Slovenia declared sovereignty. A last-ditch effort by the federal government to maintain constitutional control floundered in a brief "war" that sent the army in disgraced retreat and mobilized international sentiment in favour of Slovenia.[7] Drawing comfort from the federal debacle in Slovenia and support from Germany, Croatia, too, declared sovereignty. Macedonia and Bosnia reluctantly followed, leaving only tiny Montenegro with Serbia in what was left of the federal state. The stage was set for disaster.

Yugoslavia had been founded on two constitutionally recognized notions of sovereignty. One was based on common membership in a territorially defined civil society and the other on ethnic identity. While a republic like Slovenia, most adamant in demanding dismantling of the country, was ethnically homogeneous within well-accepted borders, others were not. The refusal of Croatian Serbs and, later, Bosnian Serbs and Bosnian Croats to accept incorporation as minorities into newly independent states sparked two interrelated but distinct wars. One occurred between republics contesting borders, the second inside republics between groups contesting the legitimacy of their inclusion within those borders. The inability of the international community to understand that, in the Yugoslav context, both forms of sovereignty could claim legitimacy, led it to embark on one of the most misdirected programs of economic sanctions in its already undistinguished career.

In 1991 there were clashes between the Yugoslav army and the Croatian militia, and Serb insurrections in economically vital areas of Croatia (Krajina, commanding access to the tourist facilities on the Dalmatian coast; and Slavonia, containing much of Croatia's oil). In response, the UN imposed an arms embargo on all of Yugoslavia. The next year the war shifted. Although the borders had been arbitrarily drawn, mainly at Serbia's expense, the European Community (EC) and the United States decided that sovereignty of republics within given frontiers took precedence over sovereignty of national communities, and recognized the independence of the republics. In so doing they encouraged a revolt by Bosnian Croats and Bosnian Serbs against the Muslim-dominated government. Bosnia descended into a three-sided civil war in which the objectives became grabbing strategic assets (arms factories, power plants, communication facilities, etc.) and creating links between localities populated by the same ethnic group. Since in a battle to create nation states out of multi-ethnic communities there could be no distinction between civilians and combatants, other ethnic groups were cleared out in the process.

The Western powers then decided that, since the worst atrocities were committed by Serb militias, the republic of Serbia was the aggressor. In reality, Serb rebels in Croatia and Bosnia largely set their own agenda, and the fact that Serbs committed more atrocities reflected not morality but opportunity. Where the other sides gained the upper hand, they matched the record. The Western powers further convinced themselves that the remnants of the old Yugoslav army was Serbia's tool in aggression, even though it had stood against disintegration rather than for Serbia until well into the conflict. As a result, the UN added to its arms embargo against all republics general sanctions against only Serbia and Montenegro, sidestepping the fact that Montenegro had tried to play peacemaker and was so economically dependent on Serbia that it was less an accomplice than a captive.

Misfire

Serbia was the least affected by the arms embargo. Its arms factories continued production with little interruption, even developing a new long-range artillery piece modelled on Gerald Bull's. The Yugoslav military had been created to be self-sufficient in wartime conditions. It maintained underground stockpiles throughout the country. Since Yugoslav defence strategy had been premised on the notion of falling back on mountainous areas where the main factories were located, the embargo gave contestants an added incentive to grab slices of Bosnia. Serbian units in the federal army stationed in Croatia also seized machinery and inventories.[8] To the limited extent Serbia needed to import weapons, the post-Cold War context made the job easy. Arms reduction agreements had meant that the U.S.S.R. dumped 11,000 tanks, 12,000 armoured personnel carriers and 1,600 fighter planes, along with masses of small arms. Then, with the demise of the U.S.S.R. and the disintegration of the Red Army, ex-Soviet republics, even cities, grabbed arsenals, armouries were looted, unpaid units dumped their inventories, and soldiers sold the tanks in which they were riding. Into this lethal flea market wandered armies of would-be gun-runners.[9] Although Russia officially stood by the arms embargo, historical ties to Serbia meant that factions within the government and army were happy to see the Serbs quietly equipped.

Others, too, lent a hand. Serbia announced its first arms acquisition from Israel within a month of sanctions. Israeli officers, many veterans of Lebanon, reputedly trained the Serbian army and militias in "counterinsurgency and anti-terrorism."[10] There were also barter deals with Iraq, formerly a leading customer for Yugoslav military equipment. Serbian know-how and parts were exchanged for oil in two-way sanctions-busting deals. Serbia continued to cooperate with Libya, another old trading partner and long-time subject of international sanctions.[11] With stockpiles, manufacturing capacity and foreign assistance, Serbia was so well endowed that it could still export weapons. In 1994 the Greek-flagged *Maria* (a.k.a. the Honduran-flagged *Varna I*), already notorious for carrying banned Serbian goods to Nigeria, ran out of fuel, water and food off the Seychelles. Aboard, the authorities discovered Serbian weapons bound for Somalia, also under a UN arms embargo.[12] The Seychelles authorities impounded the arms, then quietly sold them off to a German broker who, undeterred by another UN arms embargo, peddled them to the Rwandan army then engaged in the ethnic cleansing of the country's Tutsi minority. As long as relations with Milošević and his generals remained good, Serbian rebel forces in Croatia and Bosnia, too, were well equipped. When the Yugoslav army pulled out of Bosnia, it turned over heavy equipment and arms factories to the Bosnian Serbs, while dismantling or destroying facilities where it expected Muslims or Croats to take over.[13]

The rebel Serbs also opened up their own arms supply system. It was not always a brilliant success. In 1994 a British arms dealer offered Serbian forces in Croatia £1 million worth of British-made Starburst anti-aircraft missiles. Money was wired from Switzerland to an account in London. Before the deal could be consummated, Scotland Yard arrested the main plotters.[14] Nor were Serb rebels more successful in their alleged quest for the ultimate ethnic-cleansing device.

One of the more fabulous items to enter the arms market has been "red mercury," a hot commodity even though no one is sure it exists. Touted as everything from a means to extract oil from drying wells to a technology for making undetectable counterfeit money to a tool for triggering miniature nuclear explosives, red mercury, much like the UFO, has produced dozens of sightings but no interceptions. The stuff of bush-league scams, like a red-mercury rush in the Kenya outback in the mid-1980s, it even turned up on documents unearthed by UN weapons inspectors in Baghdad after the Gulf War. But the trail was like quicksilver — touched in one place, it divided into subsidiary channels ending nowhere, until taking a more ominous twist in 1991.

That year the dismembered body of the sales director of a chemical company that imported mercury waste turned up in the trunk of his car outside Johannesburg. It was the first of a series of murders, all popularly ascribed to red mercury, of people linked to the arms trade. There were several reasons the red mercury trail had led to South Africa. Since the end of the apartheid police state, South Africa had become one of the world's great contraband centres. Drugs, arms, ivory, gemstones and stolen cars crossed its borders.

South Africa, too, had had its own covert nuclear program, into which red mercury, supposedly a key component for miniature weapons, appeared to fit. And it still had its apartheid-era arms trafficking network of ghost companies and procurement fronts, along with a small army of former intelligence agents willing to sell their talents to the highest bidder.[15]

Apart from this flurry in South Africa, the main action was in Russia, where red mercury had supposedly been invented. Stories of one secret deal followed another, with the world's most legendary terrorists and most notorious rogue states supposedly in the market. In 1993 a scientist claimed to be making the stuff in a secret lab owned by his otherwise unprofitable environmental services company. He was ready, he said, to meet export orders for a modest $300,000 a kilogram. His three-year exclusive right, he insisted, was a gift from President Yeltsin himself. If anyone needed further proof, the scientist could show potential buyers a contract for eighty-four tons of the stuff (worth about $250 billion!) signed with a California company whose operating address was an auto-parts shop. Those who insisted that red mercury did not exist drew from the scientist a derisory rebuke. His detractors, he said, were a bunch of criminals, ex-KGB types and former Communist apparachniks exporting the stuff illegally and not wanting their monopoly challenged.[16]

Time after time red mercury was denounced as a sham, and often a cover for bank frauds and resource rip-offs in Russia. Each "sample" turned out to be common mercury compounds, tinted with everything from brick dust to red nail polish. Yet there were still those with faith. According to his political opponents, one such believer was Bosnian Serb leader Radovan Karadjić. In the closing months of the Bosnian war when the Muslims were making great gains, Karadjić assured his followers about the pending arrival of a secret weapon. Karadjić's agents reputedly met a supplier on a windswept bridge to swap a suitcase containing $6 million for a brass container said to hold the fabled substance. This was to be the first step in the acquisition of a small neutron bomb — popularly dubbed the landlord's bomb, for it emits intense radiation, killing everything in its range, while leaving physical structures intact and usable within a few hours. But when Karadjić opened the container, it was full of an innocuous red goo. By then the $6 million was long gone.

By contrast to Serbia, Croatia started the period of conflict with a handicap. Not only had most of the army's weapons been grabbed by Serbia, but so too the bulk of the federal treasury. Apart from one case early in the war when a Yugoslav general surrendered a garrison with more than 100 tanks, Croatia took few stockpiles. Therefore imports were essential.

In theory they were blocked by sanctions. In practice getting arms was relatively simple. First, many countries were eager to help. Germany and Austria resurrected a historical alliance with Croatia against Serbia; Hungary aided Croatia to weaken Serbia's position in Vojvodina; and Slovakia was eager to peddle products of the only really functioning industrial sector inherited from its break with the Czech Republic. Second, while the great majority of Serbian and Montenegrin émigrés were recently arrived working people, Croatia's diaspora was well entrenched, prosperous and eager to contribute. Third, Croatia controlled the Dalmatian coast with its myriad harbours, making it easy for arms to slip past UN monitors. Fourth, there was sheer hypocrisy. Although Croatia had taken the lead in ethnic-cleansing campaigns, not only was the arms embargo never seriously enforced against it, there was no effort to punish it through the sort of general sanctions under which Serbia laboured.[17]

Arms smuggling into Croatia actually predated the collapse of Yugoslavia. Even before Franjo Tudjman, who led Croatia's independence drive, was elected president, he made several trips to North America to solicit money. An Ottawa pizza-parlour operator and soon-to-be minister of defence set up the Croatian National Fund. Money from émigré businessmen was collected in Toronto's Croatian Credit Union, sent to Switzerland, then wired to an Austrian bank to pay for Soviet arms a British gun-runner had obtained in southern Africa. The plotters chartered a Ugandan Airways cargo plane, filed a flight plan to Botswana, and landed in Bophutaswana. There the plane took on a cargo of "technical equipment." After a brief refuelling stop in Uganda, paid for by a wire transfer from Switzerland, it left for the Balkans. However, Yugoslav intelligence had infiltrated the ring, and federal jets forced the plane down.[18]

After independence, Croatia's arms smuggling became more extensive — from Poland, Germany, Austria and even Russia where, despite its government's sympathy for Serbia, ex-KGB officers were reputedly permitted to use Croatia as a staging point for trafficking in nuclear materials in exchange for assistance in obtaining arms.[19] Croatia set up front companies to whom it would pass shopping lists. Obliging governments accepted fake end-user certificates, and complicit companies disguised cargoes, for example, by labelling detonators as "mining equipment." Weapons were stowed on trucks with foreign and frequently changed licence plates or they were put on freighters that made unscheduled stops, followed circuitous routes or offloaded to small boats able to mix with the thousands of pleasure craft that frequented the Dalmatian coast. Payments passed mainly through Austrian banks with the double protection of tight secrecy laws and Austria's sympathy for Croatia.[20]

The suppliers were certainly eclectic. As part of its peace terms, Lebanon required its militias to shed their heavy weapons. Apparently the Lebanese Forces shipped to Croatia $20 million worth to equip fellow crusaders for Catholic Civilization. There were impolite rumours that the Vatican covered the bill.

Another supplier was the Croatian Resistance Organization, an ultra-right spin-off of an organization created by the CIA from refugees facing death sentences for World War II crimes.[21] Originally a Cold War tool, by the 1990s it had become a vehicle for foreign-born Croats nurtured by ideological venom and infused with anti-Serbian racism. Apart from contributions from wealthy donors, it ran extortion rackets in North America and bought arms with the proceeds.

Yet another was Italy's Sacra Corona Unita. After investing profits from cigarette smuggling in casinos located in Croatia's tourist zone, members of the crime fraternity were required to kick back to Croatian intelligence part of the money skimmed from the casinos. Hence they decided to earn it back by selling weapons. Completing the circle, arms profits were reinvested in the Dalmatian-coast tourist facilities.[22]

The origins of the weapons were as diverse as their suppliers. Most were Soviet models from state-owned companies in Poland, ex-Czechoslovakia or Hungary. Others originated through Austrian and Swiss dealers from stocks of the former East German army: the arms were either stolen or listed as "unaccounted losses" in official inventories.[23] Yet others were Russian. In 1992 the search of a UN-authorized plane carrying humanitarian relief aid in Zagreb airport disclosed a disassembled MiG-29 fighter, part of a consignment of fighters and attack helicopters purchased from the Russian manufacturer, shipped via Germany and Italy, and brought to Croatia to be reassembled by Iranian army officers. A MiG-29 engine had already turned up hidden in a truckload of salt.[24]

Although Croatia was mainly in the market for Soviet-type weapons, it was quite willing to accept American ones. Sometimes they came strictly through entrepreneurial activity. The Croatian Resistance Organization bought weapons stolen from U.S. National Guard armouries or obtained them from licenced arms dealers willing to divert legal stock to the black market. The experience was not always happy; several members of the organization, along with a suitcase stuffed with cash, were busted in a U.S. Customs sting while trying to acquire anti-aircraft missiles.[25]

Sometimes American weapons were obtained with the covert assistance of governments. One source was Chile, which had both a wealthy Croatian émigré community willing to foot the bill and vintage American arms. The weapons were originally sent to South Vietnam, captured by the North, then bartered to Cuba for pineapples and sugar. Cuba sneaked them to a Chilean leftist insurgent group, which lost them in an army raid. When the Chilean armed forces declared the weapons surplus, they were bought, using a Sri Lankan end-user certificate, by a Swiss-based firm whose partners included the son of Chilean military strongman Augusto Pinochet. The weapons were sent to Santiago airport labelled "state equipment" and waved through Customs. Someone with a twisted sense of humour relabelled the containers "humanitarian aid" and rerouted them to Budapest. From Budapest they were to be trucked to Croatia. But a Hungarian Customs officer opened the crates.[26] That permitted Hungary to appear vigilant in enforcing the UN embargo by capturing weapons competing with its own arms pipeline to Croatia.

The Croatian diaspora was also prominent in Argentina, with the result that Croatian irregular militiamen, many recruited from ultra-right exiles or local unemployed youth, were spotted with Argentine-made assault rifles. This time the financing allegedly came from traffickers running cocaine through Dalmatian ports and washing drug money through Croatian banks and casinos.[27]

Indeed, so cosmopolitan was the emerging Croatian army that it was happy to accept weapons from South Africa's Armscor, whose covert sales wing was still functioning efficiently despite the transition to black majority rule. During 1992 two ships owned by a Danish ship owner previously fined for breaking the arms embargo to South Africa loaded ammunition, mines and mortar shells that had been purchased by a German-based Lebanese arms dealer, for delivery supposedly to Lebanon. One went directly to Croatia; the second, anticipating trouble from UN monitors, ended up in a small Italian port whence the cargo was apparently whisked across the Adriatic.[28]

None of these black market deals from government stocks could take place without the right documents. Though many countries had their paperwork, and their officials, for sale to the highest bidder, one of the most popular in Balkan arms deals turned out to be a place better known for coups and cocaine than international arms deals.[29]

Strange Bedfellows

Modern forays into the weapons black market by little landlocked Bolivia owed much to a prominent citizen of German origin named Klaus Altmann. Like the paperwork of his arms deals, Altmann was not what or whom he seemed. His real name was Klaus Barbie, and his CV included a stint as Gestapo chief of Lyon, where he gained fame for conducting interrogations with a blowtorch.[30]

After World War II, when the French were searching high and low for "the Butcher of Lyon," American Military Intelligence picked up Barbie, gave him a new identity and put him on the payroll. For a while he ran anti-Soviet espionage operations in eastern Europe. One of his handlers later insisted that Barbie charged them lots of money for worthless information from a ring of 100 agents that existed mainly in Barbie's imagination. When his operations were penetrated, the United States redeployed him to Bolivia to keep an eye on un-American activities while the country was convulsed by a populist revolution. For a time Barbie maintained the façade of a hard-working businessman. But in 1964 Air Force General René Barrientos ousted a civilian government and appointed Barbie his "counter-terrorism" expert. He almost had a second job. When Cuban revolutionary hero Ernesto "Che" Guevara started his hopeless campaign to promote a leftist insurgency among the ultra-conservative Bolivian peasantry, U.S. Military Intelligence considered reactivating Barbie.

Although Guevara was killed before Barbie's services were required, the peripatetic Nazi kept busy giving locals a practical lesson in the superiority of free enterprise. One of his fellow Third Reich exiles and Fourth Reich aspirants was Friederich Paul Schwend, former chief of the SS unit charged with converting counterfeit British banknotes from Operation Bernhard into genuine currency before depositing the money in SS accounts in Switzerland. Like Barbie, Schwend had fled to Latin America after the war, helped by a Croatian fascist priest who provided Schwend and his wife with phoney Croatian-refugee ID papers. He settled in Lima, where he and Barbie teamed up on a number of projects. One was a plan to resettle in Bolivia 30,000 white families who might be forced out of southern Africa with the fall of the Portuguese empire and, subsequently, the end of white Rhodesia. Another, which began earlier, was to sell German, Austrian and Israeli weapons to military dictatorships ruling Peru, Bolivia, Chile and Paraguay. The Barbie and Schwend gun-running business was facilitated by a special piece of infrastructure.

After losing a war with Chile in 1887, Bolivia had been stripped of access to the sea. Subsequently, restoring to Bolivia its maritime grandeur became a cardinal political objective. In the mid-1960s, Bolivia set up Transmaritima Boliviana, the first step in the creation of a merchant marine, even if it had to accept the indignity of operating out of a Peruvian port. Barbie and friends held half the shares; the military government the other half. The government gave free enterprise another boost by requiring that 50 per cent of Bolivia's exports use Transmaritima. Apart from hauling tin from Bolivia's state-run mining combine, Transmaritima was also servicing the Barbie-Schwend arms trafficking consortium when a new customer came calling.

Following the 1967 Middle East war, Israel faced an international arms embargo. It approached Bolivia's ambassador to Spain with a proposition. For a 10 per cent commission (paid to the leaders, not the country) Bolivia could broker the purchase of $50 million of Swiss and Belgian arms, which ships chartered by Transmaritima would divert to Israel. The first of three planned shipments went without a hitch. Then General Barrientos was killed in a plane crash. His successor replaced the ambassador to Spain with a crony. On returning to Bolivia, the former ambassador was angry enough to forget that in the arms trade, discretion is the better part, not of valour, but of longevity. He publicly denounced the deal while he privately demanded his share. A short time later his accounts were closed — by a bomb blast. But cover for the deal had also been blown. Israel had to find other partners.[31]

Although Transmaritima went bankrupt in 1972, Barbie went on to greater things. He became security chief to Roberto Suarez Gomez, the country's biggest drug baron and one of the architects of the 1980 "cocaine coup" in which a group of officers overthrew a civilian government and attempted to convert the cocaine business into a de facto state monopoly. But in 1982 the junta crumbled. A short time later Barbie was arrested on (probably bogus) charges of stealing export revenues from the state tin mines many years before and was quietly turned over to French intelligence, who hauled him back to face trial. However his spirit lived on.

When a Portuguese arms dealer wanted to sell assault rifles to Croatia, one Bolivian Ministry of Defence official wrote the EUC; another provided the seals; a general issued a certificate authorizing the deal; and an official at the Portuguese consulate-general in Chile provided on-site "authentication." When the documents were duly filed, the Portuguese government granted permission for a state-owned arms maker to export assault rifles to "Bolivia."[32] A short time later "Bolivia," whose heavy weapons were all of American origin, went shopping again, for eight Russian tanks in a deal worth double Bolivia's annual arms acquisition budget. Although some eyebrows were raised at the Russian Foreign Ministry, they were not raised high enough to stop the sale. Only after "Bolivia" began buying weapons from Bulgaria did trouble strike.

Even before the Portuguese and Russian deals were finalized, two different arms dealers, one Portuguese and the other Hungarian, approached Kintex, the Bulgarian state trading company, and presented Bolivian end-user certificates. The first requested $25 million worth of mortars, rocket launchers and Kalashnikovs for the Ministry of Defence, and the second $15 million in similar equipment for the Ministry of the Interior. Based on the EUCs, Bulgaria issued an export licence. The fact that Bolivia used only U.S. material and, in any event, had not made a major arms purchase for over a decade apparently rang no alarm bells. The weapons were loaded on ships flying Maltese and St. Vincent flags of convenience. That the ships were equipped with their own cranes, suggesting the weapons were more likely to be discharged off a deserted beach or in a small fishing village rather than in a modern port, also attracted no attention. Once at sea, the ships were diverted to Croatia. Three loads got through before U.S. pressure forced Bulgaria to block a fourth and take a closer look at the EUCs. On some the signature of a Bolivian officer had been forged, while on another the signature may well have been real — it was hard to tell, since the "general" had never enlisted in the Bolivian army or, for that matter, taken Spanish-language spelling lessons. However, at least one thing was genuine. The EUCs were written on authentic letterhead peddled by a Bolivian official for $300 a sheet.

In the uproar, the Portuguese dealer insisted that he had been merely a middleman. He pointed the finger for both the Kintex deal and the one involving Portuguese assault rifles at an Israeli gun-runner who, the Portuguese dealer insisted, put up the money, owned the ships and provided the EUCs. But that gun-runner was safe in Israel, apparently enjoying cosy relations with the intelligence services in an extradition-free environment. He dismissed the accusations as "absolute rubbish," threatened to sue and denounced his critics as "anti-Semites."[33]

Brothers in Arms

Fake paperwork was essential to obtain the weapons. But they also had to reach their destination. Apart from controlling the Dalmatian coastline, Croatia was aided by the pro-Croatian tilt of the United States and many Western European countries, and by Customs officials in neighbouring countries who were variously overworked, under-trained, corrupt or complicit. Since the Croatian-controlled areas of Bosnia were contiguous to and economically integrated into Croatia proper (using the same trade routes and adopting Croatian currency), they were similarly kept well supplied, directly or indirectly. In 1994 the United States brokered a truce between Bosnian Croats and Bosnian Muslims to stand together against the Serbs. Because most weapons bound for landlocked Bosnia had to cross Croatia, it could charge a transit fee sometimes as high as 50 per cent of the load.[34]

Besides geography, Bosnia had many disadvantages. While it had inherited more than its share of federal arms factories, it lost many to insurgent Croats and Serbs early in the conflict; others were incapacitated by looting or shortages of materials. Although towards the end of the conflict it managed, with technical assistance from some Muslim states, to reactivate light weapons production, Bosnia remained dependent on outsiders for heavy arms.[35] Nor could it depend on a wealthy diaspora as Croatia did. To some Bosnians returning from Germany, Sweden or Switzerland, defending Muslim Bosnia took second place to trafficking in rationed commodities, drugs and foreign exchange.[36] Indeed, one of the reasons the Bosnian government played up its Muslim identity (even though Muslims were only 40 per cent of the population) was to attract financial support from the Middle East.

During the early stages of the conflict, there was much sympathy for Bosnia but little action. Some ammunition was smuggled on UN trucks carrying relief rations, and weapons were sold by sympathetic Turkish and Malay troops with the peacekeeping missions.[37] But it was never sufficient. The Muslims swiftly lost large swaths of territory, particularly to the Serbs who increased their hold from 50 per cent (the amount of Bosnia largely Serb inhabited before the war) to 70 per cent. Then, when the United States brokered a Muslim-Croat alliance of convenience, weapons, minus the heavy toll charges, began to flow regularly.

Arms for the Muslims were purchased from Bulgaria by a Belgian firm run by a Hungarian gun-runner using an end-user certificate from Mali. The paper was genuine; the signature was forged. Munzer el-Qassar celebrated a recent acquittal in Spain on terrorism and arms trafficking charges (aided by the fact that a prosecution witness fell out of a window before he could testify) by resurrecting old ties to the Polish state-run arms producer. To help the deal, the Paris embassy of Yemen thoughtfully provided an end-user certificate.[38] In Kuwait four people, including an army officer, were arrested for trying to send to Bosnia Soviet-model weapons, including anti-tank and anti-aircraft missiles, captured from the Iraqis during the Gulf War.[39] And some deals truly represented a "new world order."

Robert Breiner, an Austrian with British citizenship, lived in Marbella on Spain's Costa Del Sol, while operating a company out of Gibraltar, through which he ran Balkan arms shipments using Bolivian EUCs. However, for his biggest coup, he looked elsewhere for the right paper. Breiner had a Franco-Italian business partner; that partner had a close friend who was consul-general of Panama in Barcelona. The consul-general personally accompanied Breiner's partner to Panama, where he introduced him to a law firm run by some relatives. It was no ordinary law firm. One of its senior members was temporarily on leave — sworn in as Panama's president during a ceremony on an American military base after the overthrow of Noriega. Breiner's partner arranged for the law firm to set up a shell company. The partner also paid a courtesy call on Panama's president. Beguiled, the president said, by tales of millions to be invested in Panama, he arranged meetings between Breiner's partner and senior government officials. Subsequently the partner arranged for his new Panama company to charter "fishing" ships to troll the Mediterranean. One of them was stopped at sea by Italian police, perplexed at the absence of nets or tackle. However, a hasty call from the Panama consul-general in Barcelona led them to release the ship to continue its course.

Just what kind of business the ships were on was discovered by accident. In the wake of an attack on UN peacekeeping forces in Bosnia, the militia responsible was found to be equipped with Czech weapons. A query to the Czech Republic turned up an application to buy 25,000 sub-machine guns, 5,000 pistols and millions of rounds of ammunition. It looked legitimate — the end-user certificate requesting the material on behalf of the Panamanian army was signed by the Barcelona vice-consul. The problem was that Panama had abolished its army after the overthrow of Noriega, and the vice-consul had no authority to sign for arms shipments. Indeed, she insisted that she had really signed an authorization to import diesel refrigeration equipment and that the documents were altered after the fact.[40]

Yet another supplier of Bosnia's Muslim army was Iran. It funded the Muslim president's re-election campaign and provided Pasdaran (and Afghan mujahideen) support to his beleaguered forces. One of its arms shipments was arranged by Austrian and Danish gun-runners who flew the weapons into Bosnia on planes painted with UN insignias. Iran also bought weapons from the ex-Soviet republics of Central Asia, sometimes working through Pakistani buyers to reduce any reluctance to deal with Iran.

Since Bosnia is landlocked, weapons had to cross Croatia by road, with the connivance of the United States, or arrive by air. That may explain why, in 1993, a group of Iranians purchased a money-losing small private airport near Hamburg at double its original price. One of the buyers was a former deputy oil minister who had run the London office of the National Iranian Oil Company when it was financing arms procurement during the Iran-Iraq War. Another was an arms dealer whose name had surfaced in the Iran-contra investigations. To run the airport, they hired as manager someone expelled from Spain on suspicion of smuggling weapons to Croatia and Bosnia.[41]

Reflecting the fact that the steel of capitalism is often forged in the heat of war, there was another more informal source on which Muslim forces could sometimes rely. In 1993, before the Muslim-Croat coalition, a Muslim officer exchanging artillery fire with a Croat unit ran out of shells. He negotiated for a supply from nearby Serbs. After the two commanders settled the terms, the Muslim chief had a better idea. For a higher price he got the Serbs to deliver the artillery shells in the most efficient way, directly onto Croat positions. However, the next year a Bosnian-Croat paramilitary force that usually devoted more energy to looting and smuggling than combat, evened the score — it paid a Serbian artillery unit 2 million Deutschmarks to blow holes in a Muslim defence line. Aware it was onto a good thing, in 1995, during another period of Muslim-Croat hostilities, the same gangster-militia sold fuel at a mark-up of more than 100 per cent to the Bosnian Serb army in return for it protecting Bosnian-Croat areas from Muslim attack.[42]

Even more important than the direct supply of arms (which may have been exaggerated by both sides for public relations purposes[43]), Islamic states also assisted the Muslim side in solving its second logistical handicap: money. While some countries bragged of the contributions they made, the actual sums arriving in Bosnia may have been considerably smaller. Large sums were raised from citizens in Turkey, upset over atrocities against Bosnian Muslims, through a charity run by an official of the Islamist Refah Party, only to be embezzled by party officials, lost in a couple of bank crashes or siphoned off to aid the electoral hopes of that party in its high-profile anti-corruption campaign.[44]

Somewhat better luck attended the efforts of Elfatih Hassanein, a Sudanese diplomat who had studied medicine in Yugoslavia and who had been a close friend of the man who became first president of independent Bosnia. In 1987 Hassanein opened the Third World Relief Agency to do Islamic charitable work in eastern Europe and the Soviet Union. In 1992 he changed somewhat his definition of charity. With the foreign minister of Bosnia in tow, he opened a Vienna bank account into which large sums (some claimed $350 million) flowed from Saudi Arabia, Iran, Sudan, Pakistan, Turkey, Brunei and Malaysia. Much was diverted into arms. Some of the rest was hauled in cash to pay off Slovenian and Croatian officials. In 1993 Hassanein bought from a group of European arms brokers Soviet-model weapons. They were shipped to the Ukraine, put on a cargo plane and flown to Khartoum, either to break the trail or to load more weapons. From there the plane went to Budapest where the weapons were inspected. Once Hassanein authorized payment, their next stop was the Slovene airport of Maribor. From there they were to be hauled by truck across Croatia to Bosnia. While that was in progress, the Bosnian Croats broke their alliance with the Muslims. That forced a change in plans. The remaining weapons were to be airlifted by heavy helicopter directly to Bosnia. But while they were sitting in a warehouse waiting for the helicopters, the intricacies of Slovenian politics got in the way.[45]

Slovenia had become a hub of the regional arms trade. Through the front of trading companies supervised by the secret intelligence wing of the

Ministry of Defence, weapons crossed Slovenia en route to Croatia and Bosnia. To make it clear there were no hard feelings, several of those corporate fronts were also put at the disposal of Serbia for acquisition of strategic materials. Just for good measure, the same intelligence force reputedly arranged for Slovenian firms to sell embargoed military technology to Iran and Libya. Officials pocketed millions, and the minister of defence used the proceeds to advance his political ambitions.[46] However, his rivals had connections with the Customs department, which raided the Maribor stash and unleashed a scandal that forced the resignation of the minister.

All these factors — a glut of Soviet-era weapons, outside sponsors willing and able to pick up the bill and gun-runners skilled in covert commerce — worked to make the arms embargo an embarrassing failure. Victory went not just to the biggest battalions, but to the most successful evaders. And what occurred with respect to weapons — smuggling, bribery and corrupt double-dealing — was replicated with the general economic sanctions against Serbia-Montenegro.

Chapter 23

PARAGONS VERSUS PARIAHS?

Under the 1992 sanctions, UN member states were forbidden any commercial relations with Serbia-Montenegro except the provision of food and medicine. Each shipment of those exempted commodities required explicit UN authorization. To limit diversions, companies shipping through Serbia-Montenegro to other destinations had to apply for permission on a case-by-case basis. In 1993 sanctions were tightened with a naval blockade and a freeze on assets held abroad.[1] The sanctions were not only tough, they were the first in history to be backed by a sophisticated, American-run electronic espionage system comprising everything from satellite surveillance of barge traffic on the Danube to tagging devices attached to suspect vehicles to trace their itineraries. UN monitoring teams were further supported by U.S. Customs officials who could apply against sanctions-busters the type of sting operations they used in drug smuggling cases.[2]

On the surface, prospects for enforcement looked good. Granted, nearly half a century of military preparation meant an arms embargo was largely futile. Serbia, too, had a diversified agricultural base, and no ban on kiwi fruit (which remained available in fancier restaurants) was likely to lead to a re-evaluation of political options. Still, Serbia should have been vulnerable on other fronts. It had made no serious preparation for sanctions.[3] Its financial position was weak; it produced only 25 per cent of its fuel requirements; its industries depended on imported parts and machinery; its coastline (Montenegro's) was short and easy to blockade; and it was surrounded by potentially hostile states.

Indeed, the impact of sanctions seemed enormous. GNP plummeted, unemployment soared, wages fell below subsistence, and public transportation ground down. As the economy shrank, so did the tax base, forcing the government, in its efforts to maintain both social spending and the war effort, to print more money. Hyperinflation further disrupted production, distorted distribution and drove down living standards.[4] But in reality, Serbia's countermeasures and lack of enthusiasm for enforcement among neighbours meant that, while sanctions were certainly effective in impoverishing the population, corrupting the public service and creating a *nouveau riche* class of profiteers, they never seemed to have much impact on Serbia's political and military decisions.

Embargo-Busting and the Spirit of Capitalism

Much of the fighting was done not by the disciplined Yugoslav army but by irregular forces, recruited among the unemployed and uneducated who were easiest to seduce into the Greater Serbia cause. Their leaders were often ex-émigré gangsters who had been sent abroad during the 1970s and 1980s by the federal intelligence services to infiltrate and harass political opposition groups. They returned in the late 1980s and early 1990s, pushed by law enforcement crackdowns in western Europe and pulled by the opportunities for business created by the collapse of the Yugoslav federal state. Back home they had two functions. One was carrying out sensitive jobs for the Serbian secret police. The second was organizing paramilitary forces to fight in Croatia and Bosnia.[5]

Irregular forces provided Belgrade with deniability by taking the heat for ethnic-cleansing campaigns and for looting. VCRs, television sets, jewellery, foreign currency, liquor and cigarettes were the prime targets. But also taken were furniture, motor vehicles and even humanitarian aid from UN convoys. Captured civilians were herded into internment camps and stripped of possessions. Equipment was grabbed from Croatia's oil refineries. A Volkswagen plant near Sarajevo was emptied of machinery and inventory — Volkswagens briefly became the car of choice of Serbian war profiteers. Meanwhile, apparently invisible to the international media, Croatian gangster-militias were doing likewise, then getting into gunfights over division of the spoils.[6]

Although in Belgrade flea markets had captured goods on display, looting could provide only a small and temporary cushion against sanctions-induced shortages. Furthermore, most plundering was the work of rebel Serbs in Croatia and Bosnia who were not only exempt from sanctions, but grabbed basic goods for their families rather than making them available to Serbia. There were "brokers" who collected art, antiquities and other valuables for international sale, reputedly depositing the proceeds, less their fees, in the bank accounts of arms suppliers. However looting, and the destruction of towns and villages that followed, was more important in helping to preclude the return of refugees than in alleviating shortages. For that, Serbia turned to a special evasion apparatus.

In much the way Rhodesia had used its special Customs advisor, South Africa its Secretariat of Unconventional Trade and Cuba its Departamento MC, the Serbian government appointed as head of Customs a trusted aide to Milo-šević who had facilitated smuggling of weapons to rebel Serbs in Bosnia. His new job was to move exports past UN monitors and to dole out import permits (essential to buy scarce foreign exchange) to those best situated to sneak back strategic goods.[7] Serbia also privatized the distribution system into small operations whose new owners repaid the favour by sanctions-busting. Although most big companies remained state-owned, the government acquiesced when powerful functionaries, whose aid was essential for keeping the regime in power, stripped the assets and hid them abroad. There was one place happy to give them sanctuary.[8]

Another Sunny Place for More Shady People

Europe's first major twentieth-century ethnic-cleansing campaign took place immediately after World War I when Thrace was emptied of most of its Greek-Christian inhabitants and many Aegean islands of their Turkish-Muslim population. Only Cyprus, a British colony, was spared. But in 1974, several years after independence, its government was overthrown in a coup backed by a military regime in Greece. Placed briefly in power was Nicos Sampson, a militant of EOKA, the group that had previously waged a guerrilla war against Britain to achieve union with Greece. The 20 per cent of the population of Turkish origin, already treated as second-class citizens, feared that it would suffer the fate of so many before. Shortly after the coup Turkey invaded, seizing the northern third of the island and precipitating a flight of the Greek population, while the Turkish population from the south took refuge in the Turkish-controlled north. Fortunately, the Turkish invasion did not precipitate a broader war. Reputedly Greece had covertly sold off enough of its U.S.-supplied weaponry to Nigeria and, perhaps, Rhodesia, that it was in no position to confront Turkey.[9]

Never as prosperous as the Greek areas, northern Cyprus faced a de facto international boycott. Its economy consisted mainly of importing Turkish subsidies, exporting fruit from orchards seized from fleeing Greek farmers, and, after 1990, operating as a platform for sanctions-busting trade to Iraq. On the other side, after the initial shock of partition, the Greek area prospered.

Since achieving independence from Britain in 1960, Cyprus had been gradually putting in place the infrastructure to create one of the world's hottest hot money havens. It had become a major flag-of-convenience centre, aided by proximity to Greece with its huge merchant fleet, and to the Suez Canal. By the mid-1990s, 1,700 ships flew the Cypriot flag, a popularity not unrelated to "its" ships leading the world in accidents and violations of international operating standards.[10] And there were further attractions to footloose entrepreneurs or their money.

The year after the Turkish invasion, two events neatly coincided. One was the start of civil war in Lebanon that sent businesses in search of another Middle Eastern home. Cyprus, a short hop from Lebanon, soon hosted banks, insurance companies and import-export firms as well as wealthy refugees. The second was the introduction by Cyprus of new tax breaks for foreign-based businesses, and the easing of exchange controls. Then, in 1982, Cyprus established offshore banking facilities protected by tight bank-secrecy laws. Together with favourable tax treaties with post-Communist eastern Europe, these factors gave Cyprus a role in international political and economic intrigue rivalling that of Tangiers a generation before.[11]

The Lebanese were the first to appreciate what Cyprus had to offer. Refugees arrived in waves after each upsurge of fighting, while the militias used Cypriot companies and banks to run their rackets. By the time the Lebanese conflict abated, the Gulf War and sanctions on Iraq provided a new impetus. Perhaps inspired by Somerset Maugham's description of Monaco as a "sunny place for shady people," Russian flight capitalists and mobsters were intrigued to find an even sunnier sanctuary closer to home, rendered more hospitable by the Orthodox faith and the Cyrillic alphabet. Most of the enormous profits from resource rip-offs, illegal arms deals, antiquities smuggling and the plunder of the public sector pouring out of Russia at the rate of about $1 billion per month headed for Switzerland. But Cyprus was a popular way station and, for some of the money, part of which arrived in cash still bound in official U.S. Federal Reserve Bank wrappers, a permanent place of domicile.[12]

Then came the Serbs. In the first six months of 1992, about 500 Serbian-owned firms joined the island's roster of 8,000 offshore companies. Some were fronts for officials stealing state-owned assets but others were created specifically for sanctions-busting. They were protected by a triple wall of secrecy. In Cyprus only the central bank and the accountant or lawyer setting up an offshore company knew its shareholders. Serbia obscured the trail by having trusted individuals front for state agencies. And many Greek-Cypriots shared with Serbian chauvinists a loathing for both Muslims (Turks in one case, Bosnians in the other) and Catholics. Cyprus also became a home-away-from-home for offshore units of Serbian banks. The Serbian government moved money from the compromised safety of pro-Croatian Austria to Cyprus, and, just before the 1993 international asset freeze, it transferred there much of its foreign exchange holdings. Through Cyprus-based companies, vehicles, machinery, parts and oil could be ordered from all over the world, nominally for non-embargoed destinations, and diverted to Serbia-Montenegro. Through them, too, Serbian-Montenegrin goods could be sold with their origins disguised. Letters of credit were negotiated through Cyprus banks without interference as long as the bills of lading indicated that the origin or destination was Greece, Macedonia, Bosnia, Slovenia or Croatia.[13]

Shipments That Pass in the Night

The tricks were almost unlimited. UN authorization forms for shipments to Serbia were falsified. Plant and equipment were moved to neighbouring countries such as Bulgaria, where Serbian semi-finished products could be completed and the goods exported as "made in Bulgaria."[14] Romanian fishermen on the Danube hauled in nets during the day and ran cargoes to and from Serbia by night, while barges plying the Danube had banned items stashed under loads of legitimate merchandise. The rundown Romanian city of Timisoara, not far from Vojvodina, suddenly burst into life. Hundreds of trading companies, many Serbian owned, set up shop along streets lined with gasoline stations. They were watched by Romanian Customs officers who were content to supplement their meagre salaries by picking up a little hush money. From Romania the trucks, frequently switching licence plates en route, would set off accompanied by paper showing the destination or origins of their loads to be Bosnia or one of the other ex-Yugoslav republics.[15]

Of those former republics, the most important for sanctions-busting was Macedonia. Its capital, Skopje, had once been the main stop on the truck route from the Greek port of Thessalonika to Belgrade. Not only did Macedonia still act as a transit point, but companies set up there by Serbian brokers specialized in faking paperwork, charging a fixed fee per truck.[16] Sometimes they counterfeited certificates of origin; sometimes they bought real ones from corrupt officials. Either way Serbian-made goods posing as Macedonian found foreign markets. Similarly, they concocted bills of lading stating Macedonia as the destination of goods that actually stopped in Serbia.[17]

To accusations of complicity, Macedonia had an easy reply. Eighty per cent of its trade had been within Yugoslavia, its only rail outlet ran through Serbia, and it still depended on Serbia for coal and electricity. It would have been economic suicide to cut off commercial relations. As well, the UN bureaucracy proved unwieldy despite its fancy electronic equipment. Macedonia sometimes had to wait months for replies to requests for permission to export its products via Serbia.[18] In addition, generalized poverty meant Macedonian officials would be unable to control smuggling even if they had wished. These commercial problems were exacerbated by one of the pettiest political disputes in modern history. Too weak to take out its cultural inferiority complex against Turkey, which hosts the most important ancient-Greek archaeological sites, Greece decided to vent its frustrations on one of the most vulnerable states in the region. Accusing Macedonia of harbouring designs on Greek territory, Greece, probably in quiet consultation with Serbia, slapped on its own trade embargo, leaving Macedonia's only viable commercial outlet northward to Serbia. Nor did there seem to be any good reason for Macedonia to suffer when others were so flagrantly enjoying the inflated profits of blockade-busting. One of them was a politically eccentric region of Bosnia.

The Bihać enclave, butting into Croatia and bordering the Bosnian Serb-held areas, was always a place apart. Although Bosnia's Muslims had tended to sympathize with the pro-German Croatian puppet state to which Bosnia was attached during World War II, even joining special SS units, those of Bihać had largely sided with Tito's partisans. It was in the Bihać area, too, that the first serious stirrings of Islamic militancy showed up in the 1960s. Bihać had been an economic backwater while Yugoslavia grew in the early decades. Then, during the 1980s, when the rest of the country was in recession, Bihać took a great leap forward. Unlike much of Bosnia, the motor force of its success was not the arms industry but Agrokomerć Corporation. Formerly a small agricultural cooperative, by the middle of the 1980s Agrokomerć had become a huge conglomerate with outlets in every major urban centre and interests in every sector from agribusiness to tourism to construction.[19]

One reason for its success was the Yugoslav credit system. Yugoslav companies needing working capital issued promissory notes, had them guaranteed by a local bank, then either traded them to other business firms for supplies or sold them to another bank for cash. When the promissory notes came due, whoever held the notes would try to collect from the original issuer, or, failing that, from the guaranteeing bank. Frequently the only collateral was the capacity of the issuer to coax the buyer into believing that notes could be met, or that the issuing firm was so politically connected it seemed prudent to buy the paper. Although far from alone, Agrokomerć was the biggest beneficiary. It had such close relations with the local bank in Bihać that the bank handed over to Agrokomerć the stamp used to authenticate paper, permitting Agrokomerć to effectively guarantee its own notes. Then Agrokomerć would send itself telexes supposedly representing big new orders and use them to reassure potential buyers of its notes that its cash-flow position was sound.

A second advantage the firm had was the skill with which its founder, a Bihać businessman named Fikret Abdić, used his political connections. He was an influential member of the federal parliament, had the backing of top people in the Central Committee of the Communist Party and cultivated powerful figures on the Bosnian political scene. While in theory local government regulators were supposed to monitor dangerous financial practices, Abdić secured their acquiescence through political influence and pay-offs. And his chum, the federal Secretary of Finance, pressured banks throughout Yugoslavia to buy the notes. In the final tally, Agrokomerć had borrowed without collateral the equivalent of nearly $1 billion from sixty-three banks. One of the largest holders was the unfortunate Ljubaljansk Bank, soon to be caught up as well in the BNL scandal.

Some of the borrowed money was recycled into bribes. Some went to buy gifts ranging from low-income housing to an Olympic-sized swimming pool for the hamlet where Agrokomerć was headquartered. But most was reinvested. The faster the firm grew, the safer its financial position appeared to be, reassuring creditors and permitting it to float yet more paper. Then, late in 1987, catastrophe struck. While on another investigation, police stumbled across falsified bank paper in Agrokomerć's financial records, much to the delight of political factions eager to undermine Abdić's political supporters in the federal and Bosnia governments.[20] He was jailed, Agrokomerć collapsed, and the scandal badly weakened the Communist Party just when the nationalist forces that would pull the country apart were gaining strength. However, Abdić, Agrokomerć and Bihać soon found a new vocation in the ruins of Yugoslavia.

On his release from prison, Abdić returned home. When Yugoslavia disintegrated, he declared himself president of an autonomous Bihać, backed by a militia composed mainly of army deserters. He appointed a prime minister and senior functionaries whose offices were in the Agrokomerć headquarters. Then he negotiated peace treaties with Croatia and the Bosnian Serbs. Until Bihać was overrun by the Bosnian army, it was as ideal a location for sanctions-busting as Swaziland was for South Africa or South Lebanon for Israel. Everything from Iranian arms to Ecuadorian bananas, from Brazilian coffee to American cigarettes passed through Bihać, while Abdić's "government" collected taxes and transit fees.[21] Abdić's chief aide said of the enclave's role, "We see ourselves as the Cayman Islands of the Balkans." Eschewing politics, he declared, "We are interested in business, finance, making money."[22]

Striking Oil

However, the really big money was in a commodity in which Bihać played no role. Facing an oil embargo backed by a naval blockade, Serbia took drastic action. Rich in generating capacity when not hampered by a shortage of spare parts, Serbia encouraged people to switch from oil to electricity for heating and introduced gasoline rationing.[23] It also had access to some of Croatia's oil fields, occupied by rebel Serbs.[24] But Serbia still needed imports. While the state company continued to service the public sector and military, in an early concession to incipient capitalism, it leased gasoline stations to private entrepreneurs (mostly party officials), leaving to them the job of securing oil for the general population. Petroleum and its derivatives were imported into Europe mainly by Greek, secondarily by Italian companies, then sold through fronts, usually in Cyprus, to Serbian traders. When the United States protested to Greece about sanctions violations, the Greek government responded by arresting one oil broker who had irritated the ruling party by publishing critical comments in a newspaper he owned. The oil smuggling went on otherwise unabated.[25] Yet more came from Russia, which sold to the Ukraine at 30 per cent of the world price, allowing the Ukraine to resell at a handsome profit to sanctions-busters.

Buying oil was no problem — the real challenge was getting it home. The most obvious route was through Montenegrin ports. Greek tankers used to call there regularly even after sanctions were imposed. In theory that stopped in 1993 when the naval blockade was imposed. However, once a Greek ship with 6,000 tons of petroleum coke claimed to have to stop for repairs in a Montenegrin port. Naturally, a proper repair job required unloading the coke. By the time the ship was ready to sail again, the cargo had magically turned into Serbian timber. A small amount of oil also came surreptitiously from Croatia. Since Serbia contained most of ex-Yugoslavia's electrical capacity, Croatia covertly pumped oil to Serbia in exchange for electrical power. It was one of many manifestations of the rule that the ex-republics of Yugoslavia were so economically interdependent that they covertly cooperated in undercutting sanctions.[26]

Oil could also be trans-shipped through Serbia, nominally on its way to embargo-exempt Serb-held areas of Bosnia and Croatia, then be "lost" en route. This was especially popular for oil coming from the south since the trip was shorter than to the nominal destinations. This saved time and fuel costs for tanker-trucks, while the oil could be sold for a higher price in Serbia.[27]

A safer option was to pretend oil was bound for Macedonia, particularly since the United States, worried over the state of the Macedonian economy, pressured the EU and UN to ignore the smuggling. Before Greece banned trade with its northern neighbour, oil arrived in Greece by tanker, then went north by tanker-truck or train. Once it was in Macedonia, officials were bribed, and the oil run across the border. While railways could carry much more, the rail routes were better monitored, and the bribes much higher. Still, sometimes money could be saved by entertaining a Macedonian border official in a local restaurant, perhaps in the company of a prostitute, while the illegal load went through. So heavy was the traffic, U.S. army monitors on the Macedonian-Serbian border complained of being kept awake at night by convoys of tanker-trucks running by their encampment.[28]

Another route went through Albania, much of whose border with Montenegro consisted of a lake whose shoreline was dotted with Serbian-financed fuel entrepôts. Fuel was legally imported into Albania (which developed a remarkable propensity to use aviation fuel for heating houses and offices) and turned over to local companies who hauled it to "gasoline stations," many just shacks in the woods. Then it was pumped into Serbian trucks or loaded in barges that chugged across the lake at night. This practice had the open complicity of the Albanian government. Not only was the largest oil company run directly by the ruling Democratic Party and chaired by its chief, but taxes on the transit trade became one of the most important sources of public revenues. When, under U.S. pressure, the Albanian government introduced a pre-shipment inspection system to verify the destination of oil before it left Greece or Italy, the main result was to raise the extra-curricular incomes of Albanian functionaries.[29]

Yet another route was along the Danube. Oil from Romania or Russia could be diverted in tanker-barges to Serbian river ports. However effective U.S. spy satellites were in spotting the movements, sanctions monitors had no legal power to stop the barges. When challenged, captains sometimes threatened to set the barges afire. The Danube even saw its own version of the *Salem* affair. In 1994 river pirates hijacked an oil barge carrying 6,000 tons of diesel fuel in Bulgarian waters and unloaded it inside Serbia. Similarly with tanker-trucks along the Romanian-Vojvodina border. So much money could be made from fuel smuggling that Romanians who had fled the old regime returned to participate in the "benzina bizness." At a time when the average wage in Romania was $100 per month, a single tanker-truck could yield a profit of $2,500. The penalty for getting caught was a small fine or a smaller bribe. Furthermore, the border villages often contained cooperative Serbian minorities.[30]

In addition to smuggling by state agencies or entrepreneurs running the newly privatized gasoline stations, ordinary citizens, facing high prices and rationing, crossed the Hungarian, Romanian or Bulgarian borders with special tanks slung under their car or plastic jugs or jerrycans in the back. (From impoverished Macedonia people entered Serbia with a few jerrycans of petrol slung on the backs of donkeys.) Guards assessed the appropriate bribe by looking at how low the car was riding. It was often dangerous — makeshift containers exploded, killing or badly burning drivers, and cars were hijacked at gun-point. But the money involved kept recruits coming. The result was that by 1994 Serbia's taxis, buses, agricultural machinery and private cars were able to function normally provided they could pay treble pre-sanctions prices.[31]

Inside Serbia fuel sold for rapidly depreciating dinars. But abroad it could only be obtained with serious money, or its equivalent. Individual smugglers might offer Deutschmark cash, jewellery or Serbian brandy, especially popular in Romania, where alcohol taxes were high. But big companies importing wholesale needed foreign exchange. That was where export sanctions were supposed to bite. Porous though borders were, Serbia's foreign exchange earnings were far lower, while the prices it had to pay for strategic goods were much higher. The desperate search for foreign exchange encouraged the state to support a massive financial fraud against an already desperate population.[32]

Warriors and Smugglers, Gangsters and Spies
For the ordinary population, the shift from legal to illegal means of earning a living was a matter of simple need. Farmers bypassed state marketing outlets to sell on the black market. Ration coupons were traded openly. Workers unable to subsist on existing wages depended increasingly on bartering valuables, trading in the "informal economy" or receiving emergency aid from relatives in the countryside. Wage declines also encouraged workers to steal supplies from factories, which made production bottlenecks worse. The most difficult-to-replace and therefore easily marketable items were taken first. It was, in a sense, a shop-floor equivalent of the "privatization" of state assets undertaken by and for officials.[33]

For the legitimate business class, small though it was, entrepreneurship came to mean smuggling and war profiteering. Merchants seeking to hoard merchandise to drive up prices rented storage space in army-run nuclear war shelters to avoid the scrutiny of the Serbian fiscal police. And for gangsters, service to the state became one of the surest ways of securing cover for rackets. Across Europe, pickpockets, auto thieves, extortionists and drug traffickers either brought their merchandise or their profits back to Serbia to sell or launder.

Sometimes they invested proceeds in smuggling embargoed commodities to reap a double profit. Meanwhile traffickers in perfume, cigarettes and other heavily taxed goods made deals with the Serbian officials to import duty-free into Serbia, pay a kickback into Cyprus bank accounts, then use the Serbian underground trading nexus to smuggle them out to surrounding countries.[34]

The most notorious of the new gangster-capitalists was Željko Ražnjatović, better known by the *nom de guerre* "Arkan." After breaking out of a Belgian jail where he was serving time for bank robbery, Arkan returned home. In 1986 he beat a Belgrade citizen with his gun butt for no apparent reason. When he was hauled into court, he flashed papers indicating he was a serving member of the Yugoslav secret police whom, he claimed, had issued him with the gun. He was quickly freed. When the war broke out, he established the Serbian Voluntary Squad, better known as the Tiger militia. Sharing a name and a modus operandi with the most notorious of Lebanon's old gangster-militias, these cut-throats in Mad Max gear were the most notorious practitioners of looting and ethnic cleansing in Serb-held Croatia and Bosnia, and later in Kosovo. As a national hero and member of the Serbian parliament, Arkan ran cash and fuel to the Serb rebels in Croatia and Bosnia, sold smuggled gasoline and trafficked in drugs, black market foreign exchange, counterfeit currency and war booty. All of this was protected by the Serbian intelligence services, which collected a share.[35]

Bridging the shrinking gap between the state-supported sanctions-breaking system and the black economy was the private financial system. Part of it was informal. With financial transfers from outside blocked, the state impounding hard currency deposits and hyperinflation eroding the local money, most remittances came into the country in clandestine forms, mostly by smuggling Deutschmark notes. The government started to print dinar notes almost non-stop. Hundreds of street money changers used the new notes to sop up the black market foreign exchange, which they resold to government agencies. The money changers were soon displaced by two officially supported pyramid banks that offered high enough interest rates — about 15 per cent per month on dollar and DM deposits and 200 per cent on dinar ones — to pull in hard currency hoards. Withdrawals were discouraged, not only because nowhere could such rates be matched, but also because the banks imposed on clients who pulled out before maturity a penalty of 10 per cent of the principal and all of the interest, including that already paid.

Some of the hard currency was lent or sold to the government. But most had another use. When the government privatized the gasoline business, it had leased 40 per cent of the stations to the two banks. Hence, much of the foreign exchange was used to buy embargo-busting oil. That oil was resold at huge mark-ups, and the profits were used to meet interest payments on deposits to keep the cycle going.

The largest, Dafiment Bank, was owned by a woman with a prison record who got her banking licence as a reward for contributing publicly to high-profile charities and privately to low-profile sanctions-busting. She was central to efforts to sneak weapons, food and oil to rebel Serbs in Croatia and Bosnia. Close to Slobodan Milošević, she was also paymaster for, as well as sometime business partner of, the infamous Arkan.[36]

The other, Yugoskandic Bank, was the domain of Jezdmir ("Jezda the Boss") Vasilijević. Along with Israeli associates, he set up an institution that, at peak, collected more than $2 billion in savings from more than 2 million people.[37] Besides banking and oil smuggling, from his headquarters on the Montenegrin island of Sveti Stefan, a former fishing village converted into a luxury resort, Jezda the Boss entertained war profiteers, smugglers and black market *nouveaux riches* who came to relax; hosted an embargo-busting chess match between Bobby Fischer and Boris Lassky; helped arrange the sale of luxury yachts stolen by the Yugoslav navy from the marinas along the Croatian coast; and supervised a business manufacturing counterfeit Pall Mall and Marlboro cigarettes.[38] His dream was to convert Sveti Stefan, for which he had signed a twenty-year lease, into a sort of Adriatic financial paradise, free of the nuisance of taxes, and therefore an ideal location from which to run contraband even after sanctions ended.

However, Jezda the Boss was viewed with suspicion because of his ethnic-Romanian roots, and lacked the political patronage enjoyed by his rival. When he fell seriously in arrears on his rent for Sveti Stefan, a Montenegrin court impounded a load of his smuggled oil worth $38 million. At the same time, the Serbian government proceeded against him for back taxes. In the midst of a corruption scandal in which both the Serbian minister of foreign trade and the federal deputy minister were arrested, and two of Jezda's business associates murdered, Jezda fled. After stopping at his safety deposit box in Budapest to stuff a million dollars in his suitcase, Jezda found haven in Israel. From there he threatened to unleash hit squads, accused high officials of diverting millions into their foreign accounts and claimed he would reveal to the West all the secrets of Serbian sanctions-busting unless he was paid $60 million in compensation for the seized oil. His bank, which had in its vaults $12.5 million in foreign currency and gold to meet $2 billion in deposit liabilities, came crashing down. In the general panic, Dafiment Bank, too, was swept up in a wave of demands for withdrawals. It crumbled a short time later. The only depositors repaid (after the bank had officially closed) were government officials and militia leaders.[39]

Scattergun Diplomacy

When Serbia finally came to the bargaining table and stopped overt assistance to the Serb rebels in Croatia and Bosnia, there was the usual flurry of self-congratulations among Western politicians eager to credit their sanctions program with ending the war. The reality was rather different.

The Serbian economy had bottomed in 1993, the year the bank crashes had transferred the public's foreign currency savings to the government and to black market operators who never repaid. But within a year the dinar had been stabilized, inflation disappeared, the psychology of hoarding was broken, foreign exchange reserves began rising and trade started to recover, even though sanctions were still in place.[40] Shelves in private shops were packed with goods varying from Italian-designer kitchen sets to French perfumes and champagne. Meantime, much to the irritation of the United States, which saw a replay of the Cuba situation, European companies began signing commercial contracts with Serbia to get a head start once sanctions were lifted. Unemployment remained high, and the level of national income was well below its 1980s level. However, those difficulties were probably as much the result of the fracturing of the country and the impact of war as of sanctions. Far from prompting internal political reappraisals, sanctions made it easier for a regime to blame problems on outsiders. Furthermore, whatever their government's sins, Serbs could feel genuinely aggrieved at the rush to recognize the breakaway states with no consideration of the minorities, and they could feel a justified anger that sanctions applied only to them, despite the human rights record of, and repeated violations of the arms embargo by, Croatia.

The notion that externally induced economic hardship will work against some target regime has been proven time and again to be at best simplistic, more often simply wrong. This is especially true when sanctions, in Serbia as much as in Iraq, enhanced government control over most people by forcing them to depend on their government for basic necessities. At the same time, sanctions and hyperinflation helped wipe out the Serbian middle class or sent it fleeing abroad. That had the effect of undermining the principal group capable of providing an organized opposition. Sanctions simultaneously created a politically powerful class of black marketeers with a strong vested interest in maintaining the status quo.[41]

What finally produced a truce was not sanctions but Serbian military reverses in the hands of both the U.S.-trained Croatian army and the Bosnian government forces bolstered by volunteers, money and military aid from Muslim states. That was combined with a falling-out between Serbia and the Serbian rebel leaders in Croatia and Bosnia who wanted to continue to battle.[42] The key to the end of the conflict was the very failure of sanctions to stop the inflow of arms.

That is not to suggest sanctions had no effect. They corrupted public officials in neighbouring states and progressively criminalized the Serbian economy. Out of the deals to link Serbian intelligence to professional smugglers emerged new networks dealing in stolen cars, cigarettes, arms, illegal aliens and heroin that were the scourge of Europe.[43] Government functionaries who had begun smuggling to earn money to prop up the regime, continued to smuggle to prop up their own bank accounts. One of Slobadan Milošević's sons, chairman of a state company with a monopoly of the import of foreign cigarettes, stood accused of smuggling them, in conjunction with Italian mobsters, from Montenegro to Italy and on to northern Europe with Serbian police and Customs taking a cut. And Serbia also became reputedly the number one supplier of counterfeit cigarettes, rolled from cheap local tobacco but packaged in brand name boxes, to the rest of Europe. In a classic case of sanctions-blowback, the same cigarette smuggling networks that assisted Serbia in getting its own goods to neighbouring countries reversed their role and began dumping smuggled cigarettes inside Serbia. In the first year after sanctions were lifted, the federal government reckoned it was losing nearly 20 per cent of its potential revenues to cigarette smugglers.[44]

Similarly, Serbian-controlled Bosnia used the old infrastructure from trafficking in oil, arms and humanitarian aid to become an entrepôt for smuggling cigarettes and liquor through to the rest of Bosnia and on to Croatia. The police protected the convoys, and the Ministry of the Interior of the Bosnian Serb Republic collected 10 per cent through state-owned trading companies.

Not least of the effects of sanctions was to create to the south of Serbia something the world assuredly did not need: yet another state in which political power and criminal profit had become interchangeable currencies and in which arms smuggling, drug trafficking and financial fraud became the backbone of the economy.

Chapter 24

FAMILY BUSINESS

$\mathbf{C}$ontrary to the stereotype of grey authoritarian sameness, in its half century, Communist Europe proved quite capable of spawning idiosyncratic regimes rooted in national cultural traditions. The management style of the Ceausescu family of Romania, for example, owed less to Vladimir Lenin than to Count Dracula.[1] Still, Albania was a case apart. The last holdout of orthodox Stalinism, Albania's creed of international proletarian solidarity was pasted hastily onto a society where loyalties were determined primarily by extended families linked in networks of mutual trust, clan obligation and suspicion of outsiders. If Sicily had its *omertà*, the vow of silence essential for the Mafia to thrive, Albania boasted *besa*, an absolute respect for oral commitments so entrenched that, after Communist rule ended, people were killed for breaking pledges made fifty years earlier.[2]

Ominously for a region in which ethnic nationalism was on the rise, only about half the ethnic-Albanian population lived in Albania. After the 1912 Balkan war, the other half was divided among Serbia, Macedonia and Montenegro with a small minority in Greece. Although most were briefly united under Italian tutelage during World War II, after the war the divisions were re-established, and with them, an underground yearning for Greater Albania, which northern neighbours saw as a territorial threat. On the other side, revanchist elements in Greece coveted the Albanian-controlled portion of the ancient Greek province of Iprios, even to the point of sponsoring, in the 1990s, a North Iprios Liberation Front to launch raids across the border.[3] If the fracturing of Yugoslavia set off the twentieth-century's third Balkan war, the Albania question had the potential to bring about a fourth in which Serbia, Montenegro and Macedonia might contest Albanian unification while Bulgaria joined in carving up Macedonia into Bulgarian, Serbian and Albanian spheres.

The Magic of the Market

At the time of World War II, Albanians had the lowest living standard and shortest life expectancy in Europe, no educational system and an economy based on subsistence agriculture and a few chromium mines. In 1944, Enver Hoxha's Communists expelled the Axis forces and began social reconstruction. While Albania remained the poorest part of Europe, over the next four decades life expectancy nearly doubled, education and medical care became universal, electrification reached the most remote villages and industry made substantial strides. Still, it was a society wrapped in an ideological cocoon. Foreign travel was strictly forbidden; private cars were banned; and trading by individuals was a serious crime — unless it was conducted by Italian gangsters who, in the 1980s, struck a modus vivendi with the regime to use Albania as a base for cigarette smuggling. Although genuine reverence for Hoxha and spartan egalitarianism papered over fundamental divisions, they failed to eradicate them.[4] For Albania was less a police state than a family business in which the southern clans controlled the Party, the secret police and the public infrastructure and used them to keep their northern rivals at bay.[5] That fatal divide would return to haunt the country when the Communist regime crumbled in 1992.

The economy went first. Already in crisis with shortages of investment and parts, when the fall of Communism elsewhere deprived Albanian industry of markets, unemployment shot up, reaching 80 per cent in some areas. As state authority progressively disintegrated, formerly crime-free Albania was swept by robberies; smuggling exploded; emergency food and medical aid from abroad was looted; and the population began to interpret democratization as a licence to steal public property. The suppressed tradition of blood feuds sprang back. To conduct them, men dug out rifles buried since the end of World War II. And over everything hung the pall of the civil wars raging in Yugoslavia.

In 1992, elections brought to power the Democratic Party, which was dominated by the long-excluded northern clans. Committed to radical privatization, the new government slashed state subsidies and threw Albania open to the "magic of the market." Remaining industries closed en masse. Since the mines, the only thing attractive to outsiders, were within artillery range of the Yugoslav army in Kosovo, foreign investment failed to materialize. Privatization and redistribution of land shut down old agricultural cooperatives, while the peasants were bequeathed tiny plots without the means to buy seeds, machinery or fertilizer. The state finances were in chaos. Bills for public services went unpaid, while Customs revenues plummeted as the secret police, formerly guardians of Communist purity, threw themselves enthusiastically into the new free-enterprise order. One of the sectors hardest hit was tobacco farming, which was ruined as smuggled cigarettes flooded the country. Fortunately, some Greek entrepreneurs, concerned over the plight of the farmers (and the suppression of the cannabis crop back home), came bearing gifts of seeds for high-grade marijuana. Coca was later added to Albania's newly diversified crop base.[6] Aside from drugs, largely produced in the south, the only flourishing sector was sanctions-busting, which the northern clans, bolstered by their new hold on the government, geographic position and trans-border family connections, could dominate.

Albania became so essential to the flow of contraband, especially oil, into Serbia-Montenegro that at peak sanctions-busting was reckoned to yield at least 10 per cent of national income.[7] Each time sanctions were tightened elsewhere, more business passed through Albania. To breaking the embargo against Serbia-Montenegro was soon added the job of evading Greek sanctions against Macedonia. The police and Customs either ignored the contraband or used it to supplement their meagre salaries, while complaining in public that they lacked personnel or equipment to stop it. Thousands of ordinary people, left without legal sustenance by the industrial collapse, found temporary relief running small loads of oil into Montenegro. It was tolerated by the authorities, first, because it helped keep a lid on popular discontent, and, second, because it diverted attention from the serious smuggling. Small operators relegated to remoter areas were arrested from time to time to show the West how serious Albania was about respecting sanctions. Meanwhile, at night vessels owned by people tight with the regime would meet Montenegrin tankers at the international boundary on Lake Scutari, link hoses and pump fuel across.[8]

Although oil for Serbia was Albania's principal clandestine export, there were others. Via Albania, arms reached Bosnia from Iran; looted Western humanitarian aid was sold in Serbia and Macedonia; cigarettes evading Customs and excise taxes transited Albania to destinations as varied as Romania and Italy; even the legendary red mercury made one of its ephemeral appearances.[9] Another big business was alien smuggling, from which police and public officials took their cut. Albania became a way station for Asian refugees en route to Europe — though some destined for Italy found themselves picked up on one Albanian beach by day and dumped on another at night.[10] The traffic was assisted by a passports business. Ordinary ones were sold to refugees while diplomatic and state-service ones were passed out to political cronies, smugglers and secret police officers. The aliens business boomed when Turkey made a massive incursion into Iraqi Kurdistan in pursuit of the PKK, sending thousands of Kurds fleeing. However, its importance in the new free-enterprise era was easily surpassed by a commodity with a long and peculiar history in that twilight zone where crime, insurgency and intelligence intersect.

Birth of the Albanian Connection

Shortly after World War II ended, American troops poured back into Europe to counter a largely imaginary Soviet threat. Complementing its role in restoring the Mafia to power in Sicily, U.S. military intelligence and, later, the CIA, ran money and guns to allow Corsican gangsters in Marseilles, discredited by their collaboration with the Gestapo, to redeem themselves by busting Communist Party-led waterfront unions. Both sides were happy. The United States could move in military supplies without danger of interference by Communist agents, while the Corsicans could use control of the port to demonstrate the practical superiority of free enterprise. Opium grown in Anatolia was diverted from legal pharmaceutical use to underground morphine refineries in Turkey, Syria and Lebanon, run to Marseilles, further refined into heroin, then shipped to the United States by three main routes. One went to South America where it linked up with the Uruguay-to-Panama-to-Miami *contrabandista* system to give those running American cigarettes, whisky, blue jeans and electrical products south by light plane a return cargo. A second went via Montreal hidden in cars. That trade was supervised by a former Gestapo informant and trafficker in counterfeit ration coupons facing a death sentence back in France. A third went directly by ship to New York.

In New York much of the heroin was controlled by another World War II veteran. Vito Genovese had moved to the United States in the 1930s, apparently as a hit man for Mussolini's intelligence service, then bolted back to Italy to escape a murder rap. He cemented relations with Mussolini by generous donations of money to the fascist party and of cocaine to the dictator's son. When the Allies invaded Sicily, he switched sides. On the recommendation of Charles "Lucky" Luciano, he was recruited into the U.S. Army as a guide and interpreter. Then he teamed up with American quartermasters to run black markets in cigarettes, food, alcohol, petroleum and weapons. Their profits were stashed in Switzerland. On his return to the United States, Genovese soon took over as don of the most powerful New York Mafia family, the first one to be heavily implicated in the transatlantic heroin trade.[11]

Meanwhile back in France, the position of the Corsican gangsters was consolidated by the Algerian war. When President Charles de Gaulle conceded independence to Algeria, dissident French settlers, army officers and secret service agents grouped in the Organisation d'armée sécrete plotted his assassination. To counter the threat, de Gaulle created a new intelligence force, drawn heavily from the Corsican underworld, to search out and destroy opposition forces. The Corsicans took advantage of their new respectability to strengthen their old business, so much so that when the French Connection heroin network was finally dismantled, more than half of those arrested were or had been members of one or other of France's intelligence services.[12]

The closing down of the French Connection occurred at much the same time as a NATO-sponsored coup in Turkey that saw a military government, in exchange for U.S. arms and money, agreeing to stamp out an opium poppy crop that had been essential to the Anatolian peasant economy for hundreds of years. But together they did less to end the heroin trade than to change the beneficiaries.

In Southeast Asia in the 1950s, French forces battling to preserve the empire had faced a double threat — from an increasingly successful Communist insurgency and from a war-weary population back home, fed up with high taxes to finance a losing cause. Hence French military intelligence tried to shift part of the cost of the war onto the opium trade. To fund local mercenary units, it taxed opium harvests and collected protection money from proprietors of opium dens. When the French gave up and passed South Vietnam on to the Americans, they also bequeathed to them the drug trade, with one twist. Opium produced by the hill tribes fighting as CIA mercenaries during the Vietnam War was sometimes flown to urban markets on cargo planes owned by CIA-proprietary companies. Part of the crop, though, was refined into heroin by Chinese mobsters in Hong Kong, then sold, first, to the burgeoning GI market, and, later, directly in the United States.[13]

But that source of heroin was soon eclipsed by another. From the late 1970s, more and more of the world's opiates came from the Golden Crescent, particularly Afghanistan and Pakistan's North West Frontier Province. Initially the main opium-morphine route lay across Iran and Turkey, then to Sicily where Mafia chemists, some veterans of the French Connection, refined it into heroin prior to shipment to western Europe and the United States. In the U.S., the most ingenious trafficking ring ran the merchandise and washed the money through a network of Sicilian-owned pizzerias. By the time the Pizza Connection was broken, heroin refineries, protected and taxed by mujahideen commanders, had been established in Afghanistan itself.[14]

At that stage trade routes proliferated. Some went by ship from Karachi, by dhow from the Makran coast or by land down to Bombay and then out to markets around the world. A big share still took the overland route across Iran, in heavily armed convoys whose guards, thanks to the U.S. arms for the mujahideen, could outgun the Iranian and Pakistani border patrols, even to the point of shooting down police helicopters with anti-aircraft missiles.[15] The fall of the Soviet-backed government accelerated Afghanistan's opium production, while victory of the ultra-fundamentalist Taliban over the old mujahideen warlords turned opiates into a virtual state industry.[16]

Although networks of Russian mobsters carted Afghan heroin, along with the product of ex-Soviet Central Asia, to market via eastern Europe, Turkey remained the main transit route. There it was handled by a curious alliance, the nature of which was exposed in 1996 by an auto accident in the little town of Susurluk. Killed in a limousine crushed by a truck were a powerful Grey Wolf activist-cum-heroin smuggler long sought internationally on drugs and murder charges, and the former deputy chief of the Istanbul police. Critically injured was a Kurdish member of parliament on the government payroll to run a thousand-man militia fighting the PKK. Found in the car were several revolvers with silencers and electronic espionage equipment. In a brief flurry of excitement, the minister of the interior was accused of being part of an extreme rightist *maffya* engaged in extortion, ransom kidnapping and drug trafficking across Europe and Central Asia. Once he was forced from office, the affair was swept under the oriental carpet, and Turkey went back to business as usual.

In fact a government riddled by corruption and subverted by *maffya* connections soon discovered the truth of the old adage that patriotism is the first refuge of the scoundrel. When the exiled head of the PKK was arrested in Italy and Italy hesitated to extradite him to face possible capital punishment in Turkey, the Turkish government slapped on sanctions. It embargoed all Italian firms from participating in state and military contracts and encouraged the population at large to shun Italian goods. In response trendy shops in the urban centres that formerly featured Italian fashions began draping their dummies in black.[17]

From Turkey the main flow of heroin had long passed through Bulgaria to Yugoslavia to take the Brotherhood and Unity Highway into central Europe or Italy. During the upheaval in Yugoslavia this traditional Balkan route shifted. Some drugs went north of the Black Sea to Romania and then Hungary, partly to service the new demand in eastern Europe where capitalist vices became the rage, but also en route farther west. Some were sent overland from Bulgaria to Macedonia, then passed north through Kosovo or east to Albania. From there drugs might take several routes depending on the state of war and the mood of the intelligence services. Some entered Serbia to pass, again via Hungary and Romania, to western Europe. Some ran up the coast to Croatian ports that balanced their imports of cocaine with exports of heroin. In addition, drugs were sent by ship directly from Turkey to Albania, offloaded, then stashed on speedboats already busy running contraband cigarettes and illegal immigrants to Italy. There was even an eccentric route running the other way. Heroin arriving in Italy directly from Asia was loaded into luxury cars, mainly Mercedes-Benzes, being sold off for cash by Italian politicians and functionaries, frightened into reducing their profile by the "Clean Hands" anti-corruption investigation. The cars, with false papers, looped north, then east, then south, discharging loads of heroin at different points and picking up electronic goods, for final delivery to Albania, where the cars and the (duty-free) electronics were sold to the *nouveau riche* class of Democratic Party cronies, sanctions-busters and drug smugglers.[18]

The Albanian connection went far beyond the immediate area. Although Albanians had long been forbidden to emigrate, Kosovars were not. By the end of the 1980s there was a large émigré community in Switzerland, Germany and Austria, attracted by economic prospects. In the 1990s it was swollen by political refugees. The great majority held unskilled jobs and struggled to remit savings back to their families. With the local economy flattened by war and sanctions, scarcely a family in the Kosovo capital of Priština did not depend on "Swiss funds." But with their close family trust, underground financial institutions and language beyond the comprehension of law-enforcement agencies, the Kosovars were ideally placed to run heroin. Their ascent was facilitated by a racist backlash against Turks in central Europe. Thousands of Kosovars acted as Balkan route couriers. Each carried a tiny load to minimize the damage should anyone get caught. And caught they were. In 1991 Swiss police made their first major Kosovar bust. Two years later more than a thousand Kosovars had been jailed in Switzerland on drugs charges.[19] Some were in it just for the money. But after Serbia stripped Kosovo of autonomy, others found a higher purpose.

The first major challenge to Serbian rule in Kosovo came with strikes and protest marches in the Trepca mines. Returning émigrés took the lead in bringing the historic mining and metallurgical complex to a standstill. Serbia struck back by pushing out most ethnic-Albanian miners, replacing them with Serbs, Montenegrins and even Bosnian-Muslim prisoners. Kosovar nationalists reacted to Serbian repression by creating parallel institutions, including their own health and education system, and by refusing to pay taxes to Serbia. Soon the struggle turned military. Émigrés sponsored the Kosovo Liberation Army. Although the big traffickers had been indifferent to politics, to maintain community standing they provided cash, even investing drug money to buy land along the Kosovo–Albania border in preparation for re-unification, and used their networks to move weapons from central Europe.[20] Then developments in Albania provided a cheaper and much more convenient source of arms.

Building Pyramids

Banks in Communist Albania had functioned almost exclusively as instruments of the central planning system. They had had little to do with ordinary savers, and nothing to do with commercial lending. After the regime changed, the old banks tried to adapt to the new economic environment. They made business loans. But no one bothered to repay. Nor were their interest rates attractive to savers. However, new institutions emerged, particularly investment banks, credit co-ops and "charitable" foundations that pulled in deposits, sometimes in local currency, sometimes in foreign, by offering interest rates of 8 to 12 per cent per month. They were cheered on by Democratic Party leaders who posed publicly on billboards or on state TV with the bosses of the banks, while privately accepting suitcases of cash to meet their political and personal expenses. To the politicians, maintaining the high-interest schemes was a way of keeping the public on side, while the population took political endorsement as an assurance the government would protect their money. To further enhance the appeal, the banks falsified their assets and engaged in advertising gimmicks — one sponsored a Miss World contest while another donated money to create a local soccer team, complete with an Argentine coach and Brazilian players.[21]

Attracted by high interest rates, local people mortgaged their property, sold their livestock and hocked their valuables as well as turning over savings sent back by relatives abroad. Because the banks that posed as charitable foundations limited the amount any depositor could put in, people had family members front for them; there was a trade in fake ID cards. In addition to ordinary savings, there were new earnings from smuggling oil, arms and drugs. Because some of the investment banks accepted deposits in Italian lira, cash arrived courtesy of mobsters of the Sacra Corona Unita, the product of, among other things, trafficking in Albanian cannabis or using Albania as a springboard for running cigarettes into Italy. The money was sometimes smuggled into Albania in coffins bearing the remains of émigrés who had died abroad. It was also couriered back and forth by bank bosses using their Democratic Party-supplied diplomatic passports, which made them immune to search. Italian mob money would be washed through the banks and be repaid as proceeds of phoney trade deals.[22]

A few of the new banks were genuine investment companies, capable of generating at least part of the money necessary to pay interest to depositors. Others were scams from the start. Almost all degenerated into pyramid schemes: they paid out interest on old deposits by attracting new ones. And they were soon in trouble.

First, the IMF forced the government, as part of the terms for a desperately needed loan, to issue a public warning. Then police probes from Italy and Greece scared off criminal money. But the really fatal blow was the lifting of sanctions on Serbia-Montenegro. With the profits of sanctions-busting gone, the banks were desperate for fresh cash. For a time they engaged in a vicious interest rate war to attract money from each other. But in the summer of 1997, a deal in black market Iraqi oil went sour, causing the owner of one bank to abscond with $13 million. The resulting panic brought them all down. The only people who got their money out before the collapse were smugglers and gangsters close to the regime. Many thousands lost their homes, cars, livestock and life savings. Outrage over the collapse, and the refusal of the government to guarantee the deposits, provided the spark for a revolt of the south against the northern-controlled government.[23]

Government authority in the south vanished. Police stations and army depots were stripped of weapons. Customs revenues, always problematic, effectively ceased as southern ports, under the leadership of militias loyal to the old Communist Party bosses, decided to taste the fruits of real capitalism. In poured consumer goods duty free, along with stolen cars, alcohol and tobacco. At least 80 per cent of cigarette imports entered without paying Customs duties or taxes, while Albanian frugality apparently enabled the population to drink annually some 1,500 tons of coffee out of official imports of 70.[24] And shipped out through those same ports was the cannabis crop on which 80,000 people depended. Out, too, went another commodity for which the Albanian minorities in neighbouring countries had developed a remarkable appetite.

Brothers in Blood or Partners in Crime?

Despite long-standing suspicions in Serbia that its southern neighbour had been fanning the nationalist flames, during the Communist era, the Greater Albania cause held little political appeal. The tightly closeted regime had no interest in opening itself to external influences. And it was the northern clans, excluded from power, who had the most extended family ties in the Yugoslav republics. Even the post-1992 northern-dominated government downplayed the nationalist line. The Democratic Party energetically adopted the Kosovo cause only after the 1997 rebellion restored to power the southern-dominated Communists, tactfully renamed Social Democrats. Then the Democratic Party opposition could accuse the Social Democratic government of failure to aid the Kosovars. The fact was that, contrary to appearances, Albanians and Kosovars had little in common. Kosovars were more cosmopolitan and wealthier. Abroad, they ran the heroin trade, while Albanians worked the business only as cheap labour, beholden to Kosovars to provide them with phoney passports or ID cards. Back home, after the fall of Communism, Kosovars, with their Swiss nest eggs, were among the first outsiders to arrive in Albania to take over privatized businesses, earning resentment for their money and the contempt they showed for their Albanian kinfolk.

But during the revolt, something more practical than ethnicity united them. More than a million weapons had been snatched from armouries. And with the profits of sanctions-busting gone, the smuggling networks were happy to find new commodities to sell abroad, to earn the foreign exchange to buy the consumer goods, alcohol and tobacco they were bringing home.

One market was Macedonia. It was no stranger to gun-running, though historically it had been members of the Macedonian majority, not the Albanian minority, who had dominated the trade. In the late nineteenth and early twentieth centuries, the Internal Macedonian Revolutionary Organization, a radical independence movement, raised money by kidnapping, extortion, counterfeiting currency or robbing banks, post offices or the homes and businesses of rich Muslims (who were often murdered). Farmers had their crops and livestock confiscated, and merchants sometimes paid more in protection money to the *komitas* (brigands) than in taxes to the state. The movement supplemented the proceeds with secret subsidies from Bulgaria, which hoped to use the nationalists to annex Macedonia. Most of the money was used for arms. Those arms came from a variety of sources. Some, financed by contributions from émigré businessmen, were purchased in England. Then they were sent to Portugal where ships would change registry, captain and cargo manifests, before continuing into the Mediterranean to offload in Greece, thence to travel north. Some were spirited overland from Bulgaria or across the Albanian frontier, on occasion using priests or diplomats as couriers.[25] Although dormant for decades, this ultra-nationalist current resurfaced after the Communist era. Armed and increasingly dangerous, it had a strong influence on the government, which saw the Macedonian ethnic movement as a counterweight to militant nationalism among the Albanian minority.

The Macedonian economy had been badly hurt by the collapse of Yugo-slavia, and further battered by sanctions. But the impact was not evenly felt. The Albanian-populated areas, traditionally the poorest, started to account for an increasingly large share of Macedonia's dwindling GNP. Partly it was an accident of geography — those areas were ideally located for sanctions-busting trade. Partly it was ethnicity — Albanian gangsters took the lead in post-sanctions trafficking, in heroin, cigarettes and arms. The foreign exchange earned from smuggling helped arm the Macedonian-Albanian nationalist formations with Albanian weapons as they prepared for a show-down with Macedonian radicals.[26]

Even more arms went to the Kosovo Liberation Army. Increasing num-bers of émigré Kosovars left menial jobs in Europe to stop over in Albania, purchase looted weapons from drug dealers, secret police agents and gov-ernment functionaries, and trek across the border into Kosovo.[27] As armed insurrection spread across Kosovo, Serbia responded by the ethnic cleans-ing of border villages, by embargoes on food and fuel to areas held by rebels and by Israeli-style tax raids on villages. And the West reacted to a mess created in good measure by its own previous sanctions — by impos-ing yet more.[28]

. . . Then came the inevitable sequel.

The Gang That Couldn't Bomb Straight

The Kosovo crisis began in December 1998 with another Anglo-American bombing raid on Iraq. Although air attacks, in which strategic targets included herds of sheep and camels, had become an almost daily routine, this one was different in two ways: intensity and Russian response — namely, anger that its opposition had been brushed aside. This reaction was reinforced by NATO's apparent intent also to beat up on Serbia, a country to which post-Commu-nist Russia felt close ties. Russian assertiveness encouraged Milošević to hang tough on Kosovo.

Kosovo was no stranger to intercommunal violence. Although by the twen-tieth century ethnic Albanians had become a majority in Kosovo, there was still a large Serb presence. That had changed by the 1980s. Partly it was the result of relative birth rates. Partly it was due to a "natural" outflow of Serbs, helped along in mid-decade by rapes, murders, burning of Orthodox churches and destruction of property.[29] In the face of rising tensions, the Communist leadership in Belgrade stood mute for fear of igniting an ethnic tinderbox throughout the country. That left the podium to Milošević, with catastrophic results. Nor did anti-Serb attacks end with his ascent to power.

Indeed, they worsened in the late 1990s when the Kosovo Liberation Army set out to provoke a backlash from Belgrade.

When the West responded to Serbia's clampdown and anti-insurgency campaign by the threat of intervention, Serbia offered major concessions. But when the time came to put signatures to a deal, Milošević balked. For the so-called Rambouillet Agreement demanded that the Kosovo Liberation Army be given full status as a signatory — a little like the U.S. forcing Britain, at the start of the Ulster "troubles" in 1969, to grant political legitimacy to the IRA. Other terms insisted that Kosovo's future be determined by referendum, which demographics guaranteed to favor independence; that NATO, rather than the UN, police Kosovo; and that NATO have the right to military maneuvers throughout Yugoslavia. There was even a codicil that stated that "the economy of Kosovo shall function in accordance with free market principles." Those long on conspiracy theory and short on geology took this as part of a Western plot to seize the ancient Trepca mines and Kosovo's huge deposits of lignite (a particularly dirty and undesirable fossil fuel).

In fact, the terms may have been written to provoke rejection. A senior American official was reported to have said, "We intentionally set the bar too high for the Serbs to comply. They need some bombing, and that is what they are going to get."[30] Then came a PR blitz claiming that a systematic mass-murder campaign was under way against ethnic Kosovars. The media, on cue, once again forgot the old adage about the first casualty of war.[31] With the public mood prepared, NATO could celebrate its recent fiftieth anniversary by lighting up Serbia (and Kosovo) with things much more lethal than birthday candles.

Initially the targets were the usual ones — roads, bridges, petrochemical and fertilizer factories, the country's sole auto plant and the electrical grid; electricity, NATO military spokesmen insisted, was a "dual purpose" commodity. The list of what was "strategic" lengthened as the Serbs, to the surprise of the U.S., did not capitulate quickly. It came to include everything whose destruction might (on the oft-disproved but still popular theory) break the popular will and spark opposition to the regime.[32] The extension of the air campaign brought inevitable accidents: schools, hospitals, a retirement home, convoys of refugees, the Chinese embassy, and so forth. It also brought deliberate atrocities — for example, the destruction of the state television offices, which killed several journalists, on the rationale that the station was important for regime propaganda. Along with direct destruction came environmental disasters, such as poisoned water, the spread of toxic chemicals from bombed-out plants and the aftereffects, already widespread in Iraq, of ordnance made from depleted uranium. Blackmail followed the bombs as the United States told the population that there would be no aid for reconstruction until Milošević was gone.[33]

The air campaign was supplemented by tighter sanctions, particularly the oil embargo, which proved as leakproof as the *Exxon Valdez*. While NATO blasted away at refineries and distribution facilities, oil flowed in via Montenegro; and from Ukrainian ports, barges chugged across the Black Sea, then up the Danube. Exhortations to Ukraine to turn off the tap and to Cyprus to freeze the accounts that paid for the oil were made in vain.[34]

Not only did the strategic bombing and sanctions have just the opposite effect to that predicted, discrediting the opposition and consolidating the regime, they also had little impact on the combat capabilities of the Serb army. However, they had considerable effect on Kosovo, from which the population fled en masse — driven out both by Serbian forces, including the paramilitaries that had proven their mettle in Bosnia, and by the very bombing that NATO claimed was being launched in defense of the Kosovars.

Since NATO was skittish about confronting the Serbs on the ground, it subcontracted the job to the KLA. Much as it had with the contras and the Afghan mujahideen, the U.S. had to convert a fragmented collection of bickering groups (denounced variously as heroin traffickers, terrorists, unrepentant Marxists, and standard-bearers of an Islamic fundamentalist assault on Christian civilization) into something resembling a proper armed force before they could be re-anointed as freedom fighters. Effective leadership was turned over to a Kosovar who had risen to brigadier general in the U.S.–trained Croatian forces, and who had spearheaded the campaign to cleanse Krajina of its Serb population.[35] Even then, the KLA made little headway. It was really the wooing of Russia with $4.5 billion in IMF money that led to a cease-fire agreement — on terms Serbia would likely have accepted months before. NATO entered Kosovo via Albania and Macedonia, without the right to free movement through Yugoslavia; there was no mention of a referendum on Kosovo's future, and NATO committed itself to disarm the KLA. It was an odd "victory" for a military alliance whose *raison d'être* was to defend members against outside aggression, not to rearrange the internal affairs of non-members to favour one ethnic group over another.

Furthermore, in Kosovo, NATO won a booby prize. Kosovo quickly became an arms-and-drugs trafficking hub, boasting 20 to 25 per cent more cars than before the war; the most popular newcomers were luxury vehicles with no license plates. This new Kosovo threatened to displace Bosnia (where half the economy operated underground — the most lucrative parts run by government officials and police) as the Balkans' premier smuggler's paradise.[36] It was a vocation whose development the occupation authorities assisted when they converted the monetary system from the Yugoslav dinar to the deutsche mark (while encouraging the free circulation of dollars, Swiss francs and other hard currencies). That shift was facilitated further by charging taxpayers a premium if they paid in Yugoslav currency.[37] In came the usual coterie of camp followers and carpetbaggers seeking to profit from reconstruction, including a British firm chasing the contract to run the central prison in Pristina.[38] Meanwhile, the former guerrilla groups dissipated their energies in internecine battles over the division of the spoils or in terror campaigns against remaining Serbs and Gypsies.

Given that NATO had reneged on its implicit deal with the KLA, relations between the guerrillas and their erstwhile air force quickly deteriorated. In a tone similar to that heard after the U.S. abandoned the Miami Cubans, NATO was denounced by KLA militants because it "failed to keep its part of the *besa*." Indeed, one KLA spin-off, the Liberation Army of Presevo, Medveja and Bujanovac, began raids across the NATO–guaranteed border into Albanian-populated areas of Serbia proper.

However, by the time NATO began taking a second look at its erstwhile allies, the shock waves from its apparent legitimization of the KLA had already spread through the region. What seemed an implicit endorsement of Albanian reunification threatened to upset domestic politics in Macedonia and Montenegro, with their large ethnic Albanian minorities bolstered by Kosovar refugees and black market arms networks. In Albania itself, though, the war paid immediate dividends. Squabbles between Southern and Northern clans were suspended, partly in solidarity with the Kosovars (who were ethnically related to the Northerners) and partly because the war brought new economic opportunities. Among them was the chance to loot refugee relief aid — some was stolen on arrival at the airport under the eyes of U.S. troops, while trucks hauling cargo from the port just vanished. There was also a boom in alien smuggling: some 180 commercial speedboats, each capable of carrying twenty to forty people, represented the largest commercial investment in Albania. But after the war, with the Kosovars safely under NATO's protection, internal ethnic tensions rekindled to the point where Albania effectively fell apart again.[39]

Then there was Serbia. The world watched closely in anticipation of the imminent fall of the house of Milošević, the brutal dictator humiliated in war, then scratched its head when that did not happen. With the population at large feeling itself a victim of NATO aggression and emotionally committed to Kosovo, the only opposition figures with mass credibility were those who attacked Milošević for not standing firmer. In reaction, the West stepped up sanctions, deftly changing their objective, much as had happened with Iraq, from stopping military aggression to collectively punishing the population. That, too, failed to produce a powerful anti-regime backlash.

Then dawned the idea of a switch from sanctions against the country at large to sanctions against individuals — beneficiaries or supporters of the regime. In the spirit of Allied measures against German sympathizers in World War II, European countries and the United States produced a blacklist of firms and persons with whom their citizens were not to do business. The notion of targeted sanctions was an intriguing theory, flawed by only three facts. One was that businesses in the hands of genuine opposition figures had already been marginalized, if not destroyed. The second was that the regime had deliberately compromised the leading business people: if they cooperated, they got rich; if they did not, the regime could easily launch tax-evasion or anti-corruption investigations against them. The third was that the country still had in place a sophisticated sanctions-busting apparatus, while more and more countries anxious for business to return to normal were as disinclined to enforce personalized embargoes as generalized ones.[40]

Finally, the West, again following the Iraq model, decided to encourage a palace coup, sowing division in the ranks of regime supporters. But, unlike the case in Iraq, this time they were "successful"— in removing the most obvious symbol of their continued failure to address the real problem.

This change of tactics coincided with a series of murders of people implicated in black market activity. The victims ranged from powerful regime-linked businessmen to the minister of Defense to paramilitary leaders only marginally less notorious than Arkan. Indeed, Arkan himself soon joined their ranks.[41] There were many explanations offered — the killings were the work of the (hitherto impotent) opposition; they were done by Kosovars defending their Balkan arms-and-drugs routes from attempts by prominent Serb gangsters to muscle in; they were the work of foreign (that is, American and German) intelligence services; and, most realistically, they were the result of disputes within the regime over the division of the spoils at a time when there was growing suspicion the party was soon going to end.[42]

Just as the United States had personally so demonized Saddam Hussein as to forget that any Iraqi regime with a modicum of national pride would have difficulty accepting the independent existence of Kuwait, so too it chose to ignore the fact that any effective successor to Milošević would be bound to keep the Kosovo question alive. Following a stormy election campaign,

Milošević was replaced by Vojislav Kostunica, a firm nationalist who had already decreed there would be no retreat from Serbian claims on Kosovo.[43]

Aftershocks

Behind the Serbian sanctions and the Kosovo air campaign was a dual myth that had emerged from World War II. One part pointed to the supposed importance of economic measures such as asset freezes and trade embargoes in defeating Hitler. Not in the least daunted by numerous instances in which sanctions immiserized the populations of weak and isolated countries while their regimes hung tough, the world continued to impose sanctions in a promiscuous way, particularly in the last two decades of the twentieth century.

Iraq was the most appalling case — its sanctions were micro-managed with a totalitarian efficiency that put the Baathist regime to shame. Even books and paper were banned as non-essentials — which, given the number of Iraqi children who quit school to scramble for food in garbage heaps, they probably were. With the advent of a new U.S. administration heavily staffed by veterans of the "victory" over Iraq in 1991, the incoming secretary of State announced his intent to "re-energize" the sanctions.[44]

But Iraq was far from alone. Even Afghanistan, ravaged by twenty years of war and the worst drought in recent memory, faced sanctions that could destroy its already marginal legal sector while bolstering the drug trafficking and smuggling from which the ruling Taliban drew its financial lifeblood.[45] Intriguingly, one of the pretexts for those sanctions was the refusal of the Afghan regime to surrender to the United States Osama bin Laden, a Saudi fundamentalist formerly lauded by the U.S. for his role in assisting the mujahideen to overthrow the pro-Soviet government in Kabul. By the time of the sanctions, bin Laden's networks had reputedly managed to secure a beachhead in Kosovo.

World War II had also produced the enduring myth of the effectiveness of strategic bombing of economic targets. The apparent failure of high-tech air power in the Kosovo war to settle things neatly from long distance at no cost of American lives led not to a reconsideration of the foundations of the doctrine, but to the plea that the U.S. military was overextended, short on training and badly deficient in spare parts, and that it was time to reverse the reductions in military spending that had accompanied the end of the cold war.[46] Fortunately for the military-industrial complex, another aftereffect of the Kosovo campaign might soon help rationalize another global arms race.

A further casualty was the Western honeymoon with China — it saw in

Kosovo a possible dress rehearsal for an intervention in Tibet (which had a history of CIA meddling) or Singkiang (where Muslim separatists were flexing their muscle). Even more ominously, in Russia, frustration at being treated as a Third World player, the public spectacle of a pro-Western clique of financial oligarchs looting national assets, and deepening economic and demographic crises combined to swing the political pendulum backwards. Virtually every faction agreed that the disintegration of Russian power and influence must stop. When Russia negotiated an arrangement with Iraq to give Russian firms privileged access to Iraqi oil fields, then began to upgrade Iraqi air defenses with the same technology that had permitted Serbia to shoot down a U.S. Stealth bomber, there was clearly much more afoot than simply a business deal.[47]

EPILOGUE

In 1568 the Spanish Crown borrowed from Genoese bankers enough gold and silver to meet the payroll of a Spanish army struggling to put down a rebellion in Flanders. As the five ships carrying the treasure entered the English Channel, they were threatened by French privateers and fled into English ports. Their admiral asked Elizabeth I to guard the treasure. Instead she "borrowed" it herself. Unable to pay the near-mutinous troops, the Spanish commander in Flanders had to extort money from local burghers. The angry Flemish merchants responded by supporting the rebellion the Spanish were using the extorted money to suppress. Elizabeth was not left smiling for long. The Spanish retaliated by stepping up financial support for rebels battling English rule in Ireland.[1]

Economic warfare has probably existed almost as long as war itself. Its manifestations varied from destroying crops to plundering merchant ships to, on occasion, counterfeiting the other side's currency. However, since the Napoleonic era most economic wars have been fought on three main fronts.

The first involves attempting to stop the target country's exports. That can dry up its foreign exchange earnings and cause unemployment in the export industries, fuelling social discontent perhaps to the point of sparking rebellion. That, in turn, might shake business confidence, decrease investment and make the unemployment problem even worse. On the second front there could be efforts to deny the target strategic imports particularly of arms, fuel and food, the three commodities whose loss will do the most damage. Access to state-of-the-art technology, too, might be embargoed, particularly if that will further hamper military preparedness. On the third front, financial measures can be deployed to cut the target off from international loans and investments and, perhaps, freeze any assets it has stashed abroad. Apart from hurting the country's ability to pay for essential imports, financial warfare can have powerful indirect effects. As people begin to fear that the national currency will lose value, they try to spend money faster. As those with goods to sell worry that inflation will erode the value of the money in which they will be paid, they jack up prices in anticipation. The cycle could eventually degenerate into a self-sustaining hyperinflation. Citizens might panic to convert cash or bank deposits into gold or U.S. dollars, or even into sacks of soybeans on the assumption that wealth held in physical commodities might be safer from inflation, depreciation or expropriation. If this happens on a sufficient scale, it will drain banks, drive up interest rates and cause the black market value of the national currency to plunge.[2]

Economic warfare can also provoke capital flight. If the wealthy attempt to shift their money abroad on a sufficient scale, it will force the country to further cut back imports of essentials, drive down investment yet more and slow, stop or even reverse economic growth. Fears of negative growth, and resulting political unrest, cause the process to feed on itself, inducing yet more money to take flight.[3] Since it is the rich who move their wealth abroad, a higher tax burden falls on the poor at a time when development has been blocked and unemployment driven up. That can cause a scramble for survival in the underground economy. If the state reacts to shortages by rationing and price controls, the underground economy grows even faster. Black market trading, smuggling and property crime soar, while legal economic activity sags. Tax receipts fall further, forcing the government to either slash social spending, cut investment in essential infrastructure or find unorthodox means of paying obligations. If it responds by printing more money, that can further discredit the national currency. These results can be exacerbated by covert forms of economic warfare — currency counterfeiting, industrial sabotage and directing rebel forces against economically strategic targets.

The most important test of the efficacy of economic warfare probably came during World War II. Against Nazi Germany an Allied army of investment bankers and commodity traders, academic economists and corporate lawyers directed blockades and embargoes, asset freezes and pre-emptive buying, sabotage and counterfeiting. The presumed success of these measures fed the post-war belief that countries could substitute measures of economic reprisal for military, and that a newly emerging United Nations could use economic warfare as a tool for enforcing collective morality.

The new optimism ignored a fundamental lesson of history, that economic warfare has often been not an alternative to, but a cause or, at a minimum, an exacerbating factor in military conflict. The need to seal Europe against British goods drove much of Napoleon's conquests in Europe. Reich Marshall Hermann Goering attempted to use in his own defence at his war crimes trial the notion that it was the British blockade, illegal, his lawyer claimed, under international law, that forced Germany into an economic emergency and justified the plundering of other nations. Needless to say, the court was not impressed. Nevertheless it remained true that the search for strategic materials, many cut off by the Allied blockade, tipped Hitler's decision to invade the Soviet Union, and exacerbated, though certainly did not cause, much less excuse his exploitation of conquered Europe.[4] The American decision to apply oil sanctions against Japan in response to its invasion of China caused Japan to redirect its war effort to Southeast Asia where oil could be obtained. That required a pre-emptive strike against Pearl Harbor.[5] Sanctions therefore helped turn limited conflicts, which could perhaps have been settled with limited military responses, into global ones.

The same has been true in more recent years. Offsetting the impact of sanctions was one motive for much South African aggression against its neighbours and for the Israeli invasion of Lebanon. Even the Iraqi grab for Kuwait was prompted in good measure by Baghdad's conviction that it was the target of a campaign of economic warfare.

Moreover, the reassuring presumption that the UN could be the enforcer of a new age of international morality ignored the fact that, even when economic sanctions seem to be the result of multilateral decisions, they are imposed only when the major powers want them to be, for their own purposes. Although a wide consensus eventually emerged for sanctions against South Africa to register opposition to its human rights violations, military aggression against neighbours and development of "weapons of mass destruction," precisely those activities earned Israel "sanctions" in the form of regular increases in U.S. economic and military aid. And behind the lofty rhetoric frequently hides baser motives. While UN inspectors, often acting as little more than spies for American and British intelligence, engaged in largely fruitless but highly publicized searches for further caches of "weapons of mass destruction," the real reason for maintaining against Iraq sanctions that have ravaged a generation with malnutrition-related disease was to keep its oil from flooding an already soft market. Even when the oil allowance was raised, it was a deliberate illusion. As the United States was fully aware, the ban on the import of spare parts meant that Iraq's pumping equipment was so dilapitated that it could not meet the previously permitted levels. Further price drops would menace the American oil patch with the spectre of massive bankruptcies; threaten to produce financial chaos and political revolution in Venezuela, where weak oil prices had already caused mass destitution and encouraged the rise of a populist, left-wing opposition; erode the ability of America's main Middle East client-regime, that of Saudi Arabia, to buy off religious and secular discontent and buy more American arms; and render financially unfeasible an American-led effort to run oil-and-gas pipelines from former Soviet Central Asia into Turkey in order to keep Russia from re-establishing its economic hegemony over the region. To be sure, the Iraqi regime is a thuggish one that merits censure. But it is impossible to avoid recalling the opinion of Yossarian in *Catch-22*. Lying in a hospital bed with shrapnel in his leg, he commented on war raging outside: "Between me and every ideal I see people cashing in, and that sort of spoils the ideal."

The conviction that economic warfare could be so effective was based on a misreading of its impact on Nazi Germany, extrapolated into a modern context in which circumstances were even less propitious. During World War II, the target was apparently sealed by an unprecedented naval blockade and subjected to massive strategic bombing. Yet at the war's end, its productive capacity was likely greater than at the start. Partly that reflected Germany's ability to mobilize resources from conquered territories. Partly it reflected its skill in finding substitutes for embargoed products. Partly it reflected its sheer determination. But it also reflected holes in the blockade. Always present, they inevitably get worse the longer sanctions are in force.

How much damage sanctions do depends on the willingness and ability (two separate things) of countries imposing them to ensure they are respected. Sanctions that for some are an expression of international moral outrage are viewed by others as golden opportunities — in more ways than one — to make friends and influence balance sheets. Even if they are willing in principle, governments riddled by corruption or with minimal resources to commit to enforcement will be in no position to match moral pronouncements with concrete action. While warships belonging to members of the Organization of American States sternly scrutinized ocean-going traffic bound for Haiti during its recent period of disfavour, the military elites of Haiti and the Dominican Republic toasted the embargo, and the black market profits from smuggling fuel across their border, with imported champagne.[6] Meanwhile fuel shortages forced the Haitian masses to cut down the few remaining trees, even to the point of digging up the roots, completing the transition of Haiti from the eighteenth-century jewel of the French colonial empire to the contemporary world's ultimate environmental disaster zone.

Even if sanctions do produce serious economic damage, they are a success only if they force the target to change *political* behaviour in some pre-determined way. But economic hardship rarely leads to the targeted state's leaders making "rational" political decisions — with "rational" generally defined as "them" doing what "we" want them to do. U.S. sanctions against Chile did not precipitate the fall of the Marxist president — it took a vicious military coup to do the job. Few countries could be more vulnerable to American economic wrath than Panama — yet ultimately it required a full-blown invasion to oust the regime. The United States squeezed Cuba for thirty years without causing the government to seriously modify its policies; it was only the fall of the Soviet Union that forced any radical reconsideration. To be sure, American Cold Warriors were quick to claim credit for that latter event. But in the disintegration of the U.S.S.R., American economic warfare played at best a secondary role, and the mess left behind should be further proof against any self-congratulations. Sanctions probably contributed less to the dismantling of apartheid in South Africa than strictly internal struggles combined with South African big business simply outgrowing the system put in place initially to raise business profitability. Nor did years of destructive sanctions over Bosnia deter Serbia from accepting yet further sanctions as the price of consolidating control over Kosovo.

In virtually every case, sanctions have been countered, at least partially, sometimes substantially, by a sanctions-busting machine. If a regime under siege is strong and in command of its resources, it organizes smuggling through parastatal corporations. If its capitalist class is advanced and on side, it privatizes the job — legal business becomes, in effect, criminalized with the approval and support of the state. If the economy is weak and the business class poorly integrated into the world economy, the target state will have to create a new entrepreneurial class that gains experience in industrial espionage, exchange control evasion, money-laundering, smuggling and maritime fraud. Gangster-capitalism flourishes in an environment of contrived shortages, financial chaos and rampant black-marketeering. Economic war profiteers cosy with the political elite gain in power and influence, reinforcing the regime's commitment to the very policies that led to the sanctions being imposed, while the costs fall on those without the means of making alternative political choices.

Nowhere is this clearer than in modern Burma, which has now surpassed Afghanistan as the world's leading opium producer. In 1988 a military junta grabbed power and attempted to legitimize itself with phoney elections two years later. In response the United States cut off all financial aid, including that slated for counter-narcotics operations, and the EU banned weapons sales. Ten years later the regime is as strong as ever. It has successfully tamed a series of revolts by minority ethnic groups and offset lack of foreign investment (except by French oil companies) by integrating the profits from the heroin trade into the legitimate economy. Khun Sa, the former "opium king," not only gave up his rebellion against Rangoon, but, in exchange for a licence to do business, put his contraband apparatus at the regime's disposal. In return the military regime touted his "surrender" as proof of their commitment to eradicating the drug trade, while it protected his heroin refineries against competitors and laundered the drug money through banks owned by the army. The regime's cut was then mixed with legitimate earnings from things like oil exports and used to purchase weapons, mainly from China.[7]

Although sanctions rarely accomplish their avowed short-term objectives, they do leave a menacing long-term legacy. As a result of arms embargoes, Israel in the 1960s, South Africa in the 1970s and Iran in the 1980s became in succession epicentres of embargo-busting operations that succeeded in trans-forming the world arms black market from a marginal entity catering to the light weapons requirements of a few guerrilla groups into a veritable global supermarket selling everything from chemical weapons components to avionics systems for fighter planes. On the other side embargoes encourage targeted states to create their own production capacity, with the result that today countries incapable of providing electricity to their masses can shock their neighbours with successful intermediate range missile tests.

Once an economic war is over, the supporting infrastructure also remains in place, simply democratizing its client base. So it was with the emergence of Liechtenstein as a haven by which Germany could evade the provisions of the Treaty of Versailles after World War I, and the growth of Tangiers as a place where intelligence operatives could work the currency black market and smuggle strategic materials during World War II. So it was when massive black markets during the Vietnam War gave Hong Kong its impetus to become an international financial centre and when U.S. intelligence encouraged the spread of bank secrecy facilities in the Caribbean during the "secret war" against Castro. So it was when South Africa sponsored offshore facilities in Indian Ocean island states as sanctions-busting platforms, and when Cyprus emerged as the favourite haven of everyone from Lebanese gun-runners to Russian flight capitalists to Serbian oil smugglers.

Because economic warfare involves economic crime, much of its conduct is delegated to the intelligence services. Contrary to public belief based on generations of spy stories, most intelligence work is not. Usually career intelligence officers spend their time shifting haunches, shuffling papers and revising opinions to reflect what they judge their superiors want to hear. Even in the glamorous aspects, the "spy" is usually someone trained to tune in with a multimillion-dollar surveillance gizmo rather than pay a seventy-five-cents general admission charge and walk through the front door.

However, there are a few, whose identity is often hidden even from the official services, who are different. They traffic in restricted technology and run guns, smuggle strategic materials and play currency black markets, forge credit instruments and bribe public functionaries. During economic wars they become, in effect, criminals with a security clearance.[8] Simultaneously, criminals become clandestine agents of national policy. Subcontracting smuggling or sabotage, arms trafficking or assassination to the underworld permits the intelligence service to deepen its cover as well as obtain proven talent for the task, while working for or with an intelligence service gives career criminals the three indispensable I's — information to prepare a job, infrastructure with which to do it, and indemnification if things go wrong.

Consider in this regard the career of Edwin Wilson. Recruited by the CIA in the 1960s to infiltrate, manipulate and inform on Communist activity in European unions, to monitor cargoes bound for Cuba and to courier cash to the Corsican mobsters who kept Marseilles dock workers in line, Wilson later became an expert in setting up and operating front companies. He mixed his corporate and covert responsibilities with sufficient enthusiasm as to be cashiered for financial defalcation. Then he was picked up by the U.S. Office of Naval Intelligence to do much the same job, with much the same results. Taking his talents private, he began advising besieged heads of state on security, selling mercenary services, and running guns — in partnership with another ex-CIA man with a talent for playing foreign exchange black markets, smuggling gems and training hitmen. In "private" business, Wilson was implicated in a scheme involving the padding of invoices on a U.S. government contract to transport arms to Egypt. He was finally brought down when he was caught smuggling embargoed explosives to Libya. Sentenced to life, he missed out on what might have been the crowning point of his career. When the Iran-contra scandal broke, he ruefully observed, "If I wasn't in jail, I would have headed up this operation."[9]

ACKNOWLEDGEMENTS

During more than ten years required to research and write this book, the author built up far more debts than it is possible to even remember, much less properly acknowledge. Among the many who shared opinions, provided information or criticized portions of the manuscript are: Abbas al-Nasrawi, George Archer, Roksanna Bahramitash, Carlos Batista, Issa Boulatta, Rex Brynen, Alexandra Canisius, Kirsten Crain, Jacques Courtois, Mihailo Crnobrnja, Allan Fenichel, Andrew Fischer, Aaron Karp, Azfar Khan, Michael Klare, Leo Kolivakis, Rafy Kourouian, Alain Labrousse, Kari Levitt, Christina Litt, Roberto Ludovico, Jonathan Marshall, Dan O'Meara, Jonathan Nitzan, Sam Noumoff, Anthony O'Sullivan, Nikos Passas, Varouj Pogharian, Alberto Rabilotta, Israel Shahak, Howard Skutel, Wendy Thomas, Marie-Joëlle Zahar, Assad Zakka and Eliah Zureik. Thanks to my editor, Jonathan Webb, who endured author's angst, untangled convoluted sentences, mercilessly culled present participles, and put up with too many last-minute changes. Others who provided specific points of information are thanked in the reference notes. Yet others requested that, for obvious reasons, their names not be revealed. And there are three other individuals who deserve a very special mention: Alan Block, who knows where the bodies are buried; Jack Blum, who buried many of them; and Jane Hunter, who, more than anyone else, helped dig them up! Thanks also to the John D. and Catherine T. MacArthur Foundation of Chicago and the Social Science and Humanities Research Council of Canada for financial support.

NOTES

PROLOGUE

1 Cited in John Prados, *Presidents' Secret Wars*, New York: William Morrow & Co. Inc., 1986, 317. The phrase was recorded in notes of then-CIA director Richard Helms. See Robert J. Schoenberg, *Geneen*, New York: Norton, 1985, 294, and the biography of Helms by Thomas Powers, *The Man Who Kept the Secrets*, New York: Pocket Books, 1979.

2 For a radical critique of U.S. responsibility, see Lawrence Birns (ed.), *The End of Chilean Democracy*, New York: Seabury Press, 1973. For a more sceptical view, see Robert Alexander, *The Tragedy of Chile*, Westport, Conn.: Greenwood Press, 1978.

3 For the theory of economic warfare see Yuan-li Wu, *Economic Warfare*, New York: Prentice Hall, 1952.

4 Gary Hufbauer, Jeffrey Schott, and Kimberley Elliott, *Economic Sanctions Reconsidered: History and Current Policy*, 2nd ed. Washington: Institute for International Economics, 1990, a comprehensive survey.

5 See R. T. Naylor "The Insurgent Economy: Black Market Operations of Guerrilla Organizations," *Crime, Law and Social Change* 20, 1993.

6 A distinction is sometimes made that "economic warfare" is part of a military campaign to defeat an enemy and "economic sanctions" are to dissuade and deter (e.g., M. P. Doxey, *Economic Sanctions and International Enforcement*, New York: Oxford University Press, 1971, 9, and Miroslav Nincic and Peter Wallensteen (eds.), *Dilemmas of Economic Coercion: Sanctions in World Politics*, New York: Praeger, 1983, 2). This is naive. The techniques and objectives are the same whether or not a shooting war is also occurring.

7 This is the central theme of R. T. Naylor, *Hot Money and the Politics of Debt*, 2nd ed. Montreal: Black Rose Books, 1994.

8 For an overview see R. T. Naylor, "Loose Cannons: Covert Commerce and Underground Finance in the Modern Arms Black Market," *Crime, Law and Social Change* 22, 1995.

9 There is a large literature on drugs and intelligence. See especially Alfred McCoy, *The Politics of Heroin: CIA Complicity in the Global Drug Trade*, New York: Lawrence Hill Books, 1991.

10 See M. Edwardes, *Asia in the European Age 1498–1955*, London: Thames and Hudson, 1961; M. Greenberg, *British Trade and the Opening of China*, Cambridge: Cambridge University Press, 1961; E. Holt, *The Opium Wars in China*, London: Putnam, 1964.

11 Thanks to Dr. Peter Lock for this phrase.

12 On Sicilia-Falcon's career, see Henrik Kruger, *The Great Heroin Coup: Drugs, Intelligence and International Fascism*, Montreal: Black Rose Books, 1980, 177–79, 182–83; and James Mills, *The Underground Empire: Where Crime and Governments Embrace*, New York: Doubleday, 1986, 88, 99, 325, 357–59, 360–64, 548–51. Both take Sicilia-Falcon's own version of events too much at face value.

CHAPTER 1

1 There are numerous biographies of Drake, most idolatrous. See A. E. W. Mason, *Life of Sir Francis Drake*, London: Hodder and Stoughton, 1941; E. F. Benson, *Sir Francis Drake*, London: John Lane, 1927; George Thomson, *Sir Francis Drake*, London: Secker and Warburg, 1972; John Sugden, *Sir Francis Drake*, London: Barrie and Jenkins, 1990; and John Cummins, *Francis Drake: The Lives of a Hero*, New York: St. Martin's Press, 1995. More methodical are K. R. Andrews, *Drake's Voyages*, London: Weidenfeld and Nicolson, 1967, *Elizabethan Privateering*, Cambridge: Cambridge University Press, 1964, and *The Last Voyage of Drake and Hawkins*, Cambridge: Cambridge University Press, 1972.

2 Eli Heckscher's *Mercantilism: A Study*, revised edition, London: Allen & Unwin, 1962, examines the political economy of power in the seventeenth and eighteenth centuries.

3 A. Hyatt Verrill, *Smugglers and Smuggling*, New York: Duffield & Co., 1924, 28.

4 W. R. Scott, *Constitution and Finance of English, Scottish and Irish Joint Stock Companies to 1720*, Vol. 1, New York: P. Smith, 1951, 74–75.

5 See Donald MacIntyre, *The Privateers*, London: Elek, 1975, and C. M. Senior, *A Nation of Pirates*, London: Newton Abbott, 1976.

6 Andrews, *Privateering*, 25.

7 Richard Kaufman, *The War Profiteers*, New York: Bobbs-Merrill, 1970, 5.

8 See Richard Lewinsohn, *The Profits of War Through the Ages*, New York: Dutton, 1937, for a survey.

9 Geoffrey Parker, *The Military Revolution*, Cambridge: Cambridge University Press, 1988, 58–59. There is an excellent treatment in H. Langer, *The Thirty Years War*, New York: Hippocrene Books, 1980, 127–38.

10 Murray Bloom, *Money of Their Own: The Great Counterfeiters*, New York: Scribner, 1957, 236.

11 Cited in Heckscher, *Mercantilism*, Vol. II, 17.

12 The pioneering work is Eli Heckscher, *The Continental System*, Oxford: Clarendon Press, 1922. For an interesting regional perspective, see Geoffrey Ellis, *Napoleon's Continental Blockade: The Case of Alsace*, Oxford: Clarendon Press, 1981. On the British side, see Judith Williams, *British Commercial Policy and Trade Expansion 1750–1850*, Oxford: Clarendon Press, 1972.

13 See W. P. Galpin, *The Grain Supply of England During the Napoleonic Period*, New York: Macmillan, 1925.

14 This thesis was first expounded by Eric Williams in his *Capitalism and Slavery*, London: André Deutsch, 1964, and elaborated in his *From Columbus to Castro: A History of the Caribbean 1492–1969*, London: André Deutsch, 1970.

15 D. T. Jack, *Studies in Economic Warfare*, London: P. S. King, 1940, 21.

16 René Sedillot, *Histoire des Marchés Noirs*, Paris: Tallandier, 1985, 92.

17 See David Phillipson, *Smuggling: A History 1700–1970*, Newton Abbott, Devon: Albert & Charles, 1973.

18 Heckscher, *Continental System*, 194.

19 On the wartime role of merchant banks, see Leland Jenks, *The Migration of British Capital to 1875*, New York: Knopf, 1927, Chapter 1.

20 Amos Elon, *Founder: A Portrait of the First Rothschild and His Time*, New York: Viking, 1996, 166–69.

21 Ellis, *Napoleon's Continental Blockade*, 201.

22 On this transformation, see François Crouzet, "Wars, Blockades and Economic Change in Europe, 1792–1815," *Journal of Economic History* 24, No. 4, 1964.

23 See Karl Polanyi, *The Great Transformation*, New York: Farrar & Rinehart, 1944, on the creation of the "free market" economy in the nineteenth century.

24 F. W. Hirst, *The Political Economy of War*, London: J. M. Dent, 1915, 15.

25 The best general work on the blockade is Stephen Wise, *Lifeline of the Confederacy*, Columbus: University of South Carolina Press, 1988. See also Robert Browning Jr., *From Cape Charles to Cape Fear: The North Atlantic Blockading Squadron During the Civil War*, Tuscaloosa: University of Alabama Press, 1993, and Craig L. Symonds (ed.), *Charleston Blockade: The Journals of John B. Marchand, U.S. Navy 1861–1862*, Newport: Naval War College Press, 1976.

26 Yuan-li Wu, *Economic Warfare*, 11–12.

27 Alan Milward, *The New Order and the French Economy*, Oxford: Clarendon Press, 1970, 15.

28 Daniel Yergin, *The Prize: The Epic Quest for Oil, Money and Power*, New York: Simon & Schuster, 1991, 180–81.

29 See the wartime memoirs of the British consul, M. W. W. P. Consett, *The Triumph of Unarmed Forces (1914–1918)*, New York: Brentano's, 1923.

30 Murray Bloom, *The Man Who Stole Portugal*, New York: Carroll & Graf, 1969, 50.

31 The classic on the war reparations and their likely consequences was John Maynard Keynes, *Economic Consequences of the Peace*, New York: Harcourt Brace and Howe, 1920.

32 T. R. Fehrenbach, *The Swiss Banks*, New York: McGraw-Hill, 1966, 44 et passim.

33 David Cordon and Roydon Dangerfield, *The Hidden Weapon: The Story of Economic Warfare*, New York: Harper, 1947, 150–51.

34 Nicholas Butler et al., *Boycotts and Peace: A Report by the Committee on Economic Sanctions*, New York: Harper & Brothers, 1932, 13.

35 Robin Renwick, *Economic Sanctions*, Cambridge, Mass.: Harvard University Center for International Affairs, 1981, 21.

CHAPTER 2

1 On U.S. involvement in the covert economic war, see R. Harris Smith, *OSS: The Secret History of America's First Central Intelligence Agency*, Berkeley: University of California Press, 1972; Bradley Smith, *The Shadow Warriors: O.S.S. and the Origins of the C.I.A.*, New York: Basic Books, 1983; William Casey, *The Secret War Against Hitler*, New York: Simon & Schuster, 1988; Joseph Persico, *Piercing the Reich*, New York: Viking, 1979; Joseph Persico, *Casey: From the OSS to the CIA*, New York: Penguin, 1990; and especially Cordon and Dangerfield, *Hidden Weapon*. One interesting memoir from the British side is by former SOE operative Edward Wharton-Tigar, *Burning Bright*, London: Metal Bulletin Books, 1987.

2 Alan Milward (*The New Order and the French Economy*, Oxford: Clarendon Press, 1970) suggests that Germany could only economically sustain a series of short wars while striving to limit the amount of economic adversity on its civilian population. Yet R. J. Overy (*War and Economy in the Third Reich*, Oxford: Clarendon Press, 1994) insists that civilian consumption was steadily declining even before the war as Germany shifted resources into the military and that the slow start in armaments production was mainly due to technical failures, not any wish to insulate the civilian sector.

3 Alan Milward, *War, Economy and Society 1939–1945*, Berkeley: University of California Press, 1979, 297.

4 John Kenneth Galbraith, *A Life in Our Times*, Boston: Houghton Mifflin, 1981, 204.

5 Cordon and Dangerfield, *Hidden Weapon*, 111; W. N. Medlicott, *The Economic Blockade*, London: Her Majesty's Stationery Office, 1978, 527–29.

6 Cordon and Dangerfield, *Hidden Weapon*, 52.

7 Anthony Cave-Brown, *Treason in the Blood*, Boston: Houghton Mifflin, 1994, 256.

8 Wharton-Tigar, *Burning Bright*, 45; Harris Smith, *OSS*, 16.

9 Anthony Cave-Brown, *The Last Hero: Wild Bill Donavan*, New York: Vintage Books, 1982, 436–41.

10 Casey, *Secret War*, 90.

11 Stanley Lovell, *Of Spies and Stratagems*, New Jersey: Prentice-Hall, 1963, 27; Murray Bloom, *The Brotherhood of Money*, Port Clinton: 1983, 26; Persico, *Casey*, 74; Persico, *Piercing the Reich*, 27–31.

12 Paul Murphy (with R. R. Arlington), *La Popessa*, New York: Warner Books, 1983, 252–55; Avro Manhattan, *The Vatican Billions*, Chino, Calif.: Chick Publications, 1983, 140–43; Larry Gurwin, *The Calvi Affair*, New York: Macmillan, 1983, 11.

13 There is an excellent survey of Tangiers in Alain Vernay, *Les Paradis Fiscaux*, Paris: Editions du Seuil, 1968.

14 Wharton-Tigar, *Burning Bright*, 87.

15 See Nicholas Faith, *Safety in Numbers: The Mysterious World of Swiss Banking*, New York: Viking, 1982, Part III, for Switzerland's role as the financial fulcrum of occupation economics.

16 Harris Smith, *OSS*, 15.

17 Anthony Sampson, *The Sovereign State: The Secret History of ITT*, London: Coronet, 1973, 29–39.

18 Wharton-Tigar, *Burning Bright*, 44.

19 The position taken, for example, by Charles Higham, *Trading With the Enemy: An Exposé of the Nazi-American Money Plot, 1933–1949*, New York: Delacorte Press, 1983.

20 Casey, *Secret War*, 40.

21 American agents accused the diamond giant De Beers of complicity and the British government of deliberately blocking investigations (Edward Jay Epstein, *The Rise and Fall of Diamonds*, New York: Simon & Schuster, 1981, 91). Similar allegations were made in a 1995 BBC program, prompting a libel action (*Guardian*, 6/23/95). Given the difficulty De Beers has today in controlling theft and black markets (see Chapter 11), it is hardly a surprise that in wartime conditions serious leaks occurred.

22 *Times* (London), 9/8/94.

23 Milward, *War, Economy and Society*, Chapter 9; Cave-Brown, *Last Hero*, 442. When Hitler's generals wanted to retreat from the Crimea, he overruled them on the assumption, which proved correct, that as long as Germany was ensconced on the Black Sea, Turkey would continue to resist Allied pressure and sell chrome. After Germany was ejected from Crimea, Turkey cut off the ore (James Pool, *Hitler and His Secret Partners: Contributions, Loot and Rewards*, New York: Pocket Books, 1997, 300).

24 Klaus Knorr, *The Power of Nations: The Political Economy of International Relations*, New York: 1971, 140; Croydon and Dangerfield, *Hidden Weapon*, 9–11; Henry Wallich, *Mainsprings of the German Revival*, New Haven: Yale University Press, 1955, 7; Galbraith, *Life*, 226; private communication from Professor Kari Levitt, who worked in the British wartime office calculating the impact of the strategic bombing campaign. Casey (*Secret War*, 77) differentiates between British bombing, which he dismisses as useless and causing much civilian damage, and American, which he claims was far more accurate. Needless to say, there are analysts who agree with his first observation while disagreeing with his second.

25 Albert Morsomme, *Anatomie de la Guerre Totale*, Brussels, 1971; Poole, *Secret Partners*, 174, 181, 184–89, 196–99, 204 et al.

26 Poole (*Secret Partners*, esp. 49–50, 123–29) provides a good summary. On the recent discovery of the tax files containing the details of participation by ordinary Germans, see *Globe and Mail*, 7/11/98.

27 J. Debû-Bridel, *Histoire du Marché Noir (1939–1947)*, Paris: Jeune Parc, 1948. See also Thomas Reveille's *The Spoil of Europe*, New York: W. W. Norton, 1941, for a very early account of what was in progress.

28 See Ian Sayer and Douglas Botting, *Nazi Gold*, New York: Congdon and Weed, 1984; Arthur Smith, *Hitler's Gold*, Oxford: Oxford University Press, 1989; Cave-Brown, *Last Hero*, 760–64; Cordon and Dangerfield, *Hidden Weapon*, 167. There has been recently much attention paid to the role of Swiss banks in laundering World War II loot. See, for example, Adam LeBor, *Hitler's Secret Bankers: The Myth of Swiss Neutrality During the Holocaust*, Seacaucus, N.J.: Birch Lane Press, 1997, and Isabel Vincent, *Hitler's Silent Partners: Swiss Banks, Nazi Gold and the Pursuit of Justice*, Toronto: Knopf, 1997. Though containing fresh detail, the recent books shed no fundamental new light. That the Swiss were aware the gold was stolen is hardly a recent revelation. See Faith, *Safety in Numbers*, Parts II and III.

29 See Theo Schulte, *The German Army and Nazi Policies in Occupied Russia*, Oxford: Oxford University Press, 1989.

30 Yergin, *The Prize*, 334; Poole, *Secret Partners*, 241–52.

31 Yergin, *The Prize*, 329–32.

32 Milward, *War, Economy and Society*, Chapter 5.

33 Albert Morsomme, *Anatomie de la Guerre Totale*, 202–3.

34 See Marshall Clinard's *The Black Market*, Montclair, N.J.: Patterson Smith, 1952. See also Louis Helbig, "Discontent on the Home Front: The Black Market in Canada During and After the Second World War," *Historical Discourses*, McGill University, Vol. VIII, Spring, 1994.

35 *New York Times*, 4/5/44, identifies the offenders as former bootleggers, gamblers, narcotics dealers and "white slavers." In fact, counterfeiting seems to have been an equal opportunity employer involving amateurs and professionals, legitimate printers turning a quick buck on the side and underworld engravers plying their normal craft.

36 The racket is described in detail in Peter Maas, *The Valachi Papers*, New York: Pocket Books, 1968, 154–58. See also *New York Times*, 4/5, 6, 22, 27/43, 5/1, 23/43, 6/4, 6, 12, 20, 25/43, and 2/24/44, 3/16/44, 4/5/44. I am indebted to Richard Zavala for references on this topic.

37 See Louis Helbig, *Black Markets in the United Kingdom During the Second World War*, London School of Economics Master of Science Thesis, August 29, 1996, and Edward Smithies, *Crime in Wartime*, London: Allen & Unwin, 1982.

38 Interestingly Clinard (*Black Market*, 27) stresses the extent of the problem. ("A black market of immense proportions engulfed our country. . . ."); while Galbraith (*Life*, 171), who ran the price control office, insists that black market activity was very limited.

39 Richard Lukas, *The Forgotten Holocaust: The German Occupation of Poland 1939–1944*, Lexington: University of Kentucky Press, 1986, 31.

40 See René Sédillot, *Histoire du Franc*, Paris: Sirey, 1979. I am indebted to Julien Vaast.

41 Debû-Bridel, *Marché Noir*, 59–60.

42 While the Gestapo pioneered this "official clandestine sector," virtually every other intelligence branch of the occupation forces was soon in the business — the Luftwaffe, Naval Intelligence, the SS, and especially the Abwehr, which effectively took over from the others. See Jacques Delarue, *Trafics et Crimes Sous l'Occupation*, Paris: Fayard, 1969.

43 Jean Cathelin and Gabrielle Gray, *Crimes et Trafics de la Gestapo Française*, Paris: 1972, Vol. I, 50, 71. Delarue, *Trafics et Crimes*, 102; and Sédillot, *Marchés Noirs*, 140.

44 Kruger, *Great Heroin Coup*, 33.

45 Bloom, *The Man Who Stole Portugal*, 88n.

46 Fenton Bresler, *Interpol*, London: Penguin, 1992, 73; Andrew Tully, *Treasury Agent*, New York: Simon & Schuster, 1958, 264; Bloom, *Money of Their Own*, 251–67; Galbraith, *Life*, 203.

47 Murphy, *La Popessa*, Chapter XI.

48 The details are recounted in Sayers and Botting, *Nazi Gold*. Though the bearer bonds kept resurfacing for years, few were successfully negotiated because of a postwar German law requiring holders to prove legitimate ownership as of January 1, 1945.

49 Kenneth Alford, *The Spoils of World War II*, New York: Birch Lane Press, 1994, passim.

50 Yergin, *The Prize*, 386; Sayer and Botting, *Nazi Gold*, 228–29; Sédillot, *Marchés Noirs*, 142.

51 Bloom, *The Man Who Stole Portugal*, 18n.

52 The mechanics are explained in Walter Rundell, *Black Market Money: The Collapse of the U.S. Currency Control in World War II*, Baton Rouge: Louisiana State University Press, 1964.

53 Galbraith, *Life*, 204–6, 211; Wallich, *Mainsprings of the German Revival*, 7.

54 Phillip Knightley, *The Second Oldest Profession*, London: 1986, 238.

55 Tully, *Treasury Agent*, 260–64.

CHAPTER 3

1 For an interesting overview, albeit flawed by being too much a Reagan puff-piece, see Peter Schweizer, *Victory: The Reagan Administration's Secret Strategy That Hastened the Collapse of the Soviet Union*, New York: Atlantic Monthly Press, 1994.

2 According to ex-CIA chief Robert Gates, from the late 1950s the agency was telling U.S. governments the opposite, that the U.S.S.R. was facing growing economic chaos that would force it to moderate its behaviour and strike deals on the West's terms (Robert Gates, *From the Shadows*, New York: Simon & Schuster, 1997, 37). In fact, the U.S.S.R. expanded rapidly until the end of the 1960s. CIA analysts made similar claims at the end of the 1970s (Gates, *From the Shadows*, 173). This time they were right, perhaps by accident.

3 Bloom, *Portugal*, 194–95n; Arnold Krammer, "When Stalin Counterfeited American Dollars," *American History Illustrated*, May 1984; W. G. Krivitsky, *In Stalin's Secret Service*, New York, Harper, 1939.

4 In general see Linda Melvern, David Hebditch and Nick Anning, *Techno-Bandits: How the Soviets Are Stealing America's High-Tech Future*, Boston: Houghton Mifflin, 1984.

5 Thanks to Jack Blum for bringing this to my attention.

6 Timothy Green, *The World of Diamonds*, London: 1981, 102; Timothy Green, *The Smugglers*, London: Michael Joseph, 1967, 182; and especially Daniel Kempton, "Soviet and Russian Relations with Foreign Corporations: The Case of Gold and Diamonds," *Slavic Review* 54, No. 1, Spring 1995.

7 See Gunnar Adler-Karlsson, *Western Economic Warfare 1947–1967*, Stockholm: Almquist & Wiksell, 1968, for a critique.

8 Persico, *Casey*, 58.

9 Cited in Schweizer, *Victory*, 6. This was from an entry in Reagan's diary early in 1981.

10 *Euromoney*, August 1981; *Financial Times*, 9/15/82, 7/24/84, 12/2/84, 8/8/85, *Wall Street Journal*, 8/4/84.

11 Some facets of the interface between Pope John Paul II, the CIA and the Polish dissident movement are examined in two works by Gordon Thomas and Max Morgan-Witts: *Pontiff*, New York: Doubleday, 1983, and *The Year of Armageddon*, New York: Granada, 1984.

12 Gates, *From the Shadows*, 237; Schweizer, *Victory*, 76.

13 Schweizer, *Victory*, 42.

14 *Wall Street Journal*, 3/13/87.

15 The most comprehensive account is by Michael Saba, *The Armageddon Network*, Brattleboro, Vt.: Amana, 1984. Ultimately the Justice Department refused to proceed against Bryen.

16 See John O'Neill, *Prodigal Genius: The Life of Nikola Tesla*, Albuquerque: Brotherhood of Life Inc., 1994.

17 See William Broad, *Teller's War: The Top-Secret Story Behind the Star Wars Deception*, New York: Simon & Schuster, 1992.

18 Schweizer, *Victory*, 135, 211; Melvern et al., *Techno-Bandits*, 29.

19 Gates (*From the Shadows*, 266) claims that it was not Star Wars per se that frightened the U.S.S.R., but what Star Wars implied about the growing technological gap.

20 Melvern et al., *Techno-Bandits*, 166–67.

21 *Business Week*, 7/29/85; *Los Angeles Times*, 5/25/89.

22 *New York Times*, 2/4/86.

23 *Los Angeles Times*, 8/12/86; *New York Times*, 8/21/87, 10/23/87.

24 John Barron, *Breaking the Ring: The Bizarre Case of the Walker Family Spy Ring*, Boston: Houghton Mifflin, 1987, 23.

25 *L'Express*, 10/23/87; *Le Monde*, 8/27, 28/87; *Wall Street Journal*, 9/11/87.

26 *New York Times*, 9/10/87.

27 *Financial Times*, 10/27/87, 3/7/88, 4/24/89, 7/7/89.

28 *Wall Street Journal*, 9/11, 14, 15/87, 10/22, 23/87, 4/25/88; *New York Times*, 10/22/87; *Financial Times*, 6/5/87, 9/10/87; *Business Week*, 5/18/87.

29 *Times of London*, 7/3, 15/87 *New York Times*, 7/2/87, 9/10/87; *The Economist*, 7/25/87; *Wall Street Journal*, 3/21/87, 6/24/87, 8/19/87; *Financial Times*, 7/6/87; *Business Week*, 9/14/87, 4/4/88.

30 *Financial Times*, 2/27/87, 7/2, 6, 11/87, 9/10/87.

31 Schweizer, *Victory*, 162–63, 165.

32 The major work is by Austrian journalist Hans Pretterebner, *Der Fall Lucona: Ost-Spionage, Korruption und Mord im Dunstkreis der Regierungsspitze*, Vienna: Politische Briefe Dokumentation, 1987. There is also a collection of background materials on Proksch in Helmut Schödel, *Ein Staat braucht einen Mörder: Udo Proksch und die "Lucona"-Obsession*, Cologne: Verlas Kieponhervrer & Witson, 1998. See also *Times of London* 4/7/88; *FBIS-WEU* 10/3, 5/89; *L'Express*, 5/6/88. I am indebted to Terry Nopper and Alexandra Canisius for background research on this topic.

33 Pretterebner, *Der Fall*, 194.

34 Melvern et al., *Techno-Bandits*; Chapter 8, contains a detailed analysis of the affair. See also Pretterebner, *Der Fall*, 122–23, 128, 149, 158.

35 *Guardian Weekly*, 5/13/90; *New York Times*, 5/7/90; Ronald Kessler, *Inside the CIA*, New York: Pocket Books, 1992, 68. Subsequent reports claimed that Poland was the biggest source, but Poland's former president is sceptical of the claim (*Washington Post*, 2/14/94).

36 *Los Angeles Times*, 4/15/85.

37 *Wall Street Journal*, 2/6/87, 3/13/87; *New York Times*, 11/10/87; Jan Feldman, "Trade Policy and Foreign Policy," *The Washington Quarterly*, Winter 1985.

38 In 1987 the U.S. government claimed that the U.S.S.R. Chamber of Commerce and Industry was headed by a lieutenant colonel of the KGB, and that one-third of all its officials were "suspected" of being KGB or GRU agents (*New York Times*, 10/28/87).

39 *Washington Post*, 6/26/98.

CHAPTER 4

1 Warren Howe, *Weapons: The International Game of Arms, Money and Diplomacy*. New York: Doubleday, 1980, 317; Lewinsohn, *Profits of War*, 109–11.

2 Gustavus Myers, *History of the Great American Fortunes*, New York: Modern Library, 1907, 569; Lewinsohn, *Profits of War*, 129–31.

3 Anthony Sampson, *The Arms Bazaar*, London: 1977, 63.

4 Kaufman, *The War Profiteers*, xx–xxi.

5 Sampson, *Arms Bazaar*, 54–55.

6 Donald McCormick, *Pedlar of Death: The Life of Sir Basil Zaharoff*, London: Macdonald, 1965, 19, 45–48, 109. This is the best of several biographies of Zaharoff.

7 R. J. Overy, *War and Economy in the Third Reich*, Oxford: Clarendon Press, 1994, 5–9.

8 Miroslav Nincic, *The Arms Race: The Political Economy of Military Growth*, New York: Praeger, 1982, 50.

9 On an early investigation of the technology question see Judith Reppy, "Military R&D and the Civilian Economy," *Bulletin of the Atomic Scientists*, October 1985. There had been a very active debate in the United States concerning the extent to which the military-industrial system really contributed to American prosperity. For the negatives, the best research was by Seymour Melman, *Pentagon Capitalism*, New York: McGraw-Hill, 1970; *The Permanent War Economy*, New York: Simon & Schuster, 1974; *Profits Without Production*, New York: Knopf, 1984; and *The Demilitarized Society*, Montreal: Harvest House, 1988. See also Robert W. Degrasse, *Military Expansion, Economic Decline*, New York: M. E. Sharpe, 1983, and Ann Markusen and Joel Yudken, *Dismantling the Cold War Economy*, New York: Basic Books, 1992. But see the critique by Doug Henwood in *Left Business Observer*, 4/17/91, 6/3/91.

10 An early critique of the system was by A. Ernest Fitzgerald, *The High Priests of Waste*, New York: Norton, 1972. Fitzgerald was brought into the Pentagon because of his experience as a cost-cutting manager. He went on to become the most celebrated of subsequent "whistle-blowers."

11 Knightley, *Second Oldest Profession*, 248.

12 The process of inflating Soviet military spending for electoral purposes was actually begun by Jimmy Carter, who used it to justify a substantial hike in military expenditure (see Victor Perlo, "The Myth of Soviet Superiority," *The Nation*, 9/13/80). But under Reagan it reached its apogee.

13 A. Ernest Fitzgerald (*The Pentagonists*, Boston: Houghton Mifflin, 1989, 76) contends that dollarization alone doubled the estimate of the size of Soviet military spending. The exercise is analyzed by Franklyn D. Holzman, "How the CIA Distorted the Truth about Soviet Military Spending," *Challenge*, March–April 1990 and "The CIA's Military Spending Estimates: Deceit and Its Costs," *Challenge*, May–June, 1992.

14 For an early warning, see *Wall Street Journal*, 9/25/85. This phenomenon was examined by Tim Weiner, *Blank Check: The Pentagon's Black Budget*, New York: Warner Books, 1990.

15 See David Boulton, *The Lockheed Papers*, New York: Harper & Row, 1978, and Sampson, *The Arms Bazaar*.

16 Sterling Seagrave, *The Soong Dynasty*, New York: Harper & Row, 1985, 334.

17 Yoshio Kodama's career is examined in Boulton, *Lockheed*, 46–48; Sampson; *Arms Bazaar*, 222–29; and in detail in David Kaplan and Alec Dubro, *Yakuza*, Reading, Mass.: Addison Wesley, 1986.

18 On Northrop's agency system in Thailand and Malaysia, see *Far Eastern Economic Review*, 1/16/76.

19 Howe, *Weapons*, 456.

20 *New York Times*, 8/29/85, 10/19, 24/88; *Business Week*, 9/26/88, 1/23/89.

21 *Wall Street Journal*, 10/29/85, 11/12/85; *Miami Herald*, 5/14/87; *New York Times*, 9/10/88, 10/13/88, 1/27/89; *Business Week*, 9/26/88, 1/23/89.

22 *Wall Street Journal*, 12/21/91.

23 In Pentagon-speak, it is called "negotiated competitive bidding" (Gregory Williams, *Defense Procurement Papers, Campaign '88*, Project on Military Procurement, Washington, 1988, 45).

24 *Business Week*, 7/4/88.

25 *Business Week*, 7/4/88; *Wall Street Journal*, 6/27/88.

26 *New York Times*, 7/7/88.

27 On Melvyn Paisley see *Christian Science Monitor*, 6/27/88; *Wall Street Journal*, 7/18/88, 11/14/89, 3/19/90; *Los Angeles Times*, 7/9/88; *New York Times*, 7/11/88, 8/18/88, 1/28/89, 3/9/89, 9/6/91, and Andy Pasztor, *When the Pentagon Was for Sale*, New York: Scribner, 1995. See also *Fortune*, 1/11/93.

28 *Christian Science Monitor*, 6/27/88; *Wall Street Journal*, 7/18/88; *Los Angeles Times*, 7/9/88; *New York Times*, 7/11/88; *Aviation Week & Space Technology*, 4/3/89.

29 *Wall Street Journal*, 11/14/89, 3/19/90.

30 One of Unisys's consultants set up shell companies in Guernsey, the Isle of Man, the Caymans and the Turks and Caicos islands. Unisys paid this consultant for phoney services, then billed the cost to the Pentagon. The consultant used the shell companies to funnel bribe money back to Pentagon officials, including Melvyn Paisley, then reported the payments as the cost of contract services, deducting them from his own taxes (*New York Times*, 8/18/88, 1/28/89, 3/9/89, 9/6/91).

31 *New York Times*, 7/7/88; *Wall Street Journal*, 7/7/88, 9/30/88; *Washington Post*, 8/7/88. Even if the plane had been an F-14, it was not designed to carry anti-ship missiles. At most it would have had to attack with "dumb bombs," which would have required it to get so close that the ship would have had ample time for visual identification.

32 Northrop claimed that it had not known the money was for bribes, and that it had been cheated by the Korean businessmen involved. However, its civil suit was tossed out by a Seoul court, which ruled that Northrop had been involved in an illegal effort to influence the purchase (*Wall Street Journal*, 12/21/92). In 1993 the U.S. government formally ended its five-year investigation and brought no charges against Northrup — which had fired its CEO and started an image-rebuilding campaign (*Wall Street Journal,* 2/25/93).

33 William Hartung, *And Weapons for All*, New York: HarperCollins, 1994, 255–65.

34 Williams, *Defense Procurement Papers*, 28, 45.

35 Political contributions by arms contractors jumped ninefold from 1981 to 1986 at the time the arms spending spigot was turned on full (*New York Times*, 8/28/87).

36 *Wall Street Journal*, 10/11/90.

37 *Wall Street Journal*, 4/3/85, 5/20/87, 6/22/87, 8/13/87; *Financial Times*, 4/3/85; *New York Times*, 5/22/85, 5/30/85, 7/30/90; *Business Week*, 3/25/85, 8/22/88.

38 *New York Times*, 11/12/90.

39 Fitzgerald, *The Pentagonists*, 76.

CHAPTER 5

1 James Hamilton-Paterson, *A Very Personal War*, New York: McKay, 1972, 65–66, 69–71, 98–99, 145. My thanks to John Carey for background research on this subject.

2 Hamilton-Paterson, *Personal War*, 120–24.

3 See U.S. Senate, Judiciary Committee, Permanent Subcommittee on Investigations, "Illegal Currency Manipulations Affecting South Vietnam," Part 4, Washington: 1973.

4 McCoy, *Politics of Drugs*, 287–88 et passim.

5 Stewart Tendler and David May, *The Brotherhood of Eternal Love*, London: Panther, 1983, and Martin Lee and Bruce Schlain, *Acid Dreams: The CIA, LSD and the Sixties Rebellion*, New York: Grove Press, 1985.

6 Jonathan Kwitny, *The Crimes of Patriots*, New York: Simon & Schuster, 1987, 52.

7 Hamilton-Paterson, *Personal War*, 77, 129.

8 U.S. Senate, Judiciary Committee, Permanent Subcommittee on Investigation, "Illegal Currency Manipulations Affecting South Vietnam," Part 3, Washington: 1969; Angelina Malhotra, "India's Underground Bankers," *Asia Inc.*, August 1995.

9 Victor Marchetti and John D. Marks, *The CIA and the Cult of Intelligence*, New York: Dell, 1974, 238–39.

10 On Deak's history, see *New York Times*, 12/10/84; Tad Szulc, "The Money Changer," *New Republic*, 4/10/76, and "The CIA and the Banks," *Inquiry*, 11/21/77; Marchetti and Marks, *CIA*, 238–39; *Wall Street Journal*, 5/14/76; U.S. President's Commission on Organized Crime, *The Cash Connection: Organized Crime, Financial Institutions and Money Laundering*, Washington: 1984, 27–28.

11 U.S. Senate, PSI, "Illegal Currency Manipulations Affecting South Vietnam," Part 4, 1973, 160.

12 This is examined in detail in U.S. President's Commission on Organized Crime, *The Cash Connection*.

13 Early the next year someone walked into Nicholas Deak's New York office and shot him dead (*New York Times*, 11/19/85).

14 The pipeline is described by Brigadier Mohammed Yousaf (the Pakistani general in charge of the supply operation) and Major Mark Adkin, *The Bear Trap: Afghanistan's Untold Story*, London: Leo Cooper, 1992, 36.

15 The figures were always controversial. The CIA insisted that the loss rate was "only" 20 per cent (*Washington Post*, 1/20/85), the U.S. Senate Foreign Relations Committee put it between 30 and 50 per cent, while admitting it was just a guess (*New York Times*, 3/24/87). Others have put the diversion at 65 per cent and even higher.

16 Kurt Lohbeck, *Holy War, Unholy Victory*, Washington: Regnery Gateway, 1993, 183–84.

17 *Washington Post*, 5/1/87.

18 Lohbeck, *Holy War*, 151.

19 *Washington Post*, 2/19/89; Yousaf, *Bear Trap*, 86.

20 *The Middle East*, October 1991.

21 *New York Times*, 10/23/87; *Wall Street Journal*, 12/8/87; *Christian Science Monitor*, 12/21/87. These diversions are denied or minimized by Mohammed Yousaf (*Bear Trap*, 102).

22 For an overview of Pakistan's role, see Marvin Weinbaum, "War and Peace in Afghanistan: The Pakistani Role," *Middle East Journal*, Vol. 45, No.1, 1991.

23 *Washington Post*, 5/6/87; *La Presse*, 12/31/88; *Far Eastern Economic Review*, 2/22/90.

24 *New York Times*, 5/15/87; *Herald*, August 1986; *Far Eastern Economic Review*, 6/6/91, 10/31/91.

25 *Far Eastern Economic Review*, 3/5/87; *Financial Times*, 7/6/89.

26 Mohammed Yousaf (*Bear Trap*, 104–5) claims that the distribution was strictly according to military prowess, while virtually everyone else insisted that most weapons went to factions that Pakistan found politically reliable and that some avoided combat with the Afghan government and the Soviet military to preserve their strength for settling accounts with their resistance rivals (Wienbaum, "War and Peace," 79; *Washington Post*, 3/26/89; *Financial Times*, 6/1/89; *Guardian Weekly*, 3/12/89).

27 *Times of London*, 1/11/89; *Jeune Afrique*, 3/19/90; *New York Times*, 2/16/90.

28 There is an enormous literature dealing with BCCI, including at least five book-length studies of highly variable quality. Mark Potts, Nicholas Kochan and Robert Whittington, *Dirty Money: The Inside Story of the World's Sleaziest Bank*, Washington: National Press, 1992, was a rather quick job, but remains best on certain British aspects of the bank's activities. James Ring Adams and Douglas Krantz, *A Full Service Bank: How BCCI Stole Billions Around the World*, New York: Pocket Books, 1992, is mainly about a Customs sting that ensnared BCCI Tampa in money-laundering charges. Peter Truell and Larry Gurwin, *False Profits: The Inside Story of BCCI, the World's Most Corrupt Financial Empire*, Boston and New York: Houghton Mifflin, 1992, focuses on the American political context. Jonathan Beaty and S. C. Gwynne, *The Outlaw Bank: A Wild Rise into the Secret Heart of BCCI*, New York: Random House, 1993, is full of sensationalism and self-promotion. The most comprehensive examination is Senator John Kerry and Senator Hank Brown, *The BCCI Affair: A Report to the Committee on Foreign Relations, United States Senate*, Washington: 1992. For a good critique of these

works, see Nikos Passas, "The Mirror of Global Evils: A Review Essay on the BCCI Affair," *Justice Quarterly*, Vol. 12, No. 2, 1995. See also his "Structural Sources of International Financial Crime: Policy Lessons from the BCCI Affair," *Crime, Law & Social Change*, Vol. 20, 1993, and "I Cheat, Therefore I Exist? The BCCI Scandal in Context"; and W. Michael Hoffman et al. (eds.), *Emerging Global Business Ethics*, Westport, Conn.: Quorum Books, 1994.

29 *Illustrated Weekly of India*, 11/10/74.

30 See R. T. Naylor, "The Underworld of Gold," *Crime, Law and Social Change*, Vol. 25, 1996.

31 *Financial Times*, 11/11/91.

32 *Financial Times*, 8/15/91.

33 *New York Times*, 12/1/87; *Far Eastern Economic Review*, 6/6/91.

34 *Observer*, 5/3/92; John Fullerton, *The Soviet Occupation of Afghanistan*, Hong Kong: 1983, 59.

35 *The Middle East*, May 1983; *New York Times*, 6/14/86, 7/14/87, 9/7/88; *Christian Science Monitor*, 1/17/88, 1/2/89; *Times of London*, 9/25/89; *Geopolitical Drug Dispatch*, August 1994. Some Islamic scholars disagreed, insisting that if a jihad is funded through an activity deemed *haram*, then the jihad itself is similarly corrupted. Others made the counter-case that the Qu'ran forbids only wine, and therefore opium is legitimate (*The Middle East*, September 1991).

36 Paul Eddy and Sara Walden, *Hunting Marco Polo*, New York: Little, Brown, 1991, 47.

37 *Times of London*, 9/25/89; *Christian Science Monitor*, 1/2/89.

38 *Middle East Times*, 5/31/87; *Financial Times*, 1/19/89, 7/6/89.

39 Until the end of the Afghan war, the only important Pakistani casualty of anti-drug operations was the vice-president of the largest state-owned commercial bank and the personal banker to Zia ul-Haq and his family. A police investigation in Norway and subsequent diplomatic uproar finally forced his arrest and conviction for money-laundering (*The Nation*, 11/14/88).

40 Edward Herman and Frank Brodhead, *The Rise and Fall of the Bulgarian Connection*, New York: Sheridan Square, 1986, 45–49.

41 On the background see Mehmet Ali Birand, *The General's Coup in Turkey*, London: Brassey's Defence Publishers, 1987, and Jacob Landau, *Radical Politics in Modern Turkey*, Leiden: Brill, 1974.

42 *Le Monde*, 1/8/69; *Guardian*, 2/3/69, 8/8/72. Properly speaking, the translation should be "steppe wolves," but "grey wolves" has become standard. It comes from the legend of a wolf leading the Turks from Central Asia to Anatolia.

43 *Herald Tribune*, 3/24/83.

44 *Le Hebdo*, 12/2/88, 5/18/89, Peter Furhman, "The Bulgarian Connection," *Forbes*, 4/17/89.

45 *Wall Street Journal*, 12/20/82.

46 On Banco Ambrosiano and the P-2 scandal, see Larry Gurwin, *The Calvi Affair: Death of a Banker*, London: Macmillan, 1983, and Rupert Cornwell, *God's Banker: An Account of the Life and Death of Roberto Calvi*, London: Gollancz, 1983. On Pazienza, see *Wall Street Journal*, 8/7, 8/85 and Herman and Brodhead, *Rise and Fall*, 91–100.

47 Christian Roulette, *Jean Paul II — Antonov — Agca: La Filière*, Paris: Editions du Sorbiev, 1984, 190.

48 *Guardian*, 6/27/85, *New York Times*, 6/18, 20/85, 10/7/85; *L'Espresso*, 6/30/85, 10/20/85.

49 *New York Times*, 6/7/85.

50 *Le Monde*, 12/9/82, 12/11/82; *New York Times*, 1/25/83.

51 Roulette, *Jean Paul II*, 122–30. This work's insinuation that the attempted assassination was a CIA plot is ludicrous.

52 *New York Times*, 6/7/85.

53 *New York Times*, 1/27/83; *Wall Street Journal*, 2/1/83. The principal popularizer was the late Claire Sterling. See, for example, *Wall Street Journal*, 12/22/82. The story was elaborated in

the works by Gordon Thomas and Max Morgan-Witts cited above. Not until 1991 did it come out at U.S. Congressional hearings into the appointment of Robert Gates as CIA chief that CIA experts were dubious from the start, but, on orders of William Casey, the CIA position paper was slanted in favour of a Bulgaria–U.S.S.R. connection (*New York Times*, 10/2/91).

54 *Le Monde*, 9/21/85, 10/16/85.

55 *New York Times*, 5/29/85; *Wall Street Journal*, 9/19/85; *Le Monde*, 6/8, 14, 19/85; *Guardian*, 6/25/85.

56 Under the civil code system, the jury could arrive at one of three verdicts, innocent, guilty, or not guilty because of lack of evidence, implying there was some evidence but it was insufficient. This permitted those who had pushed the Bulgarian Connection line to exit with a little undeserved dignity still intact — e.g., Claire Sterling in *L'Express*, 2/15/85.

CHAPTER 6

1 See, for example, Gregory Grossman, "The 'Second Economy' of the USSR," *Problems of Communism*, September–October 1977; Aaron Katsenelinboigen and Herbert Levine, "Market and Plan, Plan and Market: The Soviet Case," *American Economic Review*, February 1977; Steven Sampson, "The Second Economy of the Soviet Union and Eastern Europe," *Annals of the American Academy of Arts and Sciences*, September 1987; Luc Duhamel, "Economic Criminality in the USSR," *Revue d'Etudes Comparatives Est-Ouest*, Vol. XX, No. 3, September 1989. Perhaps the best survey is by Horst Brezinski, "The Second Economy in the Soviet Union and Its Implications for Economic Policy," in Wulf Gaertner (ed.), *International Conference on the Economics of the Shadow Economy*, Berlin: Springer-Verlag, 1983. A recent survey is by Annelise Anderson, "The Red Mafia: A Legacy of Communism," in Edward P. Lazear (ed.), *Economic Transition in Eastern Europe and Russia: Realities of Reform*, Stanford, Calif.: Hoover Institution Press, 1995. One interesting implication is that the pervasiveness of such dealings meant that CIA efforts to calculate the size and vulnerability of the Soviet economy were largely in vain. If the Soviet government did not know, American intelligence was hardly in a position to find out (Kessler, *Inside the CIA*, 148).

2 There was a legal private sector limited to the cultivation of small plots of land, residential construction, some bartering of services, and a few specialized activities like panning for gold, but it was quite minor.

3 See Stephen White, *Russia Goes Dry: Alcohol, State and Society*, New York: Cambridge University Press, 1996.

4 The one exception seems to have been in the later years of World War II and just after, when shortages were especially acute and the possibilities for speculative gains greatest. However, in the late 1940s, after a series of scandals, there was a purge of corrupt officials and magistrates (Virginie Coullodon, *La Mafia en Union Sovietique*, Paris: 1990, 13).

5 See Arkady Vaksberg, *The Soviet Mafia*, London: Weidenfeld & Nicolson, 1991, 75.

6 There are accounts of the *vor* in Couillodon, *La Mafia*, and Stephen Handleman, *Comrade Criminal: The Theft of the Second Russian Revolution*, London: Michael Joseph, 1994. There is a hysterical depiction in Claire Sterling, *Thieves' World*, London: Little, Brown, 1994.

7 See Konstantin Simis, *USSR: The Corrupt Society*, New York: Simon & Schuster, 1982.

8 *Times of London*, 1/24/88. This source states that the black market offered double, but *World Currency Yearbook* the previous year put the premium at six- to tenfold.

9 Coullodon, *La Mafia*, 185. Perhaps for that reason, in 1989, when World War II hero Vice Admiral Georgiy Kholostyakov was murdered, those who killed him scooped up his medals (and dress uniform) and left behind jewellery and cash (*Washington Post*, 10/2/89).

10 Gregory Grossman, "Notes on the Illegal Private Economy and Corruption," *The Soviet Economy in a Time of Change*, Washington: U.S. Government Printing Office, 1977.

11 Grossman, "Second Economy," 35.

12 See Georgie Arbatov, *The System*, New York: Times Books, 1992, 225–28.

13 Lev Timofeyev, *Russia's Secret Rulers*, New York: Knopf, 1992, 63–64; Coullodon, *La Mafia*, 47.

14 See, for example, Gregory Gleason, "Nationalism or Organized Crime: The Case of the 'Cotton Scandal' in the USSR," *Corruption and Reform*, Vol. 5, 1990; and James Critchlow, "The Growth of Organized Crime in Uzbekistan," *Report on the USSR, Radio Free Europe/Radio Liberty*, 2/17/89.

15 On the reaction to the anti-corruption crackdown, see Cassandra Cavanaugh, "Uzbekistan Reexamines the Cotton Affair," *Radio Free Europe/ Radio Liberty Research Report*, Vol. 1, No. 37, 1992; and Elizabeth Fuller, "Azerbaijan: Geidar Aliev's Political Comeback," *RFE/RL*, Vol. 2, No. 5, 1993.

16 Yousaf, *Bear Trap*, 36.

17 Schweizer, *Victory*, 117–19.

18 *Financial Times*, 7/28/88.

19 *Far Eastern Economic Review*, 10/31/91.

20 *Wall Street Journal*, 2/16/88.

21 Steve Galster, "The Afghan Pipeline," *Covert Action Information Bulletin*, No. 30, Summer 1988.

22 *South*, January 1987; *New York Times*, 12/2/87; *Middle East Times*, 2/15/87; *Guardian Weekly*, 7/5/87; *New York Times*, 8/30/89; *Far Eastern Economic Review*, 10/17, 31/91.

23 *Financial Times*, 2/24/89, 2/15/90; *Christian Science Monitor*, 1/17/88; *Globe and Mail*, 2/24/89.

24 *Newsweek*, 4/25/88; *Times of London*, 4/11/88; *New York Times*, 4/12, 17/88.

25 *Times of London*, 4/27/94. Even Pakistan's late president Zia ul-Huq, who was an enthusiastic booster of the mujahideen, insisted that the real reason for the Soviet pull-out was the overall shift in policy associated with Mikhail Gorbachev and not the impact of military losses at the hands of the mujahideen (*Wall Street Journal*, 4/26/88).

26 *Far Eastern Economic Review*, 2/19/87; *Globe and Mail*, 5/9/88; *Financial Times*, 10/3/88, 10/10/89; *Sunday Times*, 7/5/92; *Far Eastern Economic Review*, 5/23/91; *L'Express*, 8/21/92. For an examination of some of the effects of the Afghan war on Central Asia, see Dilip Hiro, *Between Marx and Muhammed: The Changing Face of Central Asia*, London: Harper-Collins 1995.

27 *Miami Herald*, 7/13/87; *Christian Science Monitor*, 11/9/87; *Far Eastern Economic Review*, 11/5/87; *New York Times*, 3/13/89; *Guardian Weekly*, 3/19/89.

28 This has often been called the death blow of Communism. In fact, miners afterwards claimed the objective was reform, not destruction of the system (*Financial Times*, 9/7/98).

29 *Foreign Report*, 8/20/92.

30 *Montreal Gazette*, 8/21/87.

31 Coullodon, *La Mafia*, 242; *Criminal Justice International*, Vol. 9, No. 5, 1993; *The Economist*, 2/19/94.

32 *Globe and Mail*, 3/24/89; Coullodon, *La Mafia*, 210, 224–27, *Sunday Times*, 8/16/92. One Soviet gangster described the co-ops as "a gold mine. The state gives to them, and I take away from them. It's fine for them and it's fine for me" (*Primetime Live*, New York, 10/26/89).

33 *Washington Post*, 10/2, 5/89; Vaksberg, *Soviet Mafia*, 233–34; *Financial Times*, 3/2/96; White, *Russia Goes Dry*, 107–52.

34 *Financial Times*, 1/25/91, 2/1/91; *Wall Street Journal*, 1/28/91; *New York Times*, 1/23, 25/91; *Business Week*, 2/4/91. The holders of accounts were free to transfer as much as they wished from the banks to a legitimate enterprise to finance legal purchases.

35 *Globe and Mail*, 1/8/90.

36 *Guardian Weekly*, 2/3/91.

37 *Wall Street Journal*, 10/15/91; *Financial Times*, 9/11/91; *Observer*, 10/20/91; *Paris Match*, 5/26/94.

38 The worst offender was Claire Sterling in her *Crime Without Frontiers: The Worldwide Expansion of Organised Crime and the Pax Mafiosa*, London: Little, Brown, 1994. For a dissection, see R. T. Naylor, "From Cold War to Crime War: The Search for a New 'National Security' Threat," *Transnational Organized Crime*, Vol.1, No. 4, 1995.

39 Nor were the beneficiaries inevitably or even normally mobsters or ex-party officials well placed in the new self-help economy to help themselves. They certainly claimed their share but, incompetent to run businesses, resold or lost control soon after. The successful new entrepreneurial class was made up of either veterans of the black economy, the U.S.S.R.'s equivalent of a business school, or complete outsiders to the old order (*Financial Times*, 9/27/94).

CHAPTER 7

1 See Martin Short, "Trading with the Enemy," *Middle East International*, June 1976; *Middle East Reporter*, 3/24/79. For an anti-Arab view, see Aaron Sarna, *Boycott and Blacklist: A History of Arab Economic Warfare Against Israel*, New Jersey: Rowan & Littlefield, 1986, and Dan Chill, *The Arab Boycott of Israel: Economic Aggression and World Reaction*, New York: Praeger, 1976.

2 *Free Trade Area Extended to West Bank and Gaza Strip*, Office of the Press Secretary, The White House, 5/16/97.

3 Mohammed Heikal, *Secret Channels: The Inside Story of the Arab-Israeli Peace Negotiations*, London: HarperCollins, 1996, 16, 22.

4 An excellent dissection is in David Fromkin, *A Peace to End All Peace*, New York: Avon, 1989.

5 See J. Bowyer Bell, *Terror Out of Zion: Irgun Zvai Leumi, LEHI, and the Palestine Underground*, New York: St. Martin's Press, 1977, 5–11.

6 Simha Flapan, *The Birth of Israel: Myths and Realities*, New York: Pantheon, 1987, 66.

7 See Lenni Brenner's two studies, *Zionism in the Age of Dictators: A Reappraisal*, London: Zed Books, 1983, and *The Iron Wall: Zionist Revisionism from Jabotinsky to Shamir*, London: Zed Books, 1984.

8 Bell, *Terror*, 55. The British cancelled the raid, instead asking the Irgun to spy on Iraqi military installations.

9 Stephen Green, *Taking Sides: America's Secret Relations with a Militant Israel*, New York: William Morrow, 1984, 47n.

10 See, for example, the account of the personal experiences of Wilbur Eveland Crane in *Ropes of Sand: America's Failure in the Middle East*, New York: W. W. Norton, 1980.

11 See Jimmy Fratianno's memoirs, Ovid Desmaris, *The Last Mafioso*, New York: Bantam, 1981, 32–33.

12 *Times of London*, 7/25/46, 9/14/46, 12/16/46; Robert John and Sami Hadawi, *The Palestine Diary*, Vol. II, Beirut: Palestine Research Center, 1985, 340. Menachem Begin in his memoirs (*The Revolt*, New York: Dell, 1977, 80–81) brags of his role in the payroll train heist.

13 This was actually an extension of a pre-war Irgun project in which the anti-Semitic Polish government was to provide training and help smuggle weapons to a Jewish underground in Palestine as a means of reducing Poland's Jewish population (Bell, *Terror*, 28–29).

14 On Shamir's career see Brenner, *Iron Wall*, passim; *Le Monde*, 9/1/83; *Toronto Star*, 9/2/83; *Globe and Mail*, 9/2/83, 10/8/83; *Middle East International*, 9/16, 30/83. Shamir later confessed to ordering the murder, claiming that his rival had "lost his mind" (*Associated Press*, 1/14/94).

15 *Times of London*, 9/23/40, 1/23/42, 11/9/44, 12/4/46. John and Hadawi, *Palestine Diary*, II, 298–99, 337. It was not always clear which faction was behind the robberies, and in some cases they could have been the work of entrepreneurial robbers pretending to be terrorists

to throw the British police off the trail. See for example, *Times of London*, 1/24/46, 6/27/46, 11/29/46. Diamonds were also stolen by the Irgun, for example, during one of its post office robberies (Bell, *Terror*, 110).

16 The most comprehensive account of weapons procurement and smuggling is by Leonard Slater, *The Pledge*, New York: Simon & Schuster, 1970. See also Green, *Taking Sides*, 47.

17 Robert Lacey, *Little Man: Meyer Lansky and the Gangster Life*, Boston: Little, Brown, 1991, 163; Hank Messick, *Lansky*, New York: Putnam, 1973, 276.

18 John and Hadawi, *Palestine Diary*, II, 86, 302.

19 Sayer and Botting, *Nazi Gold*, 193, 196.

20 *Times of London*, 12/13/43, 9/25/45; Alan Hart, *Arafat: Terrorist or Peacemaker*, London: Sidgwick & Jackson, 1984, 72, 141; Slater, *Pledge*, passim. This book repeats many long-discredited myths about relative strengths of the two sides. In fact, there was a three-to-one majority in favour of the Zionist forces, and they had far more air power and greatly out-gunned the other side. The Arab armies were for the most part a military joke, plagued by poor morale, often trained only for the parade ground and commanded by incompetent and sometimes corrupt officers (Bell, *Terror*, 110, 264, 312).

21 Green, *Taking Sides*, 21, 55, 60–65.

22 This was confirmed by neutrals at the time, but expunged from the mainstream historical record. On the correction of the record, see the work of the Israeli historian Benny Morris, *The Birth of the Palestinian Refugee Problem*, Cambridge: Cambridge University Press, 1987, and *1948 and After: Israel and the Palestinians*, Oxford: Clarendon Press, 1990.

23 Flapan, *Birth of Israel*, 88–96. See also Sami Hadawi, *Bitter Harvest: Palestine 1914–1979*, New York: Caravan Books, 1979, esp. Chapter VII, for the recollections of a Palestinian who survived the events.

24 The Israeli authorities at the time valued the seized property at more than $1 billion, the equivalent today of about $6 billion without taking into account forgone interest or capital gains (*La Presse*, 4/19/97 citing *Ha'aretz*).

25 Central Intelligence Agency, *Israel: Foreign Intelligence and Security Services*, March 1979, 22. A copy of this document was retrieved from the shredder during the takeover of the American embassy in Teheran in 1979.

26 The story of the seizures and looting is told by Tom Segev, *1949: The First Israelis*, New York: Free Press, 1986, Chapter 3. See also Flapan, *Birth of Israel*, 100–101. Despite Ben-Gurion's concerns, in the early 1950s more than one-third of Israel's population was living in "absentee property."

27 Green, *Taking Sides*, 38–40, traces official complicity in the murder and in the escape of the perpetrators.

28 The king also noted that it was Arab custom to distribute the burden of caring for victims of war among the victorious in proportion to their ability to carry the load. Hence he failed to see why a poor country like Palestine should absorb so much of the burden of refugee resettlement when there were fifty countries, some extremely wealthy, all claiming to be part of the winning coalition (David Holden and Richard Johns, *The House of Saud*, London: Holt, Rinehart & Winston, 1981, 137).

29 Faith, *Safety in Numbers*, 266; *Le Hebdo*, 2/23/89.

30 Faith, *Safety in Numbers*, 188, 266; on the Safra history, see Bryan Burroughs, *Vendetta: American Express and the Smearing of Edmond Safra*, New York: HarperCollins, 1992.

31 There is a good account in Dennis Eisenberg, Uri Dan and Eli Landau, *Meyer Lansky: Mogul of the Mob*, New York: Paddington Press, 1979. Rosenbaum's bank collapsed in scandal in 1974. Over 8,000 French tax-evaders had their nest eggs wiped out, Meyer Lansky saw his small fortune from skimming casinos vanish, and nearly $20 million embezzled from Israeli state companies in a desperate attempt to salvage the bank disappeared with it.

32 Sarna, *Boycott and Blacklist*, 11; Heikal, *Secret Channels*, 108–13.

33 The most thorough dissection is by Charles Raw, Bruce Page and Godfrey Hodgson, *"Do You Sincerely Want to Be Rich?" The Full Story of Bernard Cornfeld and IOS*, New York: Viking, 1971.

34 On King, IOS and the Sinai oil investments, see Raw et al., *"Do You Sincerely Want,"* 288–89.

35 The most comprehensive account is by Yergin, *The Prize*, especially Part V.

36 These developments are traced by Raymond Vernon, "An Interpretation," and Edith Penrose, "The Development of the Crisis," in Raymond Vernon (ed.), *The Oil Crisis*, New York: Norton, 1976.

37 Andrew Cockburn and Leslie Cockburn, *Dangerous Liaison: The Inside Story of the U.S.–Israel Covert Relationship*, New York: Stoddart, 1991, 175.

38 See Klaus Knorr, "The Limits of Power," in Vernon, *The Oil Crisis*.

39 On an annualized basis, overall production in 1973 was still 9 per cent greater than in 1972 (Robert Engler, *The Brotherhood of Oil: Energy Policy and the Public Interest*, Chicago: University of Chicago Press, 1977, 31).

40 Stork, *Middle East Oil*, 230–31.

41 Cited in Jeffrey Robinson, *Yamani: The Inside Story*, New York: Atlantic Monthly Press, 1988, Chapter 7. The Saudi oil minister at the time, Sheikh Yamani, concurred that "the embargo was more symbolic than anything else."

42 Edward Tivnan, *The Lobby: Jewish Political Power and American Foreign Policy*, New York: Simon & Schuster, 1987; Richard Curtis, *Stealth PAC: How Israel's American Lobby Took Control of US Middle East Policy*, Washington: American Educational Trust, 1990; Paul Findlay, *They Dare to Speak Out*, Westport, Conn.: Lawrence Hill, 1985. Findlay was a congressman unseated with the help of the Israel lobby. The structure of Jewish political organizations in the United States is detailed in Lee O'Brien, *American Jewish Organizations and Israel*, Washington: Institute for Palestine Studies, 1986.

43 In 1985 Bangladesh, with a per capita income of $140, got $11 in U.S. aid per person; Israel, with a per capita income of $5,500, got $1,250 (*Al Hamishmar*, 5/10/85; *Montreal Gazette*, 7/25/87).

44 For example, they promoted the myth that U.S.–supplied air power accounted for Israel's success against Arab armour in 1967 and 1973. In fact, not a single tank was knocked out from the air. An air-to-ground missile that had already proven useless in Vietnam turned in an equivalent performance (Cockburn, *Dangerous Liaison*, 175–88).

45 Good surveys of the many special deals are in *Los Angeles Times*, 20/7/87, *Middle East International*, 4/2/88, *Financial Times*, 6/27/89, and *Wall Street Journal*, 2/3/87, 9/19/91, 1/20/92.

46 See Said Aburish, *The Rise, Corruption and Coming Fall of the House of Saud*, New York: St. Martin's, 1994.

47 See Laton McCartney, *Friends in High Places: The Bechtel Story*, New York: Simon & Schuster, 1988.

48 Patrick Seale, *Asad: The Struggle for the Middle East*, London: I. B. Taurus, 1988, 119.

49 David Yallop's biography of "Carlos," *To the Ends of the Earth: The Hunt for the Jackal*, London: Jonathan Cape, 1993, contains information on PFLP fundraising (64, 91, 331, 357, 442).

50 There is an excellent biography by Patrick Seale, *Abu Nidal: Gun for Hire*, London: Random House, 1992.

51 Most work dealing with the PLO finances is based on recycled Israeli intelligence disinformation. See, for example, Edgar O'Ballance, *Arab Guerrilla Power 1967–72*, London: Faber & Faber, 1973; James Adams, *The Financing of Terror*, New York: Simon & Schuster, 1986, Part Two; and, perhaps worst, Neil Livingstone and David Halevy, *Inside the PLO: Covert Units, Secret Funds and the War Against Israel and the United States*, New York: William Morrow, 1990. Its chapter dealing with finance asserts an Arafat-controlled secret fund supposedly gained from skyjacking ransoms, drugs and bank robbery. The authors fudge the distinction

between Palestinian groups and the PLO itself, imputing, for example, a massive bank heist in Beirut to the PLO, when it was carried out by the Saiqa, a pro-Syria group. Hijackings carried out by the PFLP are treated similarly. Even actions well known to be the work of Abu Nidal, under a death sentence from the PLO, are blended into PLO activities.

52 Adam Zagorin, "A House Divided," *Foreign Policy*, Spring 1983; *Middle East Reporter*, 8/30/80; *Wall Street Journal*, 7/25/86.

53 Ze'ev Schiff and Ehud Ya'ari, *Intifada: The Palestinian Uprising — Israel's Third Front*, New York: Simon & Schuster, 1990, 174–75.

54 *Middle East Reporter*, 3/24/79; 8/29/87.

55 Chill, *Arab Boycott of Israel*, 36.

56 *Middle East Times*, 5/7/91.

57 *Wall Street Journal*, 3/26/93, 4/25/93.

58 *Globe and Mail*, 1/19/89; *Financial Times*, 7/27/89; *Jerusalem Post*, 3/21/91.

59 I am grateful to Eliav Steiner for this example.

60 *Le Monde Diplomatique*, November 1983. For example, Tadiran, Israel's third largest exporter of industrial goods during the early 1980s, once denationalized and sold to General Telephone & Electronics, marketed its products worldwide, including in Arab states, under the trade-name of its American parent.

61 *Middle East Times*, 5/14/91; *Financial Times*, 7/6/89.

CHAPTER 8

1 David Ben-Gurion in his diary noted that Arab "commerce has for the most part been destroyed, many stores are closed . . . and prices are rising to the Arabs," and that prior to the mass flight the economic war had already driven out the 20,000 richest (Flapan, *Birth of Israel*, 92). In theory the evacuation of Haifa was "negotiated" between the Haganah and the Arab leaders (see, for example, Bell, *Terror*, 299). In fact, the population was panicked by massacres in neighbouring areas. Those who left assumed their departure was temporary. Afterwards their property was seized and they were refused the right to return.

2 A good survey is in *Middle East Reports*, Vol. 18, No. 10, December 1978.

3 Marchetti and Marks, *CIA*, 244; Eveland, *Ropes of Sand*, 217, 252; *New York Times*, 8/8/87; *Israel & Palestine*, September 1987.

4 The flavour can be caught in Said Aburish, *Beirut Spy*, London: Bloomsbury, 1989. Many of the journalists operating out of Beirut were actually spies (Cave-Brown, *Treason*, 475).

5 Jim Hougan, *Spooks: The Haunting of America: The Private Use of Secret Agents*, New York: William Morrow, 1978, 212–14.

6 Eveland, *Ropes of Sand*, 217–18.

7 Aburish, *Beirut Spy*, 111–12, 127–28.

8 *Business Week*, 10/22, 29/66; *Middle East Economic Digest*, 11/25/66, 12/2/66, 1/5, 12/67, 3/9/67, 4/20/67, 8/3/67; *The Economist*, 11/22/66, 11/12/66, 12/24/66; *Newsweek*, 10/31/66.

9 *Middle East Economic Digest*, 3/30/67.

10 *Jerusalem Post*, 7/25–31/82, 8/8–14/82, 8/15–21/82.

11 *New York Times*, 7/25/82; Heikal, *Secret Channels*, 338.

12 Three works that survey much of the political scene in Lebanon during its civil war and subsequent Israeli invasion are David Gilmour, *Lebanon: The Fractured Country*, London: Sphere, 1983; Jonathan Randal, *Going All the Way: Christian Warlords, Israeli Adventurers, and the War in Lebanon*, New York: Viking, 1983; and Robert Fisk, *Pity the Nation: Lebanon at War*, Oxford: Oxford University Press, 1990. See also Salim Nasr, "The Crisis of Lebanese Capitalism," *Middle East Research and Information Project Reports*, Vol. 8, No. 10, 1978.

13 Ties between Phalangists and Israelis date back to 1948, when the Phalangists asked for Israeli aid in overthrowing the government of Lebanon. However, apart from a donation of

$3,000 for use in a 1951 election, there was little aid forthcoming, until the outbreak of the civil war (*Globe and Mail*, 7/5/83).

14 *Montreal Gazette*, 3/25/81; *Middle East Reports*, September–October 1982; *International Herald Tribune*, 3/16/83; *Hadashot*, 8/11/89; Beate Hamizrachi, *The Emergence of the South Lebanon Security Belt*, New York: Praeger, 1987. After Haddad's death, Israel reorganized his militia into the South Lebanon Army and put a Maronite officer (Haddad had been a Greek Catholic) in charge in the hope of improving relations with the Phalangist government then ruling in Beirut. The broadcasting facilities were taken over by Pat Robertson's Christian Broadcasting Corporation (*Le Monde Diplomatique*, September 1986; *New York Times*, 10/18/85).

15 He had been recruited by the CIA while studying law in the United States in the early 1970s. The CIA later began funding his militia, as well as introducing him to Mossad. Subsequently he was a joint asset of the two services. Reliance on Bashir was not well received by the CIA station in Beirut, which regarded him as a barbarian and a murderer (Bob Woodward, *Veil: The Secret Wars of the CIA, 1981–1987*, New York: Simon & Schuster, 1987, 203–5, 217–18).

16 *Israel & Palestine*, September 1987; *New York Times*, 8/8/87.

17 Heikal, *Secret Channels*, 312, 455.

18 Randal, *Going All the Way*, 113–14, 20; *The Nation*, 6/19/82.

19 *Middle East Reporter*, 5/15/82.

20 Later discretion was abandoned — Israeli ships started directly unloading weapons in a Phalangist-controlled port in Lebanon as well as hijacking and diverting to that port ships carrying arms to the other side (Russel Warren Howe, *Weapons: The International Game of Arms, Money and Diplomacy*, New York: Doubleday, 726–28).

21 Randal, *Going All the Way*, 98, 106.

22 *Middle East Economic Digest*, 2/6/76, and Randal, *Going All the Way*, 98–99. These sources misidentify the robbers as members of the Democratic Front for the Liberation of Palestine. See also Livingstone and Halevy, *Inside the PLO*, where the take is put at $850 million! They claim that any shares in non-bearer form were sold by the PLO back to their owners for twenty to thirty cents on the dollar. This is absurd. Non-bearer shares are just scrap paper to anyone but their registered owners and are completely replaceable. Randal, who was actually in Beirut at the time, was convinced that non-bearer shares and bonds were just thrown away. The murder of the Saiqa chief was widely, and incorrectly, blamed on the Mossad.

23 *Middle East Times*, 10/1/88; *Guardian Weekly*, 9/15/85.

24 The role of Lebanon in maritime fraud during the 1980s is examined in Barbara Conway's *The Piracy Business*, London: Hamlyn Paperbacks, 1982, and her later work, *Maritime Fraud*, London: Lloyd's of London Press, 1990.

25 *Middle East Reporter*, 11/1/80.

26 Sometimes Israeli underworld figures arranged with the Bedouin for sacks to be dropped off inside Israel en route (*Israel & Palestine*, January 1988, September 1979; *Middle East Reporter*, 7/19/86).

27 See especially Sean O'Callahan, *The Drug Traffic*, London: Anthony Blond, 1967, Chapter 3; Green, *The Smugglers*, 40–41.

28 *Middle East Reporter*, 3/8/80; *Le Monde*, 11/27/83; Alain Labrousse, *La drogue, l'argent et les armes*, Paris: Fayard, 1991, 73–75. There were rumours of a cocaine-for-weapons traffic between Nicaraguan contras and the Lebanese forces, among whom coke became increasingly popular prior to battle. Unlike heroin, cocaine would have stimulated aggressivity.

29 *Christian Science Monitor*, 10/24/83; *International Herald Tribune*, 9/30/83; *Al-Nahar*, 3/21/83, 8/8/83, 6/4, 18/84; *Institutional Investor*, June 1983; *Wall Street Journal*, 3/27/84; *Euromoney*, May 1983; *Institutional Investor*, June 1983.

30 See the excellent survey by Selim Nasr in *Middle East Report*, January–February 1990.

31 *Middle East Reporter*, 4/4/81.

32 *An-Nahar*, 12/27/82; *Wall Street Journal*, 10/19/83; *Arab News*, 8/23/83, 9/12/83. The lower figure, excluding Palestinian infrastructure, was the basis of a subsequent demand by the Lebanese government for war reparations. It referred only to capital losses, excluding any calculation of lost income. See the survey of the damage in Marwan Iskander and Elias Baroudi, *The Lebanese Economy in 1981–2*, Beirut: 1982.

33 Some of the effects are surveyed in W. S. Ellis, "Beirut: Up From the Rubble," *National Geographic* 163, No. 2, February 1983. There may have been PLO weapons stored at the hippodrome, though none in the mental asylum or orphanage.

34 Michael Jensen, *The Battle of Beirut*, Boston: South End Press, 1984, 114.

35 *Middle East Reporter*, 7/24/82; *Wall Street Journal*, 4/10/84; *Toronto Star*, 8/18/85; *Davaar*, 9/3/82; *Middle East*, November 1982; *Middle East International*, 5/13/85; *Al-Nahar*, 10/18/82, 11/15/82; *Financial Times*, 1/6/83; *New York Times*, 1/17/83; *Jerusalem Post*, 11/7/82.

36 The report, *Israel in Lebanon, Report of the International Commission to Enquire into Reported Violations of International Law by Israel During Its Invasion of the Lebanon*, London: Ithaca Press, 1983, by the late Sean MacBride, Irish Nobel laureate, notes that the destruction of industrial plant was so extensive that it "could not be explained by Israel's . . . combat objectives."

37 *Guardian*, 11/7/82; *Globe and Mail*, 12/22/83; *Financial Times*, 1/6/83; *New York Times*, 11/15/83, 1/27/84; *International Herald Tribune*, 12/3/83; *Le Monde Diplomatique*, August 1985; *An-Nahar*, 10/18/82; private communication from Dr. Israel Shahak.

38 *Euromoney*, May 1983; *Al-Nahar*, 12/13/82.

39 *Arab News*, 7/1/82. In fact, while its army was still laying siege to West Beirut, the Israeli government was requesting that the Lebanese government peg the Israeli shekel at a par with the Lebanese pound and list it on the Lebanese foreign exchange market (*Middle East Reporter*, 7/24/82).

40 *Jerusalem Post*, 10/17/82. The Israelis stamped Saudi insignias on Lebanese army weapons, then showed them to the United States, claiming this was proof that the Saudis were diverting American arms to the PLO. The United States Army checked the serial numbers and reported that Saudi Arabia had never received such weapons from the United States (Findlay, *They Dare*, 163).

41 Randal, *Going All the Way*, 258–59; MacBride, *Report*, passim; *Arab News*, 9/27, 29/82; *Jerusalem Post*, 8/15/82; *International Herald Tribune*, 9/28/82; *Koteret Rashit*, 5/13/86; *Jerusalem Post*, 8/8, 14/82. While the *Herald Tribune*, which publishes in Europe in association with the *New York Times*, carried a front-page story about Israeli looting, the story was omitted from the *New York Times* itself. Disciplinary action was taken against soldiers who looted a store in areas held by Israel's Phalangist allies (the Phalangists arrested them and turned them over to the Israeli army) and in one instance where soldiers were caught bartering weapons for hashish (*Montreal Gazette*, 10/9/82). A year later it was still going on. Eight Israeli paratroopers were court-martialled in 1983 for shaking down Lebanese civilians at roadblocks (*Montreal Gazette*, 8/18/83).

42 *Intelligence Digest*, 2/9/83.

43 *Middle East Reporter*, 2/12/83.

44 He declared that since the two countries were economic rivals in almost every field, "Israel is for us the greatest danger" (*Arab News*, 9/26/82).

45 *Times of London*, 3/4/83; *New York Times*, 8/27/82; *Montreal Gazette*, 7/17/85; *New Statesman*, 9/7/84; *Middle East Reporter*, 3/21/87, 4/18/87, 12/18/89; *Christian Science Monitor*, 2/9/89. Much as in Palestine, sham companies or Lebanese middlemen were sometimes used to disguise the real purchasers.

46 Eveland, *Ropes of Sand*, 134; *South*, July 1983; *Al-Nahar*, 9/20/82; *South*, February, July 1983; *Middle East International*, 5/13/83; *Le Monde Diplomatique*, August 1985; *Middle East Reporter*, 10/30/82, 2/26/83.

47 *Middle East Reporter*, 10/30/82; *Financial Times*, 1/6/83; *Middle East Reporter*, 3/5/83; *New York Times*, 1/17/83, 8/13/83; *Le Monde Diplomatique*, November 1983; *Middle East Times*, 4/11/89.

48 *Wall Street Journal*, 11/3/82, 2/25/83, 3/3, 7/83.

49 *Financial Times*, 1/6/83.

50 Some Lebanese workers crossed the border to take up jobs in Israel under conditions graphically described by one with the words "It is like the Mexicans in America" (*Middle East Reporter*, 10/28/89).

51 Claire Hoy and Victor Ostrovsky, *By Way of Deception: A Devastating Insider's Portrait of the Mossad*, Toronto: Stoddart, 1990, 320.

52 There is a strange, only partially credible account of covert operations run by U.S. intelligence under cover of drug enforcement out of Cyprus by an ex–DIA agent, now on the run, Lester Coleman. See Donald Goddard and Lester Coleman, *Trail of the Octopus: From Beirut to Lockerbie — Inside the DIA*, London: Bloomsbury, 1993.

53 See for example, *Ha'aretz*, 2/10/84; *Ma'ariv*, 3/25/84; *Bemahane*, 3/14/84; *Al Hamishmar*, 7/14/91; *Middle East Reporter*, 7/5, 19/86; *Actuel*, November 1986.

54 One instance involved a group of Israeli reservists, veterans of Lebanon, who amazed police with their knowledge of counter-surveillance techniques. They were busted in a plot to sell cannabis to finance the purchase of arms, including anti-aircraft missiles, for resale to the IRA (*Guardian*, 1/9/88).

55 Not all the losses were due to Israeli military action. The books of Samed, the industrial complex, were reported "lost" during the invasion, permitting everything missing to be imputed to Israeli military action. In fact, part of the hole was the result of theft by officials (private communication).

56 *Middle East Reporter*, 8/4/84. The invasion helped precipitate a major economic crisis in Israel, which was met by Congress granting a massive hike in U.S. economic aid (*Wall Street Journal*, 9/11/84).

CHAPTER 9

1 For a survey, see *Middle East Reports*, July–August 1983. For some of the more gruesome aspects of Gaza policy, see *Davaar*, 11/28/85.

2 *New York Times*, 4/1/85; *Al-Fajar*, 8/2/85; *Ha'aretz*, 2/17/82, 1/24/83; *Middle East International*, 12/21/84, 9/27/85; *The Middle East*, January 1984; *Le Monde Diplomatique*, September 1984; Said Aburish, *Cry Palestine: Inside the West Bank*, London: Bloomsbury, 1991, 77–78 et passim.

3 *Middle East International*, 9/27/85; Jacques Derogy, *Israel Connection: La Mafia en Israel*, Paris: Plon, 1980, suggests that West Bank land deals were also a good way to launder criminal money.

4 In the run-up to the 1984 elections, Shamir convened a meeting of Israeli businessmen active in the occupied territories whose fortunes might have been threatened by Labour Party ambivalence, to coax out of them aid for the Likud's electoral coffers (*Al-Fajar*, 8/30/85; *Isra-Countersource*, 1/1, 15/86).

5 *Al-Fajar*, 1/4/85, 2/1, 5/85, 9/27/85. When Nablus residents did succeed in getting the local court to order settlers to stop uprooting olive and almond trees until land disputes were resolved, the settlers simply ignored the court ruling, which the police refused to enforce. And in 1984 a fire swept the Nablus court building, destroying 15,000 case files, including vital land documents, that had been dumped in the middle of the floor and ignited.

6 *Middle East International*, 1/11/85, 9/27/85; *Al-Fajar*, 3/29/85, 5/31/85; Aburish, *Cry Palestine*, 9. Beyond the local courts, civil or military, was the Israeli High Court, to which residents of the territories seeking justice had the option of appealing. In the first half of 1986, West Bank Palestinians launched fifty-nine similar appeals to the Israeli High Court, which rejected only fifty-nine of them (*Hadashot*, 6/16/87).

7 *Christian Science Monitor*, 4/14/83; *Canadian Jewish News*, 2/10/83; *Wall Street Journal*, 4/15/83; *Middle East International*, 4/18/86; *Middle East,* January 1984; *Jerusalem Post*, 10/17/87.

8 *Al-Fajar*, 6/8/84; *Middle East International*, 9/12/87, 11/7/87. Deportation is supposed to refer to sending a fugitive back to his or her country of origin. Israel uses the term to refer to the expulsion of Palestinians from a land where their predecessors lived for centuries before the first ancient Hebrews arrived.

9 The U.S. State Department was fully aware that economic aid payments ostensibly going to Palestinians were being used to make life easier for settlers stealing Palestinian land and water, but did nothing about it while maintaining in public the position that the settlements were illegal (*New York Times*, 4/7/84).

10 *Middle East International*, 2/10/84. At a time when the FBI (disregarding Rabbi Kahane's previous service as an informant against radical black groups) decided to classify his Jewish Defense League as a terrorist organization, the State of New York maintained its status as a religious institution exempt from filing any financial reports (*Middle East International*, 4/18/86; Robert Friedman, *The False Prophet Rabbi Meir Kahane: From FBI Informant to Knesset Member*, Brooklyn: Lawrence Hill Books, 1990, Chapter 13).

11 There had been in the past lawsuits against the UJA and other organizations endowed with tax-exempt status to try to prevent them from using their donations to buy up Arab land. But they had been thrown out of court on the technical grounds that individuals do not have standing to challenge administrative rulings by the IRS (*Jerusalem Post*, 1/26/88, 2/22/88; *Middle East International*, 10/21/88).

12 On the struggle over water in this period, see John Cooley, "The War Over Water," *Foreign Policy* 54, Spring 1984; *Middle East Reports*, July–August 1983; *Middle East*, February 1981; *Le Monde Diplomatique*, September 1981; *Ha'aretz*, 4/25/89; *The Washington Report on Middle Eastern Affairs*, April, July 1991; *Water Resources of the Occupied Palestinian Territory*, New York: United Nations, 1992.

13 *Wall Street Journal*, 4/11/85, 8/22/85. One evangelical oil entrepreneur, while under investigation by the FBI for defrauding American investors, set up the tax-exempt Temple Mount Foundation. It was a conduit for running evangelical money to defend Jews accused of murdering Arabs and to promote a scheme to destroy Jerusalem's Haram el-Sharif prior to rebuilding on its site the Temple of Solomon. The hope was that obliterating the third-most sacred shrine in Islam would trigger the final clash that would lead to Armageddon (*Jerusalem Post*, 6/17/84; *Arab News*, 4/27/83, 3/4/84).

14 *Le Monde Diplomatique*, September 1981; *International Herald Tribune*, 2/20/84; *Middle East International*, 6/24/83, 1/11/85; *Al-Fajar*, 9/14/84, 11/9/84.

15 On patronage, see Rex Brynen, "The Neopatrimonial Dimension of Palestinian Politics," *Journal of Palestine Studies*, 25, No. 97, 1995. On collaborators, see *Koteret Rashit*, 3/2, 16/88; *Yediot Ahronot*, 2/26/88; *Davaar*, 2/29/88; *Ha'aretz*, 2/10/88.

16 Hart, *Arafat*, 309; *Davaar*, 3/18/88.

17 *Al-Fajar*, 9/27/85, 10/4/85; *Middle East International*, 7/11/87; *Koterit Rashit*, 4/29/87; *The Washington Report on Middle Eastern Affairs*, March 1991.

18 Although one Arab-owned institution, the Bank of Palestine, was permitted to reopen in 1981 in Gaza, and a branch of a Jordanian bank allowed into the West Bank in 1987, they were confined to a single branch and had to transact business in Israeli currency. Only after 1990 were more Arab banks permitted.

19 *Al-Fajar*, 10/19/84, 11/16, 23/84, 7/5/87.

20 *Financial Times*, 2/23/87.

21 *Financial Times*, 2/23/87; *Al-Fajar*, 5/3/85, 10/4/85; *Guardian*, 12/6/87.

22 *Middle East International*, 12/7/84; *Le Monde Diplomatique*, September 1984; *Al-Fajar*, 4/19/85, 10/4/85; *Middle East Times*, 10/4/87; *Al Hamishmar*, 4/13/87. These workers were

bussed over the "Green Line" to certain town centres referred to as "slave markets." At peak
their wages accounted for 25 to 40 per cent of the territories' GNP (*Ma'ariv*, 11/18/83; *The
Economist*, 5/28/87; *Middle East International*, 4/19/91).

23 *Al-Fajar*, 2/22/85; *The Economist*, 5/28/87; *International Herald Tribune*, 5/20/83; *Yediot
Ahronot*, 7/3/87, *Jerusalem Post*, 6/7/86.

24 *Middle East International*, 10/20/89.

25 Schiff and Ya'ari, *Intifada*, 203–4, 225; Aburish, *Cry Palestine*, 99; Rex Brynen et al., *Donor
Assistance in Palestine*, Montreal: Palestinian Development Infonet, McGill University, April
1998.

26 *Le Monde Diplomatique*, November 1983; I am indebted to Eliav Steiner for several examples.

27 Heikal, *Secret Channels*, 383; Schiff, *Intifada*, 46, 80, 82–84, 101.

28 Schiff, *Intifada*, 212–13; *Middle East International*, 8/16/91; *International Herald Tribune*,
2/20/84; *Koteret Rashit*, 4/29/87; *The Washington Report on Middle Eastern Affairs*, March
1990; *The Middle East*, July 1990; *Wall Street Journal*, 3/24/93.

29 *Al-Fajar*, 5/3/87.

30 *Israel & Palestine*, September 1989.

31 *Financial Times*, 1/17/84; *North California Jewish Bulletin*, 1/26/90. The first published analysis of the phenomenon seems to have been the work of Elazar Levin in *Koteret Rashit*,
8/25/84. For translation and additional commentary, I thank Dr. Israel Shahak.

32 *Christian Science Monitor*, 8/29/88; *Middle East International*, 6/24/88; *Middle East Reporter*,
6/11/88, 7/30/88; private communication from Dr. Israel Shahak regarding the Hassidic
pipeline.

33 Heikal, *Secret Channels*, 386–87 Schiff, *Intifada*, 266.

34 *Financial Times*, 8/25/88; *Jerusalem Post*, 6/5/88.

35 There is an excellent survey in United Nations Department of Public Information, *Life of
the Palestinians Under Israeli Occupation*, New York: 1992.

36 *Financial Times*, 11/27/90; *Middle East International*, 4/13/90, 4/19/91. See also *Washington
Report on Middle East Affairs*, July 1991; Aburish, *Cry Palestine*, 12; Schiff, *Intifada*, 124.

37 *Yediot Ahronot*, 5/7/91; *The Washington Report on Middle Eastern Affairs*, October 1989, July 1992.

38 Joseph Algazy, *Tax Commando to Break Intifada*, Israeli League for Human and Civil Rights,
September 1989; *Al Hamishmar*, 8/25/89; *New York Times*, 11/1/89; *Christian Science Monitor*,
7/27/89; *Financial Times*, 3/14/89; *Middle East International*, 10/6/89, 11/17/89; *Guardian
Weekly*, 7/31/88; *Ha'aretz*, 6/12/92.

39 Brynen et al., *Donor Assistance*, 68–69; *Middle East International*, 12/11/98; Heikal, *Secret
Channels*, 10.

40 Heikal, *Secret Channels*, 511.

CHAPTER 10

1 The most comprehensive examination of the vulnerability of South Africa to sanctions is
by Dan O'Meara, *Review of Government Measures Against Apartheid in South Africa on Areas
Critical to Its Economy*, United Nations, June 1989.

2 In general, see the recollections of the former head of the Rhodesian Central Intelligence
Organization, Ken Flower, *Serving Secretly: An Intelligence Chief on Record*, London: Murray,
1987.

3 *Time*, 11/26/65, 4/14/67; Flower, *Serving Secretly*, 62, 72.

4 On imposition, enforcement and response, see Harry Strack, *Sanctions: The Case of Rhodesia*,
Syracuse: Syracuse University Press, 1978; Doxey, *Economic Sanctions*; Renwick, *Economic
Sanctions*.

5 Flower (*Serving Secretly*, 73–76) notes that Rhodesia found friends in unexpected places,
getting assistance from Taiwan, Yemen and Mauritius, as well as from corrupt regimes in
Africa such as that of Mobutu in Zaire.

6 Flower, *Serving Secretly*, 72; Renwick, *Sanctions*, 39.

7 *Time*, 6/30/67.

8 *Time*, 4/8/66.

9 Benjamin Beit-Hallahmi, *The Israeli Connection: Who Israel Arms and Why*, New York: Pantheon Books, 1987, 63.

10 This is detailed by Norman Bailey, one of the reporters who broke the story, in *Oilgate: The Sanctions Scandal*, London: 1979.

11 According to "Tiny" Rowland, boss of Lonrho Corporation, which owned the mothballed pipeline, the oil companies had assured the Rhodesians in advance that, even if an oil embargo was imposed, deliveries would be maintained (Richard Hall, *My Life with Tiny: A Biography of Tiny Rowland*, Boston: Faber & Faber, 1987, 115–16).

12 *Time*, 3/15/76; Strack, *Sanctions*, 95; Renwick, *Sanctions*, 52.

13 *Africa Confidential*, 8/20/86. The man who had headed the Rhodesian sanctions-busting operation became head of the Johannesburg Chamber of Commerce.

14 See especially David Pallister, Sarah Stewart and Ian Lepper, *South Africa Inc.: The Oppenheimer Empire*, London: Simon & Schuster, 1987. On Anglo's role in the rise of apartheid (largely born in the gold and diamond mines as a means of holding down black wages), see Duncan Innes, *Anglo American and the Rise of Modern South Africa*, New York: Monthly Review Press, 1984. Anglo was the principal covert corporate ally of the government in breaking sanctions. Yet it was also the leader among big business in criticizing the government and insisting that the apartheid system was obsolete.

15 *Guardian Weekly*, 4/1/84; see also Pallister et al., *South Africa Inc.*, 165–66.

16 Pierre Péan, *V: enquête sur l'affaire des avions renifleurs*, Paris: Fayard, 1984; see also *Le Monde*, 1/6, 10/84, 3/29, 30/84, 7/24/84, 11/22/84.

17 Cited in Norman Bailey, *Oil Sanctions: South Africa's Weak Link*, London: Africa Bureau, 1981, 23.

18 It was so successful that China at one point bartered its own oil for the technology. See Abdelkader Ben Abdullah, *La Collusion Sino–Sud Africain*, Montreal: Editions Solidarité Trois Monde, 1984, 75–77.

19 *Le Monde Diplomatique*, September 1986; *Africa Confidential*, 8/20/86. See especially Richard Hengeveld and Jaap Rodenburg, *Embargo: Apartheid's Oil Secrets Revealed*, Amsterdam: Amsterdam University Press, 1995, an insiders' account of the work by the Shipping Research Bureau in exposing sanctions-busting over the course of the 1980s.

20 *Jeune Afrique*, 2/1/89.

21 *Le Monde Diplomatique*, September 1986.

22 *Wall Street Journal*, 11/24/87.

23 *New African*, April 1984; *African Business*, May 1992. BCCI moved into a vacuum left by the 1984 scandal-racked collapse of Johnson Matthey Bank (Naylor, *Hot Money*, 239–45; Mihir Bose and Cathy Gunn, *Fraud: The Growth Industry of the Eighties*, London: Unwin, Hymas, 1989, Chapters 2, 3, 4; US Senate, PSI, *BCCI Affair*, 103).

24 *Financial Post*, 3/31/89. I am grateful to Vassilis Dalacouras for information on this topic.

25 Mark Hulbert, *Interlock*, New York: Richardson and Snyder, 1982, 65–66 et passim.

26 Aburish, *Rise, Corruption and Fall*, 187, 295–96.

27 See R. Craig Copetas, *Metal Men: Marc Rich and the 10-Billion Dollar Scam*, New York: Harper & Row, 1985.

28 *Barron's*, 9/19, 26/83; *Fortune*, 11/22/86, 8/1/88; *Forbes*, 4/30/90, 6/22/92.

29 Copetas, *Metal Men*, 120, 130–32. His first arms-for-oil deal seems to have been with Ecuador in 1978.

30 *Latin America Political Report*, 6/1/79.

31 *Latin America Regional Reports*: Caribbean, 3/27/81; *New York Times*, 6/7/81; James Dubro, *Mob Rule: Inside the Canadian Mafia*, Toronto: Totem, 1985, 291–93.

32 Jim Hougan, *Spooks: The Haunting of America*, New York: William Morrow, 1978, 225–26.

33 Arthur Herzog, *Vesco*, New York: Doubleday, 1987, 287, 300.

34 *Observer*, 11/2/86.

35 Hengeveld, *Embargo*, 275. If Saudi Arabia were caught, it would plead it had no way of disciplining firms who took oil under false pretences and diverted it to forbidden locations. Since the Saudis made a point of not keeping an official boycott list, the same firms could repeat the diversion with impunity.

36 Hengeveld and Rodenburg, *Embargo*, 192 et passim.

37 *Africa Confidential*, 1/5/83.

38 *Wall Street Journal*, 10/13/87.

39 Commonwealth Committee of Foreign Ministers on Southern Africa, *South Africa: The Sanctions Report*, London: Penguin, 1989, 45–48.

40 Of the 865 embargo-busting voyages traced by the Shipping Research Bureau, some 380 flew the Liberian flag (Hengeveldt and Rodenburg, *Embargo*, 181).

41 Godfrey Hodgson, *Lloyd's of London: A Reputation at Risk*, London: Penguin, 1986, 179–80, 187–95.

42 Arthur Klinghoffer, *Fraud of the Century*, London: Routledge, 1988; Barbara Conway, *Maritime Fraud*; Bose and Gunn, *Fraud*, Chapter 5.

43 *Latin America Weekly Report*, 2/26/82.

44 See his own account in James Mancham, *Paradise Raped*, London: Methuen, 1983. After independence he revised his plans slightly: "My dream was to turn the Seychelles into a small Switzerland, taking advantage of our geographical position and staying out of the tug-of-war of power politics."

45 *Africa Confidential*, 3/17/78.

46 *Observer*, 4/26/87.

47 *Time*, 12/14/81; *Facts on File*, 12/11/81; *Africa Confidential*, 10/1/86, 11/4/87. Although the plot had apparently been worked out by representatives of the old regime and financed by selling future shares in a luxury casino they planned to build, it had the quiet backing of the South African intelligence services.

48 *Africa Confidential*, 4/15/87.

49 On the more dubious side of the Knights of Malta, see Martin Lee, "Thy Will Be Done," *Mother Jones*, July 1983, and Françoise Hervet, "Knights of Darkness: The Sovereign Military Order of Malta," *CovertAction*, No. 25, Winter 1986.

50 *Observer*, 3/13/87.

51 *Africa Confidential*, 5/13/87.

52 *Africa Confidential*, 4/15/87.

CHAPTER 11

1 For a dissection of the merchants-of-death myth, see John Wilz, *In Search of Peace: The Senate Munitions Inquiry, 1934–36*, Baton Rouge: Louisiana State University Press, 1963. The history of arms control measures is reviewed in John Stanley and Maurice Pearton, *The International Trade in Arms*, New York: Praeger, 1972.

2 Leslie Rout, Jr., *Politics of the Chaco Peace Conference: 1935–1939*, Austin: University of Texas Press, 1970, 59, 61, 64, 91, 120.

3 Wilz, *In Search of Peace*, 89.

4 On financing of the FLN see Faith, *Safety in Numbers*, 202–3. There is an excellent account of the war in Alistair Horne's *A Savage War of Peace: Algeria 1954–1962*, London: Macmillan, 1977.

5 Eric Gerdan, *Dossier A . . . Comme Armes*, Paris: Alain Moreau, 1975, 204–5.

6 George Thayer, *The War Business*, New York: Simon & Schuster, 1969, 138–42. Horne, *Savage War*, 84–85, 261–63; Gerdan, *Dossier A . . .*, 206.

7 The pioneering work on the relationship between French intelligence factions and the "French Connection" heroin route is in Newsday, *The Heroin Trail*, New York: Holt, Rinehart & Winston, 1974. See also Henrik Krüger, *The Great Heroin Coup: Drugs, Intelligence and International Fascism*, Montreal: Black Rose Books, 1980.

8 See John De St. Jorre, *The Nigerian Civil War*, London: Hodder & Stoughton, 1972.

9 De St. Jorre, *Nigerian Civil War*, 142.

10 De St. Jorre, *Nigerian Civil War*, 187; Anthony Mockler, *The Mercenaries*, Texas: Free Companion Press, 1969, 259–60.

11 Thayer, *The War Business*, 167–68; De St. Jorre, *Nigerian Civil War*, 241. Another version of the Banque Rothschild story (Mockler, *The Mercenaries*, 229) has it offering a £5 million per week credit against security of the soon-to-be discredited banknotes, though this seems unlikely.

12 An interesting examination of their role is by Mockler, *The Mercenaries*, but see also the career guide by Paul Balfor, *Manual of the Mercenary Soldier*, Boulder, Colo.: Palladin Press, 1988. One of the most accurate accounts appears in Frederick Forsyth's classic novel *The Dogs of War*, London: Bantam, 1974.

13 De St. Jorre, *Nigerian Civil War*, 215.

14 Stanley and Pearton, *International Trade in Arms*, 29.

15 His career has been traced in Patrick Brogan and Albert Zarca, *Deadly Business: Sam Cummings, Interarms and the Arms Trade*, New York: W. W. Norton, 1983. See also Thayer, *The War Business*, 44–75.

16 Stanley and Pearton, *International Trade in Arms*, 188.

17 Gerdan, *Dossier A . . .*, 225. In fact, some planes flying Biafran relief supplies also carried arms in the (perhaps mistaken) hope that the federal side would hesitate to shoot them down.

18 On the history see Signe Landren, *Embargo Disimplemented: South Africa's Military Industry*, Oxford: Oxford University Press, 1989. See also Michael Klare, "Evading the Embargo: Illicit U.S. Arms Transfers to South Africa," *Journal of International Affairs* 35, No. 1, Spring 1981.

19 James Adams, *Bull's Eye: The Assassination and Life of Supergun Inventor Gerald Bull*, New York: Times Books, 1992, 146–47.

20 *Africa-Asia*, February 1985.

21 *Globe and Mail*, 5/1/84.

22 A slightly different version has the weapons originating in Czechoslovakia, sold to the PLO, captured by Israel and resold to South Africa, which turned them over to Protestant paramilitaries (*Toronto Star*, 4/26/89).

23 *Sunday Telegraph*, 5/14/89, 7/9/89; *Manchester Guardian Weekly*, 4/30/89; *Financial Times*, 5/6/89; FBIS-AFR, 3/27/95.

24 There are two excellent reports in *The Middle East*, April 1981, May 1983. The scandal and trial were well covered by Sam Hemingway in the *Burlington Free Press*.

25 Apart from that by James Adams cited above, there are two biographies of Bull: William Lowther, *Arms and the Man: Dr. Gerald Bull, Iraq and the Supergun*, Toronto: Doubleday, 1991, and Dale Grant, *Wilderness of Mirrors: The Life of Gerald Bull*, Toronto: Prentice-Hall, 1991.

26 For background see Robert Coram, *Caribbean Time Bomb: The United States' Complicity in the Corruption of Antigua*, New York: Morrow, 1993.

27 *Burlington Free Press*, 12/7/78.

28 *Burlington Free Press*, 1/21/79.

29 *The Middle East*, April 1981.

30 *Toronto Star*, 8/1/88.

31 *The Middle East*, April 1981; Adel Darwish and Gregory Alexander, *Unholy Babylon: The Secret History of Saddam's War*, New York: St. Martin's Press, 1991, 146.

32 Darwish and Alexander, *Unholy Babylon*, 163.

33 *Middle East International*, 4/30/88.

34 *International Herald Tribune*, 10/12/83; *San Jose Mercury*, 7/24/88.

35 *Wall Street Journal*, 3/13/92, 4/2/92; Cockburn, *Dangerous Liaisons*, 155–57.

36 Apart from Cockburn, *Dangerous Liaisons*, and Green, *Taking Sides*, two excellent works on this subject are Jane Hunter, *Israeli Techno-Crimes in the United States*, Kingston, Ont.: Near East Cultural and Educational Foundation, 1988; and Claudia Wright, *Spy, Steal and Smuggle: Israel's Special Relationship with the United States*, Boston: Association of Arab-American University Graduates, 1986.

37 Gary Milbollin, "Heavy Water Cheaters," *Foreign Policy*, No. 69, Winter 1987–88.

38 Cockburn, *Dangerous Liaisons*, 196.

39 *Washington Post*, 11/25/87.

40 *Wall Street Journal*, 1/17/92.

41 This comment reflected frustration at dozens of cases of Israeli espionage that had been swept under the rug (*Wall Street Journal*, 12/18/85).

42 Lohbeck, *Holy War, Unholy Victory*, 133–36. Lohbeck, a top CBS correspondent, was for a time quite friendly with Pollard and observed him in action; *Jerusalem Post*, 4/5/87; *Middle East International*, 6/13/86, 7/11/86, 3/20/87; *Wall Street Journal*, 6/5/86; *Sunday Times*, 4/19/87, 9/23/87; *Washington Report on Middle Eastern Affairs*, December 1989; *UPI*, 12/13/87. One American asked an appropriate question: "What I can't understand is why Israel would want to stick its fingers in the cookie jar when they probably could have gotten the cookie jar just for asking for it" (*Jerusalem Post*, 3/21/87). If Israel got the information overtly and legally, it would not be in a position to traffic with it without causing a breakdown in its relations with the United States.

43 Beit Hallahmi, *Israeli Connection*, 124; *Israel & Palestine*, November–Dececember 1987.

44 *Wall Street Journal*, 3/13/92.

CHAPTER 12

1 *The Economist*, 7/19/86, 8/9, 16/86. On the role of gold, see Keith Ovenend and Tony Cole, *Apartheid and International Finance*, London: Penguin, 1989, 164–76.

2 *The Economist*, 6/27/88.

3 Good works on diamonds include Timothy Green, *The World of Diamonds*, New York: Morrow, 1981; Epstein, *The Rise and Fall of Diamonds*; and Stefan Kanfer, *The Last Empire: De Beers, Diamonds and the World*, New York: Farrar, Straus & Giroux, 1993.

4 Epstein, *Rise and Fall*, 114–17.

5 For the early history, see R. B. Winder, "The Lebanese in West Africa," in L. A. Fallers (ed.), *Immigrants and Associations*, The Hague: Mouton, 1967.

6 See H. L. van der Laan, *The Sierra Leone Diamonds*, London: Oxford University Press, 1965; Peter Greenhalgh, *West African Diamonds: 1919–1983*, Manchester: Manchester University Press, 1985; William Reno, *Corruption and State Power in Sierra Leone*, Cambridge: Cambridge University Press, 1995. See also Wharton-Tigar's *Burning Bright*, Chapters 13 and 14.

7 The leader, "Flash Fred" Kamil, wrote his own account: Fred Kamil, *The Diamond Underworld*, London: Allan Lane, 1979. Later he was re-deployed to crack diamond-theft rings in the De Beers mines in Namibia and South Africa. When he left West Africa he worked in Europe for a private intelligence operation, which he elliptically described as "a sort of civilian subsidiary to NATO, operating in gray areas outside the law, concerned mainly with operations against communists and other subversive groups."

8 *Africa Confidential*, 4/25/79.

9 *Africa Confidential*, 11/28/84; Reno, *Corruption*, 132.

10 *Globe and Mail*, 7/14/84; *New York Times*, 10/24/87; *Africa Confidential*, 8/20/86.

11 *Africa Confidential*, 7/22/87.

12 *Jerusalem Post*, 1/3/89. On Israeli businesses in the "homelands," see *Ha'aretz*, 6/20/84, reprinted in *Al-Fajar*, 7/27/84; also *Ma'ariv*, 1/15/88.

13 It achieved infamy earlier for its role in the "Muldergate" scandal when South African intelligence attempted to purchase critical magazines to silence them (*Africa Confidential*, 6/24/87).

14 *Africa Confidential*, 9/17/86, 1/7/87; *Africa Analysis*, 6/12/87; *FBIS, Near East and South Asia*, 1/11/88; *Israeli Foreign Affairs*, October 1987.

15 *Israeli Foreign Affairs*, April 1988.

16 *Israeli Foreign Affairs*, February 1987. There were also hints of his involvement in smuggling prohibited German technology to the U.S.S.R. (*Africa Analysis*, 5/27/88).

17 The FBI claimed another $8 million worth were about to be negotiated. Kalmanovitch claimed to have sold Sierra Leone diamonds in London and accepted the cheques in good faith (*Jerusalem Post*, 10/2/87). On De Beers' possible role in the arrest, see *Africa Analysis*, 8/18/92.

18 *Africa Confidential*, 4/2/93; *Intelligence Newsletter*, 4/1/93. On the scramble for position after the fall of LIAT see *The Economist*, 12/5/87; *Africa Analysis*, 8/4, 18/89; *Africa Confidential*, 9/8/89; *West Africa*, 8/14/89; *The Globe* (Sierra Leone), 6/23/89; *Israeli Foreign Affairs*, 7/10/92.

19 Although exempt from sanctions, imports of gold and platinum attracted criticism. Japan, by 1987 South Africa's largest trading partner, promised to cut back. Its trade data afterwards claimed its gold and platinum came from Britain, which had no mines but did have the London Metals Exchange, where much of South Africa's gold and platinum was traded (*Financial Times*, 8/1/88).

20 *Observer*, 4/17/88.

21 *Ha'aretz*, 7/13/89; *Daily Dispatch*, 7/15/89.

22 *Guardian*, 8/25/87; *Labor Research*, February 1987.

23 *The Star* (Johannesburg), 12/17/86. Israel's commercial counsellor in Johannesburg denied the deal could be so used. But South African exports to Israel suddenly rose 70 per cent (*Business Day*, 12/11/86). Moreover, the South African Ministry of Trade and Industry told exporters in an official bulletin that Israel was available as a base for duty-free exports to the United States (Jane Hunter, *Israeli Foreign Policy: South Africa and Central America*, Boston: South End Press, 1987, 65). Israel Shahak, head of the Israeli League for Human Rights at the time, concurred that goods would be imported and "Made in Israel" stickers put on them (Israel Shahak, *Israel's Global Role: Weapons for Repression*, Belmont, Mass.: Association of Arab-American University Graduates, 1982, 27).

24 *Jerusalem Post*, 12/25/86.

25 *Jerusalem Post*, 11/17/86.

26 *Labor Research*, February 1987.

27 Land held by the Jewish National Fund was considered the inalienable property of the "Jewish people" and could not be transferred to a non-Jew (Alfred Lilienthal, *The Zionist Connection*, New York: Dodd, Mead, 1978, 117, 127). Recently title passed to the State of Israel, but the same rules apply.

28 Ostensibly Israel agreed to end its military contracts. In fact, it merely agreed not to sign any new ones, but insisted it would honour those outstanding, the most important of which had many more years to run (*Washington Post*, 1/22/87; *Jerusalem Post*, 1/27/87; *Washington Jewish Week*, 6/18/87).

29 *Washington Post*, 9/17, 20/87; Steven Mufson, "South African Jews," *Tikkun* 3, No. 1, 1988; *Jerusalem Post*, 4/25/88; *Financial Times*, 11/11/91. One of the most honest critics of the Israeli policy, the late Rabbi Meir Kahane, attacked Israel for its token condemnation of apartheid while it continued to accept money from South African Jews. He noted, "Racism is fine as long as it comes packaged with money" (*Middle East Times*, 6/25/88).

30 *Jeune Afrique*, 2/1/89; *Africa Report*, January–February 1989. See Alexander Yeats, "On the Accuracy of Economic Observations: Do Sub-Saharan Trade Statistics Mean Anything?" *World Bank Economic Review* 4, No. 2, 1990. See also Robert Klitgaard, *Tropical Gangsters*, New York: Basic Books, 1990, on the state of some sub-Saharan African financial administrations.

31 *The Economist*, 7/26/86; *Financial Times*, 12/15/88.

32 *Christian Science Monitor*, 6/20/88; Hengeveld and Rodenburg, *Embargo*, 272–73.

33 *Africa Confidential*, 10/1/86, 7/27/88, 4/28/89, 4/15/87.

34 *Times of London*, 2/2/93; *Jeune Afrique*, 12/18/89; *Daily Nation* (Nairobi), 12/11/89; Roger Faligot and Pascal Krop, *La Piscine: Les Services Secrets Français 1944–1984*, Paris: Editions du Seuil, 1985, Chapter 10; Mockler, *The Mercenaries*, passim. John Stockwell, *In Search of Enemies: A CIA Story*, New York: W. W. Norton, 1978, 219–22.

35 *Afrique-Asie*, 5/29/78, 6/12/78.

36 The murder charges were pressed by relatives of those killed in his 1977 Benin coup (*Independent*, 2/23/92; *Jeune Afrique*, 3/26/92).

37 South Africa took over from French intelligence (*Africa Confidential*, 10/6/82, 1/22/88).

38 The best overview is by Joseph Hanlon, *Beggar Your Neighbor: Apartheid and Political Power in Southern Africa*, Bloomington: Indiana University Press, 1986. See also *Jeune Afrique*, 10/5/88, 12/11, 18/89; *Le Monde*, 11/28, 29/89; *Africa Analysis*, 3/4/88; *Sunday Telegraph*, 11/5/87.

39 For a general overview see Alex Vines, *RENAMO: Terrorism in Mozambique*, Bloomington: Indiana University Press, 1991; and Mota Lopes, "The MNR: Opponents or Bandits," *Africa Report*, January–February 1986. See also *Toronto Star*, 9/6/87; *Montreal Gazette* 4/21/88; *Financial Times*, 8/8/92; *Africa Confidential*, 3/18/87, 6/19/92; *New African*, September 1987; *Wall Street Journal*, 4/15/87; *Financial Times*, 8/15/88; *New York Times*, 2/21/89.

40 Hanlan, *Beggar Your Neighbor*, 192.

41 On the early history of the Angolan operation, see Stockwell's *In Search of Enemies*, Chapters 2–4.

42 *Le Monde Diplomatique*, October 1986; *New York Times*, 3/27/87; *South*, June 1987.

43 *New York Times*, 1/14/85. Each time the mine was repaired and reopened, another raid wrecked it.

44 *Wall Street Journal*, 11/13/85.

45 Economist Intelligence Unit, *Angola*, 1976, 10.

46 When a large smuggling ring was cracked in 1984, the government put the loss over two years at about $140 million. The prosecution claimed two of the accused were working for the CIA, while one of the accused insisted that senior members of the governing party were involved (*Wall Street Journal*, 9/25/84; *Africa Confidential*, 7/18/84).

47 *Africa Confidential*, 3/12/86; *Africa Report*, September 1986; *New York Times*, 1/7/85.

48 *Africa Confidential*, 2/12/86. De Beers vehemently denied that it "knowingly" bought diamonds from UNITA. But the De Beers policy was to have its field offices buy all diamonds offered, no questions asked, and it was perfectly aware of who controlled the illegal diggings.

49 Economist Intelligence Unit, *Angola*, 1978, 13; *Africa Confidential*, 2/14/79, 5/25/83.

50 First the MPLA discovered piles of counterfeit Portuguese escudos. When the government decided to issue a new currency, the kwanza, counterfeit started arriving from France (*Africa Confidential*, 6/6/79).

51 RENAMO used the notes turned out by supporters in Johannesburg to buy ivory (along with rhino horn, diamonds and emeralds) (BBC *Summary of World Broadcasting*, 3/18/85; *Washington Post*, 3/17/85).

52 *Geopolitical Drug Dispatch*, May 1998.

53 This traffic began at least as early as 1978, when UNITA's Paris office started selling diamonds, gold, sapphires and ivory (Economist Intelligence Unit, *Angola*, July 1978).

54 Republic of South Africa, Commission of Enquiry into the Alleged Smuggling of and Illegal Trade in Ivory and Rhinosaurus Horn in South Africa, *Report*, 1996. Though full of details about UNITA, the commission report insisted it could find no proof of similar activities on behalf of RENAMO. Others disagreed. It seems strange that South Africa would refuse to RENAMO a service it was providing to UNITA.

55 Park staff also arbitrarily classified elephants as problem animals, then killed them to sell the ivory (*Jeune Afrique*, 3/26/92).

56 *Daily Telegraph*, 5/15/89. The senior Zimbabwe investigator who tried to expose the army's role was murdered, along with several park rangers. RENAMO for a time also used a training camp inside South Africa's Kruger National Park, ironically the same camp the park authorities used for training anti-poaching units.

57 *Times*, 2/23/92, *Mail on Sunday*, 2/9/92. One of the largest ivory traders in South Africa was a Greek émigré expelled from Zambia for drug trafficking. Once in South Africa, he avoided a similar fate when an order for his deportation from the minister of law and order was overruled by the home affairs minister, who stated that it was not in the public interest for the country to lose such an outstanding citizen. His civic accomplishments also included running a Johannesburg hotel that doubled as the city's largest black brothel and a safe house for the wing of South African police intelligence that ran death squads against anti-regime activists (*Independent*, 2/23/92; *Jeune Afrique*, 3/26/92).

58 *New York Times*, 5/28/89; *Africa Confidential*, 10/6/89; Vines, *RENAMO*, 89. After the regime fell, the former defence minister admitted that the contraband route had been opened by South African military intelligence with his express permission in 1980 (*Glasgow Herald*, 3/2/95; *Independent*, 1/19/96; *Washington Times*, 1/18/96).

59 Hanlon, *Beggar Your Neighbor*, 69; O'Meara, *Review of Government Measures*, 92–93.

60 *The Nation*, 6/4/88.

61 Western banks refusing the South African government more loans were happy to finance trade in and out of the country; the excuse was that trade credits are strictly short-term financing for private sector deals. In fact, some were for as long as five years and involved financing imports and exports by state-run companies (*Weekly Mail*, 8/30/88).

62 I am indebted to Jonathan Nitzan for this insight. See his "Israel and South Africa: The Prospects for Their Transitions," *Emerging Markets Analyst*. 4, No. 10, 1996.

63 Thomas Karis, "Revolution in the Making: Black Politics in South Africa," *Foreign Affairs*, Winter 1983–84.

64 *The Economist*, 9/6/86; *New York Times*, 6/15/86, 2/22/88; *Africa Report*, March–April 1986, November–December 1987. I am indebted to Paul Cunningham for some of these points.

65 The details of apartheid-era front companies, from pharmaceutical labs to investment groups, travel agencies and building societies, emerged in the deliberations of the Truth and Reconciliation Commission. See the joint report of *South African Press Association Agence France Presse*, 7/7/98.

CHAPTER 13

1 Actually, Fidel stopped smoking several years ago, but this has not improved American dispositions. On the early response to Fidel's regime, see Taylor Branch and George Crile III, "The Kennedy Vendetta: How the CIA Waged a Silent War against Cuba," *Harper's*, August 1975. In fact, the CIA could think of no way Castro's regime adversely affected U.S. national security. The main motive for the Kennedy clan's vendetta was explained by one former senior agent thus: "I guess they felt they had to go after it and show their manhood. I have no plausible explanation other than that" (Seymour Hersh, *The Dark Side of Camelot*, New York: Little, Brown, 1997, 284).

2 Messick, *Lansky*, 68; Robert Lacey, *Little Man: Meyer Lansky and the Gangster Life*, Boston: Little, Brown, 1991, 79–80.

3 In his earlier time in office Batista had briefly considered legalizing the Communist party. Apparently the mob boss Meyer Lansky, on behalf of the U.S. government, carried the message that he should seriously reconsider. In his second term, Batista harboured no such plans (see Dennis Eisenberg, Uri Dan and Eli Landau, *Meyer Lansky: Mogul of the Mob*, London: Paddington, 1979).

4 Alfred Freid, *The Rise and Fall of the Jewish Gangster in America*, New York: Holt, Rinehart & Winston, 1980, 257–59; Catherine Wismer, *Sweethearts*, Toronto: Lorimer, 1980, 55.

5 Ernest Volkman and Blaine Baggett (*Secret Intelligence: The Inside Story of America's Espionage Empire*, New York: Doubleday, 1989, 124) state that the victorious revolutionaries quickly sent a flying squad to the casinos. They arrived too late — the safes had already been emptied. By contrast, Wismer (*Sweethearts*, 104) states they managed to grab $17 million that was on the point of being shipped off to Switzerland.

6 For some of the effects of the Cuban diaspora, see Robert Sherrill, "Can Miami Save Itself?" *New York Times Magazine*, 7/18/87.

7 An alarmed U.S. State Department ventured the opinion that "whoever supplies petroleum to Cuba in a sense controls Cuba or makes it highly dependent" (Engler, *Brotherhood of Oil*, 107).

8 Lacey, *Little Man*, 259.

9 *Sunday Times*, 5/17/92.

10 There is a partial survey in Adler-Karlson, *Western Economic Warfare*, Chapter 17; and Donald Losman, *International Economic Sanctions*, Albuquerque: University of New Mexico Press, 1979, Chapter 3.

11 The best treatment of U.S. anti-Castro policy in the early years is by Warren Hinckle and William Turner, *The Fish Is Red: The Story of the Secret War Against Castro*, New York: Harper & Row, 1981, recently updated and reissued as *Deadly Secrets*, New York: Thunder's Mouth Press, 1992. See also Thomas Powers, *The Man Who Kept the Secrets: Richard Helms and the CIA*, New York: Pocket Books, 1979, 171–81, and David Corn, *Blond Ghost: Ted Shackley and the CIA's Crusades*, New York: Simon & Schuster, 1994, Chapter 4.

12 Victor Marchetti and John Marks, *The CIA and the Cult of Intelligence*, New York: Dell, 1974, 147.

13 The weapon also had a later career, in the hands of anti-Duvalier Haitian exiles.

14 According to Knightley (*Second Oldest Profession*, 328–29), the broker worked through floor traders to give the impression of a general selling wave. Prices did fall, but they had formerly been inflated by bad weather and storm damage. There was no evidence the short sales contributed anything. Still, the CIA apparently thought it was a great coup, well worth the million dollars it cost them. So, it seems, did the KGB who (perhaps accidentally) used the same broker to secretly unload for hard currency some of the sugar the Soviet Union had bought from Cuba for roubles. A slightly different version of the sugar escapade — the CIA buying sugar on the spot market and then dumping it in a foreign country to drive down the price — is given by ex-CIA officer Marchetti and Marks, *The CIA*, 72.

15 These problems are explained by Morris Morley, *Imperial State and Revolution: The United States and Cuba, 1952–1986*, Cambridge: Cambridge University Press, 1987, especially Appendix 1.

16 Hinckle and Turner, *Deadly Secrets*, 197–202.

17 Thus the *Rex*, one of its gun-boats, nominally ended up the property of a firm that specialized in fuelling and outfitting cruise ships. That firm leased the *Rex* back to another company with a secret CIA connection. Dockage fees were paid by yet another shell company, and the crew, recruited at the behest of the CIA by exiled officials of the pre-Revolutionary Cuban government, were paid by cheques written on the accounts of a commercial fisheries firm whose officers agreed to cooperate with the "secret war" (Hinckle and Turner, *Deadly Secrets*, 153–54).

18 Powers, *Man Who Kept the Secrets*, 187; Volkman and Baggett, *Secret Intelligence*, 125; Sam Giancana and Chuck Giancana, *Double Cross*, New York: Warner Books, 1992, 344. The mobsters also helped fund the rise of the anti-Castro Cuban exile lobby. See John Davis, *Mafia Kingfish: Carlos Marcello and the Assassination of John F. Kennedy*, New York: McGraw-

Hill, 1989. The actual mob contract to kill Castro was let before the Bay of Pigs, and the CIA just bought into the existing plans. Some of these appear to have been con jobs in which the mobsters took the money, sold off the weapons and poured the poisons the CIA gave them down the sink. See Desmaris, *Last Mafioso*, 233–38.

19 According to the mob boss Sam Giancana (as told by his son and brother), prior to the Revolution the gangs ran $100 million worth of drugs from Cuba into the United States, from which the CIA collected 10 per cent to top up its black treasury held in secret accounts in Panama, Switzerland, the Bahamas, etc. (Giancana, *Double Cross*, 334). That story is certain to be a complete fabrication. Still, Sam Giancana managed to use the alleged CIA link to keep the FBI at bay, while bragging about the existence of all kinds of mob–CIA joint ventures around the world. Sam Giancana also claimed that, at a time when the CIA was officially backing the Batista government, the mob, with CIA knowledge, ran guns to Castro in the hopes of winning his backing for their continued operations in the event he won. That seems more credible.

20 This defence was also used successfully to beat raps for smuggling arms to the IRA. See Jack Holland, *The American Connection: US Guns, Money & Influence in Northern Ireland*, New York: Penguin, 1987, 102–8.

21 *New York Times*, 12/29/84; M. C. Finn, *The Complete Book of International Smuggling*, Boulder, Colo.: Palladin Press, 1983, 83, 138. The author claims to be a former CIA operations officer.

22 One of the most notorious examples was Castle Bank & Trust of the Bahamas. Set up in 1964 by the former OSS director of special services for China, a man who, in subsequent "private" life during the early 1950s, ran a maritime agency funnelling American weaponry to support Taiwan in its confrontation with the People's Republic of China, Castle Bank became the target of what the United States Internal Revenue Service billed as the greatest tax evasion investigation in its history. A black bag job had turned up a list of 300 wealthy American depositors, ranging from Hollywood stars to prominent mobsters, from rock band legends to political bagmen. But the bank was also handling CIA money to support the continued guerrilla actions against Cuba. And when the CIA caught wind of the IRS probe, it intrigued to have the investigation shut down. The story was first broken in the *Wall Street Journal*, 4/18/80. The most comprehensive account is by Alan Block, *Masters of Paradise: Organized Crime and the Internal Revenue Service in the Bahamas*, New Brunswick, N.J.: Transaction Publishers, 1991.

23 See Felix Rodriguez and John Weisman, *Shadow Warrior*, New York; Pocket Books, 1990, 53. Rodriguez's own initial training was financed by one of the wealthy exiles.

24 This was noted with remarkable prescience about its long-term effects by Hinckle and Turner, *The Fish Is Red*, 282 et passim.

25 "Informational Letter on Contemporary Cuban-American Relations," Embassy of the U.S.S.R. to the Republic of Cuba, 4/26/79.

26 I am indebted to Kirsten Crain for research on the topic of Cuban sanctions-busting.

27 *New York Times*, 6/5/85.

28 "Report on Cuba," *NACLA Report on the Americas* 29, No. 2, September–October 1995.

29 Hinckle and Warren, *Deadly Secrets*, 350.

30 Donna Rich, "Embargo Economics Keeping Cuba at Bay," *Multinational Monitor* 10. No. 4, April 1989; *Envío* 11, Nos. 126–27, January–February 1992. To combat this, the Reagan administration demanded that companies of any nationality exporting nickel products to the United States certify their products contained no Cuban nickel on pain of being blacklisted.

31 I am indebted to Sara May for research into the Cuban cigar smuggling business.

32 In 1996 a Cohiba that cost $3 in Havana would sell for $25 in Miami and $50 in New York (*Reuters World Service*, 12/30/96).

33 For example, the trademark war with Davidoff International of Switzerland (*Latin America Regional Report — Caribbean*, 5/17/90).

34 *New York Times*, 4/10/96; *The Economist*, 3/15/97.

35 One version of his story, highlighting the apparent size of his fraudulent operations, is by Robert Hutchison, *Vesco*, New York: Avon, 1974. The more recent work by Arthur Herzog, also called *Vesco*, New York: Doubleday, 1987, suggests that the earlier stories are greatly exaggerated. See also Lester A. Sobel (ed.), *Corruption in Business*, New York: Facts on File, 1977, 163–66; *Fortune*, 7/10/95, and *New York Times*, 6/23/95.

36 Coram, *Caribbean Time Bomb*, 78–79; Erwin Strauss, *How to Start Your Own Country*, Port Townsend, Wash.: Loompanics, 1984, 56–57; Herzog, *Vesco*, 333; *Montreal Gazette*, 7/8/89.

37 Herzog, *Vesco*, 335–38; *International Herald Tribune*, 11/16/83; *New York Times*, 11/15/83, 5/10/84; *Forbes*, 9/24/84.

38 *Globe and Mail*, 5/7/92.

39 *FBIS-LAT-92-222*, 11/17/92.

40 United States Senate, *The Cuban Government's Involvement in Facilitating International Drug Trafficking*, April 30, 1983; *New York Times*, 4/4/83; *Christian Science Monitor*, 11/10/83; *Wall Street Journal*, 4/30/84, 7/25/89.

41 *New York Times*, 6/11/95; *Sunday Times*, 4/24/95, 6/11/95. Vesco's links to drug trafficking have never been proven beyond the fact that he once tried to persuade Colombian drug-lord Carlos Lehder Rivas to allow Vesco to manage his money. They knew each other because they both owned small islands close to each other in the Bahamas chain. Allegations against Vesco for drugs appear to have been invented by United States law enforcement as a means of pressuring his various host countries into extraditing him.

42 There was a massive amount of press coverage of the events. See, for example, *Latin American Regional Reports — Caribbean*, 7/20/89; *Latin America Weekly Report*, 7/3/89, 8/24/89, 11/8/90; *Wall Street Journal*, 6/29/89, 8/25/89; *Financial Times*, 7/11, 22/89. The most comprehensive account from the Cuban side is n.a., *Affaire 1/1989: Fin de la filière cubaine*, Havana: Editions Jose Marti, 1989.

43 *National Review*, 7/31/95.

44 Economist Intelligence Unit, *Angola*, 1976, 10.

45 This aspect of Cuban socialism is analyzed by Medea Benjamin, Joseph Collins and Michael Scott, *No Free Lunch: Food and Revolution in Cuba Today*, San Francisco: Institute for Food and Development Policy, 1984.

46 A general survey is by Jorge F. Perez-Lopez, *Cuba's Second Economy*, New Brunswick, N.J.: Transaction Publishers, 1995.

47 When a U.S. cruise ship operator bought an Italian firm, one casualty was a highly successful cruise-ship joint venture the Italian firm had previously run with the Cuban government tourist department (*Financial Times*, 11/28/97).

48 *The Nation*, 11/7/94.

49 *New York Times*, 7/30/93; *Hispanic Link News Service*, 7/9/95; *Miami Herald*, 4/17/97. Supposedly this tightening followed Cuba's shooting down two aircraft sent as a provocation by exiles, though in fact pressure on Clinton had been building for some time.

50 At one point the police hauled them back to their home villages and informed parents about the "office jobs" their daughters had landed in Havana. The hope was that this would shame them into desisting. But by the next day they were back on the street. Thanks to Varouj Pogharian for this observation.

51 *FBIS-LAT-93-118*, 6/22/93; *FBIS-LAT-94-041*, 3/2/94; *FBIS-LAT-95-031*, 2/15/95; *Wall Street Journal*, 7/9/93; *New York Times*, 9/26/94.

52 *Forbes*, 2/28/94; *New York Times*, 9/23/94.

53 *Forbes*, 9/11/95; Douglas Payne, "Life in Castro's Mafia State," *Society*, January–February 1996.

54 *FBIS-LAT-93-213*, 11/5/93.

55 One particular target was Toronto-based Sherrit Inc., which engaged in joint ventures in nickel mining with the Cuban government (*Maclean's*, 6/26/95).

56 *Money Laundering Alert*, October 1996.

57 *Globe and Mail*, 7/22/97.

CHAPTER 14

1 For an overview see Lawrence Birn (ed.), *The End of Chilean Democracy*, New York: Seabury Press, 1973, in particular the contributions by Tad Szulc and Joseph Collins. See also James Petras and Morris Morley, *How Allende Fell*, Nottingham: Spokesman Books, 1974. The economic war followed the contours of a plan first suggested not by U.S. intelligence but by the multinational communications company ITT, whose local assets had been expropriated by the new government. ITT called for official loan restrictions, private bank cut-offs, spare parts embargoes, deferral of U.S. purchases of Chilean copper, and setting off runs on banks to cause a financial panic, drive up interest rates, curtail investment and push up the unemployment rate.

2 For an uncritical view that imputes everything to an American plot, see Samuel Charkin, *The Murder of Chile*, New York: Everest House, 1973. Robert Alexander, *The Tragedy of Chile*, Newport, Conn.: Greenwood Press, 1978, insists that such accusations were greatly exaggerated. On the other hand, Edy Kaufman, *Crisis in Allende's Chile: New Perspectives*, New York: Praeger, 1988, supports the more traditional view.

3 *Israeli Foreign Affairs*, December 1984; *Times of the Americas*, 8/12/87.

4 There is still much about Banco Ambrosiano's Nicaraguan activities that remains shrouded in mystery, not least because, once Somoza was overthrown, it quickly established close relations with members of the new revolutionary government. When the author in 1984 asked figures in that government for clarification, the result was a series of evasions. For a summary, see Naylor, *Hot Money*, 86–87.

5 Eduardo Crawley, *Dictators Never Die*, New York: St. Martin's Press, 1979, 96–97, 142, 167 et passim. See also *Time*, 8/6/79.

6 *Sunday Times*, 4/26/87.

7 A thorough account is by Holly Sklar, *Washington's War on Nicaragua*, Boston: South End Press, 1988.

8 These issues are discussed in Beverly May Carl's "The Nicaraguan Economic System," *America*, 2/ 21/87. However, note the dissenting view of the vice-president of Nicaragua's Superior Council of Private Enterprise (*Time*, 5/27/85).

9 Though prompted by Nicaragua, this became part of a general policy — spelled out in a confidential memorandum from the administration to the State Department — that in the future all U.S.–funded loans through international financial institutions were to be seen in political rather than economic terms (*Toronto Star*, 7/19/87).

10 *New York Times*, 8/12/83.

11 Persico, *Casey*, 364; *US News & World Report*, 12/2/85. See also Magda Henriquez, "Economic Aggression: A Policy of State Terrorism" in Marlene Dixon (ed.), *On Trial: Reagan's War Against Nicaragua*, San Francisco: Synthesis Publications, 1985.

12 Roy Gutman, *Banana Diplomacy: The Making of American Policy in Nicaragua 1981–1987*, New York: Simon & Schuster, 1988, 287; Christopher Dickey, *With the Contras*, New York: Simon & Schuster, 1985, 106; *The Economist*, 6/29/85; *World Press Review*, July 1987.

13 *Financial Post*, 8/2/89; *Envío* 8, No. 95, June 1989; *The Economist*, 8/23/86; *Miami Herald*, 6/11/87; *Washington Post*, 4/3/90.

14 Dickey, *With the Contras*, 82–83, 118; *New York Times*, 7/22, 24/87; *Miami Herald*, 1/23/87; *Wall Street Journal*, 1/16/87. The support personnel also included convicted drug dealers and someone who had blown up a civilian passenger jet and killed seventy-three people.

15 *Observer*, 6/19/88; *Financial Times*, 11/12/87; *The Nation*, 10/7/91.

16 *The Nation*, 8/29/87; *Miami Herald*, 7/12/87; *New York Times*, 4/22/87, 8/15/87. The growth of an "off-the-books" military capacity in the United States during the 1980s is examined in Steven Emerson, *Secret Warriors: Inside the Covert Military Operations of the Reagan Era*, New York: Putnam, 1988.

17 *Wall Street Journal*, 5/11/87; *Far Eastern Economic Review*, 3/19/87.

18 Emerson, *Secret Warriors*, 122–23.

19 *The Nation*, 9/12/87. The Saudi–South African diversion was plausible, but never proven conclusively.

20 *Latin America Weekly Report*, 6/21/85; *Washington Post*, 3/1/87, 5/1/87; *New York Times*, 5/3, 7, 23/87; *Wall Street Journal*, 5/7/87, 8/6/87; *Financial Times*, 5/15/87; *Miami Herald*, 5/5/87.

21 See, for example, U.S. House of Representatives Select Committee to Investigate Covert Arms Transactions with Iran and U.S. Senate Select Committee on Secret Military Assistance to Iran and the Nicaraguan Opposition, *The Iran-Contra Affair*, Washington: November 1987.

22 See Peter Brewton, *The Mafia, CIA and George Bush: The Untold Story of America's Greatest Financial Debacle*, New York: Spi Books, 1992. Unfortunately, the book is a mass of undigested facts.

23 *Washington Post*, 5/2/87. There was only one taker for the bonds, who was repaid as soon as aid from Saudi Arabia became available.

24 *Miami Herald*, 5/20/87.

25 One of the more interesting sets of claims along these lines is by DEA veteran Celerino Castillo III (and David Harmon) in *Powderburns: Cocaine, Contras and the Drug War*, Oakville, Ont.: Sundial, 1994.

26 *San Francisco Examiner*, 3/16/86.

27 The literature dealing with the relationship of the contras to drug trafficking is enormous. See, for example, Peter Dale Scott and Jonathan Marshall, *Cocaine Politics*, Berkeley: University of California Press, 1991; U.S. Senate, Committee on Foreign Relations, Subcommittee on Terrorism, Narcotics and International Operations, *Drugs, Law Enforcement and Foreign Policy*, Washington: December 1988. That the drugs-contras link was well known to U.S. intelligence was confirmed a decade later by internal CIA investigations (*New York Times*, 7/17/98).

28 *New York Times*, 4/8/87.

29 *New York Times*, 6/21/86, 5/21, 26/87; *Miami Herald*, 5/4/86, 5/20/87; *Washington Post*, 5/7/87; *Wall Street Journal*, 6/8/87.

30 *Milwaukee Journal*, 1/19/87.

31 On WACL see Scott and Jon Lee Anderson, *Inside the League*, New York: Dodd, Mead, 1986.

32 *Miami Herald*, 6/11/87; *The Nation*, 6/6/87; *New York Times*, 5/22/87.

33 On Secord's alleged (though never proven) involvement, see especially Peter Maas, *Manhunt: The Incredible Pursuit of a CIA Agent Turned Terrorist*, New York: Random House, 1986.

34 See for example, *Der Spiegel*, 11/17/89, 12/18/89; *Geopolitical Drug Dispatch*, July, August 1993, September 1993, September 1995.

35 Secord's syndicate sent the *Erria* to pick up the load. Next stop was Portugal, where the cargo was topped up with 200 tons from Defex, a Portuguese "private" arms-dealing firm that seems to have acted as cut-out for Portuguese government operations, and which figured regularly on the supplier lists in U.S. covert operations during the 1980s. Just as the ship was about to set off for Central America, the contras ran into a cash-flow crisis. With the order cancelled, the weapons were dumped in the French port of Cherbourg and the *Erria* sailed away looking for business elsewhere. Once the congressional ban on official aid to the contras was lifted, the CIA, working through yet another "private" arms dealer, bought the arms, shipped them to a CIA warehouse in North Carolina, and eventually moved them to Central America (*Wall Street Journal*, 6/11/87).

36 *Miami Herald*, 4/20/87; *Observer*, 3/8/87, 4/5/87, 5/10/87, 7/26/87; *Wall Street Journal*, 2/13/87; *San Francisco Examiner*, 11/24/87; *Sunday Times*, 3/29/87.

37 *Miami Herald*, 5/29/87; *New York Times*, 5/26/87.

38 See, for example, *New York Times*, 6/21/86, 4/25/87, 5/21, 26/87; *Washington Post*, 5/7/87; *Wall Street Journal*, 6/8/87.

39 *Wall Street Journal*, 8/4/87.

40 Sklar, *Washington's War*, 125, 134, 151. *New York Times*, 9/24/87.

41 *Financial Times*, 10/8/88, 7/19/89. At one point they tried, without much success, to out-bid the government for the annual coffee crop. The theory was that they would collect the reward in the form of public goodwill, deny the government foreign exchange, and earn profits for their own cause (*Wall Street Journal*, 1/21/86).

42 *Wall Street Journal*, 3/6/85; Sklar, *Washington's War*, 150–51, 165; Persico, *Casey*, 365. This was one incident that, figuratively speaking, blew up in the administration's face. Outrage over the mining of the harbour in 1984 was a major factor leading to the congressional cut-off of funding for the contra war.

43 Future CIA chief Robert Gates claimed that the manual advising on how to commit mur-der, blackmail and terrorism was "the product of incompetence not of malign intentions" (*From the Shadows*, 311).

44 Sklar, *Washington's War*, 183–84.

45 *Financial Times*, 12/8/87.

46 *NACLA Report on the Americas* 20, No. 2, April–May 1986. See also *Newsweek*, 8/25/86, 6/22/87.

47 For a review of other countries' experiences with currency exchanges, see R. T. Naylor, "From Underworld to Underground: Enterprise Crime, 'Informal' Business and the Public Policy Response," *Crime, Law & Social Change* 24, 1996, 105–12.

48 *Envío* 7, No. 82, May 1988.

49 *Sunday Times*, 9/8/87; *Financial Times*, 9/6/88.

50 Note the contrary opinion of Gary Hufbauer and Jeffrey Schott, authors of the major survey of sanctions cited above, to the effect that the U.S. sanctions against Nicaragua were too little, too late (*Christian Science Monitor*, 5/28/85). This reflects their failure to adequately factor in the impact of covert economic war, and their insistence on taking the publicly an-nounced goals of a sanctions program to be the real ones.

51 *New York Times*, 6/15, 24/89; *Latin America Weekly Report*, 2/16/89.

CHAPTER 15

1 Technically, a new national currency, the balboa, was created to replace the Colombian peso. In fact, the balboa was fixed at parity to the dollar, the government was allowed to mint coins but no bills, and the U.S. dollar circulated freely (Mario Hernandez, "Financial System of Panama" in Robert Effros (ed)], *Emerging Financial Centers: Legal and Insitutional Frame-work*, Washington: International Monetary Fund, 1982).

2 For a survey of the "service" economy, see Stan Duncan, "The Spoils of War," *Dollars & Sense*, December 1990, though some of its assertions about Noriega and drug trafficking should be discounted.

3 See John Dingues, *Our Man in Panama*, New York: Random House, 1991; Frederick Kempe, *Divorcing the Dictator*, New York: Putnam, 1990; and Luis Murillo, *The Noriega Mess: The Drugs, the Canal and Why America Invaded*, Berkeley: Video-Books, 1995. Written by someone with inside information and a thorough knowledge of the country's history, the last book is flawed by a tendency to give credence to all anti-Noriega stories, and by downplaying the white-mestizo split. But it is an enormous compendium of information.

4 While American vessels preferred Liberia, European and Asian ships registered in Panama in sufficient numbers to generate, by the mid-1980s, $40 million in fees annually to the gov-ernment plus another $50 million for subsidiary service industries.

5 Gerhard Kurtz, *218 Tax Havens*, Hong Kong: 1995, 126–27.

6 *Wall Street Journal*, 8/5/85, 4/22/86, 1/8/87.

7 *Miami Herald*, 6/11/87.

8 R. M. Koster and Guillermo Sanchez, *In the Time of the Tyrants, Panama: 1968–1990*, New York: W. W. Norton, 1990, 61.

9 Koster and Sanchez, *Tyrants*, 124.

10 Murillo, *Noriega Mess*, 39, 54, 71, 78, 90; Koster and Sanchez, *Tyrants*, 124.

11 This is best described in Evert Clark and Nicholas Horrock, *Contrabandista*, New York: Praeger, 1973.

12 *Wall Street Journal*, 3/6/90; Koster and Sanchez, *Tyrants*, 296–97; Murillo, *Noriega Mess*, 141, 414, 566.

13 *Wall Street Journal*, 3/6/90; Dingues, *Our Man in Panama*, 116–17; Murillo, *Noriega Mess*, 142.

14 Murillo, *Noriega Mess*, 51, 276.

15 When the Panamanian company called Caz y Pesca, set up to buy weapons for the Sandinistas in Miami, got busted by U.S. Customs, back-room dealing culminated in Panama's receiving nothing more than a public rebuke for failing to get a proper end-user certificate, although Panama also made sure that in the future foreign arms purchases would be sourced in Europe (Kempe, *Divorcing the Dictator*, 97).

16 *The Washington Report on Middle Eastern Affairs*, February 1990; *Financial Times*, 5/5/88.

17 *Washington Jewish Week*, 5/18/89; *Ha'aretz*, 1/12/90; *The Washington Report on Middle Eastern Affairs*, February 1990.

18 One of the Sephardic leaders described the newcomers' business methods. "The Israelis working here," he said, "have practically gained control of the Central Avenue business district. They are engaged in contraband and money laundering. They are here to make a lot of money and get out." (*Washington Jewish Week*, 28/12/89.) On their illicit trading practices see also *Yediot Aharonot*, 12/1/90. However, that was standard operating practice of merchants in league with Guards officers, and hardly an innovation of the Israelis (Murillo, *Noriega Mess*, 250).

19 Green, *Taking Sides*, 57; Slater, *The Pledge*, 223.

20 *Middle East International*, 5/14/88.

21 *Financial Times*, 1/8/90.

22 *Wall Street Journal*, 3/7/90.

23 *Hadashot*, 1/12/90; *U.S. News & World Report*, 5/2/88; *Israeli Foreign Affairs*, May, June 1988; *Middle East International*, 1/19/90; *Guardian*, 12/30/89; *San Francisco Examiner*, 12/31/89; *U.S. News & World Report*, 5/2/88; *In These Times*, 6/8/88; *Miami Herald*, 1/19/88.

24 *Sunday Times*, 5/29/88, *Wall Street Journal*, 10/18/89.

25 United States Senate, Committee on Governmental Affairs, Permanent Subcommittee on Investigations, *Drugs and Money Laundering in Panama*, Washington: 1/28/88.

26 United States Senate, Committee on Governmental Affairs, Permanent Subcommittee on Investigations, *Drugs and Money Laundering in Panama*, Washington: 2/11/88.

27 Thanks to Darcy Crowe for this information.

28 There are conflicting versions of the story of the *Pia Vesta*. By some accounts the Peruvian Navy really intended to buy the weapons, by others it was merely acting as a front for the contras, in others it was agent for a drug trafficker's militia! It has also been claimed that the weapons never arrived in Peru because the navy, which had acted without the assent of the president, got cold feet and cancelled the deal. It was supposedly at this point that Casey intervened and arranged for Secord to buy the arms. See variously *New York Times*, 6/14/86; *Miami Herald*, 5/10, 14/87; *Latin America Weekly Report*, 5/7/87; *Newsweek*, 2/15/88; Murillo, *Noriega Mess*, 551–53.

29 *New York Times*, 6/12/86.

30 Koster and Sanchez, *Tyrants*, 323.

31 *Latin America Weekly Review*, 7/31/86.

32 *Financial Times*, 4/7/88; Murillo, *Noriega Mess*, 614; *New York Times*, 6/19/87, 8/10/87; *Latin America Weekly Report*, 6/18, 25/87.

33 *Journal of Commerce*, 3/14/88; *Wall Street Journal*, 3/24/88. SouthCom was already slated to move, and the strategic significance of Panama to the American navy had been negligible since the 1960s, when the navy adopted the strategy of grouping task forces around aircraft carriers, which are far too large to squeeze through the Panama Canal.

34 *Financial Times*, 7/28/87; *Wall Street Journal*, 5/2/88, 12/8/89; *New York Times*, 2/8/88, 2/11/89.

35 *New York Times*, 3/12/88.

36 *Globe and Mail*, 7/6/88; *New York Times*, 6/6/88; Murillo, *Noriega Mess*, 691.

37 Kempe, *Divorcing the Dictator*, 271–72.

38 *New York Times*, 4/26/88; Murillo, *Noriega Mess*, 614, 659–60.

39 Adams and Krantz, *Full Service Bank*, 82–83, 158.

40 *Wall Street Journal*, 2/8/88.

41 *New York Times*, 2/13/90. The charges were later dropped for insufficient evidence.

42 There is still controversy over precisely what happened. Some accounts blame the burning of the El Chorrillo slum neighbourhood, close to Noriega's headquarters, on the U.S. invaders, while others insist that Noriega himself ordered it torched as an act of revenge. On the looting, see *Yediot Aharonot*, 1/12/90; *Ha'aretz*, 1/12/90; *Washington Report on Middle East Affairs*, 2/90; Murillo, *Noriega Mess*, 794.

43 *The Nation*, 12/2/91.

CHAPTER 16

1 An excellent survey of the political history is Sandra MacKey, *The Iranians: Persia, Islam and the Soul of a Nation*, New York: Penguin, 1998.

2 *The Middle East*, August 1982.

3 *The Observer*, 2/2/86; *Israel Foreign Affairs*, March 1986. Iran and Israel had been close since 1950, when Israel arranged a $400,000 bribe to the Iranian prime minister for Iran to grant Israel diplomatic recognition (William Shawcross, *The Shah's Last Ride*, New York: Simon & Schuster, 1988, 80–81).

4 An excellent analysis of the ties between Chase, the oil companies and Iran is Mark Hulbert's *Interlock: The Untold Story of America's Banks, Oil Interests, the Shah's Money, Debts and the Astounding Connections Between Them*, New York: Richardson & Snyder, 1982.

5 An insider view is by Fereydoun Hoveyda, *The Fall of the Shah*, New York: Wyndham Books, 1980. The Shah surrounded himself with parasites grasping for kickbacks. As the CIA itself assessed the situation in a briefing paper labelled SECRET, NOFORN: "The royal court has traditionally been a hotbed of byzantine scheming. In the Shah's family are an assortment of licentious and financially corrupt relatives" (CIA Directorate of Intelligence, Office of Political Research, *Elites and the Distribution of Political Power in Iran*, February 1979). This document was recovered from the shredder when the U.S. embassy was seized.

6 Dilip Hiro, *Iran Under the Ayatollahs*, London: Routledge and Kegan Paul, 1987, 61–63; Robert Graham, *Iran: The Illusion of Power*, London: Croom Helm, 1978, 224.

7 Pierre Salinger, *America Held Hostage*, New York: Doubleday, 1981, 94–97, 167.

8 Hulbert, *Interlock*, makes a case that the asset freeze was the result of conniving by Chase Manhattan to ensure that Iran's loans would go into default and permit Chase to seize and offset the Iranian deposits it held before the Iranians had time to move them to other banks. However, his further contention that pressure from David Rockefeller, and from Henry Kissinger, for the United States to admit the Shah was part of a plot by Chase to provoke the Iranians into an action that would lead to a U.S. asset freeze pushes conspiracy theory too far.

9 Gary Sick, *All Fall Down: America's Tragic Encounter with Iran*, New York: Penguin, 1986, 268.

10 A good overview is in *Middle East Report*, September–October 1987.

11 For information about the internal operations of the Pasdaran I am indebted to former students and Iranian exiles who must remain anonymous.

12 Hoveyda, *Fall*, 95.

13 For the most comprehensive investigation into the Iranian arms pipeline, see Walter De Bock and Jean-Charles Deniau, *Des Armes Pour l'Iran*, Paris: Gallimard, 1988.

14 *Sunday Times*, 10/28/84.

15 *Wall Street Journal*, 1/30/87; De Bock and Deniau, *Des Armes*, 36.

16 Hodgson, *Lloyd's of London*, 126; De Bock and Deniau, *Des Armes*, 34–36. The account of this affair in Pierre Péan, *La Menace*, Paris: Fayard, 1987, 23, is very different. Péan insists that the people paid off were relatives of Parliamentary speaker and later president Rafsanjani. There is yet a third account in Samuel Segev, *The Iranian Triangle: The Untold Story of Israel's Role in the Iran-Contra Affair*, New York: Free Press, 1988, which identifies the associate as an Israeli arms dealer, insists that $200 million worth of arms of various sorts were involved, and states that the first load was flown via Portugal and then the Iranian ran off with the $56 million. Segev seems, like Péan, to confuse several different deals that went through Paris, including a 1981 one that did involve Israelis. The account of De Bock and Deniau seems the most credible.

17 *Associated Press*, 5/5/83; De Bock and Deniau, *Des Armes*, 37.

18 *Times of London*, 3/10/83; *New York Times*, 3/10/83, 6/12/83, 12/2/86.

19 *Observer*, 12/18/87; *Africa Confidential*, 12/2/87.

20 Corn, *Blond Ghost*, 373, 376.

21 On the Pizza Connection, see Ralph Blumenthal, *Last Days of the Sicilians*, New York: Pocket Books, 1988, and Tim Shawcross and Martin Young, *Mafia Wars: The Confessions of Tommaso Buscetta*, Glasgow: Fontana, 1988, Chapters 14, 15.

22 Pascal Auchlin and Frank Garbely, *Contre-Enquête*, Lausanne: Favre, 1990, Chapter 2; *Le Hebdo*, 11/11/88, 12/15, 29/88, 1/19/89, 3/2, 16/89, 5/18/89; *Le Monde*, 2/21, 26/90; Daniel Zuberbuhler, *Enquête de la commission fédérale des banques sur le comportement des grandes banques dans l'affaire Magharian/blanchissage d'argent "Libanon-Connection,"* Bern: Weltwache, 1989; Catherine Duttweiler, *Kopp & Kopp: Aufstieg und Fall der ersten Bundesrätin*, Zurich: 1990. The minister was finally absolved (*Le Monde*, 2/2/92, 9/5/92).

23 *Toronto Star*, 5/29/90. After his release Durrani fled the United States ahead of attempts to deport him. In 1998 he was again in the news when federal agents raided an aerospace company run by his wife on suspicion it was selling counterfeit parts (*Los Angeles Times*, 10/2/98).

24 U.S. Senate, *BCCI Affair*, 315.

25 See Herman Moll and Michael Leapman, *Broker of Death*, London: Macmillan, 1988, 30–31.

26 De Bock and Deniau, *Des Armes*, 156–58; Péan, *La Menace*, 42; *L'Express*, 2/13/87.

27 *Time*, 3/16/87.

28 De Bock and Deniau, *Des Armes*, 194–96.

29 *New York Times*, 10/28/87, 1/18/88; *Financial Times*, 11/4/87; *Wall Street Journal*, 10/22/87; *Jerusalem Post*, 8/9/87; *Observer*, 6/28/87.

30 *Washington Post*, 12/18/86.

31 *Wall Street Journal*, 1/30/87.

32 *New York Times*, 11/25/86, 12/5/86, 10/29/87; *U.S. News & World Report*, 8/31/87.

33 There is a thorough account in *Los Angeles Times*, 11/29/85. See also *International Herald Tribune*, 7/25/83; *New York Times*, 7/28/83.

34 Heikal, *Secret Channels*, 108.

35 Robert Sherrill, *The Oil Follies of 1970–80*, New York: Doubleday, 1993, 512ff; *Wall Street Journal*, 6/17/87. On the 1960 election see Hersh, *Camelot*, Chapter 10.

36 *New York Times*, 6/16/87.

37 Jean-François Boyer, *L'Empire Moon*, Paris: Editions la Découverte, 1986, 310.

38 *Wall Street Journal*, 3/23/87, 6/26/87; *New York Times*, 3/23/87, 6/26/87; *Miami Herald*, 6/26/87.

39 After his partner made a deal and turned state's evidence, Van Backer, a co-defendant and five machinists who manufactured machine guns in underground shops were found guilty of a string of weapons and bribery charges (*UPI*, 6/21, 27/84, *Reuters North American Wire*, 6/27/84).

40 Frank Snepp, *Decent Interval: An Insider's Account of Saigon's Indecent End*, New York: Random House, 1977, 422–23 and passim; Brogan and Zarca, *Deadly Business*, 20, 178. Howe (*Weapons*, 675) lists 529 fixed-wing aircraft, 466 helicopters, 1,200 APCs, 1,250 howitzers, 300 naval craft, 42,000 trucks, 130,000 tons of ammunition, 1,650,000 rifles, etc.

41 *Newsweek*, 10/26/87.

42 *Cambio16*, 5/3/93; *FBIS-LAT*, 3/10/93. To better cover the trail, the Swiss arms broker who set up the deal had Iran issue its LC through Union des banques suisse in London, and arranged for the LC to be paid through a Uruguayan bank.

43 *Time*, 7/25/83; *Miami Herald*, 8/9/87; *Washington Report on Middle Eastern Affairs*, January 1987; *L'Express*, 2/13/87.

44 *Middle East Perspective*, October 1982; *The Nation*, 6/20/87.

45 *Wall Street Journal*, 6/5/86. There was nothing new about this phenomenon. Once during the 1973 war the Pentagon announced it had run out of a certain kind of anti-tank ammunition. Israel located a stock in a Department of Defense warehouse in Hawaii (Findlay, *They Dare*, 141).

46 *Jerusalem Post*, 12/3/86; *Business Week*, 12/29/86; *FBIS Near East*, 9/30/87.

CHAPTER 17

1 For a partial survey of countries that supplied Iran while usually denying it, see Anthony Cordeman's analyses in *Middle East Executive Reports*, February 1986, and *Arab-American Affairs* 20, 1987. See also *Guardian Weekly*, 10/4/87; *Jerusalem Post*, 8/6/87; *Financial Times*, 8/6/87, 9/24/87; *The Middle East*, December 1991; *Observer*, 2/28/88; *Middle East Times*, 6/28/87. Ari Ben-Menashe, who claimed to be a defecting high-level Israeli intelligence operative, suggested that much of the non-Israeli purchasing system used by the Iranians was a front to deflect attention from the fact that virtually all the material Iran was buying was supplied by Israel (*The Profits of War*, New York: Sheridan Square, 1993, Chapter 8).

2 *Inside Sweden*, No. 3–4, September 1987; Wilhelm Agrell, "La Suède et les affaires Bofors: la fin d'un mythe?" in Bernard Adam (ed.), *L'Europe des Armes*, Brussels: 1989.

3 Chris Cowley, *Guns, Lies and Spies*, London: Hamish Hamilton, 1991, 109–10.

4 *Wall Street Journal*, 8/20/87; *Far Eastern Economic Review*, 4/16/87, 8/13/87; *Financial Times*, 7/18/87, 8/13/87.

5 I am indebted to Aaron Karp for this and several other points in this chapter.

6 There is an excellent treatment of the powder cartel in De Bock and Deniau, *Des Armes*, 67–148; see also *The Nation*, 7/18/87; *Wall Street Journal*, 9/4/87; *Financial Times*, 8/28/87, 9/2/87; *Africa Confidential*, 12/2/87.

7 Although one of the company's planes was registered in St. Lucia, none operated off the island (Prime Minister of St. Lucia, *Press Release*, 2/13/87).

8 *Sunday Times*, 10/4/87.

9 *L'Espresso*, 8/30/87; *Business Week*, 9/21/87; *Wall Street Journal*, 9/22/87.

10 *The Middle East*, November 1992. For an account of delle Chiaie's career, see Magnus Linklater, Isabel Hilton and Neal Ascherson, *The Nazi Legacy: Klaus Barbie and the International Fascist Connection*, New York: Holt, Rinehart & Winston, 1984, esp. 204–14.

11 *L'Espresso*, 11/23/86.

12 *Le Monde*, 9/8/87; *Financial Times*, 9/12/87; *The Observer*, 9/13/87.

13 *Wall Street Journal*, 10/15/87, claims that among his activities was arranging with the Polish government for his followers to be awarded scholarships to attend Polish universities, supposedly in exchange for his organization's activities in promoting Polish exports!

14 *Financial Times*, 9/7, 9/87; *Wall Street Journal*, 9/8/87; *The Economist*, 9/12/87; *Times of London*, 9/6, 7/87; *Facts on File*, 9/18/87; *Washington Post*, 9/8/87; *L'Express*, 9/25/87.

15 *L'Espresso*, 10/1/87; *Sunday Times*, 9/13/87.

16 *Sunday Times*, 1/27/94; I am indebted to Jens Sven Gemmel for research on KoKo.

17 There is a good survey by François Chesnais and Claude Serfati, *L'Armement en France: genèse, ampleur et coût d'une industrie*, Paris: 1992.

18 Stanley and Pearton, *International Trade in Arms*, 39–40; *L'Express*, 1/23/87.

19 *The Economist*, 10/20/84. There is a survey of government policy and the state of the French arms industry in *Le Monde Diplomatique*, March 1988.

20 *Le Monde*, 7/29/87; *Paris Match*, 11/20/87; *Montreal Gazette*, 11/18/87. The Chinese wisely spread the action. To sell some of the Silkworms they used a German broker who dealt with a British firm run by an expatriate Iranian, with the operation monitored by MI6 (*Sunday Times*, 9/4/94).

21 *Le Monde*, 11/4/87; *Le Point*, 11/9/87.

22 *Nouvel Observatoire*, 3/11–17/88.

23 *Le Figaro*, 11/4/87.

24 After the Egyptian fiasco, the money trail got even more complex. The LCs were routed through BNL branches in the Far East and eventually were cashed through the New York branch of Banque Worms ("Illegal Arms: How the Banks Broke the Rules," *Euromoney*, October 1990).

25 French investigators unearthed twelve shipments' worth, in total about 700 million francs (perhaps $175 million) on which commissions appeared to have been about 15 per cent. By contrast, the Italians claimed they had turned up at least forty shipments with a total value of as much as 2 billion francs.

26 The initial supposition was that it had been a hit contracted by Iran to help cover the arms deals. But it turned out that the radical leftist group, working on the theory that French arms exports were the key to post-colonial control of Third World countries, acted on its own (*L'Express*, 1/15/88).

27 *L'Express*, 4/6/95.

28 Moll and Leapman, *Broker of Death*, 41.

29 *Fortune*, 2/16/87.

30 *Sunday Times*, 1/9/83. Guns were not his only business. In 1987 Soghanalian put his private Boca-financed jet at the disposal of a former senior American military man and the chief American lobbyist for the Reverend Moon when they flew to Panama in a failed effort to persuade Noriega to exit gracefully. Afterwards he tried to sell the same plane to Filipino exiles plotting a comeback coup for the Marcos dynasty (*New York Times*, 1/31/87; *Newsday*, 7/14/88; *Washington Post*, 1/30/87).

31 He was reputed to be a key intermediary in France's Project Vulcan, a covert operation to sell arms to either side in the Iran-Iraq War for which the broker would collect a 6 per cent commission (*Washington Report on Middle Eastern Affairs*, November 1990).

32 Kenneth Timmerman, *The Death Lobby: How the West Armed Iraq*, London: Fourth Estate, 1992, 92–95.

33 Several books were written on the affair in India. *Bofors: The Unfinished Story* by the newspaper *The Statesman*, Calcutta: Statesman Ltd., 1987, is essentially a collection of documents. The work by S. T. Haider, *Defence Purchases: The Deals and the Drama*, New Delhi: Progressive People's Sector Publications, 1987, tries to paint the entire affair as a plot against

Rajiv Gandhi launched by Washington because of India's ties to the U.S.S.R. The book by Chitra Subramian, *Bofors: The Story Behind the News*, Delhi: Viking, 1992, is as much the story of how she broke the scandal as it is the story itself. Prashant Bhushan's *Bofors: The Selling of a Nation*, New Delhi: Vision Books, 1990, while better factually, tends to degenerate into self-promotion. Much of the Indian press coverage was superlative. See especially Lt. Col. L. Joawn's "The Smoking Gun" in *Illustrated Weekly of India*, 9/13/87, and Nikhil Lakshman's "Wanted," *Illustrated Weekly of India*, 8/2/87. Outside India and Sweden, there was remarkably little analytical material.

34 This history is reviewed in *India Today*, 12/15/87.

35 *India Today*, 4/30/88.

36 *Financial Times*, 10/23/91.

37 *India Today*, 9/15/91.

38 *Financial Times*, 7/20/87; *Illustrated Weekly of India*, 3/1/87, 5/24/87, 8/23/87; *Far Eastern Economic Review*, 6/25/87.

39 West Germany evidently expected India to keep quiet about the South African deal in exchange for West Germany's not revealing the truth about the commission payments. Sure enough, when the UN voted to condemn West Germany's sale of the blueprints to South Africa, India — the country that should have been most offended — pointedly abstained (*Financial Times*, 4/22/88, *Newsweek*, 8/3/87; *Illustrated Weekly of India*, 7/5/87, 6/28/87). Since the Hinduja family reacts to reporters' enquiries by threatening to sue, little is known about their activities. But see *Forbes*, 12/28/87, *India Today*, 6/15/90, and *The Economist*, 9/30/95.

40 *New York Times*, 11/2/89.

41 *Globe and Mail*, 11/8/89; *Financial Times*, 11/8/89. The "evidence" implicating Gandhi personally was highly speculative. Apart from the fact that "Lotus" in Sanskrit is "Rajiv," Lotus is also the name of a company in India owned by some of the cronies Rajiv had protected from V. P. Singh's investigators. One of the bank accounts was in Lugano, near the Italian border, and Rajiv's wife was Italian, something that was also supposed to be reflected in the choice of the name "Ciaou anstalt" of AE Service's parent company. Eventually it was found that an Italian businessman close to Gandhi had been the mysterious recipient of $12 million of Bofors money although he had no official connection to the company. That raised suspicions, never proven, that he was fronting for Gandhi (*Far Eastern Economic Re-view*, 27/2/97).

42 Bhushan, *Bofors*, 162.

43 *Economist*, 12/15/84; *Financial Times*, 9/8/87, 1/27/88; *New York Times*, 1/20/86.

44 Thanks to Andrew Fischer, Terry Nopper and Alexandra Canisius for help with this section. There was massive coverage of the affair in the Viennese magazine *Profil*, for example, on 6/22/87, 10/5/87, 2/13, 20, 27/89, 3/14/89, 6/26/89, 7/17/89, 9/4/89, 10/9/89, 11/27/89, 1/2/90, 2/5, 19, 26/90, 3/26/90, 11/4/91, 3/8/93, 5/17/93, 6/28/93. See also De Bock and Deniau, *Des Armes*, 179–84.

45 *Profil*, 9/4/89.

46 *Profil*, 10/9/89. It was never proven that Proksch had any real role in the arms sales to Iran, but he was often hovering in the background.

47 While the trial of the Voest directors was in progress in 1988, Libya insisted publicly that all the paperwork was correct and that it had received the weapons (*Kurier*, 2/13/88).

48 *Sunday Times*, 7/28/91.

49 *Observer*, 3/8, 15/87, 4/5, 12/87, 5/10/87; *The Independent*, 3/23/95, *Observatoire Géopolitique des Drogues*, August 1992, September 1993, September 1995.

50 *Profil*, 1/4/88.

51 See, for example, Philip Jenkins, "The Assassination of Olaf Palme: Evidence and Ideology," *Contemporary Crises* 13, 1989.

52 It was probably a suicide. The inspector realized that Bofors had lied to him and was convinced he would be made the scapegoat (Agrell, "La Suède et les affaires Bofors: la fin d'un mythe?" in Adam (ed.), *L'Europe des Armes*).

53 *Financial Times*, 6/8/88, 8/5/88; *San Francisco Examiner*, 6/27/88; *La Presse*, 12/6/97. Sweden at the time did host a fair number of the ANC's exiled leadership.

54 See the critical appraisal of the trial by Gunnar Pettersson in *Guardian Weekly*, 8/6/89. Shortly after the suspect's arrest a former justice minister blurted out, "It would be such a relief if it turned out to be him."

CHAPTER 18

1 *Le Monde Diplomatique*, January 1985; *Guardian Weekly*, 9/15/85; *Middle East Report*, January–February 1990.

2 *Guardian Weekly*, 9/15/85; *Middle East Times*, 8/23/87; *Israel & Palestine*, February–March 1988.

3 *Le Monde*, 8/16/87; *Middle East Reporter*, 6/16/84, 4/18/87, 10/28/89; *Middle East Times*, 4/11/89; *Middle East International*, 7/22/83.

4 *Middle East Reporter*, 5/19/84, 6/29/85, 9/20/86, 7/8/88, 7/22/89; *L'évenement du jeudi*, 4/20–26/89; *Financial Times*, 6/17/87.

5 One militia group was rumoured to have got "active war insurance" for its members on the London market (*Financial Times*, 3/8/90). There is an excellent discussion in Élisabeth Picard, "Liban: la matrice historique," in François Jean and Jean-Christophe Rufin (eds.), *Économie des guerres civiles*, Paris: Hachette, 1996.

6 *Globe and Mail*, 7/17/87.

7 *Middle East Times*, 11/13/90.

8 *The Middle East*, August 1988.

9 *L'évenement du jeudi*, 4/20–26/89.

10 *Israel & Palestine*, December 1987.

11 *Middle East Times*, 9/20/87; *New York Time*, 10/29/87; *Middle East Reporter*, 11/7/87; 9/10/88, 11/26/88. In 1987 a West German industrialist fetched $2 million and a South Korean diplomat $1 million.

12 Pierre Péan, *La Menace*, 131, 159, 231; *Middle East International*, 5/14/88; *Observer*, 5/8/88.

13 *Observer*, 12/6/87; *Guardian Weekly*, 12/6/87; *Montreal Gazette*, 5/8/88; *Jeune Afrique*, 1/6/88.

14 *Davaar*, 11/29/85.

15 *Israel & Palestine*, May–June 1986, January 1987; De Bock and Deniau, *Des Armes*, 59–60. Segev in *Iranian Triangle* asserts, to the contrary, that Nimrodi sold no weapons until 1985.

16 Ghorbanifar had been the intermediary between royalist plotters and army mutineers in the abortive 1980 coup to open the border to the Iraqis. Subsequently he became a weapons supplier for the Islamic Republic. That led to the suggestion that Ghorbanifar had been a double agent who leaked to the Iranian government plans for the coup (Kenneth Timmerman, *The Death Lobby*, 79; *Washington Report on Middle Eastern Affairs*, April 1988. Segev, *Iranian Triangle*, 17, 21).

17 For an overview see Jane Mayer and Doyle McManus, *Landslide: The Unmaking of the President, 1984–1988*, Boston: Houghton Mifflin, 1988.

18 On Khashoggi's career see Ronald Kessler, *The Richest Man in the World*, New York: Warner Books, 1986. For his arms business, see Holden and Johns, *House of Saud*, 362–26, and Sampson, *Arms Bazaar*.

19 This issues are explored by Aburish, *Rise, Corruption and Fall*.

20 See *Cambio16*, 8/20/90, on the denizens of Marbella.

21 *Afrique-Asie*, 1/5/81, 5/25/81, 10/26, 12/81, 12/7/81; *South*, December 1982; *New York Times*, 12/8/86; *Time*, 1/10/87.

22 *Wall Street Journal*, 1/14/87, 8/11/87; Kessler, *Richest Man*, 251; *South*, December 1983.

23 "We are not going to pay billions of dollars to be insulted," the Saudis had unconvincingly responded (*New York Times*, 7/10/88).

24 *Financial Times*, 7/9/88; *Business Week*, 9/12/88; *The Engineer*, 6/29/89.

25 Aburish, *Rise, Corruption and Fall*, 187, 295–96.

26 *Sunday Times*, 10/9/94.

27 *Wall Street Journal*, 5/8/87; Segev, *Iranian Triangle*, 261–62. Even old friends like "Tiny" Rowlands, the British tycoon who headed Lonrho Corporation, turned him down. Khashoggi was already in his debt for several millions and one of Israel's top spooks pressed Rowlands to refuse.

28 *Toronto Star*, 8/13/89. The insider also contends that there was a scheme to salvage the Khashoggi empire by its acting as a laundromat for major Colombian cocaine barons. This is so palpably incredible that it casts some doubt on the whole story. He also contended that the cash was being collected to finance both a counter-coup and a comfortable retirement haven in Panama. Why would the Marcoses do both? However, there is no doubt about the cozy relations between Khashoggi and Marcos that earned Khashoggi a criminal indictment for helping them hide assets. He was acquitted.

29 *Observer*, 4/26/87; *Los Angeles Times*, 12/18/86.

30 *Middle East International*, 1/20/89. For evidence of official complicity, see *Israel & Palestine*, May–June 1988.

31 President's Special Review Board, *Report*, Washington: 1987, B-90.

32 Mansur Rafizadeh, *Witness: From the Shah to the Secret Arms Deal*, New York: William Morrow, 1987, 378–80.

33 There is a good account of U.S. efforts to fine-tune the Iran-Iraq War to its own ends in Murray Waas and Craig Unger, "In the Loop: Bush's Secret Mission," *The New Yorker*, 11/12/92.

34 The prosecution abandoned the case, arguing that without testimony from Hashemi, they could never prove beyond a reasonable doubt that the defendants did not genuinely believe they had government backing. See the *Nolle Prosequi* filed in the U.S. District Court, Southern District of New York, RH:jcj, DV-327/1.

35 *Observer*, 3/15/87; Segev, *Iranian Triangle*, 141. See also *Israel & Palestine*, August 1986.

36 *Wall Street Journal*, 5/19/75, 7/9/75, 8/22/75, 12/22/75.

37 For the strange story of Come-By-Chance, see variously *Atlantic Advocate*, August 1977; *Maclean's*, 3/20/76, 8/8/77, 4/22/78, 11/27/78; *Financial Post*, 7/21/79, 11/10/79, 4/14/85, 7/20/85, 5/24/86.

38 I am indebted to Walter Stewart for much of this information. Stewart, at the time a journalist with *Maclean's* magazine, exposed the deal and attracted a $40-million lawsuit from Shaheen — it was dropped.

39 *New York Times*, 12/10/88, 9/15/89; *Business Week*, 10/31/88; *Financial Times*, 9/11/88; *Wall Street Journal*, 9/10/88, 12/13/88.

CHAPTER 19

1 In twenty years Iraq bought over $19 billion worth from the U.S.S.R. and $5.5 billion from France (*Le Monde Diplomatique*, September 1990).

2 *Middle East International*, 9/27/85.

3 The apt title of Laton McCartney's *Friends in High Places: The Bechtel Story*, New York: Simon & Schuster, 1988.

4 *New York Times*, 2/4/88; *The Middle East*, April 1988.

5 Israel was not to get oil directly but rather about $70 million in cash per year plus the opportunity, arranged by Rappaport, to obtain cheap oil through swap agreements (*Jerusalem Post*, 8/13/88). The Israeli prime minister angrily denounced the idea there had been any pay-off and Rappaport also denied it. The idea appears in one of the secret memos written by Wallach.

6 There are three excellent accounts of the WedTech affair: William Sternberg and Matthew Harrison, *Feeding Frenzy: The Inside Story of WedTech*, New York: Henry Holt, 1989; Marilyn Thompson, *Feeding the Beast*, New York: Scribner, 1990; and James Traub, *Too Good To Be True*, New York: Doubleday, 1990. On Wallach's legal career, see *Wall Street Journal*, 7/21/87, 2/12/88, and *New York Times*, 4/29/87.

7 *New York Times*, 9/8/87.

8 *New York Times*, 5/15/87.

9 *Wall Street Journal*, 6/25/87.

10 *New York Times*, 6/22/87, 7/3/87; *Business Week*, 3/14/88.

11 *Wall Street Journal*, 6/25/87.

12 Found guilty in 1989 after a long legal battle, Wallach finally got influence-peddling charges dismissed, and the government decided not to pursue further charges against him (*Associated Press*, 9/15/93).

13 *New York Times*, 10/16/87, 1/26/88, 2/24, 25/88; *Jerusalem Post*, 3/6/88, 7/7/88; *Wall Street Journal*, 2/16/88, 7/11/88; *Los Angeles Times*, 4/19/88; *Business Week*, 2/22/88.

14 On Abu Nidal's operations see Seale, *Abu Nidal*; *L'Express*, 7/31/87; *New York Times*, 1/24/88; *Middle East International*, 12/20/91.

15 Potts, *Dirty Money*, 162–66.

16 Hearings of the U.S. House of Representatives, Committee on Banking, Finance and Urban Affairs, *Iraq and Banca Nazionale del Lavoro Participation in Export-Import Programs*, Washington: 4/17/1991, 29.

17 Thanks to Anthony O'Sullivan for research on BNL.

18 Friedman, *Spider's Web: The Secret History of How the White House Illegally Armed Iraq*, New York: Bantam, 1993, 85. There is an account of the interrelations of various Italian underworlds with the banks in Judge Carlo Palermo's *Il Quarto Potere*, Rome: 1996.

19 *Globe and Mail*, 10/10/92.

20 *Euromoney*, October 1990.

21 Hearings of the U.S. House of Representatives, Committee on Banking, Finance and Urban Affairs, *Banca Nazionale del Lavoro*, Washington, 4/9/91, 13, 36, 44.

22 *New York Times*, 5/22/90; *Congressional Record — House,* 3/2/92, H 861, House, 5/9/91, H 2935. This trick earned the commodity trader who handled the swaps an indictment for lavishing cash, jewellery and expense-paid vacations on BNL employees.

23 *La Republica*, 9/2/89; *Euromoney*, October 1990; *The Banker*, April 1991.

24 *Congressional Record — House*, 2/4/91, H849; *Wall Street Journal*, 10/9/92.

25 See House Republican Research Committee, Task Force on Terrorism and Unconventional Warfare, "Iran, Syria and the Trail of Counterfeit Dollars," 7/1/92. See also Frederic Dannen and Ira Silverman, "The Supernote," *New Yorker*, 10/23/95, and a hysterical report by Robert Kupperman and David Andelman in *Washington Post*, 3/6/94.

26 *Boston Globe*, 1/14/93.

27 Bloom, *The Brotherhood of Money*, 37.

28 Interestingly, once U.S.–Syrian relations improved, the secondary villains suddenly changed. The new threat became a deal between North Korea and Iran to swap Iranian counterfeiting expertise for North Korean missile technology (*BBC Summary of World Broadcasts*, 4/30/96; *New York Times*, 6/18/97).

29 *The Middle East*, August 1987, April 1988; *Middle East Reporter*, 4/2/88. For example, the Iranians arranged for a California firm run by an Israeli with whom they had previously conducted embargo-busting operations to buy surplus F-104 fighter planes from Belgium. The company removed all identification numbers and shipped the motors to Europe for forwarding to Iran. The remaining parts were junked. Since Iran did not use that type of plane, no one investigated the shipment; the motors were modified to fit one of Iran's own hybrid aircraft types (De Bock and Deniau, *Des Armes*, 169).

30 *Financial Times*, 5/27/88; *Wall Street Journal*, 7/22/88.

CHAPTER 20

1 There are many works dealing with Iraqi arms procurement. The best is Adel Darwish and Gregory Alexander, *Unholy Babylon: The Secret History of Saddam's War*, London: Victor Gollancz, 1991. The worst is Kenneth Timmerman's *The Death Lobby*, a book full of gratuitous insults against Arabs and Germans. There are three others containing useful information. Alan Friedman's *Spider's Web*, although excellent on some items, is also marred by anti-Arab rants. Peter Mantius, *Shell Game: A True Story of Banking, Lies, Spies and Politics — and the Arming of Saddam Hussein*, New York: St. Martin's Press, 1995, is a solid work, but still contains some nonsense, especially with regard to the supergun. Finally, there is Mark Phythian's *Arming Iraq: How the U.S. and Britain Secretly Built Saddam's War Machine*, Boston: Northeastern University Press, 1997. Although ill-digested, this book was able to draw on deeper research and presents a more thorough account of the British side than the others. Interesting too are the memoirs of the former managing director of Matrix-Churchill, Paul Henderson, *The Unlikely Spy*, London: Bloomsbury, 1993. There is good information in the several works dealing with the life and career of Gerald Bull cited previously.

2 By one theory, after Bob Denard's misadventures in the Comoros, South Africa was looking for a more secure method of supplying the weapons to Iraq and chose to use Industrias Cardoen as subcontractor (*Israeli Foreign Affairs*, 2/21/91).

3 *Washington Post*, 8/6/90; *Observer*, 1/3/93; *FBIS-LAT*, 12/11/92. The assumption was the murder was the handiwork of Iraqi intelligence.

4 The sections in Friedman's *Spider's Web* dealing with the cluster-bomb story (Chapters 4 and 5) are the best in the book. See also *New York Times*, 1/16/87; *Time*, 12/10/90.

5 On James Guerin's career see *Wall Street Journal*, 1/23/90.

6 *Financial Times*, 5/24/9; *Observer*, 4/26/92.

7 *Guardian Weekly*, 9/24/89; *Financial Times*, 2/5/90, 8/30/90, 10/31/91, 6/12/92; *Wall Street Journal*, 11/20/91.

8 *Independent*, 6/16/91; *New York Times*, 6/11/92, 5/17/94. Not so lucky was Teledyne, which had to face criminal charges and was repeatedly frustrated in its efforts to obtain for its own defence a secret CIA report, based on its own tip-offs, that would have demonstrated agency complicity.

9 This was well summed up in Hearings of the U.S. House of Representatives, Committee on Banking, Finance and Urban Affairs (*Banca Nazionale del Lavoro*, Washington, 4/9/91, 24), subsequent to the Iraqi invasion of Kuwait, when one of the experts testified that "unlike many Third World countries, Iraq was trying to develop autonomous production facilities. That means that, not only were they trying to make a finished product, but they were trying to make the components that went into the finished products, and in some cases were trying to go all the way back to manufacturing the raw materials. *This meant that it posed particular problems, different from those of other kinds of countries*" (italics added).

10 This is the main message of William Burrows and Robert Windrem, *Critical Mass: The Dangerous Race for Superweapons in a Fragmenting World*, New York: Simon & Schuster, 1994. For example, they argue (p. 5), "Unlike Western or Soviet bombs that were produced to end the political scourge of communism, capitalism and fascism, Third World nuclear weapons are genocidal."

11 There are rather lurid descriptions in *Congressional Record — House*, 2/3/92, H 208, and *Wall Street Journal*, 1/19/93.

12 Henderson, *Unlikely Spy*, 126–27, 134–35; *Sunday Times*, 11/15/92, 10/10/93; *Financial Times*, 11/12/92, 2/13/96; *Wall Street Journal*, 11/10/92.

13 Hearings of the U.S. House of Representatives, Committee on Banking, Finance and Urban Affairs, *Banca Nazionale del Lavoro*, Washington, 4/9/91, 28. American congressmen later charged that this was a device taught to the Iraqis by East German intelligence agents, who supposedly developed the technique as a way to evade West German controls on technology exports (*Congressional Record — House*, 2/3/92, H 208).

14 As in Mantius, *Shell Game*, 89.

15 Cf. Hearings of the U.S. House of Representatives, Committee on Banking, Finance and Urban Affairs, *Banca Nazionale del Lavoro*, Washington, 4/9/91, 35–37.

16 Hearings, House of Representatives, *Banca Nazionale del Lavoro*, 4/9/91, 52.

17 *The Middle East*, March 1991. In fact, the European brokers operating on behalf of Iraq might be more prone than the Iraqis to hide what they were doing. Typical was a British businessman who resided in Monaco while working out of Geneva through a Turks and Caicos company. He started doing deals for small arms, moved to mortar and artillery shells, then to missile components and machine tools, buying the essentials from Italian, French and German firms. But in such cases the motivation is usually more to evade taxes than strategic export controls.

18 *Congressional Quarterly*, 6/6/92; Timmerman, *Death Lobby*, 240.

19 *Washington Post*, 7/18/92.

20 *Sunday Times*, 3/27/88; *Observer*, 4/9/88.

21 Palermo, *Quarto Potere*, 148.

22 Darwish and Alexander, *Unholy Babylon*, 86–87; *FBIS–LAT*, 11/18/92.

23 Subcontractors included a division of Italy's Fiat (half owner of Valsella) and Sweden's Bofors. *Financial Times*, 4/12/89, 7/31/89. Naturally, to Burrows and Windrem (*Critical Mass*), the network was a "spiderweb" and the parent company "ghostly."

24 *Financial Times*, 11/21/89; *Middle East International*, 1/19/90; Timmerman, *Death Lobby*, 292.

25 Howe, *Weapons*, 14.

26 *Wall Street Journal*, 9/15, 16/88; *Financial Times*, 8/19/88.

27 The spectre of poisonous gas being used in an exchange with Israel led to nonsense about how Saddam's chemical arsenal was the moral descendant of Nazi gas ovens. (See especially Timmerman's *Death Lobby* and Burrows and Windrem's *Critical Mass* for some of the most hyperbolic examples.) That so many German firms were involved in Iraqi petrochemical projects was further grist to the propaganda mill. See note 32 below.

28 Hearings, House of Representatives, *Banca Nazionale del Lavoro*, 4/9/91, 59.

29 See the sensible appraisal in *World Press Review*, March 1989.

30 Although two of them are supposedly restricted, they have so many industrial uses that control is virtually impossible. On these issues see Kathleen Bailey, "Problems with a Chemical Weapons Ban," *Orbis*, Spring 1992.

31 *The Middle East*, April 1991; *Business Week*, 1/23/89; *New York Times*, 3/2/89. In fact, that can work two ways. After a long chemically fuelled anti-Libya campaign, whose main role was to prepare the public mind for the United States to bomb Tripoli and tighten trade and financial sanctions, the U.S. was able to declare victory, even though the facility was still in operation, by claiming that the Libyans had been intimidated into using the plant to make medicine instead of nerve gas.

32 That simply reflected Germany's pioneering role in the modern synthetic-organic chemical industry. On the German role, see *Middle East Report*, January–February 1991.

33 Burrows and Windrem, *Critical Mass*, 202–3.

34 *Jerusalem Post*, 3/18/90. Nimrodi acknowledged knowing Bazcroft and advanced the opinion that Bazcroft was naive and would have been a terrible spy. On the other side, Mantius (*Shell Game*, 148) still thinks Bazcroft might have been someone's spy. Others, too, share that opinion based on his background and bank records. See *Washington Report on Middle Eastern Affairs*, November 1990.

35 They included intermediating the sale of night-vision equipment made by a British company. Soghanalian was apparently rewarded by both his commission and an introduction to Mark Thatcher, which Soghanalian claims he took as a sign of government approval (*The Independent*, 8/16/94). Soghanalian was also broker in a deal (involving Spiro Agnew, the disgraced Nixon-era vice-president, and John Mitchell, the attorney-general who had tried

to cover up the Watergate scandal) to provide Iraq with army uniforms made in Romania. The quality was so bad the Iraqis withheld payment. The entire mess bogged down into a protracted lawsuit (*Washington Post*, 5/7/92; *Newsday*, 5/14/92).

36 *New York Times*, 12/4/87, 10/23/89; *Los Angeles Times*, 10/22/91; Mantius, *Shell Game*, 55.

37 *Observer*, 4/15/90; *Sunday Times*, 10/10/93; Timmerman, *Death Lobby*, 332.

38 *Financial Times*, 4/17/90, 5/26/90; *Globe and Mail*, 4/21, 23/90; *Guardian*, 5/25/90; *Middle East Times*, 5/15/90; *Daily Telegraph*, 4/16/90.

39 However, there was some evidence that Bull was also involved in a parallel project of long-distance artillery, for huge rail-mounted guns to be stationed along the Iranian border. They would be able to reach targets deep inside Iran — though not the capital, much less Tel Aviv (Darwish and Gregory, *Unholy Bablyon*, 188–89).

40 The silliest such allegations appeared in the *Globe and Mail* (1/19/91), where it was claimed that Bull was "almost certainly murdered by an Arab execution squad."

41 These theories are well surveyed by James Adams in *Bull's Eye*. The killing led to predictable media distortions in which Bull, who was notoriously up-front, was referred to routinely as a "shadowy" or "mysterious" figure. See for example *Wall Street Journal*, 2/5/91.

42 Darwish and Alexander, *Unholy Babylon*, 122. Timmerman, *Death Lobby*, 70, tells a considerably sanitized version of the story.

43 It is possible Bull had been recruited to give some assistance to the Iraqi missile program, partially to fill the void left by the discomfiture of the Egyptians working on the Condor missile. And Israel occasionally murders engineers and scientists working on Arab arms projects, not for their work per se but as a warning to others (Adams, *Bull's Eye*, 272–73; Grant, *Wilderness of Mirrors*, 193; Lowther, *Arms and the Man*, 281). But Bull's son denied that their company had been involved in the Iraqi missile program, insisting that if it had been, Bull would have taken security precautions — he did not (*Washington Post*, 4/6/90).

44 *The Economist*, 6/7/94.

45 *The Economist*, 5/7/94; *Guardian*, 11/12/94.

46 Cowley, *Guns, Lies and Spies*, 234–36.

47 *Tendances*, 2/27/95; Palermo, *Quarto Potere*, 146.

48 *Le Monde*, 5/10/96.

49 *Commission de la défense nationale*, Chambre des réprésentants de Belgique, 3/11/93. Stephen Bornstein of McGill University has suggested that the reason for the electoral funding scandals surrounding Socialist parties in Europe is that they lack the "natural" financial support vehicles of both right-wing (business funded) and left-wing (labour-union backed) parties.

50 *Le Soir*, 2/18/95, 3/13/95, 4/7/95.

51 *Le Soir*, 2/20/95.

52 *Le Soir*, 3/1/95, 4/8/95. The head of Agusta stated his belief that the Belgian ministries were making sure Agusta won over the German competitor. The French one was a frequent partner with Agusta in other deals and realized that Agusta desperately needed the Belgian contract (*Le Monde Diplomatique*, May 1995; *FBIS-WEU*, 3/2/95).

53 *Le Soir*, 2/23/95.

54 *Le Soir*, 1/18/94, 2/1/94, 4/13/95.

55 *Le Soir*, 3/2/95.

56 *Le Soir*, 1/3/95, 5/1, 26/95.

57 Even that did not go smoothly. The Mafiosi located two agricultural labourers in Sicily willing to trade pruning hooks for pistols for $35,000. Then, safely back in Sicily, they started demanding more money for their silence. There was not enough petty cash in the minister's office. So the gang arranged to steal $15 million worth of securities from Brussels airport, had them driven to Liechtenstein in the minister's car by his chauffeur, and sold them with the assistance of an uncle-in-law of the private secretary who had learned how to handle such matters during his former career as a bank robber (*Le Soir*, 9/12, 16/96).

58 *Financial Times,* 10/19/95.
59 *Financial Times,* 9/2/98.
60 "Ça n'a rien à voir avec la corruption," *Le Soir,* 5/15/95.
61 *FBIS-WEU,* 3/2/95.

CHAPTER 21

1 For a good overview see Alan Dowty, "Sanctioning Iraq: The Limits of the New World Order," *Washington Quarterly,* Summer 1994.

2 See Nikos Passas and Jack Blum, "Intelligence Services and Undercover Operations: The Case of Euromac," in S. Field and C. Pelser (eds.), *Invading the Private: State Accountability and the New Investigative Methods in Europe,* Dartmouth: Aldershot, 1998. Burrows and Windrem in *Critical Mass,* 451–65, repeat the official line uncritically.

3 *Wall Street Journal,* 5/17/85, 12/19/85; *New York Times,* 5/17/85, 5/16/85; *Middle East Report,* May–June 1987.

4 *Globe and Mail,* 5/9/90. Previously, Iraq had received permission to purchase lower-grade capacitors, and there was speculation that the Iraqis had succeeded in raising them to military specifications (*New York Times,* 5/8/90).

5 Cited in Darwish and Alexander, *Unholy Babylon,* 267.

6 Heikal, *Secret Channels,* 364–65.

7 *Financial Times,* 9/24/93; *Wall Street Journal,* 11/24/92.

8 There is an excellent overview of the issues in Darwish and Alexander, *Unholy Babylon,* 238, 254–57, 267.

9 Aburish, *House of Saud,* 172–74. The author tends to take the Iraqi point of view at face value. However, see also Mohammed Heikal, *Illusions of Triumph: An Arab View of the Gulf War,* London: Fontana, 1993, Chapter 12. Kuwait gave seemingly reasonable grounds for refusing to write off the Iraqi debts. Iraq rejected them as insincere. Kuwait was richer per capita than Saudi Arabia, which had wiped the slate clean.

10 *Times of London,* 2/26/93.

11 Contrast the views of Gary Hufbauer, who believed sanctions would work quickly (*New York Times,* 1/14/91), and those of Meheran Nakhjavani (*Iraq: What If Sanctions Fail,* Economist Intelligence Unit, London: October 1990), who forecast that they would not.

12 Wallich, *Mainsprings,* 66.

13 On the enormously successful effort to twist public opinion, see John MacArthur, *Second Front,* Berkeley: University of California Press, 1993, Chapter 2.

14 *Middle East Times,* 9/18/90, 10/2/90; *Financial Times,* 11/5/90; 12/15/90; *Middle East Economic Digest,* 8/31/90; *Globe and Mail,* 9/20/90.

15 On this secret cooperation see Scott Armstrong, "Eye of the Storm," *Mother Jones,* November–December 1991.

16 That version seems to have won at least some favour among Spanish judges, who three times rejected the KIO's claim of criminal fraud by the management of Grupo Torras (*Financial Times,* 7/7/93; *New York Times,* 9/28/93; *Wall Street Journal,* 12/7/92; *Middle East International,* 6/11/93). Late in 1998 a fraud case opened in London that promised to finally shed some light over the politics behind the missing money (*Financial Times,* 10/5/98).

17 Quoted in MacArthur, *Second Front,* 164.

18 *New York Times,* 1/24/93.

19 *Middle East International,* 8/21/98.

20 *Globe and Mail,* 9/14/90; *Financial Times,* 11/20/90; *Wall Street Journal,* 10/30/90. Originally Iraq allowed the traders to handle only basic food and a restricted list of parts, but over time relaxed those restrictions and began allowing in many forms of foreign consumer goods (*Reuters World Service,* 10/27/96).

21 *Financial Times,* 11/14/96, 12/5/96.

22 *Wall Street Journal*, 4/2/91; *New York Times*, 4/2/91; *Financial Times*, 4/2/91. The U.S. Treasury published a blacklist of fifty-two "Iraqi front companies" and thirty-seven "agents" with whom it became illegal for Americans to do business. Of course, any individual or firm on the list had, by definition, already been discovered to have been dealing with Iraq and therefore, almost by definition, had ceased to do so.

23 *Financial Times*, 11/10/96.

24 *Compass Newswire*, 3/10/97.

25 *Journal of Commerce*, 9/12/96.

26 *Observer*, 7/26/91; *Times of London*, 9/4/92; *Wall Street Journal*, 1/16/92.

27 *Financial Times*, 3/25/91.

28 *Observer*, 3/31/91; *Time*, 4/8/91; *Wall Street Journal*, 1/16/92; *The Middle East*, June 1991; *Financial Times*, 3/25/91.

29 *L'Espresso*, 8/30/87, 1/17/93. Eventually, the Italian firm went looking for other buyers. An Italian court declared that Iraq had to forfeit its down payment.

30 None of the published sources agree on what happened, differing on the role of BNL, on the amount of the Iraqi payments and on the fate of the money. See, for example, Darwish and Alexander, *Unholy Babylon*, 147–48; Timmerman, *The Death Lobby*, 328; Henderson, *Unlikely Spy*, 154–56; Mantius, *Shell Game*, 187.

31 *Le Monde*, 9/5/92.

32 Auchlin and Garbely, *Contre-Enquête*, 406–10.

33 *Observer*, 7/27/91.

34 *Los Angeles Times*, 12/8/91; *Financial Times*, 9/31/92; *Time*, 8/3/92.

35 *Financial Times*, 8/31/90, 10/4/90.

36 *Times of London*, 2/14/97.

37 *New York Times*, 9/14/90.

38 *Financial Times*, 12/6/96; *Middle East Times*, 8/29/97, 1/23/98, Arab Press Service, *Diplomat Recorder*, 2/15/97.

39 *Middle East Reporter*, 10/11/80.

40 Michael Gunter, "The KDP-PUK Conflict in Northern Iraq," *Middle East Journal*. See also *Middle East Reporter*, 10/11/80.

41 *Middle East Report*, July–August 1988; *L'Express*, 9/11/92; *Libération*, 5/5/92; *Financial Times*, 10/15/93.

42 *The Economist*, 7/11/92.

43 *Middle East Times*, 9/10/91.

44 *Time*, 6/8/92; *Newsweek*, 6/8/92. The CIA denied any involvement, claiming that it was the work of Arab states in the anti-Iraq coalition.

45 *Middle East Reporter*, 2/20/93; *Middle East International*, 4/14/93; *Washington Post*, 5/6/93; *Financial Times*, 5/28/93.

46 *Middle East Times*, 3/26/91. See Hamit Bozarslan, "Kurdistan: Economie de Guerre, Economie dans la Guerre," in François Jean and Jean-Christophe Rufin (eds.), *Economie des guerres civiles*, Hachette, Paris: 1996.

47 *Middle East International*, 5/1/92; *New York Times*, 8/12/92; *Middle East Times*, 3/26/91.

48 *Financial Times*, 12/8/94.

49 *European Energy Report*, 3/3/95. There was a parallel trade in cigarettes. Tobacco smugglers would buy cigarettes inside Turkey, nominally for export and therefore tax exempt, send them openly over the Iraqi border and then sneak them back again (*Agence France Presse*, 1/27/97).

50 *Middle East International*, 12/5/87; *New York Times*, 8/12/92; *Times of London*, 8/3, 19/92. Whenever the PKK, either to pressure the Turkish government or to express its displeasure to its Iraqi kin, chose to close the truck route — destroying trucks and murdering drivers to make its point clear — the Kurdish autonomous authority found itself in a fiscal crisis, unable to pay its civil servants and soldiers. And whenever Saddam Hussein felt the Kurds

were becoming too assertive, he could squeeze the autonomous region by curtailing the number of trucks with diesel fuel allowed to transit the zone.

51 *Middle East International,* 1/20/95. Saddam pledged that once sanctions were lifted and oil began to flow through the pipeline to Turkey again, the KDP would be compensated for any lost revenue from the end of the truck route by regular protection payments for making sure no one sabotaged the pipeline (*Wall Street Journal,* 9/11/96). Thanks to Eric Rosenberg for research on this topic.

52 MacArthur, *Second Front,* 75.

53 *Wall Street Journal,* 1/21/91.

54 Kevin Page, Greg Williams and Charles Broll, *High Tech Weapons in Desert Storm: Hype or Reality?,* Washington: Project on Government Procurement, 1991; *New York Times,* 4/17/91; MacArthur, *Second Front,* 163; *Wall Street Journal,* 1/21/91, 4/15/91, 1/15/92.

55 Hartung, *And Weapons for All,* 15. Saudi Arabia, Kuwait and the Gulf states paid the United States, Britain and France directly for their military participation $84 billion. This was on top of the $51 billion they had kicked in to create the infrastructure to support the Allied expeditionary force.

56 *Middle East Times,* 11/26/91; *Jerusalem Post,* 4/10/92.

57 *Al Hamishmar,* 5/22/91. Israel had already refused another offer, of an end to the boycott in exchange for simply stopping its settlement drive (*Washington Report on Middle East Affairs,* March 1992).

58 *Middle East Times,* 8/21/90.

59 Heikal, *Secret Channels,* 10.

60 Heikal, *Secret Channels,* 17.

61 *New York Times,* 9/8/92.

62 *Middle East International,* 1/20/95, 1/21/97, 11/27/97; *Financial Times,* 2/22, 25/98; 1/3/98.

63 *Observer,* 5/18/97; *Agence France Presse,* 2/2/97; *Deutsche Presse-Agentur,* 6/23/96; *New York Times,* 6/23/96, 3/15/98.

64 *Middle East International,* 3/31/95, 11/27/98; *La Presse,* 12/17/97; *Financial Times,* 3/21/98; *Globe and Mail,* 5/18, 19, 20/98, 6/29/98.

65 Cited in Burrows and Windrem, *Critical Mass,* 59.

CHAPTER 22

1 In the colonies, of course, armed land grabs, forced tribute payments and debt slavery were the norm. A classic old account is Parker T. Moon, *Imperialism and World Politics,* New York: Garland, 1926.

2 There are two outstanding works analyzing the background: Susan Woodward's *Balkan Tragedy: Chaos and Dissolution After the Cold War,* Washington: Brookings Institution Press, 1995; and Mihailo Crnobrnja's *The Yugoslav Drama,* Montreal: McGill-Queen's University Press, 1996. See also the account of the last American ambassador to Yugoslavia, Warren Zimmerman, *Origins of a Catastrophe,* New York: Times Books, 1996, and David Owen's *Balkan Odyssey,* London: Victor Gollancz, 1995. On-the-spot observations are provided by Misha Glenny in his *The Fall of Yugoslavia,* London: Penguin, 1993. Some works seem marred by an anti-Serbian bias. See for example, Sabrina Petra Ramet, *Balkan Babel: The Disintegration of Yugoslavia from the Death of Tito to Ethnic War,* 2nd ed., Boulder, Colo.: Westview, 1996.

3 Glenny, *Fall of Yugoslavia,* 141–42. FBIS-EEU, 9/24/93.

4 These factors are best surveyed in Crnobrnja, *Yugoslav Drama,* 65–70.

5 *Congressional Record — House,* 4/25/91, H-2549–50. The chairman of LBS was cleared but the bank itself was found guilty.

6 *New York Times,* 1/10/91; Woodward, *Balkan Tragedy,* 129.

7 Contrary to popular impressions, the Yugoslav army had neither the gumption nor the authorization to really attempt to maintain control. Far from an act of Serbian aggression,

the army was ordered in by a Croatian federal president; Slovenia had already hatched a deal with Serbia's boss to secede, further tilting the balance in Serbia's favour and providing a pretext for a purge from the army of senior officers more committed to Yugoslavian unity than to Serbian national aspirations.

8 *FBIS-EEU*, 9/24/93.

9 *Washington Post*, 8/29/93; *Washington Report on Middle Eastern Affairs*, August 1992; *Sunday Times*, 1/26/92; *Financial Times*, 4/29/92, 2/6/93; *Commersant*, 6/9/92.

10 *FBIS Near East and South Asia*, 9/29/92; *Saudi Gazette*, 5/1/95.

11 *Observer*, 7/4/93.

12 *FBIS-AFR*, 3/9/94.

13 Crnobrnja, *Yugoslav Drama*, 180.

14 *Sunday Times*, 2/20/94.

15 See Edward Badolota and Dale Andrade, "Red Mercury: Hoax or the Ultimate Terrorist Weapon," *Counterterrorism & Security*, Spring 1996.

16 *Wall Street Journal*, 12/6/93; *Barron's*, 2/15/93; *FBIS-SOV*, 7/2/93.

17 Glenny, *Fall of Yugoslavia*, passim; Owen, *Balkan Odyssey*, 74.

18 *Toronto Star*, 8/29/91, 9/15/91. All Ugandans involved, including a former prime minister, were acquitted by a Kampala court (*FBIS-AFR*, 2/3/94). A later shipment of arms of North American origin financed by the same group was seized at the Toronto airport. I am indebted to Stephen Smith for information on this case.

19 *Cambio16*, 2/22/93.

20 *FBIS-EEU*, 3/26/92.

21 There is a useful background account of the anti-Yugoslav Croatian exile forces in Anderson and Anderson, *Inside the League*, 25–27, 38–42 et passim.

22 I am grateful to Vibor Miocevic for information on this topic. See also *Espresso*, 1/17/93, for one abortive deal in Croatia supposedly involving Italian mobsters and Israeli secret service agents.

23 *Defence & Foreign Affairs Strategic Policy*, October 1992.

24 *Aviation Week & Space Technology*, 5/30/94.

25 *Sunday Times*, 9/1/91; *Chicago Sun-Times*, 10/30/94.

26 *Foreign Report*, 12/19/91; *New York Times*, 1/11/92; *World Press Review*, February 1992. Later Croatia may have succeeded in getting Short's Blowpipe missiles from Chile, again using Sri Lankan EUCs.

27 *FBIS-EEU*, 7/29/92. This report was based on the Argentine daily *Pagina 12*, though filtered through Serbian radio.

28 *Weekly Mail & Guardian*, 6/2/95.

29 *New York Times*, 9/2/93.

30 *International Herald Tribune*, 3/29/83, 8/19/83; *Guardian*, 2/14/83; *Le Monde*, 3/29/83, 8/19/83; *Observer*, 8/21/83; *Miami Herald*, 3/12/83; *Observer*, 8/21/83.

31 See the account by Linklater, Hilton and Acherson, *The Nazi Legacy: Part II*. In one later deal Barbie showed his commitment to restoring Bolivia's national pride by using Transmaritima to smuggle weapons to Chile.

32 *New York Times*, 9/2/93; *Latin America Weekly Report*, 7/8/93.

33 The most thorough account is by Peter Fuhrman in *Forbes*, 5/10/93; see also *FBIS-WEU*, 10/21/93, 3/1, 26, 29/93; *Latin America Weekly Report*, 7/8/93; *BBC Monitoring Service: Latin America*, 10/11/93; *FBIS-LAT*, 6/19/95; *Inter Press Service*, 10/19/93; *Jerusalem Post*, 4/25/93. It was possible that the Israeli was also behind the deal in which "Bolivia" ordered the eight Russian tanks. The scandal led to the arrest of three Bolivian generals and ten civilians.

34 *BBC Summary of World Broadcasts*, 4/29/94; *Periscope Daily Defence News Capsules*, 8/8/95. A U.S. security company headed by a former chief of the U.S. Defense Intelligence Agency also provided former military personnel to train Croatian forces.

35 *Globe and Mail*, 4/21/94.

36 This did not prevent them from sometimes becoming public heroes, especially in the defence of Sarajevo; and they did use their underworld ties to acquire weapons (Glenny, *Fall of Yugoslavia*, 218).

37 *New York Times*, 4/10/92; *Washington Post*, 10/5/93.

38 *Geopolitical Drug Dispatch*, September 1993; *Agence France Presse*, 8/3/95. Swiss prosecutors tried to seize $6 million in profit from el-Qassar's bank.

39 *Washington Post*, 2/14/93.

40 *Latin America Weekly Report*, 8/12/93; *Inter Press Service*, 8/20/93; *Chicago Tribune*, 8/13/93; *Cambio16*, 8/23, 30/93, 9/6, 13/93; *FBIS-LAT*, 7/29/93, 8/20, 23/93, 9/3/93.

41 *International Herald Tribune*, 3/16/95; *Washington Times*, 2/2/97.

42 Owen, *Balkan Odyssey*, 384; *L'Express*, 4/27/95. One of the reasons for the breakdown of the alliance was precisely Muslim resentment of profiteering by Croats in supplying strategic goods to besieged Sarajevo (Glenny, *Fall of Yugoslavia*, 219).

43 Gregory Webb, "Ancient Enmities, Modern Guns," *Bulletin of the Atomic Scientists*, December 1993. The Muslims exaggerated to win more Middle East support, the others to paint Muslim Bosnia as a European bridgehead for Islamic fundamentalism. After the war, the Bosnian government revealed that Russian black market dealers were far more important than Iran.

44 *Financial Times*, 1/30/96.

45 *Washington Post*, 9/22/96; *BBC Summary of World Broadcasts*, 1/28/94.

46 *Jane's Intelligence Review*, 11/1/94; *BBC Summary of World Broadcasts*, 10/8/94.

CHAPTER 23

1 Some countries, the United States in particular, did attempt to search out and seize Serbian-Montenegrin assets. But most went no further than to stop financial transfers to and from rump Yugoslavia. Some explicitly refused to attempt to block assets because of their bank secrecy laws or the possibility of harming legitimate trade (U.S. General Accounting Office, *Serbia-Montenegro: Implementation of UN Economic Sanctions*, Washington, April 1993, 6).

2 These gizmos are examined in *Aviation Week & Space Technology*, 5/30/94.

3 Some Serbian foreign exchange deposits had been shifted from a German to an Israeli bank in 1990. That was not to prepare for sanctions (the interpretation of *Haaretz*, 2/10/92). Rather, it reflected the view of Serbia's leadership that by currying favour with Israel it would win the support of some mythical cabal of Jewish magnates who, Serbia's bosses were convinced, controlled international finance. I am indebted to Mihailo Crnobrnja for this correction.

4 See the excellent survey by M. R. Palairet, "How Long Can the Milosevic Regime Withstand Sanctions?" *RFE/RL Research Report* 2, No. 34, August 1993. See also *The Econ-omist*, 2/12/94.

5 *Reuters North American Wire*, 3/9/95; Uros Komlenovic, "Crime and Corruption after Communism: State and Mafia in Yugoslavia," *Eastern European Constitutional Review* 6, No. 4, 1997.

6 Glenny, *Fall of Yugoslavia*, 133; Nouvel Observateur et Reporters Sans Frontières, *Le Livre Noir de L'Ex-Yugoslavie*, Arléa: 1993, 5, 6, 168; *New York Times*, 3/26/95.

7 *Washington Post*, 11/21/96.

8 *New York Times*, 5/21/93.

9 Howe, *Weapons*, 457.

10 *La Presse*, 1/24/98.

11 *Management Review*, July 1990; *Financial Times*, 10/11/93; *New York Times*, 6/15/95; *L'Express*, 4/6/95; *Bulletin for International Fiscal Documentation* 46, No. 4, 1992.

12 *New York Times*, 2/1/93; *The Independent*, 8/3/94; *FBIS-WEU*, 6/29/93, 5/25/94; *Times of London*, 6/17/93.

13 *Washington Post*, 6/7/92; *Times of London*, 9/12/92; *Guardian*, 9/12/92; *Montreal Gazette*, 4/29/93.

14 *New York Times*, 4/30/93; *Financial Times*, 5/5/93; *The Economist*, 2/12/94.

15 *Wall Street Journal*, 6/7/94.

16 *FBIS-WEC*, 8/13/93.

17 *New Statesman & Society*, 10/21/94.

18 *Swiss Review of World Affairs*, June 1993; *Globe and Mail*, 7/7/94.

19 *Le Monde*, 8/31/87, 9/17/87, 10/8/87; *Wall Street Journal*, 9/14/87; *Financial Times*, 9/8, 24/87; *Observer*, 9/27/87; *Time*, 9/28/87; Branka Magas, *The Destruction of Yugoslavia*, London: Verso, 1993, 110–12. I am appreciative of Mark Vujicic for research on this topic.

20 *Time*, 9/28/87. My thanks to Mihailo Crnobrnja for his observations on the Agrokomerć crisis.

21 After the defeat Abdić moved to Croatia with thousands of his followers, where they settled in refugee camps awaiting their chance to go back and re-establish their Balkan Cayman Islands (*BBC Summary of World Broadcasts*, 9/13/93, 12/30/93, 6/14/95, 8/3/95).

22 On the Bihać enclave see Glenny, *The Fall of Yugoslavia*, 152–53, *New York Times*, 7/4/94.

23 *Los Angeles Times*, 4/12/93; *Inter Press Service*, 10/6/94. Even before UN sanctions, Croatia, as part of its economic war against Serbia, cut off oil through the main pipeline from the Dalmatian coast to the interior, which Serbia offset by smuggling via Bosnia (Glenny, *Fall of Yugoslavia*, 103).

24 The oil was pumped under the Danube, refined in Serbia proper, then used locally or shipped back to the Serb-held areas of Croatia or Bosnia. (Owen, *Balkan Odyssey*, 310).

25 *Reuter Asia-Pacific Business Report*, 11/13/92; *Lloyd's List*, 7/16/93; *New York Times*, 11/18/92, 4/30/95. The Greek broker was acquitted.

26 *New York Times*, 3/23/93; *The Economist*, 5/7/94; *Central European*, April 1995.

27 *FBIS-EEU*, 8/25/92; *The Economist*, 11/21/92.

28 *Euromoney*, October 1995; *FBIS-EEU*, 8/17/92, 9/16/94; *New Statesman*, 10/21/94.

29 *Reuters News Service — Western Europe*, 6/18/94; *Montreal Gazette*, 4/2/95; *Globe and Mail*, 12/7/95; *New York Times*, 4/15/95; *The Independent*, 2/14/97. During 1994 Albania imported twice as much fuel as it used.

30 *The Economist*, 8/29/92; *Agence France Presse*, 1/25/93; *Wall Street Journal*, 6/7/94; *Euromoney*, October 1995.

31 *Reuters North American Wire*, 7/6/94, 3/9/95. To aid the entrepreneurial smugglers and reduce risks to the general public from impromptu sales points on city roadways, Serbia set up semi-official gasoline markets.

32 The fact that prices of fuel in Belgrade were, at the peak of the sanctions, just about normal for eastern European capitals was only partly due to the success of sanctions-busting. To try to keep the population on-side, the government offset the higher cost of fuel imports by reducing the tax rate it charged the retail customer.

33 See the excellent survey by Jelica Minic, "The Black Economy in Serbia: Transition from Socialism?" *RFE/RL Research Report* 2, No. 34, August 1993.

34 *The Economist*, 10/9/93.

35 *Maclean's*, 12/14/92; *Wall Street Journal*, 6/7/94; *Washington Post*, 11/21/96; Komlenovic, "Crime and Corruption . . ." *Eastern European Constitutional Review*, op. cit.; *Daily Telegraph*, 11/14/92; *The Economist*, 3/20/93; *Geopolitical Drug Dispatch*, August 1996; *Los Angeles Times*, 1/12/97.

36 *Guardian*, 4/16/93; *New York Times*, 4/6/93.

37 *Guardian*, 3/10/93.

38 *Observer*, 3/14/93, 8/30/93; *Montreal Gazette*, 3/12/93.

39 *Globe and Mail*, 3/10/93; *Times of London*, 3/11/93; *Sunday Times*, 3/14/93; *The Economist*, 3/20/93; *Le Monde*, 3/13/93; *Eastern Europe Insurance Report*, March 1993; *Washington Post*, 4/2/93; *Guardian*, 5/3/94.

40 *The Economist*, 5/7/94.

41 See Susan Woodward, "Yugoslavia: Divide and Fall," *Bulletin of the Atomic Scientists*, November 1993, for one of the few sensible analyses of sanctions.

42 *Guardian*, 5/3/94; *Daily Telegraph*, 4/30/94. When Serbia had supposedly cut off assistance to rebel forces in Croatia and Bosnia, each night Serbian police would secure a stretch of the Drina River and wave tanker-trucks across it with enough fuel to keep Bosnian Serb tanks rolling (*The Independent*, 7/26/95).

43 *Vreme*, 7/12/97; *FBIS-EEU*, 7/3/97, 8/8/97, 12/8/97, 9/21/98.

44 *Eurobusiness*, June 1995; *FBIS-WBU*, 11/5/98; *Sunday Times*, 10/18/98.

CHAPTER 24

1 On the plunder of Romania see Mario Posomai, *Money on the Run*, Toronto: Viking, 1992, Chapter 10.

2 In fact, some gave credit to Albanian émigrés for introducing *omertà* into Italy's Mezzo-giorno, laying the foundations for the Mafia (Misha Glenny, *The Rebirth of History*, London: Penguin, 1993, 149).

3 The name had last been used by a rightist Greek resistance group during World War II (*Financial Times*, 4/15/94). Conceivably it began operating again under the joint sponsorship of Greek extremists and Serbian intelligence.

4 For an overview see Miranda Vickers and James Pettifer, *Albania: From Anarchy to Balkan Identity*, New York: New York University Press, 1997.

5 A good account of the *fares* (clan) system is in *Geopolitical Drug Dispatch*, September 1994.

6 *The European*, 2/13/97.

7 The three together produced about 75 per cent of Albania's hard currency (*Eurobusiness*, June 1995).

8 *Reuters North American Wire*, 10/20/95; *BBC Monitoring Service, Eastern Europe*, 6/21/95; *BBC Summary of World Broadcasts*, 5/16/95; *Deutsche Presse-Argentur*, 11/25/94; *The Independent*, 2/14/97.

9 *The Independent*, 2/14/97.

10 *The Economist*, 4/1/95; *Eurobusiness*, June 1995; *Reuters North American Wire*, 2/16/97.

11 Luigi DiFonzo, *St. Peter's Banker*, New York: Watts, 1983, 25; Shawcross and Young, *Mafia Wars*, 38–39; Claire Sterling, *Octopus*, New York: Simon & Schuster, 1990, 56–57.

12 See *Newsday, The Heroin Trail*, New York: Souvenir Press, 1974; Pierre Galante and Louis Sapin, *The Marseilles Mafia*, London: W. H. Allen, 1979; Alain Jaubert, *Dossier D . . . Comme Drogue*, Paris: Alain Moreau, 1973; and Jean-Pierre Charbonneau, *The Canadian Connection*, Montreal: Optimum Publishers, 1976.

13 The classic work remains McCoy, *Politics of Heroin*, esp. Chapter 5.

14 On the Pizza Connection, see Blumenthal, *Sicilians*, and Shawcross and Young, *Mafia Wars*.

15 *AsiaWeek*, 2/17/93.

16 *Far Eastern Economic Review*, 4/16/98.

17 *Financial Times*, 11/4/97; *Geopolitical Drug Dispatch*, December 1996, March 1998, April 1998, November 1998; *Middle East International*, 11/27/96.

18 Excellent material on the changes in the Balkan route is in *Geopolitical Drug Dispatch*, November 1991, February 1993, June 1994, September 1994, June 1996, and August 1996. See also Observatoire géopolitique des drogues, *Géopolitique des drogues 1995*, Paris: La Découverte, 1995, 16–29; *The Independent*, 12/9/93; *Washington Post*, 11/6/93.

19 *The Independent*, 12/10/93; *Defense & Foreign Affairs' Strategic Report*, 8/31/94; *Jane's Intelligence Review*, 11/1/95.

20 *Eurobusiness*, June 1995; *Washington Post*, 11/21/96; *Washington Times*, 3/25/96. One reason the United States, in its anti-drug propaganda, may have downplayed the significance of the Kosovar traffic was precisely because it put pressure on Serbia (*Defense & Foreign Affairs' Strategic Report*, 8/31/94).

21 I am indebted to Thi Vu for information on this topic. See *Christian Science Monitor*, 2/13/97; *Deutsche Presse-Argentur*, 2/21/97; *Agence France Presse*, 2/24/97.

22 *FBIS-EEU*, 2/8/98; *The Independent*, 1/31/97.

23 *Reuters North American Wire*, 2/14/97; *Guardian*, 2/25/97; *Reuters European Business Report*, 11/26/96; *Geopolitical Drug Dispatch*, April 1997; *Deutsche Presse-Argentur*, 2/4, 12/97; *Boston Globe*, 6/12/97.

24 *Albanian Daily News*, 3/15/97, 10/1/97, 11/14/97.

25 See Duncan Perry, *The Politics of Terror: The Macedonian Revolutionary Movements, 1893–1912*, Durham, N.C.: Duke University Press, 1988, and *Financial Times*, 11/3/98.

26 *Jane's Intelligence Review*, 2/1/95.

27 *Reuters*, 7/5/98.

28 *Financial Times*, 12/20/97.

29 *New York Times*, 11/9, 28/82, 11/1/87; *Washington Post*, 1/29/86; *Financial Times*, 7/20/82, 7/22/86; *Reuters*, 7/30/88.

30 *The Nation*, 6/14/99; *FAIR Fairness & Accuracy in Reporting*, 6/2/99.

31 See the observations of the former Canadian ambassador to Yugoslavia in *Globe and Mail*, 1/10/00, and of the retired Canadian general who commanded UN forces in Bosnia in *Globe and Mail*, 11/9/99. A UN team of pathologists confirmed in early 2001 that claims of ethnic cleansing had been greatly exaggerated, while an independent Finnish forensic team concluded that there was no evidence of the supposed mass execution in the village of Racak, which had reputedly been the inaugurating event of the campaign in January 1999 (*Globe and Mail*, 1/29/01).

32 Senior military spokesmen admitted this openly (*Globe and Mail*, 5/26/99).

33 *Financial Times*, 6/22/99, *New York Times*, 5/25/99.

34 *Financial Times*, 4/20/99.

35 *Financial Times*, 5/3/99; *Mother Jones*, 6/21/99.

36 *Washington Post*, 12/26/99.

37 *La Presse*, 9/4/99

38 *Financial Times*, 7/5/99; *Times of London*, 3/24/99; *Montreal Gazette*, 4/3/99; Stratfor.Com, *Weekly Global Intelligence Update*, 3/20/00, and Special Report, *Kosovo: One Year After*, 9/5/00.

39 *Financial Times*, 5/5/99; 4/18/99; *La Presse*, 4/21/99.

40 *Financial Times*, 11/28/99, 6/16/00.

41 *Financial Times*, 1/17/00; *Globe and Mail*, 1/19/00.

42 "Murder in Belgrade: An Elite Feud or a Drug War?" Stratfor.Com, *Weekly Global Intelligence Update*, 2/10/00.

43 Stratfor.Com, *Weekly Global Intelligence Update*, 6/26/00, 10/9/00.

44 *Middle East International*, 12/22/00.

45 Stratfor.Com, *Weekly Global Intelligence Update*, 12/18/00.

46 *Newsweek*, 6/14/99.

47 Stratfor.Com, *Weekly Global Intelligence Update*, 4/19/00.

EPILOGUE

1 Sugden, *Drake*, 41.

2 An excellent examination of the economic impact of embargoes on weak targets is by Pierre Kopp, "Embargo et criminalisation de l'économie," in Jean and Rufin, *Économie des guerres civiles*.

3 See especially Miguel Rodriguez, "Consequences of Capital Flight for Latin American Debtor Countries," in Donald Lessard and John Williamson, *Capital Flight and Third World Debt*, Washington: Institute for International Economics, 1987.

4 *New York Times*, 7/6/46.

5 This is the position taken by certain "revisionist" historians. However, see the recent work by Jonathan Marshall, *To Have and Have Not: Southeast Asian Raw Materials and the Origins of the Pacific War*, Berkeley: University of California Press, 1995, in which he argues that the United States moved to total oil sanctions only after it became convinced that Japan was going to make its move southward. Still, once the sanctions were in place, Japan faced the options of capitulation or total war.

6 *Time*, 3/21/94; *Financial Times*, 6/9/93; *Wall Street Journal*, 6/24/94.

7 These aspects of Burmese covert financial diplomacy are rarely discussed in the mainstream media. See *Geopolitical Drug Dispatch*, April, December 1992, March, October, 1993, March, June, November 1994, April, September, October 1995, May, September 1996, January, May 1997, February, April 1998.

8 Thanks to Alan Block for this apt phrase.

9 *Newsweek*, 3/9/87. Two works cover Wilson's career: Joseph Goulden's *The Death Merchant*, New York: Simon & Schuster, 1985, and, far better, Peter Maas's *Manhunt*.

INDEX

The letter "n" following a page number indicates a note; for example, "435n.41" indicates note 41 on page 435.